Politics in
East Asia

Politics in East Asia

Explaining Change and Continuity

Timothy C. Lim

LYNNE
RIENNER
PUBLISHERS

BOULDER
LONDON

Published in the United States of America in 2014 by
Lynne Rienner Publishers, Inc.
1800 30th Street, Boulder, Colorado 80301
www.rienner.com

and in the United Kingdom by
Lynne Rienner Publishers, Inc.
3 Henrietta Street, Covent Garden, London WC2E 8LU

Library of Congress Cataloging-in-Publication Data
Lim, Timothy C., 1960–
  Politics in East Asia : explaining change and continuity / Timothy C. Lim.
    pages cm
  Includes bibliographical references.
  ISBN 978-1-62637-051-7 (hardcover : alk. paper) — ISBN 978-1-62637-055-5
(pbk. : alk. paper)
  1. East Asia—Politics and government. I. Title.
  JQ1499.A58L56 2013
  320.95—dc23

                                                          2013039852

British Cataloguing in Publication Data
A Cataloguing in Publication record for this book
is available from the British Library.

Printed and bound in the United States of America

          The paper used in this publication meets the requirements
  ∞   of the American National Standard for Permanence of
          Paper for Printed Library Materials Z39.48-1992.

        5 4 3 2 1

Contents

Figures

Acknowledgments

Politics in East Asia has been a very long time in the making. The idea for writing the book first came to me in 2006, but I never seemed to have the time to make any progress. Around 2011, in conversations with James Kim, a colleague who teaches in the Department of Political Science at Cal Poly Pomona, I was encouraged to make the project a priority. Originally, James and I were going to coauthor *Politics in East Asia,* but our schedules never quite meshed. Still, my early discussions with him were invaluable; he also commented on several draft chapters and made direct contributions to Chapter 6. So, while we did not end up as coauthors, I am grateful to James. In addition, I would like to thank Patrick Thompson, a publisher's representative at Oxford University Press, who put me in contact with James, since he knew that both of us were contemplating writing a similar book. I would also like to thank Stephen Ma, a colleague in my department at California State University, Los Angeles, who provided helpful advice and a lot of enthusiastic support for my discussions of China.

I am also grateful to the many students from my undergraduate Politics in East Asia course, which I have been teaching for more than a decade. Many students gladly volunteered their time to read and comment on early chapters, and two full classes of students served as guinea pigs for draft versions. Feedback from students—who, after all, are my core audience—has been essential to writing and developing *Politics in East Asia.* I should also note that it is entirely because of my course on East Asia that I wrote the book. In teaching the course, I always faced a difficult challenge in finding "just the right book" for both my own teaching preferences (i.e., an emphasis on a systematic approach that integrates theory, method, and history) and my students' usually limited background in East Asian studies and in theories of political and economic "development." Thus, I decided to simply write the book I wanted.

Special thanks goes to Lynne Rienner, who did not hesitate in offering to work with me in getting this book published. Lynne was an enthusiastic supporter of my project and, in some respects, had more confidence in its possible success than I did. Lynne was also very helpful in her editorial role, making a number of suggestions and giving useful advice. Shena Redmond and Lillia

Gajewski also deserve my heartfelt thanks for doing an extraordinarily meticulous job of copyediting my manuscript.

Finally, I would like to thank my family. My wife, Atsuko Sato, an adjunct professor of political science at California State University, Los Angeles, provided valuable assistance (especially on those parts of the book dealing with Japan). She also gave me much-needed personal support while I was working many long hours on the book. Finally, I would like to thank my daughter, Ailani, well, for just being my daughter.

A Note on Romanization (and Related Issues)

The romanization of Asian words (that is, the transliteration of words from Asian languages into the Roman or Latin alphabet) has become extremely confusing over the years. A variety of romanization systems have been developed for Chinese and Korean in particular, which can result in very different spellings for the same word. Consider, for example, the name of China's most famous leader, the spelling of which has two primary versions: *Mao Zedong* and *Mao Tse-tung*. Both versions are still used widely, although the former version (*Mao Zedong*) is now, by far, the more common one. *Mao Zedong* is based on the Pinyin system, formerly called the Hanyu Pinyin system, which has also become the accepted international standard. Thus, this book will generally follow the Pinyin system for the romanization of Chinese words. The main exceptions will be a few historically entrenched names for which the Pinyin spelling is still not dominant. The most salient examples are proper names such as Chiang Kai-shek and Sun Yat-sen. Another exception is for organizations such as the Kuomintang (in Pinyin the spelling is Guomindang), which is the political party that dominated Taiwan's political and economic systems for much of the postwar period.

Korean romanization is in some respects more confusing. In 2000, the South Korean government introduced a new system as the official standard for Korean-language romanization. Partly because the system is relatively new and partly because some resistance has been encountered to the revised rules on romanization, the official system has not been consistently applied. Many scholars, in particular, prefer an older version known as the McCune-Reischauer system. Another source of confusion is the government policy that allows family names to be written according to informal, but commonly accepted, practices. For example, the general who staged a coup in 1961 is typically referred to as Park Chung Hee. In the Korean pronunciation, however, the name has no "r" sound; the proper pronunciation is "Pak." Even more confusing is the name 이 (李), which may be romanized as *Lee, Yi,* or *Rhee*. In this book, the most commonly used and recognized transliteration of Korean names and other words is used. Thus, for example, despite having the same family name, 이, *Rhee* is used to refer to Syngman Rhee (South Korea's first president) and *Lee* is used to refer to Lee Byung-chull (the founder of Samsung, one of South Korea's largest firms).

The Japanese language has no significant similar issues. The transliteration of Japanese words is generally straightforward and consistently applied both inside and outside of academia.

A couple more points are worth mentioning: In the five countries covered in this book, family names are almost always listed first. Thus, for Mao Zedong, Park Chung Hee, and Chiang Kai-shek, *Mao, Park,* and *Chiang* are the respective family (or "last") names. The only major exception is South Korea's first elected president, Syngman Rhee. His family name is Rhee, but almost all references to Rhee are in the traditional Western style. Exceptions are also made when referring to scholars and authors whose works are cited in this book. Specifically, citation of scholars' full names will follow the way in which an article or book cites the author. For example, in the book *Prisoner of the State,* the author's name is listed in the traditional Asian style: Zhao Ziyang. Zhao is the family name and so references to the author's full name will follow the Asian style. Most academic articles published in US or European journals, however, follow the Western convention (e.g., the article "Labor Migration in Taiwan" lists the author as Ji-Ping Lin). Ji-Ping is the given name, so in referring to the author, I follow the Western convention of putting the given name first when using the full name. (Of course, all bibliographic entries follow the convention of listing the author's last name followed by a comma, then the first name.)

Finally, in using italics to indicate foreign words, I follow the standard practice of italicizing only unfamiliar foreign words such as *bafuku* or *amakudari*. Foreign words that are more generally known and found in *Webster's Collegiate Dictionary* and the proper names of organizations, movements, and so on, however, are not italicized.

1

Explaining Change and Continuity in East Asia

Change does not just happen. It is not merely an accident of history, a random or arbitrary event. Rather, it is the product of decisions, both great and small, made by individuals, individual societies, and individual **states**. Similarly, change—especially large-scale political, social, and economic change—does not occur in a vacuum. What happens, say, in South Korea reflects not only the decisions made by Koreans, but also, and perhaps even more important, decisions made by other national, international, and transnational actors. In addition, change is almost certainly influenced, even partly determined, by powerful structural forces and underlying global processes, some of which may be invisible to the casual observer. This book, in part, is about how to better understand, explain, and evaluate the changes that have occurred and are occurring in East Asia, especially since the end of World War II in 1945 (in this book, for reasons explained below, East Asia is construed narrowly to include Japan, China, South Korea, North Korea, and Taiwan). Many of these changes have been profound. Today, for example, Japan is a stable, prosperous, and peaceful democracy. But this has not always been the case. Indeed, from the beginning of the **Meiji Restoration*** (1868–1912) to the end of World War II—and despite a short-lived experiment with limited democracy (which developed during the **Taisho period**, 1912–1926)—Japan was dominated by decidedly illiberal and nondemocratic political regimes. Even more, Japan's foreign policy during the entire pre–World War II period was aggressively militaristic and expansionary, as the country used its industrial might, first, to subjugate its East Asian neighbors (Korea, Taiwan, and **Manchuria**) and, later, to challenge Western imperial dominance throughout Asia. Since 1945, by contrast, Japan has embraced an almost pacifistic stance toward the outside world.

Japan's prewar industrial might, of course, also marked a significant economic change. For centuries, during the **Tokugawa** era and before, the country

---

*Terms appearing in boldface are defined in the Glossary at the end of the book.

1

was locked into a quasi-feudal system based on a self-sufficient and decidedly nonindustrial economic **structure**. As William W. Lockwood (1968) explains, as recently as the early nineteenth century, Japan "remained at a stage of economic development hardly more advanced than that of Western Europe in the late Middle Ages. Of her 28 to 30 million people the overwhelming majority were unfree, poverty-stricken peasants. They lived mostly in self-sufficient rural villages. The foundation of the economy and chief source of wealth was the cultivation of rice, carried on by primitive methods little changed over the centuries" (p. 3). With the beginning of the Meiji era, however, "there set in a feverish process of modernization" (Lockwood 1968, p. 12), which laid the groundwork for a highly industrial and commercialized economy that would eventually compete with the most advanced Western economies of the time—although, as Lockwood carefully points out, the process of modernization was more gradual and spatially limited than is generally assumed. Nonetheless, by the early part of the twentieth century, Japan had achieved a major economic transformation.

Change in South Korea and Taiwan has, in some respects, been even more dramatic both politically and economically. Politically, for example, both countries emerged from decades of colonial domination only to be embroiled in an intense and long-lived postwar struggle between the former Soviet Union and the United States—or more broadly, between the **communist** world and the West. In the case of Korea, this struggle resulted in the wrenching division of the country into two extremely hostile regimes—the pro-US Republic of Korea (hereafter, South Korea) and the pro-Soviet Democratic People's Republic of Korea (hereafter, North Korea). South Korea's affiliation with the United States led to the establishment of a democratic government in 1948, but the country still faced a series of major difficulties, both internal and external, including an anemic economy, a devastating war against North Korea, heated domestic ideological rivalry, and intense political factionalism. Indeed, these difficulties led to a turn away from democracy and toward **autocracy** and **authoritarianism**. Ultimately, a rigged presidential election in 1960 set off a firestorm of popular protests that led to the downfall of South Korea's so-called First Republic[1] led by **Syngman Rhee** and to the imposition of military-authoritarian rule in 1961 under **Park Chung Hee**.

In Taiwan, the Cold War struggle also had both immediate and long-lasting effects as the island's "native" population was subjected to yet another invasion—this one, though, was sanctioned and given legitimacy by outside powers. Prior to the end of World War II, an agreement (the Cairo Declaration of 1943) was reached by the United States, the United Kingdom, and the Republic of China (which was then based on mainland China and led by the anticommunist **Chiang Kai-shek**). The three parties agreed that Taiwan, or the island of Formosa as it was then called, would be "returned" to mainland China after the war or after Chiang's nationalist forces defeated the Chinese communists, who were led by **Mao Zedong**. In 1949, though, Chiang's forces lost to the Chinese communists, and Chiang, along with more than 2 million fellow nationalists, fled to Taiwan and established their own, strongly authoritarian regime on the island. (One should take notice of the significant debate over the political status of Taiwan and more specifically of the issue of Taiwan's legitimacy as a state. Figure 1.1 provides a very brief discussion of this issue.)

The change or transformation that has garnered the most attention for South Korea and Taiwan has been in the realm of economics (or, more accurately, political economy). In the 1950s, both countries were desperately—and seemingly irredeemably—poor: they were quintessential **third world** countries with per capita incomes comparable to or below most other countries in the world, including those in Asia, Latin America, and Africa. In 1950, for example, **per capita GDP** in South Korea and Taiwan was less than half that in Mexico, Guatemala, Bolivia, and Ecuador, and it was significantly lower than in Morocco, Jamaica, and Honduras. In addition, Sri Lanka, Ghana, and the Philippines all had higher per capita GDPs than either South Korea or Taiwan, while Egypt's per capita GDP was about the same (see Figure 1.2). Yet, in a little less than one generation, Taiwan and South Korea had caught up with or surpassed all the aforementioned countries except Mexico. But Mexico's lead, too, vanished by the mid-1980s; by 1990, moreover, per capita GDP in Mexico was only 70 percent of South Korea's and about 60 percent of Taiwan's. Even more, both Taiwan and South Korea had essentially caught up (again, in terms of per capita wealth) with Western Europe by 2008 (see Figure 1.2)—an utterly remarkable achievement. Consider, on this point, that other countries mentioned above all

---

Figure 1.1 Is Taiwan a Country?

Taiwan's political status is subject to intense debate. Most international organizations, including the United Nations, and the large majority of states do not formally recognize Taiwan as a sovereign **state** or country. Under international law, recognition by other states and state-based organizations (such as the UN) is considered a core attribute of statehood. From a strictly legal perspective, then, one can fairly safely conclude that Taiwan does not possess all of the necessary requirements for statehood (for an in-depth discussion of this issue, see Shen 2000). For the purposes of this book, however, Taiwan's strict legal status is not a critical issue, since the government of Taiwan, or the Republic of China as it is formally known, has, in practice, clearly exercised authority over a specific territorial space and population. The capacity of Taiwan's government to exercise internal sovereignty means that it has had the same basic control over its economic and political systems, in practical terms, as any other fully recognized sovereign state. In this view, Taiwan can reasonably be treated in the same manner as South and North Korea, Japan, and China.

fell much farther behind Western Europe during the same period. The Philippines, for instance, started off with a per capita GDP that was about one-fourth (23 percent) of Western Europe's in 1950, but by 2008, the proportion had fallen to just a little more than one-tenth (13 percent).

More than sheer economic growth, however, both South Korea and Taiwan also developed a strong degree of domestically based technological and industrial capacity, which is reflected in their ability to compete head-to-head against the most advanced and largest Western corporations. South Korea, in particular, has a number of world-class corporations, including Hyundai, Samsung, and LG. Each of these companies has established a strong—and, in some cases, a dominating—presence in major international markets, and each is engaged in sophisticated, often cutting-edge production. Taiwan's strongest companies, while less well known to the general public (at least outside of Asia), are equally formidable. These include, among others, Acer, Taiwan Semiconductor Manufacturing Company (TSMC), Quanta Computer, Hon Hai Precision Industry (also known as Foxconn Technology Group), Kingston Technology, and United Microelectronics Corporation. As in South Korea, each of these companies has

---

Figure 1.2 Comparative per Capita GDP Figures (in international dollars, for selected countries and years)

	1950	1970	1980	1990	2000	2008
Mexico	2,365	4,320	6,320	6,085	7,275	7,979
Guatemala	2,085	2,919	4,005	3,240	3,927	4,461
Bolivia	1,919	2,176	2,572	2,197	2,561	2,959
Ecuador	1,863	2,845	4,129	3,903	3,219	3,987
Morocco	1,455	1,616	2,272	2,591	2,652	3,465
Jamaica	1,327	3,849	3,121	3,786	3,598	3,688
Honduras	1,313	1,556	2,062	1,857	1,912	2,323
Sri Lanka	1,253	1,499	1,830	2,424	3,597	4,895
Ghana	1,122	1,424	1,157	1,062	1,265	1,650
Philippines	1,070	1,764	2,376	2,197	2,377	2,926
Taiwan	916	2,537	5,260	9,938	16,872	20,926
Egypt	910	1,254	2,069	2,523	2,936	3,725
South Korea	854	2,167	4,114	8,704	14,375	19,614
Western Europe (avg.)	4,569	10,169	13,154	15,908	19,176	21,672

Source: Maddison (2008).

Note: The international dollar, also known as the Geary-Khamis dollar, is a hypothetical unit of currency that has the same purchasing power that the US dollar had in the United States at a given point in time. In the data above, 1990 is used as the benchmark year for comparisons that run from 1950 to 2008. While the international dollar is not widely utilized, for per capita GDP comparisons across a range of countries over a relatively long period of time, it is a useful statistic. The World Bank and the International Monetary Fund (IMF) use the international dollar in some of their published statistics.

become a major global player: Quanta Computer is the world's largest maker of notebook personal computers (PCs) and a key supplier to Dell and Hewlett-Packard, TSMC is the biggest semiconductor chip producer in the world, and Hon Hai Precision Industry is a major producer of consumer electronics for Apple (the iPhone, iPad, and iPod) and Sony (PlayStation), among others.

Significantly, too, rapid economic development in both countries also seemed to lead to another major political transformation: by the late 1980s, the two countries were well on their way toward the establishment of sturdy—albeit far from perfect—democratic political systems. In many respects, the transformation of South Korea and Taiwan into "full-fledged democracies" (I specify what I mean by this phrase in Chapter 6) is as remarkable as their economic ascendances. For in both cases, the timing of the transition was unexpected and, more significantly, unexpectedly smooth. Indeed, many observers assumed that the initial transition from authoritarianism to democracy was more illusion than reality or, at the least, subject to reversal at almost any time—especially if the interests of the most powerful social and political actors were to be threatened. In the beginning, these assumptions seemed accurate, as the initial phase of the democratic transitions in South Korea and Taiwan were dominated by the same groups and parties that had been in power during the authoritarian era. Eventually, however, once-subordinated opposition parties and groups won political power through the ballot box, and contrary to the predictions of many, their right to rule was not challenged or summarily usurped through extraconstitutional means (e.g., a military **coup d'état**).

There is, of course, far more to the story of political, economic, and social transformation in Japan, Taiwan, and South Korea than presented here. But telling this story is, in large part, the objective of this book, so I save additional discussion for later. For now, we need to turn our attention to two other East Asian countries, both of which are also very important in their own rights: China and North Korea. In China, the world is witnessing a reoccurrence of the stunning postwar economic ascendance of Japan, South Korea, and Taiwan. Once a slow-moving, industrially and technologically backward leviathan, China has become—since the 1990s—one of the fastest growing, most dynamic capitalist economies (another issue that I examine at much greater length in subsequent chapters). The significance of this change is hard to exaggerate, for unlike its East Asian neighbors, China is a country of immense proportions: its population of over 1.3 billion people is the largest in the world and accounts for fully 20 percent of the Earth's people. Thus, while China remains a relatively poor country in per capita terms, it is already a tremendously powerful country in terms of its overall GDP. In 2011, China's GDP in **purchasing power parity (PPP)** terms was, according to the **World Bank**, over $9.1 trillion, larger than any other single country except for the United States. On its present growth path, moreover, China's overtaking the United States is only a matter of time, as soon as 2025 according to many economists' predictions. However, no one can guarantee China's continued ability to reproduce its remarkable record economic growth. In the 1980s, in fact, many scholars predicted that Japan would overtake the United States, but it did not due to long-standing economic difficulties in Japan that began in the early 1990s. Still, China's sheer size means its continued growth will provoke changes throughout the rest of Asia and the entire world, even if that growth slows considerably.

Despite its embrace of capitalist and market principles, China is still dominated by an authoritarian, decidedly nondemocratic, and ostensibly communist political regime. In light of political changes experienced by its East Asian brethren, China's ongoing economic transformation raises a number of important questions: Will rapid capitalist development in China necessarily lead to significant political change, that is, to democratization? Or will something unique about China prevent this political transformation from taking place? These questions lead to broader inquiries about the nature of the relationship between economic and political change. Can a direct causal connection be established between economic and political processes? If so, what is the basis of this connection, and how exactly does it work? Or, as others might argue, are the two processes largely unconnected or, at best, tangentially related? Whatever the answer is, one also needs to consider what other processes, **institutions**, and actors might be relevant to an explanation of the prospects for major political change in countries such as China.

Whether—or more pertinently—*why* China may or may not democratize is a crucial question, and one that I address at some length. At the same time, one should also recognize that, like China's heretofore resilient political system, dramatic and profound change is not evident everywhere in East Asia. The most obvious case is North Korea, which has seen remarkably little political, social, and economic change since its official birth as a communist state and society in 1948. While not frozen in time, both North Korea's political and economic systems have remained remarkably untouched. Consider that in 2010—more than fifty years after its establishment—the country had experienced only a single leadership change, and that only because North Korea's first leader and president, **Kim Il-sung**, died of natural causes in 1994. Kim Il-sung was replaced by his son, **Kim Jong-il**, in 1997, in the first "dynastic" succession ever in a communist regime. Notably, Kim Jong-il's accession was not a foregone conclusion; in fact, he did not assume complete control until three years after his father's death. On December 17, 2011, Kim Jong-il died. He was succeeded by his son, **Kim Jong-un**, whose credentials for leadership are shaky, at best. The key point, however, is that the accession of Kim Jong-un further underscores the continuity of the regime and system in North Korea.

The longevity and stability of the North Korean political system are not unique, but they are highly unusual. As such, they call out for an explanation, particularly in light of the country's extremely poor record of economic growth since the 1970s. In many countries, long-term and serious economic difficulty provides the basis for political instability and regime change. While North Korea's isolation and extreme secretiveness—it remains one of the most isolated countries in the world—make accurate assessment of its level of economic development difficult, the country's **centrally planned** or **command economy** has clearly suffered from debilitating inefficiencies for several decades and has been unable to sustain sufficient production, especially agricultural production, for the population. The evidence of this situation is clear: in the mid-1990s, to cite a particular salient example, nearly 1 million North Koreans—in a population of about 24 million—died as a result of one of the worst famines of the twentieth century (Haggard and Noland 2007). The country's abysmal economic performance has led to some market-based reforms, but for the most part, these reforms have been limited and carefully controlled. In short, both North Korea's political and economic systems (except for their inception) have seen precious little change for well over a half-century.

Continuity is not limited to North Korea or to China's political system. The other East Asian countries have not, by any means, been completely remade. In particular, the social, institutional, and cultural features that have made each a distinct society have not simply disappeared with changes in their economies and political systems. Understanding continuity, I should stress, is equally as important as understanding change. For no less than change, continuity does not just happen. It is often, if not almost always, the product of intense but varied political, social, and economic forces: keeping things from changing can take a lot of effort and power. In this book, therefore, I examine both change and continuity in East Asia—although, I should stress at the outset, the emphasis is decidedly on the former. Still, as will become evident, both are critical to understanding the political, economic, and social dynamics of individual countries within East Asia and of the region as a whole.

Beyond the "Usual Suspects"

So far, the discussion in this chapter has revolved around the two most conventional topics in studies of change and continuity in East Asia: high-speed capitalist industrialization and democracy versus authoritarianism. Good reasons, of course, can be found to focus on these topics. Yet a number of other issues—albeit strongly related ones—of great import and interest also deserve equally serious attention. One of these has to do with a common corollary of capitalist industrialization, namely, labor repression. As Frederic Deyo (1989) forcefully puts it, "a preoccupation with the sources of [economic] growth diverted attention from a dark underside of the East Asian 'miracle': the extreme political subordination and exclusion of workers" (p. 1). Just how "extreme" has the political subordination and exclusion of workers in East Asia been (especially in the four capitalist economies of Japan, South Korea, Taiwan, and China)? Does East Asia as a whole, or as individual countries, stand out from the rest of the world, or do the experiences of workers in East Asia largely mimic the experiences of workers in any industrializing economy? If differences can be found between East Asia and other parts of the world, what are the sources of or reasons for these differences? Whatever the answers to these and similar questions, understanding or explaining change and continuity in East Asia requires that one not just consider the ostensible economic triumphs of the four capitalist economies, but that one also think very carefully about the shortcomings. Labor repression, some argue, is one of the most important of these shortcomings, which is why I devote space to an examination of this issue—albeit in the context of the discussion of political change (especially in Chapter 6).

The adverse implications of China's burgeoning economy also deserve special attention. As should already be apparent, China's rapid economic ascendance is not all "wine and roses." Unlike the other East Asian economies, for instance, China's economic expansion has been accompanied by one of the worst cases of increasing domestic income inequality on record: over the course of about two decades from the late 1980s to the mid-2000s, China experienced a virtually unprecedented deterioration of income equality—or, as Barry Naughton (2007) succinctly puts it, "there may be no other case where a society's income distribution has deteriorated so much, so fast" (p. 218). What are the reasons for this "virtually unprecedented" deterioration of income equality? Is it an unavoidable, but temporary, by-product of high-speed economic growth? Or does it portend an essentially permanent division between the "haves" and the "have-nots" in China? In assessing the varied dimensions of economic change, these questions are clearly important to address. Another extremely important issue revolves around the larger system-wide effects of China's rapid industrial expansion on the world economy and, perhaps even more importantly, on the global environment. I only touch on these issues in Chapter 7, but the approach I introduce and apply throughout this book will give readers the means to pursue a fuller and more in-depth analysis on their own.

Over the past few decades, the world has been witnessing another significant change throughout East Asia: in-migration or immigration. For decades, East Asia was primarily a source of migration to other countries, but this outward flow has started to reverse itself. Japan, South Korea, and Taiwan are becoming significant destinations for people from around the world but especially from South Asia, Southeast Asia, and China. Comparatively speaking, the numbers are still fairly small, but they nonetheless represent a momentous change. This change is especially true for Japan and South Korea, two self-described homogenous (i.e., racially and ethnically "pure") nations. While pure homogeneity has never actually been the case, the concept of ethnic and racial homogeneity has occupied a central place in the nationalist mythologies of both countries. Increasing immigration, then, raises crucial questions about the **intersubjective** foundations of the two countries. Can Japan and South Korea maintain continuity in their respective national identities, or will migration necessarily lead to fundamental social changes? Whatever the answer, any contemporary analysis of change and continuity in East Asia needs to examine the causes and implications of this growing migration. Not surprisingly, Taiwan is undergoing the same basic experience, although the context is different (a point I discuss later). China and North Korea, on the other hand, have very different stories to tell. In North Korea, almost no in-migration can be found for obvious reasons, although North Korea is beginning to witness much more out-migration. Finally, in China, migration is a massive socioeconomic and political issue, but the migration is primarily internal, from the countryside to urban areas. Chapter 8 is devoted to an examination of these issues.

In short, I cover a lot of ground in this book, from the usual suspects to a number of equally important, equally complex issues. This task is not easy and requires a number of fairly big trade-offs. In general, the sacrifice is that adequate attention cannot be given to everything. But this problem is smaller than it may at first appear to be. For, as I have already suggested—and as I discuss more below—one of the overarching goals of this book is to give readers the conceptual and analytical tools to carry out more in-depth analysis of important issues on their own. Despite this qualification, some issues certainly deserve an independent, in-depth examination and would have added to the book but are not included. One of the most salient of these issues is regional security and regionalism (economic, political, and military) more generally. Yet, while regionalism is a crucial topic, a number of excellent sources already cover regionalism in East and Northeast Asia and could serve as useful supplements to this text.[2] By contrast, few, if any, books cover political, economic, and social change (and continuity) in Japan, China, South Korea, North Korea, and Taiwan in the manner that I do in this book.

That being said, in the following section I am going to take a step back, so to speak. Specifically, I will take a step back to engage in a brief discussion of the core concepts around which this book is organized. I have already spent the first part of this chapter discussing two of these concepts—change and continuity—but a bit more discussion is warranted. *Change* and *continuity,* after all, are basically generic terms, and while I have already clarified both to some extent, being more explicit about the use of the two terms in the context of this book behooves me. I also examine two additional concepts: "development" and "East Asia." Development is typically and closely associated with notions of change, especially progressive change. Indeed, the original title of this project was *Explaining East Asian Development.* However, the term *development* has important and generally hidden connotations, which need to be addressed. The same caveats apply to the ostensibly clear-cut geographic term *East Asia.* My use of the term *East Asia* in this book is limited to Japan, China, Taiwan, South Korea, and North Korea. But I intentionally use the term in a geographically delimited way, which I need to explain and justify.

Change and Continuity in East Asia: Key Concepts

Let's begin with the idea of change, an ambiguous concept at best. Consider the dictionary definition of *change:* "to make or become different." Based on this one definition, I, or anyone else, would find trying to explain change an impossible or, at least, an impossibly vague task. Minimally, I need to specify the type of change with which I am concerned. Thus, I could talk about "economic change," "political change," "social change," and so on. Yet I soon run into the same basic problem: What sort of economic or political or social change am I trying to explain? For researchers and others concerned with explaining or understanding social, political, or economic phenomena, such ambiguity is not a virtue. Of course, I can drill down a little further. Instead of "political change," for example, I might say "democracy," which is a type of political change. On the surface, democracy does seem to be a much more specific concept. Yet I still need to specify what distinguishes a democracy from a non-democracy. Otherwise I would have no basis for asserting a change has occurred. I also need definitional criteria against which to judge if democracy (or any other type of political change) is "weakening" or getting "stronger"; without such definitional criteria, change could easily become a static, as opposed to a dynamic, concept. Similarly, if I am to offer an adequate explanation of a political change such as democracy, I need to provide an equally concrete definition of the factors or variables that create that change. In short, I need to make sure that the **dependent** and **independent variables** in my analysis and discussion are defined with as much clarity and precision as possible.

To sum up, I need to set forth the minimal conditions and boundaries of the changes to be studied in this book. For the most part, I take up this challenge in subsequent chapters. In the examination of the East Asian "miracle" (Chapter 2), for example, I provide a full discussion of the concrete economic changes around which the chapter is organized. For now, then, I use the concept of change only as a generic marker or as a temporary stand-in for a more specific concept. The same is true for the use of the term *continuity*. Unlike the notion of change, however, continuity is an intrinsically less nebulous concept to deal with in the context of this book. Consider, again, a standard dictionary definition: "a state of stability and the absence of disruption." In this view, when I examine continuity in East Asia, I am examining those aspects of economic, political, and social life that have tended to remain relatively stable over time. The most important task, then, is to provide an adequate description of extant conditions or circumstances. Before I move on, I need to discuss one other concept that is closely associated with change and inversely related to continuity: development.

Change and Development

Change is most often associated with the notion of development. Both terms suggest movement from one condition to another, but *development* connotes a progressive (or positive) change. It also connotes an evolutionary movement from a primitive (i.e., nondeveloped or underdeveloped) state to a higher, more advanced stage. While seemingly innocuous, these two connotations, when put into the larger historical context within which the term first emerged, have made the concept of development extremely controversial. Vincent Tucker (1999) goes to the crux of the issue:

> Development is the process whereby other peoples are dominated and their destinies are shaped according to an essentially Western way of conceiving and perceiving the world. The development discourse is part of an imperial process whereby other peoples are appropriated and turned into objects. It is an essential part of the process whereby the "developed" countries manage, control and even create the Third World economically, politically, sociologically and culturally. It is a process whereby the lives of some peoples, their plans, their hopes, their imaginations, are shaped by others who frequently share neither their lifestyles, nor their hopes nor their values. The real nature of this process is disguised by a discourse that portrays development as a necessary and desirable process, as human destiny itself. (p. 1)

Tucker's language may seem overstated, but the main point is not particularly controversial: development is an **ethnocentric** concept. That is, the term is defined strictly in Western economic, political, and cultural terms. In other words, the word *development* means capitalist industrialization, democratization, and the unqualified embrace of liberal values. I agree that the concept of development reflects an insidious and potentially destructive form of **ethnocentrism**,[3] which is one reason I avoid—but not altogether eschew—using the term in this book.[4] I do not entirely eschew the concept of development for a simple reason: clearly, the most significant changes in East Asia involve the **Westernization** of the region's economic and political systems. Thus, much of the attention in this book is centered precisely on the key elements of Westernization: capitalist industrialization and democratization. I more thoroughly discuss these two concepts in subsequent chapters. However, attention must also be given to those areas in which economic, political, and social change has involved a hybridization of Western and East Asian traditions and modes of "development."

What Is East Asia?

The main title of this book, *Politics in East Asia,* suggests that the concept of East Asia itself is unproblematic. Unfortunately, this is far from true. One general reason is simply that ostensibly geographic labels often carry a great deal of disguised baggage. And, as with the concept of development, this baggage is usually the product of both overt and underlying relations of power. Patrick Ziltener (2007), for example, suggests that the "idea of East Asia as a region has been introduced to the region from the outside, by European colonial powers and the US. It has never been widely used as a self-description" (p. 112). The imposition of geographic labels does not mean that physical geography is irrelevant; East Asia is a case in point (see Figure 1.3). But it does means that other factors are often at play, as I have already suggested. As Airf Dirlik (1998) bluntly puts it, "to define, as to name, is to conquer" (p. 5). Again, Dirlik's point may seem to be overstated, but denying that the imposition of a name or label can have important implications is hard. A name implies, in particular, some coherence, commonality, or relationship among the parts that is defined *for* them, rather than *by* them. Consider, on this point, Japan's insistence on "abandoning Asia, joining the West (Europe)" (*datsu-A nyu-O*) during the Meiji era (Ziltener 2007, p. 112). Being part of Asia during this period consigned Japan to third-rate status, while being part of Europe would have underscored Japan's "proper place" in the international hierarchy. Ironically, Australia's more recent efforts to redefine itself as part of Asia—after decades of denying any connection at all to the region (Jupp 1995)—indicates that neither the meaning nor the physical structure of a geographic space is fixed; in the minds of many, Asia has moved—or will eventually move—to center stage in world affairs, and becoming part of this movement behooves hitherto and self-described non-Asian countries.

The foregoing discussion raises a number of important issues—issues that should not be blithely ignored. At the same time, one needs a way to move forward, toward a practical conceptualization, and one can begin by accepting the ideas of T. J. Pempel (2005), who writes, "No self-evident and essentialist East Asia forms a single logical and self-contained regional unit . . . [because] different problems 'create different regions'" (cited in Ziltener 2007, p. 113). My conceptualization of East Asia, therefore, is not meant to impose an essential and unchanging identity on East Asia, nor is it meant to impose other elemental qualities on any of the units in this region. Rather, it represents a convenient way of demarcating a group of geographically and historically related countries sharing a similar set of concerns. Geography is important, but it certainly is not everything. Geography has *significance* to the extent that it may play a role, although not necessarily a central one, in shaping economic, political, and sociocultural processes in a region. The same can be said of historical forces and experiences and their impact on a particular geographic space or region. In this regard, the conceptualization of East Asia in this book is also based on an assumption that

Figure 1.3 Map of East Asia

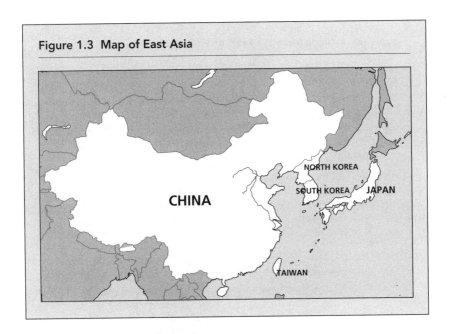

particularly strong linkages—some direct and obvious and some indirect and obscure—can be found between and among the five countries on which I focus: Japan, China, South Korea, Taiwan, and North Korea. The nature of these linkages varies among these countries, but it reflects a level of intraregional connectedness—which is not the same as affinity or a sense of kinship—that makes the notion of East Asia much more than just an arbitrary geographic label.[5]

Left out of the current conceptualization of East Asia are a number of other countries that occupy the same geographic space, including Mongolia and Russia (the latter of which borders both China and North Korea). Also left out are the ten countries belonging to the **Association of Southeast Asian Nations** (**ASEAN**)—Indonesia, Malaysia, the Philippines, Singapore, Thailand, Brunei, Myanmar (formerly Burma), Cambodia, Laos, and Vietnam—and territories controlled by China, including Hong Kong, Macau, and Tibet (see Figure 1.4). The exclusion of some of these countries is admittedly arbitrary or at least partly so (e.g., Hong Kong is typically considered part of East Asia). But this approach reflects a practical methodological choice, too: to give justice to the East Asian countries I do focus on, I needed to impose a limit. Even so, the conceptualization of East Asia used here provides a good deal of demographic, economic, political, and sociocultural diversity. At the same time, wherever relevant and practical I incorporate discussion of a number of other Asian countries.

Now that I have discussed the core concepts around which this book is organized, I need to take on another basic task, one that centers on *how* to explain

Figure 1.4 A More Inclusive Map of East Asia

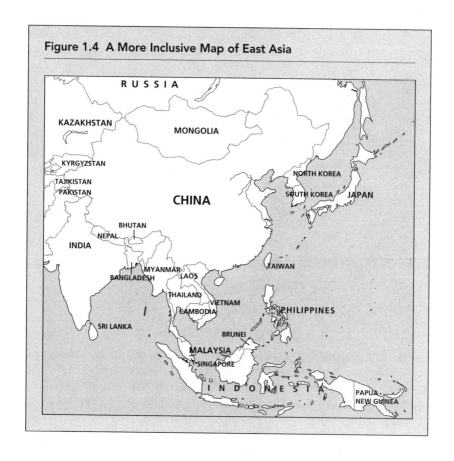

change and continuity. However, explaining change and continuity in East Asia is not something one just does "off the cuff." Explanations are not self-evident, especially explanations of complex economic, political, and social phenomena. Neither are explanations generally, if ever, the product of casual observation or facile analysis. Instead, explanations—or at least good explanations—require that one thinks carefully and seriously about theoretical and methodological issues, a task I take up in the following sections.

How to Study Change and Continuity

Before beginning to study change and continuity in East Asia, a basic question needs to be addressed: What is the best way to analyze these phenomena? That is, how does one go about identifying, understanding, and explaining those forces or factors most important to the processes of change and continuity in the region? This question is not a simple one. It is also not a question, more importantly, to take lightly or gloss over by making a few cursory comments and then moving on to the more "important stuff." Although I do not pretend to have a definitive answer, I do intend to provide a systematic, balanced, and theoretically based framework of analysis for addressing the question.

Let's begin with *theory,* a term that is often misunderstood, especially by anyone who just wants to "get to the facts." Theory, however, cannot be avoided (see Figure 1.5 for a basic definition). No matter how pragmatic or common-sensical one thinks he or she is, any time a claim or argument is made about a social, political, or economic phenomenon, the maker of the claim or argument is engaged in a process of theorizing. Consider, for a moment, the factors one might focus on if asked to answer the question, "What are the reasons for East Asia's economic success?" Some readers might emphasize a culture that puts strong emphasis on educational achievement, a strong work ethic, solid ethical values, or a combination of all three. Others might look to the free market as the main reason. If so, they would likely be persuaded by Michael Schuman (2010) of *Time* magazine, who emphatically writes, "All rapid-growth Asian economies—including China's—succeeded by latching onto the expanding forces of globalization, through *free trade* and *free flows of capital.* South Korea, Taiwan and Singapore may have had active bureaucrats, but the true source of their economic growth was exports manufactured by private companies and sold to the consumers of the world" (emphasis added). Still others might focus on far-sighted but also highly nationalistic and incorruptible political and business leaders who were absolutely committed to achieving rapid industrialization, regardless of the social costs. Or they might argue that the "special relationship" East Asian countries enjoyed with the United States—particularly during the Cold War—made the difference. The list of possible answers, while not quite endless, is cer-

---

Figure 1.5 A Basic Definition of Theory

Theory can be defined in a number of ways. For this book's purposes, I define theory as a simplified representation of reality and a framework of analysis within which facts are not only selected but also interpreted, organized, and fitted together so that they create a coherent whole (Lim 2010). Embedded in this definition are the following key points:

- Theory necessarily simplifies reality.
- Theory helps to determine what facts are important, meaningful, and relevant.
- Theory guides interpretation of the facts. (What do the facts mean?)
- Theory acts as a guide to organize the facts. (How do different facts relate to one another? Which are primary and which are secondary?)
- Theory allows for the development of "whole arguments."

tainly very long. No matter what the view, however, all possible responses are a product of theory—albeit not necessarily "good theory."

The preceding paragraph, I should note, provides purposefully oversimplified versions of four very broad theoretical approaches used to explain economic and political change: *cultural, liberal, statist-institutional,* and *structural.* Each approach emphasizes certain factors—education, values, work ethic, free markets, strong leadership, a special relationship between East Asia and the United States—while simultaneously deemphasizing or dismissing other factors. Put another way, each response posits a causally significant relationship between a specific factor, or a small set of factors, and economic growth. In this regard, one might say that each approach, albeit to varying degrees, offers a competing theoretical perspective on the specific issue of economic growth. The existence of competing perspectives can be confusing, but it also offers an opportunity for better understanding if one begins with the assumption that each competing perspective has something important to say. I began this book with just this assumption, and this assumption, in turn, is the basis for the first part of my "systematic, balanced, and theoretically based framework of analysis." Specifically, I explicitly adopt a competing-perspectives approach. In this approach, I examine contrasting arguments about major issues in East Asia: economic growth and industrialization, political continuity and change (i.e., democratization), and the dynamics of migration/immigration. Each provides indispensable insights into a proper understanding of continuity and change in East Asia, and thus each needs to be taken seriously. Moreover, the systematic juxtaposition of these competing viewpoints will allow for a more enriching and multidimensional understanding than any single perspective. In the following chapter, I dive headfirst into the competing-perspectives approach.

At the same time, I recognize that a competing-perspectives approach, while valuable, is also potentially very confusing for readers unfamiliar with the theoretical debates on economic and political change. The potential for confusion, not surprisingly, lies in the disagreement—frequently quite vehement and fundamental—among and even within the various perspectives. To put the issue simply, how is the reader or anyone else to know who is right (or which argument is right)? I cannot definitively answer this question in this book. Nor is it a question that I necessarily want to answer. What I can do is to provide, at a general level, a firm and clear basis, first, for understanding what each perspective does and does not address and the conclusions each perspective might reach. One needs to understand not only the strengths of each perspective but also of the weaknesses. In this respect, another overarching goal in this book is to provide, within the framework, a guide for critical thinking and analysis. I want readers, by the time they finish this book, to evaluate the various and varied arguments about change and continuity in East Asian on their own in order to come to their own critically informed conclusions.

Second, I endeavor through this framework to cut through some of the confusion by providing a path toward the synthesis or integration of insights from the competing perspectives. On this point, understanding that the differences among the perspectives are not just skin deep is vital. That is, the perspectives mentioned above do not have only slightly different emphases. Rather, each perspective is premised on very different assumptions both about what constitutes the fundamental processes, forces, or factors at work in the world, and how these processes, forces, or factors function to produce specific outcomes, such as rapid economic growth or democratization. For this reason, one cannot merely and unthinkingly throw together elements of the four perspectives—as many people are tempted to do.

To help illustrate this point, I ask the reader to think again about some of the stylized (or purposely simplified) arguments used above. Economic liberals assume a priori that markets function best when they are left alone. In particular, some economic liberals assert that any outside intervention in the operation of markets can only degrade, and even destroy, efficiency while inhibiting economic growth (this position is most closely associated with **neoliberalism** today). To economic liberals, the key to East Asia's economic growth, therefore, is crystal clear: getting the "fundamentals right," by allowing the forces of supply and demand to operate in an essentially unfettered manner. In sharp contrast, some statist-institutionalist scholars argue that nonmarket (i.e., state) intervention has been the key to East Asian economic success. They argue, more specifically, that East Asian economic success was, in no small measure, a product of state power, first, in building viable and strongly functioning capitalist markets and, second, in making sure business decisions contributed to national economic goals. Completely reconciling these two different arguments, as should be apparent, is not possible: the two arguments—at least in their "pure form"—cannot both be right. One or the other has to give. At the same time, however, some room may exist to link together elements and principles from both arguments—and from structural and cultural arguments—to create a coherent, integrative explanation.

Toward an Integrative Framework: The "Constructed Actor" Approach

So how can the various perspectives be brought together in a coherent and useful fashion? Is this even possible? Obviously, I think it is, although I need to emphasize at the outset that a completely balanced theoretical synthesis is not possible. Greater "theoretical weight" or primacy must unavoidably be assigned to some principles over others. Partly for this reason, any effort to develop a comprehensive and integrated perspective will be subject to criticism. I accept the validity of this criticism, but I also want to emphasize that I see great heuristic value in making the effort (one basic meaning of *heuristic* is "encouraging a person to learn, discover, understand, or solve problems on his or her own, as by experimenting, evaluating possible answers or solutions" [Dictionary.com]). After all, such an effort requires one to think more clearly, critically, and seriously about both his or her own assumptions and key operating principles and about the assumptions and principles embedded in other perspectives. It also requires one to think more openly by compelling consideration of how the pieces of a complex explanatory puzzle fit—or do not fit, as the case may be—together. In a strongly related vein, it forces one, at least temporarily, to dispense with binary or either-or thinking (e.g., "either markets are all-important or states are," "either the structures of global capitalism determine economic growth or they do not"). To be sure, binary thinking may not always be wrong, but it often results in overly narrow analysis. My purpose, in short, is not necessarily to replace existing explanations with an all-encompassing integrative one but instead to provoke and challenge readers to think about different "theoretical possibilities."

With all this in mind, I begin with a seemingly simple concept around which I organize the integrated framework: the constructed actor. The constructed actor is shorthand for a more elaborate notion articulated by Daniel Little (2005), who used the phrase "the structured circumstances of choice of socially constructed actors" (p. 2). A number of critical, and not very obvious, assumptions are embedded in this phrase. Most basically, the phrase emphasizes actors, or individual decisionmakers. In this regard, the constructed actor model begins at the *microlevel,* although Little uses the term *microfoundations.* At the same time, Little portrays the individual as a "socially constituted actor, affected by [a] large current of social facts such as value systems, **social structures**, extended social networks, and the like" (p. 10). In this view, individuals make decisions or choices, and, through these choices, certain outcomes are produced (such as rapid economic growth). Yet these choices are always conditioned or constrained by circumstances outside the direct control of the actor or actors. As Little puts it, his framework "affirms the existence of social constructs beyond the purview of the individual actor or group"; furthermore, these social constructs "have real effects on individual behavior and on social processes and outcomes" (p. 11). This discussion is a bit abstract, but the key point is not complicated: People do not exist in a vacuum. Instead, they exist in a world composed of all sorts of political, economic, and social relationships and arrangements and social structures.

Little (2005), I should note, is primarily focused on social constructs (relationships, arrangements, and structures) that exist at the mesolevel (see Figure 1.6), specifically institutions and political arrangements (property systems, legal systems, educational systems, political organizations, and the like). In principle, however, both intersubjective and macrolevel social constructs—particularly cultural milieus and the structures of global capitalism—can also be included. I argue that both are necessary in the constructed actor framework.

Figure 1.6   A Basic Analytic Tool: Levels of Analysis

In the social sciences, analysis is often focused on or located at different levels of abstraction—or levels of analysis—depending on the theoretical orientation or purpose of the researcher. The three most common levels of analysis are the microlevel, the mesolevel, and the macrolevel. For example, if a researcher believes that explanations of social, political, or economic phenomena can be primarily explained by focusing on how individuals interact or on how individuals make decisions, then as described in the table below, the researcher is focused on the microlevel (here the primary **unit of analysis** is the individual). Microlevel analysis assumes that individual actors have a significant degree of agency.

Microlevel (individual)	Mesolevel (interactional)	Macrolevel (structural/systemic)
Focuses on aspects of individual experience and on the impact that experience has on how actors behave and interact with other actors. Presumes that individual action is largely or at least significantly unstructured, that is, not dependent on external forces that compel individuals to behave in certain ways. At the microlevel, the individual is also the primary unit of analysis.	Focuses on the social, institutional, cultural, and economic environments or milieus in which individual action takes place. Presumes that individual action is shaped and influenced by social interactions or by social norms, beliefs, practices, and so on. Individuals have agency but are not entirely "free agents." At the mesolevel, society and key elements of society (e.g., social organizations, formal and informal institutions, the state) are the primary units of analysis.	Focuses on the largest or most significant processes and structures that shape and govern societies and individuals. Presumes that individual action is profoundly shaped and influenced—and sometimes determined—by overarching forces over which individuals, acting alone or in groups, have limited ability to control. At the macrolevel, "whole systems" are the primary unit of analysis. These whole systems include global capitalism and the international system.

Source: Adapted from Scott Schaffer (n.d.).
Note: No consensus exists on the dividing line between the meso- and macrolevels. The definition of the macrolevel above, therefore, reflects only one of many possible conceptualizations.

Another important aspect of Little's (2005) approach (and the constructed actor model) is a focus on the **mutually constitutive** relationship that exists between agents and institutions/structures. So, while institutions, as noted above, have "real effects" on individual behavior, they are also shaped and sustained by individual actions. Little explains the process this way: "Agents create institutions [and structures]; they support institutions; they conform their behavior to the incentives and inhibitions created by institutions; they defy or quietly defect from norms; they act opportunistically or on principle" (p. 12). More simply, institutions are not independent of human actors, nor do they wholly determine individual behavior. Even more, because institutions (and structures) do not exist independently of human action—because they are constituted by the individuals who participate in them—institutions and structures are not fixed, unchanging entities. Simply put, institutions and structures can and do change over time, which means, in turn, that the choices and opportunities available to actors are never exactly the same between any two periods of time. Thus, the repertoire and implications of institutional choices, say, for Japanese decisionmakers in the mid-1800s were significantly different from those available to Japanese decisionmakers in 1945—or Chinese decisionmakers today. This point is a basic one, but also one that is often forgotten by both novice and seasoned researchers alike.

What does all this mean at a more down-to-earth or practical level? First and most simply, people matter. Thus, the focus needs to remain on individual actors: again, what choices people make and what actions they take matter. I examine cases of individual choices made in Japan, South Korea, Taiwan, China, and North Korea that have had—and continue to have—far-reaching economic, political, and social effects. Yet one must take a step back from the actors; one cannot, in other words, ignore all those factors and forces that go into shaping an individual's attitudes, perceptions, values, and beliefs. The cultural and social milieu in which people act and interact also matters. Nor can one ignore the institutional and structural context within which individual decisions are made. To quote Karl Marx ([1852] 2008), "men make their own history, but they do not make it as they please; they do not make it under self-selected circumstances, but under circumstances existing already, given and transmitted from the past" (p. 15). The already existing circumstances, to repeat, may refer to institutions or to large-scale or macrolevel structures. Macrostructures, such as the system of global capitalism, are undeniably powerful forces in the world.

Structures both enable and constrain: they can give actors more power, or they can erect huge obstacles to the effective exercise of **agency**. As an example, consider how the dynamics and "needs" of global capitalism in the early postwar period might have opened up opportunities for Japan, South Korea, and Taiwan that helped pave the way for their rapid economic ascent. One would, in this regard, be foolish to ignore the structural processes that made East Asia's upward mobility possible (or at least more possible). I have much more to say on this issue in the next chapter. For my present purposes, the main point to remember is not merely that a reciprocal relationship exists between actors and structures, but that making sense of this relationship requires observers and researchers, as Little (2005) asserts, to "embrace the point that individuals are bearers of social structures and causes" (p. 10).

Summing Up and Breaking Down the Constructed Actor

The two words in the term *constructed actor* carry a great deal of meaning. In the model in this book, to repeat, actors have agency, which means that they have a capacity to operate independently of the determining constraints of institutions and larger social structures. Still, actors are not free-floating entities. They are, to a significant extent, weighed down by a range of social constructs, which directly and indirectly delimit the choices available to them as actors. Even more, actors themselves are "constructed." That is, their decisions and actions reflect—often quite deeply and even unknowingly—powerful cultural, institutional, and structural forces, forces that literally shape their very identities. Both the structured circumstances of choice and actors' identities, I should reemphasize, can vary widely across time and space. More simply, who actors are and what they can (or cannot) do differs from period to period and from place to place. These ideas may be little more than common sense, but they have important theoretical implications. In particular, they likely suggest a great deal of contingency and variability in any social, economic, or political process. And this contingency and variability suggests, in turn, that one needs to be very cautious in putting forth generic or ahistorical explanations of economic (or political or social) change and continuity.

I realize the foregoing discussion is probably much too abstract to make a whole lot of sense right now. As I proceed throughout the book, however, I intend to apply the constructed actor model to the various issues I explore, beginning in Chapter 2, with the economic rise of East Asia (Japan, South Korea, and Taiwan). These demonstrations of its use makes the constructed actor model more concrete and more understandable. At the same time, my intention is not to provide a full-blown theoretical and empirical account for each of these topics. One reason for not doing so is strictly practical: it would require a completely separate book or, at the very least, many separate chapters. A second and more important reason as I have already noted is heuristic. In other words, as with the discussion of the competing perspectives, the main goal is to enable readers new to the study of East Asian politics, economy, and society to learn how to theorize, or develop explanatory accounts, on their own. Accordingly, the application of the constructed actor model is, at times, far more suggestive than definitive. I provide avenues for exploration rather than complete explanatory maps. (Although, in the first application of the constructed actor model, in the following chapter, I provide a more detailed discussion.)

Studying East Asian Development: Methodological Pitfalls and Choices

Explaining change and continuity in East Asia requires more than a discussion and application of theory. One also needs to be cognizant of what researchers refer to as **method** or methodology. In the social and natural sciences, method is simply the procedures or techniques used to gather, evaluate, and analyze evidence. Despite this very basic definition, *method is vital*. In part, method provides the means for supporting and evaluating theoretical claims and arguments, which also means that it provides a basis for evaluating competing theoretical perspectives. Unfortunately, as with many terms in the social sciences, the word *method* is also the subject of much debate and dispute, both philosophical and practical. The philosophical debate is diverse, but one strand centers on a number of related questions: Are humans capable of producing objective knowledge of the social world? If so, what is the most appropriate way to produce this knowledge? If not, what type of knowledge can be produced? These are important, albeit abstruse, questions, which are best and more appropriately examined elsewhere.[6] For immediate purposes, focusing on the practical—but no less contentious—side of the debate is more constructive, particularly the question, which method should researchers use? This question, too, is regrettably complex, but I simplify the issue in the discussion that follows by proposing a basic methodological "advice column" for novice researchers and students of East Asia. Before tackling that specific issue, however, addressing an important and related question would be useful: What are the pitfalls of using method poorly?

Problems of "Bad Method"

Too often, researchers make serious mistakes because they fail to consider even the most basic methodological principles. For example, both novice and seasoned researchers examining East Asian economic growth and industrialization face a strong temptation to *compare* Japan, South Korea, and Taiwan (comparing being a basic methodological strategy in the social sciences). This approach makes sense: after all, all three countries occupy a similar geographic space, all share certain political, social, and cultural characteristics, and—perhaps most importantly—all experienced a similar and similarly rapid process of industrialization and economic growth at about the same time. Since all three countries are "essentially similar," so the thinking goes, the natural assumption is that one can learn something by comparing them to one another. And one most certainly can. But the critical question is how to go about making this comparison. Should researchers focus only on the similarities? Should they assume that, once a similarity is found among the three countries, it must necessarily be causally significant? Some researchers, in fact, do both. They may look at the three East Asian countries and say, for instance, "Aha! They all have a Confucian heritage, and they all achieved rapid economic growth in the postwar period. So there must be something about **Confucianism** that explains their rapid economic rise."

   At first glance, concluding that an obvious similarity among the three countries is causally connected to their rapid economic rise seems reasonable. Unfortunately, a fundamental problem haunts this type of admittedly stylized, although not necessarily exaggerated, example. To wit, if all three countries also share a range of other similarities in addition to a shared Confucian heritage, how do researchers know which of the many similarities are causally significant and which are not? How do researchers know if any are? Even more, how can anyone tell if instead of a single similar factor mattering, a combination of similarities interacted in specific ways that led to rapid economic growth? More concretely, what if further analysis showed that each country also had a similar type of "**developmental state**," or that each is a major exporter, or that each has a generally homogenous population? Any of these similarities could be key, but based on the foregoing comparison, one does not and cannot know which ones. The reason is well known to methodologists. When comparing countries or other units of analysis that share a range of similarities—referred to as "most similar systems" (MSS)—a somewhat counterintuitive requirement must be met: the units must be different in at least a couple of respects. More specifically, a difference must exist with regard to the outcome (i.e., the dependent variable) one is trying to explain, and differences must exist with regard to the presumed cause (i.e., the independent variable). In methodological terms, the important point is that the characteristics the systems share can, in principle, be held constant or loosely controlled for and can therefore be considered irrelevant in explaining the particular social, political, or economic phenomenon that varies between or among the systems. Having controlled for a range of similarities, the researcher can focus on finding the significant dissimilarity (or set of dissimilarities) between or among the systems, which can be put forward as the causal factor or key independent variable. Failing to understand this principle results in bad comparisons.

Badly constructed comparisons, unfortunately, represent only one of many possible methodological problems. Another very common problem, especially among novice researchers, is shallow and **ahistorical analysis**. The example of Confucian culture can be used to illustrate this point, too. When the same careless observers I describe above look at Japan, Taiwan, and South Korea, they might notice only the fact that Confucian values are present in each society. From this observation, they may jump to the conclusion that Confucianism plays basically the same role in all three countries, or that it is similarly embedded in their economies, political systems, and various other institutions. More careful and astute observation, however, may reveal significant, even profound, differences in the role Confucianism plays in each society and in the effects it has. Danny Lam and Jeremy T. Paltiel (1994), for instance, provide a narrative that contradicts the conventional view. In particular, they argue that, in Taiwan, the embrace of Confucian orthodoxy is primarily found among the political elite and the owners of large-scale enterprises. In the rest of Taiwanese society, by contrast, Confucian values are not only far less important but are actively rejected. According to the authors, this rejection of Confucian values by ordinary Taiwanese—including owners of and workers in small-scale enterprises—has had important economic implications. As they explain it, "in their market-oriented behavior, small businesses are inspired by the heterodoxy of Taoism that calls on them to challenge the established order. Freed from the constraints of orthodoxy, small firms challenge segments of industry dominated by vulnerable large-scale enterprises, question the established order of brand name products, and 'pirate' know-how and technology" (p. 211). The end result, according to Lam and Paltiel, is a vibrant, hypercompetitive domestic economy—the basis for Taiwan's amazing economic ascendance.

I examine similar arguments more closely later. For now, just remember that, while Confucian values clearly can be found in Taiwan, only in-depth or on-the-ground analysis can reveal what role these values play within the Taiwanese society and economy. More generally, shallow and ahistorical analysis—that is, analysis that fails to examine, in depth and in detail, the substance of "Confucian" culture in specific historical, sociopolitical, and economic contexts—is likely to lead to unsupported and fully unwarranted generalizations and conclusions. Good historical analysis is a type of **qualitative method**.

Method as a Tool

I realize that the foregoing discussion likely raises as many questions as it answers, but the main point is straightforward: bad method necessarily leads to bad analysis and explanation. In explaining continuity and change (including rapid economic growth) in East Asia, then, the use of "good method" is essential. As I suggested at the outset, in the social sciences especially, identifying a good method, still less the best method, is not a simple matter. Researchers have a seemingly endless number of choices: statistical analysis, comparative historical research, analytical induction, ethnomethodology, framing analysis, content analysis, discourse analysis, the comparative method, and quasi-experimental design, to name just a few. Attempting to wade through the multitude of competing methods would be an overly complicated and probably pointless task for current purposes. Instead, to make this discussion more manageable and useful, I adopt an extremely simplified and pragmatic approach, one that begins with the assertion that methods are simply tools. As tools, some methods are clearly better suited to certain tasks or objectives than others, but a certain number of basic tools and techniques can be used effectively for a wide variety of tasks. I introduce in this chapter a few tools especially appropriate to a novice but also of importance to pretty much any project. Mastering the basic tools provides a foundation for more sophisticated and challenging methodological work later. With this in mind, here are three tools that readers can begin using right away, and which I use throughout this book:

- Descriptive statistics and other quantitative data
- Case-oriented comparisons
- Historical analysis

Descriptive Statistics

A common example of a descriptive statistic is the GDP growth rate, which provides important information about the average and relative performance of an economy and also allows one to discern major trends or patterns. Figure 1.2 was focused on a similar statistic: per capita GDP expressed in international dollars for various countries and selected years between 1950 and 2008. As noted above, these statistics allow one to easily discern that the relative economic performance of Taiwan and South Korea has been remarkable during this period. From these statistics, one also knows that the two countries have reached a level of national wealth that is on par with Western European countries, which, in a discussion of economic development, is a significant outcome. Descriptive statistics, in short, are extremely useful and often necessary to support assertions of fact. They are also widely and publicly available, especially for economic issues. However, understanding their limitations is equally important.

First, while they can indicate that something significant has happened or is happening, they offer little to no information about causes and effects. More concretely, descriptive statistics indicate that a country's economy is expanding at a rapid pace, but they cannot indicate *why*. This is a crucial point to keep in mind. Second, descriptive statistics are, in an important sense, very crude (albeit still useful) measures: they reduce complex social, political, and economic phenomena to a single number or a series of numbers. Third, statistics can be misused or misinterpreted, accidentally or on purpose, and they can be dangerous if not analyzed completely.[7] Fourth, sometimes statistics are subject to serious miscalculation. A particularly relevant example are estimates of China's GDP and the important debate over how to calculate it. Arvind Subramanian (2011), for example, argues that most estimates of China's GDP are far off the mark either because they use the market exchange rate to value goods and services or because they use the wrong starting point for PPP-based calculations. Correcting for these errors, Subramanian argues that China's GDP in 2010 was not $9.12 trillion as the World Bank estimated (or $10.1 trillion according to the **International Monetary Fund**, a pretty big discrepancy in itself), but $14.8 trillion. Subramanian also argues that Chinese officials have been complicit in this underestimation since "China likes to exaggerate its growth rate (to showcase its strength and dynamism) and simultaneously understate its level of GDP (being seen to be poor may have advantages internationally, such as not being expected to contribute financially to global institutions or global **public goods**)." Whether or not Subramanian is right, his warning underscores the care that must be taken when using statistics.

Can the limitations of descriptive statistics—and of quantitative data more generally—be overcome? The short answer is yes. Some scholars would say the best approach would be to use more sophisticated statistical analysis (inferential as opposed to descriptive statistics). While I agree that inferential statistics have their place, I argue that, for current purposes, a qualitative approach is a much better complement to descriptive statistics. Qualitative research, in general, eschews statistics and numbers for in-depth analysis of whole cases. Perhaps the best model of qualitative research is the case study, or case-oriented comparisons.

Case-Oriented Comparisons

Case-oriented comparisons are holistic comparisons of events, decisions, institutions, policies, outcomes, and the like that typically occur within a specific geographic space (e.g., a country). Many important and even essential reasons can be given for holistic case-based analysis. However, most important among them is that it allows one to deal with causal complexity (Ragin 1987), which might be defined as the combination and interaction of a bunch of different (and varying) conditions producing a specific outcome. Consider, on this point, the process of democratization. How does democratization happen? Is only one factor at play, or are numerous factors coming together in a particular time and place that lead to this type of political change? Almost certainly, the latter is true. And perhaps the best way to deal with that level of complexity is through analysis of cases "as a whole" (Rueschemeyer and Stephens 1997, p. 58). Examining cases as a whole allows researchers to take into account specific historical experiences, institutional and societal configurations, and cultural influences, as well as varying relationships of power at the domestic and transnational levels. The importance of all this will be become more apparent as I proceed, so for now, just keep in mind that case-oriented analysis is very different from variable-oriented or statistical analysis.

Comparing cases is equally important. Most basically, comparisons bring a critical disciplinary element to our analysis. Recall the example I used earlier about the supposed role of Confucianism in East Asia's rapid industrialization. If a researcher looks only at one country or case, say Japan, and concludes that Confucian values played a central and even primary role, assessing the validity of this conclusion is very difficult, if not impossible—that is, the researcher cannot know if the argument is right. By examining postwar Japan in relation to other cases, however, the researcher is immediately given a stronger basis for evaluation. Even the addition of just one more case study (Taiwan) allows the researcher to see that Confucian culture has not played the same role everywhere. The in-depth analysis of both countries and societies makes this conclusion possible by giving the researcher a more comprehensive and deeper (i.e., a qualitative) understanding of the individual cases.

"Comparing cases," however, does not always mean direct comparisons. In the example from the preceding paragraph, the researcher does not necessarily have to directly compare Japan to Taiwan; instead, the principal aim might be, say, to assess the impact of Confucian values on economic growth. To accomplish this goal, the researcher might first carefully examine the case of Japan in its own right. After completing the analysis of Japan, the researcher turns his or her attention to Taiwan, again looking at Taiwan as an individual case. Once the two case studies are complete, the researcher could compare the results of the analysis. Are the results similar or are there significant differences? What do the similarities or differences in results suggest about the relationship of Confucianism to economic growth? I realize that the distinction between directly comparing cases, on the one hand, and comparing results from individual case studies, on the other hand, may be confusing. The key point, however, is fairly simple: cases can be compared in several ways, and not all involve a direct comparison of Case A to Case B.

I could say much more about case-oriented comparative analysis, but I want to keep this discussion as uncomplicated as possible. Nonetheless, especially in light of the foregoing example, concluding this section with a brief overview of two basic approaches in comparative analysis would be useful. I have already introduced one, namely, the MSS design. Keep in mind, as I present these two strategies, that they underlie a lot of actual research, sometimes explicitly but often implicitly. Keep in mind, too, that awareness of the logical principles upon which comparison is based is crucial. Failing to do so generally results in "bad comparisons."

MSS design. To most easily understand the logic behind this approach, consider a set of identical twins. Identical twins obviously share an extremely wide range of genetic similarities, and they also typically share a range of social-environmental similarities, assuming they grow up in the same household. Thus, identical twins can be thought of as exemplars of MSS. Yet, as is frequently the case, identical twins will exhibit differences, both minor and major, over time and sometimes even at birth. When an observable and significant difference occurs between the twins (or MSS) such as illness or disease (e.g., arthritis, breast cancer, multiple sclerosis, or diabetes), the main task is to find out what factor or factors (the independent variable) might have caused one twin to develop the disease. In this real-world scenario, one can assume that the many similarities between the twins are irrelevant to the explanation; the similarities, in short, can be eliminated from the analysis (this is the same point I made earlier). Elimination of similarities allows for a more focused examination of the phenomenon or outcome the researcher is trying to explain.

As I suggested above, though, some studies of Japan, South Korea, and Taiwan are seriously flawed from a methodological standpoint because they assume the three countries are MSS but only search for similarities among the three. Does all this mean that the MSS design is unusable in studies of change and continuity in East Asia? The short answer is no. As I discuss and highlight in subsequent chapters, many opportunities exist in which an MSS design can be fruitfully used in a study of change and continuity in East Asia. One of these is the "within-case comparison" (which is a misnomer, since two cases are used). Briefly put, a within-case comparison takes the same basic unit but then divides it into two separate cases based on the added dimensions of time and change. Consider this example: Between 1948 and 1960, South Korean economic growth was anemic. From 1961 to 1987, by contrast, the country grew at a dramatically faster pace. These two timespans provide a near-ideal basis for an MSS comparison because of the strong "variance on the dependent variable" (that is, the outcome I am interested in explaining—the rate of economic growth—is very different between the two periods). The question then becomes, what else changed between the two periods? The answer to this question could go a long way toward providing an explanation for the country's economic transformation. Of course, I am not limited to just the single issue of economic development. Other important aspects of change and continuity can be found in South Korea and East Asia more generally, for which a comparison based on an MSS design could be extremely valuable.

Method of agreement. The method of agreement, which is a comparative strategy described first by John Stuart Mill in 1843 but still used today is very simple (see Mill [1843] 1967). It can be best understood through an example. Suppose a researcher is interested in explaining instances of successful mass uprising (the type that recently occurred in North Africa and the Middle East). Now consider this list of possible causes:

- Long-standing economic malaise with attendant problems (e.g., high unemployment and underemployment, low incomes, and pervasive poverty)
- Persistent and rising levels of socioeconomic inequality
- Emergence of strong, class-based identities in the working and middle classes
- Splits within the ruling elite
- Loss of international support
- Emergence of prodemocratic "mass culture"
- Increasing levels of urbanization, education, and social activism
- Aging dictator
- Weak military or independent military

The basic strategy in the method of agreement is to find commonalities among the cases under examination. Do any of the factors mentioned below appear in all cases? If so, the researcher can tentatively conclude that the common factors help to explain a common outcome. On the surface, this conclusion is reasonable, but the researcher needs to be very careful. As Charles Ragin (1987) points out, the method of agreement can lead to faulty empirical generalizations for two reasons. First, a cause-and-effect relationship cannot be firmly established. Second, "the method of agreement is completely incapacitated by multiple causation" (p. 37). For example, from the list of reasons above, a successful mass uprising may be the result of either Factor 5 or Factor 6, or the presence of Factor 5 or Factor 6 and a third contingent factor, such as an economic crisis or natural disaster.

The method of agreement is a popular method of comparison and is often used in comparisons—usually implicitly—of Japan, South Korea, and Taiwan. It is a viable substitute for the MSS design, but it should never be relied upon as an exclusive method of analysis for the reasons just stated in the preceding paragraph. Instead, the method of agreement might be best employed in conjunction with other methods or as a starting point of analysis.

Historical Analysis

Historical analysis begins with the premise that what happened in the past continues to affect what happens today. Even more, how and when things happened in the past—the sequence in which particular events unfolded, when specific institutions were first created, the historical timing of large-scale processes (such as capitalist industrialization), and so on—are often key to explaining contemporary outcomes and processes. Thus, to adequately explain East Asia's rapid economic ascent or the manner in which political change came to the region, one would likely have to know about the specific histories of each country. Why did Japan become the first non-Western nation to successfully industrialize in the late nineteenth century? Almost certainly, its industrialization had something to do with more than two centuries of centralized political rule and the bureaucratization and professionalization of the government structure—historical features that stayed largely in place in the postwar period. As a further issue of interest, why were South Korea and Taiwan able to reproduce Japan's economic success? Here, one might point to over four decades of Japanese colonial rule—a period of time in which the social, political, and economic landscapes of both countries were completely reconfigured by the Japanese. What role did the particular historical configuration of the Cold War rivalry between the United States and the Soviet Union play in the process? This question highlights the importance of timing: East Asia's postwar economic rise, some argue, is at least partly a function of the Cold War structure. On this point, consider what the end of the Cold War has meant for still-poor countries today.

Historical analysis requires the researcher to move well beyond a mere listing of historical events and processes. History, in this regard, cannot be treated as a static or dead set of facts. Nor is history simply a well of wisdom—an example of which can be found in the oft-quoted statement of George Santayana, "Those who cannot remember the past are condemned to repeat it." Historical analysis, instead, treats history as a process and as an integral part of the present. This approach, in turn, requires that a researcher adopt a long view, especially in the specific cases I address in this book. In other words, historical analysis compels examination of cases over long stretches of time, to trace how particular events or issues unfolded and how they influenced and shaped societies.

Conclusion

I have covered a lot of admittedly abstract, academic, and even abstruse material in this chapter. Some risk is involved in providing such a broad overview in a book meant for students engaged or interested in **area studies**, if only because those who want to learn about the specific history, politics, geography, culture, and so forth, of particular regions (such as East Asia) will be immediately bored or turned off by a long-winded discussion of concepts, theory, and method. But the risk is well worth taking, and even necessary, for reasons I have already made clear. Even more, a focused discussion of concepts, theory, and method will make the study of East Asia more interesting and stimulating, since it seamlessly leads those interested in East Asia to think more seriously about how to relate experiences in the region to broader events and processes throughout the world. It engenders more open and critical thinking about economics, politics, and social change and continuity in general. Ultimately, this deeper examination is my overarching goal.

Notes

1. In South Korea, each time a change in leadership occurred between 1948 and 1987, a new republic was declared; after the 1986 elections, however, this practice was abandoned.

2. Some examples of books on regionalism in East or Northeast Asia include *Cross Currents: Regionalism and Nationalism in Northeast Asia,* edited by Gi-wook Shin and Daniel Sneider (2007), *Regionalism and Globalization in East Asia: Politics, Security, and Economic Development* by Mark Beeson (2007), *Asia's New Regionalism* by Ellen Frost (2008), and *The Making of Northeast Asia* by Kent Calder and Min Ye (2010).

3. Some scholars go further and argue that the term *development* not only represents a "particular form of ethnocentricity [but] is also closely linked to racist theories" (Mehmet 1995, p. 90).

4. A better approach would, of course, be to come up with an alternative concept. But this task would be extremely difficult to accomplish. As Munck (1999) explains, "the language of development is all-pervasive . . . [and] consequently it is most difficult for alternative conceptions to break out of the prison of that language" (pp. 202–203). Indeed, Munck himself, while devoting an entire chapter to the possibilities of alternative conceptions, concludes by suggesting that the task ahead is "to *imagine* a postdevelopment era that avoids likewise the restrictions of modernism and the excesses of anti-modernism" (p. 208; emphasis added). In other words, he implicitly admits that a viable alternative to the concept of development does not exist.

5. According to one study, only 26 percent of Japanese and 30 percent of mainland Chinese considered themselves to be East Asian. On the other hand, 77 percent of Koreans thought of themselves as East Asian (cited in Ziltener 2007, p. 112).

6. One nicely balanced and fairly accessible discussion of the philosophical issues surrounding method in the social sciences can be found in Sayer (1992, see especially Chapter 2).

7. For a general discussion on the misuse of statistics, see Dodhia (2007).

2 From Poverty to Prosperity in One Generation: Explaining the Economic East Asian "Miracle"

The contours of East Asian economic growth and industrialization are generally well known. With only a few notable exceptions, most observers acknowledge that economic growth and industrialization in the three East Asian economies of Japan, Taiwan, and South Korea has been remarkable, even astounding. Among these observers is the **World Bank**, which published a major report in 1993 titled *The East Asian Miracle: Economic Growth and Public Policy.*[1] Although the World Bank included nine "high-performing Asian economies" in its definition of East Asia (Japan, Hong Kong, South Korea, Singapore, Taiwan, China, Indonesia, Malaysia, and Thailand), the Bank's analysis focuses on Japan, South Korea, and Taiwan. Looking back over the thirty-year period between 1960 and 1990 (the primary focus of the chapter being roughly 1945 to 1990), the World Bank underscored a number of important changes in the region in terms of (1) economic growth, (2) income equality, and (3) human welfare. Here are the basic assessments:

- *Economic growth.* Relative to other major regions in the world, the East Asian economies grew at a significantly faster pace between 1960 and 1990; real **GDP** per capita (real GDP is GDP adjusted for inflation) in East Asia grew roughly three times as fast as that in Latin America and South Asia, twenty-five times faster than sub-Saharan Africa, and more than twice as fast as the **Organisation for Economic Co-operation and Development (OECD)** average. Between 1960 and 1985, moreover, real per capita GDP more than quadrupled in Japan, Taiwan, and South Korea (World Bank 1993).
- *Income equality.* The World Bank report noted that Japan, Taiwan, and South Korea (as well as the other high-performing Asian economies) were the only economies in the world to have both high growth and declining income inequality between 1960 and 1980 (World Bank 1993).
- *Human welfare.* Rapidly increasing wealth and relative income equality also led to significant improvements in the major indicators of human

welfare. In all three East Asian countries, for example, life expectancy, access to education, literacy rates, and quality of individual health significantly increased (United Nations Development Programme 2009).[2]

Economic change, moreover, tends to lead to political and social changes, which certainly seems to have been the case in the three East Asian countries, a key topic of discussion for later chapters. For now, though, the focus is on the undeniable economic transformation of Japan, Taiwan, and South Korea. One should acknowledge at the outset, however, that over the past two decades or so (roughly 1990 to 2011), the region has experienced a number of serious economic difficulties—a different kind of change—beginning in 1990 with Japan's "lost decade" (a long-term period of economic malaise), moving next to the **Asian Financial Crisis** of 1997 (which had a particularly devastating impact on South Korea), and extending to the global financial crisis, which began in 2008. I discuss, in detail, the region's economic difficulties in Chapter 4. In this chapter, though, the goal is to examine, through competing perspectives and constructed actor approaches, the reasons for the East Asian economic "miracle." I begin with an examination of liberal explanations of East Asian growth.

Liberal Explanations of East Asian Growth

No single, liberal economic explanation exists for the growth seen in East Asia. Instead, a variety of theoretical positions have arisen, some of which can differ quite significantly from others, even with regard to some fairly basic assumptions, as is most evident in competing liberal views on the relationship between the **state** and markets, a very important issue that I explore shortly. For now, though, I focus on identifying those core features on which most liberal economic analysts agree. In this regard, a good place to start is with the market, and more specifically the free market. A market, in the most general sense, is any place where the sellers of a particular good or service can meet with the buyers of that good or service to conduct an exchange or transaction. A free market has the same basic arrangement but is conditioned on voluntary and unrestricted exchanges, including those between and among countries, in other words, international trade. A key assumption in the liberal view is that voluntary exchanges in free markets generally result in mutual benefit, whether between individuals or between countries. Murray N. Rothbard (2007) puts it this way: "Trade, or exchange, is engaged in precisely because both parties benefit; if they did not expect to gain, they would not agree to the exchange."

Applied to the issue of economic growth, liberal analysts agree that the functioning of markets ultimately determines the economic fate of countries. Thus, countries with underdeveloped or poorly functioning markets, or even worse, no viable markets at all, will achieve little or no sustainable economic change (i.e., growth or development on a long-term basis). They will almost certainly also lack the foundation for dynamic growth and economic transformation—that is, economic growth that is the product of constant improvements in efficiency and productivity. The focus on efficiency and productivity is important because, as a number of liberal economists have highlighted, nonmarket economies can often achieve impressive growth, even if only over the short term, by mobilizing **economic inputs**. The former Soviet Union and other **centrally planned** economies, including North Korea, are cases in point. Such growth, however, is strictly limited since the mobilization of, say, labor inputs is finite. That is, once the labor force is fully mobilized, additional labor input will be dictated by population growth (see Figure 2.1 for additional discussion). By contrast, countries with well-developed and generally free or open markets (the freer the better for liberal economists) do not depend only or primarily on inputs; instead, their growth is based on technological advances, managerial innovation, the more productive use of labor, and so on. This expansion is made

---

Figure 2.1 Miracle? What Miracle?

As late as the mid-1990s, not all liberal economists even agreed that East Asia's record of economic growth was particularly impressive. Nobel Prize–winning economist Paul Krugman, in particular, famously argued for the unremarkableness of East Asia's economic growth in "The Myth of Asia's Miracle" (1994). Krugman's argument centered on the issue of **total factor productivity** (**TFP**), which refers to the portion of output or production in an economy not caused by inputs. More to the point, TFP is taken as a measure of an economy's long-term technological improvement (although nontechnological variables, such as good weather, are also included in TFP). To Krugman, TFP is the key statistic for measuring the potential for sustained and dynamic economic progress. A lack of TFP growth, therefore, indicates a lack of such potential. TFP was the jumping-off point in Krugman's analysis. As he put it, "the newly industrializing countries of Asia, like the Soviet Union of the 1950s, have achieved rapid growth in large part through an astonishing mobilization of resources. Once one accounts for the role of rapidly growing inputs in these countries' growth, one finds little left to explain" (p. 70). Based on his analysis of TFP, Krugman foresaw a Soviet-style economic collapse among *all* the East Asian economies once the mobilization of resources could no longer be sustained, which, he suggested, was virtually a sure thing. The reason was clear to Krugman: since rapid economic growth in East Asia was based "largely on one-time changes in behavior that [could not] be repeated" (p. 71), once input growth leveled or fell off, economic growth would stall, if not go into free fall.

possible because exposure to market forces compels firms to constantly look for better, more efficient ways to produce goods in order to continue earning profits. If firms fail to innovate, to put it simply, they die.

The free market, in short, is the starting point for a virtuous economic circle. This assumption leads back to a key point: whatever their liberal stripe, most liberal economists agree that free markets and private enterprise—and not nonmarket actors, such as the state—are the one and only fulcrum of a growing and dynamic economy. If one applies this basic logic to East Asia, then, one can conclude that the region's rapid economic growth was necessarily and primarily the product of market-based economic policies. More specifically, the liberal view posits that East Asia's economic rise was the product of a basic set of interconnected economic policies, including:

- Integration of the domestic economies into international markets.
- Lowering or elimination of trade barriers and other forms of **protectionism**.
- Relatively limited state or government intervention in economic affairs (including no regulation of economic activity and attempts to overcome **market failures**).
- Elimination or reduction of barriers to market entry (so that new players—entrepreneurs, foreign or domestic corporations, and other economic actors—are free to move into any market).
- Creation of a stable **macroeconomic** environment.

Where Liberal Analysts Disagree

Despite broad consensus, liberal economists do not agree on everything. A main source of debate revolves around the question of what happens when a market experiences difficulties, such as a sustained downturn in consumption and investment (i.e., a recession). Some economists—especially those associated with **neoliberal** economic thought—argue that the market will always self-correct. In other words, while the free market can and does experience problems, the market process itself will automatically resolve these problems. No outside intervention is necessary to "get things back on track" (or, as an economist would put it, "to restore equilibrium"). In this view, self-correction or self-regulation works only when markets are left alone. Furthermore, any intervention in the market (e.g., a government-led policy to protect failing industries or to temporarily increase demand through a fiscal stimulus) is likely to exacerbate and prolong a recession or other economic difficulty. Other liberal economists, by contrast, argue that government-based macroeconomic policy can play a positive, even essential role in getting through economic difficulties. This contrast is epitomized in the disagreement between advocates of **Keynesianism** and proponents of **laissez-faire economics** today. This critical debate has been playing out for well over half a century in various forms, but it is one that need not occupy us here. The key point is that, in the debate between advocates of a laissez-faire approach and advocates of government intervention, a window was left open. The opening gave credence to the idea, among at least some liberal economists, that government intervention was not, by definition, always a bad thing for a market economy and free enterprise. This opening is reflected in what might be called the market-*friendly* explanation, which sharply contrasts with the market-*only* explanation as reflected in the principle of the self-regulating market.

Market-Friendly View

A major issue with the market-only view is that it is "aggressively deductive." This phrase means, in part, that the view begins with general principles that are not only assumed to be axiomatic (i.e., undeniable or irrefutable) but also timeless and virtually absolute regardless of particular social, institutional, or political contexts. If the facts on the ground do not comport with the general principles, the facts are essentially ignored or simply "assumed away." (See Figure 2.2 for examples of "aggressively deductive" market-only accounts.) Market-friendly views, on the other hand, are much more empirically grounded;

Figure 2.2 Market-Only Explanations of East Asian Economic Growth

For many decades, many economists who examined the rapid economic rise of East Asia were convinced that it could only be due to the region's capacity to conform to the principles of the free market. This view, for example, was plainly expressed by David Henderson (1997), previously a senior economist on President Ronald Reagan's Council of Economic Advisers, who wrote, "Contrary to much scholarly and popular opinion in the United States, the chief economic lesson of East Asia is not that judicious intervention by wise bureaucrats produces high rates of economic growth. Rather, the lesson of East Asia's success is that economic growth is due either to low government intervention or to reductions in government intervention" (p. 427). Edward Chen (1979), in a much more dated but even more absolute manner, asserted that state intervention was not only low or reduced but "largely absent." Instead, according to Chen, "what the state provided [was] simply a suitable environment for the entrepreneurs to perform their functions" (cited in Wade 1990, p. 2). Any real-world analysis of the East Asian economies, however, would clearly show that state intervention was pervasive and, in many instances, highly intrusive. Thus asserting the absence of state intervention requires "assuming away" inconvenient facts.

that is, they pay attention to what has actually happened in East Asia. Significantly, the World Bank—a traditional bastion of liberal economic theory and practice, led the way for market-friendly explanations of East Asian economic growth. In the World Bank's (1993) view, activist or interventionist governments or states can and do play important roles in the economy. Specifically, they can (1) provide the basis for macroeconomic stability, (2) generate higher levels of human capital formation, (3) encourage greater openness to international trade, and (4) nurture an environment that encourages private investment and competition. According to the Bank, each of these roles, moreover, is interrelated: "Effective policy in one dimension (such as human capital formation) improves the results from effective policies in others (such as openness or macro-economic stability)" (p. 85). From this perspective, the World Bank concludes, "The success of many economies in East Asia has been due to reinforcing policy feedbacks. No single policy has ensured success; strong and effective policies in all four critical areas, and over a sustained period, have been key" (p. 85).

From a methodological and empirical perspective, I should reemphasize that the World Bank's (1993) view is clearly informed by an analysis of what has actually been happening in the East Asian economies, at least at a general level. The Bank's view is not, in other words, based on axiomatic principles that could not be connected to empirical reality (such as the arguments by Henderson and Chen presented in Figure 2.2). This rejection of market-only views is evident in the Bank's discussion of market failures, which are a bane to many developing capitalist economies. One market failure common to newly industrializing, capitalist economies is clear: **information asymmetry**. For markets to function efficiently, information about prices of inputs and outputs needs to be conveyed to all market participants. If this information is not available to some market participants, then resources cannot be efficiently allocated. In mature economies, information asymmetry may exist, but the problem is fairly limited, as market participants tend to cooperate for self-interested reasons. The Bank recognizes, however, that "institutional arrangements for cooperation and information exchange in developing economies are weaker than in industrial economies, yet the need for these forms of coordination are undoubtedly greater" (p. 91). In such cases, state intervention often is necessary, as one sees in Japan, South Korea, and Taiwan. In each country, for example, the Bank argues that the government "helped establish and aggressively supported development banks and other financial **institutions**" to address the lack of coordination and cooperation in capital markets (p. 91).

This sort of intervention, however, can cause even bigger problems down the road: if firms cooperate too much, cooperative behavior may lead to collusion and **rent seeking**—even greater banes to newly industrializing economies. The solution, in the East Asian economies, was to combine cooperative behavior with state-guided competition, in a process the World Bank (1993) refers to as "creating contests." For example, to ensure firms would not collude with one another, the state developed "institutional **structures** in which firms competed for valued economic prizes, such as access to credit" (p. 93). The state also prohibited monopolies and set up relatively transparent criteria for "winning"— such as meeting export targets. Importantly, the World Bank also acknowledges that state-guided contests have the potential to create even better results than laissez-faire or "free play." The Bank explains:

> Organizing contests is a more complicated way to run an economy than relying on laissez-faire, just as organizing party games is more complicated than providing a level playing field and letting children do as they please. Laissez-faire and free play both work. *But a well-run contest, like a well-run party game, can generate even better results, by providing a focus for competition and inducing participants to cooperate as they compete.* (p. 94, Box 2.2; emphasis added)

Again, worth repeating is that the World Bank's (1993) argument, unlike unqualified market-only or laissez-faire arguments, has a firm empirical basis. More specifically, the Bank is describing, through a tacit comparative framework, what actually took place in Japan, South Korea, and Taiwan. The Bank's analysis is also clearly taking into account the specific institutional/historical contexts of capitalist industrialization in these three countries. The Bank, in short, uses case-oriented comparative and historical analysis. Also worth repeating is that the Bank in its account of East Asia's rapid economic ascent acknowledges that, at least in the early stages of industrialization, certain market processes needed assistance to get going, and that states are usually in the best position to provide the necessary "push." At the same time, the Bank implicitly rejects the view that states can effectively displace or replace the market mechanism. Indeed, "beyond these roles [the four listed above in the opening paragraph of this section]," the Bank asserts, "governments are likely to do more harm than good" (p. 84).

Export-Led Industrialization: Liberal Centerpiece of East Asian Growth

I would be remiss if I did not emphasize one last, but very important, element of most, if not all, liberal explanations of East Asian economic growth, namely, the strong emphasis on export promotion or an "outward-looking industrialization strategy." As William James, Seiji Naya, and Gerald Meier (1989) explain, outward-looking policies involved a decisive integration of East Asia's domestic economies into the world market. The benefits of this integration were manifold, but the overarching impact was to "set bounds on how far an economy can stray from the market. If an economy is subject to competition, the costs of supporting an inefficient industry and the strain this puts on the government budget are more readily apparent than they are in a closed and heavily protected market" (p. 19). Market-only explanations are apt to attribute the shift toward export-led growth as a natural or inevitable by-product of capitalist industrialization. If this shift does *not* occur, the culprit is easy to identify: the state. If, for example, a state protects the domestic market from imports (or foreign competition), local firms can sell their products at a much higher price than would otherwise be the case. In other words, they can benefit from economic rents and would have little incentive to compete internationally.

Followers of the market-friendly view, however, believe that domestic firms sometimes need to be pushed into international markets. Left to their own devices, many local manufacturers in East Asia would likely have preferred to remain insulated from international competition. By creating contests and otherwise motivating domestic firms to compete in international markets, the East Asian states oriented their national economies toward exports on a faster and more systematic basis, thus helping to ensure a high rate of economic growth.

Liberal Views:
Concluding Remarks and Methodological Reminders

Obviously, in this brief overview, I cannot do justice to the full range and complexity of liberal economic arguments on rapid economic growth in East Asia. Still, I have presented large enough slices to get a good sense of the basic principles and basic approaches. The liberal economic focus on markets not only is clear but also cannot be ignored. *Markets matter.* This admittedly banal statement is one worth highlighting. At the same time, as has been revealed in debates among liberal economists themselves, the relationship between markets and states can be and is quite complex, interactive, and mutually beneficial, rather than unequivocally antithetical. This point is important to keep in mind as we move into the next section.

Something worth remembering is that the better analyses of market-state relations are based on concrete, empirical analysis and in-depth, often comparatively oriented research on the East Asian economies. The weakest liberal arguments, by contrast, ignore inconvenient facts and fail to engage in the type of on-the-ground research that can identify and properly evaluate key differences and similarities between and among East Asian economies, or between the East Asian economies and other economies around the world. A perfect example of this flawed analysis is the argument propounded by Krugman (discussed in Figure 2.1), who asserted that the record of East Asian economic growth,[3] while impressive at a superficial level, was essentially no different from the short-lived economic achievements of the former Soviet Union, which endured decades of economic malaise and deterioration after reaching an economic high point around 1970. Krugman's analysis, however, was essentially based on a single set of aggregate and largely abstract statistics (i.e., total factor productivity [TFP]). On that basis alone, he asserted that he could find essentially no meaningful difference between the Soviet Union and the East Asian economies. This conclusion was and is absurd. Even the most cursory case-based (and historically oriented) research would have easily uncovered major differences between what happened in the Soviet Union and what was happening in the capitalist economies of East Asia. Looking inside South Korea, Taiwan, and Japan—and especially looking inside specific industries and firms—would have immediately revealed that much innovation and technological progress were going on. To fully understand East Asia's remarkable record of industrial growth, however, one also needs to look inside the state. Or, at least, this is what other scholars suggest. These scholars recommend, more specifically, that one understand what made the East Asian states distinctive—different from most other states around the world, and especially different from other states in the so-called developing world. Reaching for this understanding is the starting point for the second competing perspective, the statist (or institutional) explanation.

State and Economic Growth in East Asia

To begin, one must recognize that statist scholars do not reject the productive power and efficiency of markets. Indeed, perhaps all would agree that integration into international markets is necessary to achieve sustained economic growth and industrialization. In this respect, statists would fully agree with liberals in rejecting the idea that inward-looking policies by themselves, such as **import-substitution industrialization (ISI)**, are a viable way to achieve sustained economic growth. (At the same time, statists recognize that ISI in conjunction with or as precursor to outward-looking strategies can be a very effective economic strategy, a point I return to shortly.) The statist view also accepts liberal injunctions against rigid central planning and **autarky**, such as North Korea's policy of *juche* (which is discussed in Chapter 4). Again, many liberal economists—particularly those who have examined the East Asian cases in depth—acknowledge that states can and do play important and beneficial roles in market economies.

What, then, is the key difference between liberal and statist views? Unfortunately, this question can be answered in no single way, for just as liberal economists disagree on key issues, so do statist scholars. At a general level, however, one can identify one basic difference: in the liberal view, as has been mentioned before, the market is always at the center of the analysis. One less-than-obvious assumption underlying this market-centered view is that a clear and real separation of economics from politics can and should be achieved. In other words, the liberal economist's assumption is that markets can operate in isolation from political processes. Statist scholars categorically reject this assumption. Instead, they assert that politics (defined in terms of power) is necessarily part of market processes and of the larger economy. The statist perspective, in short, is a quintessential political economy approach. And, in this view, states ipso facto play a central and necessary role. Many statist scholars, moreover, argue that the state's role is becoming increasingly more important "because of the radically altered environment in which national economies now operate" (Weiss and Hobson 1995, p. 135). This new environment is more integrated, more competitive, and more unequal than ever before, and, as a result, most national economies face challenges that only highly capable states are equipped to overcome. This disparity in ability among states is an important point of departure.

States and Markets in an Unequal World

In the real world, extreme inequality in terms of economic and military power is not only the rule but also perhaps an unavoidable "fact of international life." To put it more simply, there are advanced and very powerful countries—with well-developed economies, strong industries, and formidable military forces—and there are weak and industrially "backward" countries (and everything in between). Those countries with the most advanced market economies have a decided advantage over everyone else. Because their industries are more productive and economically competitive, the countries can easily dominate ostensibly free or open markets and international trade. If their economic interests and privileges are threatened, moreover, powerful countries can use their military and political power to protect their privileges by unilaterally imposing protectionist policies or by subsidizing their own industries. (Figure 2.3 provides a different and metaphorical perspective on this issue.) Importantly, the effects of this disparity are also keenly felt within weaker countries, as their domestic economies are often taken over and controlled by foreign corporations and capital and flooded with foreign goods. To the extent that weaker countries can develop their own industrial base—via an "organic" or entirely market-based process—it is invariably limited to unsophisticated, low value-added, and industrially backward commodity production.

In the grindingly harsh competition of an extremely uneven but "free" market, to put it in slightly different terms, weak and late-industrializing economies have little chance in making significant progress. This handicap is especially true because stronger states, including those presiding over the wealthiest economies, rarely stand on the sidelines of international economic competition completely. State intervention, in short, has always been (and will likely always be) the norm. For poorer, late-industrializing economies, state support is not an option but an absolute requirement. More specifically, interventionist states are necessary to provide space for domestic firms to emerge, survive, and develop. These states can provide crucial assistance in a number of ways. One prominent statist scholar, Alice Amsden (1989), explains:

Figure 2.3 The Level Playing Field: The Liberal Fallacy

Liberal economists often argue that the best way to ensure free and fair competition in international trade—and the best way to promote continued economic growth for all—is to create a level playing field. A former director-general of the World Trade Organization (WTO), for example, Pascal Lamy, was quite open on this point. As he put it, "the WTO provides a forum for negotiating agreements aimed at reducing obstacles to international trade and ensuring a level playing field for all, thus contributing to economic growth and development" (WTO 2013). In the **mercantilist** (or statist) view, however, a "level playing field" only contributes to the economic growth and development of the strongest economies. Why? Using the same sporting metaphor, the reason is clear to see. Think of it this way: The United States is the New York Yankees, an extraordinarily well-funded team with the world's best players. The Yankees' competitor is not another major league team but instead a bunch of Little League players, who represent poorer, "underdeveloped" countries. The playing field is level, the rules are the same, but the outcome of the game is predetermined: the Yankees will win every single game. Even more, if the Yankees' chance of winning is threatened, the team has the capacity to "rig" the game, since it has resources and connections unavailable to its competitors. Thus, the only way the Little League players can win is if the playing field is heavily tilted in their favor, if the rules give them huge advantages vis-à-vis the Yankees. In practice, then, for poorer countries to win they must *refuse* to play by the established rules of the game.

Countries with low productivity require low interest rates to stimulate investment, and high interest rates to induce people to save. They need undervalued exchange rates to boost exports, and overvalued exchange rates to minimize the cost of foreign debt repayment and imports. . . . They must protect their new industries from foreign competition, but they require free trade to meet their import needs. They crave stability to grow, to keep their capital at home, and to direct their investment toward long-term ventures. (p. 13)

Types of States: Predatory and Developmental

From the statist view, however, few states, in practice, actually have the required qualities and motivation to play such a role, partially because of the relationship states have with their societies. States that are "captured" or controlled by dominant social actors, for example, become little more than vehicles that the rich and powerful use to pursue and maximize their own narrow economic interests (i.e., a **plutocracy**). The result is typically an unbalanced, heavily monopolized, and static national economy. But "strong" and autonomous states are not necessarily any better. Indeed, within many such states, the political leadership, such as it is, often uses its power to "prey on its citizenry, terrorizing them, despoiling their common patrimony, and providing little in the way of services in return" (Evans 1995, p. 45). Such entities are best referred to as **predatory states**. States become predatory, according to Peter Evans (1995), not only because the leaders of a strong and autonomous state have the coercive means to dominate their society, but also because they do not need cooperation from social actors—including private business—to maintain their positions of political privilege. A state may not need to cooperate with societal actors for several reasons. The leaders of a predatory state, for instance, may have control over a valuable natural resource, which provides them all the funds they need to achieve their goals. Similarly, political leaders might maintain direct state control over the major enterprises and factories within the domestic economy; although not a recipe for economic dynamism, their dominance does allow state leaders access to the economic resources they need to maintain political control.

In contrast to the predatory state is the **developmental state**. According to Evans (1995) and others, developmental states represent an uncommon, but certainly not unique, combination of bureaucratic competence and coherence, autonomy from social forces, and "embeddedness" in society. The notion of an embedded state is key: it suggests that states are connected to or linked to their societies in a meaningful and mutually beneficial way. Evans refers to this combination of state autonomy and state-society linkage as "embedded autonomy." While embedded autonomy is an important concept, for present purposes explaining it fully is not necessary. Suffice it to say that most, even all, contemporary statist arguments acknowledge that the most dynamic economies generally require that state and societal actors be bound or linked together into a mutually beneficial and cooperative relationship. (I examine the developmental state throughout the rest of this section.)

Taken together, embedded autonomy and effective state intervention provide the necessary foundation—and the basic explanation—for the remarkable nature of economic change and transformation in East Asia (and, conversely, for the lack of economic progress in many other economies). This said, more detailed and in-depth arguments can be found in the statist literature. In fact, the existence of literally dozens of explanations means that I must be very selective of which ones I choose to discuss. The examination of the statist perspective needs to be kept at a fairly general level, focusing on representative accounts and on principles or features common to most of these arguments.

Proximate, Intermediate, and Deep Causes in the Statist Perspective

One representative argument in the statist perspective is offered by Robert Wade (1990), who advances a "governed market theory" of East Asian success. Wade explains his theory this way:

The governed market (GM) theory says that the superiority of East Asian economic performance is due in large measure to a combination of: (1) very high levels of productive investment, making for faster transfer of newer technologies into actual production; (2) more investment in certain key industries than would otherwise have occurred in the absence of government intervention; and (3) exposure of many industries to international competition, in foreign markets, if not at home. (p. 26)

On the surface, Wade's explanation seems almost the same as the liberal market-friendly approach. And, in fact, it is. Wade also suggests, however, that these three aforementioned factors are only proximate, rather than deep or intermediate, causes. To fully explain East Asian economic growth, one needs to dig deeper, which Wade does. At the next level of causation (the intermediate level), Wade identifies a coherent set of economic policies that enabled the East Asian governments to guide—or govern—market processes so as to produce different economic outcomes than would have occurred under a purely free market. Importantly, the development of a coherent and effective set of economic policies is premised on a particular set of political and institutional arrangements within the state, between the state and private enterprise, and between the state and society more generally. In other words, while policies are an important point of focus, their coherence and effectiveness depend on a range of other factors, which constitute the deep causes of East Asian economic success.

This third level of causation or explanation, however, is often taken for granted, or even ignored altogether. Yet it goes to the heart of the governed market theory, as well as other state-based or institutionalist theories. In Wade's view, the particular political arrangements of East Asia have provided the basis for effective market guidance. These political arrangements have two distinct features. First is the basic nature of the political regime itself. Most generally, the "basic nature of the regime" refers to whether it is democratic or **authoritarian**, but at a more specific level it refers to the manner in which the regime, whether democratic or authoritarian, is constituted. (Figure 2.4 provides a summary of the three levels of causation.)

This point takes the discussion back to the distinction between the developmental and predatory state—a distinction that hinges only partly on the question of democracy or authoritarianism. During the period of high growth, for example, both South Korea and Taiwan had authoritarian regimes (the most prominent authoritarian leaders were **Park Chung Hee** and **Chiang Kai-shek**, respectively). In many other countries, strong authoritarian states are unequivocally predatory, but this appeared not to be the case in South Korea or Taiwan. The question of why the authoritarian states of South Korea and Taiwan were not predatory is critical in the statist view. In postwar Japan, by contrast, the regime has always been democratically elected. Democracy makes state predation less likely, but it also decreases the prospect of establishing and maintaining a

Figure 2.4 Three Levels of Causation: Proximate, Intermediate, and Deep

	Proximate Causes	Intermediate Causes	Deep Causes
Simple Meaning	These are the "triggers" or the most salient causes of an event or process. Proximate causes may be planned or intended, or they may be accidental or unintended.	These may result from other factors or forces, but once created, they tend to "set the stage" for political, social, or economic change (they are triggered by proximate causes).	These are the basic or underlying forces or factors shaping events and processes over the long run; they are the starting point of a causal chain but also exert influence on a continual basis.
Examples	A specific state policy The sudden death of a leader A major economic crisis	Specific institutions or institutional arrangements A coherent set of economic policies	Long-standing historical processes that have shaped a society's economy, and its political, social, and cultural systems, and so on.

coherent set of economic policies over time. The Japanese state avoided instability of policies in part because of a remarkable degree of electoral consistency: one party—the **Liberal Democratic Party (LDP)**—essentially dominated the political system from 1958 to 1990. During this period, on only three occasions was the LDP unable to secure an absolute majority in the House of Representatives (December 1976, October 1979, and December 1983). In Japan's **parliamentary system**, the LDP's success not only meant that the party had firm control of the national government for virtually all of the early postwar period but also that it could govern in a relatively unfettered manner, at least compared to more competitive, multiparty democratic regimes. Chalmers Johnson (1995) refers to the Japanese situation as "soft authoritarianism." Understanding the basis for electoral consistency in the Japanese case is another important area of inquiry for statist scholars.

The second feature is the relation of interest groups (especially business interests and labor) to the state. In Japan, South Korea, and Taiwan, interest groups were often state sanctioned or co-opted into the regime in what political scientists refer to as a corporatist system.[4] "In corporatist systems," as Wade (1990) explains, "the state charters or creates a small number of interest groups, giving them a monopoly of representation of occupational interests in return for which it claims the right to monitor them in order to discourage the expression of 'narrow,' conflictual demands. The state is therefore able to shape the demands that are made upon it, and hence—in intention—maximize compliance and cooperation" (p. 27). This combination corporatist and authoritarian (or semiauthoritarian) political arrangement, Wade asserts, sets East Asia apart from most other regions and gave the East Asian economies a decided advantage.

Wade's focus on corporatist arrangements is not novel; in fact, he drew from a very extensive and much older literature that focused on Western Europe. In Europe, however, corporatist arrangements—with some notable exceptions—tended to be societally generated. In this environment, interest groups developed an important degree of autonomy or independence from the state at an early stage. Because of their initial autonomy, European interest groups could articulate effectively the interests of their members at the national level, allowing some societal groups to acquire a special status as the sole legitimate voice for their constituency (Pempel 1999, p. 37). Their relationship with the state, therefore, was relatively equal and reciprocal, rather than subordinate. This relationship suggests, more generally, that corporatist systems do not arise in a vacuum but are a product of particular historical circumstances and processes. In explaining the political and institutional foundations of East Asian economic growth, then, one must necessarily take seriously the influence of the region's specific historical context; one might call the specific historical context a "deep, deep" cause. On this point, taking a closer—albeit still broad—look at the historical basis of the East Asian states would lead to even more vital understanding, and most contemporary statist accounts do.

Historical Origins of the East Asian States

To fully appreciate the development of the East Asian states, one needs to go back at least to the mid-1800s, when Japan was first shoved onto the capitalist path. As mentioned in Chapter 1, political and economic continuity seemed to characterize Japan for many centuries during the **Tokugawa** era (1600–1868). This was no accident. As William Lockwood (1968) explains, "through strict controls on travel and trade, as well as over freedom of occupation and enterprise, the Tokugawa regime sought to suppress the growth of any new forces which might threaten the feudal-agrarian foundations of the state" (p. 5). E. Herbert Norman echoes this view. "This late feudalism," he notes, "represents one of the most conscious attempts in history to freeze society in a rigid hierarchical mold" (cited in Lockwood 1968, p. 5). One cannot possibly know how long this system could have survived had the West not intervened (see below)—but it certainly proved resilient, partly because the Tokugawa system was not as rigid as it ostensibly appeared. As Marius Jansen (2000) explains, a great deal of change actually did occur during the Tokugawa era, although outward forms of deference and authority—which remained intact—often masked the important changes in authority and society that were taking place. This "adaptive change," however, was gradual, evolving over very long stretches of time (recall that the Tokugawa era lasted for nearly three centuries). The important point, for current purposes, is that during the Tokugawa period, the essential features of a centralized and hierarchical state structure—although still not fully realized—became thoroughly embedded into the Japanese system.

The fall of the Tokugawa was precipitated by the expansion of Western power, which was brought home to Japan in 1853 when Matthew C. Perry's US naval fleet sailed into Edo Bay. Although Perry's visit was an outwardly peaceful one meant to establish trade relations between the United States and Japan, Perry was prepared to use force if his mission was refused by the Japanese—he even sent white flags to the Japanese negotiator indicating that, if his demands were not met, as Jansen (2000) describes it, Perry would "bring on a war that Japan would most assuredly lose, and in that case, the white flags of surrender would be useful" (p. 277). Perry's visit did not, by any means, bring an immediate end to the Tokugawa *bafuku*, but it did set in motion a host of far-reaching changes. There is literally much too much history here to cover adequately; suffice it to say, therefore, that the external pressures and threats of domination had a profound impact on the subsequent development of the Japanese state, polity, and economy. One of the main consequences was the acceleration and deepening of the centralization of the state, spurring "institutional innovation in order to build a modern nation-state, [which] involved the basic restructuring of society." "These developments," Jansen adds, "were important for Asian and in fact for world history because they brought a new and dynamic player [and the first non-Western one] onto the stage of nation-states" (p. 294).

The centralization of the Japanese state during the **Meiji** era in the context of what was perceived as an extremely threatening international environment cannot be underestimated. The foreign threat provided the justification for centralization and rapid industrialization; after all, to ensure its security, Japan needed to catch up with the West as quickly as possible. The centralization and the need for rapid industrialization, in turn, provided the basis for pushing through, at very high costs, the wrenching political, social, and economic changes Japan was required to endure to move from a feudal to an industrial-capitalist system. Japan's new leaders, moreover, were well aware of **mercantilist** principles and implicitly understood, in their view, that a free market approach was doomed to failure (Jansen 2000). For Japan's leaders, this realization had a crucial implication: the industrialization process could not simply be allowed to unfold in a "natural," bottom-up manner but had to be controlled in a top-down, hierarchical, and sometimes militaristic fashion. This approach did not necessarily result in "state capitalism," except at the very early stages of industrialization or in a few select industries (Lockwood 1968),[5] but it did mean that private enterprise was, from the very beginning, under the strong tutelage of the state. Not coincidentally, the newly industrializing Japanese economy came to be dominated by large, family-owned firms called *zaibatsu*, including Mitsui, Mitsubishi, Sumitomo, and Yasuda. While not purely creations of the state, the *zaibatsu* developed, according to Lockwood (1968), "as virtual partners of the State in establishing the industries essential to national power. Mining, metalworking, and large-scale transport all required large finan-cial resources and advanced technical know-how" (p. 562). Crucially, the eco-nomic influence and size of the *zaibatsu,* Lockwood adds, allowed them to become more than just tools of the state but also "makers of national policy, sharing privilege and authority with the military and civilian bureaucrats. . . . So close indeed was the affiliation of the State and big business that it was some-times difficult to tell where one left off and the other began" (p. 563). The close historical relationship between the state and big business, as is discussed later, would become a crucial element of the postwar economic environment, too.

One more related aspect of Meiji period industrialization needs to be high-lighted, and that is the exclusion of organized labor from the partnership between the state and big business. Given the close relationship between the state and big business, as well as the imperative for rapid, at-all-costs industrialization, un-surprisingly, labor—especially organized labor—was "subjected to systematic state and business repression" during the Meiji era (Pempel 1999, p. 38). The clearest manifestations of this oppression were the laws designed to limit political opposition to the **Meiji oligarchy** (e.g., Peace Preservation Law of 1894) and to restrict union movements (e.g., Public Order and Police Law of 1900). The Pub-lic Order and Police Law was promulgated by Prime Minister Yamagata Aritomo and specifically targeted organized labor movements. In addition to restrictions on freedom of speech, assembly, and association, for example, it also specifically prohibited workers from organizing and going on strike.

This very broad historical overview, to return to an earlier point, provides the essential context for the state-generated corporatist system that emerged in prewar Japan but which also extended, albeit in modified form, into the postwar period. More generally, an analysis of this period suggests that the political and institutional foundations of Japan are a product of powerful and quite specific historical forces. On this point, though, one should stress that these circum-stances are not unique to Japan. Indeed, one of the key impacts Japan's process of change had on other parts of Asia, especially East Asia, was the imposition of a similar set of political and institutional arrangements on the two Koreas, China, and Taiwan through Japan's foray into colonialism. Japan's attempts at imperialism could form the basis for yet another very long and detailed story,[6] but the gist is that the Meiji leaders not only implanted and institutionalized a similar political-economic system into its colonies as the one they built in Japan, but also—especially in the case of Korea—forcefully reshaped traditional, or long-standing, social and political relations (Peattie 1984). Japan, to it put more simply, introduced state-generated corporatism to the rest of East Asia, both as a practice and as an idea. In case it is not already apparent, I should emphasize that this corporatist model is the foundation—many might argue—for the de-velopmental state of the postwar period in Japan, Taiwan, and South Korea. In North Korea, too, the same basic model was adopted, but with very different results (a topic I return to later).

The Developmental State in East Asian Economic Growth

The developmental state remains the basis for most statist explanations of rapid economic growth and industrialization in East Asia. Accordingly, one should take a closer and more concrete look at just what the developmental state is. To make the task easier, I focus on an argument put forward by Linda Weiss in her 1998 book *The Myth of the Powerless State*. While I could present a number of other arguments here, Weiss provides an instructive and representative explanation that combines insights from a range of other influential studies that fall into the statist literature. These works include those by Chalmers Johnson (1982), Alice Amsden (1989), Robert Wade (1990), and Peter Evans (1995). Again, though, I only have space to present her argument in outline form.[7]

To begin, I must properly define the developmental state. Weiss (2000) notes that the term has become so loosely applied that it has lost its analytical meaning. As a corrective, she specifies three essential criteria upon which developmental states can be distinguished:

1. Their *priorities,* which Weiss refers to as "transformative goals, are aimed at enhancing the productive powers of the national economy, raising the investible surplus, and ultimately closing the technology gap between themselves and the most advanced industrialized countries.
2. Their *organizational arrangements* include a relatively insulated pilot agency in charge of that "transformative project," which in turn presupposes both an elite bureaucracy staffed by the best talent available, who are highly committed to the organization's objectives, and a supportive political system.
3. Their *institutional links* with organized economic actors entail the privileging of cooperative, rather than arm's-length relations. The locus of policy input, negotiation, and implementation is with sectors and industry associations rather than individual firms (Weiss 2000).

According to Weiss (2000), the criteria listed above are all necessary to an effective developmental state, but these criteria also suggest that the state, acting alone or by itself, is never sufficient to achieve rapid economic growth and technological progress. Consider the third criterion: institutional links between the state and organized economic actors. This criterion posits a specific type of state-society relationship, which is similar to, but also different from, the concept of corporatism discussed earlier. Indeed, Weiss (2000) differentiates her explanation—which can be more accurately classified as state-society, rather than statist—from older explanations in large part by focusing most strongly on the importance of these linkages. She suggests, more specifically, that what makes a developmental state work is the degree and quality of cooperation the state generates with societal actors, especially business firms. The types of cooperation, in Weiss's (2000) view, are manifold. They involve information sharing, negotiation and coordination of efforts on the content and implementation of policy, joint decisionmaking, and so on. In Japan, Taiwan, and South Korea, the mechanisms and channels for cooperation are dense and extensive. Consider Weiss's (1998) description of Japan (see Figure 2.5 for additional discussion of the Japanese Ministry of International Trade and Industry [MITI]):

> Japan boasts the most extensive set of institutional arrangements for reaching agreement between government and industry. The bureaucracy can count on more than 200 deliberating councils—forums for public-private cooperation on key policy issues. Of these, MITI [Ministry of International Trade and Industry] sponsors around twenty, which gives the ministry power of consultation and coordination with the private sector that is relatively smooth and rich in vital industry-related information. Arguably, there are more critical aspects of this joint decision-making arrangement. One is the highly systematized mode of continuous consultation between MITI officials and the Japanese scientific-technology community. Another is the prior informal process whereby government officials consult closely and extensively with industry experts about their products, technologies, and business environment. (pp. 55–56)

In Taiwan and South Korea, the evidence has shown, according to Weiss (1998), that "top-down, state-corporatist-style decision-making"—once thought to be the norm—was often quite interactive and collaborative, rather than dictatorial (p. 56). And, while top-down decisionmaking did take place, especially

---

Figure 2.5 Background on MITI

The Ministry of International Trade and Industry (MITI) was created in 1949 through the merger of the Trade Agency and the Ministry of Commerce and Industry. Originally, MITI was designed to coordinate international trade policy among various organizations in Japan, but it was also responsible for all domestic industries and businesses not specifically covered by other ministries. This range of responsibilities gave MITI tremendous influence within the Japanese economy. Indeed, some scholars note that MITI not only served as the architect of Japan's **industrial policy** but was also largely responsible for the country's rapid economic rise. Chalmers Johnson (1982), in particular, asserts that MITI's control over the foreign exchange budget "meant control of the entire economy. It was MITI that exercised this controlling power, and foreign currency allocations were to become its decisive tool for implementing industrial policy" (p. 25). Other scholars, especially mainstream economists, are very skeptical of this argument; they argue no bureaucratic organization is capable of supplementing the free market.

In 2001, MITI was reorganized, and its role was taken over by the newly created Ministry of Economy, Trade, and Industry (or METI).

in the early years of the regimes, Weiss (1998) asserts that the most effective plans were those in which private enterprises had been consulted beforehand. For example, the development of Taiwan's electronics industry was due to the existence of a "strong industrial association and a cooperative state" (Kuo 1995; cited in Weiss 1998, p. 57). In South Korea, a similar process unfolded with the establishment of a variety of industry-specific organizations and countrywide corporate organizations, such as the Federation of Korean Industries. All of this, however, raises an important question: Why are such institutional linkages important? Weiss (1998) provides a direct answer to the question. As she puts it, these connections are important, "in a nutshell, because they are about the state doing things not in isolation from the private sector, but in concertation with industry. In so far as public and private decision-makers get together to exchange information and to coordinate actions, information gaps are minimized and each generally ends up making better decisions than if trapped in isolation" (p. 58).

Weiss (1998), of course, provides a much fuller, much more detailed explanation of her argument, which I cannot reproduce here. Suffice it to say that, in her argument, she expects core similarities among the three East Asian economies—minimally, each must possess the key elements of the developmental state as defined above (see Figure 2.6 for a discussion of some methodological issues in Weiss's approach).

I have already discussed similarities in state-industry linkages, but Weiss (and many others) have made a similar case for systematic similarities in the other two areas. In terms of organizational arrangements, for example, government service has tended to attract the "best and brightest," or at least very talented individuals with extraordinarily high levels of esprit de corps. All three countries also established powerful, relatively insulated (but not isolated) economic pilot agencies responsible for coordinating and guiding economic activity on a national scale. In Japan, the lead agency was MITI (later replaced by the Ministry of Economy, Trade, and Industry [or METI] in 2001). South Korea and Taiwan had similar agencies: in South Korea, it was the Economic Planning Board (EPB), which was created in 1961 in the initial phases of the Park Chung Hee administration (in 1994, the EPB and another powerful agency, the Ministry of Finance, were merged into the Ministry of Finance and Economy or MOFE).[8] B.-K. Kim (1992) provides a description that dovetails almost perfectly with Weiss's argument:

> The strategic agency in Korea, the Economic Planning Board (EPB), decisively influences the overall national agenda. The presence or absence of these actors, as well as organizational character, largely explains the state's choice among possible policy alternatives. As a planner [for example], the EPB facilitated the change to export promotion. It commanded diverse resources and controlled crucial junctures in policy processes to bring secondary ministries into a common policy framework. The agency strengthened policy coherence;

Figure 2.6 Methodological Issues

As mentioned in Chapter 1, an analytic **method** that just shows similarities among three generally similar systems or most similar systems (MSS) is problematic at best, especially when no significant variance appears when scrutinizing either the **dependent** or the presumed **independent variable**. Weiss (1998) seems to recognize this fact, so, while she clearly argues that the similarities among the East Asian cases are causally significant, she does not attempt a direct MSS comparison. To buttress her case from a methodological standpoint, Weiss makes use of a number of relatively cursory but still instructive comparisons using a different region. For example, she compares the East Asian cases to the "second-generation NICs [newly industrializing countries]" of Southeast Asia: Thailand, Malaysia, and Indonesia. In this comparison, Weiss notes, in the Southeast Asian cases, a "weakness of domestic institutions" resulted in greater vulnerability to international market forces (p. xiii). In addition to her look at Southeast Asian economies, Weiss also included a number of other, more sustained comparisons in her larger study. In particular, she focuses on a comparison with select European cases and assesses different types of state capacity: distributive, transformative (or developmental), and dual (a combination of the first two). Part of her argument hinges on the hypothesis that "transformative" states do better than "distributive" states in terms of international competition. But she also argues that, in the longer run, "dual" states are likely to do best.

---

eased resource mobilization; and flexibly and rapidly equipped Korea to guard her export edge. (pp. 199–200)

In Taiwan, the Council for Economic Planning and Development (CEPD) has played a similar role as MITI and the EPB. The CEPD was designed to promote comprehensive national economic development and, according to Weiss (1998), served a key role in integrating the leadership of individual ministries. In comparison to the EPB and MITI, however, the CEPD had the weakest institutional position, although as David Ashton (2002) describes, the CEPD was nonetheless an influential agency. "This powerful ministry," according to Ashton, "helps to generate the industrial strategy and ensures that other ministries fall in line to meet the objectives of the economic plans" (p. 132).

The organizational characteristics of the three East Asian economies are the key mechanisms of change in Weiss's (1998) framework. But the third element—the priorities or transformative goals underlying the "developmental state"—also play a crucial role. One needs to understand, however, that these priorities or goals are often the product of, or at least profoundly influenced by, the larger historical and geopolitical environment. Why were all three East Asian regimes so committed to achieving rapid economic growth and technological progress?

The specific reasons are varied, but overall, they almost certainly had to do with the historical experiences discussed above and a threatening, postwar international or geopolitical environment, especially for South Korea and Taiwan, in which East Asia was at the center of the Cold War conflict. In other words, in East Asia, national economic growth and industrialization were intertwined with the *security* of the state and country. Both became national imperatives, two sides of the same coin. As Meredith Woo-Cumings (1998) puts it, "anyone growing up in post-1949 Taiwan or postwar South Korea [draws on the same experience], namely the intense, emotional loathing of **communism** that was so successfully drilled into every school child, the constant drumbeat of admonition that national survival was contingent on economic development and military preparedness that demanded personal sacrifice" (pp. 335–336).[9] Even more, the leaders that created this dynamic could not escape it themselves: they not only had to be unwaveringly committed to transformative goals but had to achieve those goals to maintain their authority and legitimacy to rule. However, in Japan after World War II, the situation was not quite the same, but the LDP and economic bureaucracy still quite clearly conflated nationalism and rapid industrialization into an overarching national purpose (Gao 2002).

Essential Roles of the Developmental States: Reprise

I began this section on the statist perspective with a discussion of economic policy. Before moving on, I think returning to a more concrete discussion of the policy role that developmental states play in the process of late industrialization would be useful. A quick overview will suffice. In late-industrializing economies, as previously discussed, domestic firms suffer from a position of relative weakness and industrial backwardness. To compete successfully in international competition, therefore, domestic firms almost always require a competitive boost, which the developmental state must provide. This boost almost always begins with some form of **infant industry** protection, which involves protecting local firms and domestic markets from much stronger, more advanced international firms. Infant industry protection ensures local firms a captive market. To successfully break into international markets, however, domestic firms need a competitive edge, which the state can provide through subsidies, favorable tax policy, advantageous labor policies (such as a prohibition against worker organization and strikes), and other policies designed to reduce the costs of exports by lowering the costs of production. Breaking into international markets, however, is not enough: firms also need access to technology. Here, too, states can play an essential role by setting up rules for **foreign direct investment (FDI)**—requiring foreign firms, for example, to form joint ventures in which a transfer of technology is encouraged, even required. In addition, as the market-friendly liberal view highlights, states may be crucial in addressing a range of market failures. These four policy roles, however, might all come to naught if states cannot maintain a disciplinary role that could effectively complement or substitute for market-based competition. Discipline, many statist analysts suggest, is a hallmark of the developmental state (Amsden 1989).

The mélange of economic policies could easily lead to ineffectiveness and incoherence. Thus, another role that developmental states play is as a "strategic planner" for the economy as a whole. This role often involves **industrial targeting**—that is, identifying and then encouraging the growth and development of industrial sectors considered to be important for the future. Finally, to reiterate a key theme of this section, an overarching role of the developmental state is to build strong linkages with societal actors, especially business, so that the public and private sectors work collaboratively and cooperatively.

State, Societies, and Markets: Summing Up

As with the discussion of liberal views, the discussion here is incomplete. In particular, I have admittedly left out much of the empirical detail that makes state (or state-society) arguments so compelling. Unfortunately, omissions great and small are impossible to avoid given the intent of this book (i.e., to provide a comprehensive and wide-ranging examination of competing perspectives). I strongly encourage readers, therefore, to consult with the numerous studies I mentioned throughout this section. This said, I cannot resist summing up the statist (or state-society) view with the same sort of pithy statement I used to sum up liberal perspectives: *states matter.* More accurately, though, society and markets matter, and even more, the nature of their relationships to one another matters most. The strength of the statist/state-society perspective is in its close linking of theory with concrete practices. The East Asian states have played an undeniably central role in their respective economies, and, equally undeniable, this intervention has been designed to impact market processes and to give domestic firms a competitive advantage both at home and in the international markets. Observers of East Asia know all this because they can "see" it. That is, they can observe actual institutions, policies, and interactions (between bureaucratic agencies and market actors, for example).

These same observers also know that all three East Asian economies achieved a rate of sustained economic growth and industrialization that was, at the time, unmatched in history. Yet, as Wade (1990) correctly points out, in methodological and empirical terms, adequately isolating the causal impact of the developmental state has been difficult, if not impossible. "Serious direct evidence" is hard to come by because, to put it simply, too many variables are in play, leaving no completely reliable or foolproof way to control for them. The real world, unfortunately, is too empirically "messy." Thus, "faced with the manifold difficulties in determining the economic effects of government attempts to steer the market, we can use more indirect evidence to take the debate forward" (Wade 1990, p. 32). One way to do this, according to Wade, is to "establish the extent to which the key neoclassical growth conditions have been present over time: to what extent trade has been free, the exchange rate in equilibrium, the labor market competitive, and interest rates high enough to reflect the real scarcity of capital" (p. 32). If observers can demonstrate that none of these conditions were present (or that they were seriously distorted) due to state policies, then they have gone some way toward supporting the statist position. In practice, this is what many if not most statist/state-society studies have done. Admittedly, such an approach still leaves open space for debate and disagreement.

If the debate was strictly between liberals and statists, I might agree that both have parts of the story right, especially since some movement by both sides has been made toward the middle: in other words, some liberal economists, on the one hand, have recognized that states can play an important role in spurring economic growth and technological progress, and statist scholars have recognized that the relationship between states and markets (or among the state, market, and society) is more reciprocal than they first posited. But, as has been demonstrated, other perspectives are at odds with both these views. I turn to these other perspectives next.

Cultural Perspectives on Economic Growth and Industrialization in East Asia

For many people, cultural arguments make intuitive sense. After all, our values, beliefs, and attitudes—which are all elements of culture—undeniably affect our behavior in myriad ways, both big and small. And, if individual behavior is affected and shaped by certain values, beliefs, and attitudes, then suggesting that larger communities and even whole societies are similarly affected is not much of a leap. A number of prominent scholars agree. David Landes (2000), for instance, writes, "If we learn anything from the history of economic development, it is that culture makes almost all the difference. Witness the enterprise of expatriate minorities—the Chinese in East and Southeast Asia, Lebanese in West Africa, Jews and Calvinists throughout much of Europe, and so on" (p. 2). Landes is suggesting that the values, beliefs and attitudes (i.e., culture) of these "expatriate minorities" dictate or at least chart a path for their economic success in spite of very different political, social, and economic contexts. He is suggesting, in short, that culture is important—that it is an independent force in the world. Saying culture plays an important role in economic change, however, is not enough. To base an explanation of economic or political change and continuity on cultural factors, I need to be more specific with regard to just how culture matters, which means asking and answering the following types of questions: What exactly does culture do to shape the behavior of individuals and large groups? Is culture a primary and causal force—that is, does it emerge and develop on its own to bring about or stifle large-scale economic or political change? More basically, to continue, one needs to know what culture is. I will address each of these questions, but I must begin with the most basic: What is culture?

What Is Culture?

Culture can be defined in a number of abstract and complicated ways. But Kathleen Dahl (n.d.) provides a not-too-complicated, albeit general, definition: "Culture is a shared, learned, and symbolic system of values, ideas, beliefs, and practices that shapes and influences our perceptions and behavior—culture is an abstract 'mental blueprint' or 'mental code.'" This definition has a number of important implications, some obvious and some quite subtle. The key element I wish to highlight, however, is the following: culture is inherently subjective or, more accurately, intersubjective (which is just an abstruse way of saying the culture is collectively shared among a significant number of individuals). The inherent **intersubjectivity** of culture, by definition, means that culture is not a fixed, objective entity that can exist on its own, outside the realm of human consciousness. Put another way, the intersubjectivity of culture means that it is, in essence, an almost purely intangible force: it exists only inside a population's collective heads. And although certain physical manifestations of culture can be found (e.g., churches, temples, texts, and other artifacts), these only have cultural significance by virtue of the subjective meaning a person attaches to them. The subjectivity of culture means, in turn, that the values, ideas, beliefs, and practices of culture, in principle, are subject to significant, even wholesale change at a moment's notice. This is not to say that the wholesale redefining of culture is a common occurrence. It is not. But the possibility suggests that culture does not resist change as much as many people assume. Understanding this point is important: if culture itself can change, then the manner and extent to which it has an impact on or shapes a society can vary over time. In this view, too, one needs to be aware that what may be described, say, as "Japanese culture" is not an unvarying set of values that has remained unchanged for centuries, or even decades. Rather, the words are a convenient shorthand for describing a general set of values, beliefs, and practices that are, in reality, in a constant state of flux.

In a very similar vein, the intangible and malleable nature of culture also means that it is continuously subject to contestation and to numerous competing interpretations. For this reason, assuming that culture is uniform or homogenous across a society, much less across a range of societies, is almost always a serious mistake: to put it more simply, a single Muslim (or Christian or Confucian) *culture* does not exist; instead, one finds a multiplicity of Muslim (or Christian or Confucian) *cultures*. The "competing interpretations" of a society's culture, moreover, are often at odds with one another and with other cognitive, social, economic, and political forces. Importantly, this view of culture complicates the process of incorporating culture into an understanding of economic change and continuity, for rather than explaining how one unchanging and monolithic set of values, beliefs, and practices shapes economic activity within a given society, one now must deal with numerous "cultural sets," not only interacting with each other but also interacting with broader economic, political, and social forces.

Power of Culture: Culture as a "Binding Agent"

Despite the inherent subjectivity of culture, it can and does have objective effects, both at the individual level and at a much broader societal and even intersocietal level (that is, the objective effects of culture can be felt across societies and across the globe). At the individual level—as the definition above already asserts—culture "shapes and influences our perceptions and behavior" (Dahl n.d.). Individuals act in the ways they do, in part, because of what they believe, and the stronger their beliefs, the stronger the impact on their behavior. This personal tendency is a potentially powerful force, particularly when scaled up to include thousands, tens of thousands, or even hundreds of millions of people all acting on the basis of a shared understanding. Picture the following scenario: tens of millions of people all acting with a single purpose and an unshakeable conviction that what they are doing is "right" or necessary. *This is real power.* But, because of its malleable nature, this power is also one that can be manipulated or exploited by social, political, or economic actors for their own purposes. Some scholars focusing on culture, in fact, argue that the manipulation of culture by the political and economic elite has helped propel, or even been primarily responsible for, the remarkable economic achievements in East Asia.

Another way to see the power of culture is to consider the notion that it can act as, what Albert O. Hirschman (1958) labels, a critical "binding agent." That is, culture acts as a kind of catalytic glue that helps bind together all the underutilized and scattered resources that most late-industrializing economies possess but are otherwise unable to fully or fruitfully utilize.[10] (I should reemphasize that I am adopting the notion of culture as a binding agent as one of several representative examples of the cultural perspective, but it is neither the sole nor necessarily a dominant argument within the perspective. It is, however, a useful way of thinking about the significance of culture in economic and political processes.) As a binding agent, the impact of culture on East Asian economic growth is hard to ignore. Many observers of East Asian capitalism have noted, for instance, the extraordinarily high degree of social cohesiveness and organization that has undergirded the region's rapid economic ascent. To put it differently, economic success in East Asia has not been viewed as an individual effort, but as a consolidated collective effort. In Japan and South Korea, in particular, one could argue that almost the entire society and state apparatus in each country were bound together through culture in a unified endeavor to achieve national economic growth and industrialization as rapidly as possible. This notion is reflected in the once-popular phrases of "Japan, Inc." and "Korea, Inc.," both of which portray the countries as akin to giant corporations in which government, business, labor, and the entire society work hand in glove. While admittedly overblown (and oversimplified), this view does make the point that culture has played a not-insignificant role in East Asian capitalism.

At the same time, most contemporary culturalists would agree that culture, as Landes (2000) concisely puts it, "does not stand alone" (p. 3). In other words, cultural factors necessarily interact with a range of economic, political, and other social factors to produce specific outcomes, such as rapid economic growth or a moribund economic system, in specific places. This factor fits in, too, with the earlier point about the malleability and inherent intersubjectivity of culture: culture is both shaped by and shapes economic, political, institutional, and social processes. In this regard, culture might best be seen as a **mutually constitutive** force. That is, it has the power to "make something possible" (e.g., a market economy, a democratic political system, the state), but it is also made possible by the economic, political, and social systems in which it exists as an integral part.

With the foregoing discussion in mind, one is still left with an obvious question: How should culture be incorporated into analyses of East Asian capitalism? Not surprisingly, no one best way exists. However, one can find "bad ways" and "better ways."

Good and Bad Ways to Use Culture

The bad ways, I should mention, tend to treat culture—or East Asian culture—in an essentialist and essentially generic manner. (*Essentialist* means that a set of attributes can be described that are considered necessary to the identity and function of an entity, such as culture.) Thus, a "bad cultural argument" might begin with the assumption, for example, that a single, all-encompassing East Asian culture affects all East Asian societies and economies in exactly the same manner. Many casual observers, and even some scholars, have argued (albeit, often tacitly) that a centuries-old, unchanging, and monolithic Confucian culture has been responsible for East Asia's rapid economic ascendance in an almost mathematical manner: Confucian values plus capitalism equals rapid growth. Admittedly, I am oversimplifying to make my point. Still, I am not necessarily too far off. Consider the following quote from *Time* magazine writer Hannah Beech (2006):

> The East Asian economic miracle was built on a number of sturdy pillars: hard work, high savings rates and Confucian values—in particular, an almost fanatical belief in the value of education. And for years, Asia could rest easy in the knowledge that its school systems were producing the best and the brightest. Rising GDPs were proof, so were the calculus prodigies and engineers churned out by the millions.

Beech goes on to discuss the costs of East Asia's Confucian educational system, but in the passage above, she clearly assumes that a fixed set of Confucian values has had the same impact throughout East Asia. And she clearly assumes a direct and causal relationship between Confucian values (especially an almost "fanatical belief in the value of education") and East Asia's economic growth. Such arguments have an intuitive appeal, but they are wrong. They are wrong because, as good cultural arguments demonstrate, the relationship between culture and capitalism is contingent, fluid, and context dependent. Good cultural arguments are also deeply empirical in the sense that they are based on a close examination of the interaction between culture and social, political, and economic processes. And close-in case studies and in-depth historical analysis are typically required to interpret how the economy actually works (Hamilton 1998). Fortunately, a number of useful studies have been done along just these lines upon which one can draw, and one of which was briefly discussed in Chapter 1.

Culture and Organization in Taiwan's Market Economy

Gary Hamilton (1998) and others (Lam and Paltiel 1994; Shieh 1992) argue that state-centered and liberal explanations do a good job of explaining the general contours of East Asian economic growth and industrialization, but they fail to capture critical features of the process. Focusing on Taiwan, Hamilton (1998) puts it this way: it is "a little like the sound of one hand clapping. On the one hand, there is the government's effort to shape the economy, and on the other hand, there is the actual shape of the economy. Not knowing the latter, how can we assess the former?" (pp. 42–43). And if one looks carefully at the "shape" (or the industrial organization) of East Asia's economies, one immediately notices a number of potentially significant differences. One of the most salient differences is well known: in Japan and South Korea, huge business groups— the *keiretsu* in Japan and the *chaebol* in South Korea—dominate the economic landscape (see Figure 2.7 for a brief discussion of the *keiretsu* and *chaebol*). They "form the organizational centers of these economies, integrating most other smaller networks of firms into some form of direct or indirect association with these large networks" (p. 43). In Taiwan, by contrast, networks of small- and medium-size companies predominate; they are the heart and soul of the economy, not the few large business networks and big government enterprises that do exist.

The question then becomes, what is the basic reason for these very different organizational or industrial structures in East Asia? Admittedly, a big part of the answer clearly lies in politics. In Taiwan, as previously mentioned, the early postwar political elite (from the **Kuomintang** or **KMT**) were outsiders. They fled to Taiwan after the communist victory, and they used their command of economic resources to invest in basic industries (also referred to as upstream

Figure 2.7 *Keirestu* **and** *Chaebol:* **A Brief Discussion**

James Lincoln, Michael Gerlach, and Peggy Takahashi (1992) give one definition of the *keiretsu:*

> The *keiretsu* concept refers to clusters of interlinked Japanese firms and the specific ties that bind them. *Keiretsu* relations among industrial firms, financial institutions, and the individual managers and officials who staff them are distinguished by their long-term, personal, and reciprocal character. Once castigated as atavistic "feudal" structures imperiling the full modernization of an ascendant economy, *keiretsu* networks, like other institutions in Japanese economic life, are increasingly credited with conferring a key competitive advantage on Japan. (p. 561)

Importantly, this description suggests that the *keiretsu* have historical roots and are based on a mixture of economic and normative ties. Japan has six commonly recognized *keiretsu:* Mitsubishi, Mitsui, Sumitomo, Fuji, Sanwa, and Dai-ichi Kangyo.

Jones and SaKong (1980) define a *chaebol* as a family-controlled organization managed centrally through a holding company. Each *chaebol* typically began in a single industry during the first years after liberation from Japan in 1945 but gradually expanded into more and more industrial and service sectors, often unrelated to one another. In other words, the *chaebol* tended to be highly diversified conglomerates. In addition to their basic economic structure, the *chaebol* were also characterized as (1) holding an oligopolistic or monopolistic position in the marketplace, (2) having a close and privileged relationship with the government, (3) having a top-down, highly centralized decisionmaking structure, and (4) inculcating a strongly paternalistic management style (Kang 1996).

industries): steel, petroleum, power generation, and the like. The KMT leaders also intentionally blocked the formation of large, private sector enterprises, in part to undermine the economic power of the native Taiwanese. But politics does not explain everything. Neither does economics, especially when comparing Taiwan to South Korea and Japan, the latter two of which, to repeat, are dominated by large firms. On this point, consider a basic reason for encouraging large firms: **economies of scale**. A similar type of reason holds for the development of conglomerates (i.e., firms that operate in a variety of industries, usually related, but not necessarily so): **economies of scope**. Yet Taiwanese companies seemed to have eschewed both of these economic advantages in favor of "rampant entrepreneurism." In fact, according to Hamilton (1998), between 1966 and 1986, the number of reported firms in Taiwan increased by 315 percent, while the average size of a firm expanded by just 15 percent. This trend is almost exactly opposite of what happened in South Korea, where average firm size increased by 300 percent and firms grew in number by only 10 percent during the same period (Biggs 1988, cited in Hamilton 1998). In other words, while Koreans tended to jump aboard the biggest economic ships, Taiwanese tended to abandon the big ships in favor of much smaller ones. On a society-wide basis, this difference in approach has far-reaching economic implications.

If politics and economics offer incomplete answers, culture helps to fill the gaps. Actually, it does much more than that: it provides the basis for a comprehensive explanation. As Hamilton (1998) explains, "politicians and state officials build upon existing social patterns, and although they may work to restructure society, they do not start with blank slates. Political actors tacitly accept and take for granted the cultural milieu as well as the organization features of the societies and economies of which they are a part" (p. 69). In Taiwan, a critical part of the cultural milieu is family-based or familial networks, which exist both between family-controlled enterprises (interfamily networks) and within families (intrafamily networks). Hamilton asserts that the interaction of these networks within Taiwan's larger political and economic landscape goes a long way toward explaining the specific structure and dynamics of Taiwan's "market culture." His argument is quite detailed, but it boils down to two basic ideas.

First, firms in Taiwan reproduce family structures. The head of the household is the head of the firm, while family members are the core employees. If the firm prospers, the family will reinvest a good part of the profits in unrelated business ventures, which allows different family members to run different companies. Moreover, when the patriarch dies, the family's assets are divided by allocating separate enterprises to the surviving sons, each of whom attempts to expand his own firm as did the father (Hamilton and Biggart 1997). "In this way, the assets of a Chinese family are always considered divisible, control of the assets are always considered family business, and decisions (in normative terms) should be made in light of long-term family interests" (Hamilton and Biggart 1997, pp. 143–144).

Second, because of the economic inefficiencies and disadvantages that come from their relatively small firm size, Taiwanese firms form horizontal networks based on **guanxi**. Roughly translated, *guanxi* means "relationship," but the term is typically reserved for types of relationships that are bound by particular norms of reciprocity that extend beyond the family to locality, surname, school, and so on. Ultimately, *guanxi* is a type of culturally based trust that allows family-based firms to transcend the impersonal nature of market-based transactions and develop long-term, mutually beneficial relationships and networks with nonrelated firms. "Such guanxi networks," as Hamilton (1998) explains, "have several economic functions; they may be a source of investment capital or a means to organize the production and distribution of commodities. Whatever the economic purpose, the typical organization is the same. People who own or who at some time may own their own firms are linked into a network in which the norms of reciprocity take a concrete form of mutual indebtedness" (p. 63).

Confucianism in East Asian Growth: Cautionary Tales

While *guanxi* has been a keen focus of research among culturalists, other aspects of Taiwan's cultural milieu warrant attention as well. One interesting argument looks at the impact of Confucian values on Taiwan's market culture. Turning the conventional view on its head, however, Danny Lam and Jeremy Paltiel (1994), whose work was discussed in Chapter 1, argue that Confucian values have been largely rejected by mass Taiwanese society. In Taiwan, **Confucianism** is seen as an alien and imposed culture of the political elite, rather than as a culture of the people. Indeed, under Chiang Kai-shek and the KMT, a major effort was undertaken to suppress Taiwanese cultural expression (Winckler 1994) and to inculcate a **Han Chinese** identity among Taiwan's native population. To this end, the school curriculum was remade along nationalist lines: Mandarin was made the official language (punishments were meted out for the use of other languages, including the native Taiwanese language, **Hakka**); students were taught to "revere" Confucian ethics; and even major thoroughfares in Taipei were given names associated with traditional Confucian virtues (Dreyer 2003). Not surprisingly, such heavy-handed policies generated deep resentment among the indigenous Taiwanese population; they also engendered a countercultural and explicitly anti-Confucian movement that emphasized populist culture and religion: Taoism, Buddhism, and folk religion. Lam and Paltiel (1994) contend that this populist "counterculture"—and not the elite-based Confucian culture—had the greater influence on the development of Taiwan's distinctive market culture, including the proliferation of small-scale enterprises.

The logic of their argument is straightforward: the efforts by the elite to impose a Confucian orthodoxy in the "hearts and minds" of the Taiwanese people led to or reinforced widespread contempt and deep skepticism of the type of impersonal and hierarchal authority around which the state-imposed Confucian culture was based. The elite's actions not only had an impact on people's attitude toward the state, and the KMT more specifically, but they also shaped attitudes toward relations of authority within enterprises. Thus, as Lam and Paltiel argue, to fully understand the prevalence of small- and medium-sized enterprises in Taiwan, one must take account of the strong anti-Confucian bias among entrepreneurs and ordinary citizens. As they explain it:

> As a firm begins to expand beyond the family, hires more distantly related persons, and forms partnerships with friends and even "outsiders," tensions and cracks begin to appear in the organizational structure of the firm. The classical Confucian reaction to these tensions is for the firm's "patriarch" to begin to act much like the Emperor in the state by replacing strictly personal, face-to-face

loyalty with the more abstract loyalty of orthodoxy and punishing "unortho-
dox" or innovative behavior within the firm as "disloyalty," especially where
it involves nonfamily members. Patriarchal behavior in the firm typically exacerbates underlying factional tensions and leads talented and innovative individuals to vote with their feet and form their own firms. . . . The tendency
for talented individuals to exit larger firms as the firms' competitiveness declines partially explains why there is a large number of small-scale enterprises
in Taiwan. (p. 209)

More than encouraging the growth of an industrial structure dominated by
small-scale enterprises, Taiwan's strongly anti-Confucian bias helped to create
a freewheeling, hypercompetitive domestic economy based on "a high intensity
of competition between firms and pressure on all firms to improve their technology and products over time" (Lam and Paltiel 1994, p. 212). The end result
is clear: Taiwan has one of the strongest, most resilient economies in Asia and
the world. The underlying cultural strength of the Taiwanese economy, to reiterate, is not adherence to Confucianism but the opposite: the rejection of Confucian values, combined with the embrace of heterodox, primarily Taoist,
values. Lam and Paltiel (1994) go even further than this. They claim that where
Confucianism is strongest in Taiwan's economy—in the largest, often state-
owned firms—dynamism and entrepreneurism are weakest. In sum, they argue
that, in Taiwan, Confucianism has been a largely dysfunctional ideology insofar
as capitalist development is concerned.

I need to emphasize, in keeping with the basic precepts of the cultural approach, that "Confucianism" in East Asia has played decidedly different roles
in different sociopolitical contexts. I enclosed *Confucianism* in quotation marks
because just as culture does not stand alone, neither does any element of a society's culture. This fluidity in meaning has already been demonstrated in Taiwan, but even in societies where Confucian values have, arguably, been more
widely and popularly embraced (as in Japan and South Korea), a complex interaction, an ongoing dialectic, has been occurring between and among different
sets of values, practices, ideas, and processes (economic, political, institutional,
and social). In different terms, no single interpretation or essential understanding
can be found in Confucianism or any other set of values.

In Meiji and prewar Japan, for example, Confucian values were consciously co-opted and reshaped by the Meiji leadership, in part to provide an
ideological foundation for modernization. Beginning in the 1880s—after a short
period of experimentation with Western libertarian and individualistic values—
major "steps in the direction of tighter control of the schools and indoctrination
and training of the young to serve the interests of the state were taken" (Hane
1986, p. 104). Of course, one of the key interests of the state was rapid industrialization, which required a massive mobilization of new workers, extremely
harsh working conditions, low pay (in 1891, Japanese textile workers made only
one-tenth the wages of English workers and were even paid less than workers

in British-controlled India), and limited labor rights (see Hane 1986 for more details, especially pp. 144–150). To inculcate the "right" set of values for these conditions, an imperial rescript on education (signed by the emperor) was issued, which emphasized Confucian precepts of **filial piety**, loyalty, and harmony. Citizens were also told that their duty was to "advance the public good," which the Meiji government defined as building a "rich country and strong military" (Ornatowski 1996). I need to emphasize the specific context of these exhortations: in Meiji Japan, the emperor held an exalted, almost godlike position. Mikoso Hane (1986) explains, "The institution of the emperor constituted the main pillar of the Meiji political system. It was the single most effective [cultural] instrument employed by the ruling elite to retain their authority" (p. 184). Significantly, this instrument was another creation of the Meiji leadership. As Hane puts it, "the transformation of the imperial court from an empty institution, virtually unknown to the masses during the Tokugawa era, into an institution that claimed unquestioned, absolute sovereignty was one of the key achievements of the Meiji leader" (p. 184).

Confucian values were also embedded more directly into Japan's economy generally and into industrial relations more specifically. For example, in an effort to transfer the concepts of loyalty and filial piety directly into employer-worker relations, Japanese workers were portrayed as loyal subjects and subordinate family members, while capitalists were portrayed as masters, who were loving toward those below, but who commanded respect, authority, and obedience (Ornatowski 1996). But not just Confucian values played a role in this new market culture. Feudal relationships were also part of the mix, especially those based on Japan's centuries-old samurai culture, which was codified in **Bushido**, the "way of the warrior." The juxtaposition of Bushido and capitalism, on the surface, was contradictory. For, as Jansen (2000) explains, Bushido provided the justification for the pursuit of virtue to the exception of all else, including ordinary work or labor. At the same time, Bushido extolled extreme loyalty (absolute subordination of the samurai to his lord), extraordinary discipline, and absolute self-sacrifice. Indeed, the samurai are most famous for their supposed willingness to commit suicide through the excruciatingly painful act of self-immolation known as seppuku (or, hara-kiri—usually mispronounced as "harry-carry") at the mere word of their lord (Jansen 2000). Together with other elements of extant Japanese culture, the Meiji leaders crafted an ideology almost ideal to the demands and imperatives of capitalist industrialization for a country trying frantically to catch up as quickly as possible to the industrial leaders.

In South Korea, a similar pattern emerged, but within a very different time and context. As in Japan, however, state and business leaders in South Korea perceived an immense economic advantage in institutionalizing Confucian norms into the workplace and into the economy as a whole. For business leaders, in particular, Confucian values were seen as an instrument to strengthen their control over subordinates, "a control that the older managers considered as serving their own and their firm's material advantage" (Janelli and Yim 1999, p. 123). And while considerable debate has taken place about the significance of Confucian capitalism in South Korea recently,[11] a number of in-depth **ethnographic** studies of South Korean large enterprises, including one prominent *chaebol,* provide a large amount of evidence documenting the impact of Confucian values in South Korean market culture, including an insistence on a moral dimension in relations to participants in a commercial transaction, a strong degree of authoritarian paternalism within the workplace, and persistent efforts to impose a Confucian-based hierarchy (Janelli and Yim 1999; see also C. S. Kim 1992). But equally clear to these researchers was a strong and mutually reciprocal interplay between and among supposedly Confucian values, capitalist principles, and other embedded aspects of Korean culture (including shamanistic rituals), such that they had difficulty isolating specific Confucian traditions. I should point out, too, that while East Asian culture is generally associated with Asian religious traditions, in South Korea, Christianity has occupied a significant role in the society's cultural milieu for at least a century. In this view, any analysis of the relationship between Korean culture and capitalist industrialization would have to incorporate a discussion of Christianity.

Confucianism and Capitalism in East Asia: A Brief Conclusion

From the foregoing and very brief discussion of Confucianism and culture, one thing should be clear: despite outward similarities, significant cultural, institutional, and political differences can, in fact, be found among Japan, South Korea, and Taiwan, differences that, I should emphasize, can only be revealed through case-oriented, historical analysis. For this reason, simplistic or generic explanations that purport to explain East Asian economic growth by focusing on a certain set of values, such as Confucian norms, are clearly unwarranted. Furthermore, cultural analysis that attempts to examine a range of societies at once is almost always doomed to failure. At the same time, the cultural explanations I have presented do not directly address issues of causation. To a certain extent, this is to be expected. As I have repeatedly stressed, contemporary cultural accounts typically do not argue a direct one-to-one connection between cultural factors and complex outcomes such as economic growth and industrialization. Cultural accounts, instead, endeavor to establish the importance of cultural factors within specific contexts.

The Structural View: A Primer

Outside of academia, structural arguments tend to get a "bad rap." The perspective's bad reputation is based primarily on a seriously flawed understanding of a prominent theory within the structural perspective, Marxism. I do not have the space to explain the flaws in people's understanding of Marxism; instead, I can more usefully begin this discussion by differentiating the structural perspective from the three preceding perspectives. Perhaps the clearest difference revolves around the level and unit(s) of analysis. The liberal perspective focuses on the individual level and the individual actor, whose voluntary decisions to buy, sell, and invest, along with innumerable other individuals, spontaneously create and sustain markets—another focus of attention for liberals. Statist arguments, of course, center on the state itself but also look at state-market and state-society interactions. These interactions, however, all reflect a strong domestic-level focus. A broader dimension can be found in the statist view insofar as states interact with other states, but, even here, primary analytical attention is placed on states—and power differentials among states—and not the overarching system in which they exist (i.e., the international system). Finally, the cultural perspective emphasizes the mutually constitutive interaction between individuals and their surrounding environment. This surrounding environment may be local, national, international, or transnational (or a combination thereof); ultimately, however, the operating assumption is that individual cultures in specific contexts shape behavior and determine outcomes.

Structural perspectives, by contrast, typically begin at the system level. The "system" may be regional, international, or global. And while one can legitimately talk of spatially and temporally limited systems existing at a local level, in the structural view the systems of the greatest interest are those that transcend a single place and time. Structuralists, for example, are fond of talking about the overarching system of world or global capitalism. The key point is that systems are assumed to be integrated or interdependent wholes, which embody a complex set of relationships that determine, in large part, the various functions and degrees of freedom that individual units within the system have. Systems, moreover, have a defined structure, which are presumed to have an objective, as opposed to subjective, existence.

In examinations of world capitalism, to cite one prominent example, some structuralists (those who are labeled world-systems analysts) assert that the system of global capitalism is defined by a trimodal structure consisting of three semipermanent zones: the core, the semiperiphery, and the periphery. For now, the distinctions and relations among these three zones are not the main concern. Instead, this trimodal structure indicates, in a broad sense, how the system is organized—where the units (individual states, societies, social classes, etc.) "fit" into the system and how they are connected to one another. In this case, moreover, it also suggests a hierarchical organization: in a pyramidal fashion, the core sits on the top of structure, and units in the core enjoy privileges and opportunities largely denied to others: "Membership," as the American Express commercial aptly puts it, "has its privileges." In the middle is the semiperiphery and at the bottom is the periphery. Not surprisingly, the periphery is characterized by poverty, extreme dependence, and economic weakness. This dearth of resources at the bottom is part and parcel of the "system"; that is, the poverty and dependence of the periphery (in relation to the core and semiperiphery) is a function of how the system operates.

Importantly, structure helps explain both change and continuity. Since the structure is hierarchical and unequal, those countries in the periphery are clearly systematically disadvantaged. A change in their economic circumstances, then, is possible only under severely restricted or exceptional conditions. These conditions, moreover, may have little or nothing to do with the individual attributes of particular countries (their states, societies, economic systems, or culture), and much more to do with structural forces beyond their control. This realization provides a nice jumping-off point for an application of the structural approach to East Asia. To put it in the simplest terms, structuralists argue that East Asia's economic rise should be seen as a product of relationships within the system of global capitalism, and of the processes and dynamics that define this system.

East Asia and Global Capitalism

For a long time, many structural analysts firmly believed that the structure of global capitalism would prevent the East Asian economies—especially South Korea and Taiwan—from achieving much economic success. In this regard, some structuralists shared common ground with liberal skeptics, such as Paul Krugman. Writing in 1984, for example, Bruce Cumings (a devotee of world-systems theory) was fairly convinced that South Korea and Taiwan were on the brink of an economic collapse due to their inability to "break into the system of economic exchange at a point other than **comparative advantage** in labor, that is, in marketing, better technology, or better organization" (p. 35). Cumings also posited that the two countries would not keep ahead of poorer states and therefore would be shut out of the export game from both "above" (by the more technologically advanced economies) and "below" (by poorer countries with lower labor costs). Interestingly, the rationale in Cumings's argument was not significantly different, on the surface at least, from Krugman's liberal view. Both agreed that a lack of productivity gains and technological progress would doom South Korea and Taiwan (or the Asian economies more generally).

Cumings's pessimistic assessment for continued economic ascent on the part of South Korea and Taiwan was primarily based on his evaluation of regional- and world-systemic dynamics, which, as noted in the preceding paragraph, were inexorably "squeezing" these two economies from above and below. Cumings (1984) was particularly pessimistic about South Korea; he suggested that the country's serious economic dip in 1980 was a sign of impending failure (I should underscore here the danger of making conclusions based on a single year of economic data). His evaluation, of course, was way off the mark:

instead of collapsing, South Korea moved very rapidly ahead, particularly in terms of technological progress. Does Cumings's mistaken prediction mean that structural arguments, in general, are wrong? The short answer is an unequivocal "no," for one should have little doubt, as I explain shortly, that much of the early economic growth in South Korea, as well as in Japan and Taiwan, was based on outside processes and forces over which the individual East Asian countries had little to no control. In other words, their adherence to market principles, their developmental states, or their unique cultural characteristics did not put them on the path of economic growth; instead, they had an advantageous position in an emerging postwar system of world capitalism led by a new hegemon, the United States.

Before I get to this story, however, hearing how another prominent world-systems scholar, Giovanni Arrighi, described the economic ascent of East Asia would be useful. Writing about a dozen years after Cumings expressed his dire predictions, in 1996, Arrighi concluded that East Asia (he included Singapore in his analysis) had risen to the "epicenter of systemic processes of capital accumulation" and had made "major advances in the value-added and financial hierarchies of the capitalist world-economy" (p. 13). Arrighi also concluded that "East Asian capitalism [had] already gone far toward setting itself free from dependence on, and subordination to, US political and economic power" (p. 13).

US Hegemony and East Asia's Economic Ascent

In the structural view, pinpointing the source of East Asia's economic ascent— the United States—is not at all difficult. The United States provided East Asia with security, capital, and, perhaps most importantly, one-way access to its vast and growing domestic market in the first few decades of the postwar period. This policy was, as one writer put it, "magnanimous," especially with regard to Japan, a country against which the United States had just completed a vicious, hate-filled war (Ozawa 1993). Even more, Arrighi (1996) suggested, this magnanimous gesture made possible a structural transformation and upgrading of the Japanese economy, and "it was this phenomenal upgrading of the Japanese economy that became the main factor of the industrial expansion and economic integration of the entire East Asian region" (pp. 14–15). The role of the newly minted world power raises an obvious question: Why did the United States not only aid in the economic recovery of Japan and East Asia but also provide the means for the region as a whole to become a major economic player and future rival to the United States? The answer goes to the heart of the structural view.

To begin, one must recognize that in the early postwar period the United States was unquestionably the most powerful economic unit (i.e., the hegemon) in the world-capitalist system. US policymakers clearly understood the country's position, and they also understood that the smooth functioning of the world-system required that they fulfill certain functions. More specifically, as the system hegemon, the United States needed to ensure that several regional centers of industrial production and capital accumulation were spread throughout the world: capitalism, as a system, requires space for constant expansion. The space allows the process of capital accumulation and profit making to move forward. Take away this space, and capitalism will grind to a halt. Ironically, the logic of this argument was spelled out very clearly and very forcefully by President Dwight D. Eisenhower, during a press conference, of the "falling domino principle" in 1954. In his response to a reporter's question about the strategic importance of Indochina (viz., Vietnam), Eisenhower stated, in surprisingly candid terms, that the United States was ultimately fighting in Vietnam to protect Japan's "trading area" (2005 [1954], p. 383), which Japan needed for its long-term economic growth. This point bears repeating: the United States fought the war in Vietnam to protect Japan's trading areas!

On the surface, this claim makes no sense. Why would the United States engage in a costly, brutal war in a country few in the United States had ever heard of at the time to protect Japan's trading areas? From a world-systems perspective, though, one already knows the answer: the United States needed Japan to anchor capitalism in East Asia. On this point, however, I should emphasize that the United States did not originally choose Japan to play this role. Until the late 1940s, in fact, the United States had pinned its hopes on China. Consider, again, Eisenhower's "falling domino" speech: "Asia, after all, has already lost some 450 million of its people to the Communist dictatorship [in China] and we simply can't afford greater losses" (Eisenhower 2005 [1954], p. 383). Of course, the Chinese were not "lost"—they remained in China where they had always been—but the country had been lost (temporarily, as it turned out) to world capitalism. This so-called loss meant a replacement had to be found, and Japan was the only viable candidate. Indeed, fears of a communist victory—and the full onset of the Cold War—had compelled the United States to reverse course in Japan prior to 1949. To reiterate, initial US policy in Japan was not designed to resuscitate the Japanese economy, and while US policy was not necessarily punitive, from 1945–1946, the United States "leaned toward a strategy that would contradict Japan's comparative advantage. Japanese industry would be decentralized and scaled down through the break-up of the prewar monopolies and the forfeit of industrial reparations to its wartime Asian victims" (McCormick 1995, p. 57). Much more attention was given to political and social reforms designed to democratize Japan, thereby making the reemergence of militaristic and fascist leaders more difficult.

US policymakers soon realized, however, that an "impoverished and enfeebled Japan . . . would not serve America's strategic interests" (Allen 1981, p. 189). The solution was to rebuild and reindustrialize Japan as quickly as possible. This shift in policy was strongly advocated by George Kennan, then director of policy planning in the administration of Harry Truman. In a top-secret planning report, Kennan wrote,

Economic recovery should be made the prime objective of United States policy in Japan for the coming period. It should be sought through a combination
of a long-term U.S. aid program envisaging shipments and/or credits . . . and
by a vigorous and concerted effort by all interested agencies and departments
of the United States Government to cut away existing obstacles to the revival
of Japanese foreign trade and to facilitate the restoration and development of
Japan's exports. (as cited in US Department of State 1948, p. 694)

Kennan and others in the administration, including Dean Acheson, not only advocated the economic revival of Japan but also argued that achieving this goal
would require creating an economic hinterland for the Japanese (the hinterland
is what Eisenhower referred to as Japan's "trading areas"). Accomplishing this
goal meant reestablishing Japan's regional economic dominance—something
the Japanese fought so hard to attain in the first half of the twentieth century,
but which was now being handed to them on a silver platter.

To this end, the United States began pouring resources into Japan, aided in
no small measure by the "fortuitous" outbreak of the **Korean War** in June 1950.
Although the war ended in 1953, the US government continued to rely on Japan
for military equipment: by 1964, the United States had spent $7.2 billion in off-
shore procurements and other military expenditures in Japan. In addition, between 1950 and 1970, US aid to Japan averaged $500 million a year (Arrighi
1996). While the Korean War may have been, in the words of then Japanese
prime minister Yoshida Shigeru (in office 1948–1954), "a gift of the gods"
(cited in Stubbs 2005, p. 66), it was only one of many "gifts." Others included
a US-backed fixed exchange rate of ¥360 to the dollar, which made Japanese
exports much less expensive than would have been the case. In addition, against
European wishes, the United States forced European allies (Britain, in particular) to admit Japan to the General Agreement on Trade and Tariffs (GATT) and,
as noted earlier, allowed Japanese products virtually one-way access to US markets. Furthermore, US security guarantees for Japan also allowed the Japanese
government to funnel "all their resources and energies into an economic expan-
sionism that has brought affluence to Japan and taken its business to the farthest
reaches of the globe" (Schurmann 1974; cited in Arrighi et al. 2003, p. 301).

The notion that Japan's economic growth was premised on "gifts" is an apt
analogy, for world-systems scholars typically argue that Japan was "invited to
develop" by the system hegemon, the United States (Arrighi 1996; Cumings
1984; Wallerstein 1974). And, just as Japan was invited, so too were South
Korea and Taiwan. Their invitations came a little later, but they, too, were show-
ered with "gifts," including security guarantees, economic and military aid,
privileged access to US markets, and, especially in the case of South Korea,
military procurement benefits. (As a chief ally to the United States during the
Vietnam War, South Korea received US help in the development of its fledgling
electronics industry by being allowed to purchase military radios and radar [So
and Chiu 1995].) In fact, US military and economic aid to South Korea and Tai-

wan was even more than Japan received: between 1946 and 1978, South Korea alone received $13 billion and Taiwan $5.6 billion (Arrighi 1996).

Flying Geese and Snowballs: Integration of East Asian Capitalism

Theoretically speaking, however, "invitations" to develop and US "gifts" are hardly adequate to explain the sustained economic ascent of the three East Asian countries and their movement into the core or near-core (in the case of Taiwan and South Korea), for once the invitation is withdrawn—as started to happen as early as the late 1960s with an "over-accumulation crisis" in the United States (Arrighi 1996, p. 20)—the entire basis for economic growth would simply disappear unless other factors or mechanisms were in play. In the structural view, these other factors or mechanisms are relatively easy to discern. Most structural analyses agree on one of the key mechanisms of sustained East Asian economic ascent: the economic integration of the East Asian countries regionally, centered on Japan. This mechanism, structuralists are quick to point out, was not strictly a postwar development; instead, it originally emerged during the colonial period, when Japan forcibly drew the economies of Taiwan and South Korea into its economic orbit. This coerced integration set up a hierarchical relationship among the economies, which a Japanese economist, Akamatsu Kaname (1935), famously likened to a flying geese formation (*ganko keitai*). In the "flying geese" model, a specific division of labor is created whereby the dominant economy, the lead goose, relies on cheap labor in the follower economies to accelerate its industrial progress. However, the follower economies benefit as well by having access to resources to "upgrade" their industries.

The logic of the flying geese model is fairly simple: any given industry, as Cumings (1984) explains, experiences a general cycle of origin, rise, apogee, and decline (this idea is also based on the work of Raymond Vernon [1966] who developed the product life-cycle theory). In the first three stages, the lead economy first exploits its domestic economy and then exports the product to other markets; as long as it maintains a comparative and competitive advantage in production, it continues to manufacture the product at home. Over time, however, as the product becomes more standardized, other countries can manufacture the same product for their domestic markets and eventually for export: competition increases and profits decline (see also Kasahara 2004). At this point, a transfer of production of the product by the dominant economy to lower-cost areas (i.e., follower countries) makes sense. Cumings and others have asserted that this is exactly what happened in the prewar period, but also in the first few decades of the postwar period, especially after the United States explicitly and forcefully pursued a policy of regional reintegration beginning in the 1960s (Arrighi 1996; So and Chiu 1995). I return to this issue shortly.

Structuralists, I might note, have also used another metaphor to describe the regional pattern of economic growth and change in East Asia: snowballing

(Arrighi 1996; Arrighi et al. 2003; Ozawa 1993). In the snowballing model, Japan's expansion is seen as generating a process of "concatenated [linked together in a chain or series], labor-seeking rounds of investment that promoted and sustained a region-wide economic expansion" (Arrighi et al. 2003, p. 301). This model—which is represented in Figure 2.8 and includes the United States—shows how successive but descending flows of "labor-seeking investment from higher- to lower-income jurisdictions and ascending counter-flows of labor-intensive exports" have created a mutually reinforcing and expanding or snowballing ring of economic growth (Arrighi et al. 2003, p. 301). Arrighi and his colleagues (2003) refer to this pattern as regional space-of-flows. They further explain:

> [In this regional space-of-flows] labor-seeking investments mobilize the cheaper or more abundant labor supplies of lower-income locales to contain costs of production and consumption in higher-income locales, while labor-intensive

Figure 2.8 Snowballing Model of East Asian Industrialization

In the 1950s and 1960s, Japan sent labor-intensive exports to the United States. During this period, however, labor costs in Japan began to rise, which compelled Japanese companies to seek lower-cost labor in South Korea and Taiwan. This was the first phase in the snowballing model. The second phase occurred in the 1970s and 1980s, as South Korea and Taiwan also began to export labor-intensive goods to the United States. As in Japan, as labor costs in South Korea and Taiwan rose, firms producing in those two countries, including Japanese firms, sought lower-cost labor elsewhere. This led to a third round of labor-seeking investment by Japan, South Korea, and Taiwan in **ASEAN** economies. After China's transition to capitalism (beginning in the late-1970s), a new pool of low-cost labor was opened up, which led to a fresh round of labor-seeking investment on the part of all the Asian economies, plus the United States.

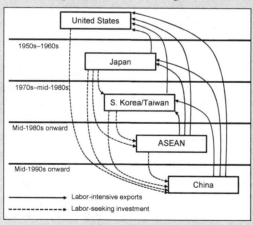

Source: Adapted from Arrighi (1996) and Ozawa (1993).

exports tap the wealthier or larger markets of higher-income locales to boost the prices fetched by the productive combinations of lower-income locales. (pp. 301–302)

Structuralists generally agree that this regional integration did not just happen fortuitously but reflected historical patterns, structural imperatives, and political intent. Politically and structurally, an important part of the regional process was based on US interests. The US effort at reintegration, in particular, was designed to ease the financial burden on the United States, a burden that was largely a product of its hegemonic role in the capitalist world-system. As Arrighi (1996) explains it, the US goal was to incorporate "Japanese business as an intermediary between US purchasing power and cheap Asian labor" (p. 19). The United States needed Japan to be a source of relatively cheap supplies, which were essential to ongoing US power pursuits both at home and abroad. "Were it not for the massive procurement of means of war and livelihood from Japanese sources at much lower costs than they could be obtained in the US or anywhere else," Arrighi argues, "the simultaneous escalation of US welfare expenditures at home and of warfare expenditures abroad of the 1960s would have been far more crippling financially than it already was" (p. 20). If US policy meant running a large trade deficit with Japan, as well as South Korea and Taiwan, then that was just the "cost of hegemony." The costs would be balanced out by even greater benefits, at least as long as the world-system as a whole was expanding and deepening.

Whichever model one uses, one thing is clear to structuralists: much of East Asia's economic ascent is due to regional integration, which was not a one-shot event; rather, it was (and is) an ongoing and expanding process. Consider, again, Figure 2.8: the snowballing effect shows the incorporation of Japan and then South Korea and Taiwan (plus Hong Kong and Singapore). But one can also see the incorporation of the ASEAN countries beginning in the mid-1980s—albeit on much less favorable terms compared to South Korea and Taiwan—and, since the 1990s, the fuller incorporation of China. This incorporation is part and parcel of the structural process. It reflects the dynamics and the demands of a system that must keep expanding to thrive and survive. This necessity suggests, however, that expansion may have limits, and once these limits are met, everything will begin to fall apart. On this point, only time will tell. For now, suffice it to say that signs of an impending breakdown are already appearing, as Japan's economic ascent began to stall in the 1990s and, twenty years later, at the time this textbook was published, has still failed to fully recover.

In the next section, I introduce the constructed actor model; in preparation, however, a quick review of the four major competing theories is in order. Rather than an extended discussion, see the summary table in Figure 2.9 for review.

Figure 2.9 Theories of Economic Change: A Summary

	Liberal	Statist	Cultural	Structural
Main theoretical proposition (example)	Self-interested actors' competition in a free market produces maximum allocative efficiency and economic growth.	For late-industrializing countries, state intervention is necessary to overcome the disadvantages of "lateness."	Culture acts as a binding agent; it brings together underutilized and scattered resources within an economy and society in a manner that promotes rapid industrialization.	National-level industrial growth is primarily a function of system-level forces and dynamics and of specific relationships between dominant and subordinate units.
Level of analysis	Micro/individual	Meso	Meso	Macro/system
Key actors or units	Self-interested market actors	States	Individuals and their societies	Social class
A basic lesson or insight	Markets and the decisions of individual market actors are fundamental to sustained and dynamic economic growth.	Huge disparities in national economic power and competitiveness make state intervention in markets necessary.	Subjective or intersubjective processes are essential in constituting market economies.	National economies do not exist in isolation; they must be understood to be part of an overarching system.

East Asia's Ascent:
Applying the Constructed Actor Model

Contemporary structuralists, such as Arrighi, are careful not to attribute everything to structure or to systemic imperatives and dynamics. They acknowledge that the state- and domestic-level institutions can and do play important roles in bringing about economic change. Consider, on this point, another basic reason Arrighi (1996) emphasizes to explain Japan's economic success: he argues that Japanese industry used regional reintegration to create a highly adaptive, highly flexible, and decentralized transnational production network that allowed it to gain a decisive competitive advantage over the United States and other advanced capitalist economies. Significantly, the model for this transnational production network was a decidedly domestic creation, namely, the *keiretsu*. The *keiretsu,* as discussed earlier, is a distinctive Japanese institution: a network of interconnected firms, revolving around a core company and many subcontracting enterprises, bound to one another by cross-shareholding, interlocking directorates, and other mechanisms. While considerable debate can be found about the efficacy of the *keiretsu* system (see, for example, Lincoln, Gerlach, and Ahmadjian 1996), Arrighi is convinced that the regional and transnational expansion of this system was key to Japan's success. He explains:

> Most important for our purposes, the Japanese multilayered subcontracting system [i.e., the *keiretsu*] has developed domestically and expanded transnationally in a close symbiotic relation with the abundant and highly competitive supply of labor of the Northeast and Southeast Asian region. *It is hardly conceivable that in the absence of such a symbiotic relation capital accumulation in Japan could have proceeded as fast as it has since 1960 without undermining, and eventually disrupting, the cooperative arrangements among enterprises on which the domestic viability and world competitiveness of the Japanese multilayered subcontracting system rests.* Inevitably, the reinvestment of an ever-growing mass of profits in the expansion of trade and production within the Japanese domestic economy would have driven individual enterprises or families of enterprises to invade one another's networks and market niches in an attempt to counter downward pressures in sale prices and/or upward pressures in purchase prices. This mutual invasion, in turn, would have dissolved the cooperating confraternity of Japanese business into a chaotic ensemble of intensely competing factions. (pp. 23–24; emphasis added)

In Arrighi's (1996) analysis, a clear conjunction of structural or system-level and institutional factors is at play. He provides, in this regard, a good starting point for a constructed actor account of East Asia's high-speed industrial growth—although he does not bring his analysis down to the microlevel. In the constructed actor model, though, analysis at the microlevel is a necessary step. Indeed, one would not be stretching to argue that, at the heart of the conjunction between structural and institutional factors, lies the choices made and actions taken by individual actors. This argument is proven by the fact that the *keiretsu* system did not emerge out of thin air; it was the purposeful creation of myriad individual actors in Japan. Nor did the transnational expansion of this system just happen as part and parcel of some predetermined structural process. Instead, it involved conscious and strategic decisionmaking on how best to allocate and organize economic resources, both within Japan and outside of Japan, by actors in a variety of countries, including the United States. Of course, none of this decisionmaking took place in a social vacuum. All the actors in this process were influenced by a large current of "social facts," including geopolitical relationships and regional-international economic dynamics, by long-standing institutional arrangements (e.g., the corporatist arrangements discussed by Wade [1990] or the state-society linkages highlighted by Weiss [1998, 2000], Evans [1995], and others), and by normative or cultural systems. These and other social facts, moreover, have real effects; they make certain choices and the achievement of economic goals more or less possible—a point that Arrighi makes quite explicit both with regard to Japan's *keiretsu* system and to the US-dominated system of world capitalism, which temporarily gave Japan privileged access to resources and markets it would otherwise not have had.

From the constructed actor perspective, all of this raises important questions. Could Japan (or South Korea or Taiwan) have achieved the economic success it did without the purposeful decisions and actions of individual actors? If so, what factors determine or influence the types of decisions that actors make? In other words, are decisions based purely on rational self-interest (as a liberal might argue), or is there an important, perhaps profoundly important, "nonrational" basis? Lastly, regardless of the motivations, would the actors' decisions and actions have had the same results were it not for the panoply of advantageous social facts, especially large-scale social facts? Anyone paying attention will already have basic answers to each of the foregoing questions—indeed, I indirectly answered each of these questions in the preceding paragraph. For the sake of clarity, however, a little repetition is in order.

First, decisions by individual actors were unequivocally key. Second, the motivations or the factors that shape decisions of "constructed actors" also clearly transcend narrow economic self-interest to include ideological-cultural and other intersubjective factors. Third, one can assume that individual actors are rarely, if ever, able to simply "do as they please" or to achieve any goal they set out to accomplish. So how does one put all this together into a coherent account of high-speed industrial growth in East Asia? As I emphasized in Chapter 1, the objective is only to provide a basic and illustrative account (rather than a full-blown explanation). To do this, I focus on a particular country, South Korea, and a single but very important industry, electronics. This more-focused approach compels one to stay grounded at the microlevel, while allowing for the assessment and careful observation of the interaction of individual, meso-, and system-level factors and processes.

Illustrative Example: South Korean Electronics Industry

I begin by considering the development of South Korea's electronics industry, which has played a key role in the country's overall record of high-speed growth. On this point, reviewing a few statistics would be useful. In 1960, South Korea had yet to sell a single electronics product overseas: export sales were zero. After less than a decade of concerted effort, sales increased to a respectable but still small $29 million in 1970 and accounted for just 3 percent of South Korean exports. But only five years later, in 1975, exports sales shot up to $453 million (a fifteen-fold increase) and became about 9 percent of South Korean export sales. By 1991, exports of South Korean electronics surpassed $20 billion and made up 28 percent of all exports for that year (see Figure 2.10). By this time, too, the electronics industry had become South Korea's leading export sector.

The rapid expansion of the electronics industry in South Korea was a product of multiple forces, which played different roles in different time periods. The early stages of the industry's development in South Korea reflected an

Figure 2.10 Exports of Electronic Products by South Korea (selected years)

Year	Electronic Products (US$ millions)	Share of Total Exports (%)
1960	0	0.0
1970	29	3.5
1975	453	8.9
1980	2,004	11.4
1985	4,285	14.1
1991	20,157	28.0

Source: Cited in Hobday (1995, p. 58). Original source is the Korea Foreign Trade Association, *Trade Yearbooks* (various years).

underlying process in global capitalism, namely, the diffusion of capital from technologically advanced and higher-cost locations (primarily in the United States and Japan) to lower-cost or low-wage locations. This diffusion is evidenced by the fact that the capital and technology required to create an electronics-manufacturing base in South Korea came primarily from outside the country. The first major foreign investment came from US firms, such as Motorola, Signetics, and Fairchild, and Japanese firms, such as Sanyo, Crown Radio, Toshiba, and Alps (Hobday 1995). US and Japanese firms, I should add, supplied more than just capital. They also brought technology, production management, and marketing expertise, while South Korean firms, for the most part, were consigned to providing low-wage workers (S. C. Suh 1978). Looked at from afar, this scenario seems to conform to both the liberal and structural arguments, which suggest that South Korea's initial economic success in the electronics industry was a result of its comparative advantage in low labor costs, and to the dynamics of the product cycle. The implication of this scenario, moreover, was fairly clear. As one well-informed observer noted at the time, "If [this] pattern of Korean development is allowed to persist in the future, there is a real danger that the Korean electronics industry may develop into a permanent satellite of a few advanced countries under the disguise of the international division of labor" (S. C. Suh 1975, p. 120). *This did not happen.*

To understand why the Korean electronics industry did not remain trapped as an appendage to more powerful economies one needs to consider what was happening inside firms, within the institutions of the state, and among workers. One also needs to understand the extent to which political and economic institutions in South Korea were effective at influencing structural dynamics, and why they were effective at all. And, finally, one needs to consider why Koreans in the public and private sectors undertook certain courses of action and not others. While this task is very big and complicated, the basic elements are not hard to identify and assess. Let us consider, first, why South Korea became a destination for foreign capital in the electronics sector. As I noted above, one reason is clear: South Korea had a comparative advantage in low-cost labor, which was attractive for foreign firms that needed to reduce production costs (for their still-profitable but older technologies). In addition, the country's close geographic proximity to Japan, and its burgeoning strategic relationship with the United States, made South Korea a good candidate for FDI. Undoubtedly, these external factors were critically important, but foreign capital does not just stream across borders in an automatic or spontaneous fashion. It must be directed, and it must have a place to coalesce. In South Korea, a ready receptacle already existed for FDI: the *chaebol.*

The *chaebol,* however, were more than just receptacles. They were run by extraordinarily ambitious and capable individuals who took advantage of whatever economic opportunities were available. During the 1950s, the *chaebol* dominated domestic industries, forged close, though also often corrupt, links with the then ruling government under **Syngman Rhee**, and built monopolistic or semimonopolistic positions in all of South Korea's most important markets. By the late 1950s, this economic and political dominance had led to a highly distorted and anemic national economy with very little room for additional internal growth. A number of *chaebol* leaders, therefore, began to look beyond the country's sated domestic markets for new opportunities. Foreign capital earmarked to build electronic products for export provided just this opportunity. For the first decade, South Korean companies were content to serve as "water boys" to far richer and immeasurably more technologically advanced Western and Japanese firms. By 1970, however, Koreans began producing the least sophisticated products on their own. At the same time, the most capable *chaebol* shifted to joint venture agreements, agreements that allowed them to absorb more readily the production, technological, and managerial know-how they needed to move beyond water-boy status.

Case Study: Rapid Rise of Samsung Electronics

One of the best examples of the above is Samsung, which, as late as 1969, had never produced a single electronics product. Instead, the company made its riches on international trade, especially of commodities such as sugar and flour (T. C. Lim 1996). Today, Samsung is one of the largest and most sophisticated producers of electronics for both the consumer and business markets, and as a diversified *chaebol,* Samsung also has major operations in financial services, engineering, machinery and heavy equipment, hotels and resorts, and chemicals and petrochemicals. In electronics, Samsung began at the bottom of the technology ladder, simply assembling transistor radios and black-and-white televisions under a joint venture with Sanyo Electric (Hobday 1995). Only a decade later, however, Samsung was ready to ascend the technology ladder and eventually move into a leadership position; in 1983, it became only the third company in the world to develop a sixty-four-kilobit dynamic random-access memory (DRAM) chip, and about a decade later, in 1992, it was the first company to produce working samples of the then cutting-edge, sixty-four-megabit DRAM chip (Hobday 1995). One year later, Samsung emerged as the world's largest maker of DRAM chips, a position it has held since then (in the fourth quarter of 2010, Samsung accounted for 42.1 percent of the global market share for random-access memory chips [Howard 2011]). The company is also the world's top producer of flat-panel televisions (including those utilizing active-matrix organic light-emitting diodes [OLEDs]), second in mobile handsets, and one of the top suppliers of "smart" home appliances, lithium-ion batteries, tablets, digital cameras, NAND flash (NAND flash memory is a type of storage technology that does not require power to retain data), and computer hard drives (D.-S. Kim 2010).

So how did Samsung achieve so much in so little time? A big part of the answer unequivocally lies in the aggressive and strategic decisionmaking that went on within Samsung. In 1983, for example, Samsung's founder Lee Byung-chull boldly announced the company's large-scale investment plans in the semiconductor business, an announcement that was dubbed the "Tokyo declaration" (C. Oh 2010).[12] Yet, at the time, the company did not possess the requisite technical know-how. To overcome this rather formidable obstacle, according to Michael Hobday (1995), Samsung contracted with a US company, Micron Technology, which had developed a sixty-four-kilobit DRAM suitable for low-end PCs and other consumer electronic products. Micron Technology agreed to license its technology to Samsung in exchange for a $5 million investment. More importantly, Samsung then "transferred young engineers from other parts of its electronics business to learn about the technology from the US firm. . . . Some of Micron's engineers were [also] dispatched to the ROK [Republic of Korea] to train Samsung's staff under the licensing deal" (p. 81). Around the same time, Samsung formed its own Silicon Valley company, Tristar Semiconductor (*samsung* means "three stars" in Korean), which directly hired US-trained Asian engineers, mostly ethnic Koreans and Chinese. Samsung's initial investment was $10 million in 1983, followed by a further $60 million in 1984. Tristar is the company that succeeded in producing Samsung's own sixty-four-kilobit chip, but it also developed a 256-kilobit DRAM in-house. The mid-1980s, therefore, marked the beginning of Samsung's rise to prominence in the electronics sector. Hobday provides a nice summary: "During this period [between 1983 and 1988] Samsung ironed out many of its process difficulties and then quickly took control of the design content of mainstream DRAMs. During this five-year period Samsung caught up with the DRAMs leaders by heavy investments, trial-and-error learning and foreign collaboration" (p. 82). This process accelerated beginning in 1989, as Samsung evolved from a technology follower to a technology leader and innovator in DRAMs of four, sixteen, and sixty-four megabits, "achieving parity with Japanese and US companies in DRAM technology and broadening the company's technology base" (Hobday 1995). Samsung soon began shipping its own brand to large users such as IBM, Hewlett-Packard, Sun Microsystems, and NEC.

In consumer electronics, a similar process took place, as Samsung developed branded products based on its own innovations in technology—although the process took much longer than the company's success in semiconductor production. By 2008, Samsung Electronics had become the world's largest technology company, with annual revenue of more than $106 billion and about 164,600 employees.[13] Of the company's employees, moreover, 42,000 work in research and development and one in every twenty-five has a doctorate degree. Of course, the full story is far more complex and detailed than described here, not only for Samsung Electronics but for dozens (if not hundreds) of other East Asian firms. Indeed, Hobday's (1995) research shows that the paths to technological progress followed by different firms in different East Asian countries varied significantly (in his book, Hobday examines Singapore, Taiwan, Hong Kong, and South Korea and employs, in broad terms, a comparative historical analytical approach). The key lesson, however, is straightforward: a full understanding of East Asian economic growth, including technological progress, requires a detailed, on-the-ground analysis at the industry and firm level.

Samsung's Ascendance in Context: Structural and Institutional Considerations

Despite earlier qualifications, the foregoing narrative makes it seem as if Samsung's economic success was almost entirely a product of extraordinary entrepreneurship and business acumen. This is hardly the case. Consider, on this point, a counterfactual question: Could Lee Byung-chull (the founder of Samsung) have achieved the same success in any country at any time? An answer to this question cannot be definitive. But fairly clear is that the particular context in which Samsung developed as a preeminent electronics company was profoundly important. I already mentioned the significance of the structural dynamics that opened the door to FDI: timing, in this regard, was crucial. South Korea, to put it very simply, was in the right place at the right time. This fortuitousness was not solely, or even primarily, because it was a good, low-cost receptacle for foreign investment, but also because the country's businesses had relatively little competition from other low-wage countries, something that was true in most other sectors as well, such as textiles. The lack of international competition gave South Korean firms an opportunity to accumulate capital (especially US dollars), which could then be used for the sort of investments made by Samsung I discussed above. To better see the importance of timing, consider what would have happened if just one other country—China—had been equally prepared for and open to FDI as South Korea was in the 1960s. One does not have a hard time imagining that South Korean firms would have had a much tougher time attracting foreign capital. Even more important, the capacity to accumulate capital would have been severely constrained by the additional competition from Chinese firms selling the same products to the same markets.

Reaffirming the importance of institutions, both economic and political, is also useful. In the discussion of Samsung, Lee Byung-chull's personal vision was made possible through the institutional power of his *chaebol*. Samsung's ability to form joint ventures with foreign firms, and then to absorb technological know-how, its ability to pursue licensing deals and to make major overseas investments ($70 million in the case of Tristar), and so on, all speak to the institutional power of the *chaebol*. Even more basically, while Lee undoubtedly was largely responsible for building his company in the first place, the rapid growth of Samsung as a *chaebol*, in both scale and scope, was also very much a product of a particular sociopolitical and economic context, one in which the state played a key role. The constructed actor model considers the state a central part of the story in the success of Samsung specifically, and of the South Korean economy more generally. In the case of Samsung Electronics, however, success was less a matter of direct assistance (if anything, state bureaucrats had little faith in Samsung's more ambitious goals) than it was of creating an environment that pushed Samsung toward positive-sum economic activity.

Samsung's is another complex story (a good deal of which I covered earlier), but it can be boiled down to the developmental state using its institutional capacity to provide South Korean firms a crucial competitive advantage vis-à-vis international competition, but also to "create contests" between and among domestic firms, especially the *chaebol*, and construct a suitable socioeconomic environment for sustained capitalist growth. On this last point, it bears repeating that prior to 1960, South Korea's domestic economy had become dominated by economic leviathans such as Samsung, which had divided the economy into noncompetitive havens for rent seeking (T. Lim 1996). In this context, an equally strong institution was required to break the *chaebol*'s unhealthy grip on the economy. Here, too, South Korea was lucky: in 1961, a military faction, led by General Park Chung Hee,[14] staged a **coup d'état** that replaced an ineffective interim regime (the previous regime of Syngman Rhee was brought down by popular protests in 1960) with an iron-fisted authoritarian system. The power of this new authoritarian system has often been greatly exaggerated in the literature (see T. Lim 2001 for further discussion), but under Park Chung Hee, a rebalancing of state-society relations clearly occurred, especially the state-business relationship, which went from one that was highly skewed in favor of big business to one that was relatively equal. The rebalancing allowed for the establishment of the sort of crucial institutional links between the state and business that Weiss (1998) and others have identified as the hallmark of a developmental state.

Actors Within Institutions: Coming Back to the Microlevel

The emergence of Park Chung Hee, I should note, brings the discussion back to the always important role of **agency** in the current analysis. On this point, I must stress that states have no agency in their own right. They do not possess intent or free will; only the individuals that constitute the state have these qualities. At the same time, the institutional capacity of the state—its military and police powers, its control over the monetary and fiscal systems, its authority for rule making and enforcement—have the potential to make the state a very powerful instrument. In the right hands, state capacity can be effectively used to exploit economic opportunities in the international/global system and even create opportunities where none may have existed. Park, in particular, was a master at manipulating the country's relationship with the United States: to ensure continued US support, for example, Park committed to sending South Korean troops to Vietnam. This commitment was very much a strategic decision. As Sungjoo Han (1978) explains, shortly after Park dispatched his troops, "the Johnson administration overcame whatever reservations it still had about [the regime's] legitimacy and instead began to praise it lavishly for its achievements and governing ability" (p. 907; originally cited in Lie 1998, p. 63).

The ascendance of Park also led to the diplomatic normalization of South Korea's relationship with Japan. Importantly, this relationship paved the way for the construction of the centerpiece of South Korea's industrial rise: the Pohang Iron and Steel Company. Building a world-class integrated iron and steel works was a top priority for Park, but all his attempts failed until normalization, which led to an agreement by the Japanese to pay reparations for "36 years of hardship under Japanese rule" (as cited in Amsden 1989, p. 295). Reparations provided the necessary capital, as well as technical assistance, which the South Koreans used as the basis to become one of the leading steel producers in the world (Amsden 1989). Worth noting is that, in 1970, South Korea had no comparative advantage in steel production; therefore, according to liberal principles, the country had no business entering the sector at all, much less in the manner that it did by building one of the largest steel mills in the world at the time, with a capacity of 9.1 million tons (Amsden 1989).

Transformative Power of Culture and Identity

The transformative potential of the state and its leaders is not limited to concrete economic projects. States also have an ability to reshape their societies at an intersubjective or cultural level. Arguably, reshaping society was one of the major achievements of the Park regime. His regime brought wholesale changes to South Korean society through educational reforms (part of which involved moral education), a rural "revitalization" project (dubbed the **Saemaul Undong** or the "New Community Movement"),[15] and the construction of a more unified, highly nationalistic, and "egalitarian" Korean identity—all of which was meant, in large part, to create a sustainable basis for collective mobilization geared toward rapid industrialization. No one, however, should find anything surprising about Park's strategy. A little comparative analysis reveals that political leaders everywhere rely on cultural strategies to shape attitudes and perceptions of the citizenry. In South Korea, this strategy was particularly effective—many observers agree—because of the overarching political context, one that included a hostile relationship between North and South Korea (recall the intersection between politics and culture). The Park regime, to put it simply, used already widespread antipathy toward North Korea to instill an especially virulent anticommunist nationalism among the South Korean people. Importantly, the objective of this nationalism was not only, or even mostly, to ensure a vigilant attitude toward the communist regime, but also to legitimize both the new military-based authoritarian regime in South Korea and its political-economic agenda.

Bringing and maintaining legitimacy was critical. To achieve the ambitious economic goals set out by his regime, Park needed the active cooperation and unquestioning loyalty of the South Korean people, especially industrial workers, who would necessarily be the backbone of the national economy. While certainly never fully achieving its goal of unflagging dedication to state (radicalism among workers is a motif of industrial relations in South Korea), the regime was successful in linking hard and self-sacrificing work to a sense of national and patriotic duty.

The Park regime also had more immediate concerns. I mentioned the Pohang Iron and Steel works above, which required Japanese financial and technical assistance. Left out of that discussion was the tremendous obstacle of overcoming domestic resistance to anything Japanese. Indeed, as Park Sang Mi (2010) notes, "the exclusion of 'Japaneseness' from Korean public discourse had been a central pillar supporting post-liberation Korean nationalism," and during negotiations to normalize relations, upwards of 60,000 students demonstrated daily against the regime's "humiliating diplomacy" (p. 72). The Park administration, however, used the strengthened anticommunist ideology as a way to justify closer relations with Japan. Park Sang Mi (2010) explains it this way:

> The Park administration manipulated the public by encouraging a softer concept of Korea's "triumph over Japan" rather than pushing hard-line, anti-Japanese exclusionary rhetoric. When the massive civil protests erupted, Park justified his position by arguing that normalization was a necessary evil because South Korea would be able to obtain Japanese loans, which would facilitate the Republic of Korea's economic development and thus prevent foreign powers and ideologies from dominating the Korean peninsula ever again. (p. 72)

The account so far presumes that Park Chung Hee and his cohorts were somehow unaffected by intersubjective factors themselves. This was not the case. Park was a "military man," inculcated with the values and principles of military culture, and infused with a strong sense of anticommunism and patriotic duty himself. A range of social facts, all of which framed his attitudes, perceptions, and decisions, constituted his own worldview. A full-fledged constructed actor account would include a detailed examination of General Park and other military-authoritarian leaders. Unfortunately, I do not have the space to undertake this full-fledged account, nor do I have the space to adequately cover the many other facets of the transformative power of culture and identity. Still, the upshot is clear: cultural or intersubjective factors played an important role in South Korea's economic rise. And while their influence is difficult if not impossible to quantify, any analysis of South Korea—or of Japan, Taiwan, China, or North Korea—that does not include cultural or intersubjective factors is bound to be incomplete.

Conclusion

The first application of the constructed actor model was quite narrowly focused and seemed to stray from a more general account of East Asia's economic rise (centering the attention, as I did, on South Korea). My approach was meant to highlight a key lesson: good explanations of economic (or political or social) change often require in-depth, close examination of events and processes "on the ground." At the same time, an in-depth, close examination of specific events and processes means that other relevant and equally important issues and cases must be left out. Such omissions are an unavoidable drawback in a book that covers a range of countries over a long span of time. As I emphasized in Chapter 1, however, this selectivity gives readers an opportunity to consider and develop their own arguments. In this regard, a range of issues can still be fruitfully addressed, including the following:

- Did the structural processes of global capitalism have the same effects—and elicit the same responses and outcomes—in South Korea, Japan, and Taiwan (as well as China and North Korea)? If not, what were the differences and what was the basis for these differences?
- From the 1950s through the 1970s, relatively poor countries in all parts of the world were subject to the same overarching structural dynamics as the East Asian economies. Yet few achieved the same economic results. Do institutional, cultural, and microlevel factors explain this divergence?
- Does the constructed actor model allow for the identification of basic similarities among the East Asian countries? Can these shared characteristics be found in other regions?

This list is not exhaustive by any means, but the questions posed above compel one to make the sort of comparisons that are necessary to develop causal or explanatory accounts of East Asian industrialization.

Notes

1. The World Bank report focused on eight East Asian economies: Japan, South Korea, Taiwan, China, Hong Kong, Indonesia, Malaysia, and Thailand. Other economies in East Asia were explicitly or tacitly excluded from this group, including Vietnam, North Korea, Mongolia, Burma, and Laos.

2. *The Human Development Report* prepared by the United Nations Development Programme does not include data on Taiwan. This deliberate omission is due to a "political issue" based on a decision by the United Nations in 1971 to expel Taiwan (the Republic of China) from the organization and to give the People's Republic of China (PRC) the "China seat" in the United Nations. This action was formalized in Resolution 2758 passed by the General Assembly on October 25. The resolution extended formal recognition to the representatives of the government of the PRC as the "only lawful representatives of China to the United Nations" while expelling "forthwith the representatives of Chiang Kai-chek [*sic*] from the place which they unlawfully occupy at the United Nations and in all the organizations related to it" (United Nations 1971).

3. Krugman's actual focus was sharply on Singapore, but he clearly implied that what was true for Singapore was true for South Korea and Taiwan as well, as is made evident in his consistent use of the term *East Asia* in his article. However, he also had separate discussions of Japan and Taiwan.

4. Corporatist systems are not limited to East Asia. Indeed, the origin of corporatist theory derives from research on European political systems.

5. One prominent exception was the Yawata Iron Works, which was established in 1896 by the national government and was considered to be vital to national security (Lockwood 1968).

6. Readers should refer to the volume *The Japanese Colonial Empire, 1895–1945,* edited by Ramon Myers, Mark Peattie, and Ching-chih Chen for further discussion.

7. I can add others to this list as well, including Calder (1993), Samuels (1987), Okimoto (1989), E. M. Kim (1997), and Gold (1997).

8. Other changes took place, too. In 1998, in response to the Asian Financial Crisis, the MOFE's functions were "separated and transferred to other Ministries so as to mitigate the over-concentration of decision making authority by MOFE. Its budgetary authority was transferred to the National Budget Administration, its financial supervision to the Financial Supervisory Commission, and its trade negotiating authority to the Ministry of Foreign Affairs and Trade." Then, in 2008, the MOFE and the Ministry of Planning and Budget were again merged to form the Ministry of Strategy and Finance (MOSF) (MOSF 2013).

9. For a more detailed discussion of this issue in Korea, see Bleiker (2005).

10. Needless to say, not everyone readily accepted Hirschman's idea about the need for a "binding agent" in late-developing economies. Writing a review of Hirschman's book, Myint (1960) asserts that the term *binding agent* is "vague and unhelpful" (p. 129).

11. See, for example, S. H. Cha (2003) and Yun (2010).

12. Notably, the South Korean government did not support Samsung's foray into semiconductor fabrication. At the time, according to a *Korea Times* article, Samsung's announcement to invest heavily in this field "generated more skepticism than excitement

from the business community and policymakers. Everybody had their own concerns. A few Japanese companies were dominating the global semiconductor market back then and many wondered whether Samsung would ever achieve the level of technology or gain the wealth of engineering talent to compete with them" (T. Kim 2010).

13. Based on *Fortune* magazine's annual listing of the world's 500 largest companies (the "Global 500"). In 2009 and 2010, Hewlett-Packard took over the top spot. The rankings are available online at http://money.cnn.com/magazines/fortune/global500/2008/full_list/. The employee figure comes from Samsung's *Sustainability Report* (2009).

14. As John Lie (1998) makes clear, Park's rise to prominence was not automatic. He was originally part of a junta (a group of military leaders), but engineered his ascendance by "skillfully manipulating alliances and ruthlessly purging his rivals," including Chang To-yŏng, who was the symbolic head of the coup (pp. 50–51).

15. For a discussion of the New Community Movement, see Reed (2010).

3 Crises and Malaise: Whither the East Asian Miracle?

The high-speed economic growth of Japan, South Korea, and Taiwan could not last forever. Even the most ardent advocates of the East Asian model knew that the collective ascent of these East Asian economies would shift to a slower pace eventually. As I pointed out in the previous chapter, too, a few naysayers, such as Paul Krugman and Bruce Cumings, were convinced that East Asian economic success was always more mirage than reality. The naysayers were not disappointed. Beginning in the early 1990s, the biggest of the East Asian economies at the time—Japan—began a long and, in the view of the vast majority of observers, tortuous period of economic decline. Bai Gao (2001) provides a basic summary of Japan's economic problems:

> In the last decade of the twentieth century . . . the bubble of the Japanese economy burst. The depth of the crisis was as astonishing as the extent of the preceding success. In the 1990s, the Japanese economy grew at a mere 1 percent per year on average. In 1997 and 1998, it even experienced negative growth. According to one estimate, Japan lost 800 trillion yen in the stock and real estate markets between 1989 and 1992; this loss was equivalent to 11.3 percent of the country's national wealth. Both markets continued to slump after 1992, sinking to (or below) levels perhaps comparable to those in World War II, during which Japan lost 14 percent of its national wealth. . . . Although the rise and fall of an economy is nothing unusual in history, the magnitude of the Japanese economy's swing within such a short period of time, in the absence of major wars, is unprecedented. (pp. 1–2)

Japan did not seem to fare significantly better in the first decade of the twenty-first century. From 2000 to 2009, the economy grew at an average annual rate of 1.4 percent, which included three years of negative real **GDP** growth (see Figure 3.1). More important, over the decade, the country's public debt also increased dramatically: from an already high debt-to-GDP ratio of 120 percent in 1999 (twice the level of the United States and Germany at the time), it almost doubled to an astounding 214.3 percent in 2012 (Central Intelligence Agency [CIA] 2013). As a result, Japan earned the dubious distinction of being the most

Figure 3.1 Selected Economic Statistics for Japan, 2000–2010

	2000	2002	2003	2004	2005	2006	2007	2008	2009	2010
Real GDP growth rate (%)	1.3	–0.3	2.7	2.9	2.6	2.2	2.0	–0.7	–5.2	3.9
Public debt (% of GDP)	—	—	—	164.3	158.0	176.2	170.0	173.0	192.9	225.8
Unemployment rate (%)	4.7	4.7	5.4	5.3	4.7	4.1	4.4	3.8	4.0	5.1
Current account balance ($US billions)	—	—	—	170.2	165.6	174.4	210.5	156.6	142.2	165.5

Source: CIA World Factbook (various years).
Note: — No data available.

indebted country in the world for that year, far ahead of the second-place country, Zimbabwe.[1]

Japan's national financial struggles, however, do not mean that Japan's industrial, financial, and technological might has disappeared. Far from it. The largest and most globalized Japanese companies—Toyota, Honda, Sony, Hitachi, Canon, NEC, Komatsu, Kawasaki, and Mitsubishi, among many others—remain as formidable, perhaps even more formidable, than ever. (However, as I discuss below, the strength of Japan's largest and most internationally oriented corporations has tended to disguise the economic weakness of the country's domestically focused manufacturing and services sectors.) Moreover, Japan is second only to China in the amount of US Treasury securities held by foreign governments: in June 2011, the figure was $911 billion (US Department of Treasury 2011); Japan's total foreign reserves were $1.3 trillion that same year (World Bank 2013a). Indeed, one longtime Japanese observer, Eamonn Fingleton (2011), argues that Japan's economic problems since 1990 have been vastly overblown (see Figure 3.2 for further discussion of Fingleton's argument). Still, Japan is fairly clearly no longer the economic juggernaut—one that many observers believed was destined to surpass the United States—it was once considered to be.

Japan was not the only East Asian economy to experience difficulties in the years leading up to the twenty-first century. South Korea, along with a group of other so-called Asian miracle or tiger economies (including Thailand, Indonesia, Malaysia, and Hong Kong) were severely affected by the **Asian Financial Crisis**, which began to take shape in the mid-1990s. The official start of the financial crisis is generally considered to be the decision by the Thai central bank to withdraw its support of the Thai baht on July 2, 1997, although the first signs of the Asian Financial Crisis appeared much earlier. The decision by the Thai central bank led to a sudden and extremely rapid depreciation of the baht, which forced a similarly severe depreciation in neighboring countries—a sort of financial contagion. In South Korea specifically, the Korean won fell from 886 won to the dollar in June 1997 to 1,822 on December 24 that same year—this disaster came only a couple of months after the Korean central bank had vowed to "never, never, never" let the Korean won fall below the 1,000 to US$1 mark (cited in S. H. Kim 2001, p. 51). Even more troubling was the collapse of several of South Korea's leading *chaebol*. Seven out of the country's thirty top conglomerates were forced to file for court-mediated protection or court-ordered receivership by October 1997 (Pyo 1999)—although one must note that several *chaebol,* including Hanbo Steel (which failed in early 1997), were experiencing difficulties long before the crisis hit. More generally, in just one month, December 1997, at least 3,000 South Korean companies of all sizes failed, a 1,000 percent increase from a year earlier (Moon 1998, p. 54). Predictably, the stock market also took a beating, falling to 376.3 points at the end of 1997, just about half what it was in 1996. Admittedly, the South Korean stock market had been experiencing periods of decline for some time already: in 1994, at its height, the stock price index was 1,027.4; the index fell to 882.9 in 1995 and to 651.2 in 1996. According to Hak K. Pyo (1999), this decline reflected long-simmering anxieties about the underlying strength of the South Korean financial sector. The fact that the South Korean economy was already experiencing difficulties was, to some observers, not that surprising. After all, Japan's still ongoing difficulties demonstrated that East Asia's economic foundation was not as unshakable as many observers had once assumed.

The greatest indignity for South Korea came with a **bailout** from the **IMF**. On December 3, 1997, the South Korean government was provided with a bailout package worth $57 billion—at the time, the largest such package ever. In return for the bailout funds, however, the South Korean government had to agree to a number of demands by the IMF, including (1) **macroeconomic** retrenchment involving high interest rates and fiscal austerity, (2) **liberalization** or opening of product and capital markets to foreign companies and investors, and (3) major structural reforms in the financial and corporate sectors (such as tightening bank supervision and monitoring and clamping down on the *chaebol*). One other particularly controversial measure was the following demand by the IMF: South Korea had to develop a more "flexible" labor market. One of the key targets was the country's labor termination law, which had protected workers against layoffs, resulting in an extraordinarily low unemployment rate of only 2.0 percent in 1997. The IMF's demand sparked large-scale popular protests, but the government pushed through the required changes. Mostly for this reason, Koreans often refer to the Asian Financial Crisis as the "IMF Crisis."

Figure 3.2 Japan's Lost Decades: Fact or Fiction?

Eamonn Fingleton (2011), former editor for *Forbes* and the *Financial Times*, challenges the taken-for-granted notion that, during the two decades between 1990 and 2010, an unremitting decline has taken place in Japan's economic status and power in the world economy. Fingleton, on the contrary, asserts that Japan's economic performance since 1990 has been, in important respects, just as impressive as the period of high-speed economic growth. He points out, in particular, that Japan's current account surplus, the widest and most meaningful measure of its trade, increased from $36 billion in 1990 to $194 billion in 2010. This accomplishment, moreover, was brought about in the face of a constantly appreciating currency: between 1990 and 2010, the value of the yen increased more than 65 percent against the dollar—meaning that, over this twenty-year period, Japanese exports became increasingly more expensive and, therefore, less price competitive in world markets. In this view, the constantly increasing current account surplus during a time of ostensible economic stagnation and malaise is remarkable and seemingly inexplicable. More generally, Fingleton argues that, despite all the "doom and gloom" stories of Japan's economic decline, between 1990 and 2010, "the Japanese people have enjoyed one of the biggest improvements in living standards of any major First World nation."

While few experts agree with Fingleton, at least one other observer echoes his main points. Writing in the *Los Angeles Times,* Steven Hill (2010) poses the rhetorical question, "How . . . should we regard a country that has 5% unemployment, the lowest income inequality [among the wealthiest economies], healthcare for all of its people and is one of the world's leading exporters?" (p. A-21). (On the issue of unemployment, worth noting is that unemployment rates in Japan have declined since 2010, from a high of 5.3 percent in July 2010, to just 4.6 percent in July 2011, about half of the US unemployment rate of 9.1 percent in the same month.) To this list of accomplishments, Hill adds the fact that Japan has one of the highest life expectancies and the lowest infant mortality rates, is one of the top performers in math and literacy on international tests, and, to top it off, has very low rates of crime, incarceration, mental illness, and drug abuse.

(continues)

The Tale of Taiwan: Crisis? What Crisis?

One more East Asian "tiger" is left to discuss, however: Taiwan. Unlike Japan and South Korea, Taiwan made it through the 1990s and the first decade of the twenty-first century relatively unscathed. An article in *The Economist* notes that Taiwan had weathered the Asian Financial Crisis "in much better shape than many of its neighbors" ("A Survey of Taiwan" 1998a). In particular, while most other East Asian countries experienced a meltdown in the value of their currencies and

Figure 3.2 continued

One additional point needs to be considered: GDP growth is a deceptive fig-ure, in part, because it does not account for population growth, which varies widely among countries. Japan, in fact, has one of the world's lowest rates of population growth. A better indicator of Japan's economic performance, then, might be **per capita GDP** growth. And on this figure, Japan has done quite well, as seen in figures compiled by HSBC (Hong Kong and Shanghai Banking Cor-poration), which show a comparison of annual growth of per capita GDP along-side overall GDP growth rates (in parentheses) for the period 2001–2010 ("Taking Lessons from Japan" 2012):

Japan	1.6% (0.8%)
United Kingdom	1.2% (1.5%)
Germany	0.8% (0.8%)
United States	0.7% (1.6%)
France	0.6% (1.2%)

Given these statistics, Fingleton (2011) poses the question: "How can such facts be reconciled with the 'two lost decades' story?" In his view, they cannot be reconciled. Instead, writes Fingleton, "If we believe the evidence of our eyes, we necessarily must look again at those economic growth figures. Preposterous though it may seem to an acclimatized Western observer, it appears that Japanese officials have been deliberately understating the nation's growth." This statement is bold, to be sure, and one that Fingleton does not provide clear and direct evi-dence to support. Still, his overall analysis should not be dismissed out of hand. At the very least, he forces one to consider the fuller picture, not to just focus on a single set of aggregate statistics (i.e., GDP growth rate) and assume that these tell the whole story. Indeed, viewed from a wider perspective, Japan's economic performance and "development" between 1990 and 2010 suggests that, while economic growth may have slowed considerably (compared to earlier periods), the country continued to "develop" in many important ways.

in their stock markets, Taiwan's were down by a modest 20 percent or so. Its economy, moreover, grew strongly in 1997 at 6.9 percent per annum, the sev-enth highest in the world (Y.-C. Chen 1998). *The Economist,* a bastion of liberal economic thought, also points out, in the article "A Survey of Taiwan: The Sur-vivor's Tale" (1998b), some seemingly obvious reasons for Taiwan's resistance to the "Asian contagion," as it was also called. The most important, perhaps, was simply a sound macroeconomic environment. Taiwan's foreign exchange reserves, for example, totaled $84 billion in 1998, exceeded only by China and Japan—two much larger economies with much larger populations. Moreover, its foreign debts were a "trifling" $250 million, while the country, "as always," had a large trade surplus. The only negative that *The Economist* could find was Taiwan's "chronic budget deficits and its relatively high national debt (about 20 percent of GDP), explained mostly by the vast sums it spends on F16s (fighter jets) and other arms to keep China at bay" ("A Survey of Taiwan" 1998b).

Taiwan's ability to brush off the Asian Financial Crisis and to avoid the sort of long-term economic malaise that has beset Japan suggests, on the surface at least, that significant causal differences exist between Taiwan, on the one hand, and Japan and South Korea, on the other hand (as well as a host of other Asian economies that suffered through the financial crisis). The key difference, as *The Economist* posits, may be as simple as Taiwan's sound macroeconomic environment ("A Survey of Taiwan" 1998b). Or less obvious and more complex factors could be at play.[2] Indeed, even if *The Economist* was spot on about the importance of Taiwan's macroeconomic environment, the conclusion raises questions as to how this environment was created and sustained, especially when so many of Taiwan's neighbors were seemingly unable to do the same. Taiwan's experience also suggests, quite strongly, that no single East Asian model will ever be found, something that is not at all surprising. After all, while clear similarities can be found among the three East Asian economies, in Chapter 2 I also discussed the range of differences. This point brings the discussion back to the key question, namely, what are the specific differences between and among Japan, South Korea, and Taiwan that might explain the divergent economic paths of the three countries since the 1990s? To find out, of course, one has to engage in empirically in-depth and methodologically sound analysis.

In this chapter, I examine the varied experiences of Japan, South Korea, and Taiwan since the 1990s, first, through the competing-perspectives approach and, second, through the constructed actor model. A disproportionate amount of space, I should note at the outset, is devoted to liberal explanations, primarily because liberal analysis in particular utterly dominates the discussion of Japan's economic troubles since 1990 and the Asian Financial Crisis. Paying closer attention to what liberal analysts had and have to say about both issues behooves anyone looking for answers. Secondarily, in the discussion of the constructed actor model, I incorporate key principles from institutional, cultural, and structural approaches to avoid unnecessary repetition (although a certain amount of repetition can be very useful).

Japan's "Lost Decades" and the Effects of the Asian Financial Crisis on South Korea and Taiwan: Liberal Arguments

Japan's long-term economic malaise and the effects of the Asian Financial Crisis on South Korea are sometimes unthinkingly lumped together as closely related events or even as reflections of the same basic process. Combining them can be a mistake. Takeo Kikkawa (2005), for one, argues that the causes of the crisis in Japan "undoubtedly differ" from those in South Korea and the other affected countries (p. 93). The most important difference, according to Kikkawa, is obvious: unlike the casualties of the Asian crisis, which suffered from a shortage of "foreign exchange holdings and a high dependency on foreign capital" (p. 92), Japan had an excess of capital and domestic savings and more than sufficient foreign exchange holdings. Almost certainly, some validity can be found in what Kikkawa says, although if one limits the focus to South Korea—which, in general economic terms, was much closer to Japan than to Thailand, Indonesia, Malaysia, and the Philippines—a little bit of "lumping," especially if done with care and reason, might be justified. Still, to start off, retaining a degree of analytical separation would be advisable. In the discussion that follows, then, I begin by examining the two economic crises separately but also endeavor to bring them together when warranted. With this basic point in mind, I begin by looking at liberal explanations of East Asia's economic woes.

Surprisingly, perhaps, no clear consensus has arisen among liberal economists on the key reasons behind either Japan's economic malaise or the Asian Financial Crisis. In the case of Japan, the situation is complicated because two separate crises or problems need to be explained. The first crisis was the bursting of the Japanese **asset bubble**, the extraordinarily rapid and dramatic run-up in domestic real estate and stock prices, which started in 1986, and their equally dramatic deflation beginning in 1990. The second crisis or problem was the long-term stagnation (or protracted recession) of the Japanese economy after the bubble burst. Of course, these two problems are tightly linked, but the factors that led up to and then triggered the major asset deflation in Japan, on the one hand, and that have sustained the country's protracted recession, on the other hand, are not necessarily the same. Liberal economists, of course, understand that Japan suffered from two separate economic problems quite well. Still, the distinction is sometimes lost in translation, especially to noneconomists trying to follow the logic of liberal arguments. This said, much less disagreement exists about the reasons behind the bursting of Japan's bubble economy than about the prolonged recession.

Japan's Bubble Economy

The beginning of the bubble is generally, albeit not universally, attributed to the 1985 Plaza Accord (see Figure 3.3), the main outcome of which was the intended depreciation of the US dollar relative to other major world currencies, especially the Japanese yen. The connection is fairly clear. With the steady but drastic strengthening of the yen (which made Japanese exports more expensive), the Japanese economy experienced a temporary and relatively mild downturn, but one that was perceived with some alarm by Japanese officials used to seeing

Figure 3.3 The Plaza Accord

The 1985 Plaza Accord, so named because the agreement was signed at the Plaza Hotel in New York, was based on negotiations among the G-5 countries: the United States, Japan, West Germany, France, and the United Kingdom. The primary purpose of the negotiations was to decrease the value of the US dollar relative to other major currencies, especially the Japanese yen. At the time, the United States was running large current account deficits—reaching 3.5 percent of GDP in 1985. The deficits were partially caused by the strength of US currency, which effectively made exports by US companies more expensive relative to exports from their major competitors in Japan and Western Europe. Devaluing the dollar, therefore, was meant to increase the price competitiveness of US goods, while simultaneously making imports from the leading international economies more expensive in the United States. The accord, in short, was designed to reduce or eliminate the US trade deficit and boost overall economic growth.

The five countries agreed to target rates: after the agreement went into effect, the US dollar declined in value by about 50 percent, while the deutsche mark, pound, franc, and yen all saw about a 50 percent appreciation (Twomey 2009). The Japanese yen, in particular, went from ¥242 to US$1 in September 1985 to ¥183 to US$1 in 1986; a year later, the value of the yen reached ¥120 to US$1.

The Plaza Accord's effects on Japan were more profound than anticipated. As Hisane Masaki (2005, n.p.) explains,

> The sharply higher yen prompted Japanese manufacturers to rush to shift production abroad, especially to Southeast Asia, to take advantage of cheaper labor there. Japanese automakers, which were particularly on the hot seat at the time amid raging trade **protectionism** in the US, also accelerated production in that country, not only to weather the stronger yen but to ease trade friction. In the early 1990s, the number of vehicles they assembled in the US exceeded that of their US-bound exports. To help cushion the impact of the stronger yen on its economy in the wake of the Plaza Accord, Japan kept its monetary policy loose to stimulate domestic demand, but did so longer than necessary, resulting in the "bubble economy" of the late 1980s characterized by inflated prices for assets such as stocks and land.

very strong growth. As a result, the Japanese government attempted—quite successfully in some respects—to stimulate domestic demand, first by halving the **discount rate** (from 5 percent in January 1986 to 2.5 percent in February 1987), and second by pursuing a policy of monetary expansion: from 1986 to 1990, the Bank of Japan expanded the money stock (or money supply) by an average of 10.5 percent per year (Powell 2002). This "extraordinary episode of monetary expansion," notes Raj Aggarwal (2002, p. 51), propelled the asset bubble forward.

In part, a rapid expansion of the money stock led to artificially lower interest rates across the board. Money became very "cheap" for both Japanese businesses and consumers, which led to a huge and sustained surge in business investments—often without due regard to future profitability—and consumer-level investment and spending (including in the stock market and real estate). In addition, as Aggarwal explains, a number of other factors "accelerated the bubble with positive feedbacks." In particular, since most lending in Japan tends to be based on collateral value, an increase in the price of assets "led to higher collateral values and higher levels of lending which then led to higher asset prices and so forth in an ever accelerating set of self reinforcing cycles" (p. 52). "Unfortunately," concludes Aggarwal, "there were few if any mechanisms in Japan at that time to discipline or stop the bubble in asset prices" (p. 52).

The general lack of disciplinary mechanisms also needs to be highlighted, for an underlying aspect of the asset bubble, most liberal economists agree, was the extremely weak foundation upon which a large number of loans rested. For many years, the Japanese financial system has been criticized for the "traditional practice of supervisory forbearance and the absence of effective prudential regulations of the banking sector" (Hutchison, Ito, and Westerman 2006, p. 10). To put it in simpler terms, the banking system was not well regulated, which—especially in an era of cheap money—made pouring huge amounts of capital into very shaky loans and other suspect financial deals easy. (One can argue that the United States experienced the same phenomenon with its housing bubble of the early to mid-2000s.) The era of cheap money, as I just mentioned, also gave rise to poorly conceived investments, especially foreign investments, made by Japanese corporations through retained earnings and equity financing (rather than bank loans). Remember, on this last point, that in the late 1980s the stock market shot virtually straight up, while the appreciation of the yen gave businesses more foreign purchasing power than ever before. The greater reliance by Japanese businesses on nonbank financing was reflected in one of the buzzwords of the time, *zaiteku* (or financial techniques). The shortcomings of the financial sector, however, were easily glossed over when the economy was growing by leaps and bounds. But, over time, the huge accumulation of nonperforming assets and bad loans proved to be an extremely serious problem, helping to ensure, first, that the bubble would burst, and second, that the said bursting would cause huge reverberations within Japan.

Japan's "Great Stagnation": Rise of the Zombies

Serious asset bubbles are not uncommon, something that most of the world came to recognize much more clearly after the global recession of 2008. Thus, dwelling too much on the causes of the financial bubble in Japan is probably unnecessary: because asset bubbles can and do happen in practically any country, one can surmise that they are not a unique malady of the East Asian economies.

More interesting is Japan's protracted recession, which raises important questions. Does the severity and length of the recession mean that some factor or set of factors are unique to Japan specifically? Even more, does some inherent flaw—one that violates liberal economic principles—explain Japan's seeming inability to recover fully from the crash of 1990? Indeed, will Japan ever recover? As noted above, among liberal economists, much less consensus has arisen on the answers to these questions. To make the task more manageable, then, I focus on two basic but contrasting explanations, with a very quick nod to a third, overarching explanation. For reasons that will become clear, beginning with the third explanation is useful. To wit, instead of allowing the market to self-correct after the bubble burst, the Japanese government did, as Benjamin Powell (2002) succinctly puts it, "everything *but* leave the economy alone" (emphasis added). This approach and its subsequent failure to bring Japan out of recession are the epitome of the liberal and especially **neoliberal** view: long-term, pervasive, and seemingly insoluble economic problems are always the product of nonmarket intervention in free markets. There is obviously more to this explanation, but a focus on the "evils" of nonmarket or government intervention as the primary reason is a fair and reasonable characterization (premised, as I mentioned before, on the deductive principles of liberal economic thought).

The two other liberal explanations are much more nuanced variations on this theme. The first is provided by Ricardo Caballero, Takeo Hoshi, and Anil Kashyap (2008), who, simply put, argue Japan's political and regulatory response to the collapse of the financial bubble "was to deny the existence of problems and delay any serious reforms or restructuring of the banks" (p. 1943). Worse still, large Japanese banks only feigned compliance with international standards governing their minimum level of capital. As Cabellero, Hoshi, and Kashyap explain,

> This meant that when banks wanted to call in a nonperforming loan, they were likely to have to write off existing capital, which in turn pushed them up against the minimum capital levels. The fear of falling below the capital standards led many banks to continue to extend credit to insolvent borrowers, gambling that somehow these firms would recover or that the government would bail them out. . . . Indeed the government also encouraged the banks to *increase* their lending to small and medium-sized firms to ease the apparent "credit crunch," especially after 1998. The continued financing, or "evergreening," can therefore be seen as a rational response by the banks to these various pressures. (p. 1944; emphasis in original)

The key point is that, throughout the postbubble, recessionary period, a significant number of "dead" (i.e., insolvent) firms were kept alive artificially—the authors called these firms "zombies." The problem with zombies is that having too many of them distorts competition throughout the rest of the economy in a number of very important ways: zombies depress market prices for their products, they artificially increase wages (by employing workers whose productivity has declined), and they depress the creation of new businesses in sectors where many of them are prevalent, which further lowers productivity since the inefficient zombie firms crowd out new, more productive firms (Hoshi and Kashyap 2004, p. 7). The problem, at the most general level, is the inability of the economy to undergo a needed restructuring (i.e., the eradication of old and inefficient elements of the economy, including, of course, unproductive zombie firms, replacing them with new and more efficient ones). Not coincidentally, this basic conclusion lines up quite nicely with Powell's (2002) analysis, for he also focuses on the lack of restructuring as the fundamental reason for Japan's long-term stagnation.

The argument put forward by Caballero, Hoshi, and Kashyap, as well as the one by Powell, reflects, albeit not necessarily in an intended manner, the idea of creative destruction as espoused by Joseph Schumpeter.[3] Schumpeter argues, in *Capitalism, Socialism, and Democracy* ([1942] 1975), that capitalism is a process, one that "incessantly revolutionizes the economic **structure** from within, incessantly destroying the old one, incessantly creating a new one. This process of creative destruction is the essential fact about capitalism" (p. 83). To Schumpeter, this process is necessary for maintaining a healthy and dynamic economy, but he also recognizes that it is a process that leads to a great deal of short-term pain: lost jobs, ruined companies, and vanishing industries. All this destruction, however, has a "saving grace." As Michael Cox and Richard Aim (2007) put it:

> Over time, societies that allow creative destruction to operate grow more productive and richer; their citizens see the benefits of new and better products, short work weeks, better jobs, and higher living standards. Herein lies the paradox of progress. A society cannot reap the rewards of creative destruction without accepting that some individuals might be worse off, not just in the short term, but perhaps forever. At the same time, attempts to soften the harsher aspects of creative destruction by trying to preserve jobs or protect industries will lead to stagnation and decline, short-circuiting the march of progress. Schumpeter's enduring term reminds us that capitalism's pain and gain are inextricably linked. The process of creating new industries does not go forward without sweeping away the preexisting order.

I bring up the concept of creative destruction because of its wide, although sometimes only tacit, acceptance within liberal economic theory. As the passage above indicates, moreover, the principle of creative destruction underscores very clearly why even the most well-meaning government interference in "natural" market processes can and does lead to unintended or undesirable economic consequences.

This point brings the discussion to a second liberal explanation, one that basically extends backward, rather than forward, the argument by Caballero,

Hoshi, and Kashyap. In a study conducted by the McKinsey Global Institute, the authors of the study argue that the Japanese economy "was never as strong as it appeared to be during its glory days" (Kondo et al. 2000, pp. 21–22). The basic problem was clear: throughout the postwar period, Japan has suffered from a hollowed-out **dual economy**. One very successful economy is composed of world-beating exporters, and the other, much larger economy is composed of "laggardly locals hidden from public view" (p. 22). The former economy accounts for about 10 percent of Japan's total economic activity, while the latter accounts for fully 90 percent. Given this vastly unbalanced distribution of economic activity, one wonders how Japan was as successful at it was. Indeed, according to the McKinsey authors, the productivity level of the localized economy is a mere 63 percent of US levels, and even worse in four key sectors: retailing, health care, housing construction, and food processing (Kondo et al. 2000).

Guessing why this productivity gap exists is not difficult: large exporters are subject to continuous and intense competition in international markets while local producers are effectively insulated from competition by government subsidies and rules that block the entry of new competitors, foreign and domestic. In the retailing sector, for example, M. James Kondo and colleagues, writing for the McKinsey Global Institute, indicate, "The tiny mom-and-pop stores remain in business because the government has lavished subsidy after subsidy upon them. They have been given guaranteed loans of over $40 billion with almost no credit evaluation" (p. 26); in addition, small-scale stores receive $10 billion worth of rent subsidies, grants to buy computers, and access to infrastructure programs. Just as important, zoning and others laws were designed to make competition by large-scale retailers directly with mom-and-pop shops difficult. The McKinsey report points to the Large-Scale Retail Location Law,[4] or Large Stores Law, as a key factor limiting competition in the retail sector. Indeed, the Large Stores Law, first implemented in 1974, was very clearly designed to preserve struggling small and medium-size retail stores at the cost of increased efficiency and competition. Not only did the law restrict the opening or expansion of retail stores with a total retail floor space in excess of 1,500 square meters, but it also established a labyrinth of regulatory hurdles, including restrictions on operating hours, days of operation, number of holidays, and so on. Between 1974 and 1990, the Large Stores Law was revised numerous times, but in most cases, according to a complaint filed against Japan by the United States, these changes only served to strengthen the law's regulations of large stores. The upshot, again, is seemingly unequivocal: the Large Store Law effectively undermined productivity growth in a major segment of the Japanese economy. However, one important empirical caveat can be found in the analysis by McKinsey Global Institute: during the 1990s, productivity in the retail sector actually experienced strong growth, in part because of a series of reforms undertaken during the decade culminating in the scrapping of the original law and the establishment of a new law, the Large-Scale Retail Store Location Law in 2000.

Still, the overarching point remains largely unchallenged: Japan's economic woes between 1990 and 2010 have been due primarily to ill-conceived and even unnecessary government interference in the market process. This intervention has encouraged and sometimes created allocative inefficiencies on a wide scale, through an army of zombie firms, or in whole sectors of the national economy. In an important respect, then, this point brings the discussion back to where it began: to many (but certainly not all) liberal analysts, Japan would have been much better off if the government had simply done nothing. Allowing thousands of banks and businesses (whether large or small) to fail and millions of workers to lose their jobs—no matter how painful—would have wiped away the most debilitating inefficiencies and allowed stronger, more productive and dynamic firms to emerge and thrive. Workers, too, would have been forced to retool, acquiring new skills and increasing their personal productivity. At the same time, what the government should or should not have done after the bubble burst, I should emphasize, is subject to great debate among liberal analysts. So, while some argue that doing nothing was the best option (Powell 2002), others argue for a different kind of policy intervention, including far more dramatic banking reform, "unconventional monetary expansion" (Krugman 2001), and deregulation leading to an increase in **FDI** (Paprzycki and Fukao 2004), among others. While the various sides to the debate warrant careful consideration, for current purposes, understanding that liberal prescriptions all revolve around the issue of how best to return the market to its "normal," competitive equilibrium is enough. This last point provides a nice segue into a discussion of the Asian Financial Crisis.

Liberal Explanations of the Asian Financial Crisis: Overview

Earlier, I made sure to differentiate between Japan's economic problems and the Asian Financial Crisis. Generally this precaution is necessary, although one can fairly point out, in the liberal view, that the distinction may not be that critical after all. Thus, while clear differences can be found between the two crises, particularly in terms of the immediate effects and proximate (or triggering) causes, most liberal analysis focuses on "poor fundamentals" as the underlying reason for the crisis. So what are these poor fundamentals? To many liberal analysts, this question is fairly easy to answer: outdated and often corrupted financial systems rife with **moral hazards**. In South Korea, in particular, the problems began with a financial system that allowed for and even encouraged excessive borrowing by already overleveraged companies (in other words, firms borrowed more than was prudent and then could not cover the interest payments on their debt). Long before the crisis hit, for example, the **debt-to-equity ratios** of the top thirty *chaebol* were between 2.5 and 85.0 (Pyo 1999), with an average of 4.4 in 1997 (Lee and Han 2006). In the United States, a debt-to-equity ratio between 0.5 and 1.5 is the generally accepted standard, so the South Korean figures were considered by many economists and financial analysts to be unsustainably and even absurdly high. But the numbers raise a more important question: How did the average (not to mention the upper extreme) debt-to-equity ratio reach such a high level in South Korea?

One answer is simply that borrowing in South Korea, especially for the largest and most powerful firms (i.e., the *chaebol*), was not subject to market discipline or, really, to discipline of any kind—including, most importantly, discipline by the visible hand of the **state**. If anything, the situation was just the opposite: borrowers and lenders were afforded special protection by the state against failure. Lenders and investors, in other words, assumed that the South Korean conglomerates were immune to bankruptcy because they had the implicit backing of the South Korean government. Even more, financial intermediaries themselves were perceived as having the same implicit government guarantee. Herein lies the fundamental problem: with no disciplinary mechanisms to speak of for either lenders or borrowers, a tremendous moral hazard problem was created. The lack of repercussions led to excessive and often very risky lending, which generated the sort of asset inflation also witnessed in Japan. The overpricing of assets, moreover, "was sustained in part by a sort of circular process, in which the proliferation of risky lending drove up the prices of risky assets, making the financial condition of the intermediaries seem sounder than it was. And then the bubble burst" (Krugman 1998, n.p.).

The moral hazard problem, of course, was not unique to South Korea. It was, however, exacerbated and deeply embedded in the economy by a history of heavy-handed state intervention, or so liberal analysts argue, which distorted South Korea's industrial structure and financial system. The story here is a long one, but it boils down to an effort by the South Korean government, beginning in the 1970s, to rapidly construct an array of heavy industries (e.g., steel, shipbuilding, automobiles, machinery, and petrochemicals) so that it could establish a self-sufficient military and industrial capability. But heavy and chemical industries, as Song Yong Park (2001) explains, are highly capital intensive, requiring more than $1 billion on average per project. Typically, because of the time required to recover the initial investment, these types of projects in other capitalist economies are funded by long-term risk capital financed through the equity or stock market. Yet, in the case of South Korea, the major source of funding has been debt, mainly in the form of credits from bank and nonbank financial institutions (S. Y. Park 2001). There is a reason for this approach, too: unlike the stock market, financing through credit allows the government to maintain control of the companies and specific projects that receive funding. And while the South Korean government did not prohibit or even inhibit the development of bond and equity markets, the growth of these markets was, for a very long time, stunted by the availability of plentiful, cheap, and preferential credit, most of which was expressly funneled to the *chaebol* (for further discussion on this issue, see Lukauskas 2002). This arrangement, liberal economists might concede, worked reasonably well during the high-speed growth period, but it was absolutely bound to fail—as happened in the 1990s. So, once again, the culprit and the cause is clear to liberal analysts: a meddling government that distorted and undermined the market process and market-based institutions.

South Korea's Rapid Recovery: "Killing the Zombies"

The account above is admittedly cursory and stylized, but the logic of the liberal position is clear. Thus, while variations and sharp disagreements may be found among different liberal analysts, broad agreement exists on the folly of "messing" with market fundamentals. Significantly, however, South Korea did seem to recover from the Asian Financial Crisis extremely quickly: after a one-year contraction of 6.7 percent in 1998, GDP started growing in the first quarter of 1999 and then accelerated: from 5.8 percent, to 11.2 percent in the second quarter, to 13 percent in both the third and fourth quarters, resulting in an annual growth rate of 10.9 percent. This trend continued into 2000, with a growth rate of 9.3 percent for that year. Not surprisingly, the IMF and its supporters took credit for this rapid turnaround. In December 1999, for example, Michel Camdessus (then managing director of the IMF) gave most of the credit to sound macroeconomic policies "cherished by the IMF," the promotion of the free market and an outward orientation of economic policies, and the establishment of laws, regulations, standards, and norms advocated by the IMF that support the functioning of markets (Camdessus 1999). No doubt, Camdessus and other liberal analysts would also point to the bitter medicine the country was forced to swallow in the form of corporate restructuring, which I discuss in the following section.

Corporate Restructuring in South Korea

A major part of the IMF program centered on the need to deal decisively with insolvent and financially unstable firms. To this end, hundreds of companies—including the largest and most powerful *chaebol*—were either liquidated or "rehabilitated" through forced reorganization. The biggest to fall was Daewoo in 1999 (which had debts of 60 trillion won and $10 billion), but Daewoo's collapse was followed by more than half of the then top thirty conglomerates (not all were dissolved—many were subject to forced merger or consolidation), including four of South Korea's five carmakers.[5] As I mentioned earlier, thousands of small and medium-size firms also went out of business. In an important respect, then, South Korea went through the sort of corporate bloodletting that Japan assiduously avoided. To put it very simply, South Korea killed off its zombies. This process helped to wipe out inefficiencies and restore rationality to the economy, which explains, from the liberal perspective, why South Korea avoided its own lost decade. As usual, the foregoing account is only part of the liberal analysts' story, and this explanation is only representative rather than definitive. Indeed, several alternative accounts exist, including one which gives almost no credit to the IMF program and instead focuses on Keynesian policies—in other words, an aggressive reduction in interest rates and a huge increase in public spending (see Shin and Chang 2005).

Weathering the Storm: Taiwan's Stability in a Sea of Trouble

Thus far, I have said little about Taiwan. The main reason, as I suggested above, should already be clear: Taiwan was relatively, although not completely, unaffected by the Asian Financial Crisis or any other major economic downturn. Taiwan's seeming immunity raises the question, why? That is, what made Taiwan seemingly impervious to the economic difficulties experienced by South Korea and Japan? I have already provided a basic liberal answer to this question, namely, a sound macroeconomic environment. The key elements of this environment included substantial foreign reserves, a relatively low external debt burden, a current account surplus, an effective system of bank regulation, and sound monetary policies. In addition, unlike its Asian neighbors, Taiwan had already moved to a floating exchange rate (as opposed to a **dollar-peg scheme**). I should emphasize that, in the liberal view, all the aforementioned factors are mutually reinforcing. For example, a current account surplus means that the country as a whole is accumulating assets, particularly foreign ones, which reduces the need for foreign borrowing. Obviously, too, consistent current account surpluses allow countries to build larger foreign reserves: Taiwan's foreign reserve was approximately $90 billion in June 1997, more than three times its external debt of $25.3 billion. Tellingly, in this regard, South Korea, Indonesia, Malaysia, the Philippines, and Thailand all had current account deficits throughout the 1990s, and all had significant external debt burdens and relatively meager foreign reserves, ranging from $9.8 billion to $34.1 billion (all figures cited in Y.-C. Chen 1998).

Another important difference between Taiwan and the Asian economies affected by the Asian Financial Crisis, including South Korea, was Taiwan's greater reliance on the stock market for investment: in 1997, Taiwanese firms raised $15.3 billion in equity, an amount that is quite significant given the fact that Taiwan's industrial structure consists primarily of small and medium-size firms (Y.-C. Chen 1998). The relative lack of large and extremely large enterprises in Taiwan—and the political clout and influence that often comes with size—has meant, too, that nonprofitable firms can and do fail, a boon to economic efficiency, and a practice that stood in stark contrast to South Korea prior to the Asian Financial Crisis and to Japan even during its lost decade.

To sum up, in the liberal view, Taiwan was not necessarily a model of free market economics or a paragon of market fundamentals in the 1990s, but it definitely came much, much closer than either Japan or South Korea. And, for this reason, Taiwan avoided the ravages of the Asian Financial Crisis or a similar fate (at least, this argument would be the one that liberals would make). Indeed, Taiwan has also made it through the recent global recession relatively unscathed. Following the onset of the global recession, the economy did experience a slump, with real GDP growth falling to –1.1 percent in 2009. Yet, by 2010, the GDP growth rate was back up to a remarkable 10.7 percent, while the current account was a healthy $39.9 billion (all figures cited in CEPD 2012).

Before one accepts the liberal account, of course, one must consider a range of other possibilities, of which there are many. Methodologically, too, I need to reemphasize a key point: overreliance on aggregate statistics and "faraway" analysis can be problematic. Even when essentially accurate, such analysis can leave out the most important elements of the explanation. Thus, while macroeconomic factors might very well be a critical part of the explanation for Japan's economic malaise, South Korea's problems following the Asian Financial Crisis, or Taiwan's admirable stability, one also needs to know why some societies can build and sustain a sound macroeconomic environment while others cannot. At the same time, closer, comparative historical analysis might reveal that macroeconomic factors were not nearly as important as they seemed.

Statist Explanations of Economic Crises in East Asia

As I have just presented, liberal analysis suggests that a commitment to free market principles—especially to the liberalization or opening of financial markets—is a key to both economic stability and dynamic, sustainable growth in a more fluid and open global economy. But statist analysts tell a different story. On the one hand, statists generally recognize that the **developmental state** cannot remain unchanged in a context of increasing globalization and burgeoning democracy, the latter of which purportedly makes state leaders' development of and follow-through on coherent economic plans far more difficult. The reason for this is simple: in a democratic political system, political leaders are more strongly subject to the "will of the people," or at least to more political pressure and influence from groups outside the government. Thus, they cannot rule by fiat, as generally is the case in authoritarian systems. On the other hand, many statist analysts suggest that the dismantling or erosion of the developmental state—particularly the control it exercises over certain types of economic activity—has led to the most serious problems. Linda Lim (1998), for example, argues that, "if openness was an essential ingredient of the Asian economic miracle, too much openness too fast was responsible for its downfall" (p. 28). More specifically, Lim writes, "In particular, rapid and sweeping . . . capital market liberalization that began in the late 1980s led to a massive influx of foreign capital, especially short-term loan and equity capital, which contributed to the boom economy and over-investment bubble of the 1990s" (p. 28). To put it more simply, the problem was not too much state intervention but not enough. Or, more accurately, states did not exercise enough of the "right kind" of control over economic activity, especially in financial markets.

Financial Liberalization in Taiwan and South Korea: Continuing Importance of the State

Linda Weiss (2000) and Yu-Shan Wu (2007) provide a complementary and useful perspective, one that explains why Taiwan largely avoided getting swept up in the Asian Financial Crisis, while South Korea was directly engulfed by the same meltdown. As Weiss explains, Taiwanese authorities—primarily through the Central Bank of China—exercised a great deal more caution in opening up the country's financial market than did the South Koreans. The Central Bank of China, Weiss writes, was "the embodiment of financial caution, keeping a vigilant eye on the disruptive potential of capital flows, insisting on 'emergency powers' of intervention as a *quid pro quo* for opening up the currency and stock markets, and indeed intervening before and after the Asian crisis to prevent currency speculation and stock market manipulation" (p. 30). In addition, new controls were added after Taiwanese officials witnessed what was going on around them. For example, Weiss (2000) notes that, following Taiwan's decision to deregulate the corporate bond market in 1989 (which allowed Taiwanese companies to raise funds abroad by issuing bonds), the Central Bank of China implemented new rules limiting the proceeds of such overseas issuances to the support of offshore investment and the purchase of raw materials. This rule was relaxed four years later, but this "relaxation" was accompanied by new rules requiring all domestic remittances to be invested in plant expansion (Weiss 2000). Taiwan's financial "liberalization," in this regard, was anything but a free-flowing, unregulated process. Instead, each step of liberalization seemed to be followed by some sort of reregulation, or at least by a careful consideration of the implications of the changes that increasing liberalization was likely to bring to Taiwan. This reregulation, moreover, was part of an overarching plan to maintain and enhance state capacity so that political authorities could continue to pursue their goals of industrial upgrading (Weiss 2000).

Taiwan followed this path, Weiss (2000) asserts, for two basic historical reasons. The first was the "insecurity factor": while both South Korea and Taiwan faced so-called existential security threats (i.e., threats that could lead to the extinction or destruction of a whole society), for Taiwan this threat was increasing with every passing year as China, unlike North Korea, was (and is) a growing military and economic power. Even more, unlike South Korea, Taiwan faces a significant degree of diplomatic isolation and does not enjoy the same level of security commitment from the major powers, especially the United States, should China follow through on its always implicit threat to reincorporate Taiwan. "The Taiwanese therefore cannot afford the luxury of feeling more secure from military threat, and since national security and economic security are nowadays so heavily intertwined, all the more reasons to remain vigilant in regard to the disruptive potential of short-term money markets" (Weiss 2000, p. 31). Second, Taiwan's relative diplomatic isolation has a flip side: because the Taiwanese are effectively barred from joining major international organizations, such as the **OECD**, they have been less subject to—although not immune from—external political pressures to liberalize their financial markets. This insulation is not an insignificant factor given the hoops that South Korea was forced to jump through in its efforts to join the OECD beginning in 1993. In fact, in order to join the OECD, South Korea had to agree to financial market liberalization and to opening its domestic market to foreign investors (Kalinowski and Cho 2009).

Moreover, despite historical differences between Taiwan and South Korea, in both countries, the state played a key role in the liberalization process. In Taiwan's case, as I have discussed, the state fairly clearly remained cautious about the liberalization process in general and endeavored to exercise control whenever and wherever officials deemed necessary and appropriate. But this caution was also true, for the most part, in South Korea. The key distinction, however, was that South Korean authorities focused their attention on long-term credit inflows and equity participation, while allowing and even encouraging short-term credit inflows to unfold in relatively unregulated fashion. In retrospect, the lack of regulation was a strategic miscalculation, but it was one that reflected the underlying political dynamics of South Korea and existing institutional relations, particularly between a fledgling democratic state and the still-powerful *chaebol*. More specifically, the dual strategy of loosening regulations on short-term credit while maintaining control of long-term credit inflows "served the interests of the *chaebols'* strategy to become 'global players' and provided them with easier access to international financial markets and the foreign credits needed to finance this endeavor. At the same time, the policy reflected the fear of *chaebol* families and the government about the increasing influence of foreign investors through long-term involvement and equity participation" (Kalinowski and Cho 2009, p. 225). This policy helped lead to the economic disaster that South Korea experienced as a result of the Asian Financial Crisis. Thomas Kalinowski and Cho Hyekyung explain the basic dynamic this way:

> Because of liberalization, the state lost control over the inflow of short-term credit, but at the same time the actors still expected the government to guarantee private credit, just as it had done during the time of tight financial market control. The withdrawal of the state left the financial market in a control vacuum in which huge amounts of short-term foreign capital flowed into Korea. This capital was mainly channeled through the *chaebol*-owned non-bank financial institutions (NBFI), which mushroomed in the 1990s. The NBFI were neither subject to the restrictions on *chaebol* involvement in the banking sector

nor as closely monitored as the deposit-taking commercial banks. This liberalization and loose regulation were exploited by the *chaebol*-owned NBFI to borrow short-term from abroad and lend long-term to their sister companies. Equally important for the expansion of credit was the government's withdrawal from active industrial policies, investment regulation, and supervision. The consequence was that the *chaebol* aggressively expanded and diversified their operations in fields such as steel and car manufacturing, where there was already an overcapacity in Korea. (pp. 225–226)

In the foregoing passage, one can clearly see key elements of the liberal argument, especially the moral hazard generated through the implicit state guarantee of private credit and the self-generating cycle of asset inflation that guarantee tends to create. And viewing these factors in isolation (that is, noncomparatively), one might easily conclude that, for South Korea, the liberal view is correct. Yet, viewing these circumstances in relation to a similar process in Taiwan, one can come to a very different conclusion. To repeat, throughout the 1980s and 1990s, the developmental state in Taiwan endeavored to control or manage the liberalization process, an effort that proved to be quite successful. More important, the unwavering purpose of this effort was to enable the country to achieve a clear set of developmental goals: to protect the national economy and domestic industries from the vicissitudes of the global market, from speculative forces, from powerful foreign competitors, and so on. This effort continued into the 2000s, even as international pressures for liberalization grew stronger.

Interestingly, part of this increased pressure was due to the decision by Taiwan to gain accession to the WTO. Taiwan actually made this decision in 1990, when the country first submitted an application to join the WTO (at the time, the organization was known as the GATT). Significantly, perhaps, Taiwan's application to the WTO took a very long time to be approved, almost twelve years. Thus, during the 1990s, Taiwan faced relatively little external pressure for liberalization. Once approval came, however, the Taiwanese government was required to commit to and implement a wide range of market-opening and liberalizing measures going forth. The key commitments centered on liberalization of international trade (reduction or elimination of tariffs and nontariff barriers) and services, including financial services. In the financial services sector, Taiwan committed to

- Deregulation of requirements restricting foreign banks from establishing branches and representative offices in Taiwan.
- Elimination of the ceiling on the level of deposits denominated by the New Taiwan dollar that foreign banks may hold.
- Elimination of bans prohibiting banks from providing underwriting and certification services for commercial paper.
- Allowing foreigners to establish billing companies in the financial services sector.

- Relaxing limitations on foreign investment in foreign currency broker-ages (Board of Foreign Trade 2001).

Despite making these commitments, the Taiwanese government was still not ready to cede control to the "impersonal" dictates of the free market. For example, the government adopted a plan designed to ensure that Taiwanese firms would be large enough to compete with major international players. This policy meant mergers and consolidation of domestic firms; however, the government did not leave it up to the market to decide how the combining would be done. Instead, as Wu (2007) describes it, the government simply "announced that by the end of 2005 at least three financial holding companies should each hold more than 10% of market share, that the number of public financial institutions should be reduced from 12 to six, and that the total number of financial holding companies should be halved, to seven" (p. 990). This "liberalization" was by government dictate, in a top-down approach, "redolent of good old **industrial policy**" (p. 990). Wu notably suggests that the old statist model had become outdated—primarily because of a new domestic political context, one which was no longer **authoritarian** but democratic—and that Taiwan's economy could easily suffer the same fate as the economies of South Korea, Japan, and other Asian countries. Wu's reason is a bit ironic: because an authoritarian developmental state is less beholden to societal, and especially corporate, interests, it can pursue policies that reflect the broader national interests. However, in a democratic context, societal actors generally have more influence over economic policymaking, which means that they can sway policies in their favor. Democracy, in other words, compromises the autonomy of the developmental state; thus, the raison d'être of the developmental state—a commitment to the public good—is lost. Wu may be right, although Taiwan's recent economic performance does not necessarily support his view, but one should not lose sight of the larger statist argument, which is that in any explanation of the effects of the Asian Financial Crisis on Taiwan (and South Korea), states continue to matter: their decisions and actions deeply influence economic outcomes both in positive and negative ways. To repeat, in the statist view, the lack of effective state intervention—combined with too much reliance on unfettered market forces—creates problems, not the other way around.

The Still Perplexing Case of Japan: Statist View

Statists recognize that Japan is no longer the economic juggernaut it once was. At the same time, viewing Japan's economic difficulties in wider perspective is crucial, which liberal analysts almost universally fail to do. Part of this wider perspective suggests that Japan's inability to recover immediately after its financial crisis is not unusual. As Weiss (2000) points out and as I have already mentioned, other wealthy capitalist economies have experienced similar asset bubbles, usually following a period of deregulation, and, more importantly, other capitalist economies have experienced equally long periods of economic malaise. Significantly, this stagnation was true for the United States following the Savings and Loan Crisis, the effects of which were felt for at least a decade (1982–1992).[6] Weiss also notes that, in several cases—Sweden, Norway, Finland, and Italy—the extent of financial and economic difficulties (measured as the ratio of nonperforming loans at their peak to gross national product [GNP]) was even greater than in Japan. I could even point to the recent global recession, a product in no small measure of the 2007 subprime mortgage and credit crisis in the United States, from which many countries are still suffering years later. Indeed, it would not be a stretch to argue that this crisis will affect the United States for a decade or longer (in 2013, for example, the United States had still not fully or even mostly recovered from the crisis). Finally, Weiss reminds readers that just prior to the outbreak of the Asian Financial Crisis, Japan seemed to be on the path of economic recovery, recording a growth rate of 3.8 percent in 1995–1996. Were it not for the financial crisis, then, Japan could have possibly gained the momentum necessary to complete its recovery (admittedly, no one will never know).

On this last point, one must understand that the Japanese state, through the Ministry of Finance and other agencies, was consciously pursuing a wait-and-see solution, and that the policy appeared to be working. The consensus within the state, according to Weiss (2000), was that Japan could "grow out" of the financial crisis fairly quickly, largely by allowing asset values to increase and bad loans to decrease in value through a more "natural" process of inflation (p. 45). In addition, domestic political conditions made this approach the most reasonable and viable choice at the time. And while the "growing out" strategy ultimately did not work, its failure does not mean that the Japanese state had become the problem rather than the solution (or, as liberal analysts might argue, was always the problem). It only meant that the state was less than perfect and that the complexity of domestic, international, and global political-economic dynamics made the decisionmaking process highly contingent. Furthermore, important mitigating factors need to be considered. In Japan, the developmental state has not been solely focused on rapid economic growth and technological advancement; it has also been focused on equity.

The Japanese state's focus on equity is reflected in such outcomes as high secondary school completion rates, high levels of employment, and relatively equal distribution of income (Weiss 2000). Consider some of the following figures. First, Japan is only one of three countries in the world (France and Sweden are the other two) with a secondary school enrollment of 98 percent or better. Second, during its so-called lost decade, the unemployment rate in Japan never exceeded 5 percent, and for most of the decade (until 1998) was less than 3.6 percent—a remarkably low level by international standards. Third, Japan has long had the lowest level of inequality (as measured by the **Gini coefficient**) in

Asia, and one of the lowest among the wealthiest capitalist economies. These outcomes do not happen automatically or by chance but instead are products of conscious government policy. In this regard, one can argue that the Japanese state is purposefully trading off greater equity for less growth; this trade-off is a normative choice. In addition, the prioritization of equity is not just a matter of state policy but is also connected to culture. This point provides a nice segue into an examination of culture and, more specifically, into an examination of how cultural factors influence policy choices.

How Cultural Factors Contributed to Japan's Economic Malaise

That states pursue multiple and often competing goals is a simple yet very important point to keep in mind. Let us consider this in more concrete terms. Earlier I discussed Japan's dual economy and the striking lack of productivity among workers in the domestically oriented sectors. Liberal analysts strongly suggest that this lack of productivity represents an unwanted and unintended flaw in the Japanese system. After all, what country would purposely allow for and even encourage low productivity? The liberal view, however, reflects an unstated normative position, one that prioritizes allocative efficiency over equity and employment security. Thus, in the liberal view, large-scale unemployment and a massive wave of bankruptcies are better because these help to wipe out economic inefficiency (for instance, by getting rid of zombie workers and zombie firms). This adjustment may involve a great deal of pain and destruction because, after all, workers and employers are not really zombies but instead are living, feeling human beings. For liberals, however, the end result will be a stronger, more efficient and competitive national economy. The human costs, in short, are worth the economic gains. In the statist view, by contrast, market values are not always considered sacrosanct. In other words, statist analysts and others understand that what is good for the market is not always good for society as a whole. Thus, economic inefficiency can be and often is a desirable outcome, if it means, for example, greater social cohesion and protection of domestic groups (be they workers, firms, or families). This differing view may help to explain why Japan maintained a relatively low unemployment rate following the collapse of the asset bubble, a stark contrast to the level of unemployment in the United States following the 2007 subprime mortgage and credit crisis. In short, sustaining high employment was (and is) a conscious policy choice (see Figure 3.4). On this last point, consider that, after the collapse of Japan's asset bubble in the early 1990s, domestic unemployment increased, but never exceeded 5 percent. In the United States, by contrast, the collapse of the real estate bubble led to an unemployment rate of almost 10 percent. In early 2013, the US unemployment rate was still much higher than Japan's peak unemployment

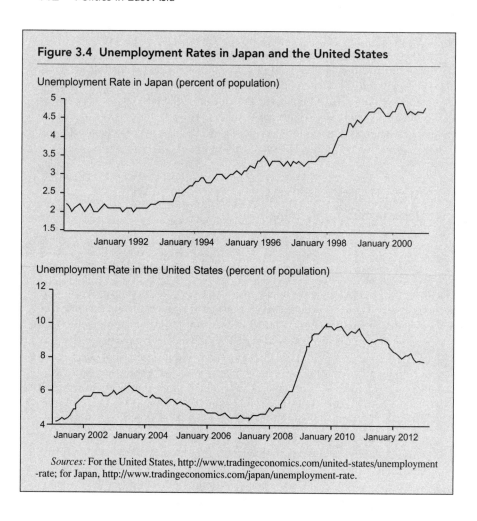

Figure 3.4 Unemployment Rates in Japan and the United States

Unemployment Rate in Japan (percent of population)

Unemployment Rate in the United States (percent of population)

Sources: For the United States, http://www.tradingeconomics.com/united-states/unemployment
-rate; for Japan, http://www.tradingeconomics.com/japan/unemployment-rate.

rate throughout the 1990s. Of course, the comparison is very crude, but it is suggestive of important differences between the two countries. The statist view may also explain why Japan "suffers" from perennially low productivity: low productivity, too, is an acceptable trade-off in achieving a greater degree of equity and social protection.

The distinction between the liberal and statist views, as I already suggested, reflects two different normative positions. Put another way, the liberal and statist views, in addition to being an amalgam of supposedly impersonal economic principles, represent contrasting cultural models as well, something that should not come as a surprise, for economic systems do not exist in a vacuum. For better or worse, they reflect the unique social, cultural, and political contexts of the societies of which they are a part. An economic structure, in short, mirrors the characteristics of the nation to which it belongs (Williams 1994). I have already discussed the "better" part of this equation for the East Asian economies—cultural factors contributed, perhaps profoundly, to the economic successes of Japan, South Korea, and Taiwan. However, the equation has a "worse" part, a part that may provide an important insight into Japan's prolonged economic difficulties since 1990.

In Chapter 2, I discussed culture as a sort of binding agent or catalytic glue that helps connect all the underutilized and scattered resources that most late-industrializing economies possess but are otherwise unable to fully or fruitfully utilize. This binding agent, to repeat, is the "better" part of culture: the part that is a functional, highly productive, and dynamic force within a national economy. However, culture can have the opposite effect. That is, it may block change, or, in keeping with the theme of this book, it may become a powerful force for continuity. Thus, even while culture always remains **intersubjective** and malleable, once certain norms, values, beliefs, and practices become entrenched within a society—once they take root, so to speak—they can become very difficult to uproot. More important, entrenched cultural forces can, over time, easily lead to "path-dependent" situations. The basic concept of **path dependence**, while the subject of a complex debate,[7] can easily be boiled down to the following: Past decisions often have a lock-in effect. In other words, once certain decisions or choices are made, they tend to keep people, institutions, and whole societies on particular paths regardless of changing circumstances. Importantly, while the initial decisions may have been productive and even necessary, lock-ins generally lead to negative, or less than optimal, outcomes (Liebowitz and Margolis 1999).

In Japan, for example, consider a well-known feature of the labor-business organization: the **three pillars**. The three pillars are (1) enterprise-based union, (2) seniority-based wages and promotion, and (3) lifetime employment. All three are found in most large firms and some smaller firms.[8] As a group, these three pillars had a clear economic and political rationale: while mostly associated with the post–World War II era, the origin of the latter two pillars can clearly be found in the prewar period when severe labor shortages among skilled and semiskilled workers and job hopping by Japanese workers more generally made maintaining stable production schedules difficult for companies. To attract and keep workers, therefore, Japanese companies had to implement new "attachment-inducing measures," including "longevity-based compensation systems to encourage long-term attachment" (Stone 2009, p. 7). Although originally intended primarily for white-collar or managerial workers, seniority- and age-based compensation and lifetime employment were eventually extended to all regular (i.e., blue-collar) employees beginning in the 1950s. The expansion of the job security to regular employees, in other words, was primarily a rational economic and political decision, too; it reflected an effort by Japanese employers to build a stable workforce and, even more importantly, to thwart the radicalization of workers in the early postwar period.

The upsurge of labor militancy in the early postwar period is a complex story unto itself; suffice it to say that it was the product of myriad factors,[9] including a decision by General Douglas MacArthur, the **supreme commander for the Allied Powers**, in the late 1940s, to give workers the right to organize, engage in collective bargaining, and strike. Workers took full advantage of these newfound rights and, in fact, pushed them to their limits. One key tactic of union activists (in lieu of the conventional strike) was to take over and then run factories, railroads, and mines—a practice referred to as "production control" (Jeong and Aguilera 2007). This practice, which subsequently became a widespread movement, helped give rise to the third pillar of the Japanese employment system, enterprise unionism. Dae Yong Jeong and Ruth Aguilera (2007) explain, "The plant union became crucial to carrying out production control for survival. Organizers felt that it was too time-consuming to distribute handbills to individuals at the factory gate and encourage each individual to join the union, as they had done in the prewar years. Instead, they organized the employees altogether at once in the factory yard" (p. 25). These initial factory-based organizing efforts also encouraged cooperation between white- and blue-collar workers, since both midlevel managers and factory-floor workers were important to the success of the production control movement, and both had something to gain from this cooperation.

Ultimately, the production control movement was eradicated by the state, which used the courts to outlaw the strategy (Stone 2009). Enterprise-based unionism, however, survived and was even encouraged by large companies and state leaders since it was less threatening than industry-wide unionism. The trade-off for the companies was the extension, as noted earlier, of job security (lifetime employment and seniority-based wages and promotion) to all workers, not just white-collar employees. Once established in the 1950s, the three pillars gradually became an accepted and expected norm within the Japanese employment system. And for several decades, many scholars argue, the three pillars served Japan's overall economic interests very well.[10] They helped to ensure long-term industrial stability, they encouraged firms and employees to invest in human capital, and they paved the way for cooperative and productive relations between labor and management. More broadly and more significantly for current purposes, the three pillars became part of Japan's larger institutional and cultural milieu. (The point here runs counter to some older accounts, which viewed Japanese culture itself as the source of the three pillars; instead, I argue that the three pillars helped to shape the larger culture.)

Despite the rationality and economic contributions of the three pillars, clear economic drawbacks can be found in an employment system that limits the ability of capitalist enterprises (1) to lay off or fire workers during economic downturns—still less, when a workforce reduction might simply benefit a company financially; (2) to promote and pay workers based on merit rather than seniority; or (3) to "poach" the best workers from other, competing firms. Indeed, such "hand-tying" limits are, as I have already suggested, at least partly responsible for the relatively low productivity of the Japanese labor force and can have detrimental effects on the competitiveness of Japanese firms in the global marketplace (see Figure 3.5 for further discussion). Yet, until very recently, Japanese firms have largely abided by the normative principles of the three pillars. Attributing the staying power of the three pillars entirely to culture would be too simplistic, not to mention downright wrong. Scholars, in fact, point to a number of reasons for the persistence of the three pillars, especially of lifetime employment. These include court-imposed limits on layoffs and firing (Moriguchi and

---

Figure 3.5 "In Japan, Secure Jobs Have a Cost"

"When the sheet metal orders coming into his small business . . . fell by half last October [2008], it never occurred to Masaaki Taruki to lay off his workers. Instead, he set about brainstorming new projects to occupy them. An indoor vegetable garden? A handicrafts workshop? Because of government subsidies, Mr. Taruki in the last three months installed rows of parsley, watercress and other plants, using factory space that has been empty since the company disposed of unused machinery. . . . [Similarly, when] sales at the machinery maker Shinano Kogyo in central Japan plunged some 70 percent late last year, the company started dispatching its idle workers to sweep the streets and pick up trash in the wider community, while remaining on the payroll" (Tabuchi 2009).

While admittedly anecdotal, these vignettes, from Hiroko Tabuchi's (2009) article in the *New York Times,* suggest that Japan has a very different way of dealing with economic crisis than countries such as the United States. Less anecdotal are the unemployment statistics—a point I made earlier but which bears repeating. In the first quarter of 2009, the same article notes, Japan's economy suffered its worse contraction in more than a decade, declining 15.2 percent on an annualized basis; yet the country's unemployment rate rose to only 4.8 percent. According to analysts, as cited in the article, this paradox was "because lifetime employment is alive and well in Japan."

As one expert on Japanese employment commented to Tabuchi, "job tenure in Japan remains remarkably long. Companies get rid of the buffers first. They'll get rid of temporary workers, reduce overtime, reduce bonuses. They would squeeze their suppliers. They would do anything before considering cutting regular workers." But the cost of doing so, the *New York Times* reporter notes, is clear: "Companies slash wages, which reduces consumer spending. Businesses become more reluctant to take on new recruits, shutting young people out of the labor force. And productivity plummets, hurting Japan's competitiveness in an increasingly aggressive international market."

Ono 2004) and substantial subsidies by the Japanese state. On this last point, significantly, in 2009, the Japanese government budgeted ¥60 billion, or about US$624 million, to reimburse companies for keeping workers (the government pays half the cost); in March 2009, about 48,000 companies sought subsidies for 2.38 million employees (Tabuchi 2009).

At the same time, arguing that culture is irrelevant would be equally remiss. To understand why, one should consider the issue from a societal standpoint: Japanese of all stripes consider lifetime employment a basic right, and something that is good for both employees and their companies. In a 2011 survey, for example, more than 87.5 percent of respondents to a national survey agreed with the question, "Do you support lifetime employment?" This figure was fairly consistent across gender and age but reflected a significant increase in approval since 1999, when 72.3 percent agreed with the question (Japan Institute for Labor Policy and Training 2013, p. 9). One should also note, in this regard, that a large proportion of Japan's workforce is not explicitly or implicitly guaranteed lifetime employment. According to an analysis by Hiroshi Ono (2005), for instance, only about 20 percent of Japan's labor force can expect lifetime employment in practice, although other researchers argue that the figure is higher. In addition, lifetime employment is unevenly distributed, with male university graduates being the primary beneficiaries (Ono estimates that 55 percent of this group have lifetime employment). Given these statistics—and from a US cultural viewpoint—one might expect widespread opposition to lifetime employment, which would be widely viewed as "wasteful," "inefficient," and even "corrupt" by the large majority of the working population that does not benefit from lifetime employment or the other pillars. But as the survey indicates, this is not the case among most Japanese. As a result, in practice, lifetime employment, even if limited to a relatively small proportion of the labor force, has remained a core feature of the Japanese employment system, something that has continued to be true even during Japan's two "lost decades," which brings the discussion back to the key point of this section: institutional, legal, and governmental policy have combined to transform a contingent employment practice into a deeply entrenched social norm. This combination is a powerful one and also one that seems to reflect the lock-in effect of path dependence. In an era of slower growth and increasingly intense global competition, moreover, adherence to this pillar certainly contributed to Japan's long-term economic malaise. At the same time, however, dedication to this principle underscores one of the general cultural traits of postwar Japan: the emphasis on equity and social protection over economic efficiency.

The argument here could easily be extended to other aspects of the Japanese economy, but the point is clear: underlying many "irrational" or economically inefficient practices may be an important cultural foundation that is difficult to ignore.

A Structural Explanation: The Problem of Overcapacity

While liberal, statist, and cultural accounts may provide useful and even necessary insights into aspects of East Asia's economic difficulties in the recent past, structural accounts suggest, most generally, that one needs to begin with an understanding that East Asia's troubles are part and parcel of a larger global pattern—in other words, that region after region (or country after country) has experienced a similar set of economic crises is no accident. The consistent recurrence of economic and financial crises indicates that these crises are not primarily domestic or mesolevel phenomena, although mesolevel factors certainly play a role, but are instead indicative of system-level dynamics. On one level, nothing should be surprising about this realization, as researchers of all theoretical stripes acknowledge the cyclical, boom-and-bust nature of capitalism. At the same time, liberal economists and statist analysts, in particular, have a strong tendency to assume that any crises can be managed, minimized, or even avoided (à la Taiwan) through a "freer market," good policy, some sort of domestic-level "adjustments," or some combination thereof. For many structural analysts, however, that view is myopic—albeit not irrelevant. Consider one view expressed by Jeffrey Winters (1999):

> The course of the [Asian financial] crisis lay in systemic changes in international capitalism—specifically, in who controlled capital flows to developing countries and in the growing prominence of highly mobile and volatile forms of capital and transactions. But equally important, the vulnerability of particular countries varied with the nature of their linkages and with their exposure to external capital flows that could change course more rapidly than ever before and on a scale that could easily overwhelm all but a few countries economically. (p. 79)

Other researchers have focused on deeper causes, in particular, the "classic crisis of overproduction, over-investment, and over-capacity, meaning the emergence of too much productive capacity globally relative to global demand, resulting in a decline in the rate of profit" (Bello 2006, p. 1347). To put the issue in simpler (and admittedly even simplistic) terms, many structural analysts argue that capitalism has reached a stage in which it can produce too much "stuff" on a long-term basis (the so-called B-phase of the **Kondratieff cycle**). While this conclusion may not sound particularly ominous, the implications are clear, and clearly negative: if productive capacity consistently exceeds consumptive capacity, prices for goods must fall, which means firms—even or especially in the core economies—will find earning profits from "normal" economic transactions (i.e., from industrial production) harder. In this situation, production tends to move from core zones to other parts of the world-system, a phenomenon about which one should already be familiar (recall the discussion from the previous chapter on the product cycle and flying geese model). More significantly, capitalists have a strong tendency, even need, to turn increasingly to speculative and other "value-creating" activities in the financial arena (Wallerstein 2008). Certainly, the dramatic shift to and even dependence on finance capitalism has become readily apparent to both careful and casual observers alike. Less recognized, however, is how this shift has profoundly altered the dynamics of global capitalism, including its effects on national and regional economies.

As I noted above, the cyclical nature of capitalism is well understood. Less well understood is how finance capitalism, overproduction, and the secular decline of corporate profits from the "real economy" are tied together, and how these are ultimately responsible for the economic crisis in Japan, for the Asian Financial Crisis, and for myriad other crises (past, present, and future). To repeat, all of these crises are cut from the same cloth (another point of disagreement with liberal analysts); they all reflect the inherent instability and volatility of a global capitalist system that has become increasingly reliant on financial speculation for profit making. To be sure, some actors will always make huge sums of money from the speculative bubbles that finance capitalism produces, and these individual successes can create the illusion that everything still works. "But," as Immanuel Wallerstein (2008) succinctly puts it, "speculative bubbles always burst, sooner or later." In fact, not only do they burst with unnerving regularity, but they also emerge time and time again with the same unnerving regularity. The reason, to repeat, is clear: the traditional avenue for generating large-scale corporate profits is choked off by excessive production, investment, and competition; thus, financial speculation serves as one of the few major and "reliable" roads still open to capital accumulation on a sufficient scale. Indeed, one can expect an acceleration of this trend since the world's productive capacity will continue to outpace its consumptive capacity.

East Asia and the Overcapacity Problem: "Falling Geese"

One should already have a good sense of how the structure-based overcapacity argument applies to East Asia, but taking a slightly closer look would still be useful. To begin, one absolutely must recognize that the region's heavy reliance on export-oriented growth strategies has meant an even greater exposure to the problems caused by overcapacity. In this regard, the "more relevant question to ask," according to Korkut Erturk (2001–2002), is not why their economies failed, but rather "how the East Asian economies could [have been] successful for so long" (p. 259). One should note Erturk is referring to the larger collection of East Asian economies, which include Thailand, Malaysia, Indonesia, the Philippines, and Hong Kong (in addition to South Korea and Taiwan). Typically, as one country after another begins producing for export, the intensity of competition increases, revolving almost solely around price, since late-developing economies tend to export similar goods. Increasing price competition, in turn, invariably means deterioration in the **terms of trade**, which makes maintaining strong economic growth harder and harder for most export-dependent countries. Yet this problem was avoided among the East Asian economies for longer than expected. The countries could avoid this deterioration, as Erturk explains, for two basic reasons: first, a regional division of labor and a harmonization of industrial policies minimized intraregional competition in export markets, and, second, the countries benefited from early exporter status.

Fittingly, Erturk points to the flying geese model as the basis for the division of labor and harmonization of industrial policies. Structurally speaking, however, the flying geese model always had a limited life span. The reasons are clear enough to see, according to Erturk: for the model to work, the East Asian economies needed the time and the opportunity to accumulate profits, upgrade their production capabilities, and increase productivity in a relatively orderly, step-by-step fashion. Their early exporter status helped make all of this possible, as the major East Asian economies (first Japan and then Taiwan and South Korea) were among the first "new economies" to penetrate markets in developed countries at a time when the latter enjoyed higher growth rates. In addition, as Japan, Taiwan, and South Korea began to abandon low-cost, labor-intensive exports in the 1970s and early 1980s, the remaining East Asian economies were ready to take their places. Not coincidentally, often Japanese, Korean, and Taiwanese investment (in the form of FDI) provided the initial capital for the transfer of production. Fortuitously, competition from other regions was still largely absent, so the flying geese model continued to work fairly smoothly. Eventually, however, competitive pressures on and within the region would have to grow, economic growth rates in major export markets (i.e., the United States and Western Europe) would slow, and the "orderly" industrial-technological progression of the East Asian economies would break down—meaning that the major East Asian economies would begin to compete against one another in markets that were not growing fast enough to ensure sustained and rapid economic growth for all. This all began to take shape toward the end of the 1980s and into the 1990s.

"The Party's Over"

The key point, to repeat, is that the breakdown of the flying geese model was, in structural terms, inevitable. At the same time, other forces were at play that would help to ensure there would be no reprise of the East Asian miracle. In Chapter 2, I discussed the notion of development by invitation. The conditions that led to Japan, South Korea, and Taiwan being invited to develop, as I noted, had begun to disappear beginning in the 1960s. This disappearance was due, in part, to the first signs of the overaccumulation crisis. Equally important, however, was the concomitant weakening of US hegemony. In this regard, as Stephen Gill

(1999) argues, the economic ills that have fallen on East Asia are also a product of geopolitical factors, and specifically of efforts by the United States—acting in its role as a declining hegemonic power—to rewrite the "rules of the game" for capitalism at both the regional and global levels. One of the new rules was as follows: no more invitations would be extended to develop, and those invitations already sent out would be revoked. The desire to change the game was manifested in the central strategy of the United States since the early 1980s, namely, the imposition of a "specific neoliberal model of restructuring" (Gill 1999, p. 1).

The contours of neoliberalism are well known. The principal objectives involved deregulation (especially the deregulation of finance capital), privatization, and the restoration of free market or neoliberal trade regime on noncore economies—or, more accurately, on a few core economies, such as Japan's, which had benefited from nonreciprocal access to US and European markets during most of the Cold War. While the principles of neoliberal restructuring were most strongly applied outside of East Asia, they were also a motif of US–East Asian relations. In US-Japan relations specifically, the large and persistent bilateral trade deficits between the two countries were a constant source of friction. Thus, throughout the 1980s, the United States pressured Japan to open its markets in a number of areas, including telecommunications, medical equipment, tobacco, beef, citrus products, and semiconductors (Mastanduno 1992). During this time, too, the United States pushed for an exchange rate adjustment (making the Japanese yen stronger to reduce the competitiveness of Japanese exports). One of the most interesting US efforts, however, was the **Structural Impediments Initiative** (SII), which was designed to eliminate "anticompetitive practices" and "major structural barriers" in Japan, including savings and investment policies, land use, domestic pricing mechanisms, the distribution system (which favored smaller distributors), *keiretsu* relationships, and exclusionary business practices (Mastanduno 1992, p. 248). In many respects, the United States was demanding a fundamental reorganization of Japan's politico-economic system in a manner that primarily reflected US interests. Notably, while the SII talks were ostensibly a give-and-take (or two-way) negotiation, Japan's participation was essentially coerced. Consider, on this point, that in announcing the SII, the United States concurrently named Japan as an unfair trading nation under the **Super 301** provisions in the Omnibus Trade and Competitiveness Act of 1988. Thus, if Japan had not agreed to the SII talks, the United States would have almost certainly unilaterally imposed "retaliatory" trade sanctions.

US–South Korean relations have far less drama, but the United States was clearly intent on liberalizing South Korea's economy as well. Martin Hart-Landsberg (2004) provides a nice summary:

> In 1983, [the United States] began pressing South Korea to drop its tariffs, end its quantitative restrictions on imports, liberalize its service sector, and

improve protection of international property rights. That same year it initiated anti-dumping suits against South Korean color TV exports and forced South Korea to agree to so-called voluntary restrictions on its steel exports. By the middle of the decade, it was forcefully demanding that the South Korean government open the country's beef, rice, and cigarette markets to U.S. goods. In 1988, with South Korea's bilateral trade surplus growing rapidly, the U.S. government demanded that South Korea revalue its currency. . . . In 1989, the U.S. trade representative threatened South Korea with trade penalties if it continued to block imports of U.S. goods and placed the country on the special trade watch list each of the next three years. (p. 104)

On top of all these efforts, the United States also pressured South Korea to liberalize its financial markets. And while South Korean policymakers had their own domestic reasons for doing so (Chang, Park, and Yoo 1999), including a decision to apply for membership in the OECD, the United States certainly played an important role. Indeed, as Ha-Joon Chang, Hong-Jae Park, and Chul Gyue Yoo (1999) note, the basis for South Korea's financial liberalization program in 1993 was an agreement reached in bilateral talks between the two countries in March 1992.

Saving East Asia? Japan, the United States, and the Asian Monetary Fund

The opening up of these two East Asian economies—the loss of their special invitations to develop—made them more vulnerable to external or systemic dynamics (remember from the discussion earlier in the chapter that Taiwan largely escaped the pressures to liberalize). But I should also add that, from a structural perspective, the United States was intent on ensuring the continued vulnerability—or subordination—of East Asia for as long as possible, a desire that was most evident in the US reaction to Japan's proposal, during the height of the Asian Financial Crisis, to create an **Asian Monetary Fund** (AMF). The Japanese proposal, as is also important to understand, was an indirect but clear challenge to US dominance in the region: the AMF could have temporarily and perhaps permanently supplanted the IMF within Asia and perhaps in other parts of the world as well. From the US standpoint, this turn of events was completely unacceptable. The reason is clear: over a number of decades, the IMF has become an extremely effective tool of the United States in its role as global hegemon. In particular, through **conditionality**, the IMF enabled the United States to liberalize large swaths of the world economy almost at will. Beginning in the 1980s, for example, the IMF subjected more than sixty countries to austerity measures under strict conditionality (Gill 1999). In other words, while ostensibly a neutral international financial institution, the IMF was created by the United States in 1945, an era of unrivaled US hegemony, and since then, the United States has continued to dominate the institution. Not only does the United States retain the largest single share of votes—about 16.5 percent in 2010, compared to only 6.1 percent for Japan, the country with the second-largest voting share (IMF 2012)—but also the IMF was and is designed to reflect US interests primarily.

Given the central role the IMF has played—and continues to play—in the US strategy of neoliberal restructuring, the Japanese proposal (which, not surprisingly, was based on promoting Japanese interests in the region) had little chance of success. In fact, immediately after learning of the AMF, then deputy treasury secretary Larry Summers called Sakakibara Eisuke, former vice minister for international affairs, at his residence at midnight and indignantly remarked, "I thought you were my friend" (cited in Lipscy 2003, pp. 95–96). Significantly, during their heated two-hour conversation, Summers allegedly criticized the proposal for excluding the United States and allowing for action autonomous of the IMF. Sakakibara felt that the harsh reaction by the United States "was driven by its perception that Japan was posing a challenge to American hegemony in Asia though the AMF" (cited in Lipscy 2003, p. 96). Equally significant is the fact that the proposal, when first announced, was warmly received by almost all the concerned nations in Asia, including Taiwan and South Korea. Ultimately, a "compromise" was reached, but one that gave only the barest nod toward Japanese concerns. As Phillip Lipscy explains, the main benefit to Japan was an agreement to open an IMF regional office in Tokyo, but otherwise the cooperative framework failed to include an "institutional component or the regional orientation of an AMF, and the core prescriptions are designed to enhance rather than weaken the role of the IMF" (p. 96).

Crisis, Malaise, and Stability: Applying the Constructed Actor Model

The AMF, at base, represented an effort by a small group of Japanese policymakers to increase Japan's influence in East Asia and to reduce the region's dependence on the IMF and other key institutions of global capitalism, all of which are dominated by the United States and European core powers. (Keep in mind, for example, that, by "tradition," the managing director of the IMF is always a European and the president of the **World Bank** is always a US citizen.) This Japanese initiative, of course, failed. However, this failure was not predetermined, and neither did the Japanese simply give up. In fact, Japan's aborted proposal for the AMF eventually formed the basis for the **Chiang Mai Initiative** (CMI) in 2000, which, about a decade later in 2009, morphed into the Chiang Mai Initiative Multilateralization (CMIM). The CMI was a very limited arrangement; it was meant to expand a network of bilateral swap agreements between the central banks of the **ASEAN** members, plus China, Japan, and

South Korea. Under this agreement, the banks promised to provide each other with liquidity. The CMIM, as the name implies, "multilateralized" the CMI, turning the agreement into a formal, binding arrangement among all thirteen participating countries. The most salient accomplishment of the CMIM was the establishment of a $120 billion regional currency reserve, to which each country is required to contribute, and from which member countries can borrow during a financial crisis. (In March 2012, the members of CMIM agreed to raise the reserve amount to $240 billion.) The raising of the regional currency reserve, however, is not as impressive as it may seem on first glance. According to *The Economist,* in an article titled "A Rather Flimsy Firewall" (2012), the reserves remain in the individual central banks, so the CMIM is essentially a set of promises rather than an institutionalized fund. While a debate over how effective the CMIM would be in a future crisis[11] is ongoing—for example, *The Economist* suggests that it would have little to no utility as presently constituted ("A Rather Flimsy Firewall")—the more important point, for current purposes, is that the CMIM, as well as the AMF and CMI, reflect persistent microlevel efforts to build new institutional arrangements, which could have a significant effect on future crises in East Asia and the rest of Asia.

One can also see, from discussion throughout this chapter, these persistent microlevel efforts in the experiences of Japan, South Korea, and Taiwan in dealing with the same basic structural processes and maladies. Of course, their experiences diverged significantly. Japan's economy was severely shaken by the collapse of its asset bubble, and according to most analysts, the country is still struggling more than twenty years later. South Korea went through a similarly traumatic episode, but recovered fairly quickly, while Taiwan has thus far weathered every financial-economic storm with relative ease. Taken together, the divergency of the experiences of the three East Asian economies strongly suggests that the constructed actor model can be fruitfully applied to explain "crisis, malaise, and stability" in East Asia over the past several decades. This explanation is the focus of the remainder of this chapter. Unlike the approach in Chapter 2, however, in this chapter I purposely avoid presenting a detailed application of the model, for one basic reason: as suggested before, use of the constructed actor model is meant, first and foremost, to be heuristic (in other words, a tool to teach readers to solve problems on their own). The goal, then, is to enable readers to develop the conceptual skills necessary to conduct their own informed analysis. With this in mind, the following discussion of the constructed actor model is designed to suggest or point to areas and issues for further research and analysis.

Without too much effort, one can discern a number of significant lessons from the experiences of Japan, South Korea, and Taiwan since 1990. First, the economic-financial problems of the region are a fairly clear part of a broader pattern, a pattern that is the product of structural forces over which individual

East Asian actors and actors elsewhere have little direct control. Second, and at the same time, these structural forces are necessarily mediated by a variety of institutional, cultural/normative, political, and other mesolevel factors. To come to this conclusion, from a methodological perspective, one only has to consider, again, the divergent experiences of the three East Asian economies when faced, by and large, with the same set of structural forces: without significant differences at the domestic level, one should have expected to see the same outcomes in all three cases, and the same (or at least very similar) progression of events. Third, while institutions, norms, political arrangements, and the like can become deeply rooted themselves, they are never entirely fixed. New institutions, new norms, and new political arrangements are always possible, but changes are not self-generated. An institution, for example, does not have a mind or will of its own, so it cannot change itself. Instead, changes originate from and are sustained by socially constituted actors, individuals such as Sakakibara Eisuke or Larry Summers. At the same time, Sakakibara and Summers, just as other individuals do, operate within particular contexts (institutional, cultural, geopolitical, and so forth); the power they have (or do not have) to bring about change is therefore contingent upon a host of factors both large and small. In sum, in applying the constructed actor model to an explanation of "crisis, malaise, and stability" in East Asia, one must remember to think very carefully about the relationship between structure and **agency** (both individual and collective), about the ways in which actors are socially constituted, and about the **mutually constitutive** relationship among structures, institutions, culture (as well as other mesolevel factors), and individuals.

Let us consider these lessons in slightly more detail. The first lesson underscores the always important role that structural or systemic forces have played in shaping economic outcomes in East Asia (and the rest of Asia). In Chapter 2, I explained how the dynamics of global capitalism and the particular geopolitical context of the Cold War opened a huge window of opportunity for Japan, South Korea, and Taiwan. In this chapter, by contrast, I have examined how "open windows" (or invitations) are invariably closed shut (or withdrawn) in accordance with shifting dynamics—but a consistent logic—in the broader system of global capitalism. Indeed, the very success of the East Asian economies, plus the other fast-growing economies elsewhere in Asia, was partly responsible for the region's subsequent difficulties: as each economy moved up the technological-industrial ladder, competition intensified, profits declined, and Asia's "flying geese" were squeezed tighter and tighter. The success of each economy, moreover, accelerated the pace of industrial and manufacturing growth on a global scale, as other countries both inside and outside the region (including, most importantly, China) began copying the East Asian model of export-oriented growth. The industrial progress of successive economies in Asia not only contributed to and exacerbated the overaccumulation crisis but also made Asia a focal point of overproduction, overinvestment, and overcapacity. Any analysis that ignores these structural processes is bound to be seriously incomplete at best.

The second lesson, to repeat, suggests very clearly that structural forces, while almost always important, are not all-important. One cannot simply assume that the same structural forces will have the same impact everywhere—a point that should be readily apparent, but which is oftentimes forgotten. Applying the constructed actor model with this lesson in mind, then, requires that one dispenses with generic or overly general analyses that, in particular, treat the East Asian economies as a single, essentially similar entity or model. Instead, one needs to look very carefully inside each country, at its particular (and unique) political, institutional, social, and cultural contexts. This level of examination can be an admittedly difficult and even overwhelming process. In this chapter, however, I have reviewed a number of useful and concrete examples that make the process more manageable. For example, in the case of Taiwan, key elements of the developmental state were left largely intact into the late 1990s, while in Japan and South Korea, a stronger move was made toward liberalization. In Japan and South Korea, in other words, the apparatus of the developmental state, while not completely dismantled, was altered in important ways. Statists argue that these differences are key to explaining Taiwan's ability to weather the structurally based economic-financial crisis of the past few decades. Culturalists, in the same vein, suggest that, despite outwardly similar normative/institutional structures, sharp distinctions can be found among the three East Asian countries. One of these distinctions—an extraordinarily strong emphasis on "lifetime employment"—likely contributed to Japan's long-term economic malaise. The discussion here, I need to emphasize, is still quite general, but the point is clear: the constructed actor model takes structural forces seriously but warns that the intersection between structural forces and domestic social, political, economic, and cultural factors must be considered to understand and explain differing outcomes among the East Asian economies.

The third lesson brings the focus back to the microlevel, on individual actors. In and outside of East Asia, one can easily see that socially constituted actors were not just reacting unthinkingly and powerlessly to structural, institutional, and cultural forces, nor were they merely representing their positions—hegemonic, subordinate, and otherwise—within the overarching system of global capitalism (e.g., one might argue that Larry Summers was representing the interests of the hegemon in opposing Japan's proposal for the AMF). By the same token, equally clear is that the actors in East Asia are not simply rational and narrowly self-interested beings (the *homo economicus* of liberal economic theory) but are indeed "socially constituted." Thus, while individual actors in Japan, South Korea, Taiwan, the United States, and elsewhere certainly reacted to the various economic crises in rational or self-interested manners, their specific reactions were shaped by a "large current of social facts such as value systems, **social structures**, extended social networks, and the like" (Little 2005, p. 10). Consider, again, the "zombie problem" in Japan, which can be tied to the relatively high value the Japanese place on equity (over efficiency) and to the institutional-cultural norms of lifetime employment. From this perspective, a purposeful yet socially conditioned choice was made to save firms and maximize employment, which gave rise to zombie firms and prolonged Japan's economic problems. Notably, plenty of evidence can be found that the Japanese commitment to equity and high employment is coming under increasing strain, and may one day be abandoned. Even if the latter were to happen, the constructed actor model provides an ideal framework for analyzing this process; at the least, it explains why resistance to such change, at the microlevel, was so strong and consistent for so long.

Conclusion

Explaining "crisis, malaise, and stability" in East Asia is an admittedly difficult task. Seasoned scholars and economic experts continue to disagree—often quite vehemently—on the basic causes of Japan's long-term economic problems, on South Korea's vulnerability to the Asian Financial Crisis, and on Taiwan's ability to remain relatively unaffected. Examining the competing views with an open mind, however, leaves one with the conclusion that all have merit. Unfortunately, by focusing on or giving overarching priority to a single set of factors or forces, each of the competing approaches—the liberal, statist, structural, and cultural—narrows the field of vision, perhaps to an unacceptable degree. For instance, the liberal emphasis on zombie firms, combined with the empirically valid observation that productivity in Japan is persistently low by international standards, is an important part of explaining Japan's long-term economic malaise. By itself, however, the liberal explanation is inadequate. In a similar vein, statist, structural, and cultural arguments provide equally useful and valid points, but again they provide only part of the picture. The structural argument, in particular, suggests that contemporary economic-financial crises should not be analyzed as discrete, isolated events, but that they instead reflect a new dynamic in global capitalism. This observation is critical, but it cannot explain different outcomes in similarly situated economies. Nor do structural approaches generally pay any attention to microlevel factors and, especially, to decisions made by individual actors.

An integrated, comprehensive approach is therefore necessary. The constructed actor model is, of course, designed to fulfill this role. In the discussion above, I provided a very rough and admittedly incomplete guide. But it was enough (combined with more extensive "application" elsewhere) to give readers a good idea of how to develop their own "constructed actor" argument.

Notes

1. However, Japan's overwhelming debt burden, which broke the $1 trillion mark in 2009, is mitigated by the sheer amount of domestic savings in Japan, which is about $7.7 trillion kept mostly in very low interest-bearing bank deposits. Those savings, according to *Forbes* magazine, equal two-thirds of the total household wealth of Germany, France, and the United Kingdom combined (cited in Fisher 2010).

2. *The Economist,* I should also point out, identifies a number of other reasons for Taiwan's ability to resist the ill effects of the Asian Financial Crisis. One of these was just "good luck." *The Economist* explains it this way: "For one, Taiwan is fortunate in that it trades mostly with America and China rather than the rest of Asia" ("A Survey of Taiwan" 1998a). This relationship shielded Taiwan from the disruption in trade that occurred as the crisis unfolded. Second, "Taiwan is also lucky that its business cycle happened to be out of phase with the rest of the region. It has seen mad property inflation and stock market booms, just like Thailand, Hong Kong, and the rest, but that was in the late 1980s and early 1990s" ("A Survey of Taiwan" 1998a). Another reason for Taiwan's success was, as *The Economist* colloquially put it, due to "paranoia" ("A Survey of Taiwan" 1998b). By "paranoia," *The Economist* suggests in the article "A Survey of Taiwan: The Survivor's Tale" (1998b), that a lot of what goes on in Taiwan is based on anxiety about the intentions of China, or on the perception that "China is really out to get [Taiwan]." "This fear," according to *The Economist,* "permeates everything Taiwan does." Most basically, it has compelled Taiwan's leaders to pursue economic policies premised on a very conservative, worst-case scenario line of thinking. This so-called paranoia is precisely why Taiwan's banks "have the lowest bad-loan ratios in Asia, and its companies have the lowest debt-to-equity ratios." It is also why the Taiwan government has "never fully abandoned currency controls" ("A Survey of Taiwan" 1998a).

3. Although widely and approvingly used by neoliberal economists, the term *creative destruction,* ironically, originally comes from Marxist economic theory. It was used to describe the way in which capitalism is, by nature, an evolutionary—or more accurately, revolutionary—system. Marx described capitalism's revolutionary role as "constant revolutionizing of production" (cited in Elliot 1980, p. 47). Elliot (1980) provides a very nice discussion on creative destruction in both Schumpeter's and Marx's writings.

4. The McKinsey report does not specify the version of the law to which it refers. The original law went into effect in 1974, but over the years, it was subject to a number of significant revisions, especially in the 1990s. Then, in 2000, the original law was essentially replaced with a new law, the Large-Scale Retail Store Location Law. Riethmuller and Chai (1999) provide a useful summary of the changes to the Large-Scale Retail Store Law.

5. For a more detailed discussion of corporate restructuring in South Korea during the Asian Financial Crisis, see Sohn (2002).

6. For a fuller discussion of the US Savings and Loan Crisis, particularly in relation to Japan's financial crisis, see Friedman (2000) and Posen and Mikitani (2000).

7. For an example of the ongoing debate, see Martin (2012).

8. Some disagreement can be found on which practices constitute the three pillars. Most everyone agrees on seniority-based wages/promotions and lifetime employment, but instead of enterprise unionism, some scholars assert that the third pillar is profit-sharing bonuses. See, for example, Price (1997). The term *enterprise unionism* refers to the organization of a single trade union within one plant or multiplant enterprise, rather than within a craft or industry—an organizational form that is common to the United States. Enterprise unions, moreover, usually include both regularly employed white- and

blue-collar workers and even low-level managers. Functionally, these types of unions engage in direct bargaining with the management of their particular company (e.g., workers in Toyota's union will bargain directly with Toyota management).

9. For a more detailed discussion of these factors, see Jeong and Aguilera (2007).

10. A few examples include Aoki and Dore (1996) and Garvey and Swan (1992).

11. For a more detailed discussion of the CMIM, see Ciorciari (2011).

4

Capitalism or Bust?
China's Rise and North Korea's
Economic Decay

The economic rise of China, on the one hand, and the seemingly relentless decay of North Korea's economy, on the other hand, provide an interesting study in contrasts. For the first three decades of their existence as **communist states**, the two countries seemed to be traveling the same basic economic and political paths. Both countries embraced **central planning** and both countries achieved early economic success followed by serious economic decline. Both were also led, even dominated, by charismatic leaders: **Mao Zedong** (1893–1976), in the case of China, and **Kim Il-sung** (1912–1994), in the case of North Korea. Despite their cult-like following, both leaders also helped to build a centralized, highly effective **party-state system** in their respective countries. Mao and Kim, too, were both deeply influenced by **Marxist-Leninist** thought but also developed their own indigenous versions: Maoism and *juche*, respectively (see Figure 4.1 for a brief overview of Maoism and *juche*). While a more in-depth inspection would certainly reveal significant differences between the two countries (not the least of which is their relative size in terms of population), in the early postwar period, the political, economic, and ideological similarities between the two countries made them at least partial clones, with North Korea being the "Mini-Me" version of China.

All this changed when the paths followed by China and North Korea started to diverge in the late 1970s; China turned gradually but decisively toward a market-oriented economy, while North Korea took only a few hesitant steps in the same direction. In China, the transition was not immediate, nor did it mean an end to the country's **authoritarian** one-party rule. It did, however, lay the groundwork for a remarkable economic transformation, which is continuing to this day. Part of the impetus for this change was the death of Mao Zedong in September 1976. His death, combined with the excesses of the **Cultural Revolution**, allowed the country's more pragmatic leadership, with **Deng Xiaoping** in front, to finally assume firm control of the economy. In North Korea, the death of Kim Il-sung in 1994 did not have the same results. Instead, Kim's son—**Kim Jong-il**—largely followed in the footsteps of his father. For a short

---

Figure 4.1 Maoism and *Juche*

Maoism

According to William Joseph (2010), one way to think of Maoism (also known as Mao Zedong Thought) is as a practical ideology to complement the "pure ideology" of Marxism-Leninism, upon which Maoism is clearly based. In Marxism-Leninism, two principles are put forward: (1) **class struggle** is the key to understanding the development of human history, and (2) class struggle can be manifested through the construction of a vanguard proletarian (or workers') party to lead the revolution against capitalism. Mao deviated from the orthodox view by insisting that peasants, rather than workers, would be the leading force in advancing China's revolution. To achieve this end meant building a strong organization around peasants or the rural masses. Given China's still-strong rural roots, this approach made practical sense, but it nonetheless contradicted Marx's view. Marx had seen the peasants as "a class of barbarians standing halfway outside society, and a class combining all the crudest and most primitive forms of society with the anguish and misery of civilized countries" (cited in Joseph 2010, p. 136). The emphasis on the peasantry was also embedded in the Maoist idea that industrialization could take place in the countryside, rather than in urban areas exclusively: this belief was the basis for the **Great Leap Forward** (discussed later in the chapter).

Juche

Often translated as "self-reliance," *juche* is a difficult concept to describe. In the words of Kim Il-sung himself, "establishing *juche* means, in a nutshell, being the master of revolution and reconstruction in one's own country. This means holding fast to an independent position, rejecting dependence on others, using one's own brains, believing in one's own strength, displaying the revolutionary spirit of self-reliance, and thus solving one's own problems for oneself on one's own responsibility under all circumstances" (cited in G. Lee 2003, p. 105). The foregoing passage suggests another translation for *juche*: "self-determination." But any simple English translation is bound to fall short. Instead, Bruce Cumings (1993) suggests that we should think of *juche* as "a state of mind." As he explains, "the term literally means being subjective where Korean matters are concerned, putting Korea first in everything" (p. 213). The term, Cumings adds, "is really untranslatable" (p. 214). At the same time, one should not conclude that *juche* is a mere slogan, with no significant impact in North Korea. It has been and is an integral, perhaps *the* integral, element of North Korean culture. It has, one might argue, shaped the worldview of North Koreans in profound ways.

time, though, foreign observers speculated that a behind-the-scenes power struggle had occurred following the elder Kim's death: several years passed before Kim Jong-il was officially named general secretary of the **Korean Workers' Party**. (In most communist countries, the party leader is considered the most powerful person in the country.) Bruce Cumings (2012), a noted expert on Korean history, suggests, however, that this delay did not signify a power struggle but was instead a reflection of Korean tradition. As he explains, "actually he was doing what the heir-apparent prince was supposed to do under the *ancien régime*: mourn his father for three years. By the 50th anniversary of the DPRK's [Democratic People's Republic of Korea's] founding in 1998, it was clear that Kim Jong-il was in full charge of the country" (p. 218).[1]

Indeed, Kim Jong-il's smooth accession to power was assiduously planned: as early as 1972, preparations had already begun for the younger Kim to succeed his father. In other words, for twenty-two years, not only was Kim Jong-il an understudy to his father, but his path to "supreme leadership" was carefully plotted and constructed (D.-S. Suh 1995, p. xiv). Unsurprisingly, then, no radical changes were made under the younger Kim's watch, although indications could be found that he hoped to reenergize the North Korean economy à la the Chinese model; he even thought he could create a North Korean version of California's Silicon Valley (Scobell 2006). Unfortunately, the situation only got worse. One might even say that it *could* only get worse as long as the North Korean leadership retained its totalitarian control over the country and especially the economy. Another opportunity for change arrived with the untimely death of Kim Jong-il in December 2011. Yet Kim Jong-il's death led to another hereditary succession, as his son, **Kim Jong-un**, was quickly appointed to the key leadership positions. Thus far (as of December 2013), the second succession has not signaled any turnaround in North Korea's economic or political policies, although there have been rumblings of a change.[2]

Given the divergent paths of the two countries, a number of questions arise: What explains the economic rise of China, on the one hand, and the steady decline of North Korea, on the other hand? Is China merely reproducing the East Asian model, or is it charting its own unique, or at least individualized, path? As for North Korea, the question is not so much why the economy is failing, but why the regime has, so far, seemed incapable of implementing effective reforms. After all, other still-communist countries—most notably China, but also Vietnam and Laos (discussed later in this chapter)—have, with varying degrees of success, made the transition to a market-oriented economy. What, in other words, explains the seemingly unassailable continuity of North Korea's political economy? In this chapter, I address each of these questions, beginning with an examination of North Korea. Unlike in Chapter 2 (and in the rest of the book), however, the analysis of North Korea does not utilize the competing-perspectives approach, at least not fully, primarily because I intend to focus on the question of reform, or rather the lack of effective market-oriented economic reform, in North Korea. This analysis calls for a different approach than the one used in Chapter 2. In addition, as I analyze the reform process in North Korea, I immediately center on the constructed actor model.

Following the discussion of North Korea, China becomes the focus of attention. Here I return to the basic competing-perspectives approach, although I place a very strong focus on the statist (or political economy) and structural perspectives. I address the reasons for this more narrow focus as I proceed. Suffice it to say, for now, that the deductive principles in the liberal view can be applied to China in a manner that does not differ in any significant way from the liberal explanation of Japanese, Taiwanese, or South Korean economic growth. This fact makes the analysis short and sweet. As for the cultural perspective, one can find precious few analyses applying a cultural framework to China's economic rise. This dearth does not mean that culture is irrelevant. It almost assuredly is not. However, for current purposes, applying cultural principles within the context of the constructed actor model makes more sense—something I also do in the case of North Korea.

One more point before I begin: the pairing of China and North Korea requires some additional explanation. Discussing the two countries in the same chapter might suggest that they are still similar types of regimes with similar experiences, which is emphatically not the case. The differences between North Korea and China today—and for quite some time now—are quite significant. Indeed, China likely shares many more similarities with Japan, South Korea, and Taiwan today than it does with North Korea. At the same time, as I noted above, China and North Korea clearly started off on a very similar path, with a very similar type of political and economic system. In this regard, the fact that they are so different now makes their pairing particularly useful from a pedagogic and methodological perspective. Why? Because their remarkable divergence is exactly what allows one to more clearly see and highlight the factors that lead to dramatic change, on the one hand, and to stubborn continuity, on the other hand. In other words, a lot can be learned by examining two countries that started off under similar circumstances but ended up, thus far, in very different places (recall the principle of the MSS design, too: in a comparison of two similar units, the differences are key). With this in mind, let's begin with a focus on North Korea.

North Korea's Downward Spiral

In many respects, North Korea remains an enigma to the world. Its reputation as "the most closed society on earth" was (and still is) well deserved. For a long time, North Korea's isolation made writing about the political, economic, and social dynamics of the country a very tricky task, and one that was necessarily subject to a great amount of speculative analysis. Still, over the past decade or so, scholars and other observers have learned more about North Korea, in part through the tens of thousands of migrants or refugees leaving the country and through a slightly more "open-door" policy on the part of the regime itself (Armstrong 2011). Nonetheless, reliable hard data—especially on the economy—remains difficult to come by, so any analysis of the North Korean economy necessarily contains an unsubstantiated element and is subject to revision. Even with this caveat, the major contours of North Korea's economic performance and problems are reasonably well known. Little doubt can be found, in particular, that the economy has been suffering for a very long time, and no doubt exists about the serious famines that swept the country in the 1990s, although estimates of the number of people who died from the famines differ significantly, from a low of 900,000 to a high of 3.5 million (Noland, Robinson, and Wang 1999). Beginning in 2008, signs of another serious food shortage were appearing, although a full-fledged famine on the scale of the 1990s famine was largely avoided; North Korea, however, remains on the brink. To better understand how North Korea got to where it is today, one can usefully take a quick look at where the country started and what has transpired since the 1950s.

As with many centrally planned or **command economies**, North Korea started off strongly. Following the end of the **Korean War** in 1953, the North Korean leadership focused on developing the country's heavy industries: iron and steel, shipbuilding, mining, electrical power, chemicals, and machine tools. The results, according to official statistics, were impressive: from 1954 to 1956, gross industrial production increased at an annual rate of 41.8 percent; this success was followed by a 36.6 percent annual increase from 1957 to 1961 (H.-S. Lee 1988). While the figures are likely exaggerated, most outside observers agree that the North had made impressive industrial strides at least until the early 1960s; indeed, through the 1950s, North Korea's growth rate was higher than South Korea's, a point on which one can find almost universal consensus. Where analysts begin to disagree is with the 1960s. Estimates vary widely. According to the CIA (see Figure 4.2), for example, North Korea experienced average annual growth rates of 9.8 percent from 1961 to 1965, 5.5 percent from 1966 to 1970, and 10.4 percent from 1971 to 1975. Byung-Yeon Kim, Suk Jin Kim, and Keun Lee (2007), however, provide much lower estimates of 3.3 percent, 3.3 percent, and 4.6 percent, respectively. If these lower figures are accurate, they would have indicated per capita growth rates of less than 1 percent for the entire decade of the 1960s (see Figure 4.2 for details). Even more telling are the fairly consistent and significant declines in both labor and capital productivity. These declines suggest that North Korea's early growth was primarily the product of an increase in labor inputs rather than an increase in efficiency—a phenomenon common to all command economies. To reiterate, as mentioned previously in Chapter 2, many countries, especially those with coercive states, achieve immediate spurts of economic growth by a rapid and dramatic mobilization of inputs, especially labor, in the early stages of industrialization. North Korea, by most accounts, was no exception. Over time, however, this strategy peters out as resources become scarcer and more difficult to mobilize; North Korea appears to fit this model to a T.

The statistics in Figure 4.2 suggest that North Korea was already beginning to experience economic difficulties as early as 1960. Still, to the outside world at the time, North Korea's economic difficulties were not necessarily obvious. Writing in 1981, for example, Jon Halliday (a prominent historian specializing in modern Asia) had the following to say: "North Korea has articulated a comprehensive strategy for economic, political, military, ideological and cultural independence, with sustained high growth (*juche*). Self-reliance, not self-sufficiency, is the stated goal and has been achieved to a high degree, especially in food, machine-tools, and energy, in spite of the country having no oil. . . . *[North] Korea is probably the most successful economy in any post-revolutionary society*" (p. 889; emphasis added). The North Korean regime was equally boastful: it projected an image of immense economic strength, claiming in 1984 that the country had produced 10 million tons of grain, 50 billion kilowatt hours of electricity, 76.5 million tons of coal, 7.4 million tons of steel, and 4.7 million tons of chemical fertilizer, among other accomplishments (Jin 2012). Despite such claims, by the mid-1980s, the North Korean model was clearly faltering, made evident, in part, by the actions of the North Korean leadership itself, which introduced market-oriented measures into the national economy for the first time in 1984. If the economy was doing well, the North Korean regime would not likely have felt a need for any market-based reforms. Yet in the same year that it boasted of high production, North Korea's Supreme People's Assembly announced a plan to begin foreign joint ventures. Another major reform, also

Figure 4.2 Economic Indicators for North Korea, 1954–1990 (annual growth rate, percentage)

	GNP (CIA est.)	GNP	GNP per Capita	Labor Productivity	Capital Productivity
1954–1960	—	9.3	5.7	3.5	−3.2
1960–1965	9.8	3.3	0.7	−1.8	−3.4
1965–1970	5.5	3.3	0.6	−0.5	−0.8
1970–1975	10.4	4.6	1.6	0.5	−2.5
1975–1980	4.1	2.2	0.4	−1.3	−4.2
1980–1985	4.3	4.0	2.3	0.9	−4.2
1985–1990	—	2.7	1.5	0.1	−4.5

Sources: CIA estimates from National Foreign Assessment Center, *Handbook of Economic Statistics* (Washington, DC: Government Printing Office), various years (as cited in H.-S. Lee 1988); all other statistics from Kim, Kim, and Lee (2007).

announced in 1984, was the "August 3 Consumer Goods Movement," part of which allowed for small groups of workers to produce basic necessities (made from waste or other unused materials from heavy industry) and sell them directly to consumers at unregulated prices (H.-S. Lee 1988).

Over the next few years, the government allowed for the further expansion of small-scale "free market" activities, but these efforts were extremely limited in scope. The joint venture law, too, attracted little attention and even less investment: between 1984 and 1997, the total amount of foreign investment was perhaps $200 million, but almost all of this came from the pro–North Korean community in Japan, the **Chongryon** (Nanto and Chanlett-Avery 2008). Understandably, perhaps, this first effort at reform was limited. Prior to the 1980s, as I discussed above, the economy had done relatively well, so a strong belief still probably prevailed that the economic difficulties were temporary and contingent, rather than permanent and structural. Thus, while a little bit of "tweaking" may have been in order, wholesale reform was not viewed as necessary by the North Korean leadership.

Of course, the lack of serious reform meant that basic problems in the economy were not addressed. Not dealing with these issues would prove to be particularly damaging for North Korea, as the end of the Cold War seriously exacerbated the accumulating domestic problems of the 1980s. Most saliently, the end of the Cold War meant an end to North Korea's privileged trade relations with the Soviet Union. For decades, the North Korean regime enjoyed favorable trade terms with the Soviet Union and China in the form of subsidized barter trade, patron aid, and debt-financed trade (V. Cha 2012). Even more, the Soviet Union was North Korea's main source for essential imports, most notably food and oil, the latter of which was sold to North Korea at concessionary prices. Beginning in 1991, everything changed. Russia no longer provided trade credits and concessionary prices; it also started requiring North Korea to pay for its goods with hard currency—something that was in very short supply in North Korea. Then China imposed the same requirement in 1992. These new requirements had an especially dire impact on North Korea's energy situation: oil imports from the Soviets went from a high of about 3.5 million tons per year to just 45,000 tons in 1991. As Victor Cha (2012) points out, the drop in oil imports also had a ripple effect throughout the North Korean economy: "The reduction in oil imports hurt domestic coal production, because the ammonium nitrate necessary for explosives in blast mining required petroleum products that were now in short supply. The lack of oil hurt annual crop production, because it led to a decline in the production of chemical fertilizers."

In combination, then, the lack of effective reforms and the dismantling of favorable trade relations led to a severe and prolonged economic downturn in the 1990s—general agreement can be found that the North's economy shrank for at least nine consecutive years from 1990 to 1998. The famines were the most overt sign of this decline,[3] but another telling sign was in the rhetoric of the North Korean regime, which likely reflected the dire economic situation: the years from 1995 to 1997 were named "the period of the arduous march," and 1998 was labeled "the desperate march for socialism" (Hong 2002, p. 98).

Given the depth of North Korea's economic problems, that the leadership again turned toward reforms in the early 2000s is not surprising. The first major reforms were announced in July 2002 and were dubbed the "Economic Adjustment Policy." The "adjustments" included an end to the rationing system for daily commodities (food was excluded), a major increase in the prices of essentials and in wages, a major devaluation of the currency, the abolishment of the foreign exchange coupon system, an increase in enterprise autonomy, the authorization for markets and trading centers, and a further opening of the economy to foreign investment (Nanto and Chanlett-Avery 2008). Unlike earlier reforms, the newer reforms were designed to deal, in a more forthright manner, with basic inefficiencies and distortions in the existing system. But as with the older reforms, the regime was willing only to slightly loosen its grip on the national economy. Thus, while the regime legalized farmers' markets in 2003—allowing individuals to earn and keep profits—it began to clamp down on these markets as their popularity grew. In Pyongyang (North Korea's capital city), for example, two markets became extremely popular, the Pyongyang Central Market and the Tongil market, the latter of which sold everything from locally grown and imported fruit to Chinese-made televisions and washing machines to imported beer from Singapore (Lintner 2004). After witnessing several years of relatively unfettered growth in these markets, however, the government began to grow very wary. The government's concern led, in 2007, to an announcement by Kim Jong-il that "markets have become anti-socialist, Western-style markets" and needed to be reined in (cited in Nanto and Chanlett-Avery 2008, p. 17). I should emphasize, too, that during the 1990s, an underground and unsanctioned, quasi-market economy had emerged as a result of the regime's inability to feed its own people.

At the same time, the regime exercised much more tolerance for foreign investment. Indeed, in sharp contrast to its earlier efforts, the North Korean leadership has allowed foreign investment—usually through **FDI**—to grow at a relatively significant pace. For political and historical reasons, Chinese investment has been particularly strong, although even it took some time to develop. For most of the 2000s, Chinese investment was relatively small: it was limited to minor investments made by profit-seeking, private sector Chinese investors (Shepard 2010). In 2010, though, the North Korean and Chinese governments signed a major deal involving two projects: the Agreement on Joint Development and Management of the Rason Economic and Trade Zone and the Hwanggumpyong and Wihwa Islands Economic Zone. These large-scale projects were designed to "improve North Korea's overall level of industrialization, raise the competitiveness of North Korean products, and expand North Korea's **comparative advantage** from labor, land and minerals" (M.-H. Choi

2011, p. 131). The Rason project calls for $3.5 billion to be invested over five years, with China spending $2 billion on infrastructure, while the Hwang-gumpyong project will cost $3.7 billion ($500 million has already been invested by the Chinese government, and the remainder will come from private investors). I should note, though, progress on the projects has been extremely slow by Chinese standards. At Hwanggumpyong project, for example, a bridge to the area was (in December 2013) still unfinished thirty months after construction began, "mostly because," as Adam Cathcart put it, "of North Korea's failure to get its economic house in order" (cited in Rauhala 2013, n.p.). Even more, the North Korean official with primary responsibilities for the Hwang-gumpyong project, Jang Song Taek (the uncle of Kim Jong-un), was suddenly and somewhat mysteriously arrested, then executed, in December 2013 for "dreaming different dreams." North Korea observers have surmised that this phrase means Jang's ideological vision was at odds with the official ideology (cited in Rauhala 2013).

South Korea has also become a major investor in North Korea, although many projects are motivated by nonfinancial goals (i.e., building the basis for inter-Korean cooperation). One of the most important areas of South Korean investment is the Kaesong Industrial Complex (see Figure 4.3 for further discussion). North Korea has also attracted FDI from Egypt, Norway, Italy, France, Japan, Germany, Singapore, Sweden, and elsewhere. And while investment from the United States is essentially nil due to US economic sanctions against North Korea, US companies have used North Korean labor. For example, the North Korean company, Scientific and Educational Film Studio of Korea, sub-contracts with over seventy companies from around the world, including US companies, and has worked on such US films as *The Lion King 2: Simba's Pride* and *Pocahontas,* as well as the television series, *The Simpsons* (S. Lee 2007; Tija 2012). Altogether, foreign investment in North Korea reached $1.475 billion in 2010 but will increase dramatically once the joint development project between China and North Korea is fully implemented.

Despite the strong uptick in foreign investment, how effective or significant these reforms will be remains to be seen; however, the rapid economic slide of the 1990s did appear, at least for a short time, to be halted. In particular, most sources show positive, albeit still anemic, growth beginning in 1999 (well before the 2002 reforms were announced) and extending until 2005. By 2006, however, the economy had moved back into negative territory, and only recovered again in 2011 (in that year, the Bank of Korea [2012] estimated a growth rate of 0.8 percent). Before this upturn, though, ordinary North Korean citizens had to endure a drastic government-mandated devaluation of the currency: in November 2009, in an effort to curb "unofficial economic activity" and to suppress inflation, the regime summarily reduced the value of the North Korean won to practically nothing. Specifically, the value of the won was slashed by 99 percent: a 1,000 won note was reduced in value to 10 won. This effectively wiped out the savings of every North Korean household, especially since the

Figure 4.3 Kaesong Industrial Complex (KIC)

The KIC was established in 1998 in an initiative led by the Hyundai Group, a major South Korean conglomerate (or *chaebol*). It was part of larger initiative by the South Korean government known as the "sunshine policy." Located about 100 miles southeast of Pyongyang and forty miles north of the Seoul, the KIC is situated across the demilitarized zone (DMZ) in North Korean territory. For the South Koreans, the KIC was an opportunity to ease tensions with the North through economic cooperation. At the same time, the KIC operated as most **special economic zones** (SEZs) in that it provided South Korean manufacturers with a low-cost production center: the KIC is a duty-free zone, with no restrictions on the use of foreign currency, and South Korean companies operating in the Kaesong receive incentives from the South Korean government. The corporate tax rate, in particular, is 10 to 14 percent, with an exemption for the first five years after generating profits and a 50 percent reduction for the ensuing three years. Companies also have access to low-interest loans.

For the North Korean leadership, the KIC offers an opportunity to earn foreign exchange. The wages of North Korean workers are paid in US dollars (or other hard currencies), although they are remitted to the Central Special Direct General Bureau, a North Korean government agency, which then pays the workers. Estimates are that the North Korean government keeps as much as 45 percent of the

(continues)

regime also limited the amount of money that could be converted at the old rate to 100,000 won, or about US$40. After the devaluation, the same 100,000 won would be worth only 4¢ (later, the limit was raised to 150,000 won in cash and 300,000 won in savings).[4]

Despite a few positive signs (but many more negative ones), then, the upshot is apparent: the North Korean economy remains in tatters with no clear prospect of recovery. Even more, the failure of the formal economy has meant

Figure 4.3 continued

wages paid by South Korean companies. The monthly minimum wage in 2010 was $60.78, or between $2 and $3 a day. Although extremely low by South Korean standards, the wage is much higher than the average pay for regular North Korean workers. (All figures and other information cited from Manyin and Nanto 2011.)

Key Statistics for the Kaesong Industrial Complex

	2005	2006	2007	2008	2009	2010
South Korean manufacturing firms	11	15	65	93	118	121
North Korean workers (est.)	6,000	11,000	23,000	39,000	42,000	47,000
South Korean workers (est.)	n.a.	700	800	1,500	960	500
Annual production value (in $US millions)	$15	$74	$185	$250	$256	$323
Exports to third-party countries (in $US millions)	n.a.	$20	$40	$36	$29	$37

Source: South Korean Ministry of Unification (cited in Manyin and Nanto 2011, p. 1).

that ordinary North Korean citizens have had no choice but to turn to the informal or underground economy to eke out a living. While partly allowing the informal sector to serve as safety net (albeit, a far-from-perfect one), the regime has also demonstrated strict limits to its tolerance and to its concern for ordinary citizens. The abrupt and destructive currency devaluation in 2009 was only one of the more recent manifestations of this limit.

Continuity or Change for North Korea? Problems of Reform

One needs to understand that North Korea's leadership is not in a unique position. As I briefly mentioned in the introduction, not only has China implemented successful, market-based reforms, but so too have Vietnam and Laos. I discuss China at length in the second part of this chapter (and so reserve further comment until then), but the experiences of Vietnam and Laos may also be instructive. Figure 4.4 provides an overview of the reform process in these two countries, but the main point is that both Vietnam and Laos have achieved relatively strong levels of economic growth and industrialization through market-oriented reforms while

Figure 4.4 Market-Based Reforms in Vietnam and Laos

Vietnam

As in North Korea, the communist regime in Vietnam based its economy on the Soviet model, and as in North Korea, Vietnam experienced serious economic difficulties stemming from reliance on central planning. Unlike North Korea, however, Vietnam's communist regime undertook a largely successful and far-reaching reform of the economy—dubbed *doi moi* (or "major renovation") beginning in 1986. The need for reform was recognized and debated during preparations for Vietnam's Sixth Party Congress. The debates produced a broad consensus, and *doi moi* was officially launched in December 1986. Although the details of the reform took some time to be implemented, the main thrust was clear: the elimination of central planning and a turn toward the market. Accordingly, over a number of years, the government relaxed controls on private sector activity, introduced price reforms that allowed the cost of nonessential consumer goods to reflect market prices, recognized private property rights, eliminated centrally planned targets in agriculture, encouraged foreign investment and joint ventures, removed or reduced government controls on the foreign exchange market and on international trade, and so on (for a detailed list of reforms, see Brian Van Arkadie and Raymond Mallon [2003, especially Chapter 6]). The results were impressive: between 1991 and 1998, the Vietnamese economy grew at an average annual rate of 8.6 percent, which increased per capita income from $707 to $1,263 (in **PPP** terms). In 2010, per capita income had increased to $3,142. Equally important, the reform process solved Vietnam's chronic food shortage problem. In fact, in only a couple of years following the introduction of *doi moi,* Vietnam began to export food for the first time—in 1989, the country exported 1.4 million tons of rice. Since then, Vietnam has not only remained a rice exporter but has become the second-largest rice exporter in the world after Thailand (Tuan 2009).

Laos

Laos has experienced a great deal of turbulence since it became an independent state in 1953. In only the first decade of its existence, it held elections, saw its elected government fail, witnessed a **coup d'état**, saw another government collapse, and was then enmeshed in the war between the United States and Vietnam. During the war, Laos was subject to heavy bombing by the United States and repeated invasions by Vietnam. Vietnam's presence, in fact, led to the emergence of the country's communist government on December 2, 1975. Not surprisingly, then, once relative peace returned to the country, the new communist regime introduced central planning, nationalized all major enterprises, and attempted to introduce agricultural collectivization (Bird and Hill 2010). The results were predictable: the economy largely failed, living standards declined, and poverty

(continues)

Figure 4.4 continued

increased. Fortunately, the communist regime in Laos, as in Vietnam, had a pragmatic attitude and followed the Vietnamese model of *doi moi* under the banner, the "New Economic

Mechanism." Under this program, according to Bird and Hill (2010), "reform has been gradual and reasonably consistent, with three broad episodes apparent. In the first and most important phase, about 1987–94, most domestic trade barriers were relaxed almost immediately, private companies were permitted to trade domestically and internationally, and much of the transport sector was opened up to the private sector" (p. 120).

Laos remains a poor country, but the reforms did lead to significant changes. Most importantly, the poverty rate has dropped from a high of between 72 and 76 percent below the poverty line in 1992–1993 to between 48 and 53 percent in 2002–2003. The infant mortality rate and life expectancy showed similar signs of improvement: in 1990, the infant mortality rate dropped from 120 per 1,000 live births to 70 in 2005, while life expectancy at birth increased from fifty to sixty-one over the same period (all figures cited in Hill and Bird 2010). Per capita income has also increased significantly, going from $1,300 in 1999 to $2,500 in 2010.

eschewing major political reform, in other words, a breakup of their single-party, authoritarian regimes (both countries had a "not free" rating in the Freedom House index in 2013).[5] The relative economic success of Laos is particularly noteworthy given the tremendous economic obstacles this very small, very poor, and landlocked country faced and continues to face. Kelly Bird and Hall Hill (2010) describes the early prospects for Laos this way: "It is difficult to imagine a country with more unfavourable 'initial conditions' than Laos. . . . The legacy of 60 years of colonial neglect and more than a decade of vicious conflict resulted in it being one of the poorest countries in the world in 1975, when it then turned Communist. About three-quarters of its small educated elite, comprising its entrepreneurial class and senior policy-makers, fled the country, were killed, or imprisoned. Thirty years later, only 14% of is population had completed primary education" (p. 118). And yet, while far from rich, Laos has made tremendous economic strides since the mid-1990s. Its per capita income in 2011 was $2,700 in PPP terms, compared to an estimated per capita income of US$1,800 in North Korea. At the risk of being flippant, I might say, "If Laos could do it, anyone can."

So why hasn't North Korea been able to do the same? What makes North Korea, in other words, so different from other single-party communist dictatorships? Before discussing what the answer to this question might be, one should first consider what the answer is *not*. First, the answer is not that single-party communist dictatorships are incapable of implementing far-reaching, market-oriented economic reform. China, Vietnam, and Laos quickly put that myth to rest. Second, the answer is not insurmountable structural obstacles at either the regional or global levels. Indeed, if North Korea were to pursue genuine market-based reform, its integration into the world economy would almost certainly be encouraged by South Korea, Japan, and China. Even the United States would likely welcome the economic transformation of North Korea. To be sure, North Korea is regarded as a pariah and rogue state, but the major capitalist powers, including the United States, have consistently demonstrated a willingness to negotiate with the regime. Third, it is not that North Korea has a dearth of individuals with the skills, motivation, knowledge, or willingness to make a market-based system in the country work. Again, if Laos and Vietnam can reform their markets, so can North Korea. Laos, in particular, suffered from a massive "brain drain" when the communists came to power, and its population was severely undereducated at the time reforms began. Yet the lack of a skilled and educated workforce did not prevent the reforms from working. North Korea, by contrast, has a well-developed compulsory educational system. Moreover, according to a number of sources, beginning in the mid-2000s the regime began to "revolutionize" the educational system by emphasizing creativity over rote memorization, and the development of higher-order analytical, mathematical, and logical thinking skills. The regime has put particularly strong emphasis on computer and information technology (IT) education. Furthermore, the failure of the formal economy has already created a quasi-market economy in North Korea.

To explain the lack of effective reform in North Korea, then, one should begin by focusing on the **agency** of North Korea's leaders, whose power over the country is still largely unquestioned, although not necessarily unassailable. At the same time, one must remember to see North Korea's leaders as constructed actors—actors who are, to repeat, affected by a larger current of social facts and whose decisions and choices are conditioned and constrained by social constructs. So what are the key social facts and constructs that have shaped the decisions of the North Korean regime? One fact is crystal clear: North Korea has a rigid single-party system, a system that privileges loyalty over all else (I return to this point below). Underlying this system, however, is the ideology of *juche,* which I introduced in Figure 4.1. While it is difficult (even impossible) to say exactly how much this ideological construct influences North Korea's leaders, to argue that it is a powerful social-cultural force that colors, to a significant extent, every decision and choice they make is not unreasonable. Consider, for example, the regime's basic approach to reform. According to Young Chul Chung (2004), the regime denies that it is engaged in market-oriented reform at all. Instead, it uses the terms *rebuilding* (*kaegon*) and *improvement* (*kaeson*) and claims that the "rebuilding and improvement" efforts are geared toward creating a more powerful state and a self-reliant economy. Self-reliance is the core of *juche*. Of course, North Korean leaders' simply referring to *juche* does not necessarily mean that this philosophy is actually shaping the decisions and actions of the regime. But, thus far, the reform measures have fairly clearly been designed by the regime to preserve the tenets of *juche* as well as the power of the state.

The main point, to be clear, is that the North Korean regime has been hemmed in by its still strong devotion to *juche* and the North Korean–style socialism it entails. The constraint is, in many respects, self-imposed, but one should also understand that, over the years, *juche* has become a central—perhaps the central—source of legitimacy for the regime. It also remains as the basic framework for policymaking, even as the country continues its economic decline. The regime has essentially rejected the type of far-reaching economic reform that could reverse the decline of the economy because of *juche*. Instead, North Korean leaders continue to hold fast to the idea that economic revitalization can be achieved through a tightly constrained reform process that stays true to their ideological principles. Consider, on this point, the approach by North Korea to the IT sector (IT refers to anything related to computing technology, including networking, hardware, software, and the Internet).

Ideological Constraints and the IT Industry in North Korea: A Comparative Perspective

As I alluded to above, North Korea's leaders believed that they could solve the country's economic difficulties by developing an indigenous IT sector. North Korea's strategy, for the most part, has been to gradually develop software-engineering and computing skills though a heavy emphasis on IT-related education among its own people. To this end, the regime began to develop IT research organizations and an IT faculty at the university level as early as the mid-1980s. In addition, the entire school curriculum was revised in the mid-1990s to include computer training from the elementary school level to the university level (Y. H. Kim 2004). Recognizing that some external help is necessary, the regime has also selectively established joint projects with technology firms outside of North Korea. One such project is with South Korea's Samsung Electronics, and another is with a German company (the joint company is named KCC Europe),[6] the latter of which is providing a pay service for e-mail to foreign embassies in North Korea (Kim 2004). Surprisingly, perhaps, the regime has had some success with its strategy. According to Paul Tija (2012), founder of GPI Consultancy (a Dutch company specializing in outsourcing), North

Korea now has a well-trained corps of IT professionals—about 10,000—many of whom have the skills to do advanced work in programming for enterprise-resource-planning systems, business process management systems, e-business applications, computer security, gaming, and animation.

Apparently, then, IT is a promising economic sector for North Korea, but its development remains seriously and perhaps fatally hobbled—particularly as an engine of economic growth for the country as whole—by *juche,* the regime's inward-looking tendencies, and fear of openness. The Internet, for example, remains heavily regulated allowing ordinary citizens almost no access; even for North Korea's IT "corporations," access is limited to a "local Internet" (i.e., an "intranet" that is not connected to the outside world). As a result, potential foreign clients cannot communicate directly with North Korean IT companies. In general, even e-mailing or calling a North Korean company directly is not possible: everything must be done in person or through a well-connected intermediary (Tija 2012). So far, too, all of North Korea's IT companies are state owned. This lack of connectedness and openness, especially if it remains unchanged, will almost certainly doom North Korea's IT sector to a very small niche. Perhaps the best way to appreciate the limitations of this strategy is to compare it with another communist player in the IT sector, China. Quite unlike North Korea, China has eschewed an inward-looking, self-sufficient strategy and has instead opted for a more open and interdependent one. Although I focus on China in the second part of this chapter, taking a quick look at the contrasting development of China's IT industry right now would be useful for comparative purposes.

The development of China's IT industry, from the early stages, depended heavily on foreign participation and private entrepreneurship, as opposed to state entrepreneurship. To a significant extent, this approach was and is necessary, especially in the IT sector. Globally, the IT sector is a hypercompetitive, extremely fluid, and highly dynamic industry; latecomers in particular are at a severe disadvantage, particularly if they try to rely on a go-it-alone strategy. Significantly, as with North Korea, Chinese leaders clearly wanted to develop domestic production capabilities in IT hardware and software; they wanted, simply put, to be "independent." However, they understood from the beginning that integration into the global production network, along with close and strong reliance on foreign companies, was essential. Thus, the Chinese state strongly encouraged and actively promoted foreign participation, something it did through a variety of incentives, from low-cost to no-cost financing, to land grants in the form of long-term leases, to tax credits and rebates. Significantly, the regime also allowed privately owned Chinese firms to occupy an important position in the industry. This approach allowed China to become a major player very quickly: in 2006, China emerged as the world's largest producer of IT hardware, and by 2010, the country accounted for 29 percent of global IT production. As early as 2004, China also became the world's largest exporter of information and communication technology (Jeong 2012). One should note, however, that these figures hide the fact that roughly 90 percent of China's technology exports are made by foreign firms operating in China; thus, as James Lewis (2007) and others have pointed out, China's "success is not the conquest of a global industry but rather [is a result of] being absorbed by it" (p. 2). However, Lewis's statement is likely an exaggeration, for as China is being absorbed, it is also absorbing the knowledge and technical know-how to develop its own independent footing in the IT industry. Whatever the case, the "absorption" of China's IT sector underscores openness to the outside world that is sorely lacking in North Korea.

I might also note that, although the Chinese state is well known for its efforts to censor the Internet for Chinese citizens, its efforts have been only partly successful. On the one hand, the state has an effective censorship policy to control access to specific online content: it uses website and Internet protocol (IP) address blocking and keyword filtering; regulates and monitors Internet service providers, Internet cafés, and university bulletin board systems; requires registration of websites and blogs; and occasionally arrests high-profile "cyber-dissidents" (Lum, Moloney Figliola, and Weed 2012). On the other hand, with 500 million Internet users (including 300 million people with accounts on Twitter-like microblogging sites, such as **Weibo**), complete surveillance is, in practical terms, impossible. Moreover, for active "dissidents," circumventing government controls is relatively easy through the use of special software, proxy servers, and virtual private networks (Lum, Moloney Figliola, and Weed 2012). The Chinese state, of course, recognizes the limitations on its ability to censor its citizens, but—unlike the North Korean regime—understands and accepts the trade-offs: a fully functioning Internet and free flow of most information are necessary for a thriving IT sector.

Back to the Problem of Reform

The foregoing discussion provides an indication of the concrete impacts that the ideological commitment of the North Korean regime has had on the development of the country's IT industry. (However, that security concerns play a prominent role, too, is apparent. But the manner in which North Korea's leaders perceive security is also a reflection of their ideological positions.) I realize that the argument may not be entirely convincing, if only because one cannot demonstrate a direct causal link between *juche* and North Korean economic reforms. On this point, though, one more comparison with China might be helpful. I mentioned Deng Xiaoping earlier. He is widely considered the primary political force behind China's successful embrace of capitalism. He also helped to rebuild the Chinese economy after the disastrous famines—during which an estimated 15 to 30 million people died—caused by the Great Leap Forward. At that point, in fact, Deng put forth his so-called **cat principle** (see Figure 4.5), which implicitly argued against Mao's ideology and for the adoption of any economic practice, including capitalism, which worked to resolve the country's economic problems. His ideas and reforms were initially accepted, but very soon after, Mao began to criticize both the market-friendly policies (which included allowing for full-fledged private farming) and the leaders who backed them. Mao's disapproval forced Deng to remove his quip about black and white cats from the record (Teiwes 2010). But it was too late. The remark marked Deng as a **capitalist roader**, a label that was used against him during the Cultural Revolution, when he was stripped of his party and government posts and sent to the countryside to work in a farm-machinery repair shop. (Significantly, though, Deng was not expelled from the Communist Party, which allowed him to return and eventually take power.) The main point, to repeat, is the following: during the Mao era, ideological commitment was a powerful constraint against reform—a constraint that was only overcome after Mao died. In North Korea, however, the death of the "supreme leader" does not result in change. One reason, perhaps, is the practice of hereditary succession—a practice that makes the son's repudiation of the father difficult.

Undoubtedly, other social facts and constructs are important in the North Korean context. One such factor, as I pointed out above, derives from the institutional dynamics of North Korea's totalitarian single-party system. Earlier, I asserted that single-party communist dictatorships are clearly capable of implementing effective market-based reforms; one sees this capability demonstrated in other cases. One must conclude that something about North Korea's single-party system will not allow for this change. I already identified the

---

Figure 4.5 Deng's Cat Principle (or Cat Theory)

The cat principle grew out of a famous saying by Deng Xiaoping in 1962: "It does not matter if it is a white cat or a black cat, as long as it catches mice." While seemingly innocuous, this statement was significant in the context of Chinese politics during the Mao era. In essence, Deng was suggesting that China's political leadership should be pragmatic rather than ideological; more concretely, his cat principle was premised on the idea that policy results were more important than ideological purity or "correctness." Thus, if market-based policies worked, then market-based policies should be used rather than policies that reflected socialist principles. For Deng, the quip would return to haunt him: he was later branded a capitalist roader and was compelled to renounce his cat theory and instead emphasize the collective economy (Teiwes 2010).

importance of the regime's ideology and the practice of hereditary succession, but another important aspect of North Korea's system is the privileged position of the military. That the military occupies a central position in a single-party authoritarian regime is in no way unusual. After all, party leaders ultimately depend upon the coercive capacity of the military. For this reason, though, strong efforts are made to subordinate the military to the party and to depoliticize the military as much as possible. Under Kim Il-sung, the military's subordination to the party was unequivocal; following his death, however, Kim Jong-il purposely turned the **Korean People's Army** into a political tool, which he used to counterbalance the party. Kim Jong-il's approach was manifested in his military-first policy (known as **Songun**), under which the Korean People's Army was made the center of the government and the "repository of all political authority and power" (H. S. Park 2007, p. 6). Not surprisingly, this change in policy meant that the military would be first in line for economic resources, and that the defense industry, through emphasis on heavy industry, would become the core of the national economy. Military leaders were also elevated to positions above most party officials and were given more and more decisionmaking authority in policy matters (Jeon 2000a).

Kim Jong-il clearly recognized the danger of putting so much power into the hands of the military; he understood, as Jeon (2000a) puts it, that a powerful military is like a dangerous tiger, which could turn against and devour its master at any time. For this reason, Kim did his best to check the power of the military through an extensive use of institutional devices and other methods, including the use of his secret-police network to ensure that military commanders were under constant surveillance. But military leaders had little reason to scheme against Kim while he was in power; after all, they were getting everything they wanted. Herein lies the basic problem of reform: a meaningful move toward a market-oriented economy will almost invariably mean a major shift in resources away from the military. And while military endorsement of such a shift is certainly conceivable,[7] during the years of economic decline and devastating famine, the military largely stood by while the economy crumbled and millions of civilians died of starvation.

Tellingly, the military-first policy was supposed to rescue the North Korean economy. Instead, the elevation of the military as a central political **institution** in North Korea makes the issue of economic reform even more complicated, and for fairly obvious reasons. The material, security, and ideological interests of the military may clash with a significant **liberalization** and opening of the national economy. Consider, on this point, that Kim Jong-un, in one of his first public declarations after taking over after his father's death, reconfirmed the central position of the military. As he put it, military strength should be the country's "first, second, and third priority" (cited in Ramstad 2012).

Brief Conclusion: The Underlying Importance of Structure

Despite its deep-seated and severe economic difficulties, North Korea has proven highly resistant to implementing far-reaching, market-oriented economic reform. North Korea's refusal to make any truly substantial change stands in sharp contrast to other single-party communist dictatorships, which arguably had less compelling reasons for reform when the process first started. In the discussion of the reform process in North Korea, I identified a number of probable obstacles to reform while using, at least very generally, the constructed actor model. I did not, however, explicitly discuss the underlying structural processes at play. With only minimal reflection, however, one can see that structural forces have and are clearly playing a role. North Korea's entire economic trajectory evinces the presence of these forces. From its initial withdrawal from the capitalist world-system, to the collapse of its economy, to its still tentative movements toward reincorporation, North Korea's economic fate has been largely determined by underlying structural processes. In the first phase, North Korea's withdrawal from global capitalism was premised on similar withdrawals by the Soviet Union and China and their attempt to create an alternative world-system (I discuss this issue in more detail below in the examination of China). On this point, it is enough to say that without military and economic support from the Soviet Union and especially China, North Korea would have ceased to exist as early as 1950, when the Chinese intervened during the Korean War to save North Korea from almost certain military defeat. In the second phase, while command economies clearly have inherent limitations, cooperative relations with a network of other command economies can allow for extended survival. The Soviet Union's and China's decisive turns to capitalism, however, left North Korea too economically isolated. In the third phase, the inexorable expansion of capitalism has left North Korea only one viable economic option: integration into a system its leaders abhor.

Structural forces, in short, cannot be ignored. They help explain why the menu of economic reforms from which North Korea's leaders (and people) can order is ultimately limited to only one selection: capitalism. In applying the constructed actor model, therefore, one absolutely needs to remember that, while individuals make their own decisions—oftentimes in defiance of structural conditions and imperatives—those decisions are never made in a vacuum. Those decisions also have very clear, very real consequences. For North Korea, the consequence of choosing to delay and strictly limit incorporation into the capitalist world-system has meant, at best, a slowly deteriorating economy. On the other hand, choosing or, more accurately, being forced into full-fledged integration may consign North Korea to peripheral status for many decades—although the constructed model suggests other possibilities á la South Korea and Taiwan. With this in mind, I will now turn to China—a country that, like

North Korea, insisted on following a socialist economic path for the first three decades of the PRC's existence; unlike North Korea, however, China chose a capitalist path at a relatively early stage.

China's Economic Transformation: An Introduction

On the surface, one can hardly ignore the strikingly similar economic trajectories of China's economic rise, on the one hand, and the rise of Japan, South Korea, and Taiwan, on the other hand. The most salient aspect of this similar trajectory is the rate of economic growth. One should already be familiar with the basic statistics: over a thirty-five-year period, from 1960 to 1995, South Korea and Taiwan experienced annualized and, at the time, unprecedented average growth rates of over 8 percent (Japan's was lower, but only because its economy was already relatively large). Since 1979, China has grown at an even faster pace, averaging 9.9 percent over a slightly shorter span (1979–2008). Even during the depths of the global recession, from 2009 to 2011, China continued with high growth rates at an average of 9.5 percent per year (see Figure 4.6). For much of the rest of the world, by contrast, the period between 2009 and 2011 was marked by either negative growth or low growth, with 2009 being a particularly bad year. According to the United Nations, the developed economies as a group contracted by 4 percent in 2009, while developing economies as a whole showed positive growth of just 2.4 percent (United Nations 2011). On a per capita basis, I should point out, an economic growth rate of 2.4 percent just barely outpaced the average population growth of 1.5 percent for low-income countries (or 1.2 percent for middle-income countries). A comparison of **GDP** growth rates, unfortunately, really reveals very little, except that something is definitely unusual about China and the other East Asian economies. So, are there any other important similarities?

The short answer is yes. In fact, one does not have to look very hard to find another similarity—and one that is likely far more significant. The similarity is the role of the state. Japan, South Korea (after 1961), and Taiwan were all governed by strong, highly effective, developmentally oriented leadership—at least according to some observers. In China, one can see a very similar type of state, although in the prereform era (that is, the period during which Mao Zedong was in control), the state was clearly not effective at building a basis for sustained and dynamic economic growth. But this difference pre- and postreform points to another obvious but easy-to-overlook similarity: during their periods of rapid and sustained economic growth and industrialization, all four East Asian economies (China, Japan, South Korea, and Taiwan) had adopted an export-oriented, capitalist system. These two similarities raise a few deceptively simple questions: Is China's economic success primarily due to its being a strong

Figure 4.6 China's Average Annual Real GDP Growth Rate, 1960–2012

Time Period	Annual Growth Rate (% per year)
1960–1978 (prereform)	5.3 (average)
1990	3.8
1991	9.3
1992	14.2
1993	14.0
1994	13.1
1995	10.9
1996	10.0
1997	9.3
1998	7.8
1999	7.6
2000	8.4
2001	8.3
2003	9.1
2004	10.1
2005	9.9
2006	11.1
2007	13.0
2008	9.0
2009	9.1
2010	10.3
2011	9.2
2012	7.8

Sources: For the years prior to 2009, official Chinese government data and data from the Economist Intelligence Unit (cited in Morrison 2009); for the years 2009–2012, *CIA World Factbook* (https://www.cia.gov/library/publications/the-world-factbook/).

developmental state, or is it the product of the dismantling of its centrally planned, **command economy** and the embrace of the free market? Or perhaps China's success is based on a combination of these factors? From the structural and cultural perspectives, one might also ask these questions: Was China's integration into the capitalist world-system inevitable, and did structural forces largely determine how this integration would play out? Has the legacy of Maoism or other elements of China's broader historical culture shaped the country's economic path? These questions, one might surmise, are meant to highlight the various competing interpretations of China's transformation, as I wrote in Chapter 1, from an industrially and technologically backward leviathan, to one of the most dynamic and fastest-growing capitalist economies in the world. Before I move on to the theoretical debate, I should provide some background on China's transition from a command economy to a market-oriented one.

Political Economy of China's Economic Rise

While Chinese civilization goes back thousands of years, the PRC itself goes back just to 1949, when the **Chinese Communist Party (CCP)**, led by Mao Zedong, came to power. As with any new revolutionary regime, the CCP was immediately confronted with the need to build a viable and sustainable economy. This need was all the more imperative given China's huge population of 541.7 million people in 1949, a population that was growing at a rate of about 2 percent a year (Jowett 1984). Mao and the CCP adopted a Soviet-style **Stalinist model** for the economy, but the adoption of this model was not immediate. Instead, the CCP initially planned a moderate program of economic reform, which would have left the private economy alone in the hope that China's remaining capitalists would continue to invest in their own firms (Zweig 2010). The CCP also implemented **land reform**, which is a common practice even in noncommunist regimes—Japan, South Korea, and Taiwan all pursued sweeping land reform in the early postwar period (see Figure 4.7 for further discussion of land reform). In China, land reform redistributed more than 40 percent of arable land from richer farmers to approximately 100 million peasants (Klein 1961); the primary goal was to destroy the landlord class and other supporters of the **KMT**.

By the early 1950s, the goal of moderate economic reform was replaced by a desire to achieve more rapid industrialization. At this point, the Soviet/Stalinist model was embraced in earnest by the CCP. The implications of this decision were immense. In particular, the state had much stronger control over the entire economy, including the agricultural sector, since any available economic surplus needed to be directed to the industrial sector. In turn, the land that had been given to individual peasants—which had resulted in a highly inefficient agricultural system because of fragmentation—needed to be reaggregated. The CCP accomplished this goal by first creating mutual aid teams, then producers' cooperatives and collectives. While more efficient, the surplus produced in these new collective farms did not go to the farmers but was instead expropriated by the state. The CCP then used this agricultural surplus to invest in heavy industry. Significantly, farmers not only had to turn their crops over to the state but were also forced to surrender almost everything else they owned, collectively and individually, to their cooperatives. In the cities, too, anyone who owned a business, large or small, was forced to turn over his or her assets to the state. Despite achieving some success through these collectivist policies, the CCP leadership was unhappy with the pace of industrial progress under the Stalinist model. This dissatisfaction was the basis for the ironically named Great Leap Forward (1958–1960).

The main goal of the Great Leap Forward was to rapidly increase production in both heavy industry and agriculture at the same time. On the agricultural

Figure 4.7 The Importance of Land Reform

Land reform (or agrarian reform) typically involves measures that redistribute ownership and control of agricultural land from large landowners to peasants, small-scale farmers, or tenants. In the case of communist countries, however, land reform usually means transferring ownership of the land from private landowners to the state. In either case, one of the objectives of land reform is to curtail or eliminate the power of traditional landed elites, who are often hostile to economic, political, and social change. In societies making the transition from a primarily agricultural mode of production to a capitalist-industrial or planned-industrial one, moreover, land reform (or agrarian reform) is often considered a necessary step. Under traditional landholding arrangements, agricultural productivity is typically low, since the people who work the land have little incentive to invest capital or expend significant effort to increase yields, yet industrialization plans often rely on surplus agricultural production to create sufficient investment capital for industry. Land reform is seen as an important way to address this problem. For example, through private ownership, new small-scale farmers will have a stronger incentive to maximize production, as was the case in South Korea. As the transformation of tenants into owners created a major incentive for an increase in efficiency and production, the state, as Christóbal Kay (2002) notes, was able to "cream off" a significant proportion of this increased efficiency to finance the industrialization process (p. 1080). Even more, Kay argues that the success of land reform efforts in South Korea and Taiwan specifically was largely responsible for the overall economic success of the two countries.

Not coincidentally, perhaps, significant land reform took place in all five East Asian countries: Japan, South and North Korea, Taiwan, and China. In the cases of Japan and South Korea, land reform took place under the auspices of the United States.

front, this policy called for even larger farms, or **communes**: by the end of 1958, 120 million family farms had been reduced to 26,500 communes—a stupendous feat. With these new "supersized" farms, the CCP assigned extremely high output targets; the intent was to produce enough surplus to finance a rapid expansion of industry. For a while the plan seemed to be working as local cadres reported extraordinarily—really impossibly—high levels of production: based on their reports, grain production for 1958 was projected to increase to 525 million metric tons from only 195 million metric tons in the preceding year. The problem, however, was that the reports were wrong (actual grain production was 200 million metric tons). The cadres, to put it bluntly, had lied. Unfortunately, Mao and the CCP were easily duped, perhaps blinded by their own ideological fervor: in fact, they believed that collectivization had basically solved China's food problem once and for all. This false understanding had disastrous consequences. As Wei Li and Dennis Tao Yang (2005) explain, the exaggerated outcomes encouraged the CCP leadership to redouble its efforts in industrialization at the expense of agriculture. Believing that fewer people were needed to farm the land, for example, 16.4 million peasants, roughly twice the size of the industrial workforce in 1957, were relocated to cities; another 100 million peasants were ordered to undertake large irrigation and land reclamation projects, as well to build backyard iron furnaces. Most ironically of all, because the CCP believed the year 1958 would see a food surplus, it ordered communes to reduce production of food grains and switch to cash crops. However, instead of a surplus, China experienced a serious decline in grain production: in 1959, grain output fell to 170 million tons; in 1960, to 143 million tons; and in 1962, 148 million tons.

Although these and other policies were not entirely responsible for the decline in grain production between 1959 and 1961—severe weather also played a role—they certainly contributed to it in a significant way. Moreover, because so much grain had been sent back to the state, many villages simply had not been left enough food. The result was the Great Famine, which claimed the lives of an estimated 15 to 30 million people (no completely reliable statistics exist).[8] The famine—and the underlying political reasons for it—compelled the CCP to begin moderating and even reversing some of its economic policies. Mao himself temporarily withdrew from day-to-day management of the economy and allowed **Liu Shaoqi** and Deng Xiaoping, two of the CCP's more pragmatic leaders (see Figure 4.8 for a list of key political figures in the PRC), to chart a more moderate path. Millions of workers were sent back to the countryside, the size of communes was reduced, unreasonable output targets were abolished, and the government began to import rather than export grain. The return to moderation, however, was only temporary. Mao quickly became unhappy with the direction the country was moving, not just economically but politically, socially, and ideologically as well. As Frederick Teiwes (2010) explains it, "Mao saw signs of a possibly degenerating revolution: widespread corruption and self-seeking behavior, significant social inequality, and the emergence of what he called a 'new bourgeoisie' privileged stratum that benefitted disproportionately from China's socialist system" (p. 82). The solution for Mao was another revolution, the Great Proletarian Cultural Revolution (or Cultural Revolution for short). Although the full dynamics and meaning of the Cultural Revolution are too complex to cover here, suffice it to say that it had a tremendously disruptive effect on China: the economy, which had been recovering in the aftermath of the Great Leap Forward, went back into decline, China's educational system was destroyed, moderate political leaders and their ideas were marginalized, the regime and CCP leadership fragmented into hostile factions, and at least 1.5 million essentially innocent people were killed.

When Mao died in 1976, the country—and especially the economy—had still not recovered from the Cultural Revolution. His death also left a power

Figure 4.8 Key Figures in China's Political History

Name	Key Positions	
Chen Yun (1905–1995)	CCP Vice Chairman, 1956–1966, 1978–1982 PRC Vice Premier, 1949–1966, 1979–1980	Became one of China's leading economic planners after 1949.
Deng Xiaoping (1904–1997)	CCP General Secretary, 1956–1966 CCP Vice Chairman, 1975–1982 PRC Vice Premier, 1952–1966, 1973–1976, 1977–1980	Was instrumental in launching China's turn toward the market in the late 1970s; ordered the assault on peaceful demonstrators during the Tiananmen Square movement.
Hu Jintao (b. 1942)	CCP General Secretary, 2002–2012 PRC President, 2003–2013	Former leader of the Fourth Generation of the CCP's leadership; presided over a decade of strong economic growth in China; introduced the idea of building a "harmonious society."
Hu Yaobang (1915–1989)	CCP Chairman, 1981–1982 CCP General Secretary, 1982–1987	Played an important role in implementing market-oriented reforms in the 1980s; his death in 1989 sparked the Tiananmen Square movement.
Hua Guofeng (1921–2008)	CCP Chairman, 1976–1981 PRC Premier, 1976–1980	Handpicked by Mao to succeed Zhou Enlai as premier in 1976; played a key role in dismantling the Gang of Four.
Jiang Qing (1914–1991)	Deputy Director, Central Cultural Revolution Group, 1966–1969 Member, CCP Politburo, 1969–1976	Wife of Mao Zedong and member of the Gang of Four; became an important figure during the Cultural Revolution; sentenced to life in prison and committed suicide in 1991.
Jiang Zemin (b. 1926)	CCP General Secretary, 1989–2002 PRC President, 1993–2003	Came to power following the Tiananmen Square protests of 1989; promoted economic reform and helped to rebuild ties with the United States; presided over the peaceful return of Hong Kong and Macau to Chinese control.
Li Xiannian (1909–1992)	PRC President, 1983–1988 CCP Vice Chairman, 1988–1993	One of the key architects of China's economic policies after the Cultural Revolution; considered one of the Eight Elders of the CCP.
Liu Shaoqi (1898–1969)	PRC Vice Premier, 1949–1959 PRC President, 1959–1966 CCP Vice Chairman, 1956–1966	Purged as a capitalist roader during the Cultural Revolution; posthumously rehabilitated in 1980.

(continues)

Figure 4.8 continued

Name	Key Positions	
Mao Zedong (1893–1976)	CCP Chairman, 1945–1976 PRC President, 1949–1959	One of the principal founders of the CCP; occupied the preeminent position in China from 1949 until his death in 1976.
Wen Jiabao (b. 1942)	PRC Premier, 2003–2013 Member, CCP Politburo Standing Committee, 2002–2012	Served with Hu Jintao; advocated for a more balanced approach in China's economic policies.
Xi Jinping (b. 1953)	CCP Chairman, 2012–present PRC President, 2013–present CCP Vice President, 2008–2013	Selected to succeed Hu Jintao as PRC president in 2012; known as an economic reformer.
Zhao Ziyang (1919–2005)	PRC Premier, 1980–1987 CCP General Secretary, 1987–1989	Close associate of Deng Xiaoping and one of the architects of China's market-oriented reforms; purged after the 1989 Tiananmen Square movement and forced to live under house arrest.

Sources: Tiewes (2010) and Gilley (2010).

vacuum, despite the fact that Mao had clearly designated a successor, **Hua Guofeng**. Fortunately, perhaps, Mao's proclivity to favor, and disfavor, other potential leaders based on an ambiguous set of personal preferences and attitudes meant that several contenders existed for the position, including Deng Xiaoping, another moderate, and the much more radical, prorevolutionary **Gang of Four**, which included Mao's wife, Jiang Qing, and three others (Zhang Chunqiao, Yao Wenyuan, and Wang Hongwen). The Gang of Four problem was resolved by Hua, who decided simply to arrest his four rivals. In the end, this decision turned out to be an easy and popular one, but also one that was fraught with unpredictable danger. The emergence of Deng Xiaoping was a more subtle and complicated affair, the details of which are not important for current purposes. It is enough to say that the death of Mao had finally freed China's leadership from the constraints of Maoism and especially from their hitherto blind adherence to Mao's economic principles. This newfound freedom gave the pragmatists a chance to prevail.

As Bruce Gilley (2010) notes, one of the more important "economic" reforms of the late 1970s was actually a political reform: the party's repudiation of **class struggle** as its primary objective. While seemingly unimportant—class struggle, after all, is "only" a concept—the repudiation of this idea opened the ideological door for concrete political and economic reforms, which otherwise may not have been possible. In particular, it opened the door for the adoption of market-based economic policies, or more simply, it opened the door to capitalism. Significantly, though, the shift to capitalism was framed as a choice fully consistent with the principles of socialism and communism. This shift required a bit of backtracking on the part of the CCP, but the party returned to the classical Marxist idea that capitalism is a necessary historical stage on the road to socialism. In Marx's view, capitalism provided the material foundation necessary for a civilization to progress to the next higher stage, socialism. (Mao, by contrast, argued that China could compress or skip the capitalist stage through the collectivization of agriculture and state control of industry.) The new view, to repeat, was that capitalism would provide a better pathway toward achieving socialism (Gilley 2010). Indeed, from the beginning of the reform period, Deng and his allies were careful to frame all their actions and policies as a way to save, rather than to destroy, communism. Even the characterization of market reforms reflected this position, as the reform process was dubbed "socialism with Chinese characteristics." While this language may appear little more than window dressing, good reason exists to believe that this verbal dance was necessary for the reform process to proceed and succeed. As **Zhao Ziyang** (one of Deng's top deputies and a key, but often neglected, architect of reforms) explains, a justification for market reforms was necessary since they contradicted more than thirty years of past practices; thus, without a strong, believable justification, the reform process could easily have been "killed in its infancy" (Zhao et al. 2009, p. 205).

The reform process itself was complicated, as it resulted in changes to almost every aspect of China's economic policies, big and small, domestic and foreign. One of the earliest changes was decollectivization in the countryside: communes and collectives were dismantled, although collective ownership of land was maintained, and individual households were given far more autonomy. They could decide what crops to plant, how to allocate labor, and how to dispose of or sell their goods. Private markets were encouraged, and the state raised the price it would pay for agricultural products—initially, the state set a quota, and only surplus crops (i.e., crops remaining after the quota was fulfilled) could be sold in private markets; in 1984, however, the quota system was eliminated entirely. The result was a very rapid increase in grain production; wheat production, for example, more than doubled between 1978 and 1985. Another major reform in the early years was the establishment, in 1980, of the first **special economic zones** (SEZs) in Shenzhen, Zhuhai, Xiamen, and Shantou. Establishment of the SEZs marked the first major opening of the Chinese economy to the outside world and the first major step toward integration into global capitalism. The SEZs provided tax incentives for foreign investment, fewer restrictions on international trade activity, a streamlined approval process, and access to "cheap land and labor" for foreign companies. In 1984, the CCP opened fourteen additional coastal cities to overseas investment and foreign trade and further expanded the SEZs in 1985.

In the early years of reform, the CCP also began to ease control over **state-owned enterprises (SOEs**; see Figure 4.9). The process began very slowly, with only six SOEs in 1978, but accelerated quickly: by the end of 1981, about 80 percent of all SOEs were involved in the reform process (for details, see Lin and Li 2006). The reform process was gradual, and it was initially based on the same "two-tier" (or dual-track) strategy used in the agricultural sector. That is, the SOEs were still obliged to meet state-mandated production targets at a price determined by the state, but these targets were generally kept very low; the SOEs were then encouraged to sell their surplus production at unregulated prices on the open market. The firms were also given some autonomy over how to use the profits generated from their sales (some of which could be used for managerial bonuses). Over time, the targets became lower and reliance on market prices and autonomous decisionmaking increased; the idea was for the SOEs to "grow out of the plan" (Naughton 1995). In addition, financing arrangements were shifted such that the old system, which was based on direct government funding, was steadily replaced with bank financing. As in the private market, SOEs were required to pay back their loans with interest; the goal was to require SOEs to finance their growth based on the "real cost of capital." In general, the transition from a planned system to a market system for SOEs was successful, but not without a number of difficulties (I should also note an intense debate is ongoing about the overall success of the reforms for SOEs).[9]

The story of reform in China is obviously a much larger one than I have covered here. However, the foregoing review provides a good sense of some of the more significant changes that took place in China beginning in the late 1970s. Unlike North Korea, these changes were dramatic and profound. In the countryside, in particular, the regime moved very swiftly. But small-farm households could adjust more quickly to a market system than large industrial enterprises. In fact, the reform process for SOEs was much more incremental. Almost two decades passed as the state gradually disposed of (or sold off) some of the smaller SOEs via a policy dubbed "grasping the large and letting go of the small." And although thousands of smaller SOEs were effectively privatized beginning in the late 1990s, SOEs still play a very prominent role in China's economy today.

Debating China's Economic Rise

In thinking about China's economic transformation, everyone can agree upon one point: the shift from central planning and rigid state control to a market-oriented economy was an essential ingredient. Simply put, *no market, no turnaround*. Even

Figure 4.9 State-Owned Enterprises (SOEs) in China

State-owned enterprises, or SOEs, "are business entities established by central and local governments, . . . whose supervisory officials are from the government" (Szamosszegi and Kyle 2011, p. 6). SOEs, however, are only one of a number of other types of state-controlled enterprises. Thus, in addition to SOEs, one can find joint-operation enterprises, limited liability corporations, shareholding corporations (with the state owning the majority of shares), and public organizations. In 2010, China was home to 9,105 SOEs and another 11,405 enterprises in which the state held a controlling share of the company (Szamosszegi and Kyle 2011). Despite the relatively small number of SOEs (and other state-controlled companies), their influence in the national economy remains significant. Accurate figures, unfortunately, are not available, but various analyses have put the SOEs' share of China's GDP at between 30 percent and 50 percent. In addition, SOEs and state-controlled enterprises account for as much as 48 percent of urban employment and 54 percent of total wages paid to urban employees.

Equally if not more important, the Chinese state has designated defense, electric power, petroleum and petrochemical, telecommunications, coal, civil aviation, and shipping as strategic industries, and the state has also designated equipment manufacturing, automobiles, IT, construction, iron and steel, nonferrous metals, chemicals, and surveying as pillar industries. In strategic industries, the state has declared that SOEs or state-controlled enterprises must maintain either sole ownership or absolute control, while in pillar industries only a "strong control position" is required. All SOEs, but particularly those in strategic and pillar industries, receive preferential treatment from state-owned banks. For example, they have access to capital and favorable interest rates or, if unable to repay their loans, their debts may be forgiven. In addition, some "uncreditworthy" SOEs are extended loans.

The greatest benefits are provided to the so-called national champions, which are among China's largest SOEs. These include:

- China National Petroleum Company (CNPC)
- Sinopec
- China National Offshore Oil Corporation (CNOOC)
- Aluminum Corporation of China (CHALCO)
- China Minmetals Corporation
- China State Construction Engineering Corporation (CSCEC)
- China Ocean Shipping Group (COSCO)
- China Communications Construction Company Limited
- ZTE Corporation (telecommunications)
- Lenovo (IT)
- Haier (consumer goods)
- CITIC (formerly the China International Trust and Investment Corporation)
- China Investment Corporation (CIC; a sovereign wealth fund)

(The statistics and other information cited here come from Szamosszegi and Kyle [2011].)

more, a very strong consensus generally can be found that China's export-oriented policies allowed for more rapid and dynamic economic growth than would otherwise have been possible. Once observers of the Chinese economy get beyond these two points, however, disagreements start to crop up rather quickly. Not surprisingly, these disagreements are divided along the same set of theoretical lines discussed in Chapter 2: liberal, statist (or institutional), structural, and cultural. Even more, the arguments about China are not significantly different from the arguments about the other East Asian economies, Japan, South Korea, and Taiwan, as is to be expected. Nonetheless, one can make some subtle and some not-so-subtle distinctions, which I try to highlight in the discussion that follows.

Why Is China Growing So Fast? The Liberal Argument

The liberal explanation of China's rapid pace of economic growth since 1979, not surprisingly, focuses primarily on market dynamics and on increases in key economic indicators, particularly capital inputs and productivity. A good representative example of the liberal perspective is provided by two **IMF** researchers, Zuliu Hu and Moshin Khan, in their aptly titled booklet, *Why Is China Growing So Fast?* (1997). Their answer is quite simple. According to Hu and Khan, a significant proportion of China's rapid growth can be attributed to an unexpectedly large increase in productivity. Their finding, at least partially, contradicted the then prevailing notion among economists that China's growth was primarily based on increases in capital. To be sure, the authors note, capital stock did grow significantly in China—about 7 percent a year over 1979–1994. However, the capital-output ratio "hardly budged" (p. 3). In other words, the production of goods and services per unit of capital remained almost the same throughout the first sixteen years of China's economic takeoff. Even more, the other major factor of production—labor—also declined in relative terms during the same period. The upshot is that China's post-Mao economic growth did not fit the classic Soviet model discussed in Chapter 2 (and earlier in this chapter with regard to North Korea). In fact, increased capital and labor inputs accounted for only 58 percent of China's overall economic growth between 1979 and 1994. The "residual," then, is due to an increase in productivity.

According to Hu and Khan, China's **TFP** increased at an annual rate of 3.9 percent during 1979 to 1994. Now, 3.9 percent may not sound particularly impressive, but in relative terms it represents "explosive growth" and puts China "in a class by itself" (p. 4). To see this statistic in context, consider the statistics on productivity published by the **OECD**. For the period between 1990 and 2008, the average TFP growth rate in the United States, Japan, Germany, Britain, and France was around 1 percent a year. For a few other large "emerging" capitalist economies—those economies that are much closer to China in terms of level of industrialization—the rate was even lower. Specifically, in

Russia, Mexico, and Brazil, TFP growth was less that 0.5 percent. Assessing these statistics, *The Economist* magazine concurs fully with Khan and Hu. "Probably no other country in history," the magazine notes, "has enjoyed such rapid efficiency gains" ("Secret Sauce" 2009). In a more detailed analysis by Barry Bosworth and Susan Collins (2008), the results were largely the same. Looking at a series of different time periods, they show that China's TFP growth rate between 1978 and 2004 was 3.6 percent per year, compared to 0.9 percent for Indonesia, South Korea, Malaysia, the Philippines, Singapore, Taiwan, and Thailand as a group, over roughly the same period (see Figure 4.10).

Merely pointing to economic statistics, however, does not provide sufficient explanation. One also needs to know how and why China could achieve such remarkably high rates of productivity growth and overall economic growth. The answer, according to Hu and Khan, is quite simple: China's market-oriented economic reforms, which introduced profit incentives to rural enterprises and small private businesses, unleashed a productivity boom. In particular, the authors credit decollectivization in the agricultural sector along with an increase in agricultural prices as encouraging the more efficient use of labor. They also point to the growth of "village enterprises," which drew tens of millions of people from traditional agriculture into higher value-added manufacturing. In the industrial sector, they focus on the increased autonomy given to enterprise managers, which allowed them—for the first time—to sell products on the open market at competitive prices, get rid of unproductive employees, reward the best workers with bonus pay, and retain earnings for future investment (all points that were discussed in the previous section). The authors also give credit to China's newfound open-

Figure 4.10 Sources of Growth: China and East Asia (annual rate of change, in percent)

Country and Time Period	Physical Capital[a]	Education[b]	TFP
China			
1978–2004	3.2	0.3	3.6
East Asia, excluding China			
1960–1980	2.2	0.5	1.2
1980–2003	2.2	0.5	0.9
1993–2003	1.8	0.5	0.3

Source: Bosworth and Collins (2008).
Notes: The East Asia comparison includes Indonesia, South Korea, Malaysia, the Philippines, Singapore, Taiwan, and Thailand.
    a. Physical capital refers to any manufactured asset that is used in production, such as machinery, buildings, and vehicles.
    b. Education refers to average years of schooling.

ness to FDI and foreign trade, which encouraged the adoption of new technologies and improvements in the organization of production.

As noted at the outset, nothing is surprising about this liberal account of China's economic transformation. But perhaps even more than in the previous analysis of Japan, South Korea, and Taiwan, a critical question is left unaddressed by Hu and Khan. The liberal explanation suggests, in essence, that China's success was and is due to market reforms that unleashed the productive power of millions of Chinese workers and entrepreneurs. This idea undoubtedly contains a good deal of truth. At the same time, as Hu and Khan readily admit, China's economic performance—specifically with respect to productivity—has been in a class by itself. Yet Hu and Khan offer no explicit explanation as to why China is outperforming other countries. What differentiates China from other countries that have also pursued wide-ranging market reform and that have opened their economies to the outside world? On this last question, one should recall that, while China's turn toward the market has been dramatic and profound, it has also been limited. China, in short, is very far from being a **laissez-faire economy**. As described above, for example, SOEs still account for a significant proportion of output in China's national economy. Moreover, a general consensus can be found that the role of centrally controlled SOEs (of which there are 120, with some being the largest companies in China and among the largest in the world) has started to increase as the CCP has sought to foster national champions in the strategic industries of the future. The dominant role of the state in the country's economy raises the possibility that China's economic success is not only due to freer and more open markets but also to state control or state guidance of the economy. At the very least, the still heavy involvement of the Communist Party in the national economy problematizes the notion that China has a primarily market-based economic system. This conflict in theory provides a perfect segue into the statist or institutional perspective.

State and Economy in China:
The Political Economy Approach

To the statist scholar, one fact is unambiguously clear: the process of reform in the post-Mao era has involved a very heavy dose of state action and constant state intervention in the economy. Part of this action, of course, has been centered on marketization (i.e., introducing market forces into specific sectors of the Chinese economy). Marketization has been most apparent in the agricultural sector—as evidenced by the process of decollectivization, which happened early on and which was implemented fairly quickly. On the other hand, the state has, to a significant extent, been true to its word that the reform process would not immediately remake the entire economy into a laissez-faire capitalist one but would instead be "socialism with Chinese characteristics" (later the phrase was revised to a "socialist market economy," a point I return to below). The most obvious evidence of socialist principles at work can be seen in the still strong presence of SOEs. Even more important, the willingness of the state to directly intervene in the economy has not decreased over the years but instead has become more focused, more coherent, and more purposeful.

So how does all of this information translate into a specific argument about the centrality of the state in China's economic transformation? There are, as one might guess, several variations of the statist argument, many of which focus on the idea of China as another developmental state. While a good case can be made for China as a developmental state, I think one would find it more fruitful to eschew that specific terminology and the analytical framework it implies, at least at the outset, and instead look more broadly at the role of the state throughout the process of economic transformation in the post-Mao period. This approach allows one to see the inextricable connection between the state and the economy in China. This political economy approach, in turn, is absolutely essential for an adequate understanding of China's industrialization and growth since the mid-1980s. One of the best guides for this approach is Barry Naughton, considered to be a leading expert on the Chinese economy. And whereas Naughton is not a statist scholar per se, his examination of China's economic transformation clearly puts the state at the center of the analysis. In addition, Naughton does consider China to have a type of developmental state. As he puts it, "China today is more of a centralized developmental **autocracy**" (2007b, p. 8).

Naughton (2008) divides China's reform period into two distinct phases. The first phase, or period of transition, ran from 1978 to 1993; the second phase began in 1993 and continues to this day. The main difference between these two phases revolves around the structure of power at the top of China's political hierarchy, and how changes in the structure of power affected and shaped the decisionmaking process, specifically in relation to economic reform. In contrast to the conventional wisdom, which portrays the CCP hierarchy as largely unified following the emergence of Deng Xiaoping as China's top leader, Naughton argues that the first phase was characterized by fragmentation and dispersed authority. Instead of one unchallenged, paramount leader making and enforcing decisions, throughout the 1980s at least a dozen leaders had "effective veto power over some aspect of economic policy. Moreover, most of the important veto players . . . had extensive patronage networks extending down through the hierarchical system, further complicating policy implementation" (p. 101). The leaders were divided by age (an older and younger generation), by ideology, and by expertise. Not surprisingly, varied opinions were voiced on the appropriate need for and pace of reform. In his memoir, for example, Zhao Ziyang (2009) writes that **Chen Yun** and **Li Xiannian** (both part of the old guard) were extremely skeptical of the reform process, and while they could not stop it, they could slow things down. Indeed, precisely because of the fragmented power structure, the first period of reform was characterized by cautious incremental-ism or gradualism (Naughton 2008). If Deng and his supporters had had their way, by contrast, the reform process would have unfolded much more quickly.

In hindsight, the gradualism of the first period may have served China quite well, as it created a much more stable political environment than might other-wise have been the case. On this point, one needs to understand that the reform process threatened entrenched and often powerful interests. A far-reaching and immediate reform program, therefore, could easily have led to internecine con-flict, thereby derailing the program before it ever got started. Instead, those who had the most to lose compromised and accepted the reform grudgingly—as long as their interests were at least partly protected. At the same time, if vested in-terests had been allowed to dictate the entire reform process, then "China's eco-nomic reform would have been smothered in its crib, and there would be no Chinese economic miracle to write about" (Naughton 2008, p. 106). Fortunately for China, the key advocates of reform—especially Zhao Ziyang—were brilliant tacticians who knew how to achieve both political and economic goals at the same time. Thus, instead of full marketization, a dual-track strategy of reform was adopted, whereby firms operated on both a planned and a market track. Second, incentivization was used throughout the hierarchy: enterprise managers were allowed to keep profits above a base figure (between 50 and 100 percent); bureaucrats and even military units were also offered cash bonuses as incentives for, for example, cutting costs on existing operations. A third major reform was decentralization, which brought budgetary and "extra-budgetary" decisions down to the local level (p. 107). These reforms (and a few others, including the opening of SEZs), while limited, were enough to propel the Chinese economy forward, while also providing clear benefits to practically every privileged group. The rural reforms, moreover, brought significant benefits to hitherto poor farming families, who were used to living hand to mouth. In fact, overall income equality actually improved during this period—a sharp contrast to more recent times, when inequality has shot up.

If China had remained on the same track of limited reform, however, the rapid pace of industrialization and growth would have likely petered out. In-deed, as Naughton describes, by the early 1990s, the country was "facing a gathering crisis of effectiveness" (Naughton 2008, p. 114). Around this time, however, the old guard was, quite literally, beginning to die off. Most were al-ready in their late eighties and were becoming increasing less relevant even be-fore their deaths. The passing of the old guard allowed a reconsolidation of power at the top of the hierarchy, which in turn allowed for more aggressive and more decisive decisionmaking. The new center of power was **Jiang Zemin**, who presided over the **Politburo Standing Committee**, the formal apex of the political system. Under Jiang, the CCP adopted the goal of a "socialist market economy"—the first time that the party acknowledged that reforms were actu-ally leading toward a market-based economy (Naughton 2008). One of the most dramatic reforms during this second phase was the Company Law (1993), which began the phased process of "corporatizing" SOEs; at the same time, the dual-track system was eliminated. Given the economic weight and importance of the SOEs, the Company Law's significance should not be underestimated; for the first time, a large proportion of SOEs were subject to market discipline, which meant that some closed down and others were forced to lay off redundant or unnecessary workers. As a result, 30 million workers were laid off, 18 million workers were reassigned to restructured corporations, and another 20 million workers in urban collectives lost their jobs. This undertaking was truly massive. Other important reforms occurred during this period, too. In 1994, new fiscal reforms were implemented, and these reforms dramatically revised the tax system, allowing the central government to collect a greater share of tax revenue and thereby strengthen its policymaking authority. Reforms also took place in the foreign exchange and banking systems.

China's Industrial Policy

During the two phases of reform, in sum, politics and economics were clearly and inextricably intertwined. Since the beginning of the second phase, moreover, the Chinese state has been very strongly involved in **industrial policy**; it has targeted both traditional industries (e.g., shipbuilding, automobiles, steel, petrochemicals, and textiles) and emerging "strategic" industries, including nanotechnology, biotechnology, high-end manufacturing equipment, aerospace, "new energy" (nuclear and renewable), IT, and new materials. Established industries have been restructured so that they might become globally competitive, while emerging industries were protected from foreign competition. Here is where the Chinese state most closely resembles the other developmental states in East Asia. As with the Japanese, South Korean, and Taiwanese states, in other words, China has not been content to rely solely on static or passive comparative advantage. Instead, the Chinese state "wields industrial policy to help improve the competitive standing of Chinese firms" (Linden 2004, p. 1). State intervention has meant, in particular, the strategic use of foreign investment.

For a long time, the Chinese state has published an "investment catalogue," which lists specific areas in which FDI is "encouraged," "accepted," and "discouraged." Investors in the first category have access to a range of preferences: tax subsidies, preferential access to land and labor, a simplified regulatory process, and so on. The offer of preferences, however, is generally contingent on the foreign firm's willingness to transfer technology to Chinese firms. In the high-speed rail sector, for example, foreign firms were restricted to joint ventures and, as a condition of their investment, required to transfer important technology to their Chinese partners. The result? Chinese firms quickly absorbed the technology and then proceeded to compete directly against US, European, and Japanese firms for contracts outside of China (Sally 2011). Another salient example is the steel industry. The Chinese government imposes strict guidelines on acceptable foreign investment. China's "Iron and Steel Industry Development Policy," for instance, lists the following criteria for foreign investors: "[They] must possess iron and steel technology with independent property rights and should have produced at least 10 millions tons of carbon steel or a least 1 millions tons of high-alloyed special steel in the previous year" (cited in Heiden 2011, p. 20). As in the high-speed rail sector, the Chinese state (through the National Development and Reform Commission) requires joint ventures in which the Chinese partner maintains at least 50 percent ownership in the firm. The state's involvement, it is important to note, goes well beyond the issue of foreign investment; the state also manipulates the prices of vital inputs, imposes export restrictions on important raw materials (such as coke) and semifinished products, selectively promotes exports of high value-added, technology-intensive products, and subsidizes outward investment by Chinese firms (Heiden 2011). The goal, of course, is to make China into the largest and most profitable steel producer in the world. The first part of this goal was achieved in 1996, when China surpassed Japan as the world's leading steel producer; ten years later, China also surpassed Japan as the largest exporter.

China's industrial policy has many other aspects—too many to cover here. Suffice it to say, then, that China's state seems to have followed the same basic economic and institutional path as the other East Asian states. So is China simply another developmental state? This question is a complicated one. On the one hand, that the Chinese state has pursued developmental goals throughout the reform period is unequivocally clear: rapid industrialization has been a strong and consistent priority of the Chinese leadership. On the other hand, China's gradual, dual-track approach to economic reform has resulted in pervasive corruption in the form of **rent seeking** and predatory behavior, especially at the subnational level. Much of the blame for this behavior, according to most scholars, centers on the same policy of gradual reform discussed earlier. Another major source of corruption is fiscal and administrative decentralization (i.e., the transfer of revenue-raising power from Beijing to the provinces) and the devolution of decisionmaking power concerning routine administrative matters to the local level (Pei 2006).

On the first point, asserting that gradualism has both helped and hindered the Chinese economy may seem odd, if not contradictory. The explanation, though, is straightforward. As I indicated above, a major reason the SOE sector was not immediately broken up and privatized was the political importance of SOEs as a source of patronage. Without a political compromise allowing SOEs to survive, the entire reform process could have easily stalled. Yet failing to dramatically remake or eliminate the SOE sector entirely has, in an important sense, embedded it even more deeply in China's political economy, mostly due to the sheer amount of resources and money flowing into this sector, in an era of high growth, the latter of which has increased exponentially.

Between 2002 and 2010, for example, the total assets of China's 121 largest SOEs went from $360 billion to $2.9 trillion ("State Capitalism's Global Reach" 2012). Indeed, despite the earlier "crackdown" on inefficient, profit-losing SOEs in the 1990s, the sector has actually started to grow again in terms of overall revenues: in 2007, SOE revenues accounted for about 40 percent of China's GDP, but in 2012 that figure had grown to more than 50 percent (Roberts 2012). Much of this growth, however, is the product of monopolistic or oligopolistic power and not higher efficiency, higher productivity, or innovation. This fact raises the specter of a major and sudden collapse in the Chinese economy, as the largest SOEs, because of their dominant positions and political connections, receive the lion's share of state investment (and 85 percent of all bank loans) and have started "pumping easy credit into risky property and feeding other **asset bubbles** while private companies struggle" (Roberts 2012).

At the same time, decentralization combined with an inability to effectively monitor and discipline local officials has created an untenable situation in the provinces. In this environment, local officials exercise a great deal of unchecked power through control over such "mundane" decisions as granting a business license, approving contracts and land leases, allocating capital, regulating commercial activities, and so on (Pei 2006). Without accountability, local officials are free to demand bribes, kickbacks, and other forms of graft. According to Minxin Pei (2006), the lack of oversight of local officials has not only resulted in widespread corruption but has also spawned "numerous mafia states": areas in which local officials collude with criminal elements. In Shenyang, for example, "practically all key local officials . . . took bribes from the city's mafia boss, Liu Yong, in return for protecting his criminal activities, which included extortion, murder, assault, and fraud" (p. 161).

The upshot is that China is a paradox. It has elements of both a developmental and **predatory state**; it has a powerful, developmentally oriented, centralized decisionmaking apparatus, but decentralization allows for endemic corruption. The structure of power is far more coherent and extensive than it was in the 1980s, but solid control of major economic players and vested interests remains elusive. The state has been effective at building national champions, which generate huge profits. For example, China Mobile and China National Petroleum Corporation made more profits ($33 billion) in 2009 than China's 400 most profitable private companies combined ("State Capitalism's Global Reach" 2012). But these same companies are the most unproductive in the country. This paradox suggests that China's future will depend mightily on the quality of governance and on the capacity of political leaders to adapt to changing circumstances. Equally important to understand, though, is that the Chinese state will not likely ever leave the market alone. The experiences of China's East Asian brethren make clear that state capitalism works, and China's vast market gives Chinese leaders leverage that Japanese, South Korean, and

Taiwanese leaders have always lacked. Understanding China's economic future, then, will always require an understanding of the relationship between the state and the market.

China in the Capitalist World-System: The Structural Approach

I have devoted considerable space to the political economy approach, and more specifically to the role of the state in China's economic rise in the post-Mao period. And I have a very good reason for allotting this approach so much space, since one cannot possibly ignore the central role the Chinese state has played in the country's economic transformation since the 1980s. Even many critics of state intervention (i.e., those who believe that excessive meddling by the state will ultimately ruin the Chinese economy) acknowledge the vital role the Chinese government has played in that country's success so far. So is this the end of the theoretical story? That is, is the state-centered political economy theory the obvious and only choice to explain China's economic rise? The short answer is no. As I have already suggested, structuralists are certainly not willing to concede the explanatory high ground. At the same time, their devotion does not mean that the two sides lack areas of agreement. Recall that structural analysis does leave room for agency; states and other institutions and actors can and do play important roles in bringing about and sustaining economic change (or, in the case of North Korea, preventing that change from taking place). Still, to focus solely on the *agents of change* while neglecting the *circumstances of change* is a serious, even fatal analytical error. In structural analysis, one absolutely must properly understand and take into full account the circumstances, or the structural context, within which national economies and individual actors exist. With this in mind, let us now consider a structural explanation of China's economic ascendance.

Explaining China's Economic Ascendance: China's Integration into the Global Economy

The first thing to note about China's economic ascendance as a capitalist system is the following: for about three decades (from 1949 to 1979), the country's leaders attempted to chart an intentionally noncapitalist path. Obviously, their efforts failed. To most observers, this failure is primarily, if not entirely, seen as the product of an inherently inefficient and unproductive socialist system that was destined to collapse. To structuralists, this observation is not entirely or even mostly wrong, but it misses the larger point: China's socialist economy was, from the very beginning, firmly situated within the dominant capitalist world-system. As a potential, and potentially essential, part of the capitalist world-system, China's attempt to withdraw from that system necessarily provoked efforts to undermine and eventually reverse this decision. Not surprisingly, these efforts were led by the core powers and especially by the hegemon, namely, the United States. Accordingly, immediately following the communist victory in China, the United States sent warships to patrol the Taiwan Strait and attempted to undercut the new government in China by freezing Chinese assets in the United States, imposing an embargo on Chinese products, and waging an intense ideological war against the Chinese (and Soviet) "menace" (So and Chiu 1995). None of these actions came about because communist China represented a military threat to the United States or other core powers. This was hardly the case. Instead, China's attempted withdrawal from the capitalist world-system represented a threat to the continued and future expansion of global capitalism. As a case in point, consider President Dwight Eisenhower's "falling domino" argument again (which I examined in Chapter 2). In referring to China, Eisenhower asserted: "Asia . . . has already *lost* some 450 million of its peoples to the Communist dictatorship, and *we simply can't afford greater losses*" (Eisenhower 2005 [1954], p. 383; emphasis added).

To repeat, no Chinese were "lost"; Eisenhower and everyone else knew exactly where they were. What he obviously meant was that China's immense market was "lost" to the United States and to world capitalism. On this point, recall also that the United States helped Japan reindustrialize, radically reversing its stance against Japan precisely because China was "lost" to the communists. The communist victory in China also made "saving" the rest of Asia by whatever means necessary an imperative. This ideology helps explain why the United States fought a number of wars in Asia, beginning with the Korean War and extending to the war in Vietnam and other parts of Southeast Asia, including Cambodia and Laos (McCormick 1995). These wars, to be clear, were not fought to protect the United States from any military threat; instead, they were fought "as part of a general strategy to integrate the periphery more effectively into core economies and [as] part of a specific strategy to sustain Japanese economic recovery, insure its participation in the world-system and keep open the option that China itself might someday be restored to that system and led down a capitalist path" (McCormick 1995, p. 111). China, as has been discussed throughout this chapter, was eventually "led down a capitalist path." And although China's decision appeared voluntary, unremitting pressure by the United States and other core economies made following a socialist path an increasingly difficult and eventually untenable choice (the same thing happened to the Soviet Union). The failure of China's socialist system, in this sense, was at least partly predetermined.

China's failure as a socialist nation, however, helps explain its subsequent success as a capitalist one. The capitalist world economy, to put it very simply, needed China to become an integral and integrated part of the overall system. The early stages of this integration, for example, invariably provided opportunities for greater wealth creation in core and near-core economies (including the economies of Japan, South Korea, and Taiwan), as literally hundreds of millions of as yet unexploited, low-paid Chinese workers became part of the global production process. Unsurprisingly, then, as China's post-Mao leaders began to open up the economy, foreign investment quickly poured in. The first significant surge began in 1992, after Deng Xiaoping confirmed the regime's continued commitment to reforms. From 1982 to 1991, the net annual inflow of FDI remained relatively low, growing from just $430 million to $4.366 billion—an average of $2.26 billion a year. In 1992, by contrast, FDI shot up to $11.15 billion and then more than doubled to $27.5 billion in 1993. Between 1993 and 2002, FDI averaged almost $40 billion a year (all figures cited in http://data.worldbank.org/). By the late 1990s, China had become the second-largest destination for FDI in the world, behind only the United States; in 2002, China temporarily passed the United States, and since then, the two countries have been neck and neck. Among late-industrializing countries, though, China has been by far the largest recipient of FDI. The most impressive growth began in 2005: that year alone, China attracted $117.2 billion in FDI, breaking the $100 billion mark for the first time (OECD 2012). In 2011, China broke the $200 billion mark with a total of $280 billion—about $23 billion more than the United States.[10]

In the 1990s, the bulk of FDI went to manufacturing (about 60 percent), and about half of manufacturing investment was directed to labor-intensive manufacturing (Tseng and Zebregs 2002). In other words, foreign companies were clearly taking full advantage of low-cost and low-skilled labor in China: in the early 2000s, low-skilled urban workers were earning about 60¢ an hour (and rural workers were earning only a third of that). At the same time, because China already had a more skilled and well-educated workforce and a relatively advanced supply chain infrastructure (compared to other low-cost locations) in the 1990s, foreigners also made large investments in technology- and capital-intensive manufacturing. Labor costs were higher in these areas but still much lower than in more advanced capitalist economies. A Chinese autoworker, for example, received about $5 an hour in total compensation in the early 2000s. The comparable costs in the United States and Germany, by contrast, were about $53 and $65, respectively (Malkiel, Mei, and Yang 2005). Even the most highly skilled Chinese workers, such as engineers, could be hired for a small fraction of the cost for comparably trained workers in the West. According to Burton Malkiel, Jianping Mei, and Rui Yang (2005), "this explains the enormous growth of foreign direct investment in China, as foreign firms attempt to exploit the labor-arbitrage opportunities" (p. 3).

While no one can dispute China's tremendous overall economic growth since the 1980s, structuralists will also point out that, in keeping with the inherently exploitative nature of capitalism, China's growth has been tremendously unequal. This inequality is particularly apparent in the gap between the urban and rural areas and, more generally, between the rich and the poor in China. As Naughton (2007b) describes it, "since the early 1980s . . . inequality in China has increased steadily and inexorably" (p. 217). The country's **Gini coefficient**—a scale on which zero is perfect equality and 1.0 is perfect inequality—increased from 0.28 in 1983 to 0.447 in 2001. This unprecedented deterioration has turned a country that was once one of the most equalitarian in the world to one that is "now similar to the most unequal Asian developing countries, such as Thailand, 0.43, or the Philippines, 0.46" (p. 218). From a structural perspective, the deterioration in equality indicates that China is reproducing a core-semiperiphery-periphery structure within its borders. Thus, while a new, relatively prosperous **middle class** in China has also emerged—along with the rise of a class of economic elites—a huge and almost assuredly permanent underclass of hyperexploited, low-skilled workers has also been created. Capitalism, after all, requires inequality.

The growing polarization of Chinese society, one must understand, can become a source of tremendous political and social instability; a huge and growing gap between the "haves" and the "have-nots" is often a recipe for widespread discontent, labor strife, and civil unrest. A strong, coercive, and usually authoritarian state is needed to ensure that popular discontent—whether over rising inequality, low wages, unemployment, corruption, environmental destruction, and so on—does not get out of hand. In this regard, structuralists will also suggest that the central role the Chinese state has played in the country's economic transformation was and is utterly predictable. The reason is clear: in the increasingly competitive environment of global capitalism, late-industrializing economies must compete largely on the basis of low-cost and "disciplined" labor. To keep labor costs down and to ensure a disciplined (i.e., obedient) labor force, state repression is usually necessary. Workers are typically not allowed to organize or otherwise freely engage in collective action. Political opponents of the regime must also be kept in check, since their advocacy of political and human rights stirs unrest and threatens the legitimacy of the state. In the case of China, unions are allowed, but only those that are affiliated with the state and the CCP. These labor unions do not bargain for higher wages, advocate for better working conditions, or otherwise represent the interests of workers; instead, they are essentially tools of management and of the CCP. More generally, the Chinese state has adopted a policy of "selective repression." Outspoken dissidents are often targeted, but instead of simply brutalizing them, "the state security apparatus has skillfully employed a wide range of tactics to intimidate, control, and neutralize key political activists" (Pei 2006, p. 82). Many, for example, are offered a "choice": long prison terms or exile. In 2012, for example, blind Chinese dissident Chen Guangcheng was allowed to leave for the United States. "This tactic," according to Pei (2006), "has successfully decapitated China's fledgling dissident movement and even allowed China's government to deflect international criticisms of its human rights practices" (p. 82).

In the structural view, a strong state is also necessary because it provides a "buffer" against the power of core economies, who would otherwise dominate weaker economies and their societies. Moreover, since the mechanisms of domination are well known, the few states that have the capacity to challenge or stand up to core economies will generally employ the same economic policies and approaches (i.e., industrial policy), which is the primary reason for the similarity between China and the other East Asian "success stories." In other words, China's restrictions on FDI, the manipulation of its currency (albeit, stronger in the past than today), the identification and targeting of strategic industries, the heavy use of subsidies, the reliance on national champions, and so on, are all tried-and-true methods of overcoming the disadvantages of late development in the capitalist world economy. The specific mix of policies used by China certainly differs from that used by Japan, South Korea, and Taiwan, but the general approach, and the logic underlying that approach, are substantially the same. China, though, is extremely fortunate, or fortunate in a way that most other late-developing economies are not. It has a state with the capacity and the opportunity—given China's advantageous position in the capitalist world economy—to achieve a significant degree of economic growth and industrialization.

China's Impact on the Structure of Global Capitalism: Beginning of the End?

Before I conclude the structural analysis of China's economic rise, I should examine, even if only cursorily, the broader structural impact that China's rapid capitalist industrialization is having and is likely to have on the world. Let's begin with a key point: China is not just another capitalist economy. In terms of population, it is the largest capitalist economy on the planet. But it will also soon become the largest capitalist economy in terms of sheer productive output. The immense size of China and its continuing development have any number of serious structural implications. One of the most salient is as follows: as the last major outpost of global economic expansion (along with India), China's integration into the capitalist world-system means that the system has essentially reached its geographic or spatial limits. Within the next three to five decades, in other words, no more mass reserves of cheap labor and underexploited natural resources will be left to plunder. What the final outcome will be is not entirely clear, but at least two major possibilities stand out. First, the world can expect significant, even fundamental, changes in the dynamics of global capitalism and a reordering of the global hierarchy. Second, the planet will likely be faced with a deepening and potentially disastrous environmental crisis (M. Li 2005).

An important fact: China's labor force—approximately 780 million workers—is larger than the total labor force in all the core economies combined. Indeed, for every four workers in the entire world, one is Chinese. China's full integration into the **global division of labor**, therefore, will potentially have a major impact on the cost of labor everywhere. There are multiple scenarios, according to Li Minqi (2005). In one, China will cause a downward convergence of wages; in this situation, competition from China "will completely undermine the relative monopoly of the existing semi-peripheral states. . . . The value added will be squeezed, forcing the traditional semi-peripheral states to accept lower wage rates close to China" (p. 436). Nor is this problem one that only low-skilled, poorly paid workers will face. China along with India is turning out hundreds of thousands—soon to be millions, perhaps tens of millions—of skilled and highly skilled workers, too; this flood of skilled workers will reduce middle-class wages in all core economies, including the United States. This oversupply is a problem for global capitalism, for as wages decline worldwide so does effective demand. And without sufficient demand, capitalist economies can easily fall into recession or depression. Economic decline, in turn, can lead to political instability, both in the core and the semiperiphery. The problems in the semiperiphery, however, are likely to be more serious. For as once comfortable workers fall into destitution, their demands will be stronger and more radical. The entire semiperiphery, as Li (2005) notes, "will be threatened with revolution and political turmoil" (p. 437).

On the other hand, however, China might become a fully "modern" economy with a much higher wage level. This scenario is, in fact, far more likely as China is already showing signs of becoming a major destination for technology- and capital-intensive investments. Indeed, in contrast to most countries in the periphery/semiperiphery, wages in China have steadily risen in the reform period. Between 1978 and 2003, real wages grew from about 500 yuan (annual wage) to 3,000 yuan, an astounding sixfold increase (Cai, Park, and Zhao 2008). But a modern China with higher wages is equally dangerous to world capitalism. "The problem, again, lies with China's huge size" (Li 2005, p. 437). Most simply, as higher wages are paid to China's vast workforce, less surplus will be available for the rest of the world. Remember, on this point, that China's full incorporation in the global economy will mean a near complete depletion of the world economy's **reserve labor force** (or **reserve army of labor**)—thus, no more readily available outlets will exist for capital to find a vast pool of "cheap labor." The upshot is clear: a rise in Chinese wages will mean a decline in wages for much of the rest of the world, but especially for semiperipheral economies. In other words, to reiterate the point, the global economy will be further polarized, creating greater political instability and likely more violence. I should point out that this discussion is not a **zero-sum** argument but instead is a recognition of the demands on capital to continue generating profits. In a world with untapped and unexploited labor reserves, relocating production to bring costs down and keep profits up has always been easy. But without labor reserves, maintaining profits becomes harder and harder.

China, Capitalism, and the Global Environment

Blaming China for much of the world's environmental problems has become fashionable. After all, since China began its industrialization drive, it has become a "world leader" in environmental pollution and destruction. In 2007, China overtook the United States in aggregate carbon dioxide emissions, although, on a per capita basis, its emissions are still relatively low. In 2009, according to the International Energy Agency, China also overtook the United States in total energy use (2.252 billion tons of oil equivalent, compared to 2.17 billion tons in the United States). Sixteen of the twenty most polluted cities in the world are in China. Finally, not surprisingly, China is the world's top emitter of sulfur dioxide (a noxious gas with a pungent, irritating smell). Even more, the average daily discharge of polluted water in China is comparable to that of the United States, Japan, and India combined, which has resulted in the serious contamination of over 70 percent of China's rivers and lakes, exacerbating a water shortage in China to a "critical threshold." Desertification is also accelerating, which is largely responsible for annual dust storms that spread toxic clouds of fine soil (called "yellow sand") throughout East Asia every spring. The toxicity is from industrial pollutants contained in the dust (all figures cited in Morton 2009). China's environmental issues, however, are all symptomatic of the economic imperatives driving capitalism as a system. The **commodification** of nature and the sloughing off of environmental preservation and protection as a hindrance to profit maximization are part and parcel of the capitalist process. China is simply the latest in a long line of capitalist economies that have already followed (and are still following) this path.

Capital accumulation is a basic cause of global environmental degradation, but an underlying cause is intense capitalist competition within the framework of an interstate system: individual national economies are in competition with one another for markets and profits. As a result, no individual economy can act to reduce its damage to the global environment without incurring costs that would make its industries less competitive, a situation that is especially true for late-industrializing economies that compete primarily on the basis of price. China, of course, is just such a country, but even the most "advanced" capitalist economies are often unwilling to incur the costs associated with environmental protection. The best example is the United States, which failed to ratify the **Kyoto Protocol** in large part because of the costs it would impose on US industry. This is not to say that international cooperation on global environmental issues is impossible, but no international agreement can resolve the problem of global environmental destruction without a fundamental restructuring of global capitalism. Consider, on this point, another central aspect of capitalism: the unremitting need to produce more and more things to continue the process of capital accumulation. In China, this general process of accumulation is exacerbated by the need to meet still unsated consumer demand. In 2011, for example, there were 35 million cars in China; in ten years, that number is expected to grow to 150 million! China is already the world's largest market for cars—it passed the United States in 2009. By 2015, it is expected to exceed the United States, Japan, and Germany combined. The addition of tens of millions more automobiles (even hundreds of millions) will necessarily have a huge impact on the global environment. But automobiles are only one product: as the Chinese increasingly adopt "Western" (i.e., capitalist) lifestyles, their consumption of everything will increase, putting more and more strain on both the domestic Chinese and global environments.

The Western solution has always been to export environmental problems to poorer countries; indeed, China has been a major, and perhaps *the* major, recipient of these "environmental exports" over the past few decades. China is the world's workshop. It produces 70 percent of the world's toys, 66 percent of its shoes, 50 percent of its color TVs and digital cameras, and 33 percent of the world's computers and refrigerators (A. Wang 2012). The production of these and other products—all of which are exported, mostly back to the West—creates significant environmental degradation. But China is now starting to export its environmental problems to other, poorer countries, too. As problems worsen within China, and as public outcry grows, this process will likely accelerate. Of course, simply shifting environmental problems from one location to another is not a solution. Moreover, China's sheer size makes this solution increasingly untenable. China's emergence as a center of global capitalism, in short, may push the world past the tipping point of global environmental catastrophe.

Change and Continuity in China: The Role of Constructed Actors

The three perspectives on China's economic ascendance—the liberal, political economy/statist, and the structural—all suggest something observers need to know. First, China's economic rise clearly could not have been achieved without the adoption of a market, or at least a quasi-market, economy. Years of economic stagnation and decay under a centrally planned command economy made this shift unequivocal. Second, equally clear is that the transition to a "socialist market economy" required a skillful and committed state leadership who had the institutional capacity and tools to effect far-reaching economic reform. For despite all the difficulties, missteps, and halfhearted measures, the transition from a rigid command economy to a market-oriented one was, in fact, carried out with a remarkable degree of efficacy. The wrong leadership and a less capable and developmentally oriented state could have easily led China down a very different path: one need only look to North Korea for evidence of this potential outcome—or to China's earlier experiences with central planning. Even more, despite all the quite reasonable criticisms of and concerns about the reform process, with little doubt, China has, in about one generation, made tremendous economic strides—strides that have lifted hundreds of millions of ordinary Chinese citizens out of absolute poverty. Third, despite the achievements of the market and of the state, China's economic rise cannot be adequately understood without an appreciation of the underlying structural forces and processes that have shaped the country's economic destiny. On this point, too, one needs to understand why China—a hitherto untapped and underexploited market at the end of the 1970s—almost had to be incorporated into the capitalist world-system. At the same time, structural analysis indicates profound systemic implications to China's full incorporation, implications that suggest very clearly that the economic success of China is not all "wine and roses" but could instead have dire consequences for the entire planet.

Role of Human Agency

To repeat: all the three competing perspectives need to be taken seriously. The next step, though, must be to bring insights from the three perspectives together. Fortunately, the constructed actor model provides a useful and even necessary starting point: individual actors. At the center of each of the three competing perspectives are purposeful agents who clearly shaped the process of economic change and transformation. The market-oriented system in China, as has been demonstrated, was unequivocally the product of purposeful action. It did not just magically or automatically appear but was put in motion by specific and identifiable leaders: Deng Xiaoping, Zhao Ziyang, Chen Yun, and Li Xiannian played instrumental roles. Perhaps even more important was the role of Mao Zedong, who seemingly single-handedly prevented fundamental reforms from moving forward while he was alive. In addition, one must not forget the role of tens of millions of ordinary Chinese peasants, workers, party members, and so on. When presented with opportunities, they undertook the actions that made the reforms real; conversely, they also helped to make real the principles of Maoism, especially during the Cultural Revolution. Other institutional factors—especially the structure of power within China's state apparatus and the CCP—certainly and significantly shaped the actions of those individuals leading the reform process (as well as those who opposed it), yet these institutions could not, by themselves, dictate every decision and action. The persistence, determination, and specific decisionmaking of the reformers simply cannot be dismissed as tangential or unimportant. Just as important, China's key institutions have, over time, been remade to support an economic and social system radically different from the prereform era.

Structural forces and processes, by their very nature, are much less amenable to human agency. Nonetheless, within any structural framework are many paths and possible outcomes. Despite its immense size, for example, China had no guarantee or even reason to believe that it would ever transcend the periphery of the capitalist world economy. Although huge segments of China's vast economy remain firmly embedded in the periphery, China has in many ways transcended the margins of the world-system. On the other hand, despite its success so far, there is no guarantee that China will emerge as a transcendent economic power, or hegemon, as some observers predict. To a large extent, China's economic fate hinges on the agency of its leaders and people and, conversely, on the agency of leaders and individuals in other countries. Similarly, while China's economic rise is bringing the Earth closer to an environmental tipping point, humans have shown a capacity to overcome crises. In this case, however, no one country can solve the problem; the people who constitute states, businesses, nongovernmental organizations (NGOs), social movements, and so on, must create frameworks for effective global and transborder cooperation, which may be manifested in international regimes and institutions, treaties, and other agreements. Technological solutions are also possible, but, of course, technological advancement is also a product, in no small measure, of human agency. One additional point: overarching structures, too, are not impervious to change. As discussed in Chapter 1, an essential **intersubjective** element can be found in any **social structure**, which makes even the most powerful structure malleable.

Constructed Actors and Frameworks for Action

In China as well as North Korea, one can readily see the enduring power of nonmaterial (i.e., intersubjective) forces. Mao's version of Marxism-Leninism helped to create and then undergird a framework for action—a social and institutional structure—that had a profound impact on the lives of hundreds of millions of people. The Maoist system, however, proved to be no match for the much more powerful forces of global capitalism, a much more encompassing framework. Yet, while structural forces and processes inexorably pushed China toward capitalism, choices still mattered. What those choices would be and how effectively they were implemented depended on actors both inside and outside of China. Within China, the CCP leadership—at least those pushing for reform—made choices that reflected economic, political, and ideological-cultural imperatives: they could not do anything they wanted to do. Instead, they were clearly constructed actors whose choices were constrained by a range of social facts. A full-fledged embrace of laissez-faire capitalism, for example, was decidedly not one of those choices, but neither was staying the course with a rigid, centrally planned economy. Instead, they purposefully chose a hybrid path, "socialism with Chinese characteristics" or a "socialist market economy."

This hybrid path involved (and still does involve) a heavy dose of state intervention; it also includes an important element of the old socialist system: five-year plans. In fact, since the beginning of the reform period until today, the CCP has developed new five-year plans continuously without interruption. The latest is the Twelfth Five-Year Plan for National Economic and Social Development (2011–2015), which continues to include a strong emphasis on industrial policy. The plan, for example, focuses on developing "strategic emerging industries" in biotechnology, new energy, high-end equipment manufacturing, environmental protection, clean energy vehicles, new materials, and next-generation IT (I mentioned these areas earlier). The persistence of state planning in China's capitalist economy, to be clear, reflects the specifics of China's institutional and sociopolitical context (i.e., "social facts"). Within this context, Chinese leaders largely take for granted the need for detailed national economic planning and, much more importantly, active and sustained intervention in the economy as a whole, but also in specific industries and sectors. Contrast this intervention with what takes place in the United States. In the United States, national-level economic planning, still less industrial policy, carried out by the political leadership is considered anathema—although, admittedly, the issue is much more complex, as industrial policy is practiced in the United States but in a less open and direct way. This reluctance is due, in large part, to the fact that the very idea of industrial policy is subject to intense political challenges. In China, state leaders do not have to justify economic planning and intervention. Thus, they have a choice that US policymakers largely lack.

Arguably, the option to engage freely in **dirigiste** economic planning and policy has given China's leaders an economic advantage they might not otherwise enjoy. As one assesses the impact of economic planning and of specific policy choices, moreover, one must keep in mind the governing power of China's party-state system, a system in which the institutions of the party and the state are inextricably intertwined. This system has survived tremendous turmoil and overseen far-reaching changes while remaining firmly in control of China for the better part of the twentieth century and into the twenty-first. One has a harder time imagining a stronger political institution in the world than the CCP, with between 60 and 76 million members and an institutional structure that affords no formal means of checks and balances, while being situated in a still weak civil society. Those who sit at the pinnacle of China's party-state system—the three top layers are the general secretary (in 2012 **Hu Jintao** was replaced by **Xi Jinping**), the Politburo Standing Committee, and the Politburo—therefore wield almost unmatched political power. With little wonder, then, China's leaders have "gotten things done" in a manner that few other late-industrializing capitalist economies have been able to replicate. Add to this China's structurally advantageous position as the last major area for expansion in the capitalist world-system, and the reasons for China's unprecedented economic ascendance become much clearer.

Chinese leaders, however, also had to contend with a number of serious disadvantages and challenges within their particular framework of action. Most important, perhaps, is the seeming contradiction between maintaining a closed, authoritarian political system while actively promoting a more open, free-flowing economic system. Indeed, over the first ten years of the market reform period, the expectations for corresponding political reform had grown quite strong among segments of China's population. Open political protests took place in 1985 and 1986, with students and others calling for faster political reform. Significantly, sympathy could be found for the students' demands even among the

CCP leadership—most notably, **Hu Yaobang** and Zhao Ziyang. The incipient movement for **political liberalization** came to a head in 1989 after the death of Hu Yaobang. Students immediately began to gather in Tiananmen Square to honor Hu; their congregation led to the **Tiananmen Movement**, which spread to 341 of China's cities and was joined by 100 million people (Gilley 2010). The movement lasted about seven weeks but was eventually put down by military force and was then followed by "some of the most politically repressive years in China since 1949" (Zhao 1998, p. 289). I discuss this issue in more depth in Chapter 7, but the key point here is the following: since the reform period began, China's leaders have consistently faced the problem of legitimacy— of maintaining their control, not of the economy per se but of the country as a whole.

The issue of political liberalization, however, was only one challenge. The Chinese state's problems or disadvantages were compounded by at least two other, albeit closely related, factors: first, tremendous socioeconomic inequities, especially between the urban and rural areas, and, second, periodic, but very damaging, episodes of high inflation and mass unemployment. Another related problem was and is China's huge and still largely poor and ethnically diverse population (fifty-five minority nationalities can be found in the country). Each of these problems, too, threatened to undermine the reform process and the state's legitimacy. The fundamental problem, in short, was how to create centripetal force to counter the centrifugal tendencies of China's often brutal, growth-at-any-cost economic model. The solution, as a number of observers have argued, was found in a reconstitution or reconstruction of a Chinese identity, one that could not completely contradict the Maoist identity of the communist era—for the Maoist identity was part and parcel of the legitimating ideology of the party—but that could justify the continued dominance of the party in an era of immense and often confounding change. The effort to create a new Chinese identity led to a renewed emphasis on nationalism. Thus, in the years following the Tiananmen Movement, as Suisheng Zhao (1998) puts it, "Deng Xiaoping and his successor, Jiang Zemin, began to wrap themselves in the banner of nationalism which, they found, remained the one bedrock of political belief shared by most Chinese people in spite of the rapid decay of Communist official ideology" (p. 289).

Deng, Jiang, and others, however, faced a problem. Under Mao, nationalism was decidedly antimodern. That is, Chinese nationalism was partly defined as a rejection of modernization. A major reason for this ideology stems from China's very complicated relationship with the West during the colonial era. The story is too long to cover here; suffice it to say, then, that an embrace of "modern values" (and even most of China's "traditional culture") was construed as incompatible with the goals of revolutionary China, which helps to explain why China's post-Mao leaders were very careful to eschew capitalism as an idea while embracing it as a concrete practice. The dilemma they faced in the

1990s was how to reconcile the abandonment of Maoism with the embrace of the market, while at the same time justifying the continuation of authoritarian rule under the Communist Party. State-led nationalism was the answer. In this version of nationalism, Deng and other Chinese leaders recast modernization as "material civilization" and emphasized that only the Communist Party could lead China down the right path. In this view, moreover, the communist party-state became the embodiment of the entire nation's will and desires (Zhao 1998): modernization, nationalism, and the party-state became one. To a certain extent, the strategy worked. While not forgotten, the Tiananmen Movement has not been repeated, although there have been thousands of small-scale demonstrations, and the Chinese economy has grown even faster and become far stronger since the mid-1990s.

State-led nationalism, however, is very "thin." That is, it lacks a substantive and enduring core because it is essentially based on the partisan political views and policies of China's current leadership (Pye 1993; Zhao 1998). In other words, Chinese nationalism is a fragile and unstable ideological base for both the party-state itself and the country as a whole. The weakness of Chinese nationalism makes the possibility of myriad groups within China's burgeoning civil society developing their own, more organic forms of nationalism or ideological positions far more likely, and some of these more individualized nationalisms could sharply clash with the official ideology. Because the state continues to suppress and restrict the development of civil society and alternative ideologies in an effort to uphold its own orthodoxy, knowing with any certainty how effective or ineffective "Chinese nationalism" will be is difficult. One can easily surmise, though, that the issue of legitimacy will not simply disappear. In fact, some signs can already be seen that China's leadership recognizes the growth-at-any-cost model is beginning to seriously undermine its authority and ideological legitimacy. Thus, in 2005 Hu Jintao and **Wen Jiabao** made the development of a "harmonious society" a key priority (a priority that was repeated in the 2011 Five-Year Plan). The specific goals of the "harmonious society" were to narrow the wealth gap, increase employment, reduce corruption, and protect the environment. While many critics dismissed the new emphasis as nothing more than propaganda or empty sloganeering, at the very least it reflected an awareness of pervasive popular discontent about the economic direction of the country. From a constructed actor perspective, moreover, one can argue that the notion of a "harmonious society" is meaningful. In the context of Chinese politics, the introduction of new national development concepts marks an important shift in discourse, which in turn has typically had a concrete impact on policy decisions. More basically, it redraws, at least to some extent, the framework of action within which Chinese leaders, in particular, must act. By introducing the concept, in other words, they have tied their future legitimacy to achieving the goals set forth in a harmonious society (for further discussion, see Joshi 2012).

Conclusion

Unlike Chapter 2, the discussion in this chapter of the constructed actor model was quite general and open ended. This method was intentional and is the basic approach I take in the remaining chapters. The intent, to repeat, is to use the constructed actor model heuristically, meaning that I want readers to try applying the model, as much as possible, on their own. At the same time, my duty is to provide guidance, to give readers a clear and concrete sense of some of the issues and evidence they need to consider, and to provide a starting point—but not the end point—for analysis. I did use this approach in the foregoing section and in the discussion of the stalled reform process in North Korea. Recall, too, the intention is not to lead anyone to a specific theoretical conclusion; that is, I am not asserting that the constructed actor model always yields the best answers. But the constructed actor model does require one to think in a more integrative and comprehensive manner than might otherwise be the case. Thinking in this way is a good practice, even or especially if one thinks one of the competing perspectives offers a better or perhaps the best framework of analysis, for putting on "theoretical blinders" and seeing only a narrow slice of a very complex situation is very easy. Similarly, some observers may look through a theoretical lens that colors the world in a very specific way; they may be right, but they would still find putting on a different "lens" extremely useful to make sure that nothing important or critical is being missed.

Notes

1. Another scholar, Jeon (2000b), while agreeing with Cumings that the three-year delay in Kim Jong-il's formal assumption of political power in North Korea reflected the traditional Confucian principle of an extended mourning period, also argues that more was going on. Specifically, the three-year period was strategically used by Kim Jong-il to make up for his political shortcomings and to strengthen his power base. In this regard, Jeon suggests that, in fact, a behind-the-scenes power struggle was taking place following the death of Kim Il-sung.

2. Writing for the *Telegraph* (London), Mike Firn (2012) reported Kim Jong-un as saying, "When I go to Europe or Japan, I see overflowing products and food, but when I return to the North, there is nothing. Do we need to study China's policies?"

3. Some debate exists on whether the famines were a product of North Korea's failing economy or were primarily a product of severe weather conditions. For two contrasting views, see Haggard and Noland (2007) and Woo-Cumings (2002).

4. For a discussion of the devaluation and its aftermath, see McNeill (2009).

5. The most recent Freedom House ratings for Vietnam and Laos can be found on the Freedom House website at http://www.freedomhouse.org/country/vietnam and http://www.freedomhouse.org/country/laos, respectively.

6. For a detailed discussion of the development of North Korea's IT sector, see Mansourov (2011).

7. Alexander Vorontsov (2006), for example, argues that the military-first policy has already led North Korea to a mixed economy, and that the Korean People's Army could play an important role in the ongoing process of privatization.

8. Peng (1987) provides a detailed demographic analysis of "excess deaths" during the period of the Great Famine and concludes that the total may have amounted to 23 million. Still, Peng cautions, "this is a very rough estimate that should be interpreted with great caution" (p. 649).

9. For a general discussion on the success (or failure) of the SOE reforms, see Li and Putterman (2008).

10. Figures are from the **World Bank's** online data bank (2013a). The OECD (2012) provides different figures, showing that China had $228.8 billion of FDI in 2011, which was about $5 billion less than the United States.

5 Political Change in Japan, South Korea, and Taiwan

Writing in 1991, prominent Harvard political scientist Samuel Huntington asserted that "only two countries [in East Asia], Japan and the Philippines, had *sustained* experience with democratic government prior to 1990. . . . In both cases [however], democracy was the product of an American presence" (p. 24; emphasis added). Were it not for direct US intervention, in other words, Huntington implied that there very well might not have been any democracies in East Asia for the first four decades of the postwar period. Huntington, however, was certainly not ruling out the possibility of additional democratic advances in the region. After all, both South Korea and Taiwan had started down a democratic path in the latter part of the 1980s. Indeed, Huntington thought that the twenty-first century would see wider democratization in Asia primarily because of growing incomes. As he put it, "fewer relationships between social, economic, and political phenomena are stronger than that between the level of economic development and the existence of democratic politics. Most wealthy countries are democratic, and most democratic countries—India is the most dramatic exception—are wealthy" (p. 30). Still, Huntington was pessimistic that advances in East Asian democracy would lead to the type of presumably superior democratic systems prevalent in the West. Instead, he argued that East Asian democracy would likely see the reproduction of "dominant-party systems" in which one could find nominal competition between opposing political parties but no alteration in political power. This type of political system, as Huntington bluntly put it, "offers democracy without turnover" (p. 27).

In retrospect, the picture has changed substantially. In 1993, for example, Japan's **LDP**, by a substantial margin, lost its absolute majority in the important lower house of Japan's bicameral **parliamentary system**, known as the **Diet**, and for the first time since 1955 was forced to sit in the opposition.[1] While its minority party position lasted only a year (after which, the LDP again held on to power for another fifteen years), a second, even more stunning defeat occurred in 2009, when nearly 60 percent of LDP incumbents were turned out, and many sitting and former ministers lost their seats in the Diet (Krauss and

Pekkanen 2010). In South Korea, an important milestone in the democratization process was the election of Kim Dae-jung in December 1997; this event marked the first time in South Korea's short history that an opposition presidential candidate defeated a ruling party candidate. Kim, I should add, was a leading dissident during the authoritarian period. Significantly, Roh Moo-hyun, another longtime dissident, succeeded Kim in 2003 (sadly, Roh committed suicide a year after leaving office). After the election of two "opposition" candidates, the erstwhile Grand National Party—the traditional ruling party—won back the presidency in 2007 with the election of Lee Myung-bak (the Grand National Party renamed itself the Saenuri Party before the election). In the most recent election in South Korea, which took place in December 2012, another Saenuri candidate, Park Geun-hye, won. Park, the daughter of **Park Chung Hee**, also happened to be the first woman elected as president of South Korea. Despite a slightly later start in Taiwan (the first multiparty legislative elections were not held until 1991–1992), relatively quick progress was made there as well: in 2000, Chen Shui-bian won the presidential race as a candidate for the proindependence Democratic Progress Party, which effectively ended fifty-five years of rule by the **KMT**. Notably, the KMT had dominated Taiwan since 1949. Thus, despite Huntington's pessimism, ample evidence can be found that East Asian democracy is more than a dominant-party system.

None of this is to imply that East Asia has reached a state of "democratic nirvana." Far from it. As many critics have pointed out, democratic progress is not guaranteed to equate to good governance or a just society. Consider what Choi Jang Jip (2005), a highly regarded Korean sociologist, had to say about the state of Korean democracy in the early 2000s: "Democracy in Korea is failing to perform its primary function, which is to politically express and represent a variety of social conflicts and interests, and thereby organize alternatives to both expand the foundation of public participation and contribute to the stabilization of the political system. Democracy in Korea has become a mere façade decorating . . . the conservative monopoly" (p. 21). One could easily apply the same critique to Japan and Taiwan, as well as to other democracies in Asia and around the world. Importantly, Choi's critique and its relevance to democracies worldwide raise questions about how to define democracy itself. Choi has his own point of view: "Democracy is not a political system that should be understood from the perspective of the 'minimalist conception of democracy,' which is based on conformity to procedural standards and on whether or not certain **institutions** and rules exist" (p. 93). These procedural minimums (in his book, Choi used the term *mini-mums*) include universal suffrage, free and fair elections held on a regular basis, competition among parties, and an effective framework of civil rights and liberties.

Not coincidentally, the characteristics Choi (2005) points to are the main criteria that many scholars use in their definitions of democracy, which helps explain Choi's criticism of the democratic minimums: he believes too many

scholars are too easily satisfied with simply identifying and explaining superficial political change. At the same time, Choi recognizes that a minimalist conception is not all together useless since it "makes comparative studies possible,
and that, from the perspective of a social scientific discipline, it renders analytical accuracy and rigor" (p. 13). Beyond this rather narrow purpose, however,
Choi is convinced that procedural democracy marks an essentially unimportant
or substantively empty political change. Choi's position is understandable. But
many scholars, including me, do not entirely agree. The procedural minimums
are just that: minimums. That is, they represent the minimal—not ideal—conditions for democracy to exist. Yet even these minimal conditions mark a clear
distinction between a democratic and a nondemocratic political system. On this
point, I should emphasize that the notion of democracy need not have any normative implications, although it is admittedly hard to ignore normative issues.
A democratic political system, in other words, is not necessarily better than,
say, a dictatorship. It is simply different. (For a fuller discussion of this issue,
see Figure 5.1.)

Explaining Democratic Transition in East Asia

However one defines democracy, one thing is clear: political change has taken
place in East Asia. This change raises a number of basic questions. What were
the main reasons behind East Asia's postwar political transformation from **authoritarianism** to democracy? Was the transformation primarily a function of
increasing wealth, as Huntington implies, or were there other, more important
processes at play? Not surprisingly, the answers to these questions vary, sometimes dramatically, among scholars and other observers. Even less surprisingly,
perhaps, the answers can be divided along similar (albeit not exactly the same)
lines as the discussion and analysis of economic change. One finds, to use
slightly different terminology, micro-, meso-, and macrolevel accounts. Macrolevel accounts correspond quite strongly with the structural perspective. The
emphasis, in both older and more contemporary versions, is on the interaction
and relations of power between and among social classes or groups. Capitalism,
along with "modernization" in some versions, as an overarching structural process, occupies a central position and is said to create the conditions—or preconditions—for democracy to emerge. Mesolevel arguments are quite diverse
but generally focus on the role of institutional, cultural-religious, and ideological
factors. Significant actors in this perspective may include social movements,
organized groups (e.g., labor unions and other civic organizations, including
religious organizations), and student groups. Some scholars have focused on
the institutional characteristics of the political regime itself.

By far the most prevalent—and arguably the most dominant—line of research on democratic transition is geared at the microlevel. "Proponents," as

Figure 5.1 The Case for a Formal Definition of Democracy

Democracy is a contested concept. Many scholars, however, have had a strong tendency to adopt a minimal or formal definition of democracy, which, as I noted already, includes the following core characteristics: (1) near-universal suffrage, (2) a competitive multiparty system, (3) free and noncorrupt elections, and (4) an effective framework of civil liberties and human rights. Many scholars also borrow from a more extended set of "institutional guarantees" or conditions proposed by Robert Dahl (1956) in his classic *A Preface to Democratic Theory.* Dahl (1972) also coined the term *polyarchy* to be used as a substitute for democracy. For current purposes, I will use the initial definition.

The key question, however, is whether a formal definition, in general, has any meaning beyond its "analytical accuracy." To many scholars who study and think about democracy, the answer to this question is an unequivocal, albeit often implicit, "yes." One set of scholars who address this question explicitly is Dietrich Rueschemeyer, Evelyne Huber Stephens, and John Stephens (1992). In their book *Capitalist Development and Democracy,* these authors ask, "Why do we care about formal democracy if it considerably falls short of the actual rule of the many?" (p. 10). Their answer is simple: "We care about formal democracy because it tends to be more than merely formal. It tends to be real to some extent" (p. 10). In other words, Rueschemeyer and colleagues believe that formal democracy matters, because once the most basic institutions, practices, and components of democracy are established in a society, they almost invariably create a "promising basis for further progress in the distribution of power and other forms of substantive equality" (p. 10). Specifically, the authors contend, "The same factors which support the installation and consolidation of formal democracy, namely the growth in the strength of civil society in general and of the lower classes in particular, also support progress towards greater equality in political participation and towards greater social and economic equality" (pp. 10–11). On this last point, I should note one other criticism of formal definitions, which comes from Charles Tilly (2007). He argues that formal definitions tell us democracy is an either-or condition. To Tilly, this approach is problematic since "democracy" is an ongoing, often nonlinear process, rather than a static state of being. If one wants to compare regimes with regard to how democratic they are, or if one wants to follow individual regimes through time to see when and how they become more or less democratic, one needs to move away from either-or, or "checklist," definitions (Tilly 2007, p. 10).

(continues)

Yin-wah Chu and Siu-lun Wong (2010) explain, "referred to as transitionists, usually examine the **agency** of a political elite, arguing that strategic [or rational] choice and tactical interaction among the hardliners and softliners within the regime and the opposition are more important than structural constellations of a society" (p. 3). As should be apparent from the last point, in this view, one

Figure 5.1 continued

I am quite sympathetic to Tilly's criticism. Still, his conclusions do not obviate the need to establish a baseline definition. A formal definition of democracy, even if imperfect, is designed, first and foremost, to provide a clear-cut basis for analysis—for determining, at a minimum, the basic dividing line between real-world democracies and nondemocracies. If researchers cannot or will not come up with this list of criteria, then they have little reason to even attempt an analysis of how and why countries democratize in a concrete sense, which is the topic of this chapter. After all, if one does not define what democracy is, or if the definition essentially excludes all or mostly all real-world cases, then any analysis of "democracy" will be empirically and perhaps even theoretically empty.

finds hostility toward, or at least deep skepticism about, the structural notion that democracy requires preconditions. Consider, for example, the case of India: in the 1950s, India had an extremely poor, essentially subsistence-level economy, yet it has also successfully maintained a democratic system since the 1940s (Kohli 2001). On the other end of the spectrum sits Singapore, an extremely wealthy capitalist economy with a "soft-authoritarian" **state**. Importantly, in both these cases, one can find strong evidence that individual actors—primarily elite actors—played a key role, perhaps *the* key role, in either creating and sustaining a democratic system, or in preventing one from emerging. I will continue with a discussion and application of the elite-centered approach shortly; for now, I want to emphasize that this elite-centered model finds its closest parallel in liberal economic theory. These two models, though, are primarily related in terms of shared assumptions about agency, rationality, and progress.

Given the prevalence of microlevel, elite-centered explanations, I begin the examination of the competing theories there. More specifically, I examine the argument that self-interested decisionmaking by elite actors in Japan, South Korea, and Taiwan determined the success or failure of those countries' transitions to democracy. The discussion of Japan will focus on the prewar period and the era known as **Taisho** democracy, while the discussion of South Korea and Taiwan will concentrate on the period between 1945 and the mid-1990s. Next, I turn to macrolevel or structural explanations. I tread over some of the same empirical ground as in the previous section but do so with a different purpose in mind: to see how a structural lens allows for a sharply contrasting interpretation of the set of facts and processes that mattered most in the region's experience with democratic transition. In the third major section, I examine the significance of a key **intersubjective** factor: legitimacy. Importantly, one can find the concept of political legitimacy embedded in most discussions of political stability and change, including in elite-centered and structural arguments. Not surprisingly, in these approaches the concept is not accorded much, if any, independent causal significance. A strong case can be made, however, that legitimacy is an important factor in its own right. Finally, I consider the constructed actor model. As usual, the objective is not to present a full-blown, highly detailed argument, but one that is instead heuristic.

One more note before I begin: the primary emphasis in this chapter is on the transition from authoritarianism to democracy, but I also examine the breakdown of democracy—that is, the transition from democracy to authoritarianism. These are two sides of the same coin. I do not, however, focus the discussion on the consolidation or strengthening of democracy; this topic is addressed in the following chapter (although, in the discussion of Japan, I allude to issues of consolidation).

Microlevel Approaches: A Focus on Elite Interests and Power

Microlevel research, to repeat, suggests that rationality and agency determine, at a basic level, every transition to democracy and also every reversal of democracy. To put it more simply, all transitions and reversals are an expression of actors' self-interests and power. Admittedly, this generalization is unremarkable and even trivial, but it underscores the fact that democracy is generally a product of intense and ongoing political struggle between those who want change and those who do not. Not surprisingly, particularly in nondemocratic regimes, those who oppose democracy are the political, economic, and military elites. A closed, authoritarian political system ensures that their positions of privilege—that their economic, political, and social interests—cannot be easily challenged. In this view, elites by definition have preponderant power in society, and this power is why many, although certainly not all, microlevel approaches put the elite at the center of their analyses. After all, if political change takes place, that the main agents of this change must be those with the most power stands to reason. But this conclusion raises another key question: Under what conditions do the interests of elites change such that they are willing to relinquish control, or at least some control, of the political system?

To answer the foregoing question, one needs to recognize that the elites themselves are generally not a monolithic bloc. Instead, they are a coalition of different groups or factions, each seeking to maximize their own interests, something they can do when they combine their power. Thus, as long as elite groups stay united, major political change, such as a transition to democracy, is not likely to occur. Elite cohesion is relatively easy to maintain in "ordinary times," that is, when the economy is growing or at least not in serious decline, when external or international relations are stable or positive, when no major natural or artificial disasters have occurred that might spark widespread unrest, and so on. In ordinary times, to repeat, elites have no incentive to consider any change in the status quo. In "less ordinary times," however, elite control and unity may be tested by a critical event or events that undermine the legitimacy of the regime. When these events happen, discontent and dissatisfaction can lead to mass mobilization. Mass mobilization, in turn, gives an opening to opponents of the regime to demand political reform. Under these conditions, splits (e.g., disagreements over how to deal with demands for political reform) among or between major factions of the elite are likely to materialize. Here, too, elite interests play the central role: so-called soft-liners believe that reform is the best way to protect their interests while hard-liners argue that any reform must be resisted. Other factors may come into play that tip the balance toward one or another group. For example, in the face of a mass popular uprising in 2011 (during the **Arab Spring**), international pressure, especially from the United States, helped to convince Egyptian military leaders to split with the regime of Hosni Mubarek and allow for political reform. I need to add, however, that the military elite did not simply give up power but instead implemented a "managed" transition toward a still limited and conditional type of democracy—a point that was driven home in July 2013, when Mohammed Morsi, the first democratically elected leader of Egypt, was removed from office by the Egyptian military.

Taisho Democracy

In East Asia, too, ample evidence can be found of how the elite dominate or control transitions to democracy. In the case of Japan, democratic institutions were imposed on the country by the United States at the end of the Pacific War, but this imposition did not result in a Western-style alternation of political power between or among competing parties. Instead, a conservative party, the LDP, and prewar business and bureaucratic elites dominated politics for most of the postwar period. Many observers have referred to this combination of elite interests as the **Iron Triangle**. The external imposition of democracy renders moot some of the issues I discussed above (in that the Japanese elite had no choice but to accept democracy), but the manner in which conservative leaders coalesced to control the new political system underscores the capacity of the elite to reassert their power and interests even under "unfavorable conditions." On this point, one should note that the LDP has never been a cohesive, fully united party. Far from it. Indeed, ever since the party first emerged as an amalgamation of the Liberal and Japan Democratic parties in 1955, it has been characterized by "congeries of factions" constantly engaged in internal competition and conflict over specific policy choices and programs (Ward 1978, p. 110). Yet, in spite of persistent internal tension, the LDP has been highly effective in maintaining just enough cohesion to serve the varied "interests of members, its leaders, and its interest group constituency by winning elections, formulating public policy proposals, and providing a system for recruiting party and government leaders" (Richardson 1997, p. 75).

A better example of the dynamics of the elite-centered approach in Japan can be found by going back to the prewar period, during the era known as Taisho democracy, a roughly twenty-year period between 1905 and 1925.[2] Prior to the Taisho period, the Japanese political system was highly exclusionary and nondemocratic: the right to vote was given only to landowners and capitalists who represented 1 percent of the population, freedom of speech, meeting, and association were severely restrained, and the military was largely insulated from political control (Takayoshi 1966). The political and economic systems, moreover, were thoroughly dominated by five elite groups: (1) the **Meiji oligarchs**; (2) a cadre of professionalized, high-ranking military officers; (3) the higher ranks of the civil bureaucracy; (4) an hereditary peerage; and (5) the leaders of Japan's major businesses, known as the *zaibatsu* (Ward 1978). A group of Japanese liberals—upper-class farmers, ex-samurai intellectuals, journalists, and lawyers (Takayoshi 1966)—acted as an opposition group. During the Meiji era, this latter group pressed for political reforms, including the establishment of a national representative parliament, universal male suffrage, and the abolition of the House of Peers. The influence of the elite liberal opposition, however, was extremely limited, not only because they faced intransigent resistance from conservative elite groups, but also because they had no base of popular support, which held true until a critical event, the Russo-Japanese War (see Figure 5.2 for further discussion of this conflict).

Although Japan won the Russo-Japanese War, the war required a national mobilization effort, which awakened ordinary citizens to their national rights and duties (Takayoshi 1966). Victory, moreover, was achieved at a heavy cost in lives: according to Mikiso Hane (1986) at least 60,000 Japanese were killed in battle, and another 22,000 died as a result of disease (as I noted in Figure 5.2, Jansen gives a far higher estimate). For all this sacrifice, the Japanese people, as Hane (1986) explains, "were convinced that a better life would follow the war. The amelioration of conditions did not, however, come about as anticipated, and the struggle for social and economic justice became more intense" (p. 179). Ironically, the real crisis was not the war but the conditions of peace: the Japanese public expected major concessions—including indemnity and cession of Sakhalin Island—but instead were presented with a "humiliating treaty." The result was an explosion of public anger: mobs attacked public buildings, police stations, Christian churches, and progovernment newspapers, "throwing Tokyo into a state of anarchy" (Hane 1986, p. 178). The peace terms of the Russo-Japanese War, in short, marked an awakening of the first "definite nation-wide citizen movement against the absolutist Japanese government of the Meiji era" (Takayoshi 1966, p. 619). Not to say that democracy suddenly appeared. This was hardly the case. In fact, this first "definite nation-wide citizen movement" was only the opening scene in what would be twenty years of

---

Figure 5.2 The Russo-Japanese War (1904–1905)

The Russo-Japanese War marked a significant milestone: it was the first modern war in which a European power lost to an Asian power. The war was rooted in the imperial ambitions of both Russia and Japan. With much of the world already dominated by Western countries, Russia and Japan were engaged in intense struggle to control Korea and **Manchuria**. Russia was particularly interested in finding a warm water port on the Pacific Ocean, and in 1898, it successfully pressured the Chinese government into granting it a lease for Port Arthur, which was located on the tip of the Liaodong Peninsula. The port gave Russia direct access to the seas around Korea and Japan and to the Yellow Sea. Conflict was almost inevitable as three European powers (Russia, Germany, and France)—via the so-called Triple Intervention—had forced Japan from the same peninsula in 1895. Japan had acquired possession of the peninsula in an early war with China, the first Sino-Japanese War. That war ended with the Treaty of Shimonoseki, which ceded to Japan control of the Liaodong Peninsula, including the city of Port Arthur.

Understandably, Japan found Russia's control of Port Arthur objectionable, but in 1898, the Japanese did not have the capacity to force Russia out. Thus, between the signing of the lease and the outbreak of war between the two countries, Japanese officials attempted to work out a peaceful agreement; at one point, they proposed giving the Russians primacy in Manchuria in return for a free hand in Korea (Jansen 2000). No agreement could be reached. Then, in 1902, Japan signed the Anglo-Japanese Alliance. The treaty obligated the British to fight alongside Japan if another country joined Russia in a conflict with Japan. In effect, the treaty meant that a war between the two countries would be one-on-one—a "fairer" fight that the Japanese felt was winnable. Without the treaty, other countries, as in the Triple Alliance, would likely have sided with Russia against Japan. "With its back protected," writes Marius Jansen (2000), "Japan could now enter into serious negotiations with imperial Russia" (p. 439). The result was intransigence on both sides, which ultimately led to war.

The war itself was brutal. In the battle for Port Arthur, tens of thousands of Japanese and Russian soldiers died; in the battle for Mukden, the death toll was even higher. Moreover, the Japanese dealt the harshest blows to Russia at sea, as the Japanese sank virtually the entire Russian fleet (Jansen 2000). Jansen cites a death toll far higher than most other sources: he writes that 58,000 Japanese soldiers were killed at the battle for the Liaodong base at Port Arthur alone, with another 70,000 in the "final gigantic battle" for Mukden (p. 440). Together, these amount to more than twice the number of total casualties listed by Mikoso Hane (1986) and others.

---

political struggle. Even more, the end point of this struggle was, as Matsuo Takayoshi (1966) describes, a "pseudo-democratic imperialistic ruling structure" (p. 636), one into which many liberal elites had been co-opted.

The story of how this change happened is complicated and too much to cover adequately in this chapter. Suffice it to say that the story reflects an elite-driven process of limited political change. To repeat: widespread public discontent—the clear result of a national crisis—for the first time put real pressure on the Japanese elite. Both hard-liners and soft-liners could be found, and an opposition developed that relied on mass support—support that ebbed and flowed, usually in conjunction with other critical events, both internal and external: World War I, the Russian Revolution, the death of the Meiji emperor, the **Rice Riots** of 1918, an economic crisis in 1919, and the **Great (Kanto) Earthquake** of 1923, among others. In addition, as Japan's economy continued to modernize, organized labor began to grow. Between 1921 and 1926, the number of unionized workers increased from 103,400 to 385,000 (Hane 1986). The number of strikes, too, increased dramatically: between 1906 and 1915, the average number of strikes per year was 33.9, but the figure between 1916 and 1926 was about ten times higher at 318.4 strikes annually (Garon 1987). The rise of organized labor created a more permanent base of mass pressure and support for opposition forces, including a more radicalized socialist and **communist** movement.

The elite groups were divided on the best course of action: some fought to preserve the extant system, albeit with minor changes, while others thought more significant reform was necessary, including universal male suffrage and legal recognition of labor unions. In fact, the hard-liners eventually conceded to the implementation of universal suffrage in the spring of 1925. Still, even this success was mostly an empty victory for democracy, for just ten days before the suffrage bill was passed, the Peace Preservation Law was enacted, the main objective of which was to curb "dangerous thought." A little later, too, a bill aimed at protecting the right of workers to organize and strike was blocked by the *zaibatsu* (Hane 1986). The passage of the two, essentially contradictory laws, along with the successful blocking of a prolabor law by the business elite, reflected perfectly the conflicted and split condition of the Japanese elite. Ultimately, however, even the pseudodemocratic reforms of Taisho democracy were expunged by the military elite, who manipulated the public and convinced other elite groups to back their efforts to return Japan to a militarized authoritarian system.

Rocky Road to Democracy in South Korea

South Korea, likewise, had a democratic system "imposed" on it from the outside at the end of World War II. In this case, though, the UN General Assembly—albeit clearly reflecting US interests—recommended that democratic elections be held for all of Korea. To this end, a UN Temporary Commission on Korea was established, and on January 12, 1948, it held its first meeting in Seoul. Representatives from the northern, Soviet-controlled part of the country, however, were barred from the meeting because the Soviet Union refused to cooperate—a position that the Soviets steadfastly held. Subsequently, the commission and the US government decided to go ahead with elections only in the southern, US-controlled part of Korea, and on May 10, 1948, the first general election (for the National Assembly) in Korean history was held with over 75 percent of the total potential voters and 95 percent of registered voters casting a ballot (J. K. Oh 1968). Significantly, of the men elected to the first National Assembly in 1948 and in subsequent National Assembly elections throughout the 1950s, a very large percentage belonged to the "upper strata of the Korean social hierarchy": the largest group (36 percent) were sons of landlords, a group directly tied to Korea's traditional ruling class, the *yangban* (Hahn and Kim 1963, p. 309). South Korea's first assembly, I should also mention, had fair representation from the "lower strata" (i.e., ordinary farmers, small-business owners, and laborers); however, their influence was limited.

While the composition of the assembly was important, even more important was the role of South Korea's first president, **Syngman Rhee**, whose family was also of *yangban* origin. In the early days of the Republic of Korea, Rhee had an opportunity to shape the nature of the political system in a fundamental way; unfortunately, he ruled with an **autocratic** bias from the very beginning. Rhee's ruling temperament, no doubt, was influenced by the factionalized state of South Korean politics—an understandable condition given the suddenness of the country's transition to "democratic" rule. Still, Rhee was merciless: he immediately dismissed any cabinet member who showed the slightest degree of "disloyalty," but even this purging of his closest circle was not enough. As John Kie-chiang Oh (1968) puts it, "virtually all decisions in both policy and administrative matters were made by the President himself—the beginning of a vicious circle in which Rhee quickly became so occupied with trivia that he was unable to supervise an orderly process of decision-making" (p. 16). Rhee also sought to control the police and military through the same process of purging disloyal officers and replacing them with those who followed his commands without question; Rhee then used the coercive power of the police and military to ruthlessly suppress "leftists." The one major figure who openly stood up to Rhee—Kim Ku, the former president of the Korean Provisional Government— was mysteriously assassinated by a South Korean army lieutenant in 1949. (See Figure 5.3 for brief biographies of key figures in South Korea's early political history.)

Rhee's consolidation of power was not, however, unlimited: he was curbed by outside pressure from the United States, which was intent on presenting South Korea as a showcase of democracy in Asia. This pressure kept Rhee from postponing the 1950 elections for the National Assembly—an election that promised to bring in many opponents. After the US government threatened to suspend all aid to South Korea, Rhee relented and allowed the elections to be held. As expected, his supporters were routed: only 57 of 200 seats were pro-Rhee. Under normal circumstances and with continued US pressure on Rhee, this election might have "saved" Korean democracy, but six days after the opening session of the second National Assembly, the **Korean War** broke out. Rhee

Figure 5.3 Key Figures in South Korea's Political History

Chang Myon (1899–1966). Also known as John M. Chang. Chang served in the administration of Syngman Rhee as ambassador to the United States. He returned in 1951 to South Korea and was appointed prime minister by Rhee. Despite his close connection with Rhee, Chang later decided to run on the opposition ticket for vice president in 1952, a position he won. In 1960, Chang ran directly against Rhee for president. He lost this election, but charges of vote rigging led to widespread demonstrations that eventually swept Rhee from power. After the collapse of Rhee's regime, Chang was elected prime minister of the interim government. He was ousted from office during the **coup d'état** staged by Park Chung Hee.

    Chun Doo-hwan (b. 1931). Chun was South Korea's fifth president, a position he secured after seizing control of the government in 1979 (his coup took place in the aftermath of the assassination of Park Chung Hee). Prior to his "election" as president, Chun imposed martial law on the entire country—a move that led to the **Kwangju Uprising** in May 1980. The uprising posed a serious threat to the regime, and Chun moved quickly to quell the movement by sending in military troops to "retake" the city. The rest of his rule, until 1987, was strongly colored by this violent event, but also under Chun, Seoul won the right to host the 1988 Summer Olympics. Chun stepped down in 1987—as he promised—but handpicked his successor, Roh Tae-woo.

    Kim Dae-jung (1924–2009). Kim was a leading opposition figure in South Korea who rose to prominence during the early years after the military coup led by Park Chung Hee. Kim, in fact, had won a seat in South Korea's National Assembly just two days before the coup in May 1961 and was one of many opposition figures arrested. In 1963, after being released from jail, Kim ran for the assembly again and won a decisive victory. He was reelected in 1967 and later chosen by the New Democratic Party to run for president in the 1971 elections (this was during the years of "restricted democracy"). Kim received 46 percent of the vote. A year after the election, Park imposed martial law and banned all political activity. At the time Kim was in Japan, but he immediately led an international campaign against Park. He was seen as such a threat to the regime that he was abducted by agents of the Korean Central Intelligence Agency and was placed under house arrest. Unbowed, Kim continued to fight the regime and was eventually rearrested and sentenced to five years in prison. His battles with the authoritarian regime continued; in May 1980, he was charged with treason and sentenced to death. Under heavy international pressure, the death penalty was commuted, and he was allowed to travel to the United States. Just prior to the end of authoritarian rule in 1987, Kim went back to South Korea and ran for president in the 1987 elections, this time coming in third. He ran again in 1992 but failed to win. Finally, in 1997, Kim was elected to the presidency, winning 40.3 percent of the vote.

(continues)

Figure 5.3 continued

Kim Ku (1876–1949); also spelled Kim Gu. Kim was one of the leading figures, along with Syngman Rhee, in the struggle for Korean independence during the period of Japanese colonial rule. He was also the sixth and last president of the Provisional Government of the Republic of Korea, a government-in-exile. Kim returned to Seoul after the Japanese surrendered in 1945 and endeavored to stave off the division of the country by meeting Kim Il-sung in Pyongyang (which would later become the capital of North Korea). In 1948, Kim ran for president of South Korea but was defeated by Rhee. In 1949, Kim was assassinated while in his office.

Park Chung Hee (1917–1979). Park led the military coup that toppled the interim government led by Chang Myon in May 1961. While in power, Park undertook a number of significant and far-reaching projects. Most saliently, he has been credited with turning the South Korean economy around. He did so, most generally, by pursuing a plan of state-directed capitalism and shifting the economy toward export-oriented production. Park also normalized diplomatic relations with Japan in 1965—an action that met with significant public disapproval—and forged an even stronger relationship with the United States by sending 320,000 to 350,000 South Korean troops to fight with US troops in the Vietnam War from 1965–1973. Despite taking power through a coup, Park attempted to legitimize his rule through the electoral process. In 1963, he formally resigned his position in the military so he could run as a civilian in the 1963 presidential election—an election he won by a narrow margin of 46.6 percent to 45.1 percent over his closest rival. Park was reelected in 1967 and then amended the constitution so that he could run a third time. He won reelection again in 1971, but by then, his legitimacy was being seriously questioned. To deal with dissent, Park declared a state of emergency and then imposed a new constitution, known as the **Yushin Constitution**. The new constitution was designed to give Park the authority for a "legal dictatorship." Park's rule was cut short when he was shot to death by Kim Jae-kyu, the head of the Korean Central Intelligence Agency. In 2012, Park's daughter, Park Geun-hye, was elected South Korea's first female president.

Rhee, Syngman (1875–1965). During the colonial period, Rhee was a leader in the struggle against the Japanese. He is, however, most well known for his role as South Korea's first democratically elected president, a position he held for twelve years from 1948 to 1960. While popularly elected, Rhee quickly used his position as president to consolidate power in an essentially dictatorial manner—for example, he outlawed a leading opposition party and executed its leader on charges of treason. Rhee's popularity consistently declined the longer he stayed in power. By 1960, when Rhee clearly tampered with the election results, mass demonstrations sprang up, and Rhee was eventually forced to resign. After stepping down from office, Rhee went into exile in Hawaii, where he later died of natural causes.

(continues)

Figure 5.3 continued

Roh Moo-hyun (1946–2009). Roh (also pronounced "no") was a self-taught lawyer who used his legal skills to advocate for human rights and to defend student activists during the 1980s. During this same period, he became a prodemocracy activist himself and joined a number of demonstrations, one of which cost him his license to practice law. Losing his license compelled Roh to turn to politics, and he quickly won a seat in the National Assembly in 1987. While his political career went up and down, his relative youth, personal charisma, and prodemocracy background made him an ideal presidential candidate. Roh narrowly won the 2002 presidential election and began his term in 2003. Roh's time in office was turbulent. Indeed, in 2004, the National Assembly voted to impeach Roh on charges of illegal electioneering; the Constitutional Court later overturned the impeachment. After leaving office in 2008, Roh was questioned over allegations that he had taken $6 million in bribes; he later admitted to receiving the money but insisted that it was not a bribe. In 2009, Roh jumped into a ravine while on a climbing trip; he died of massive head injuries.

Roh Tae-woo (b. 1932). Roh (pronounced "no") was South Korea's sixth president, succeeding Chun Doo-hwan in 1987 (his term in office began in 1988). Roh was handpicked by Chun to be his successor—hardly a surprise given the close relationship between the two men, which went back to their days in high school. Roh, however, stunned many in South Korea by announcing, shortly after he was elected as the ruling party's candidate for president, sweeping reforms to the South Korea political system that effectively paved the way for democracy. In particular, he agreed to restore the political rights of Kim Dae-jung, to hold a direct election for the president, and to lift restrictions on the press. Roh won the election with only 36.6 percent of the popular vote; his victory was a product of a conflict between the two leading opposition candidates, Kim Dae-jung and Kim Young-sam. The two Kims split the opposition vote almost in half, as Kim Dae-jung won 28 percent of the vote, and Kim Young-sam 27 percent of the total vote. As he promised, however, when Roh's term ended in 1993, he stepped down from power peacefully and voluntarily.

masterfully used the war—and the emergency power the war granted him—as a pretext to eliminate his opponents: many were arrested on trumped-up charges and others were intimidated and assaulted by paid ruffians. Rhee again dominated the assembly, which, in turn, allowed him to amend the constitution to ensure his continued—and increasingly autocratic—rule. In this way, the failure of South Korea's first experience with democracy was dictated by the interests and maneuvering of the elite in general, but by Rhee more specifically.

When ordinary citizens rose up against Rhee, as happened during the Student Uprising in April 1960, a split among the elite allowed the uprising to succeed.

Much like what happened in Egypt in 2011, US pressure played a key role in convincing the military elites to maintain a "neutral stance" between the Rhee government and the people. This military neutrality was easier, in part, because the United States, through the UN Command in Korea, had tactical control of the South Korean army (Oh 1968). Without the coercive power of the military at his disposal, Rhee had no way to stop the protestors, whose anger was sparked by the discovery of a nineteen-year-old boy with a tear-gas canister imbedded in his eye (he was killed during an election day riot in the small port city of Masan). The more important causes of the mass demonstrations, however, were years of corruption and the obvious and systematic rigging of the 1960 elections. Rhee resigned on April 26, 1960, but the return to democracy was short lived. After the downfall of Rhee's First Republic, the South Korean constitution was amended to "guarantee" strong democracy, a new government was elected, and a prime minister, Chang Myon, was appointed (one of the constitutional amendments provided for a cabinet system of government). Unfortunately, persistent infighting, continued economic problems, and overall political instability led to the collapse of the Second Republic after less than nine months. This time, though, a mass-based movement was not what brought the regime down, but a **coup d'état** led by the South Korean military and masterminded by Major General Park Chung Hee. The dynamics of the coup deserve careful attention, but for current purposes, the main point is the following: despite the success of the Student Uprising in 1960, another elite group—a small faction within the military—ultimately decided the political fate of the country for the next several decades.

Park and his inner circle were quintessential hard-liners. Still, after consolidating his control through direct military rule, Park returned South Korea to a type of restricted democracy, one in which formal democratic institutions and procedures were maintained, but one that also guaranteed the core interests of the military power holders (Im 1987). But why did Park even bother with the façade of democracy? The answer is fairly clear: The military junta, at the time of the coup, lacked a sufficient social base of support. The leaders, therefore, needed to acquire a degree of legitimacy. (I discuss the issue in more detail below.) At the same time, because the military was largely viewed as a "clean" institution, the military leaders were confident in winning partly competitive elections (Im 1987). For almost a decade, in fact, this strategy worked, especially since, as discussed above, Park also embarked on an ambitious economic program almost as soon as he secured power. The rapid industrialization of the country provided additional legitimacy to the regime.

Restricted democracy, however, is almost unavoidably problematic since its stability is premised on constant electoral wins by the ruling party. If an election threatens to undermine the ruling party's grip on political power, one can expect to see a quick crackdown and a shift back to undisguised authoritarianism, which is precisely what happened in 1971, when Kim Dae-jung had a surprisingly strong showing—especially given the massive interference committed by the ruling party—in the presidential election against Park Chung Hee. Kim received 45.3 percent of the vote to Park's 53.2 percent. Equally, if not more important, was the legislative election the following month, when the main opposition party (Kim's New Democratic Party) won forty-six of sixty-five seats in urban areas. Park's ruling Democratic Republican Party maintained a majority in the assembly (with 113 of 204 seats), but the electoral success of the opposition galvanized antiregime activists to demand even more. Faced with growing unrest, Park did what any hard-liner would: he issued the Emergency Decree on National Security in 1971, dissolved the National Assembly, suspended the constitution, and then rewrote it. The new constitution was named **Yushin**, which means "restoration."

The Yushin Constitution gave Park dictatorial powers and included the elimination of presidential term limits; it also gave Park the power to appoint a large portion of the National Assembly (significantly, under the Yushin Constitution, elections were still permitted). Another critical feature of the new constitution was the provision allowing the president to take extraordinary measures in times of "national crisis." The first "crisis" was over the promulgation of the Yushin Constitution itself; accordingly, Park issued Presidential Emergency Decree No. 1, which outlawed all activities or statements opposing the Yushin Constitution; Decree No. 2 allowed authorities to take all violators of Decree No. 1 into custody without arrest warrants and to mete out prison sentences of up to fifteen years (Breen 2010). The implementation of the Yushin Constitution, not surprisingly, sparked outrage throughout South Korea. However, the outrage proved futile in the face of the violence and brutality of the regime.

Under Park, both before and after the Yushin Constitution, disunity or factionalism among the ruling elite was largely held in check but certainly not eliminated, a fact that became apparent in 1979, when Park was assassinated by Kim Jae-kyu, his security chief and the head of the Korean Central Intelligence Agency. While Kim's motivations remain a mystery, the assassination took place during a time of increasing economic and political turbulence. The economy was in recession, workers had begun to demonstrate, and the opposition New Democratic Party—despite huge institutional and financial disadvantages—won a plurality (34.7 percent) in the 1978 elections for the National Assembly. The assassination of Park led to a scramble for power, which was eventually resolved when another military officer, Chun Doo-hwan, spearheaded the country's second coup. Chun's coup led to one of the most infamous events in South Korea's short history: the **Kwangju Uprising**, which took place from May 18 to May 27, 1980.

The uprising and the government's response represented a new level of social conflict, as citizens essentially took over a city in a protest against the new regime, and the government sent a full division of special forces to take the city back. The crackdown was an extreme but consistent example of hard-line decisionmaking. It had the effect of "pacifying" the population, which allowed the regime to reassert control but at a high cost. Worth noting, too, is the US role in this incident: in order for Chun to use special forces in the attack, General John A. Wickham Jr. had to release the South Korean troops from the Republic of Korea–US Combined Forces Command (General Wickham served as commander in chief from July 1979 to June 1982). While the actions of the United States are mired in controversy, one thing is clear: with no active opposition from the United States, South Korea's main strategic ally, that country's hard-liners did not have to be unduly concerned about the international costs of their decision. Indeed, Chun later used his crackdown—which also resulted in the conviction of Kim Dae-jung on charges of sedition—as leverage in relations with the United States; in return for not executing Kim and agreeing to lift martial law, Chun was given the honor of being the first foreign head of state to meet with President Ronald Reagan shortly after Reagan's inauguration in January 1981 (Wampler 2010).

The violence of the crackdown during the Kwangju Uprising, not surprisingly, could only tamp down but not eliminate public discontent and anger. Mass protests only needed another spark to ignite. This spark came with the revelation, in early 1986, that the police had tortured and killed a Seoul National University student while he was being interrogated. More fuel was added when Chun declared that an ongoing debate on constitutional reform would be suspended. Over the next few months, public unrest intensified, reaching a peak in June when the ruling party announced that no election would be held to replace Chun, but that he instead would be replaced by a handpicked successor, Roh Tae-woo. Massive street demonstrations broke out, and the hard-liners again faced a stark choice: capitulate or resort to military force. The choice seemed to be obvious given South Korea's political history.

This time, however, something different happened. First, Chun himself offered to compromise by reopening debate on constitutional reform; emboldened by the protests, however, the opposition rejected his offer. Thus, the stage appeared to be set for another violent crackdown, but in a surprising turn of events, the designated presidential successor, Roh Tae-woo, announced that he would support immediate democratization. Roh, it turned out, was a soft-liner. He understood that, while violence and repression were still viable options, the costs were becoming too great to bear, something that was true from both a domestic and international perspective. Internationally, Seoul was gearing up to host the 1988 Summer Olympic Games, and the specter of violently battling tens of thousands of demonstrators just before and even during the Games was a grave concern to the country's elite, especially Korea's business elite (i.e., the heads of the *chaebol*), whose companies had become increasingly internationalized and tied into Western markets. They certainly were not anxious to see the country's reputation—and by extension, their companies' reputations—stained by the blood of prodemocracy protestors. The late 1980s, in short, were an opportune time for a transition to democracy.

Taiwan's "Managed" Transition

As I noted above, Taiwan was the last of the trio of East Asian countries to make the transition to democracy. From the microlevel, elite-focused point of view, Taiwan's tardiness is easy to understand: the coherence and organizational strength of the KMT, the main instrument of political dominance in Taiwan, was virtually unmatched outside the communist world. The KMT's strength was no accident as the party was intentionally designed to be a Leninist-style organization—which meant, among other things, having a strong central committee, control of the military, deep integration with and control over the apparatus of the state, and an overarching revolutionary and nationalist ideology (Chou and Nathan 1987). On this point, one must understand that the history of KMT goes back to the turn of the twentieth century—a time of revolutionary change in the political sphere—and to the activities of Sun Yat-sen. (See Figure 5.4 for a discussion of key figures in Taiwan's early political history.)

Figure 5.4 Key Figures in Taiwan's Political History

Chen Cheng (1897–1965). Chen served as the governor of the Taiwan Province in 1949 (from January 5 to December 21), shortly before nationalist forces and the KMT fled mainland China. After the arrival of the KMT, Chen served as the prime minister of Taiwan from 1950 to 1954 and again from 1958 to 1963. During his years in Taiwan, Chen introduced and helped carry out **land reform**, but he was also intimately involved in the so-called White Terror. The White Terror refers to, in the most general sense, the entire period of martial law in Taiwan, which ran from 1949 to 1987 but was especially brutal in the 1950s and 1960s. During this period, tens of thousands of suspected spies and communists were imprisoned, tortured, or executed by the KMT.

    Chen Shui-bian (b. 1950). Chen served as president of Taiwan from 2000 to 2008. His election as president is especially noteworthy as it ended more than fifty years of KMT control over Taiwan's executive branch, known as the Executive Yuan. He was the first native-born Taiwanese to hold office through a direct election. During the 1980s, Chen was a member of the Tangwai movement (a movement that represented the opposition in Taiwanese politics) and was once arrested and jailed by the government for his activities (officially, he was charged with libel based on a critical argument he published as editor of the weekly prodemocracy magazine *Neo-Formosa*. After he was released from jail, Chen

(continues)

Figure 5.4 continued

helped establish the Democratic Progressive Party in 1986; he was later elected to the Legislative Yuan (Taiwan's national assembly) in 1989 and then as mayor of Taipei in 1994. In 2000, Chen won Taiwan's presidential election with 39 percent of the popular vote. He won reelection in 2004 by an extremely narrow margin: just 30,000 votes out of more than 12.9 million total votes. Shortly after stepping down from office in 2008, Chen was arrested on charges of corruption (while serving as president, Chen was immune from prosecution). Chen was later tried, convicted, and imprisoned.

Chen Yi (1883–1950). Acting on behalf of the KMT, Chen served as the chief executive and garrison commander of Taiwan following Japan's surrender in World War II (the KMT was given possession of Taiwan—then known as Formosa—in virtue of Chiang Kai-shek's participation as the legal representative of China during the Cairo Conference, which promised that Japan would be required to return—or retrocede—all its colonial possessions). Chen Yi accepted the Japanese government's surrender of Taiwan on behalf of the allied powers. While serving as the garrison commander, Chen became infamous for his handling of the 228 Incident, during which Chen ordered the violent suppression of demonstrators protesting KMT rule. Following the incident—or massacre, as many people argue—Chen was dismissed and executed for disloyalty.

Chiang Ching-kuo (1910–1988). The son of Chiang Kai-shek, Chiang Ching-kuo succeeded his father as president of Taiwan. The younger Chiang originally took over upon his father's death in 1975 but was later formally elected by the Legislative Yuan to a six-year presidential term in 1978. He was reelected to a second term in 1984. Chiang is largely credited with ending authoritarian rule and martial law in Taiwan, although, during his first few years in office, he followed the same authoritarian path as his father.

Chiang Kai-shek (1887–1975). Shortly after the KMT fled to Taiwan at the end of 1949, on March 1, 1950, Chiang formally assumed his duties of president of the Republic of China (Taiwan). He held this position until his death in 1975. Prior to leaving the mainland, Chiang played an important role in shaping the political destiny of China. In the early 1900s, more specifically, Chiang fought for Sun Yat-sen's United Revolutionary League to help overthrow China's imperial dynasty, which led to the establishment of the Republic of China in 1912. He was also an influential member of the KMT, which would eventually challenge the Chinese communists led by **Mao Zedong**. Under Chiang's leadership, in fact, the KMT and the communists fought a vicious, nationwide civil war beginning in 1927. The war between Chiang's nationalists and Mao's communists was interrupted by the Japanese invasion of China in 1937, but the animosity and distrust between the two groups remained strong. Thus, violence between the two sides reerupted after Japan's defeat in World War II; ultimately, Mao's forces won. On Taiwan, Chiang imposed martial law and governed as a dictator until his death in 1975. The first decade of KMT rule was especially repressive and

(continues)

Figure 5.4 continued

brutal and is known as the period of White Terror (for many critics of Chiang, White Terror characterized the entire period from 1949 to 1987). At the same time, Chiang is generally credited with laying the groundwork for Taiwan's economic transformation.

Lee Teng-hui (b. 1923). Lee was also the first native Taiwanese to become chairman of the KMT, a position he held between 1988 and 2000. As KMT chairman, Lee also was Taiwan's first native-born president, although he obtained this position through succession (after the death of Chiang Ching-kuo), rather than through a direct election. Lee first joined the KMT in the early 1970s and was promptly appointed to the position of minister without portfolio by Chiang Ching-kuo (his main responsibility was in overseeing the agricultural economy—a position he trained for as a Ph.D. in agricultural economies, which he earned at Cornell University). Later, Lee was appointed mayor of Taipei, which is considered an important stepping-stone for higher political appointments. Indeed, after his tenure as mayor (1978–1981), Lee was appointed governor of Taiwan, a position that is only one step below the presidency in administrative importance. A large part of Lee's early success was due to his close relationship with Chiang Ching-kuo, to whom Lee became a close adviser. That Chiang designated Lee as his heir apparent was no surprise then. Despite opposition from old guard KMT leaders, Lee assumed the presidency after Chiang's death in 1988. As president, Lee set in motion the changes required to end martial law and establish the basis for electoral democracy. On March 23, 1996, Taiwan's first free elections for president were held. Lee won 54 percent of the popular vote and thus became Taiwan's first democratically elected president. He stepped down from the presidency in 2000 in accordance with constitutionally mandated term limits—limits that he helped to enact.

Sun Yat-sen (1866–1925). Sun is, in some respects, a transcendent figure in Chinese history: he is honored as the Father of the Nation (or the Father of the Revolution) by leaders in both the People's Republic of China and the Republic of China (Taiwan). In particular, Sun's Three Principles of the People influenced the ideological development of Chiang Kai-shek and Mao Zedong, who took to heart (but differently interpreted) the principles of nationalism (*minzu*), democracy (*minquan*), and the livelihood of the people (*minsheng*).

Sun was particularly influenced by the rise and development of the Soviet Union; indeed, he allowed **Comintern** agents to help reorganize the KMT along the lines of the Communist Party of the Soviet Union (Hood 1997). And while Sun died in 1925, his reorganization of the party remained largely intact until 1990, primarily under the leadership of **Chiang Kai-shek**.

The coherence and organizational strength of the KMT allowed it to deal with potential problems efficiently and effectively—and often ruthlessly. In the years prior to its full-fledged relocation to Taiwan (the KMT had been in Taiwan since 1945, when the island was placed under the administrative control of the Republic of China by the United Nations), the KMT faced a serious uprising by the local population, dubbed the **228 Incident** (so named because it occurred on February 28). The uprising was sparked by an otherwise minor dispute— but one that clearly reflected deep tensions—between a female tobacco vendor and an officer of the Taiwan Monopoly Bureau, who beat the vendor for selling tobacco without a license. The beating ignited large-scale civil disorder and rioting, which resulted in an estimated 10,000 deaths (T. Durdin 1947). To carry out this massive violence, the KMT called in troops from mainland China and, according to one contemporary report, massacred unarmed Taiwanese protestors with machine guns and automatic rifles. Even more, the soldiers apparently demanded entry into many homes, killing the first person to appear (P. Durdin 1947). Once order was restored, however, the KMT removed the governor, Chen Yi, and replaced him with a more moderate official. Even more important, the new governor received authorization from Chiang Kai-shek to implement a program of **land reform** in early 1949, which would serve a dual purpose: first, to help restore the legitimacy of the KMT and, second, to prepare Taiwan to become the possible seat of government (Hood 1997), which happened later that year. The reform was successfully executed with relatively little difficulty, in part because it was widely supported by Taiwan's peasantry and in part because the reform received financial support and technical assistance from the United States (Barraclough 1999).

Once the KMT relocated in toto to Taiwan, a new political program was announced that emphasized economic development, the outcome of which should already be familiar. As a "political" program, the focus on economic development was another effort to firmly establish the legitimacy of the KMT. The effort largely paid off. For twenty years, rapid economic growth, combined with egalitarian policies pursued under the principle of "People's Livelihood," helped minimize domestic unrest (Chou and Nathan 1987). Strong and stable economic performance also served to maintain strong unity among the different elite groups within the KMT and to minimize the power of opposition elites, which were referred to as Tangwai (literally, "outside the party"). On the former point, Hood (1997) identifies three major groups of KMT elites: (1) the party chairman, (2) other top party leaders, and (3) other party and government leaders. No major rifts occurred within the ruling elite while Chiang Kai-shek headed the KMT and government for twenty-five years between 1950 and 1975, nor were opposition elites able to develop any significant power. Upon his death on April 5, 1975, however, the situation changed. Chiang Kai-shek was succeeded by his son, Chiang Ching-kuo, who maintained the position and power of the KMT and government in the first few years after his father's death. By the late 1970s, however, the opposition had begun to gather steam. In 1977, in particular, a riot broke out in Chungli, a town just south of Taipei, after KMT officials were caught stuffing the ballot box. The following year, another violent clash occurred between demonstrators and the police during a celebration of Human Rights Day led by the Tangwai. In response to the clash, known as the **Kaohsiung Incident**, the government arrested and tried virtually all well-known opposition leaders (more than fifty in all).

The harsh crackdown, though, did little to dissuade opponents of the regime. Pressure continued to build, and the leaders—or at least some leaders—within the KMT understood that violence and repression would not work forever. Significantly, one of those leaders seemed to be Chiang Ching-kuo himself, who adopted a somewhat open and accommodationist stance toward the political opposition from early on. Indeed, one of his first acts as president was to release political prisoners imprisoned under his father's regime. While Chiang vacillated between repression and accommodation during his first decade in office, by 1986, he seemed to have finally decided on a more democratic path. In September 1986, he formally announced that martial law would be lifted and a new national security law would be established. This said, within the KMT, many older leaders strongly opposed the pace and nature of the reform (Hood 1997), and when Chiang died in January 1988, the stage was set for a showdown between the hard-liners and soft-liners in the KMT.

The main battle was fought over who would succeed Chiang. The designated successor was Lee Teng-hui, a native of Taiwan. Lee was viewed with deep suspicion by a group of conservative (i.e., hard-line) mainlanders known as the "Palace Faction." The fight, however, was anticlimactic: by 1988, the power of the hard-liners had become limited, largely because of an infusion of younger members into the KMT, including a relatively large number of native-born Taiwanese. While the road to democracy was far from assured—Lee himself aligned with hard-liners in 1989, when social protests seemed to be getting out of hand (Hsiao and Ho 2010)—the early 1990s was a period of increasing **liberalization** overall. Yet, while pressure from below certainly played a role, politics within the KMT were clearly central to the process.

The ascendance of soft-liners, particularly Chiang Ching-kuo and Lee Teng-hui, in short, made democracy possible in Taiwan. The importance of soft-liners in Taiwan provides a nice segue back to the South Korean case. In Taiwan, as was just shown, the dominance of soft-liners—after the death of Chiang Kai-shek—allowed for a controlled and gradual transition from authoritarianism to democracy. Or, as Yangsun Chou and Andrew Nathan (1987) put, the KMT's response was a "mix of selective repression with institutional liberalization" (p. 283); one scholar goes so far as to say that the transition was "expertly planned and managed" (Eberstadt 1992, p. 85). In South Korea, by contrast, hard-liners held sway, which meant a much stronger reliance on repression and violence. As a result, political change was anything but smooth.

Seeing Beyond the Elite "Trees": A Structural Approach to Political Change

The study of elite interests and agency tells a persuasive story. And dismissing the significant and obvious role that elites played in Japan, South Korea, and Taiwan is certainly hard. Still, a narrow focus on elite interests and agency can easily be misleading. To use a trite but instructive expression, elite-centered approaches encourage observers to "miss seeing the forest for the trees." That is, when one focuses on individual actors or select groups of actors, one misses seeing the larger forces and processes that not only shape, at a deeper explanatory level, the decisions elites and others make but also, and perhaps more important, determine the success or failure of those decisions. Once one begins looking with a broader vision, however, "seeing the forest" becomes easier. As has been demonstrated, on this last point, in Japan, South Korea, and Taiwan, political shifts—unless externally imposed—were largely a product of or reaction to pressure from below. Further, as was shown, the efficacy and effects of this pressure varied widely. In prewar Japan, it produced a very limited and temporary shift to a more inclusive but extremely fragile democracy. In South Korea, pressure from below was partly responsible for the collapse of the First Republic under Syngman Rhee, but it could not prevent a reassertion of military authoritarian rule under Park Chung Hee. Another twenty-five years passed before the "pressure" was sufficient to topple authoritarian rule on a lasting basis. In Taiwan, a much smoother, more gradual process of political change occurred, but this change, too, was clearly a reaction to pressure from below. Elite-centered approaches tend to ignore the source of bottom-up or popular pressure; at best, it is the starting point of their analyses. Most structural approaches, by contrast, insist, first, that one focus on the source or origin of popular pressure or power, and, second, that one identify and explain the conditions under which such pressure is likely to lead to lasting political change, typically in the form of democracy.

Capitalist Industrialization and Political Change: An Introduction

As I suggested at the outset of this chapter, in most contemporary structural approaches, the primary source of popular pressure or power is, most simply, capitalist industrialization. The general argument, however, does not focus on increased wealth per se (as Huntington [1991] and others have suggested);

instead, the main argument is that capitalist industrialization sets in motion a structural process that brings profound, and largely unavoidable, changes in social arrangements and in relations of power within a society. One of the most important changes is a shift in the balance of power between subordinate groups, especially the working class, and the ruling elite: the more pronounced the shift, the more likely the prospects for lasting political change/democracy, and vice versa. The logic here is clear cut: capitalist industrialization generally requires increased factory production and a centralization of industry in specific locations; this, in turn, leads to increased urbanization (i.e., the concentration of people, wealth, services, and employment, particularly factory employment, in relatively small areas). Capitalism also brings major improvements in communication and transportation networks throughout a country (Huber, Rueschemeyer, and Stephens 1993). Taken together, these factors enable subordinate groups and actors (again, workers are a key group) to communicate more easily, to organize, and ultimately to unite en masse to pursue their common interests. To better understand the significance of this point, keep in mind a basic maxim, one restated by Martin Luther King Jr.: "There is power in unity and there is power in numbers."[3] The power of subordinate groups, to make the point clear, lies in their ability to act in a sustained collective manner. To be sure, capitalist industrialization is not always necessary for sustained collective action (postcolonial India is a good example of this), but it almost always produces the foundation for collective action by subordinate groups or classes wherever it unfolds.

Another important change arises from the reciprocal nature of capitalist production: in a capitalist system, workers depend on capitalists to organize capital and production, but capitalists depend on workers to, well, work. As capitalism expands and deepens, the degree of reciprocity grows. In this relationship, too, the more organized and unified workers are, the more capacity they have to exercise agency. Workers' increased agency leads to a struggle for control or influence over the state and the political system more generally, since the state can either protect and promote labor rights vis-à-vis capital or work hand in hand with capital to repress labor. In most capitalist-authoritarian systems, the state is decidedly on the side of capital and may even be little more than an instrument of capitalist domination. This factor helps one understand why democracy or **political liberalization** is generally in the common interests of workers and other subordinate groups. It also helps one understand why the structural approach tends to focus on the relationship between capital and labor, rather than on the relationship between the political elite (or state) and the "masses." (I should note, however, that many structural analysts focus more strongly on the role of the **middle class** in the democratization process.)

One should recognize that the relationship between capitalist development and democracy is not as straightforward or linear as the foregoing discussion suggests. The structural changes caused by capitalist industrialization can cut in a number of directions and are affected by a number of historically contingent factors. Thus, while the working class becomes more empowered as a function of capitalist expansion and deepening, so does a new capitalist-industrial class. Since the mid-twentieth century, moreover, capitalism has become increasingly globalized: that is, production and flows of capital have become less and less restricted by borders. As a result, the capitalist class itself has taken on a trans-national character, which makes workers' exercising their organizational power more difficult. The reason is simple: because capital no longer must occupy a fixed geographic position, it can undercut the power of organized labor by sim-ply threatening to move to another location, a process referred to as global labor arbitrage. In addition, since the 1950s, the relative size of the working class has shrunk largely due to **enclave development** (Rueschemeyer, Stephens, and Stephens 1992), producing another blow to the organization power of labor.

At the same time, other dynamics are at play. In particular, contemporary capitalism also tends to create a larger middle class, which occupies a nebu-lous but important position in the "capitalist class structure." Since the power of subordinate classes resides in "unity and numbers," political change—democratization—generally requires an alliance between the working and middle classes. The interest of the middle class, however, is variable. As Rueschemeyer, Stephens, and Stephens (1992) explain, "the very position of the middle classes, in between the elites and the masses, [makes] for consider-able ambiguity in the perception of their class interests regarding the desirability of full democracy. Moreover, the great heterogeneity of the middle classes [makes] for diversity in the perception of class interests" (p. 185). The upshot? Capitalist industrialization does not guarantee a specific political outcome, but it does, on the whole, create a strong basis for democracy to emerge.

Capitalism and Political Change and East Asia

Applying structural principles to the three East Asian cases is not difficult. In the case of prewar Japan, for instance, capitalist industrialization clearly and fundamentally disrupted and reshaped traditional—and quite long-lived—hier-archic power relations in Japanese society. Whole new classes were created, and the economy shifted from one primarily dependent on agriculture and do-mestically oriented production, to one increasingly dependent on industry and export-oriented production. This story is very familiar. As a structural force par excellence, capitalism has a similar effect everywhere it takes hold. Still, one can easily forget the power of the social and political structures in the preceding era, the **Tokugawa** or Edo period (1603–1867). A key feature of this former period was the "freezing of society" (Duus 1976, p. 103) into strict, hierarchi-cally organized classes: a hereditary ruling class composed of the samurai, and a subordinate class, or rather classes, composed of farmers and peasants, arti-sans, and merchants;[4] there were also outcaste communities, the *burakumin*,

Ainu, and *hinin*. At some risk of oversimplification, one can say that even the notion of popular sovereignty and democracy was impossible within the rigid hierarchical structure of Japan's feudal system, both before and during the Tokugawa era. This changed very quickly, however, once Japan adopted a capitalist economic system—a decision that, one should remember, was essentially forced upon Japan by the Western capitalist countries. The samurai, while still clinging to power, lost their privileged status as a class; they were replaced by the bureaucrat and the capitalist[5]—those actors who would make rapid industrialization possible. As for workers (former peasants) and smaller merchants (the petite bourgeoisie, a part of the middle class), they were gradually "released" from the structural constraints of feudal society. (I am again purposely simplifying a more complex chain of events to highlight a basic point.)

In most of the Meiji and Taisho periods, however, the agency and power of the middle and working classes was nonetheless limited. One reason is clear: despite rapid industrial growth and a not-insignificant level of urbanization, their numbers were still relatively small and their organizational capacity remained constrained by the underdevelopment of large factories. In 1909, the number of factory workers was about 1 million, although this figure more than doubled by 1929 to 2.4 million (Hane 1986). Even this larger number, however, constituted only 15 percent of Japan's working-age (fifteen to forty-nine) male population, and less than 4 percent of Japan's total population of 63.5 million people at the time (author's calculation; population data are from the Director-General for Policy Planning 2009). In addition, as late as the mid-1930s, most factories in Japan remained very small, and thus the number of workers in large factories was comparably small. According to Hane (1986), for example, in 1934, a million factory workshops employed fewer than five workers per workshop. Urbanization, as I suggested above, had long been unfolding in Japan, but by 1925, less than one-third (32.4 percent) of Japanese lived in cities with a population of 10,000 people or more.

From a structural perspective, then, subordinate classes in prewar Japan fairly clearly lacked the critical mass needed to sustain a fundamental change in the political system. As was explored above, however, their inability to force large-scale change did not mean that they were powerless to effect any change. Labor strife was an effective tactic in bringing about labor reform (such as an eight-hour workday), and, as workers combined with allies in the bureaucracy and liberal-minded "bourgeois-landlord parties" (Garon 1987, p. 121), universal male suffrage was achieved at a relatively early stage. Yet this alliance was not strong enough to withstand the entrenched power of Japan's major capitalists, who viewed the passage of the universal male suffrage law as a fundamental threat. Specifically, they saw universal male suffrage as opening the door to a major expansion of labor rights, especially the right to organize. In short order, then, Japan's industrialists organized an "unprecedented nationwide campaign to unify employers against the legal recognition of unions" (Garon 1987, p. 167).

They succeeded so well that, in 1932, Yoshioka Shigeyoshi, a strong proponent of trade unionism, proclaimed the death of liberal labor policy in Japan: "labor union legislation, which had attracted the attention of all of society as a major historical issue, has become an exquisite luxury. Having no bearing on the grave times, it has been totally eliminated from the political agenda" (cited in Garon 1987, p. 186). Shortly thereafter, Japan reverted back to authoritarianism.

I should stress that democracy's survival in Japan into the 1930s was certainly possible. The key point, however, is that workers and their allies did not have sufficient power, in structural terms, to prevent the slide back to authoritarianism. Workers' lack of power was not simply due to the increasing wealth and influence of Japan's leading capitalists but also to the specific state-capital relationship that emerged in the Meiji period. Part of this relationship was contingent on Japan's historical circumstances, the "bureaucratized warrior" **social structure** of the Tokugawa era, but a large part was due to the structural pressures of late industrialization. These pressures created an imperative for state-led industrialization. The reasons are fairly clear: in the late nineteenth and early twentieth centuries, late-developing economies required a strong state that could simultaneously fend off Western aggressors (during a period of capitalist imperialism), quickly mobilize resources for rapid industrialization, and subsidize domestic industries to compete effectively against far more advanced Western firms (Amsden 1989). This close relationship between the "late-developing state" and capital—one committed to rapid industrialization at all costs and the other to accumulation at all costs—had a deleterious effect on democratic political change. Indeed, authoritarianism is the modus operandi of the state-capital alliance, as was made especially evident in the cases of South Korea and Taiwan.

Labor Subordination and Political Exclusion in South Korea and Taiwan

For South Korea and Taiwan, the basic thrust of the structural argument should already be apparent. Still, underscoring the key points would be useful. To begin, recall that both South Korea and Taiwan were "invited to develop" by the regional hegemon, Japan, and the global hegemon, the United States. This invitation, though, was highly conditional, and one of the key conditions was that labor and other costs of production be kept as low as possible, in large part, so that Japan's industrialization could proceed unabated. Of course, for their own reasons, state leaders in South Korea and Taiwan also needed to suppress domestic wages and facilitate the exploitation of their own workers, especially female workers. This exploitation required both an effective and a repressive state apparatus. I already discussed the effectiveness of the **developmental state** in Chapter 2; if anything, the South Korean and Taiwanese states were even better at labor repression and exclusion than the Japanese state. In South Korea, brute force was typically used. After Park Chung Hee came to power, for example, he instituted a total ban on strikes, deregistered all existing unions, and arrested many union activists (Deyo 1987). Once he destroyed oppositional unionism, his regime re-created his own state-controlled union system under the umbrella of the **Federation of Korean Trade Unions**, with which all reactivated unions had to affiliate (Deyo 1987).

In Taiwan, the KMT used more finesse, in part because of the predominance of small and medium-size enterprises, which made large-scale collective action much more difficult (Koo 1989). In 1966, for example, only about 11 percent of Taiwanese workers were employed by large, typically state-owned enterprises or **SOEs** (Ho 2010). For workers in SOEs, the state's strategy was to co-opt the workers by treating them as "labor aristocrats," providing company housing, libraries, movie theaters, and sports facilities—at a time when few ordinary Taiwanese workers had access to such privileges (Ho 2010). At the same time, a heavy price was to be paid: constant and very tight surveillance, backed up by the security police, who were given sweeping powers and virtually unchecked authority over workers in and outside the factory walls (Ho 2010). In addition to the security police, the KMT "implanted an intricate security control apparatus," which included a clandestine network of informants among the workforce (Ho 2010, p. 567). In non-SOEs, nominally independent unions were permitted, but they were also infiltrated by local KMT cadres, who helped to monitor and control their activities. And, if all this surveillance and control were not enough, as an added precaution against rising labor costs, unions were not allowed to enter into collective bargaining over wages. Instead, wages were unilaterally set by management. Furthermore, newly organized unions, as well as their officials, had to be approved by local KMT committees (Deyo 1989); workers were also prohibited from going on strike. The "finesse" of the KMT, one should keep in mind, was based on a state ready and willing to use force and violence whenever necessary. As a result of these efforts, organized labor was effectively excluded from the political process, and wages were kept very low (see Figure 5.5).

Given the tight control over the working class exercised by the regimes in South Korea and Taiwan, the question of how and why labor was able to break this stranglehold—particularly from the standpoint of political change—needs to be considered afresh. Would or, perhaps more appropriately, could political change (i.e., democratization) have emerged without the structural changes brought by capitalist industrialization? The elite-centered answer to this question, as has been explored, is an almost unqualified "yes," but even advocates of the elite view recognize that, for the elites, a powerful incentive has to be present for change to occur, and, for the most part, this incentive comes from "below." As has been discussed previously, elite-centered analysts point to a key triggering event, some sort of national crisis that undermines the legitimacy of the regime. This argument, however, has a problem: many serious delegitimizing crises do not result in a breakdown of authoritarian rule. In South Korea, for example,

Figure 5.5 Hourly Compensation for Manufacturing Production Workers (in US dollars for selected countries)

	1975	1980	1986
United States	6.36	9.84	13.21
Japan	3.05	5.61	9.47
Mexico	2.00	2.96	1.49
South Korea	0.34	1.01	1.39
Taiwan	0.39	0.98	1.67

Source: US Department of Labor, Bureau of Labor Statistics (1988), cited in Deyo (1989).

the 1971 electoral crisis—a product of increasing dissatisfaction with the costs of rapid industrialization—threatened the regime. Park responded to "protestors by denying their voices altogether" (Jung and Kim 2009, p. 6). The subsequent implementation of the Yushin Constitution, which was widely reviled by labor and other opponents of the regime, effectively suppressed dissent.

Overcoming Elite Resistance: An Underlying Shift in the Balance of Class Power

To elite-centered analysts, a regime's decision to use force against a popular uprising is the end of the story, but from a structural view, the key question is left unanswered: Why were subordinate groups defeated? The short and somewhat simplistic answer, from a structural perspective, is that they did not have sufficient social power—at least at the time. On this point, one must understand that the state's opponents did not give up. They continued to struggle, bringing constant, almost unremitting pressure against the regime, year after year. This pressure and determination required the state to exercise a high level of brutality and violence, but also to make periodic attempts at "appeasement," all in an effort to quell dissent. In 1984, one such effort at appeasement in South Korea backfired: during the rule of Chun Doo-hwan, the regime temporarily eased up on repressive policies, in part to burnish the country's image for the upcoming 1986 Seoul Asian Games (as well as the 1988 Seoul Olympic Games). Instead of mollifying the opposition, however, it "gave an impetus to the explosive growth of the democratization movement in *every* sector of society" (Jung and Kim 2009, p. 10). Most important, a stronger alignment or alliance between middle-class students and labor, which had begun to emerge in the mid-1980s, was finally forged. This alignment was known as the *no-hak yondae* (or "worker-student alliance"). The worker-student alliance, in turn, was buttressed by growing support from middle-class urban professionals, intellectuals, and the self-employed

(C. J. Choi 1993). In short, by 1986, a massive coalition of subordinate groups had formed in opposition to the regime. And while the method of dealing with this coalition provoked a division among hard-liners and soft-liners within the ruling elite, the regime as a whole had little choice but to accede to demands for political reform. This acquiescence was not the end of the conflict, as the regime used a number of "divide-and-conquer" tactics to limit the extent of political reform (C. J. Choi 1993). Still, the dynamics of the process suggest that underlying the political changes that transpired in the late 1980s was a structural process that had fundamentally shifted the balance of class power in South Korean society.

Other important aspects can be found in the structural argument as well. By the late 1980s, the rapid and sustained pace of South Korea's industrialization, the increasing reliance on exports, and the heavy dependence of foreign loans worked together, in interrelated fashion, to, first, undermine the utility of coercion and violence against labor specifically, and mass movements more generally, and, second, weaken the hitherto strong alliance between capital and the state. Let us briefly consider each of these points. First, rapid and sustained industrialization creates a constant demand for labor. The existence of surplus labor weakens the organizational potential and power of workers, in large part because it allows companies to easily replace recalcitrant workers. However, in high-speed growth economies—and especially those with relatively small populations, such as South Korea—the surplus labor pool quickly dries up. For this reason, even in traditional, patriarchal societies, women are quickly drawn into the labor force; initially, the inclusion of this hitherto excluded group into the formal labor market allows a significant expansion of surplus labor. But incorporating women is only a stopgap measure. Eventually, as José Alemán (2008) explains, "lower levels of surplus labor reduce the asymmetry between the organizational power of wage earners and [capital]" (p. 8). The rapid shrinking of South Korea's surplus labor pool can be seen, albeit indirectly, in statistics on unemployment, specifically nonagricultural unemployment, which dropped from 16.3 percent in 1962 to a scant 3.8 percent in 1987 (see Figure 5.6). In addition, as demand for higher-skilled industrial workers increases, capital's reliance on a cooperative workforce also increases, since skilled workers, too, are difficult to replace. These factors make capital more amenable to the economic and political demands of labor.

Second, while the strong relationship between labor repression and export-oriented industrialization is unequivocal, as countries move up the technological ladder—and as labor becomes scarcer and more skilled, and production processes more complex and capital intensive—the utility of repression and coercion tends to decrease (Sharma 1985). As with a shrinking pool of surplus labor, capital-intensive, export-reliant economies are vulnerable to work stoppages and other disruptions. And when capital (i.e., the *chaebol*) and the state become

Figure 5.6　Economic Structure of South Korean Economy
(selected years)

	1962	1972	1982	1987
Unemployment rate	8.2	4.5	4.4	3.1
Nonagricultural unemployment rate	16.3	7.5	6.0	3.8
Employment structure (%)				
Agriculture	37.0	26.8	14.7	10.5
Mining and manufacturing	16.4	23.5	30.4	33.0
Other	46.6	49.7	54.9	56.5
Export (% of GNP)	2.4	15.0	30.7	36.7
Heavy industry in manufacturing (%)	28.6	36.1	54.9	56.5
Heavy industry goods in exports (%)	n.a.	21.3	50.8	52.9

Source: Cited in SaKong (1993).
Note: n.a. = data not available.

heavily dependent on exports for their very survival, this vulnerability can only increase. On this point, consider South Korea's steadily growing reliance on exports: in 1962 exports accounted for only 2.4 percent of GNP, but this figure increased more than fifteen times by 1987 to 36.7 percent (see Figure 5.6). Third, for the same basic reasons, increasing dependence on foreign capital also puts a premium on smooth capital-labor relations and a stable political environment. Significantly, for almost two decades after Park Chung Hee took power, South Korea maintained a cautious—even suspicious—policy toward **FDI** and instead relied heavily on foreign loans. This approach resulted in an ever-increasing debt load, measured in total debt to GNP, reaching a high of 52.1 percent in 1985 (see Figure 5.7 below). The unabated growth of foreign debt (a combination of a number of factors)[6] put greater pressure on firms to maintain strong export growth, which proved to be a very difficult task in the turbulent years of the early 1980s. A huge jump in exports in 1987—a 36.2 percent increase from the previous year (combined with a stabilization in the cost of imports)—allowed the country to reduce its foreign debt considerably. But this set of events simply underscores the importance of maintaining strong and uninterrupted export growth. Beginning in the mid-1980s, one might note, FDI started to replaced foreign loans: between 1982 and 1986, more than $1.7 billion in FDI, mainly from Japan, flowed into South Korea. In the structural view, then, little doubt can exist that the dynamics of capitalism significantly undermined the power of the political and economic elite, while simultaneously empowering the subordinate classes. But can the same basic analysis be used to explain political change in Taiwan? On the surface, this explanation seems

Figure 5.7 South Korea's Foreign Debt and FDI (selected years)

	1972	1976	1981	1985	1987
Total foreign debt (millions of US$)	3,587	10,520	32,433	46,762	35,568
Total debt to GNP (%)	33.9	36.7	49.0	52.1	27.6

Source: SaKong (1993).

	1962–1966	1972–1976	1982–1986	1987	1987–1991
FDI: total approvals Number of cases	42	1,260	948	551	2,584
Amount (thousands of US$)	47,411	879,620	1,767,729	1,063,327	5,634,966

Source: SaKong (1993).

difficult to apply, but just a little structural digging tells us that Taiwan is not necessarily much different.

In Taiwan, the microlevel, elite-centered argument suggests that one can naturally assign primary responsibility for that country's democratization to elite leaders, especially Chiang Ching-kuo. Indeed, even among skeptics of elite-centered explanations, strong agreement can be found that he played a role in the *timing* of the democratization process in Taiwan. Yet while timing is important, it is not all-important. Again, one must consider the underlying changes that were taking place in the economy and society that made Chiang's decision "natural" in the first place. On this point, worthwhile noting is that **single-party states** with authoritarian systems rarely make a peaceful transition to democracy; in fact, most show remarkable stability and longevity. The reasons, according to Barbara Geddes (1999), are clear:

> Single-party regimes . . . have few endogenous sources of instability and, in addition, can usually weather the death of founders and leaders. Through their control over the allocation of educational opportunities, jobs, and positions in government, single parties can typically claim the loyalty . . . of many of the most able, ambitious, and upwardly mobile individuals in society, especially those from peasant and urban marginal backgrounds. . . . In the absence of exogenous shocks [i.e., national crises], they are unlikely to be destabilized by either internal rivalries or external opposition. (p. 134)

The key point, to repeat, is that, in the absence of a severe national crisis (or crises) that destabilizes and delegitimizes the regime, those at the top of a single-party system will have no incentive to dissolve the system. Thus, if one sticks to the elite-centered view, Taiwan's democratization is utterly inexplicable (admittedly, I am purposely adopting an exaggerated stance here to distinguish the structural and elite-centered approaches). Again, though, if one looks under the surface, almost immediately apparent is that KMT rule—strong and repressive as it was—was built on a foundation of sand. The main structural reason is clear: the KMT built its single-party regime, in part, not only by excluding labor but also by excluding large swaths of the indigenous business sector. (On this point, recall that the KMT is a nonnative ruling party.)

The reasons for this exclusion are historical and contingent, one of the most important of which is simply that the KMT has, until recently, ruled Taiwan as outsiders. As outsiders, the KMT not only failed to forge ties with Taiwanese-owned businesses but also intentionally institutionalized an economic division between itself and the local business class. The division one sees between large businesses (which are mostly SOEs or owned by Chinese who fled with the KMT from mainland China), on the one hand, and small and medium-size businesses, on the other hand, is a reflection of a KMT policy designed to minimize the economic and, therefore, political power of the indigenous Taiwanese population. This approach worked for a long time, but the rapid expansion of the local business class—which, ironically, was spurred on by the exclusionary tactics of the KMT—gradually led to a shift in the balance of power in Taiwan. A particularly important indicator of this shift can be found in the relative share of exports controlled by small and medium-size enterprises: in 1981, this size of business accounted for more than 68 percent of all exports (Wu and Huang 2003). The ability of the local business class to dominate export markets, which also made them the dominant earners of foreign exchange, gave them added importance in the structure of Taiwan's export-oriented economy and made them a largely independent and potent political force (Cheng 1989).

The power of the local business class, however, needed to be activated. But here, too, one finds structural forces at play. For at the same time as the local business class was emerging as a powerful class actor, so too was Taiwan's middle class. As Tun-Jen Cheng (1989) explains, "the main activists for political change in Taiwan were the newly emerging middle-class intellectuals who had come of age during the period of rapid economic growth" (p. 483). This new group, Cheng continues, were Taiwanese mainly from the countryside who not only demanded a liberal democracy but also had a concrete sense of how to apply "democratic procedures, institutional design, political techniques, and legal frameworks" (p. 483). By themselves, however, they lacked the power necessary to effectively challenge the regime: they needed upper-class allies. They found their key ally, Cheng suggests, in the local business class. This alliance did not lead to an immediate breakthrough by any means, but it did create a more level playing field from a structural standpoint, which allowed opponents of the regime to exert continuous and effective pressure for political change. In other words, instead of a one-sided game in which the KMT would simply, and sometimes literally, beat down or destroy its opponents, the two sides became "locked into a continuous process of bargaining wherein communication was possible and actions were observable" (p. 490). This process is likely the primary reason for the gradual and largely peaceful transition to democracy in Taiwan, a transition, to be clear, that was born of structural changes brought about by capitalist industrialization.

Mesolevel Explanations: Institutions and Culture

The Significance of Regime Type

Mesolevel explanations, as noted above, cover a wide range of often overlapping possibilities, including institutional, cultural-religious, and ideological factors. In the foregoing discussion of Taiwan, for example, I mentioned a particular type of authoritarian institution: the single-party state. In this argument, institutional forces are assumed to play a central role; they shape, in a basic and systematic way, the self-interests of political elites (Geddes 1999). In single-party regimes (again, predemocracy Taiwan under KMT rule is a prime example), the overriding interest of party members is to hold office. According to Geddes, "some value office because they want to control policy, some for the pure enjoyment of influence and power, and some for the illicit gains that come with office in some countries" (p. 129). Geddes's statement may not appear to be particularly insightful, but she also suggests that not all authoritarian regimes are alike. In a military-authoritarian regime, the leaders are less interested in holding office and far more interested in ensuring the survival and efficacy of the military itself; in other words, they take power (e.g., stage a coup d'état, as General Park did in South Korea) when they feel the military as an institution or the primary mission of the military (i.e., ensuring national security) is threatened. The upshot of this insight is that military-authoritarian leaders are much more likely to give up political power, often through a negotiated process. Some evidence of this trend can be found in the early years of the Park regime, when he returned the country to restricted democracy, but as was pointed out, he was unwilling to cede power through the ballot box when push came to shove.[7] In Taiwan's single-party system, by contrast, one did see a negotiated process— but this process, too, was not predicted by Geddes's rational-institutional framework. Although the experience of Taiwan, in particular, seems to problematize Geddes's argument, thinking about the influence and power of institutions— and other mesolevel factors—is clearly important. The importance of these elements does not mean that mesolevel factors, and specifically culture, explain everything. With this qualification in mind, I again focus attention on culture, and more specifically on the significance of legitimacy.

The Importance of Legitimacy

Centuries ago, Jean-Jacques Rousseau wrote, "The strongest man is never strong enough to be master all the time, unless he transforms force into right and obedience into duty" (cited in Kane, Loy, and Patapan 2010, p. 386). Looking at the world today, one would be hard put to dismiss Rousseau's observation. To be sure, one can find political regimes that seem to rule by force alone, but a peek under the surface of even the most brutal regime will likely reveal a systematic effort by that regime to "transform force into right and obedience into duty." North Korea, perhaps, is a case in point: despite the brutality of the regime, almost no effort has been spared by the country's leaders to legitimize their autocratic rule. But why bother? That is, why do autocratic regimes endeavor to legitimize their power? The simple answer is that legitimacy matters, both to elites and the masses. But what exactly is legitimacy? Legitimacy, most simply put, is a *belief*. In Max Weber's view, legitimacy is "the basis of every system of authority, and correspondingly of every kind of willingness to obey, [it] is a belief, a belief by virtue of which persons exercising authority are lent prestige" (Weber 1964, p. 382). This is a descriptive definition of legitimacy but also one that leaves out what others argue is an essential normative element. Normative views often link legitimacy to the moral justification of political authority (Fabienne 2010). Peter Fabienne explains, "Political bodies such as states may be effective, or *de facto*, authorities, without being legitimate. They claim the right to rule and to create obligations to be obeyed, and as long as these claims are met with sufficient acquiescence, they are authoritative. Legitimate authority, on this view, differs from merely effective or *de facto* authority in that it actually holds the right to rule and creates political obligations."

The debate between descriptive and normative definitions—while important—need not detain us. For our purposes, the primary point is the following: legitimacy is a precious political resource, albeit one that is fundamentally subjective rather than objective. To repeat, legitimacy is ultimately a belief; it is not a concrete object or good, such as economic performance. Despite its subjective nature, legitimacy is a key element of a regime's power, whether the regime is authoritarian or democratic. Conversely, it is equally key to opponents of the regime. For these reasons, without surprise, a constant struggle can be witnessed over and for legitimacy, a struggle that has been clearly manifested in East Asia. In particular, the political and economic elite in all three countries endeavored to legitimize their rule through a process of cultural construction. At the same time, opponents to the regime attempted to define legitimacy in very different, often contradictory terms. "This constant contestation," as John

Kane, Hui-Chieh Loy, and Haig Patapan (2010) put it, "means that legitimacy issues are seldom settled once and for all" (p. 388).

Political Legitimacy and Political Change and Continuity in East Asia

The argument here is not that legitimacy or a lack of legitimacy is the principal reason for regime survival, but instead that legitimacy plays an important role in the level of popular opposition to or support of the regime, regardless of whether the regime is authoritarian, democratic, or something else. In addition, one must understand the intimate connection between legitimacy and regime performance: regimes must "deliver the goods." The goods may be (as I suggested above) rapid and sustained economic growth, internal stability, external security, social justice and equity, or any number of other things (in practice, preferences are not expressed in dichotomous terms but instead reflect a mixture of different goals and priorities). The relationship between legitimacy and goods, I recognize, suggests that legitimacy is ultimately based on strictly objective criteria: in other words, a regime that delivers strong economic performance is automatically "legitimate." But this conclusion ignores a key question: What determines societal preferences in the first place? For instance, why does a society prefer economic development over equity or social justice, or domestic security over individual freedom? More generally, one might even ask, "Why do people prefer authoritarianism over democracy?" (That is, why might most of a society's population consider authoritarian rule more legitimate than democratic rule?) The general answer to all these questions brings the discussion back to a fundamentally intersubjective/cultural process, the elements of which I discuss below. Judging legitimacy in terms of how well a regime fulfills its functions, one should note, is only one side of the legitimacy coin. The other side of the coin is whether most of a country's population sees a viable alternative to the existing regime (Matveerva 1999). As might be apparent, this issue is particularly significant for opponents of a regime. With all this in mind, let us now look more carefully at the issue of legitimacy in East Asia.

In all three East Asian countries, the governments—in the Meiji and Taisho eras in Japan, and during the Park and Chiang eras in South Korea and Taiwan, respectively—strongly relied on industrialization or the achievement of sustained economic growth as symbols of legitimacy. They also all went to great lengths to bind industrialization and national security together inextricably. This linkage was critical because it helped to justify—or legitimize—repression, violence, and exclusionary policies. To fully appreciate the importance of legitimacy for these regimes, though, one needs to go back to the years when the regimes first came to power. This step back is especially relevant for Taiwan and South Korea, since the authority of the Chiang and Park regimes to govern was in serious question from the moment the men came into power. In Taiwan, as was discussed before, the legitimacy of the KMT was in doubt even prior to the party's exodus from mainland China: the 228 Incident and the corruption of Chen Yi's administration of the island had turned many Taiwanese against the KMT. Chen Yi was replaced by Chen Cheng who, according to Steven Hood (1997), "understood the KMT needed legitimacy in Taiwan to be successful. He believed economic reform, in particular land reform, was a necessary prerequisite to build support for the KMT" (p. 30). Significantly, Chen Cheng and the KMT's focus on land reform was simultaneously meant to deprive a major rival of the KMT, namely the Chinese communists, of legitimacy. Chen Cheng put it this way:

> The life of ease and happiness enjoyed by the landlord was built entirely on the miseries of the tenant. This led to irreconcilable opposition between the two and created internal unrest in the rural districts and made them susceptible to external propaganda. This provided the communist agitators with an opportunity to infiltrate the villages. It was one of the main reasons the Chinese mainland fell to the communists. . . . With the implementation of rent reduction, the livelihood of the masses . . . was immediately improved. The communists were effectively deprived of propagandistic weapons by a new social order that had arisen in the rural areas. (quoted in Hood 1997, pp. 30–31)

At a more fundamental level, the KMT held fast (in principle, if not in practice) to an ideology known as the **Three Principles of the People**, which was originally articulated by Sun Yat-sen. These principles, which can be roughly translated into nationalism (*minzu*), democracy (*minquan*), and social welfare (*misheng*), were meant to underscore the KMT's ultimate commitment to the people. However, the KMT leadership also sought to justify a very gradual realization of the three principles on the premise that the conflict with the communists required the party to exercise a high degree of control over the political system. For this reason, restrictions on political and other rights—including the imposition of martial law—were portrayed as necessary but temporary measures (Chou and Nathan 1987). Another early effort at building legitimacy involved efforts to implement local self-rule at the provincial and lower levels through local elections. Not surprisingly, in the early years, these local elections did not and could not threaten the KMT's hold on power, but they allowed the KMT to recruit local party leaders—mostly Taiwanese—into the party, thus buttressing the notion that the KMT was a truly representative organization (Hood 1997). On this point, one should recognize that local elections were "comprehensive, institutionalized, and quite real"; they were real in the sense that they were competitive and open to non-KMT candidates, who could and did win (Cheng and Lin 2008, p. 164).

In South Korea, the failed legacy of democracy under Syngman Rhee and the short-lived Chang administration helped to create an aura of ambivalence; nonetheless, Park's seizure of power through a military coup could not help but undermine the legitimacy of his regime. He wasted little time, therefore, in articulating a meticulous and thorough justification for the coup: in 1962, Park published *Our Nation's Path: Ideology of Social Reconstruction,* a 240-page book devoted to his ideas. The coup, Park asserted, was designed to save the country from all the ills that had plagued Koreans for centuries—factionalism, indolence, vassalage, "malicious selfishness," political incompetence and corruption, backwardness, and so on. Even more, the military revolution, as he described it, was not meant to destroy democracy but to save it. As Park himself wrote, the revolution "is a surgical operation intended to excise a malignant social, political, and economic tumor. The Revolution was staged with the compassion of a benevolent surgeon who sometimes must cause pain in order to preserve life and restore health" (C. H. Park 1962a, p. 189). Park's interpretation of democracy, however, was skeptical of Western, liberal democracy—which he likened to "borrowed clothes" that "did not fit" South Koreans (pp. 191–192). A key reason for the poor fit was South Korea's economic backwardness; thus, until South Korea could catch up economically with the West, the pursuit of liberal democracy would be futile. His responsibility as South Korea's leader, then, was to focus on building a strong economy. In this way, Park echoed the logic of the KMT in asserting that "undemocratic emergency measures may be necessary" to improve the people's living conditions (p. 195). To top all of this off, Park argued that a premature embrace of democracy would open the door to the "pressures of Communist regimes" (p. 195).

As I noted above, both the KMT and Park understood that solemn pronouncements and words on paper needed to be buttressed with observable results, namely, rapid industrialization. And both, as demonstrated earlier, were very successful. In this view, the lack of widespread popular movements against either regime in their early years is not surprising. In Taiwan, little indication could be found of widespread domestic dissatisfaction or unrest for more than two decades. To be sure, this lack of protest was also a reflection of repressive state policies and "watchful surveillance" of even the most benign social gatherings, including religious festivals (Hsiao and Ho 2010, p. 46), yet these sorts of policies have certainly not stopped organized opposition movements from forming in other countries. In South Korea, Park had a much rougher road to travel because the groundwork for an organized and vocal oppositional and democratically oriented movement had already been created and achieved success in overthrowing the Rhee regime. This established opposition was demonstrated in a massive campaign that sprung up to oppose Park's efforts to normalize diplomatic relations with Japan in 1964–1965. For Park, his efforts to define legitimacy were subject to constant and intense contestation virtually every moment of his regime. From this perspective, that he did find, for a time, a significant degree of public support is remarkable. In 1963, before many of his economic polices had been implemented and borne fruit, Park won the presidency by a small margin with less than 50 percent of the vote (Park won 46.6

percent while the second place finisher had 45.1 percent). The results suggest that a large segment of the South Korean population "believed in" Park's message and the legitimacy of his regime. In 1967, Park won 51.4 percent of the vote, more than ten points higher than his nearest opponent. The large margin of victory was almost assuredly a product of the regime's success at "growing the economy" and in demonstrating genuine competence (C. J. Choi 2005, p. 120).

These elections, one should remember, occurred under conditions of restricted democracy, which represented another element in Park's effort to legitimize his regime. Ironically, but not surprisingly, the allowance for restricted democracy also helped lead to the first major crisis in legitimacy. Specifically, once Park began to openly manipulate the electoral system—in 1969, the ruling party passed a constitutional amendment that allowed Park to run for a third term—the "belief" in the regime's legitimacy began to ebb, a feeling that was manifested in the results from the 1971 election, which I discussed above. The upshot from the 1971 elections is clear. As Choi (2005) explains, "the 1971 election results show that no matter how great the regime's [economic] achievements were, the voters opposed the regime when the regime's industrialization project could not coexist with democratic values, and when it became clear that it was an authoritarian development plan" (p. 120). Choi also points out another telling aspect of this voter shift in 1971, which was the change in middle-class support for the regime. Up until 1971, the middle class tended to support the Park regime, in no small measure because they were the direct beneficiaries of industrialization. They would continue to benefit from industrial growth after 1971, but this factor did not seem to matter when they lost their belief in the regime's legitimacy.

The existence of a vocal and often fearless opposition, combined with the Park regime's contradictions, created a highly combustible political environment that put the question of legitimacy front and center from the time Park seized power until the day the authoritarian regime came to an end in 1987. In Taiwan, as discussed elsewhere, the environment was far less combustible, but the issue of legitimacy was never far from the surface. Tun-Jen Cheng and Gang Lin (2008), for example, argue that the implementation of local elections combined with the promise of a transition to constitutional democracy in the future, after a period of tutelage, was instrumental to political institutional change (i.e., democratization) in Taiwan. Local elections were important in that they gradually and inexorably increased the pressure to expand the scope of electoral competition from the local to the national level. Political self-interest was, of course, a major factor in local-level officials' wanting to move up to higher-level elected offices, but in terms of regime legitimacy, denying these opportunities became increasingly difficult. A contradiction was beginning to appear. By the 1970s, opponents of the regime were beginning to voice their dissent, albeit very cautiously, as the regime remained vigilant against any signs of trouble.

An outlet was found in the publication of magazines (Hsiao and Ho 2010), in the creation of ostensibly nonpolitical study groups, and in "informal" meetings during election periods (Cheng and Lin 2008). The contradiction began to grow bigger as the promise made by the KMT was delayed again and again. As Cheng and Lin (2008) explain, a "promise arouses expectation. . . . If a political promise has been given but not lived up to, the expectation will be frustrated, and the party giving the promise will lose credibility" (pp. 168–170), or, more pertinently for our purposes, legitimacy.

Second, when the regime runs out of viable reasons (e.g., building the economy, retaking the mainland, or providing sufficient "tutelage") for fulfilling a promise, eventually the promise (i.e., achieving constitutional democracy) becomes the only remaining task to be done. Third, the unfulfilled promise forced the KMT into a defensive position: "As the standard arguments for postponing democracy—Communist insurrection on the mainland and economic development on Taiwan—increasingly lost their marginal utility, the opposition had become more innovative and audacious in making a case for democratization in Taiwan" (Cheng and Lin 2008, p. 170). As the opposition became more innovative and audacious, their "audience" began to grow. (One might even argue that this contradiction was responsible for the rise of soft-liners within the KMT; after all, their ideas had to come from somewhere, too.) Dissent, whether or not directed against the regime itself, became more common and Taiwan civil society finally gave rise to bona fide social movements (Hsiao and Ho 2010). This shift made the cost of repression higher and finally encouraged political opposition activists to organize a political party—the Democratic Progressive Party—in clear defiance of the regime. Importantly, their social power was still extremely limited; in fact, most members of the new party assumed that they would be immediately arrested (Chou and Nathan 1987).

The weakening of the KMT's legitimacy did not directly lead to the dismantling of Taiwan's authoritarian system, but it almost certainly played a role in coalescing and emboldening opponents of the regime, and, as I suggested above, likely affected members of the KMT itself. On this last point, notably, in 1987, the KMT still had ample capacity to destroy any domestic opposition, and even the need for negotiation was, at best, limited. So why did the KMT—and more specifically, Chiang Ching-kuo—adopt a soft line? Some analysts argue that Chiang's actions were due, in large part, to growing international pressures (Cheng and Lin 2008). This conclusion is probably true, but even here questions of legitimacy play an important role. For example, Chiang saw democracy as a way to legitimize the regime during a period when China was gaining the upper hand in diplomatic relations. In an interview with the *Washington Post* (October 7, 1986), Chiang had the following to say:

> Especially today when the communist bandit regime is near the end of the road, with its vile reputation known to everyone . . . it is more important than

ever for us to strengthen the construction of constitutional government to demonstrate clearly that the strong contrast between the two sides of the Taiwan Strait is basically due to the fact that one side has implemented a constitution based on the Three People's Principles while the other has not. (cited in Nathan 1997, p. 96)

To repeat the central point of this section: the argument here is not to say that legitimacy determined the outcome in Taiwan, or that it, by itself, led to Taiwan's democratization. This is not the case. Fair to say, however, is that the question of legitimacy undergirded the political dynamics of Taiwan from the earliest days of KMT rule until today. It is a factor that should not be ignored in any discussion of political change in Taiwan or East Asia more generally.

Interests, Power, and Ideas: Building a Constructed Actor Model

Despite the many avowed differences among the competing perspectives, discerning some significant areas of agreement is not difficult. All three approaches, more specifically, fairly clearly recognize that interests, power, and ideas invariably play a role in explaining both political change and continuity. The trick, of course, is figuring out how to bring all these factors and forces together into a coherent and comprehensive framework of analysis. While always challenging, this task is not necessarily overwhelming. To give a sense of how one can get going, let's first consider a statement by Michael McFaul (2002), a prominent scholar and US ambassador to Russia, appointed by President Barack Obama in 2011:

> Inert, invisible structures do not make democracies or dictatorships. *People do.* Structural factors such as economic development, cultural influence, and historical institutional arrangements influence actors' preferences and power, but ultimately these forces have causal significance *only if translated* into human action. Individuals and the decisions they make are especially important for explaining how divergent outcomes result from similar structural contexts. (p. 214; emphasis added)

With a little tweaking, McFaul's statement provides a very nice starting point for the constructed actor model. While McFaul's own microlevel, rational choice position is clear, he is careful not to dismiss structural, institutional, and cultural-ideational factors and forces altogether. In his view, these are all a part of an explanation for political change and continuity, although they are, it seems, clearly secondary to "individuals and the decisions they make." This point is the one that requires tweaking. McFaul's assertion that structural factors, cultural influences, and historical institutional arrangements "have causal significance only if translated into human action" may be true, but keep in mind that no translation is meaningful or even possible without an original source. This requirement suggests, quite clearly, that focusing primarily, still less solely, on the "translators" (i.e., individuals making decisions and actions) will allow one to see only the surface of a much deeper process. To be fair, McFaul may not have completely thought through his metaphor, but it is a particularly apt way to conceptualize the issue. That is, when one examines the process of political change and continuity, one needs to understand that individual decisions and actions cannot be analyzed separately from structural, cultural, and institutional variables: these are the "original sources"—the essential foundation—of any agent-driven "translation." This idea is also a basic starting point for explaining political change and continuity in East Asia from a constructed actor perspective. Put simply, the explanation must begin by contextualizing the decisions and actions of individual actors.

The Essential Context of Individual Decisions and Actions

As has been discussed, actors are socially constituted. Their decisions are central to the political process, but every decision is conditioned. Why do people struggle for democracy in the first place? Why do the political elite of today worry about legitimacy defined in terms of the public good? It has not always been this way. Indeed, for most of human history, it has not been this way at all. In the Tokugawa period, the ruling elite had little regard for the people. As Jansen (2000) points out, "official documents left little doubt of the purpose with which the authorities viewed the peasants; they should be squeezed like seeds, one statement had it, in order to extract as much as possible from them. Another held that farmers should be worked so that they would neither live (to consume) nor die (and stop producing). Major edicts, especially those of the seventeenth century, bear this out" (p. 114). While the actual life of peasants and villagers was far more complicated than these official documents portray (a point Jansen emphasizes), the social facts (e.g., value systems, social structures, prevailing ideas) of that time fairly clearly did not merely "influence actors' preferences and power" but shaped them in a deep and profound manner. No one advocated, for example, for social justice, popular sovereignty, women's rights, and so on, in feudal Japan. One might even say, with only slight exaggeration, that such ideas were beyond the ken of Japanese, elite and peasant alike.

As the "social facts" began to change, however, so did the thinking and actions of the Japanese. Taisho democracy, in an important sense, was a product of the new social facts. Consider, on this point, that the Meiji era brought far-reaching changes to Japanese society—and not just structural changes. I have already discussed the change in the status of various groups (or classes) in Meiji Japan, particularly the samurai and merchants, but also worth noting is that modernization brought formal education to almost all of Japan: in fact, by the end of the Meiji era, four years of compulsory education was virtually universal throughout the country. In addition, a network of girls' schools began to sprout up (Jansen 2000). Women also began to join the formal workforce in increasing numbers. At the same time, liberal ideas were flooding into the country for the first time—a reflection, in part, of Meiji Japan's initial embrace of all things modern. In this context, Japan's first women's movement emerged in the years around World War I, even before similar movements arose in other capitalist countries (Jansen 2000). On this point, one does not stretch to say that the social facts of Meiji Japan essentially created the preference for equal rights among some Japanese women; their decision, in other words, was conditioned by a new sociopolitical and economic environment. This first women's movement, I should add, did not succeed. Its failure suggests that the decisions and actions by some Japanese women were not only conditioned but also highly constrained. Wanting a change and achieving that change are two very different things. Of course, when one speaks of subordinate groups, groups with little power, this point seems to be a banal one, but one should also keep this point in mind when speaking of "the rulers": What enables the ruling elite to get what they want? What enables them to keep what they want? And the big question is, why do they give up something—such as authoritarian rule—they have had for a long time, and which has served their interests well? The answers, to repeat, require a careful look at the context of individual decisions and actions.

This set of questions leads directly to another key point: namely, the changes that took place during the Meiji and Taisho eras were part and parcel of a larger, structural process. I have already discussed the major elements of this process, so I will not repeat myself here. Suffice it to say that these changes have to be incorporated into any explanation of political change or continuity. However, I am not saying that structural variables determine outcomes—a common and mostly undeserved criticism of structural arguments. Instead, I am saying (as I noted above) that they condition outcomes (i.e., they make democratization more or less likely, but sometimes very unlikely). They allow for large-scale, organized collective action, or they make sustained mass mobilization extremely difficult to achieve. Peasants in Tokugawa Japan, from a structural view, had little to no chance to overturn the political system because they lacked organizational power. As I discussed above, for this reason, Japan saw 300 years of rigid hierarchical rule during the Tokugawa era. The rigidity of the Tokugawa era does not mean that changes were not taking place. Indeed, a careful analysis will reveal the Tokugawa social structure was not "frozen." Still, the changes were slow because the structures of Japan's feudalism did not allow for dramatic and sudden social transformation. Even after several decades of industrialization under Meiji rule, the organizational power of the underclasses was largely absent (but clearly coalescing): the new structures of capitalism allowed for much faster changes. In a similar vein, structural conditions, both at the domestic and transnational levels, worked against South Korean and Taiwanese opponents of dictatorship in the 1960s and 1970s. I have not said much about transnational structural forces, but these often play a central role in domestic political processes. The integration of South Korea and Taiwan into the capitalist world-system as manufacturing-based, export-oriented peripheral economies at the height of the Cold War, in particular, had a dramatic impact on both the balance of class power within those two countries and, even more so, the balance of state-society relations.

Structural variables, in short, cannot be ignored. They are a critical part of any sociopolitical context. They indicate how power is distributed in society; they determine the balance of power between and among different social groups or classes. Their necessity is the primary problem with consigning structure to secondary status. But McFaul is right: human agency is required to "activate" or to transform structural forces into democracy or dictatorship or some other political arrangement. One reason is clear: social power is often latent, as is particularly the case for subordinate groups. Thus, without individuals to tap into the organizational power that exists, the potential for political change may never be realized. Equally, social power can also be produced by nonstructural sources, including culture. For this reason, individuals and groups can sometimes rise above structural conditions, or, because of the inherently **mutually constitutive** relationship between structure and agency, individuals as agents can reshape structures in subtle but important ways. The latent power of individuals returns the discussion to a focus on the microlevel. The "trick" here, however, is to keep firmly in mind this one oft-repeated point: individuals are socially constituted actors. In thinking about political change and continuity, and in thinking about democracy more specifically, an additional "trick" is to focus on the crucial importance of the idea of democracy itself in shaping the identities of citizens and rulers alike.

The Importance of Identity in the Constructed Actor Model

A little earlier, I posed two questions: Why do people struggle for democracy in the first place? And why do the political elite of today worry about legitimacy defined in terms of the public good? I alluded to an answer but did not directly provide one. The answer or answers, though, go to the heart of the constructed actor model and its explanation of political change and continuity. As one should recall, the constructed actor model is vitally concerned with the characteristics and motivations of the actors themselves—as opposed to simply identifying who the key actors are (e.g., the ruling elite, subordinate social classes, or mass publics). Getting to know the actors requires not only looking carefully at the broader forces that have shaped or influenced the preferences of actors but also identifying the principal elements of actors' identities and how these identities govern their decisions and actions. To put this issue more concretely, one can say that mass publics struggle for democracy, in part, because the idea of democracy has become a deeply rooted aspect of people's belief systems. Of course, the embeddedness of the idea of democracy is highly variable within and among societies and across time, and people oftentimes have very different conceptions of democracy. Still, adequately explaining why, for instance, South Korean students were willing to risk their lives and futures in a fight against a repressive and violent dictatorship would be difficult without reference to their identification with and commitment to democracy. Consider, on this point, that as rational, self-interested actors, they would have been better off waiting for others to take action, or, to use a term in rational choice theory, they should have attempted to **free ride** off the efforts of others. Granted, plenty of "free riders" could be found in South Korea (and in Taiwan and Japan), but an explanation still must be made for those who undertook the difficult task of "translation."

On the other side, from a historical perspective, elite identities in East Asia also changed dramatically. Of course, a great deal of diversity continued to be found among the elite in how they defined or identified themselves and their roles in society. Still, beginning in the late nineteenth and early twentieth century, a strong shift was made toward a Westernized, liberal identity and all that goes with it: nationalism, rationalism, industrialism, individualism, popular sovereignty, and so forth. This shift, however, was far from total, nor was it made without an intense struggle, something that is particularly evident during transitional periods, such as the Meiji and Taisho eras in Japan. During periods of immense and rapid change, identities are often in flux: as "modern" (or Western) ideas, values, and beliefs stream into society, they necessarily clash with traditional ideas, values, and beliefs. The result, in Japan, was a hybrid identity that endeavored to reconcile the "traditional" with the "modern." As Jansen (2000) explains it, "Meiji culture . . . had its contradictions: on the one hand there was the urgency of a program of modernization that took the West as its model, and on the other was the commitment to adapt Japan's oldest myths to modern uses to bolster the authority of the emperor—and, of course, those who stood at his elbow" (p. 493). For some Japanese elite, the embrace of a modern identity seemed much stronger. One former aristocrat, Hara Takashi, "showed little doubt about his commitment to representative government and in particular the House of Representatives"; he not only voluntarily gave up his classification as a "former samurai," but also turned down offers of peerage (Jansen 2000, p. 503). For Hara and others, their newfound identity made the achievement of constitutional party government a must. Consider, too, the identity and mindset of men such as Chiang Kai-shek, Chiang Ching-kuo, Park Chung Hee, Roh Tae-woo, and other authoritarian political leaders in East Asia. One can argue that all were driven by something much more than personal ambition and simple self-interest. In the cases of Chiang Kai-shek and Park Chung Hee, a virulent anticommunism permeated their views of the world. At the same time, both were highly nationalistic, making for a powerful combination. For Park, these motivations were his justification for the military coup and the formation of a "revolutionary government," justifications he detailed in his books *Our Nation's*

Path (1962a) and *The Country, the Revolution and I* (1962b). As the Meiji leaders did, Park drew on a discourse of traditional patterns and the imperatives of modernization to legitimize the military's intervention and takeover of the government. Although one can very easily dismiss such writings as self-serving propaganda—one can find similar writings by many dictators, including Kim Il-sung in North Korea—one does not have a hard time imagining that Park's decisions and actions were intimately and unshakably connected to his identity as a nationalist, a soldier, and a new type of modernizing leader whose solemn duty was to lead the entire country to freedom, prosperity, and peace.

Conclusion

Interests, power, and ideas. As I stated at the outset of this section, these are common elements—albeit often only implicit—of most micro-, meso-, and macrolevel analyses of political change and continuity. Most frequently, the three factors are hierarchically organized in a causal sense; they are also analytically separated, but in manner that sometimes delinks them from each other. This need not be the case. The first step, to repeat, is to contextualize individual decisions and actions. Historical institutional arrangements and "big" structural processes are the main parts of this contextualization. Through these arrangements and processes, one can answer questions about the distribution and balance of power within societies. In the dynamics of these arrangements and processes, one can find the potential for political change in the form of democratic transition, or the likelihood of political continuity, typically in the form of authoritarian political rule. Understanding the context allows one to assess the significance or efficacy of the decisions and actions that individuals make. Individuals and groups—whether the ruling elite, the opposition elite, subordinate classes, military officers, capital, or mass publics—certainly pursue their own interests and attempt to "get what they want," but explaining why some succeed and some fail depends largely on the context of their decisions and actions. Power and interests cannot be separated.

Interests, too, cannot be separated from ideas and identity. Actors may be "self-interested," but self-interest is not always self-evident. To put the issue more concretely, explaining the decisions and actions of Park Chung Hee, Chiang Kai-shek, or the many political leaders in Japan requires knowledge of the broader cultural-ideational values, beliefs, and attitudes they embraced. In other words, they are all constructed actors. The same applies to elite opponents and, perhaps even more so, to the thousands or hundreds of thousands of ordinary citizens who were willing to put their lives and bodies on the line to achieve political change. This last point also suggests a strong relationship between identity and social power. As discussed previously, structural processes can provide the basis for subordinate groups to exercise power through self-organization and collective mobilization, yet, in an increasingly interconnected world, in techno-logical terms, organizational capacity is no longer primarily a function of heavy urbanization and the concentration of an industrial workforce. Instead, it can be achieved through an identity premised on shared goals, beliefs, and ideas.

The key to the constructed actor model, then, is to focus on the inextricable interconnectedness of "interests, power, and ideas," and how these shape, con-dition, enable, and constrain decisions and actions. In practice, bringing inter-ests, power, and ideas together in a coherent manner is much easier said than done. But it is a task well worth doing if one wants to develop strong analyses of political change and continuity in East Asia.

Notes

1. The 1993 election, however, was not the first lower house election in which the LDP lost its majority. On three other occasions (1976, 1979, and 1983), the LDP lost its majority, but in each of these cases, the margin was slim. More important, in each of these losses the LDP was able to co-opt independent conservative politicians or a minor party in order to form a governing coalition (Jain 1993).

2. Scholars disagree on the specific dates of Taisho democracy, but three basic pe-riods are used: (1) 1918–1932, (2) 1905–1925, and (3) 1913–1925. For further discussion on the debate over when to date Taisho democracy, see Takayoshi (1966, especially pp. 614–615).

3. This statement can be found in a speech made by King in May 1963, delivered at St. Luke's Baptist Church in Birmingham, Alabama, and entitled, "Keep on Moving." Excerpts from the speech are available from the *Morning Edition* program on the NPR (National Public Radio) website. Here is the first main passage from the address: "Never in the history of this nation have so many people been arrested, for the cause of freedom and human dignity. You know there are approximately 2500 people in jail right now. Now let me say this. The thing that we are challenged to do is to keep this movement moving. *There is power in unity and there is power in numbers.* As long us we keep moving like we are moving, the power structure of Birmingham will have to give in" (National Public Radio 2002; emphasis added).

4. Despite occupying the lowest rung in the feudal hierarchy, during the Tokugawa period, the social position and power of the merchant class (especially those who would later become the *zaibatsu*) began to shift. That is, members of the merchant class were able to transcend their "lower class" status. This shift, however, can also be attributed to structural changes in Japan; in many respects, the Tokugawa era can be seen as a tran-sitional period between feudalism and capitalism—a type of protoindustrialism or proto-capitalism (Howell 1992). As such, the status and position of the merchant class were bound to improve.

5. During the Tokugawa period, one should note, the samurai were largely con-verted from warriors to bureaucrats. In this sense, the samurai continued to occupy a privileged position in Japanese society following the collapse of the Tokugawa system; however, their privilege was no longer based on a strictly hereditary criterion but instead was based on their functional utility within a new type of economic and social system.

6. SaKong (1993), for example, argues that both domestic and international factors contributed to relatively high borrowing. Domestically, the government encouraged for-eign borrowing by providing loan guarantees; South Korean firms especially responded

to this encouragement when the country's inflation rates and nominal interest rates were much higher than the respective rates of their main trading partners, which was true throughout the 1980s and 1970s. Oil price "shocks" also spurred foreign borrowing because of the rapid and sudden rise of an essential commodity, oil. Oil prices spiked twice, first in 1972 and again in 1979. The government's emphasis on the rapid development of a heavy chemical and industrial sector also necessitated foreign borrowing.

7. To be fair, Geddes (1999) argues that authoritarian regimes often morph from one type to another, or take on a hybrid characteristic. In this view, although Park's regime had a clear military-authoritarian character in the early years, by the end of the 1960s, the regime had taken on a strong "personalist" element. (A personalist regime is one in which "access to office and the fruits of office depends . . . on the discretion of an individual leader" [p. 121].) In fact, Geddes argues that coups often lead to personalist regimes. As she puts it, "it is common for military interventions to lead to short periods of military rule followed by the consolidation of power by a single military officer and the political marginalization of much of the rest of the officer corps. These are personalist dictatorships, even though the leader wears a uniform" (p. 124).

6 Democracy After Transition: Consolidating Political Change

In Chapter 5, I discussed the process by which Japan, South Korea, and Taiwan made their transitions from nondemocratic or **authoritarian** regimes to democracy. Transitions to democracy, I should reemphasize, are not necessarily permanent, nor do they guarantee the development of "strong democracy." As Charles Tilly (2007) makes clear, democratization is generally a nonlinear, highly volatile, and eminently reversible process, one that frequently oscillates between democracy and nondemocracy or between "weak" and "strong" democracy. To illustrate this tendency, Tilly points to the European period between 1900 and 1949. During this period, he notes, "17 regimes underwent at least one period of accelerated democratization . . . [but of] those 17, 12—Austria, Finland, France, Germany, Greece, Hungary, Italy, Portugal, Romania, Russia, Spain, and (if we count the Nazi occupation) the Netherlands—also underwent even more rapid *de-democratization* at least once" (p. 44; emphasis added). Similar patterns of democratization and de-democratization have occurred with regularity in every region of the world, from Africa to Latin America. As I mentioned earlier, too, in the previous chapter, both Japan and South Korea experienced de-democratization or democratic reversals—reversals that lasted for several decades. Readily apparent, then, is that the initial transition to democracy is not the end of the story. More to the point, the oscillation between democratization and de-democratization suggests that explaining transitions to democracy is not enough. Instead, one also needs to explain why democracy becomes embedded—or consolidated—within a political system and society. To be sure, explanations of transitions and consolidations are bound to overlap, but significant differences are likely to be revealed. The broad goal in this chapter is to explore what these differences might be.

This chapter was written with the help of J. James Kim (California State University, Pomona).

231

The three East Asian democracies raise a number of interesting and important questions. What prevented consolidation from taking place in Japan in the 1920s and in South Korea in the late 1940s? Or, to put the issue in slightly different terms, what were the key differences between these two earlier periods and the subsequent periods of democratic survival? Why did Taiwan avoid the same sort of democratic reversal in that country's first experience with democracy in the 1990s? At the same time, one should not take for granted that the survival of democracy necessarily entails a deepening and strengthening of democratic principles and practices in the three East Asian countries, or anywhere else. Indeed, basic comparative checking suggests that a relationship cannot necessarily be found between democratic survival (or continuity) and democratic quality. These are, as I discuss in the next section, two distinct concepts. In this chapter, the primary focus is on the former concept, although I do not ignore the issue of democratic quality. That is, I must also ask the following question: To what extent has the quality of democracy improved in Japan, South Korea, and Taiwan? I address each of these questions to varying degrees throughout this chapter. To begin, I need to spend some time discussing and clarifying the focal point of this chapter, namely, the concept of democratic consolidation.

What Is Democratic Consolidation?

Recall that democratic transition can loosely be defined as a process by which a political system moves from one based on a severe limitation (even a complete absence) of political rights and liberties, on a lack of free and fair elections, on **single-party** or one-man rule, and on restricted suffrage, to one in which all these elements are significantly weakened or eliminated. Logically, the process of democratic consolidation can begin only once a transition has already been achieved. Democratic consolidation requires, minimally, the holding of free and contested elections on a repeated or regular basis, but elections alone are never sufficient, since a newly elected government may possibly either lack effective power or authority to govern the country (e.g., unelected leaders, say, in the military, often hold ultimate political power) or may use its success in the election as a pretext for subverting other core democratic principles—as happened after South Korea's **Park Chung Hee** was elected in a "fair and contested" election in 1963 (or **Syngman Rhee** before him). Thus, consolidation also requires that freely elected officials abide by the constitution or act within the rule of law more generally, refrain from violating the political rights of individuals and groups, and allow the courts and legislature to fulfill their legitimate functions.

Meeting these requirements, however, is not particularly meaningful if freely elected officials reserve the "right" to violate them whenever their interests are threatened. Again, one can point to the experience of South Korea, where both Park and Rhee were willing—at least to some degree—to abide by democratic principles and norms as long as these principles served their respective interests. But when their hold on political power was threatened, they both moved quickly to implement changes designed to guarantee their continued rule. Thus, Juan Linz and Alfred Stepan (2010) add another important element to the definition of democratic consolidation:

> In most cases after a democratic transition is completed, there are still many tasks that need to be accomplished, conditions that must be established, and attitudes that must be cultivated before democracy can be regarded as consolidated. What, then, are the characteristics of a consolidated democracy? Many scholars, in advancing definitions of consolidated democracy, enumerate all the regime characteristics that would improve the overall quality of democracy. We favor, instead, a narrower definition of democratic consolidation, but one that nonetheless combines behavioral, attitudinal, and constitutional dimensions. Essentially, by "consolidated democracy" we mean a political regime in which democracy as a complex system of **institutions**, rules, and patterned incentives and disincentives has become, in a phrase, "the only game in town." (p. 4)

The specific behavioral, attitudinal, and constitutional dimensions, as Linz and Stepan explain, are as follows: Behaviorally, consolidation is achieved when significant domestic actors stop attempting to undermine the regime by creating a nondemocratic alternative. Attitudinally, democratic consolidation is reflected in strong public support of democratic procedures and institutions even in the midst of major economic problems or deep dissatisfaction with incumbents. Constitutionally, a regime is consolidated when every domestic group, including the government itself, willingly and habitually submits to the rule of law. This characterization of consolidated democracy intentionally leaves open the possibility of different types of consolidated democracies and of the quality of these various types varying considerably. This definition, therefore, has the advantage of avoiding the perhaps irreconcilable debates over exactly what a consolidated democracy should or must look like or what specific characteristics it must have, at least beyond the basic elements discussed earlier.

Beyond finding an appropriate definition, a great deal of disagreement remains over the notion of consolidated democracy at all. Guillermo O'Donnell (2010) is a particularly harsh critic. As he puts it, there is "little analytical gain in attaching the term 'consolidated' to something that will probably though not certainly endure—'democracy' and 'consolidation' are terms too polysemic [i.e., having multiple possible meanings] to make a good pair" (p. 26). This extremely contentious debate is further complicated by a plethora of competing definitions, which has resulted in conceptual confusion and disorder. This confusion and disorder are, in turn, "acting as a powerful barrier to scholarly communication, theory building, and the accumulation of knowledge" (Schedler 2010, p. 60). Unfortunately, one cannot just throw up his or her hands and give up. As I noted at the outset, the transition from an authoritarian system to a democratic one is rarely, if ever, the end of the story. Minimally, scholars and other observers—including the people who live in "new democracies"—want to know how and why democracy endures, even if they have difficulty agreeing on much else.

With respect to the last point, Andreas Schedler (2010) offers a tantalizingly simple alternative. He argues that scholars and observers should restore the classical meaning of democratic consolidation, which is based on "securing achieved levels of democratic rule against authoritarian regression" (p. 70). More specifically, the definition of consolidation should be restricted to two negative notions: avoiding democratic breakdown and avoiding democratic erosion (the latter term refers to a gradual or incremental process whereby basic democratic procedures and principles devolve into a "fuzzy semidemocracy" [p. 64]). This definition portrays consolidation as an expectation of regime continuity and, as Schedler bluntly and succinctly notes, "nothing else." This barebones definition raises a number of questions, but Schedler himself asks and answers the most obvious: "Why should one restrict the use of 'democratic consolidation' in this particular way and not another?" (p. 71). The answer, according to Schedler, is simple: "The main reason is that all other usages of democratic consolidation . . . are problematic and can be replaced by superior alternative concepts" (p. 71). On this point, Schedler is particularly wary of definitions that associate consolidation with improvements in the quality of democracy or with democratic deepening. Both these concepts, he suggests, open the door to any and all "kinds of goals and criteria that one deems to be indispensable for a high-quality and thus 'consolidated democracy' (which becomes just another vague label for 'real' democracy)" (p. 72).

While Schedler's basic definition of democratic consolidation is not by any means universally embraced,[1] his "back to the basics" definition is probably sufficient for current purposes. I should note, too, that it dovetails with the idea of democracy as the only game in town. However, one more problem remains: how to **operationalize** the concept of democratic consolidation. That is, how can one measure the expectation of regime continuity? In a second study, Schedler (2001) tackles this question and argues that the most reliable measurement of consolidation is based on behavioral evidence: What matters is what actors do. In this regard, "playing by the rules" is key. More specifically, following the rules means rejecting violence as a means to achieving political power; accepting and abiding by electoral procedures; and adhering to the rule of law, the constitution, and norms of acceptable political conduct. With all this in mind, I can now turn to a discussion of democratic consolidation in East Asia, specifically in Japan, South Korea, and Taiwan.

Democratic Consolidation in East Asia: An Overview

In Chapter 5, I provided a very brief overview of major political developments in Japan, South Korea, and Taiwan, including, in all three cases, a peaceful transfer of power between ruling and opposition parties through the electoral process. Peaceful transfers of power are, to repeat, a useful indicator of democratic consolidation, since they demonstrate a willingness on the part of electoral losers to observe (or play by) the rules of the game even when adherence to the rules means a loss of political power, at least temporarily. In all three countries, however, a peaceful transfer of power did not materialize immediately, especially in Japan. Once the Liberal and Democratic parties merged into the **LDP** in 1955, the newly formed LDP stayed in political power (that is, held on to an outright electoral majority, or a majority through a governing coalition, in the **Diet**, Japan's parliament) until 1993. So how did the LDP achieve such electoral dominance? There are a number of explanations—one of the most common of which centers on the notion of **clientelism** (for an example of this type of argument, see Scheiner 2005). This issue is an important one, but also one that is beyond the scope of this chapter. Suffice it to say, then, that the ability of a single party to dominate the electoral process for such a long period raises questions about the nature of Japanese democracy.

Indeed, given the long-lived and uninterrupted tenure of the LDP, unsurprisingly, many scholars and other observers have had no problem in suggesting that democracy in Japan was incomplete, not a "real" or fully consolidated democracy, during the period of uninterrupted LDP rule. Recall, for example, Samuel Huntington's (1991) notion of East Asian democracy as a type of dominant-party system. Others have referred to post-1955 Japanese democracy as a "one-and-a-half party system," which suggests some sort of deficiency compared to a more "proper" two-party or multiparty system. Still others have put the issue in much blunter terms. In particular, Chalmers Johnson (1995), a well-known expert on Japan, used the phrase "soft authoritarianism" to describe the postwar Japanese political system. The criticisms of Japanese democracy are not without merit. Yet to suggest that Japan was still in a transitory or non-consolidated stage until 1993 (or 2009) is unreasonable. For all its imperfections and faults, both real and imagined, Japanese democracy was clearly never in danger of breakdown or regression back to authoritarianism at any time during the entire postwar period. In this regard, just imagining that an LDP loss in the 1950s or 1960s could have threatened to overturn the democratic framework in Japan is hard.

From a different perspective, some scholars assert that Japanese democracy during the period of LDP dominance simply reflected a different way of doing things. Bradley Richardson (1997), for example, suggests that Japan had a version of democracy that differed from the accepted Western norm—in other words, the British model of democracy in which parties compete on the basis of platforms, and electorates choose the party that best represents their interests. Moreover, where the British version of democracy centralizes decisionmaking in the parliament itself, in Japan, the democratic process has been far more decentralized, such that "interests and policy choices are bargained over at many decision points in a political system, rather than being negotiated solely through the mechanism of alternating, responsible parties" (p. 9). At the same time, Richardson contends that elements of both models are present in most modern democracies, so Japan is unusual only insofar as its political system is tilted much further to the decentralized, "bargaining" side. Here remembering the point by Linz and Stepan (2010) is useful: consolidation does not require a specific type or quality of democracy. What matters is that everyone accepts the rules of the democratic game. On this point, one can clearly see evidence of consolidation. During the period of one-party dominance and after its electoral defeat in 1993, the LDP and opposition parties played by the rules: violence and intimidation were essentially absent from the electoral process, electoral procedures and outcomes were always accepted, and the rule of law was followed. However, one should note that corruption and political scandals were a constant and even endemic problem. (See Figure 6.1 for an overview of three major political scandals in Japan.)

In South Korea and Taiwan, the consolidation process was more conventional. South Korea's first opposition leader, Kim Dae-jung, was elected a decade after the 1987 transition to democracy; since then South Korea has witnessed a smooth alternation of political power between ruling and opposition parties—after Kim, another opposition candidate, Roh Moo-hyun was elected president, and after Roh, the traditional ruling party candidate, Lee Myung-bak, won. Most recently, another conservative candidate, Park Geun-hye, was elected president in 2012. (Figure 6.2 lists South Korea's presidents since 1987.) No hints can be found of extraconstitutional activity (especially of the type experienced under Rhee and Park), and political, military, and civilian actors have clearly come to accept and respect the electoral process. One can fairly say that South Korea has achieved democratic consolidation, even if the quality of democracy in the country leaves much to be desired.

On this last point, recall that I introduced one critic in Chapter 5, Choi Jang Jip (2005), who argues that democracy in South Korea is a mere façade decorating a "conservative monopoly" on political power. Choi's criticism of South Korean democracy is not the only one. Another prominent Korean scholar, Byung-Kook Kim (1998), for example, echoed a widely held sentiment: despite the fact that the electoral system in South Korea has become secure, a key facet of that system—party politics—has become increasingly incoherent and unstable. "Since 1987," Kim writes, "Korean political parties have encountered profound difficulty in developing political discourse that can aggregate diverse societal demands and interests into coherent programs with clear priorities and

---

Figure 6.1 Three Major Political Scandals in Japan

Lockheed Scandal (1976). One of the first major corruption scandals in Japan was the Lockheed bribery scandal, which involved an ongoing series of bribes and illicit contributions—totaling $12.3 million in "agent fees"—made by officials representing Lockheed Corporation (now Lockheed Martin). This scandal led to the resignation of Prime Minister Tanaka Kakuei, who was arrested in 1976 for taking bribes in return for helping Lockheed sell L-1011 TriStar jets to All Nippon Airways. Altogether, sixteen Japanese politicians, including Tanaka, were indicted. Tanaka was convicted in a lower court but died in 1993 while he was appealing his case to the Japanese Supreme Court.

Recruit Scandal (1989). In this scandal, government and LDP officials—including Prime Minister Takeshita Noboru, former prime minister Nakasone Yasuhiro, and Chief Cabinet Secretary Fujinami Takao—were accused of accepting preflotation shares of Recruit Cosmos Corporation, a real estate subsidiary of the Recruit group. When the shares were listed on the Tokyo stock market, their value skyrocketed, and the recipients of the preflotation shares made tremendous profits. After the scandal became public, Takeshita resigned, and one of his top aides committed suicide.

Sagawa Kyubin Scandal (1992). As a leading transport company in Tokyo, Sagawa Kyubin was intent on expanding its service network across Japan, but to do so, it needed a special license. At the time, however, the Ministry of Transport had suspended all new license applications in advance of deregulation of the industry. To get by this barrier, Sagawa's management approached leading LDP politicians with offers of large donations and lavish dinners. Between 1988 and 1991, the company distributed at least ¥2.5 billion in "donations" (and perhaps much more, up to ¥70 billion) to 200 Diet members and local politicians; the largest sum was paid to the vice president of the LDP, Kanemaru Shin (he received about ¥500 million). However, the lack of a clear connection between the payments and specific policy decisions led to all cases against the Diet members being dropped without charges (details in Blechinger 2000).

---

consistent internal logic, and in the process transform naked power politics into struggles over ideas, values, and public policies. In fact, they have acted in a diametrically opposite way" (p. 117). Even more, Kim continues, the South Korean people's understanding of democracy is as shallow as the party system is chaotic. Despite these and other harsh indictments of the quality of democracy in South Korea, few see any danger of democratic regression or collapse.

In Taiwan, the situation was very similar. Writing in 1998, while Taiwan was still in the midst of its transition to democracy, Chu Yun-han (a leading political scientist from Taiwan) argued that the country faced a series of difficult challenges before its democracy could be considered consolidated. These challenges

Figure 6.2 South Korean Presidents Since 1987

Name	Year Elected	Term	Party Orientation[a]	Popular Vote (%)
Roh Tae-woo	1987	1988–1992	Conservative	36.6
Kim Young-sam	1992	1993–1998	Conservative	42.0
Kim Dae-jung	1997	1998–2003	Liberal/progressive	40.3
Roh Moo-hyun	2002	2003–2008[b]	Liberal/progressive	48.9
Lee Myung-bak	2007	2008–2013	Conservative	48.7
Park Geun-hye	2012	2013–2017	Conservative	51.6

Notes: Since 1987, South Korean presidents have been limited to one five-year term.
 a. In this table, the label *conservative* refers to those parties most closely associated with the ruling party during the authoritarian period from 1961 to 1987. *Liberal/progressive* refers to political parties most closely associated with the opposition during the same period.
 b. President Roh was impeached early in his term, and for a short period (between March 2004 and May 2004), Prime Minister Goh Kun served as acting president.

included establishing consensus among the three major parties (the **KMT**, the Democratic Progressive Party, and the New Party) "over the nature and logic of the emerging constitutional order" (Chu 1998, p. 138), which was designed to move Taiwan away from a **parliamentary system** and toward a semipresidential one (I discuss this transition in more detail below). A second major challenge was the removal of authoritarian elements from the political terrain. Opposition parties were concerned with the potentially deleterious influence of the military and national security apparatus in the political process. In this regard, a particularly important issue was the still close connection between the KMT and the military: throughout the authoritarian period, the KMT had party cells embedded in the military, and active duty generals had always been members of the KMT's Central Standing Committee (Chu 1998). Until and unless the linkage between the KMT and the military was broken, the ability of Taiwan to move from transition to consolidation would remain doubtful, according to Chu.

The first major test for Taiwan came in March 2000, when the opposition Democratic Progress Party candidate, Chen Shui-bian, won Taiwan's second direct presidential election, albeit with only 39.3 percent of the popular vote. Chen's victory, I should note, was the product of a split in the conservative bloc, which came about when James Soong, a very popular former provincial governor, was passed over by the KMT leadership; he decided to run as an independent. Soong received 37 percent of the vote, while the KMT candidate Lien Chan won 23 percent. Chen's electoral win—which ended fifty-five years of uninterrupted KMT rule—proved that the military would not immediately intervene on behalf of the KMT in the case of an electoral defeat. The military's restraint did not mean, however, that his rule would be smooth. In fact, six months after Chen became president, the KMT tried to impeach him, and "in the ensuing months, the political processes were gridlocked" (Copper 2003, p. 328). Yet even the attempt to impeach Chen reflected an acceptance by the KMT to work within the rules dictated by the constitution. Indeed, when the party leaders failed in their efforts, no attempt was made to remove Chen through extra-constitutional means (i.e., a military **coup d'état**). Moreover, despite his early difficulties, Chen won reelection in 2004, this time getting 50.1 percent of the vote, while the KMT candidate received 49.9 percent. (See Figure 6.3 for a list of Taiwan's presidents since 1996.) Although extremely unhappy with the results, the KMT again accepted the decision of the electorate, and Chen went on to serve his second term. However, one potentially disruptive incident did occur: the day before the election, Chen survived an assassination attempt. To this day, the facts surrounding the assassination attempt remain unclear. While Chen blamed the KMT, the KMT charged that Chen himself staged the shooting to boost his electoral chances. In any case, the incident did not seriously interrupt the democratic process in Taiwan. Thus, one can reasonably conclude that Taiwan, too, has become a consolidated democracy.

Studying Democratic Consolidation in East Asia

In studying or explaining democratic consolidation, considering both negative and positive cases is useful. Negative cases are those in which an initial transition to democracy is reversed. Positive cases are those in which democracy becomes "the only game in town." Based on these criteria, Japan, South Korea, and Taiwan present us with six total, useful cases for examination: the three cases of nonconsolidation or democratic reversal that were first discussed in Chapter 5 (Japan in the 1920s, and South Korea in the 1950s under Syngman Rhee and in the 1960s under Park Chung Hee), and the three cases of successful consolidation (postwar Japan, South Korea after 1987, and Taiwan in the latter part of the 1990s). A renewed discussion of negative cases, I readily admit, runs the risk of repetitiveness. But the context of the discussion of these cases is different, as are the key points I make. I am also careful, in this chapter, to avoid covering the same empirical ground. This said, I am now going to confront the same basic set of theoretical questions as in the last chapter: What are the key factors that explain successful democratic consolidation? Are these factors rooted in individual-level interests and rational behavior? Or do they primarily reflect institutional, cultural, or structural forces and processes?

I begin the competing-perspectives analysis from a different starting point than in Chapter 5. Instead of a microlevel, elite-centered approach, I examine democratic consolidation from a rational institutionalist perspective, a perspective that focuses primarily on institutional design and is premised on the assertion

Figure 6.3 Taiwan's Presidents Since 1996

Name	Year Elected	Term	Party Orientation[a]	Popular Vote (%)
Lee Teng-hui	1996	1996–2000	Conservative (KMT)	54.0
Chen Shui-bian	2000	2000–2004	Liberal (Democratic Progressive Party)	39.3
Chen Shui-bian	2004	2004–2008	Liberal (Democratic Progressive Party)	50.1
Ma Ying-jeou	2008	2008–2012	Conservative (KMT)	58.5
Ma Ying-jeou	2012	2012–2016	Conservative (KMT)	51.6

Note: Since 1996, in Taiwan, presidents serve a four-year term and may be reelected once.

that specific types of institutional arrangements play a direct role in determining the outcome of democratic continuity.

Institutions as the Building Blocks of Democracies in East Asia

Institutions are a useful place to begin a discussion on democracy and democratic consolidation since they are, in many respects, the defining feature of any political system. As I pointed out in Chapter 1, institutions are traditionally equated with concrete public and private organizations or agencies, such as the legislature, the presidency, the **state** as a whole, or a corporation. This traditional view refers to formal institutions. As I demonstrate, this formal definition is particularly relevant in a discussion of democracy, but it is nonetheless important to understand that this is a constricted definition. More broadly, institutions are "systems of established and embedded social rules that structure social interactions," where rules are understood as "socially transmitted and customary normative injunctions" (Hodgson 2006, pp. 17–18). According to this broader definition, institutions, both formal and informal, play a key role in shaping actors' interests and decisions: rules and norms of behavior, in other words, provide incentives for compliance and disincentives for noncompliance. In this regard, institutions lend a certain level of predictability to the outcomes of interactions between and among actors, a major reason why I use the phrase "rational institutionalism" to describe this approach.

More specifically, some scholars argue that certain institutional designs or frameworks, as well as the degree to which specific institutional arrangements are embedded in a political system and society, have an important effect on the sustainability of democracy. In particular, scholars have argued that causally significant differences exist between the two most salient types of institutional arrangements in democracies: the presidential and the parliamentary. While not exactly self-explanatory, the two terms are easy enough to understand. A presidential system is one in which significant political and constitutional power is vested in a chief executive, the president. In this system, the power of the president is separate from, but not necessarily superior to, the legislature; presidential systems typically are characterized by the separation of powers among different branches: the executive, the legislative, and the judicial. In addition, in a presidential system, presidents are elected by popular vote. The United States is often pointed to as a quintessential presidential system.

A parliamentary system, by contrast, is one in which the powers of the executive and legislative branches are not only interconnected but also hierarchical, with parliament occupying the top position. That is, in a parliamentary system, the executive branch is accountable to the legislature (or parliament). Parliamentary systems may have popularly elected presidents, but executive authority resides primarily with the prime minister—who, in turn, is selected by the majority party in the parliament. Britain provides a good example of a parliamentary system. The more important question is how and why the different institutional arrangements influence the consolidation process. The answer is fairly simple. One of the leading proponents of the institutionalist approach, Juan Linz (1990), explains, "Perhaps the best way to summarize the basic differences between presidential and parliamentary systems is to say that while parliamentarism imparts flexibility to the political process, presidentialism makes it rather rigid" (p. 55).

Both institutional forms of democratic governance have their advantages and disadvantages, but for newly formed democracies, presidentialism is particularly "perilous" (the title of one of Linz's most well-known articles on the subject is "The Perils of Presidentialism" [1990]). One of the key reasons for this, according to Linz (1990), is its winner-take-all format, "an arrangement that tends to make democratic politics a **zero-sum** game, with all the potential for conflict such games portend" (p. 56). This zero-sum mentality contrasts sharply with a parliamentary system, where "losers" (i.e., political parties that lose a majority of seats in the national legislature) are still "in the game" and almost always have a realistic chance of returning to the majority. Moreover, even incumbents who lose their particular seats can return to a nonelected position within their party and continue to exercise political power; opportunities can also be found to join the ruling party or create a new party. The arrangements of a parliamentary system, in short, create rational incentives for both losers and winners to continue to play by the rules.

In the presidential system, as I have already suggested, the rules create a very different set of incentives. In addition to the winner-take-all format, fixed presidential terms create a definite end point for individual rule; sitting presidents who are determined to stay in power, therefore, will often attempt to revise the electoral rules by whatever means possible, including subverting and even "shredding" the constitution. If institutional or other obstacles to doing so are limited—a not uncommon situation in new democracies that give disproportionate power to the chief executive—one can easily see why presidential systems frequently collapse. That new presidential systems are easily manipulated does not mean that newly formed parliamentary systems do not break down, too. They certainly do. Still, as Minxin Pei (1998) notes, the "breakdown of democracy tended to be more complete and the subsequent authoritarian regime more dictatorial in presidential systems [compared to parliamentary systems]" (p. 63).

Presidentialism, Parliamentarianism, and Democratic Reversals in East Asia

How well does the institutional argument explain patterns of democratic consolidation and de-democratization in East Asia? If one considers the three negative cases, the institutional argument appears to have some support. In 1948 and 1963, a very strong executive branch characterized the political systems under both Rhee and Park. A slightly closer examination of the two regimes also reveals that the dynamics of de-democratization largely reflected the predictions of the rational institutional perspective. As explored in Chapter 5, when Rhee was faced with a loss of political support in the National Assembly, he attempted to postpone the elections and only relented after strong pressure from the United States; as he expected, his party lost in a landslide. The **Korean War**, however, allowed Rhee to reassert control over the assembly; he then used this control to manipulate the constitution to ensure he could remain in office. Under Park, one can see a similar process, although Park was wary of democratic principles and procedures from the very beginning. Thus, he allowed for a restricted democracy, which meant holding "fair and competitive" elections on a regular basis, but he was clearly not willing to cede political power through the ballot box. When electoral support began to shift to the regime's opponents, therefore, he moved quickly and forcefully to suspend the constitution and replace it with his own—the **Yushin Constitution**. In sum, South Korea's first experiences with democracy, both of which resulted in unequivocal reversals, seem to reflect quite clearly the "perils of presidentialism."

In **Taisho**-era Japan, however, the situation is less clear. Taisho democracy, to begin, was not based on presidentialism but was instead a parliamentary system. (Although under the **Meiji** Constitution, the parliament was not the supreme authority in the Japanese political system; instead, the constitution rested on the principle of imperial sovereignty. In practice, though, the relationship between the parliament and the emperor was not strictly hierarchical.) Moreover, the parliamentary system was dominated by the elite. As Robert Scalapino (1968) describes it, "The participating citizen still came from the upper socioeconomic brackets. Even with the widening of the suffrage, more-over, at least initially, the government could count upon the common core of values and political principles implanted via universal education and nationalist indoctrination cutting across class lines" (p. 263).

In addition, Japan's first parliamentary system had, by 1915, evolved into a relatively stable two-party system, one in which the two dominant parties were not only roughly balanced in terms of elite representation but also shared the same basic philosophy with regard to political and economic policies. Equally important, perhaps, in Taisho-era Japan, no "strong-man monolithic political organization" dominated the political system (Scalapino 1968, p. 272). One can fairly say, then, that Taisho democracy had most of the institutional elements needed for consolidation, yet consolidation did not happen. I could cite a plethora of reasons (as I did in Chapter 5) for the failure of democracy in the Taisho period, but I should also reemphasize that the institutional argument makes no claims that parliamentary systems cannot fail, especially in the face of a serious crisis. Still, the failure of Taisho democracy suggests that institutional arrangements alone provide an insufficient basis for explaining the political dynamics of de-democratization.

Democratic Consolidation in East Asia: Positive Cases

Taken together, the three negative cases of democratic consolidation are inconclusive, but they do not necessarily contradict the institutional argument. To complete the analysis, one needs to take a careful look at the three positive cases. In so doing, however, one is immediately presented with a problem of classification: while Japan's postwar democracy is clearly based on a parliamentary system, the South Korean and Taiwanese political regimes in the 1990s had elements of both parliamentary and presidential systems. More specifically, both South Korea and Taiwan have dual executives—a president and a prime minister (or premier). The distribution of power between these two executives positions, however, has been different in the two countries. In the case of Taiwan, the premier (or president of the Executive **Yuan**) is the head of government, while the president is the head of state. The distinction is important, as the head of government exercises executive power (or supreme administrative authority), while the head of state is commander in chief of the armed forces and has authority over foreign affairs. The premier and the Executive Yuan can also serve as an important check against the president in that the latter must obtain the support of the premier and other cabinet members to promulgate laws or issue mandates. Moreover, while the president nominates and appoints the premier, his appointments originally required the approval of the Legislative Yuan. After his election in 1988, for example, President Lee Teng-hui was compelled to appoint premiers who had initially opposed his ascension to power. Only after his reelection in 1996—the first by popular vote—could President

Lee appoint a premier of his own choosing (the power of the Legislative Yuan to approve the president's choice of premier was removed during this period). Since then, and especially after 2000, the institutional power of the president has increased. Nonetheless, the premier is not a mere figurehead.

Unlike Taiwan, the South Korean Constitution has always guaranteed greater authority for the president. Aside from the power to ratify treaties and declare war, the president can, among other things, proclaim martial law, appoint and remove public officers, issue presidential decrees, and issue national referendums on matters related to diplomacy, national defense, and unification. The sitting president is also immune from prosecution for criminal offenses except in the case of insurrection and treason. I should also point out that the South Korean president, because he is elected for single term, is not necessarily beholden to the electorate after being inaugurated into office, while the first-term president in Taiwan is. Accountability partly derives from the demands of reelection in the case of sitting presidents. In theory, reelection places greater restriction on what the sitting president is willing to risk in his first term as opposed to a president who knows that his or her days are numbered. With respect to the relationship between the prime minister and the president, the South Korean Constitution is clear that the prime minister's duty is restricted to simply "assisting" the president (Article 86). Also somewhat different from the Taiwanese system, the South Korean Constitution only allows the National Assembly "to recommend" to the president the removal of the prime minister (Article 63). In other words, unlike in Taiwan, the legislature has little power to act unilaterally on matters dealing with the removal of the prime minister.

The hybrid institutional arrangements in Taiwan and South Korea can be described in a number of ways, but the simplest term, and one that has been around for more than three decades, is simply *semipresidentialism*. The original definition, developed by Maurice Duverger (1980), defined semipresidentialism as a political regime with three core elements: (1) a president elected by universal suffrage, (2) a president with "quite considerable powers" or constitutional authority, and (3) "a prime minister and ministers who possess executive and governmental power and can stay in office only if the parliament does not show its opposition to them" (p. 166). Based on these three criteria, South Korea does not easily fit into the semipresidential category (Shugart 2005); however, subsequent and more expansive definitions have classified South Korea as semipresidential. For example, Robert Elgie (2007) defines semipresidentialism as a "regime where there is both a popularly elected fixed-term president and a prime minister and cabinet responsible to the legislature" (p. 60). Under this definition, South Korea fits the category, as does Taiwan.

This discussion raises an obvious question: Is semipresidentialism more likely to lead to democratic consolidation, or is it more likely to lead to a breakdown? The answer is fairly simple: in semipresidential systems with very strong presidents and weak prime ministers (à la South Korea), democratic breakdown is more likely. In semipresidential systems with weak or ceremonial presidents and strong prime ministers, democratic consolidation is more likely. As has been demonstrated, though, both South Korea and Taiwan have successfully consolidated. For South Korea, Elgie (2010) suggests that the country's successful consolidation, while unexpected, nonetheless reflected serious tensions inherent in highly presidentialized systems. "In particular," he notes, "the attempts of successive South Korean presidents to assert their powers have sometimes brought them into sharp conflict with the legislature, especially when that body was controlled by the opposition" (p. 297).

One illustrative example of these "serious tensions" can be found in the impeachment proceedings against Roh Moo-hyun, a former human rights lawyer, without a college degree, and political activist who succeeded Kim Dae-jung as president in 2003. The problem began when Roh and his supporters left Kim's Millennium Democratic Party to form the Uri Party. The split with the Millennium Democratic Party reflected a generational rift between the old guard (followers of Kim) and a younger generation of legislators, who identified more closely with Roh (Y. Lee 2005). The upshot was that Roh could not count on the members of his previous party for legislative support. Not surprisingly, once Roh left the Millennium Democratic Party, his erstwhile party, the Uri Party, not only turned against him but also formed an anti-Roh alliance with the Grand National Party; importantly, this set of events gave anti-Roh forces a supermajority in the National Assembly (Y. Lee 2005). A series of other problems—from illegal campaign contributions to a declining economy—further weakened Roh's power. To address the situation, Roh understood that his new party would need to do well in the upcoming elections for the National Assembly, which is where he ran into difficulties: by voicing support for the Uri Party, he technically violated a constitutional provision mandating presidential impartiality. His opposition used this technicality as a pretext to impeach Roh, and with a supermajority in the assembly, the motion for impeachment was successful; thus, Roh was temporarily removed from office. Ultimately, the Constitutional Court ruled that the impeachment motion was invalid, and Roh resumed his duties—which also came with stronger popular and legislative support as the Uri Party gained a majority of assembly seats after the legislative elections.

In Taiwan, a similar tension emerged during Chen Shui-bian's term as president (coincidentally Chen was also a self-educated human rights lawyer turned politician). Chen, as I noted above, encountered serious opposition, including an unsuccessful impeachment, during his presidency. Chen's problems continued even after his party won an impressive victory in the 2001 elections. This victory, which made the Democratic Progress Party the largest party, still did not give Chen and his party a majority in the Legislative Yuan. As a result, his relationship with the KMT remained confrontational and largely unproductive. Interestingly, when Chen first took office, the institutional basis of Taiwan's political system was in flux—it had presidential, parliamentary, and cabinet components, among which the relationships were still not clearly and solidly defined (Copper 2003). Thus Chen was largely responsible for forging Taiwan's semipresidential system. Outside of the government, too, the potential for serious conflict existed. In particular, Chen's relationship with the military was also strained. Just a few weeks into his presidency, in fact, a number of high-ranking officers refused to pledge their fealty to the Chen government and resigned; Chen's advisers returned the favor by accusing the military, security, and intelligence agencies of being manned by traitors (Copper 2003). Despite these problems, the military "stayed in the barracks," so to speak, and did not directly interfere in the political process.

The key point is as follows: while the semipresidential systems in South Korea and Taiwan created the basis for serious tension and political conflict, the essential rules of the democratic game never seemed to be fundamentally threatened. The democratic system, in other words, worked as it was supposed to by confining conflict within prescribed constitutional limits—limits that were no doubt tested but never broken. To be sure, these arrangements made the task of opposition-cum-ruling parties' achieving their desired policy objectives difficult, but their challenges are largely irrelevant to the question of democratic consolidation. These cases do, however, illustrate how inefficient and ineffective democracy can sometimes be. Part of the reason that the administrations of Kim Dae-jung, Roh Moo-hyun, and Chen Shui-bian were less than successful in implementing their visions can be attributed to the strengthening of the checks and balances within their respective democratic systems.

Parliamentarism in Postwar Japan

However one slices the institutional argument, the argument itself clearly does a poor job of explaining democratic consolidation in South Korea and Taiwan specifically—even if it does a seemingly much better job of predicting democratic outcomes at a more general level. This failing suggests, then, that one needs to look elsewhere for an explanation of democratic consolidation in two of the three East Asian democracies. But what about the third case, Japan? Here a much better match seems to exist between prediction and reality. Unlike South Korea or Taiwan, Japan has operated under a Westminster parliamentary system since the end of World War II. In this system, the parliament or the Diet, as it is referred to in Japan, is the "highest organ of state power" (Article 41 of the Japanese constitution) and the "sole lawmaking organ of the State" (National Diet Library 1947). The importance of the Diet marks a fundamental distinction between the pre- and postwar periods: under the Meiji Constitution, the emperor was designated the "head of the Empire," combining in himself the rights of sovereignty, and all laws were issued in the "name of the Emperor" (Constitution of the Empire of Japan 1889). The postwar "demotion" of the emperor, of course, reflected US demands that Japan's postwar constitution be grounded in liberal principles of popular sovereignty. Moreover, according to Ray Moore and Donald Robinson (2002), the US framers of Japan's new constitution— after the end of the war, the United States occupied Japan from 1945 to 1952— carried with them a strong conviction that "constitution making was a matter of distinguishing the functions of government, ensuring that basic institutions had the means and incentive to check one another, and then balancing them properly, securely harnessing those that had gotten out of control in the past, fortifying those that tended to be weak in the Japanese environment, and grounding it all in accountability to the electorate" (pp. 98–99). The framers took one more important step: to limit executive power, presidential veto power was not included in the constitution, and the Diet was consciously strengthened so that it would have "decisive and ultimate power over all legislation" (p. 99). US influence on these issues was important, for quite likely, if left to their own devices, Japanese leaders would not have made the Diet the "highest organ of state power" (Baerwald 1987, p. 137).

The focus on ensuring legislative power in the Diet was, in many respects, quite prescient, as the US framers seemed to anticipate scholarly arguments about the significance of constitutional and institutional design. That is, they were clearly operating on the premise that specific and sound constitutional arrangements could help prevent the rise of another military-fascist or otherwise nondemocratic regime in Japan. Whether they were right about this danger is the key question. To wit, did the US-designed institutional framework for postwar Japanese democracy play a central role—*the* central role—in the process of democratic consolidation? Determining the answer is, unfortunately, impossible. As has been discussed, the evidence provided by two other positive cases (i.e., South Korea and Taiwan) and the three negative cases (Taisho Japan and South Korea under Rhee and then again under Park) is, at best, inconsistent. At worst, it strongly contradicts the institutional argument by showing that no relationship, causal or otherwise, can be found between institutional design and democratic consolidation or failure. In addition, too many potentially significant differences between the Taisho era and the postwar period leave observers unable to make any sound methodological judgment. Put another way, one cannot apply the principles of a MSS comparison between the two periods because one cannot control for all the potentially relevant **independent variables**.

Political Attitudes and Political Culture: Microfoundations of Democratic Consolidation

So where does this leave us? The East Asian cases do not, by themselves, prove the institutional argument wrong, but they do unequivocally show that the institutional argument cannot, by itself, adequately explain the processes of democratic consolidation and reversal in Japan, South Korea, and Taiwan. Again, this lack of direct evidence does not mean that institutional factors are unimportant. This is almost certainly not the case. But it does means that one needs to look elsewhere for the missing pieces. One alternative can be found in approaches that focus on individual attitudes or beliefs and political culture. A number of scholars, in particular, argue that political beliefs and values—microlevel factors that are arguably shaped by mesolevel processes—serve an essential role in embedding institutions and institutional practices into a political system such that they become the only game in town (see, for example, Fukuyama 1995 and Shin and Wells 2005). The theoretical premise in this view, as expressed by Doh Chull Shin and Jason Wells (2005), is that "democratic consolidation is absent until a majority of the citizenry embraces democracy as the only legitimate form of government. Citizens must accept the structure of the new system, support the practices of the newly constructed democratic institutions, *and* reject the old authoritarian systems and its practices" (p. 90; emphasis in original). This argument, not surprisingly, reflects the same principles I discussed in Chapter 5 regarding the importance of legitimacy. In this case, though, the question is not only one of regime legitimacy (that is, the legitimacy of a specific government in power) but is instead one about the legitimacy of one type of political system over another.

Some proponents of this view, including Shin and Wells (2005), I should emphasize, define consolidation in terms of or equivalent to a strong societal preference for democracy over its alternatives. To put it more simply, they argue that until a majority of citizens embrace democracy as the only acceptable type of government, consolidation, by definition, cannot have taken place. This definition differs considerably from the one I laid out in the beginning of the chapter. I do not argue that my definition is better, but consider the following: The focus of the discussion is why democracy survives over the long term. One reason might be the strong societal preference for democracy. Thus, if the citizenry believe firmly in the values of democracy, and if these beliefs are one of the reasons a democracy survives, then they are a cause—and not an effect—of democratic consolidation.[2] The mechanism here is easy enough to see: a population that is committed to democratic norms and values is more likely, for instance, to defend against any efforts to reverse democratic achievements. Finding direct evidence to support this argument is, unfortunately, difficult. But some studies provide indirect support. A study by Satoru Mikami (2008), for example, found that an increase in the proportion of people who prioritize respect for plurality and political freedom as opposed to the maintenance of order and substantive economic achievement enhances the likelihood of democratic regime survival (cited in Mikami and Inoguchi 2010).

Another way to assess the significance of attitudes and political culture is through an analysis that focuses on political attitudes and public opinion. In this regard, surveys, which provide descriptive statistics, are particularly useful, albeit limited, methodological tools. They can provide an important glimpse into the political attitudes, opinions, and beliefs held by specific populations, although I must add that they cannot reveal everything one needs to know. Fortunately, since the early 2000s, a cross-national survey project—the East Asia Barometer Survey—has been conducting face-to-face interviews with randomly selected citizens in several East Asian countries, including Japan, South Korea, Taiwan, Mongolia, Thailand, the Philippines, and China.[3] So what do the survey data indicate? On one level, the data suggest strong popular support for democracy. In a direct question asking respondents to indicate the type of regime they found most desirable, 97 percent of Japanese, 95 percent of South Koreans, and 87 percent of Taiwanese indicated that democracy was the most "desirable" regime type. The large majority also agreed that democracy was "suitable" (89, 86, and 70 percent, respectively) for their respective countries. Interestingly, on the question of preference, the figures went down significantly in South Korea and Taiwan; thus, while 79 percent of Japanese still considered democracy "preferable" to other regime types, only 49 percent of South Koreans and 45 percent of Taiwanese felt the same (see Figure 6.4 for a summary of results). To repeat, in these two East Asian democracies, less than a majority of respondents expressed unconditional support for democracy over authoritarianism. The result from these two questions indicates that the level of citizenship attachment to democracy is very strong as an abstract or ideal concept, but weaker when considered as a practical system of governance.

Examining just two questions can be deceiving. And, although I do not have the space to conduct a comprehensive analysis of the East Asia Barometer Survey results, I can draw from others who have already taken up the task. Shin and Wells (2005), for example, conducted a thorough review of the data and concluded, "While respondents in all six countries [Japan, South Korea, Taiwan, the Philippines, Thailand, and Mongolia] prefer democracy to other regime

Figure 6.4 East Asia Barometer Survey Results: Attachment to Democratic Regime (percentage)

Country	Desirable[a]	Suitable[a]	Preferable[b]	None[c]	Full[d]
Japan	97	89	79	1	73
South Korea	95	86	49	2	43
Taiwan	87	70	45	9	37

Sources: Table reproduced from Shin and Wells (2005, p. 91). Original source is the 2002–2003 East Asia Barometer Surveys.
Notes: a. Percent answering 6 to 10 on a 10-point scale.
b. Percent answering that democracy is always preferable to dictatorship.
c. Percent scoring 0 on the 4-point index of democratic regime support.
d. Percent scoring 3 on the 4-point index of democratic regime support.

types, the magnitude of these net preferences varies considerably" (p. 94). Indeed, of the six countries, only Japan and Thailand showed a strong net preference for democracy, and South Korea and Taiwan showed positive but weaker support, while Mongolia and the Philippines demonstrated the weakest support overall. More significantly, perhaps, is Shin and Wells's analysis of support for democracy at a practical or procedural level. To gauge attitudes about democratic procedures, the survey asked for responses (i.e., whether participants agreed or disagreed) to the following statements:

- "The most important thing for a political leader is to accomplish his goals even if he has to ignore the established procedures."
- "If a political leader really believes in his position, he should refuse to compromise regardless of how many people disagree."
- "As long as a political leader enjoys majority support, he should implement his own agenda and disregard the views of the minority."
- "When the country is facing a difficult situation, it is okay for the government to disregard the law in order to deal with the situation."
- "When judges decide important cases, they should accept the view of the executive branch."
- "The government should decide whether certain ideas should be allowed to be discussed in society."

Each of these and other statements was designed to highlight certain democratic norms. Again, Shin and Wells subjected these questions to an analysis that produced a "net preference score"; according to their analysis, in Japan, South Korea, and Taiwan, democratic processes and procedures were generally favored over authoritarian ones by a two-to-one margin. In Mongolia, Thailand, and the Philippines, by contrast, more respondents favored authoritarian practices. (See Figure 6.5 for a summary of results.)

The results suggest that individual attitudes and an evolving democratic political culture have contributed to democratic consolidation in Japan, South Korea, and Taiwan. From a comparative perspective, too, the results lend support to political attitudes and culture as important factors. Consider Thailand. In 1997, Thailand went through a transition to democracy with the promulgation of the "People's Constitution." Among the important features of this constitution were the creation of a bicameral legislature with elections for both houses, recognition and acknowledgment of many civil rights, and the establishment of the Constitutional Court, the Administrative Court, and the Ombudsman. (I might note that the constitution created a parliamentary system.) Thailand seemed on its way to stable, albeit imperfect, democracy. Yet five years after the establishment of the People's Constitution, a majority of Thai citizens were—as suggested above—still extremely skeptical of democratic norms and procedures. Given this skepticism, one should not be surprised that a military

Figure 6.5 East Asia Barometer Survey Results: Types of Preferences Regarding Democracy (various countries, percentage of total responses within each country)

Favors Democracy?		Countries					
Regime	Process	Japan	S. Korea	Taiwan	Mongolia	Philippines	Thailand
1 No	No	4	6	7	18	16	9
2 No	Yes	3	3	10	3	9	1
3 Yes	No	25	28	23	57	36	51
4 Yes	Yes	68	62	61	22	39	38

Sources: Table reproduced from Shin and Wells (2005, p. 98). Original source is the 2002–2003 East Asia Barometer Surveys.

Note: The "regime column" indicates a preference (yes or no) for democracy as a type of political system; the "process column" indicates a preference (yes or no) for democratic norms and procedures and democratic decisionmaking processes. Column totals do not equal 100 percent because of rounding.

coup in 2006 did not spark huge popular protests against the military. Indeed, as one scholar put it, the coup "was well received by the majority of people in Thailand, without any of the mass protests that accompanied the 1991 coup" (Thongswasdi 2008, p. 164). The result of the coup was the suspension of democracy and return to military authoritarianism—at least for a short period. In 2008, an elected civilian government led by the People's Power Party replaced the military administration, but the military maintained significant influence and continued to restrict civil liberties and political rights (in 2012, Freedom House still gave Thailand a "Freedom Rating" of 4.0, which translates into "partly free" status).

If one continues to analyze the results from the East Asia Barometer Survey comparatively, however, one can also find contradictory evidence in the experiences of the Philippines. The Philippines has been an electoral democracy for almost twenty-five years, albeit with one brief "hiccup": in 2001, four days of mass protests, known as EDSA II,[4] peacefully overthrew President Joseph Estrada. Military authoritarian rule was not, however, reimposed; instead, Estrada was immediately succeeded by his vice president, Gloria Macapagal-Arroyo. In terms of continuity and a transfer of power between ruling and opposition parties, then, the Philippines arguably meets the limited definition of democratic consolidation. Yet, in 2002, less than a majority of Filipino citizens (39 percent) embraced democracy both as a regime and process according to Shin and Wells (2005). One can find fairly clear reasons for Filipinos' reluctance to champion democracy. As Mely Caballero-Anthony (2007) explains, democracy in the Philippines has been plagued by corruption and weak political institutions.

Political parties, in particular, have often been described as "patronage-infested" and tend to serve as "elite clubs," that is, as vehicles for political and economic elites to perpetuate their power (pp. 5–6). Given these problems, many if not nearly all observers have classified the Philippines as a "deficient" or "reduced" democracy (Dressel 2011, p. 541).

The poor quality of Philippine democracy is certainly an important issue and one that should not be dismissed. On this point, though, one might usefully consider the perspective offered by James Putzel (1999), who argues that, while democracy in the Philippines is undoubtedly shallow, "the country is far better off now than it was under authoritarian rule. . . . Competitive elections, even when dominated by the elite power brokers, offer a degree of accountability and focus incumbents' attention toward the impact of their policy decisions on society and the economy more than would be the case in the absence of competition" (p. 217). More importantly, for current purposes, the Philippine experience with democracy suggests that democratic continuity does not depend on political attitudes and political culture alone; again, as has been made evident throughout this book, other factors are at play.

Democracy After Transition:
Structural Determinants of Democratic Consolidation

One place to look for these other factors is in structural conditions. Indeed, if structural variables truly play a role in democratic transitions, then structural variables would also inevitably have an impact on democracy after a transition. Unfortunately, few structural analyses have been done of democratic consolidation per se; instead, structuralists tend to focus much more strongly on the issue of democratic quality. This lack of research complicates the discussion, since pains were taken to distinguish between consolidation and quality in the beginning of the chapter, and I do not wish to conflate the two terms now. At the same time, ignoring these structural arguments altogether would be unwise; after all, they still focus on democracy after transition and therefore can provide critical insights into the structural processes and factors that shape the path of democracy, including its sustainability, over time. Indeed, as I will present, inferring key elements of a structural account of democratic consolidation from arguments on democratic quality is not difficult. With this in mind, a useful place to start is with the writings of C. Wright Mills (1916–1962), a prominent US sociologist, perhaps most known for his book *The Power Elite,* first published in 1956. Although quite dated, Mills's ideas in *The Power Elite* (as well as his other works) continue to shape thinking about structural factors and democratic processes today.

As the title of his book suggests, Mills ([1965] 2000) argues that, in modern, industrial societies, decisionmaking power is increasingly concentrated into a "power elite." These individuals occupy leading positions in three major institutions: government, military, and corporations. These institutions are not only part and parcel of modern capitalist societies (Mills was primarily concerned with the United States) but have become increasingly centralized and even more important over time. The result is clear:

> In each of these institutional areas, the means of power at the disposal of decision makers have increased enormously; their central executive powers have been enhanced; within each of them modern administrative routines have been elaborated and tightened up. As each of these domains becomes enlarged and centralized, the consequences of its activities become greater, and its traffic with the others increases. The decisions of a handful of corporations bear upon military and political as well as upon economic developments around the world. (p. 7)

The basic relationship between the power elite and democratic quality is fairly easy to see: the dominant position of the power elite, which is premised on an integrated **social structure** created by industrialization and modernization, makes the full realization of democracy (Mills has his own six-part definition of democracy)[5] extremely difficult to achieve. Concentrated institutional and elite power, in short, make ordinary citizens having an effective voice in the decisionmaking process increasingly more difficult, albeit not impossible.

In this view, one could argue that the fear of democratic transition expressed by political, business, and military elites in still authoritarian regimes has generally been exaggerated and misplaced: a transition to democracy does not necessarily mean a loss or even serious interruption of elite power as long as the key institutions are not threatened and remain under their control. This conclusion provides the first insight into how structural factors influence consolidation or democratic continuity. Namely, in those countries in which the institutions of civilian bureaucratic, military, and corporate power remain firmly and deeply entrenched and continue to be dominated by the same basic set of elite leaders, power holders will have little need to struggle against formal or electoral democracy once a transition has taken place. A return to authoritarianism, to put it very simply, is unnecessary and potentially more disruptive than maintaining the new status quo. This is not to say that elite interests and power are unassailable under a democratic system, still less that democracy does not matter. As I indicated in the foregoing discussion of the Philippines' "shallow democracy," for example, even a clearly flawed democracy requires a degree of accountability that is largely missing in authoritarian systems. In addition, compared to authoritarianism, democracy provides much greater opportunity for subordinated groups to exercise political power in an institutionalized way, both in their own interests and against elite interests. Or, as Dietrich Rueschemeyer, Evelyne Huber Stephens, and John Stephens (1992) put it, even in its minimal form, democracy gives "the many a real voice in the formal collective decision-making of a country" and, more importantly, "is the most promising basis for further progress in the distribution of power and other forms of substantive equality" (p. 10). Further progress or improvements in the quality of democracy, however, are never guaranteed.

This conclusion leads to a second insight—or more accurately, a hypothesis—which is simply that the more secure and unified elite interests are in the period following a transition, the more likely that democracy will survive. A secure and unified elite interest, I should add, requires a strong structural foundation, one in which a high level of integration among the dominant institutional centers of power (government, military, and corporate) has been achieved. Integration is key because it leads to an important degree of reciprocity among the elite. The end result, as Mills describes it, is that

> there is no longer, on the one hand, an economy, and, on the other hand, a political order containing a military establishment unimportant to politics and to money-making. There is a political economy linked, in a thousand ways, with military institutions and decisions. . . . [T]here is an ever-increasing interlocking of economic, military, and political **structures**. . . . In the structural sense, this triangle of power is the source of the interlocking directorate that is most important for the historical structure of the present. (pp. 7–8)

Reversals of Democracy in East Asia: Structural Considerations

Consider the three cases of democratic reversals in East Asia, beginning with Japan. In the Taisho period, democratic principles gained considerable public appeal, and a parliamentary form of democracy was put into place, only to be summarily dismantled by the military in the 1930s. Structurally speaking, however, Japan was highly unbalanced in the first part of the twentieth century. Indeed, even the conditions for transition (i.e., a strong and unified working class, an increasingly large **middle class**, and relatively balanced state-society relations) were essentially missing. In addition, international factors, from the Great Depression of the 1930s to intense intercapitalist rivalry in the form of imperialism, strongly militated against the creation of democracy in late-industrializing countries such as Japan. Under these conditions, that Japan made any progress at all toward democracy in the early twentieth century is surprising. But what should be completely unsurprising is that the progress Japan did make was built on extremely shaky ground. In particular, the rise of militarism had few structural obstacles during this period. While corporate (i.e., *zaibatsu*) and military interests became increasingly interconnected and integrated during the Meiji and Taisho eras, militarists clearly occupied a dominant position.

Even more, military leaders at the time used the economic hardship brought on by the worldwide depression as an opportunity to attack business and political leaders for their selfishness, decadence, and corruption. This argument was easily accepted by a population that was, as Mikoso Hane (1986) puts it, on "the very brink of starvation" (p. 246). Equally clearly, even limited democracy represented a threat to the interests of military leaders, who were convinced that aggressive military expansion was the only way to ensure Japan's long-term security and national strength. In this regard, a clear and profound conflict grew between military and political leaders: in the late 1920s to early 1930s, the civilian government, led by the Minseito (Democratic Party), was strongly opposed to the military's aggressive policies and instead pursued diplomatic solutions. Since the military was largely autonomous from the government and could manipulate public opinion, little stood in its way. But the final blow to parliamentary democracy occurred on May 15, 1932, when military plotters carried out the assassination of the prime minister, Inukai Tsuyoshi.

In South Korea, the reversals of democracy were less dramatic, although the structural conditions were not that different from those in Taisho-era democracy. That is, in 1948, South Korea was still an agriculturally based economy (as late as 1963, 63 percent of the workforce was still engaged in agriculture, forestry, and fishing, and only 8 percent in manufacturing [Mason et al. 1980, p. 111]), the level of urbanization was still very low, and the society contained virtually no middle class. In addition, under Japanese colonial rule, the state was **overdeveloped** with a strong emphasis on developing coercive capacities. Needless to say, these conditions were not conducive to the survival of democracy, still less the development of strong democracy. Combined with a chaotic political environment, both internally and internationally, then, one can argue that there was virtually no hope for democratic consolidation under South Korea's First Republic. As has been discussed, this proved to be the case. In fact, almost before the ink had dried on South Korea's new constitution, Rhee successfully "quash[ed] the initial plan for a cabinet-responsible system and . . . substitute[d] for it a strong presidential system with the prime minister retained only as 'an assistant to the president'" (G. Henderson 1968, p. 158).

Rhee used his self-crafted presidential system to solidify his hold on power and to steer South Korean politics away from democracy and toward **autocracy**. Structurally, he found no obstacles in his way, as his reliance on other elite groups and institutions was limited. Given the poor structural foundation for democracy under Rhee, that his regime was brought down due to protests and replaced by Chang Myon, who served as premier in a reconfigured parliamentary system, is a testament to the will and power of South Korean citizens. The Second Republic, however, lasted a scant nine months, overthrown by a military faction that faced surprisingly little public resistance. I am not going to repeat the story of Park's initial rise to power, except to say that, during the first decade or so of Park's rule, the military dominated the political, economic, and social scene, and that the other institutional centers of power were only beginning to emerge.

The foregoing analysis is admittedly stylized and extremely broad. Yet little doubt can be left that the structural conditions for democratic consolidation were largely missing in Japan and South Korea during their initial experiences with democracy. Unfortunately, one cannot draw any hard-and-fast conclusions from an examination of the negative cases; the evidence is only suggestive. At the same time, unlike previous discussions of the rational institutional and attitudes/political culture approaches, the evidence is more consistent. In other words, no obviously contradictory cases have been presented thus far. With this in mind, let us see what our three positive cases can tell us.

Structural Foundations of Democratic Consolidation

The discussion here is also highly stylized and broad, in part because readers should already be familiar from past discussions with the structural changes that helped lay the groundwork for a successful democratic transition in all three East Asian countries. Shifts in the balance of class power and, especially in the case of Japan, state-society relations arguably marked the biggest changes between the periods of reversal and consolidation. In Japan, the post-1945 period saw a dramatic diminution of the military's institutional power. This shift was arguably more a reflection of contingent historical factors rather than structural factors, but it had the effect of creating a far more balanced relationship among the major institutional centers of power. Indeed, in the postwar period, the Japanese military quickly became a secondary player, while the LDP emerged as a major institutional center of power in its own right. LDP power was counterbalanced by a highly autonomous bureaucracy—which played a leading role in Japan's rapid economic recovery—and an equally formidable corporate sector.

Together, the LDP, the civilian bureaucracy, and large corporations constituted Japan's **Iron Triangle**, which I mentioned in Chapter 5. Japan's Iron Triangle, though, differed from Mills's conceptualization of the power elite; not only is the military missing from the equation, but also the movement of elites has tended to flow in a single direction, from the public sector (the bureaucracy and LDP) to the corporate sector. In fact, the Japanese have a special term for this movement: *amakudari*, typically translated as "descent from heaven" (see Figure 6.6 for additional discussion). *Amakudari*, as a number of scholars have argued, provides the key mechanism for building interinstitutional networks of cooperation (see, for example, Colignon and Usui 2001). The end result is a unified and firmly embedded elite whose interests are well protected by a system that provides strong insulation from popular demands (in the case of the bureaucracy and the corporate sector) and a proven ability to dominate the electoral process in the case of the LDP. Given this dominance, one should not be surprised at all that the postwar power elite in Japan felt little need to struggle against the US-imposed system of democracy.

In South Korea, the changes wrought by almost three decades of state-guided high-speed industrialization created a new social structure, one dominated by a powerful and pervasive bureaucracy, a massive military establishment, and

Figure 6.6 The Meaning of *Amakudari*

Most basically, *amakudari* refers to the process by which high-level bureaucrats "retire" to senior management positions in private enterprises. But the term has a deeper meaning as well. As Richard Colignon and Chikako Usui (2001) explain,

> [The] term implies a distinction between the life of the sacred and profane. Before World War II, civil servants worked directly for the emperor, who was considered a god and the embodiment of the Japanese nation. Bureaucrats were seen as in heaven by their noble and sacred work for the god and the nation. Upon retirement, bureaucrats were viewed as descending in status by their reemployment in the profane world of material self-interest. (p. 866)

Thus, the notion of "descending from heaven." The actual process of *amakudari* has become more complicated over time; a number of different paths and hierarchies are involved in these movements, which Colignon and Usui detail in their research. In addition, the two authors note that *amakudari* has been expanded to include former LDP members.

a handful of huge conglomerates, the ***chaebol*** who exercised near-unfettered control of the South Korean economy. The *chaebol,* I should note, were already powerful economic actors in the 1960s, but in the early years of Park's rule, they were viewed with deep suspicion by the government. As Jung-en Woo (1991) puts it, the leaders of the coup "were men of peasant origin and harbored, like ultranationalist Japanese officers in the 1930s, a peasants' suspicion of the wealthy. When they thought of capitalism, they thought of a conspiracy of the rich" (p. 81). At the same time, Park understood from a very early stage that he needed to rely on the *chaebol* to achieve his economic goals. These conflicting elements set the stage for a mutually beneficial but still unequal, dependent, and very tense relationship between these two institutional centers of power. By the mid-1980s, however, the *chaebol* had become too powerful for the state to effectively control.

As I noted above, during the era of authoritarian rule, the military also emerged as a center of institutional power—although, for most of these years, it was closely tied to the government. Nonetheless, as Aurel Croissant (2011) points out, the military could still develop an important degree of institutional separation, despite the fact that it staged a coup d'état in 1979–1980 (in addition to the 1961 coup). In both cases the military's interventions were "factional coups" (p. 19). That is, they were carried out by a small group of officers against the desires of their military superiors. After the democratic transition in 1987, the potential for and fear of additional military interventions certainly remained; however, efforts by President Kim Young-sam (1993–1998) helped to "depoliticize" the military and neutralize factionalism. By the time Kim Dae-jung was elected in 1998, the military had come to accept a more "normal" role in South Korean politics.

While the military's role in South Korean politics has changed, its position in the South Korean socioeconomic landscape has hardly weakened: the military remains firmly embedded. The military's entrenchment is partly reflected in the institution's deepening and increasingly interdependent relationship with South Korea's *chaebol*. Since the early 1970s, the government put heavy emphasis on developing an indigenous South Korean defense industry. This emphasis, of course, meant that the *chaebol* would play a key role in producing military goods—from uniforms to battleships. By 1990, about 70 percent of all military equipment and supplies were being produced by domestic companies, and by the late 1990s, South Korea moved toward becoming a major arms exporter (South Korean military exports rose from $147 million in 1998 to $1.03 billion in 2008 [Moon and Paek 2010]).

In sum, in the almost three decades between South Korea's democratic reversals and its successful transition to democracy, structural and institutional changes had produced an environment in which elite control has become more diverse and reciprocal and even more deeply entrenched. Whereas this change has obviated the need for elites to interrupt the democratic process, it has also meant—as critics argue—a "weak" form of democracy, one dominated by a "conservative monopoly" that fails to give voice to subordinated groups and that has exacerbated inequality (C. J. Choi 2005). Whether or not the quality of democracy can be meaningfully improved in South Korea remains to be seen. Critics are not optimistic, but neither are they fatalistic, for the forces that brought about political change (i.e., an end to authoritarianism) can also bring an end to the conservative monopoly.

Of the three countries, Taiwan was the only one not to experience a democratic reversal. Taiwan was also the last to make the transition from authoritarianism to democracy, so the fact that the country avoided "backsliding" is not particularly surprising. The delay in making the transition, in fact, was key to the relatively smooth process of democratic consolidation. As in Japan and South Korea, by the time Taiwan made its transition, the underlying structural conditions for consolidation were well established, and the highly managed nature of the transition also meant that elites in the **KMT**, the military, and the corporate sector were well prepared for the major challenges the transition to democracy would bring. In particular, unlike South Korea, by the time of the transition, Taiwan had already firmly established civilian control of the military—although, given the military's close connection with the KMT, the bigger problem was exactly how the military would react to an electoral loss by the KMT. As already demonstrated, this fear proved not to be a major issue: by 2000, the military's institutional position in Taiwan was secure enough that pro-KMT military leaders did not feel threatened by the election of Chen Shui-bian, despite a testy relationship from the very beginning. Significantly, however, Chen did not attempt to challenge the military as an institution. He endeavored, instead, to promote further professionalization of the military, while also increasing the number of native Taiwanese in the military leadership (Croissant 2011).

One other potentially disruptive factor in Taiwan—a factor not present in either Japan or South Korea—revolved around ethnic and national identity. While not a structural factor, ethnic cleavages often play a divisive role in the democratic process. For Taiwan, this point was particularly salient since the country's elite systems had long been dominated by mainland Chinese (or "mainlanders"). Democratization, therefore, had the potential of undermining the structurally embedded but not invulnerable position of mainlander elites in the political, economic, and military spheres. A sudden transition, therefore, likely would have sparked much more concern and resistance on the part of mainlander elites, but because the transition was managed, the KMT could pursue a gradual "Taiwanization" of the party, state, and military, a policy that accelerated under the leadership of Chiang Ching-kuo. The policy did not eliminate the internal cleavage between the native Taiwanese islanders and the Chinese mainlanders, but it helped to stabilize the political system, ensuring that the vested interests of the ruling elites would not be subject to a serious challenge in a democratic system. The policy, in many respects, was a resounding success. As Teh-fu Huang and Ching-hsin Yu (1999) put it,

> To many Taiwanese, the KMT has gradually become a legitimate ruling party through elections. Thanks to its policy of "Taiwanization," most of its members and cadres are now Taiwanese. It is no longer an "immigrant regime." Moreover, political reform and democratization have not only given the KMT the reputation of being a democratic party but also allowed it to reap the fruits of popular support resulting from democratization. Therefore, the KMT has been able to consolidate its support among Taiwanese. (p. 98)

Structural Determinants of Democratic Consolidation: Summing Up

Taken together, the six cases of democratic reversal and consolidation in East Asia seem to provide strong support for the argument that structural factors play a key role in democratic consolidation. From a methodological standpoint, however, one must continue to exercise caution. The comparison of positive cases, in particular, is loosely based on the method of agreement (discussed in Chapter 1); this method allows one to identify common factors between or among cases, but it can easily lead to faulty empirical generalizations. The inclusion of the negative cases gives one more confidence in the conclusions but still cannot establish a clear-cut, cause-and-effect relationship between the structural variables identified and democratic reversal/consolidation. In addition, the admittedly cursory historical analysis means that important factors might have been missed. I realize that all these qualifications may sound "too cautionary," but as mentioned throughout this book, the processes of economic and political change and continuity are extremely complex and contingent.

A Few Words on the Constructed Actor Model: A Comparative Perspective

In Chapter 5, I noted a good deal of overlap could be found among the competing perspectives on the issue of democratic transition, which in turn provided a strong basis for synthesis and integration. In this chapter, however, one sees much less overlap among the three competing models. Even more, as demonstrated earlier, two of the models—the rational institutional and behavioral (focusing on attitudes and political culture)—did not do a particularly good job of explaining democratic consolidation in East Asia specifically. However, rational institutional and attitudinal/cultural factors are still important. Indeed, the constructed actor model indicates that one cannot likely explain any complex social, political, or economic outcome adequately by focusing on only one set of factors. With this stipulation in mind, in applying the constructed actor model to an explanation of democratic consolidation in East Asia, one can follow the same general approach as for the issue of democratic transition. That is, one should begin with the assumption that interests, power, and ideas all play a significant role, and, as usual, constructed actors will be placed at the center of the analysis. Since this same basic process appeared in the previous chapter, the discussion here is brief and general. (I encourage readers to revisit the last section in Chapter 5.)

To begin, one should recall that structural factors do not determine but instead condition outcomes. Thus, the structural processes that made democratic transitions more likely in East Asia also made the achievement of democratic consolidation more likely. The structural analysis above bore this theory out, although it was limited to the three negative and three positive cases in East Asia. More broadly, other scholars have shown a strong positive correlation between development-related socioeconomic factors (**per capita GDP**, urbanization rate, level of industrialization, educational level, etc.) and the likelihood of democratic consolidation (Gasiorowski and Power 1998). This conclusion again suggests, very strongly, that structural factors are not to be ignored. Equally evident, though, is that structure cannot explain everything, something that is especially clear if one looks beyond East Asia. One particularly good example (and one I also alluded to in Chapter 5) is India, which made its "transition" to democracy in the 1940s, a time in which India had almost none of the structural prerequisites for either a successful transition to or a consolidation of democracy.

Economically, for example, India was (and still is) extremely poor with a very high rate of poverty. The level of urbanization was very low, and almost no industrial working class could be found to speak of. Even as late as 2001, almost three-quarters of India's population still lived in rural areas, and in 1991, the rural workforce still accounted for 249 million or 79 percent of the total workforce (Office of the Registrar General [India] 2002). The middle class, too, was very small in the 1950s. Yet, against all odds, from a structural standpoint at least, democracy has survived—for more than six decades now—in that country, which is not to say that many very serious concerns have not been raised about the quality of Indian democracy. Significantly, a number of scholars point to institutional and ideational factors as key to the success of Indian democracy. Institutionally, one can usefully note, a parliamentary system did not lay the groundwork for democratic consolidation; instead, India developed a unique version of **federalism**, which was designed to recognize and accommodate the varied linguistic communities in India as "legitimate political components" (Kohli 2001, p. 7).[6] Equally important, perhaps, was the early development of a well-functioning civil service and an elite-dominated but popular ruling party, the Indian National Congress. I do not have the space to examine these two institutions in detail; suffice it to say, however, that both contributed mightily to political stability following the end of British rule in India.

Still, the existence of strong institutions is not enough either: as has been shown before in the East Asian cases, all also had strong, well-functioning bureaucracies and, in the case of Taiwan especially, a dominant party before democratization. But democracy in East Asia took many decades to emerge as a viable political option. So one might conclude that here ideational factors likely played a key role in India: the leaders of the Indian National Congress were strong proponents of democratic principles and practices long before India became a democracy. Much of their devotion to this ideology had to do with the context of British colonial rule. Under British rule, an appeal to democratic principles was a useful, and perhaps the most practical, way to construct the basis for national unity among India's many disparate communities, and national unity was the most effective way to challenge the British. But the embrace of democratic principles was more than just a political strategy; it became an integral part of Indian political culture and national identity, both at the elite and popular levels. Obviously, deeper historical analysis is needed to clearly demonstrate this argument, but the basic point should be clear: cultural-ideational factors helped to determine the political and institutional choices of the Indian elite, which in turn helped make democratic consolidation possible under less-than-ideal circumstances.

From even this very cursory examination of India, one can see more easily the importance of "keeping our eyes open"—a caveat that applies to both the East Asian and Indian cases. For example, while structural factors seem unimportant in the Indian case (at least in terms of democratic continuity), one would be well advised not to dismiss structure completely. As I noted above, according to almost all analysts, the quality of Indian democracy has remained relatively low despite six-plus decades of opportunities for improvement. Additional analysis may show that structural conditions have likely contributed to the "low quality" of Indian democracy. For East Asia, one seems to encounter the opposite issue; that is, structural factors seem dominant. Yet, from the discussion in Chapter 5, clearly the infusion of democratic principles and values into the East Asian societies gradually and inexorably altered the political dynamics in each country: regime legitimacy increasingly became tied to democratization. Once the transition to democracy was made, moreover, the commitment to democracy by large swaths of the population (albeit, not necessarily the majority) made any backsliding a very dangerous proposition. To be sure, backsliding (i.e., de-democratization) was much more difficult in an environment of relative economic prosperity, but this fact demonstrates the interdependent relationship between structural and cultural-ideational factors.

The Indian case, too, encourages observers to keep their eyes open to different types of institutional arrangements. While the literature on democratic consolidation has focused very strongly on parliamentarianism versus presidentialism, in India, federalism seemed to be key. India's success with a ruling system aside from parliamentarianism raises questions about more specific institutional arrangements in East Asia, and whether these had an impact on the early reversals of democracy, on the one hand, or on the successful consolidations of democracy, on the other hand. Consider, on this point, the role of the KMT in Taiwan or aspects of the US-imposed institutional arrangement on Japan—an arrangement that dramatically reduced the institutional power of the military. In a less obvious way, the Indian case also highlights the importance of socially constructed individual actors. First, as has been shown above, India's political success shows how "unfavorable" structural conditions can, at least partly, be overcome through individual and collective human action. Second, it demonstrates the role that individual actors play in constructing specific types of institutions and institutional arrangements. Federalism, for instance, did not just magically emerge in postcolonial India but instead was the conscious creation of India's political elite.

In looking at East Asia, one can see a similar process, albeit with different results. In South Korea, as I noted above, Syngman Rhee used the chaotic postliberation environment to put an end to a proposed cabinet system and to replace it with a strong presidential one. How and why Rhee could almost single-handedly determine the institutional design for South Korea's first democracy had a great deal to do with his elevated status and legitimacy as the country's greatest "patriot," along with the lack of any other institutional safeguards. The situation was unusual, but almost all countries face some unique circumstances, which a good researcher must take into account through careful historical analysis. As political and institutional arrangements become more settled, however, the room for individuals to exercise such a high degree of personal power typically becomes much smaller. Today, one can fairly say, no South Korean (or Taiwanese or Japanese) leader could do the same as Rhee did in the 1950s. This conclusion reminds one that, while actors are socially constituted, timing is also very important: what was possible in one period may not be possible in a different period, a simple but often forgotten lesson.

In this section, I have been content to simply highlight a number of different issues and concerns that might be relevant to the application of a constructed actor model. I am, quite intentionally, leaving the heavy lifting to the reader. The "heaviest" part of the constructed actor model is integration and synthesis: bringing **agency**, structure, culture, and institutions (or interests, power, and ideas) into a coherent whole. This task requires one, most basically, to contextualize human action—a point that I have reiterated time and time again throughout this book. As I have tried to show in this section, too, good contextualization generally requires one to keep his or her eyes open. Concretely, this approach often means adopting an explicitly comparative perspective and purposefully looking for cases that force one to think more carefully about the conclusions. This approach may also require one to consider cases outside the normal purview. India is just such a case, but in this chapter, Thailand and the Philippines were also considered. As has been demonstrated, even very cursory comparisons can be extremely useful.

Conclusion

Democratic consolidation, as I emphasized in the beginning of the chapter, is never a sure thing. Throughout history, myriad countries that have made the transition from authoritarianism to democracy have found that sustaining democracy is sometimes as difficult as achieving democracy in the first place. In this regard, despite South Korea's democratic reversals, the successful consolidation of democracy in the region overall is no small feat. Taiwan's smooth transition to and consolidation of democracy is especially noteworthy since the country had no prior experience with democratic practices and procedures. Indeed, Taiwan's experience in particular gives one a lot to think about from a theoretical perspective. Clear indications exist that structural factors played a key role in the consolidation process, but what seems equally evident is the importance of the dominant institutional role of the KMT. Perhaps no less significant were cultural and ideational factors that seemed to shape the thinking of KMT elites and of the population more generally. The same combination of factors likely shaped the consolidation process in Japan and South Korea, but the on-the-ground details are undoubtedly quite different among the three cases. This is another simple lesson to keep in mind.

Notes

1. Schedler is not alone. Another set of scholars, Gasiorowski and Power (1998), define democratic consolidation as follows: "Democratic consolidation refers to the process by which a newly established democratic regime becomes sufficiently durable that democratic breakdown—a return to nondemocratic rule—is no longer likely" (p. 743).

2. Schedler (2001) argues along essentially the same lines. As he puts it, once scholars begin to measure democratic consolidation in terms of popular legitimacy, "popular legitimacy" becomes the **dependent variable**. This shift leads to a simple problem: democratic consolidation then becomes "dependent on whatever citizens demand (or we think they demand) to confer legitimacy to the democratic regime" (p. 75).

3. The East Asia Barometer Survey is part of the more extensive Asian Barometer Survey Project, which includes a larger number of countries. Thus, in addition to Japan, South Korea, Taiwan, China, Mongolia, Thailand, and the Philippines, the Asian Barometer covers Hong Kong, Vietnam, Cambodia, Singapore, Indonesia, India, Pakistan, Bangladesh, Sri Lanka, and Nepal. So far, two rounds of surveys have been held: 2001–2003 and 2005–2008 (for more information, see http://www.asianbarometer.org/).

4. EDSA stands for Epifanio de los Santos Avenue, which is a major arterial road and freeway in metropolitan Manila. The EDSA became connected to prodemocracy or "people power" movements in the Philippines because most of the demonstrations took place on a long stretch of the avenue.

5. This is how Mills defined democracy: "By democracy I mean a system of power in which those who are vitally affected by such decisions as are made—and as could be made but are not—have an effective voice in these decisions and defaults. The political structure of a modern democratic state, I suggest, requires at least these six conditions (1) a forum within which a politics of real issues is enacted; (2) nationally responsible parties; (3) a senior civil service firmly linked to the world of knowledge and sensibility; (4) an intelligentsia who carry on the big discourse of the Western world; (5) media of genuine communication; and (6) free associations linking families and smaller communities and publics on the one hand with the state, the military establishment, the corporation on the other" (1958, pp. 121–123).

6. For further discussion of the importance of federalism in Indian democracy, see Sarkar (2001) and Dasgupta (2001).

7

The Prospects for Political Change in China and North Korea

China and North Korea are two of only five countries in the world that still proclaim to be **communist**. The other three are Cuba, Laos, and Vietnam. China and North Korea also have the distinction of being the longest-lived communist regimes: in North Korea, the communist political system was established in 1948, while China followed a year later in 1949 (one should note, however, that the former Soviet Union lasted for a longer period of time, from 1922 to 1991). Yet, while the five remaining regimes all purport to be "communist," the reality has long been much more ambiguous. In particular, all five countries have adopted at least some market-based reforms, with China arguably having moved the farthest toward a free enterprise system, and North Korea having made the least "progress." To be clear, a fundamental contradiction exists between establishing a market-based system, on the one hand, and attempting to maintain communism, on the other hand. In fact, this contradiction existed even before the turn toward capitalism: in principle, communism is not only a classless but a stateless society. But all real-world "communist" regimes have revolved around an **authoritarian** and often totalitarian **state**. It might be better, then, to see China and North Korea—and the other similar regimes, both past and present—not as communist but as simply a specific type of authoritarian regime.

Although the label "communist" is misleading, China and North Korea have quite clearly developed very strong, very durable political systems (surviving, as they have, for more than six decades), both of which are built upon the same basic model. At the core of this model is a single, deeply entrenched political party, which is the center of power—political, economic, and social—within the country. In China, the **CCP** dominates, while in North Korea it is the **Korean Workers' Party**. Institutionally, the parties are organized along much the same lines, with a pyramidal structure that not only funnels political power to the top but also is designed to put the party's eyes and ears in every important area of the state, economy, and society. On this last point, one needs to recall that, in China and North Korea, the party and the state are two sides of the same coin. That is, while the two can be seen as distinct entities, the state apparatus is controlled by the party to the extent that the two countries are often referred to as **party-states**. This type of political arrangement, to repeat a basic point, is not unique to supposedly communist regimes. Taiwan's **KMT**, as has been explained, also followed this model in the decades before the country began to democratize. The reason was clear: the single-party system provides an exceptionally strong basis for exercising strong, pervasive, and sustained control over a country.

Some scholars argue that the overall design of the single-party system is key to understanding the longevity of authoritarian regimes in general and of the Chinese and North Korean regimes more specifically. This rational institutional argument was already briefly considered in Chapter 5, although in the end, the conclusion was that it did not do a particularly good job of explaining democratic transition in Taiwan, nor did it seem to adequately explain political dynamics in South Korea during its authoritarian period (although that South Korea had a primarily single-party regime is admittedly arguable). Nonetheless, revisiting this rational institutional argument would be useful to see what it can tell us about political continuity in China and North Korea and, conversely, about the prospects for political change in the two countries—specifically, the prospects for democracy. I do this in the following section.

In keeping with the framework of this book, I also revisit the other approaches. Thus, following the discussion of the rational institutional approach, I look carefully at both structural and cultural explanations. In Chapter 5, I also separately examined the microlevel focus on elite interests and power. This approach, however, can be readily folded into the rational institutional approach, which is what I do in this chapter.

Single-Party Authoritarianism in China and North Korea: All or Nothing?

As I noted above, a distinctive, although by no means unique, institutional feature of both the Chinese and North Korean political systems is the existence of a disciplined, centralized, and highly bureaucratized party. In both countries, the power and dominance of the party is unequivocal, and so too is the main ramification: with a pervasive presence throughout the country and with control of the state—including the military and internal security forces—the regime leaves little opportunity for those opposed to it to mount a significant challenge. Opponents of the regime can be easily monitored and, when necessary, imprisoned, exiled, or even killed. Mass movements, if and when they do coalesce, can be and are put down with ruthless force and violence. No doubt, the above scenario is exactly what has happened in China and North Korea. In China, the most salient example is the **Tiananmen Movement** of 1989, discussed briefly in Chapter 4 (see Figure 7.1 for further discussion). Since then, another large-scale mass protest has not taken place against the government, partly because the CCP has been even more vigilant since the 1989 protests and has moved preemptively by imprisoning, exiling, or executing any figure who might become an agent of change. The Congressional-Executive Commission on China (2012), an independent agency of the US government, found at least 7,014 cases of political or religious imprisonment in China as of October 2012: 1,484 were cases of political or religious prisoners currently imprisoned, and 5,530 were cases of prisoners who are known to have been released or executed or who died while imprisoned. The cases of three of China's most famous dissidents— Ai Weiwei, Liu Xiaobo, and Chen Guangcheng (see Figure 7.2 for further discussion)—further highlight the tactics used by the CCP to ensure that any challenge to the regime does not get out of hand.

In North Korea, the methods are harsher, even draconian. Dissidents— whether real or imagined—are given no quarter. Estimates are that as many as 200,000 people are political prisoners in North Korea, many if not most of whom are tortured and then subject to all sorts of deprivations: they are denied visits, if in fact family members know where they are (in fact, many are

---

Figure 7.1 The Tiananmen Movement of 1989

This massive, student-led movement unfolded over many weeks, and while centered in Beijing's Tiananmen Square (with over 100,000 protestors), the movement saw sympathetic protests emerge in as many as 250 cities spread across China. The movement sparked an intense intraparty debate among hard-liners (such as **Li Peng**) and reformers or soft-liners (such as **Zhao Ziyang**). In the end, however, the hard-liners won, and the decision was made to send two divisions of **People's Liberation Army (PLA)** troops into Beijing. The first "assault" took place on the morning of June 3. In this case, though, the soldiers were mostly unarmed, and those who did carry a weapon were ordered not to shoot the protestors. The protestors were able to repel the PLA with rocks and bricks and in few cases set fire to military vehicles. After the troops withdrew, a period of calm ensued, during which the students faced the choice of whether to evacuate the square or remain to face a second—likely more violent—assault. Most students decided to remain.

The second assault, in fact, was far more violent. The soldiers were now all armed with rifles and bayonets. They were supported with tanks, which not only fired at the protestors but also drove straight into the crowds. Many protestors were killed, although the exact number is not known (estimates range from 800 to 4,000). Leaders of the protest were given jail terms (up to ten years), while others were blacklisted so they could no longer find jobs. In the provinces outside of Beijing, many protestors were imprisoned or executed.

Figure 7.2   Three Chinese Dissidents: Ai Weiwei, Liu Xiaobo, and Chen Guangcheng

Ai Weiwei, Liu Xiaobo, and Chen Guangcheng are all prominent Chinese dissidents who have received significant notoriety outside of China.

Ai Weiwei is an internationally renowned artist (he helped design the "Bird's Nest" stadium for the 2008 Beijing Summer Olympic Games), but he is arguably much more famous for his pointed public criticism of the Chinese government. Ai was particularly critical of the government's handling of the devastating earthquake in Sichuan in 2008, which killed at least 69,000 people, including many schoolchildren, many of whom were buried under the rubble of collapsed school buildings. Ai produced an art exhibit commemorating the deaths of these children and also accused the government of exacerbating parents' grief with official denial. Ai has also been an outspoken critic of China's authoritarianism and has advocated for democracy. As with many dissidents, he has been subject to constant surveillance and was once imprisoned with no charge by the government and held incommunicado for almost three months (between April 3, 2011, and June 22, 2011). After being released on bail, Ai was charged with "economic crimes" and ordered to play $2.4 million in taxes.

Liu Xiaobo, literary critic, writer, and professor, was the winner of the 2010 Nobel Peace Prize, but before that, he was best known for his participation in the Tiananmen Movement and for writing **Charter 08**, a document that called for political change in China. The document called for an end to one-party rule and laid out a vision for a rights-based society, which included electoral democracy, rule of law, and freedoms of speech and expression. Shortly after release of Charter 08, on December 8, 2008, Liu was detained, subsequently charged on suspicion of "inciting subversion of state power," and then tried and convicted by the government. He was sentenced to an eleven-year term. During his prison term, Liu was awarded the Nobel Peace Prize. Not surprisingly, Liu was not allowed to accept the award either in person or by proxy. In his absence, the Nobel committee decided to place Liu's citation and medal on an empty chair during the award ceremony, making the first time since 1936 that the Nobel Peace Prize was awarded in this way.

Chen Guangcheng is known as the "blind activist" or the "barefoot lawyer." Chen is a blind, self-taught lawyer who was imprisoned in 2006 for advocating for women who were subjected to forced abortions and sterilizations as part of China's **one-child policy**. In 2005, he filed a class-action lawsuit against authorities in Shandong challenging their draconian policies. In response, local officials went after Chen and convicted him on charges of destroying property and obstructing traffic (during the trial, Chen's attorneys were forbidden access to the court). He was sentenced to four years and was released in September 2010 after serving his full sentence. Although released from prison, Chen was kept under house arrest and put under constant surveillance. Somehow, though, Chen escaped his house and found his way to the US Embassy in Beijing. Eventually, the Chinese government allowed Chen, his wife, and their two children to leave China for the United States. Chen was awarded a fellowship to study law at New York University Law School.

"disappeared," or simply whisked away with no trace of what may have happened to them and why); they are underfed and malnourished; they are forced into hard labor; and they are severely punished for even the most minor of "offenses." One escaped prisoner, Shin Dong-hyuk, tells of witnessing a prison teacher beat a six- or seven-year-old girl to death for hiding grains of corn in her pocket. In his own case, Shin's finger was cut off for accidentally breaking a machine. Later, when suspected of planning to escape with his family—Shin was born and raised in a North Korean gulag, or labor camp—he was hung by his ankles and tortured with fire. He was then forced to watch as his mother and brother were executed in front of him (he related these events in a *60 Minutes* interview ["Three Generations of Punishment" 2012]). Interestingly, Shin indicated that he felt no grief in witnessing their execution; to his mind at the time, his mother and brother deserved execution for breaking camp rules. In fact, Shin himself reported the escape plans to a prison guard.[1] It was no accident, moreover, that Shin was in prison with his family: as a way to deter even the thought of opposing the regime, and to stamp out the *potential* for dissidence, three generations of an entire family (children, parents, and grandparents) are incarcerated for the transgressions of a single person. This policy is known as the "Three Generations Punishment," a form of punishment that exists only in North Korea. In this context, imagining that anyone outside the party and regime would dare stand up in opposition is hard.

The methods of control used by the CCP and the Korean Workers' Party underscore the basic point of this section: in authoritarian systems, especially those built around a party rather than a person, the prospects for overthrowing or even meaningfully destabilizing the regime through a popular uprising are practically nil under normal circumstances. The costs are simply too clear cut and too high. At the same time, a single-party regime that rules by fear, intimidation, and force alone likely will have a difficult time achieving larger goals, especially sustained economic growth. At least a moderate degree of acquiescence and cooperation is needed from a significant part of the population, especially from those who have skills and expertise the party and state need. Gaining cooperation is best achieved by opening the party to new members and by distributing benefits to active supporters (including new cadres) and allies. In North Korea, the initial rapid pace of industrialization, particularly in the 1970s, created a demand for a better-educated and more technically competent workforce. As the demand for these workers grew, so did membership in the Korean Workers' Party: between 1961 and the late 1970s, according to estimates by scholarly and other experts, the party grew from about 1.3 million members to 2 million. Notably, party membership in the late 1980s constituted about 11 percent of North Korea's total population at the time, which was almost 17 million people (D.-S. Kim 1994). In Chapter 4, I noted that the CCP's membership, in raw numbers, is a much more impressive 60 to 76 million, but the larger number is still only about 6 percent of the total population. Still, this figure is significant. The sheer number of loyal party cadres, I should point out, makes the party's monitoring of the rest of the population easier, especially keeping tabs on potential trouble spots and "troublemakers."

The image so far is of regimes that simply cannot collapse. Clearly, however, this is not the case. As Barbara Geddes (1999) suggests (and demonstrates in her research), any authoritarian regime, including a single-party authoritarian one, can find itself in a vulnerable situation if a crisis—an exogenous shock—severely damages the economy, impedes the distribution of benefits to supporters and allies, or destroys coercive capacity. In a single-party system, such crises, which generally must be extreme, may lead to popular uprisings as people who have nothing to lose have less to fear. But if the party and state stay united, even a large-scale popular uprising can be dealt with, and often quite easily. In some situations, however, a crisis can create splits within the party leadership and the state, as the safety, security, and benefits of party rule begin to be questioned; if this split happens, popular pressure can lead to the collapse of the regime. Perhaps the most common scenario is when the military or, more likely, parts of the military decide to "defect"; without the undivided coercive capability of the military, even the staunchest party system—which might still have control of internal security forces—might be unable to put down a mass uprising. Of course, party leaders realize this vulnerability, which is why so much effort is made to keep the military loyal.

This discussion helps explain North Korea's military-first policy (known as **Songun**), first formally introduced after the death of **Kim Il-sung** in 1994. At that time, the younger Kim was unsure that he had the unquestioned support of the **Korean People's Army**. Putting the military first—first in line for scarce resources, first in line for food during the famine period, first in the lineup of political authority—helped to build and maintain its loyalty. **Kim Jong-il** also ensured the Korean People's Army's loyalty by doling out perks and special privileges to military officers and by promoting military leaders based on political allegiance instead of military competence. As a further guarantee, Kim built multiple and competing internal security agencies, and a parallel security force to protect his regime from the possibility of a military **coup d'état**. In retrospect, his efforts clearly worked—although reports have filtered out that the army's loyalty was tested in the transition from Kim Jong-il to his son, **Kim Jong-un**. For now, though, the solidarity between the military and party in North Korea appears to be strong. And as long as this remains the case, the prospect for meaningful political change in North Korea will continue to be very slim.

In China, the same issues exist with regard to the relationship between the CCP and the **People's Liberation Army** (**PLA**), although the dynamics of the relationship have differed. In the early years of the regime, the degree of integration between the CCP and PLA was very strong, in part because the first leaders of the CCP also occupied leading positions in the PLA. In particular, both **Mao Zedong** and **Deng Xiaoping**, as former supreme and active commanders of the PLA, enjoyed almost unconditional support from the military, which enabled them "to use the army as a power base in elite politics" (Joffe 1996, p. 301). Over the years, the degree of control exercised by the CCP leadership has generally remained quite firm, but increasing professionalism within the PLA has long had the potential to lead the military down a more autonomous path. During the turbulent years of the **Cultural Revolution**, for example, a number of local PLA commanders, as Ellis Joffe (1996) notes, "acted on their own in the absence of clear orders [from the party], or circumvented orders so as to suppress unruly Red Guards" (p. 307). Later, after restoring order, the PLA became the effective ruler in many provincial areas, but rather than simply cede control back to the party, military commanders remained in power until they became convinced that the radical elements of the CCP would not return to positions of authority. Another pertinent example comes from the Tiananmen crisis; in this instance, the military, and specifically senior commanders, were reluctant participants. The reason was clear: many senior military commanders questioned the legitimacy of a military assault against unarmed and largely peaceful Chinese civilians. And while the PLA ultimately followed party orders in a disciplined fashion, the initial ambivalence of the military led CCP leaders to later crack down on professionalism in the military. Military leaders, however, successfully resisted the party's efforts; the result has been a marked decline of political intrusion in military affairs (Joffe 1996). Over time, then, the contrast in basic interests, functions, and outlook between the PLA and the CCP has become sharper (Joffe 1996). The upshot is clear: the party no longer has absolute control over the PLA, and, as a result, the regime is now more vulnerable in the event of a serious crisis. However, the PLA's growing independence does not mean that the CCP is in danger of losing power any time soon, for unlike the North Korean regime, the CCP is still "delivering the [economic] goods."

In sum, from a rational institutional perspective, the prospects for sudden and dramatic political change in China and North Korea remain fairly dim, although the situation is somewhat brighter in China. The North Korean regime, in particular, has demonstrated a remarkable capacity—in the face of severe and ongoing economic crises—for maintaining solidarity both within the Korean Workers' Party, and between the party and key **institutions** of the state, especially the military. If the economy continues to fail, though, the prospects for a breakdown will grow. Pressure for change is not likely to come from the popular level, which has been thoroughly beaten down over decades of brutal dictatorial rule. Instead, the most likely source is the military. Sustained economic failure will continue to undermine military preparedness, no matter how much priority it is given through the Songun policy. If the military command believes the leaders of the Korean Workers' Party are incapable of ever reviving the economy, some action might possibly be taken against the party itself. Military action will not necessarily mean—or, perhaps more accurately worded, almost certainly will not mean—a transition to democracy. Instead, one might see the emergence of a military-authoritarian system in the vein of those created by **Park Chung Hee** and the KMT, with a strong emphasis on market-based economic reform.

Local Elections in China: A Harbinger of Democracy?

In China, one should note, political change has been taking place for some time. The pace of political reforms, of course, lags far behind economic reform, but changes are noticeable. The most salient and concrete changes are at the local level, where direct and indirect elections for a variety of offices have been held for many years (in fact, some political reforms were enacted before significant economic reforms after the death of Mao). Direct elections have been used to fill seats in the local people's congresses at the township and county levels, and indirect elections are used to select members of people's congresses at the city level and above. Indirect elections are also used to fill posts within the party leadership itself at various levels (C. Li 2008). The granting of greater autonomy at the local level, however, does not necessarily mean that the CCP leadership is intent on gradually democratizing the country. Instead, as Suzanne Ogden (2002) posits, it can be seen as an exercise in rational cost-benefit analysis by the CCP: the leadership "concluded that greater village autonomy would further the party-state's interest better than continuing a system of centrally directed government" (p. 185).

Other analysts argue that the continuing trend of political reform at the village level, or in rural areas, reflects a growing realization on the part of the CCP leadership that the status quo is becoming less and less viable. Since the 1990s and into the 2000s, unrest has become endemic and even unmanageable in parts of rural China, and village-level elections were viewed as a way to deal with growing discontent by making public officials more accountable to the people (Kennedy 2010). According to Tom Orlik (2011) of the *Wall Street Journal,* for example, 180,000 protests, riots, and mass demonstrations took place in 2010 alone—or about 500 every day. Millions of formal complaints are also made, which mainly involve petitions submitted to the State Bureau for Letters and Visits or lawsuits filed against local officials or government offices (Kennedy 2010). The large majority of these legal and illegal modes of resistance take place in the countryside, and many center on local-level corruption and repression. The continued existence and prevalence of local unrest is testament to the seriousness and deeply rooted nature of corruption in the Chinese system, which indicates that the situation has not been resolved, either through an electoral process that brings more accountability or through public protests (this conclusion does not mean that either is completely ineffectual, only that they are not sufficient to bring about fundamental political change).

Whatever the initial motivation and effectiveness of village elections, however, one can fairly conclude that they have institutionalized important aspects of procedural democracy among China's 800 million villagers, who "may register their approval or disapproval of local leaders through the elected villagers' committees and representative assemblies" (Ogden 2002, p. 189). Even this small step is helping to lay the institutional groundwork for more far-reaching political change, but with no competing political party candidates—and a still weak and inconsistent system of constitutional law (the party, not the constitution, remains the final arbiter in China)—the barriers to a fuller transition to democracy continue to be very high.

This said, the wild card in the rational institutional approach is always the "exogenous shock." And although predicting how severe a given shock will be, or when one will occur, is impossible, one can know with near certainty that such shocks happen and will have an impact on the regime. (See Figure 7.3 for an example of potential shock to the Chinese system.) Even when the impact appears minimal, a cumulative effect can become evident if the aftereffects or underlying reasons for the shock are not adequately addressed, as is the case with North Korea—although, as I just noted, the regime continues to muddle through. In China, the consistent and strong growth of the economy over the past twenty-plus years has significantly reduced popular pressure for political reform, but the real test will come when an economic or another type of crisis compels a large segment of China's population to question the viability and legitimacy of continued single-party authoritarian rule.

Will Capitalism Democratize China?
Rebalancing Class Relations

The rational institutional argument on political change and democratization in the single-party systems of North Korea and China hinges on two key factors: first, the internal strength and unity of the authoritarian regime and, second, the essentially fortuitous occurrence of an exogenous shock strong enough to significantly undermine the stability and power of a very firmly entrenched party system. No mention is made of how capitalist industrialization might redefine the interests of party leaders and cadres or produce a different type of society, with new social classes and new social actors. Nor does any discussion take place about how social-structural changes affect the prospects for significant political change or transformation. Structural factors, in short, are basically ignored within the rational institutional framework. The key question, then, is whether the dismissal of structural factors in favor of institutional ones is warranted. Before answering, consider the differences that have emerged since the

---

Figure 7.3 A Possible "Shock" to the Chinese System

China's rapid economic growth of the past several decades has been truly impressive. Rapid growth (among other economic processes), however, tends to create what Alan Greenspan (former chairman of the US Federal Reserve Board) refers to as "irrational exuberance." What he means by this term is the tendency by investors—motivated by seemingly no-lose investment opportunities—to drive asset prices up to levels that are not supported by economic "fundamentals" or are not supportable in the long run. Irrational exuberance, in other words, leads to **asset bubbles**. When asset bubbles burst, the results can be devastating to an economy and society.

In China, many observers have pointed to a particularly dangerous bubble in the residential real estate market. For the past decade or so, Chinese investors—and especially **middle-class** investors—have been pouring money into the housing market, which is viewed as one of the few safe but lucrative areas of investment. In fact, property values have skyrocketed, which has further fueled investment. A middle-class family owning multiple apartments, even as many as five to ten, is not unusual. This investment, in turn, has encouraged even more housing starts. The result has been the construction of so much "middle-class" housing that entire districts of newly built, fully paid for, but entirely unoccupied condominiums have created veritable "ghost cities." So why aren't these empty cities being filled? The most obvious reason is that the vast majority of Chinese citizens cannot afford to rent or buy middle-class housing at the current pricing level. At some point, then, the bubble will likely burst, and housing prices will collapse. This event will wipe out the investments of a large swath of China's middle class, which could then cripple the Chinese economy, in part because of the central role that construction plays in the economy. The resulting economic instability could easily lead to severe political instability. The collapse of the housing bubble, in short, could be the shock that brings an end to one-party rule in China.

---

early 1980s between the two countries. Until China's strong turn toward a market-oriented economy, China and North Korea seemed to operate along very similar political, economic, and sociocultural lines, despite the immense difference in population size. They may not have been identical twins, but they shared a lot of the same DNA, so to speak.

The transition toward a market economy, however, clearly put the two countries on diverging trajectories—not just economically but politically and socially as well. In both countries, the party still dominates the political landscape, but once one looks below the surface, one can see significant differences. Within the CCP, in particular, an increasingly outward orientation can be found among party leaders, along with an understanding that the fate of China has a great deal to do with the country's position within and relation to a strongly "liberal" global order. Outside the party, China is developing a partly autonomous entrepreneurial class—one that may still rely on state aid and protection—but also one that is increasingly cosmopolitan, with interests that may not always overlap with the party-state. One can also find a large and growing **middle class**, as well as a much more politically aware rural population. These developments, to be clear, are the direct and unequivocal product of structural changes brought on by capitalist industrialization. Their source is precisely why one does not see the same changes taking place in North Korea, a country in which the process of market reform continues to move at a snail's pace, a baby snail at that. Structuralists suggest that the now very significant differences between China and North Korea cannot be dismissed or considered somehow irrelevant or marginal to the process of political change in either country. To put the main point in slightly different terms, the structurally based differences between China and North Korea mean that political dynamics in the two countries are necessarily different; thus, the prospects for political change in the two countries are also necessarily different.

The significance of structural change in Chinese society and in state-society relations, one needs to note, has already produced some still nascent but potentially far-reaching political changes. I discussed some of these changes in the preceding section with respect to the growth of local elections. With that discussion in mind, consider some of the following questions. Why, in recent years, has the CCP leadership's agreement to more "village autonomy" through the ballot box become more reasonable? Why open a possible Pandora's box of electoral choice to almost 70 percent of China's population? After all, once the people (700 to 800 million strong in the countryside) get a taste for an electoral and democratic process, even one limited to relatively minor offices at the local level, their demands for a greater political voice in the future become much more likely. Their insistence is all the more possible given the underside of rapid industrialization in China: severe income inequality (especially between the rural and urban areas), environmental destruction, pervasive corruption, state-enforced "land takings," and so on. The destructive or negative elements of China's marketization, in other words, increase the likelihood of widespread popular unrest and citizen protests. And, although I have not yet discussed this issue, why did the top leadership of the CCP, including **Hu Jintao** and **Wen Jiabao** (both of whom stepped down from their positions in the CCP in November 2012, after ten years in power), repeatedly talk of the need for political reform—specifically democracy—to take place alongside economic reform? In other words, why would China's leaders purposely amplify societal demands for political change by expressly agreeing that such change is needed?

The rational institutional approach, again, does not offer adequate answers to any of these questions. From a structural perspective, by contrast, the answers are clear cut. Most generally, the process of capitalist industrialization, which is not only increasing wealth in China at a prodigious rate but also increasing the number and density of China's linkages with the rest of the world, has created a very different environment for the CCP. In this environment, the party-state may still be (and is) the dominant player, but it now has competition from a range of other players whose interests and growing power need to be considered. A little earlier in this section, I spoke of an emerging entrepreneurial class, an expanding middle class, and a politically aware and increasingly vocal rural population—some of the most important "new players." The entrepreneurial and middle classes are truly new (i.e., they did not exist before the era of market reform), while the rural class is new in that it has become much more assertive in standing up to the party-state, albeit most often at the local level. By most accounts, for example, the number of "mass protests" has increased significantly over the last decade;[2] these are part of the larger number of protests of all kinds, such as the 180,000 protests, riots, and mass demonstrations in 2010. (Worth noting, too, is that the total number of protests has increased dramatically over the years; in 2004, for example, the estimate was about 74,000.) The key point, to be clear, is that structural changes are slowly but surely ending the era of the unchallenged and unchallengeable party-state. Up to this point, however, China's leaders have done a good job of moderating or deflecting calls for dramatic political reform by engaging in a process of piecemeal reform. To turn a popular phrase on its head, the process of political reform in China might best be described as "democracy by a thousand cuts."

One is still left with a puzzle: If the structural changes in China are as significant as structural analysts have suggested, why is the pressure for more immediate and far-reaching political reform not stronger? Why has the party-state, in other words, been able to "get away with" piecemeal reform for so long? To answer this question, one needs to examine more carefully the dynamics of China's social and class **structure**. On this point, the reader should recall from Chapter 5 the discussion on how capitalist industrialization changes the balance of class power in society, giving subordinate groups—those groups most likely to support democratization—more social power. At the same time, capitalist development tends to change the basis of state-society relations such that the relationship itself becomes more interdependent or reciprocal. I also stressed that the relationship between capitalist development and democracy can cut in a number of directions and can be strongly affected by historically contingent factors. Keeping these points in mind, one must recognize several easily identifiable factors militating against rapid political change in China. One of these has to do with the development of the urban workforce, and a second with China's burgeoning but generally conservative middle class.

China's Urban Working Class: Mobile and Divided

China's urban population—and by extension, the urban working class—has increased significantly since 1978. At the end of the Mao era, approximately 82 percent of China's total population still lived in the countryside or rural areas. Since then, the urban population has increased rapidly. In 2008, China's urban population reached 46 percent (Banister 2009), and just a few years later, according to China's National Bureau of Statistics, the 50 percent barrier was broken for the first time: at the end of 2011, the total urban population was estimated at 51.3 percent (National Bureau of Statistics of China 2012). One should understand, too, that this increase in the urbanization rate was strongly resisted by the CCP, which wanted to restrict rural-to-urban movement and the growth of massive urban areas. The government's primary policy for urban areas in the 1980s was premised on the slogan, "leaving the land, not the villages, entering the factories but not cities." Later, China's national urbanization policy evolved into three pillars, which were later codified in the National Urban Planning Law of 1989: "controlling the big cities, moderating development of medium-sized cities, encouraging growth of small cities" (Kamal-Chaoui, Leman, and Rufei 2009, p. 9).

By itself, increasing urbanization is entirely predictable; all market economies go through pretty much exactly the same process. What sets China apart from most other capitalist industrializing countries, however, is the high degree of back-and-forth migration that accompanies this process. I discuss this issue in more depth in Chapter 8; for now, suffice it to say that China's industrial boom is fueled, in large measure, by "internal migrants" who number at least 150 million people (but the figure could be as high as 210 million).[3] This number represents about 12 percent of China's population (and about 19 percent of the country's workforce), which is a significant figure all by itself. But to put this number in better perspective, keep in mind that only a handful of countries other than China have populations exceeding 150 million: Nigeria, Bangladesh, Pakistan, Brazil, Indonesia, the United States, and India (in ascending order). Although not all internal migrants move for the purposes of work, a very large proportion does: in 2006, rural migrant labor amounted to about 132 million people (K. W. Chan 2009). As a result, workers constantly cycle between the urban factories and rural areas. A major reason for this mobility is that China's migrant workers, for all intents and purposes, are not allowed to settle in the cities due to the country's strictly enforced *hukou*, or household registration system. Under the *hukou* system, Chinese citizens are assigned a place of permanent residence and, under most circumstances, this assignment is impossible to change. The household registration system, in effect, creates a permanent class of temporary and mobile workers, who, in an important respect, are no different from "illegal" foreign migrant workers in other countries. Despite their disadvantaged status, these workers are hard to organize, and therefore are, as Dorothy Solinger (2008) puts it, "not politically relevant in any 'democratic' sense . . . because of the nature of their demands but also because of the barriers imposed by the registration system" (p. 255). The creation of this "floating population" of Chinese rural citizens, moreover, drives a wedge between them and the relatively privileged urban workforce.

From a structural perspective, the division of the industrial workforce into two large and unequal segments undermines the organizational and social power of the working class as a whole. Whether this process is by design or by accident, the result is the same. Indeed, the CCP leadership could eliminate the problem fairly quickly by dramatically reforming the *hukou* system, but it has obviously chosen not to do so (which is not to say that nothing has been done—a number of changes have been implemented over the years). The implication of doing nothing, moreover, means that China's "floating population" will continue to increase: by 2050, assuming no change in government policy, the floating population will hit 350 million. Meanwhile, the party-state continues to benefit from the lack of fundamental reform; not only does the working class remain divided, but the low-cost, extremely "flexible" rural-*hukou* labor—which can be paid at rural-subsistence wage rates—has, as Kam Wing Chan (2009) notes, become the backbone of China's export industry. Indeed, Chan argues that whereas "the first use of temporary rural migrant labor in export-processing zones such as Shenzhen might well have had an experimental or *ad hoc* character . . . the practice now has been in place for more than a quarter century, at a massive scale, and with clear support of both local and central governments. Accordingly, it must now be considered a rather conscious policy" (p. 208).

China's Middle Class: The Vanguard of Authoritarianism?

In the postwar period, the middle class has tended to play an instrumental role in the movement from authoritarianism to democracy. As I noted in Chapter 5, they have taken on this role largely because the working class has generally been too weak to bring about democracy on its own, something that is especially true in late-industrializing economies, many of which are based on what scholars refer to as an enclave economy, that is, an economy that prioritizes exporting and **FDI**. From a structural perspective, the result of **enclave development** is a working class that is typically small in proportion to the overall economy. Thus, to develop enough social power, the working class usually needs to form an alliance with other subordinate classes, which in most cases is the middle class. The middle class, in turn, has tended to side with workers for self-interested reasons: for members of the middle class in an authoritarian system, democracy gives them a greater capacity to protect their individual and property rights against potential and often arbitrary encroachment by the state and economic elites (Glassman 1995). Middle-class support of democracy, and of the working class, however, cannot be counted upon in all situations. For a variety of reasons, the attitude of the middle class toward democracy has been ambivalent or, as scholars like to put it, contingent. Here, too, the primary reason goes back to self-interest. To put it bluntly, when faced with the choice of supporting an authoritarian regime or siding with other subordinate groups, middle-class actors base their decision on a simple cost-benefit calculation. If they have more to gain materially and politically in siding with a repressive, authoritarian government, they will. If they have been shut out of the political process and subject to harsh and abusive, corrupt, and arbitrary state action, middle-class actors may "choose" democracy. Real-world cases—including South Korea and Taiwan—more than bear this conclusion out.

In China, one can find an almost perfect reflection of middle-class ambivalence toward democracy. In a study, Jie Chen and Chunglong Lu (2011) posed the question, "How supportive is the middle class in urban China of basic democratic values and institutions?" The answer to this question, the authors note, is twofold:

> On the one hand, like most of the lower-class people, most members of the Chinese middle class are vigilant about the individual rights that are closely related to their own interests. On the other hand, however, most members of this class are not willing to claim their political rights (such as engaging in public demonstrations and forming their own organizations) if such rights could possibly disrupt social order; they are not disposed to have a say in government affairs and to play a role in initiating a political change; they seem to support competitive elections only within the current one-party-dominated and -controlled electoral system. From a comparative perspective, it has also been found that the middle class as a whole is even less supportive of democratic principles and institutions in these areas than is the lower class. (p. 711)

The reasons for this ambivalence within the Chinese middle class are fairly easy to discern. Members of China's middle class have benefited tremendously, and disproportionately, from the market reform process. The party-state, for the most part, has treated them well and has given them "economic freedom of choice" in place of political freedom. They do not want their positions of relative privilege undermined by the instability and uncertainty that might ensue if the CCP were to suddenly lose power. This reluctance does not mean that the middle class is entirely against political reform. They are not. As An Chen (2002) explains, "They [the middle class] expect a system of checks and balances that could effectively constrain party power over the market and hold a tight rein over corruption. But . . . the middle classes hardly accept the complete breakdown of the CCP government" (p. 416). They want the political and economic stability the party-state guarantees, which means that they would be happy with a system that protects their interests, while "exclud[ing] the majority of the population from participating" (Chen 2002, p. 416). Another well-regarded expert on China, Jonathan Unger (2006), echoes these comments. A good portion of the middle class, Unger asserts, holds the "rural population in disdain" and fears that, if allowed to vote, the peasants would be "swayed by demagogues and vote-buying" (p. 29). The upshot is clear: China's growing middle class will not be an "agent of democratic change" in the near future. Nor will the Chinese middle class likely support a prodemocracy working-class movement.

What is the Chinese middle class? I have, up to now, taken the concept of the middle class in China for granted; that is, I have proceeded as if what the Chinese middle class is, is clear, which is hardly the case. Indeed, a number of definitions are used by scholars, journalists, policymakers, business organizations, and the Chinese themselves, though the last, for the most part, eschew the term for ideological or cultural reasons. Most definitions are compatible, but the range is still fairly broad. The *China Daily Business Weekly,* for example, defines the middle class as "a couple with one child, an urban apartment, no pets, and one car mainly used for weekend getaways" (cited in Solinger 2008, p. 258). This definition is somewhat narrow (and perhaps cheeky), but it does indicate that a middle-class family must have the financial means to buy a car and an urban house—no small feat. Most other definitions are based on a specific income range. China's National Bureau of Statistics, for example, uses a range of 60,000 yuan to 500,000 yuan (in equivalent US dollars, the range would be $7,250 to $62,500). The McKinsey Global Institute, by contrast, uses a narrower range of between $13,500 and $53,900 (both figures cited in H. H. Wang 2010). The two preceding figures define the Chinese middle class by comparing Chinese citizens to each other. Homi Kharas (2010), writing for the **OECD**, prefers a broader international approach; thus, instead of defining a *Chinese* middle class, he defines a *global* middle class and estimates the number of Chinese who fit into this broader category. For Kharas, the global middle class is defined as those households with daily expenditures between US$10 and US$100 per person in **PPP** terms. He admits, though, that the choice of a middle range is "rather arbitrary" (p. 12).

Given the wide variance over what constitutes the middle class in China, estimates on the number of Chinese who are in the middle class vary just as widely. According to the estimate by Kharas, China's middle class numbers about 157 million people, which is a very large absolute amount (second only to the United States) but only about 12 percent of China's population. Using the figure provided by the Chinese National Bureau of Statistics, however, the number almost doubles to 300 million (the figure that is most often cited in the popular media). On the other end of the scale, Chen (2002) estimates that only about 4 percent of Chinese nationwide, around 50 to 60 million people, belong to the middle class (since 2002, however, a large number of Chinese have quite likely moved from the "lower class" to the middle class, so the number is almost certainly significantly higher today).

The future role of China's middle class. From a structural perspective, a precise definition of the middle class is not altogether necessary. More important is the trend. That is, is China's middle class likely to continue growing? Will the pace of that growth accelerate or slow down? These questions also result in contrasting predictions, although a general consensus can be found that China's middle class will continue to expand in the coming decades. A report by the McKinsey

Global Institute, for instance, optimistically posits that by 2025, China's upper middle class "will comprise a staggering 520 million people" (Farrell, Gersch, and Stephenson 2006, p. 64). Kharas (2010), who does not provide a concrete estimate, is less optimistic. He notes that increasing income inequality limits the growth of the middle class in China. Kharas also points to other basic issues, such as equality of educational access and opportunity, and an economic strategy that inhibits household consumption. Nonetheless, because the size of China's middle class, according to Kharas, is still relatively small at only 12 percent, even limited growth will see tens of millions of Chinese enter the middle class in the coming decades.

The continuing growth and expansion of China's middle class is important. As it expands, its defense of an authoritarian, one-party system is likely to decline. In this regard, the previous discussion of Taiwan and South Korea in Chapter 5 is instructive. In both these cases, the middle class was also largely ambivalent about democracy during the initial stages of industrialization. Over time, however, the position of the middle class shifted toward stronger and clearer support of prodemocracy efforts. Structurally speaking, a key aspect of this shift was the growth of the middle class relative to the total population. In other words, as Chen (2002) explains, as the middle class edged closer to constituting 50 percent of the population, "socioeconomic equality improved, the likelihood of extremist politics lessened, and the threats from the lower class mitigated. Only with such a **social structure** can the middle class acquire a sense of economic security and hence care about state accountability" (p. 414). Equally important to understand is that China's rapid economic expansion, particularly since the early 1990s, will gradually begin to slow, likely sooner rather than later. From a structural perspective, moreover, China will almost certainly experience major economic downturns—just as all capitalist economies do (the discussion in Figure 7.3 pointed to a likely and potential cause of a major economic downturn). When this downturn happens, middle-class support of the regime may deteriorate even more quickly.

In sum, good reason exists to believe that social structural forces are laying the groundwork for the political transformation of China's one-party authoritarian system into a democratic one. The question is not so much "Will China democratize?" but "When will China democratize?" Structuralists, however, are not naïve. Maintaining or strengthening democracy in an era of globalization and global **neoliberalism**, in particular, is no easy task. Consider, for example, how globalization undercuts the power of the working and middle classes by allowing capital to move anywhere and everywhere, or how the capacity to accumulate vast sums of wealth on a global scale allows transnational corporations to subvert the democratic process. More generally, the imposition of the market process on economies throughout the world has undermined state control and power, while simultaneously constraining citizen participation; the mantra of neoliberal globalization—"Let the market decide!"—sounds democratic but, in reality, acts to reduce dramatically the capacity of people to exercise their collective political "voice." Globalization, however, is a complex process. Thus, although it gives corporations more tools, so too does it give new tools to civil society. However, I am beginning to go too far afield. I should return to the main point: the structural approach indicates that capitalist industrialization has begun and is necessarily reshaping China. In general, this reshaping means not only that the prospects for democratization in China are inexorably increasing, but also that China almost certainly will democratize. The "strength" and form of Chinese democracy, however, cannot be predicted in advance.

One last point: in this section I have not said much about North Korea, except to emphasize that the lack of market reform in that country means that North Korean society has seen little change. The lack of any shift toward democracy does not mean that political change is impossible. It is not. The lack of far-reaching market reform within North Korea coupled with a partial disintegration of its formerly close economic ties with its main communist allies, the Soviet Union and China, has brought the regime close to economic ruin. A sudden collapse of the North's economy would certainly undermine even further the capacity of the regime to stay in control. In the most likely scenario following the collapse of the current regime, the structural account would echo the rational institutional argument. That is, any new regime would most likely remain authoritarian but would also be more inclined to follow a stronger path of economic and market-based reform, perhaps following the Chinese model. At the same time, North Korea has its own unique characteristics and circumstances, one of which is its historical connection with South Korea. If the current North Korean regime were to fail, the country's economy would possibly be "united" with the South Korean economy, as happened with East and West Germany in 1990. The challenges of Korean unification would be immense, but at least some degree of preparatory planning has been going on for years. In this scenario, the North would undergo sweeping political change almost immediately.

Regime Stability and the Power of Ideas

Institutions, interests, structural changes, and power are all, I might readily admit, important when discussing political change and continuity. But so, too, are ideas. The significance of ideas can be clearly understood when examining a country such as North Korea. Earlier I discussed Shin Dong-hyuk, the individual who lived the first twenty-three years of his life in a North Korean labor camp, born to captivity because his uncles were deemed to be enemies of the state (during the **Korean War**, two of his uncles reportedly defected to South Korea).[4] Shin's entire life was governed by the extraordinarily restricted cultural milieu of the labor camp. He believed, for instance, that the entire world—not just his prison camp—was divided into prisoners and guards. The rules of the prison were his belief system; they were literally his gospel. Thus, when he witnessed the execution of his mother and brother, or when he witnessed a seven-year-old girl beaten to death for hiding kernels of corn in her pocket, he felt no sympathy or sadness because they had violated the rules. To Shin, the rules were sacrosanct, which is why he is the one who turned his mother and brother in for planning an escape. Shin's understanding of the world changed only when his belief system was challenged by a new prisoner who had lived in the world outside the prison camp and had even traveled to China. Until that time, however, Shin's life was almost completely governed by the rules, principles, values, and practices of his prison culture. I recognize, however, that Shin's belief system being undermined so quickly may seem odd. On this point, though, remember a key assumption in the cultural perspective: culture is inherently subjective (or **intersubjective**). The subjectivity of culture means, in turn, that the values, ideas, beliefs, and practices of culture, in principle, are subject to significant, even wholesale change at a moment's notice. Shin's sudden "conversion," then, is not at all surprising.

Admittedly, Shin's situation may be extreme, but North Korea is an extreme society. Thus, one might only slightly exaggerate in asserting, as Han S. Park (2002) did, that the citizens of North Korea as a whole "are not only physically confined but also mentally isolated within their own surroundings. Their environment is created and maintained by the government, and their minds are nourished with 'food' provided by the leadership. In this way, their minds are induced to be exactly the way the leadership designs them to be" (p. 61). With that level of control, no wonder that the devastating famines of the 1990s—which demonstrated the state's almost complete inability to take care of the needs of the North Korean people—did not lead to a breakdown of regime legitimacy and authority. Also no wonder that, after multiple and sustained economic shocks, which have essentially put the country in a near-permanent crisis since the 1990s, the North Korea regime has seemingly not budged a centimeter in political terms. Of the two, the prolonged economic crisis was and is the much greater threat. A starving population, after all, lacks the strength to wage a struggle against a regime as ruthless and as coercive as North Korea's, but a prolonged economic crisis means fewer and fewer resources to distribute to cadres and other supporters of the regime. For this reason, almost any other country, including single-party or personalist authoritarian regimes, would almost certainly have seen significant and ongoing political instability in the face of a decaying economy. Minimally, any other country would have experienced a coup d'état, or a least several serious attempts, led by a group of disaffected military or political elite, convinced that they could do a better job of governing the country. And while rumors have filtered out of one or two coup attempts in North Korea, nothing so far has generated a crisis of leadership.

To be clear, the argument thus far is that a major reason—albeit, certainly not the only reason—for the long-term stability of the North Korean regime is the ideological-cultural basis on which it rests. The North Korean party-state, perhaps more so than any other governing authority in the world, has derived its legitimacy primarily from what it claims to be rather than what it is, something that also works inside the leadership circle. As Han S. Park (2002) argues, under Kim Il-sung, the regime spent several decades "establish[ing] a political culture in which the Kims have been idolized. . . . In fact, the masses are led to believe that the two leaders [Kim Il-sung and his son] are inseparable, that one is the other" (p. 164). In this regard, one might say, according to Park, that Kim Il-sung is "still ruling North Korea under the proclamation of 'governance by the will of the deceased'" (p. 164). In this cultural context, no other North Korean leader can replace or displace any of the Kims by force, including Kim Jong-un, without provoking a true crisis of legitimacy throughout the North Korean power structure.

In Chapter 4, I mentioned the ideological-cultural touchstone of the North Korean system, *juche*. The concept of *juche* is most often translated as "self-reliance." While this translation conveys an aspect of *juche*, some scholars argue that it distorts the meaning of a term that is, in an important sense, "untranslatable" (Scobell 2006, p. 30). This view is that of Bruce Cumings (1993), whom I have referred to several times already. Indeed, Cumings argues that *juche* is "less an idea than a state of mind." Continuing, he writes, "The term literally means being subjective where Korean matters are concerned, putting Korea first in everything." (p. 213). Whether Cumings's definition is the best way to conceptualize *juche* is debatable. Not debatable, however, is the immense effort the regime has exerted to embed the concept or philosophy of *juche* into every aspect of North Korea's society, economy, and political system, and into the consciousness of the people. But the idea's entrenchment did not happen right away. In the early years of the regime, *juche* was more a political slogan than an ideology, still less a fully formed philosophy. As such, it was most often invoked in speeches and used to exhort collective effort and self-sacrificing behavior. By the end of the 1960s, it began to be reshaped as a legitimizing and nationalist ideology for the regime, particularly in the struggle against South Korea. By the 1970s, *juche* had become an important bedrock of the regime but also was increasingly connected to the personal rule of Kim Il-sung, who was "sanctified as the generator and embodiment of the ideology" (H. S. Park 2002, p. 25). During the first Kim's rule, a more intensified process of ideological-cultural indoctrination was started, as *juche* was integrated into the school curriculum and into all workplaces (at least one full day a week was set aside for "self-criticism" and study of *juche* principles).

The successful embedding of *juche* into all aspects of life in North Korea is hard to dispute. Equally hard to dispute is that it has had an important impact on political dynamics within the country, or that it is at least partly responsible—as an **independent variable** or factor—for regime stability and continuity. Certainly, the coercive and institutional capacities of the party-state and the willingness to ruthlessly suppress the North Korea people and potential opponents cannot be ignored. But these better explain the lack of a popular uprising. Left largely unexplained, as I have already suggested, is the lack of internal opposition within the regime itself. Unfortunately, no way exists to quantify, still less prove, the significance or power of ideological-cultural factors to the longevity and stability of the North Korean government, especially given the opacity of the regime. What has been proven, however, is that other **Marxist-Leninist**, single-party authoritarian systems have shown far less sustained organizational coherence and unity, especially after the death of their "revolutionary fathers," something that was true in the former Soviet Union and in China, too. China, in fact, offers a useful contrast with North Korea.

Political Change and Ideology in China

Under Mao, the ideological-cultural foundation of the regime seemed equally powerful, and equally rigid. The concern for ideological purity became a recurring theme during this period, as the CCP was constantly purging itself, although not always on a permanent basis, of "rightists" or "**capitalist roaders**," or any others who questioned the fundamental principles of Maoist ideology and thought. Yet the continued existence of rightists, especially at the highest levels of the party-state, indicates that the depth of indoctrination, while no doubt strong, was clearly not enough to extinguish "deviant" or nonconformist thought, perhaps because China is such a large country, particularly in terms of population (and especially in comparison to North Korea). During the 1950s and 1960s, extending communication, and indoctrination, to all corners of China was no easy task. Consider, on this point, the Socialist Education Movement of 1962–1966. The movement, as Frederick Teiwes (2010) explains, was aimed at ideologically reinvigorating village cadres, but it was not implemented universally; instead, it reached only about one-third of China's villages. Mao, too, was often ambivalent; after the failure of the **Great Leap Forward**, for example, he allowed pragmatists such as Deng Xiaoping to implement market-based reforms but then backtracked when he felt the reforms had gone too far. None of this is to say, however, that ideological-cultural factors are any less important in China than in North Korea. Rather, they had a different type of importance in the Chinese context.

In China, as in North Korea, ideological-cultural factors helped to create a unique and partially self-created framework within which the CCP and everyone else in China had to operate during the Maoist era. As discussed in Chapter 4, within this framework, every economic reform had to be justified in terms of Maoist ideology. Even after Mao died, an effort had to be made to frame market-based reforms as reflecting the developmental policies of the "good Mao" (Gilley 2010, p. 106). In this regard, Bruce Gilley (2010) also suggests that understanding that political reform had to precede economic reform is important, for political changes were a necessary precondition for economic ones. In particular, the party had to repudiate "**class struggle**" as its primary objective, but this shift in focus opened the door to more concrete change, including a new law (passed in 1979) that "expanded the direct popular election of people's congress delegates from the township to the county level" (pp. 107–108). Still, fundamental political reform—for example, abandoning the one-party system and moving toward liberal democracy—was off the table. The power and self-interests of the CCP leadership fairly clearly made wholesale political reform a nonstarter; still, an underlying reason for the unlikelihood of large-scale reform was the rejection of liberal democracy as an idea suitable for China. This point may seem trivial, but one way to consider the importance of the leadership's attitude toward democracy is to consider a counterfactual question: What if Zhao Ziyang's views and understanding of political reform in the 1980s, rather than being on the outside or margins of power within the CCP, were dominant?

In his memoirs (and here, for the sake of argument, I will take him at his word), Zhao was clear that he was not in favor of proceeding toward a multiparty and **parliamentary system**, but he was adamant that the CCP's method of governing had to change (Zhao et al. 2009). At the most general level, he believed that China needed to establish the rule of law. Zhao enumerated a number of changes he recommended to accomplish this task. First, as Zhao put it, "we needed to increase the transparency of Party and state decision making" because the people had a "right to know how decisions were made" (p. 258). Second, multiple channels for dialogue—with various factions, forces, and interests—needed to be established. Decisions on major issues would use these channels to ensure "ongoing consultation and dialogue with various social groups" (p. 258). As a further result of this change, social groups would be permitted to form, and they would need to be allowed or perhaps even encouraged to operate independently of the party and state; he also recommended a clear separation of the party and state. Third, he proposed the adoption of "differential quota elections" for high-level posts in the central leadership. Fourth, Zhao advocated for laws that would guarantee freedom of association, of assembly, of petitions, and of strikes, along with greater freedom of the press. While not liberal democracy, these changes would have gone a long way toward **political liberalization** in the Chinese system. Zhao, however, was clearly in the minority: his views were not the views of the large majority of the CCP leadership. In fact, because of his soft-liner views during the Tiananmen Movement, Zhao was ousted from the party and forced to live under house arrest for the next fifteen years.

Returning to the counterfactual question, if Zhao's views toward political reform were shared by the majority of the CCP leadership, China would quite likely look very different today. Keep in mind, too, that Zhao's self-interest as a member of the CCP's leadership circle should have been essentially the same as his comrades. What distinguished Zhao were his subjectively held beliefs and values about the role of the CCP and its relationship with the Chinese people. Gilley (2004) even suggests that the Tiananmen Movement had the potential to turn out very differently because Zhao was never completely alone. Gilley pointed out, in particular, that a third of the **standing committee** of the National People's Congress supported Zhao's liberal position, and that the call for political reform during the Tiananmen Movement failed was partly a matter of bad luck and happenstance. Worthwhile recalling is that, in Taiwan, a similarly situated party, the KMT, built a one-party authoritarian system quite similar to the one on mainland China. The KMT leadership, however, orchestrated a largely voluntary transition to democracy, which is one reason why the rational institutional approach has difficulty explaining political dynamics in Taiwan: no obvious exogenous shock seriously disrupted regime stability and legitimacy, thereby forcing a transition to democracy. Can the same gentle, "voluntary" turn to democracy happen in China? From a cultural perspective, answering this question hinges on understanding the attitudes, perceptions, and beliefs of China's current leaders, specifically regarding liberal democracy.

So has a significant shift taken place within the party leadership toward a greater acceptance of the need for political and specifically democratic reform? The short answer is yes. Yu Keping (2008), a professor at Beijing University and deputy director of the Translation Bureau of the CCP Central Committee, argues that especially since the mid-2000s or so, the trend toward major political reform is clear. Between 1978 and 2008, Yu writes, the CCP went from "monistic governance to pluralist governance; from centralization to decentralization; from rule of man to rule of law; from a government of regulation to a government of service; from intra-party democracy to social democracy" (pp. 8–9). Most of these new changes are the product of changes since the late 1990s, and all reflect meaningful shifts in how the party views its relationship with and responsibilities toward the citizenry. (Yu is also well known for publishing a widely read article in China entitled "Democracy Is a Good Thing," which was later published in the United States [2009].) Under Hu Jintao and Wen Jiabao, who served as president and premier, respectively, between 2003 and 2012, moreover, the CCP leadership has adopted a fairly clear position of the need for democracy in China. Hu, in particular, has repeatedly said, "If there is no democracy, there will be no modernization" (cited in C. Li 2008, p. 3). Granted, a change in rhetoric does not always lead to a concrete change in policies, still less far-reaching political change. However, in China, as has already been proven, a central importance is attached to language in legitimizing economic reform. Yu (2008) also notes that the shift in ideological rhetoric has resulted in incremental but still significant political reform. One of the most important changes has been the emergence of a civil society in China, which many scholars point to as a critical foundation for democracy.

So far, I have focused attention on Chinese elites. Equally important are ideological-cultural shifts among the Chinese people. As I suggested above in the discussion of China's growing middle class, popular attitudes toward democracy are ambivalent. Significantly, perhaps, not only the middle and upper classes have this ambivalence. Using data from a 2002 survey by East Asia Barometer Project, Zhengxu Wang (2006) notes that a remarkable 98 percent of Chinese citizens expressed "confidence" in both the national government and the CCP (and, by extension, in authoritarian rule). In his analysis of this data, Wang (2006) argues that public support of the regime is most likely based both on the success of its economic policies and on less dramatic but still meaningful political reform. Wang also posits that a good number of ordinary Chinese see a radical shift to democracy as potentially disastrous, leading to economic failure, societal disintegration, loss of public order, ethnic conflict, and so on. Does this attitude mean that the Chinese citizenry is composed almost entirely of self-interested actors who view democracy in purely instrumental terms? Gilley (2004), for one, thinks not. As he puts it, "[China] . . . has a large number of proto-democratic groups focused on women's rights, liberal intellectual thought, or public charity. More important, civic societies which grow up within a dictatorship often take on nondemocratic colors as a result, just as people do. Evidence from elsewhere shows that this changes quickly with democratic opening" (p. 75). In other words, Gilley is suggesting that a strong reservoir of latent democratic sentiment can be found among the Chinese. Unfortunately, the accuracy of Gilley's point is hard, if not impossible, to assess. But, as I discussed earlier, organized and open protests against the government (albeit usually at the local level) are an everyday occurrence. Therefore, one can conclude that the Chinese people are less afraid of voicing their complaints, in part because of a change in the behavior of the police; no longer do the police act purely as upholders of CCP dominance but, instead, act as upholders of public order. Gilley asserts that this change is monumental, a "prelude to the defection of coercive forces that is critical in democratic transitions" (p. 77). Still, at this point, democratization in China being the product of a massive upsurge of prodemocratic forces at the grassroots level remains unlikely.

In sum, from an ideological-cultural standpoint, not only is the prospect for democracy in China relatively good, but so too is the prospect for a peaceful transition to democracy à la Taiwan's top-down, guided transition. And while no guarantee can be found of this peaceful transition happening (recall that good cultural accounts include structural, institutional, and political factors), a very important discursive and attitudinal shift has clearly taken place within the leadership—Zhao Ziyang would certainly find much more company and support today than he did in 1989—and incremental changes toward a more open, democratic political system have already been made. Within the global cultural context, too, democracy has become an almost unquestioned norm, a shift that has already affected the views of Chinese leaders. This impact is likely to spread and deepen as time goes on, both at the leadership level and throughout Chinese society. At some point, democracy may become a taken-for-granted expectation, and when this change happens, what was once anathema may be embraced as a natural—but not necessarily ideal or idyllic—consequence of China's political and economic trajectory.

Political Change and the Socially Constituted Actor

I have mentioned Zhao Ziyang a number of times in this chapter, suggesting quite strongly that if his views on political reform and change had been predominant among the CCP leadership in 1989, China could very well be a liberal democracy today, or at least moving much more strongly in that direction. This conclusion, in turn, suggests that individual actors—and the ways in which they are socially constituted—play a central role in determining the political, economic, and social fate of a country. A discussion of the power of individuals is a good starting point for considering how one might apply the constructed actor model to an explanation of political continuity and change in China and North Korea. Considering, then, how Zhao's views on political reform evolved would be instructive. Fortunately, Zhao himself talked about the evolution of his views, at least in general terms, in the book, *Prisoner of the State* (Zhao et al. 2009).

Zhao did not start off as a political reformer. If anything, he took a very conservative stance regarding China's one-party authoritarian system. In his view, the political system worked effectively. Granted, he recognized a few "abnormal events" (i.e., the Great Leap Forward and the Cultural Revolution), but fundamental changes were unnecessary (Zhao et al. 2009, p. 256). He held these views without question until the mid-1980s. At that point, though, his understanding and attitude started to change. "My attention," he writes, "was aroused somewhat by events in the broader international community and problems that had emerged in the Eastern Bloc. Yet the main reason for the change was that I had come to see a need for political reform from the perspective of economic reform" (pp. 256–257). On this point, his reasoning was largely instrumental. That is, he saw political reform as a necessary corollary of economic reform, both to ensure that market-based reforms could reach their full potential and to reduce the problems of corruption, or, as he puts it, "the exploitation of power for personal gain" (p. 257). Not surprisingly, then, his political "conversion" was limited. He did not believe that China should adopt a Western-style, multiparty parliamentary system, nor did he think the dominant position of the CCP should change in any significant way. His focus, as discussed earlier, was on the manner in which the party governed China. I enumerated his specific proposals above and noted that they represented a pretty significant shift, one that would have firmly put China on a path toward democratization—if they had been implemented.

As more time passed, however, Zhao's political views continued to change (albeit in a situation in which he was isolated from the center of political power in China). While he once believed that people could be "master of their own affairs" only within a socialist system, he came to see such systems, including the one in China, as "just superficial." Socialist systems, he asserted, "are not systems in which the people are in charge, but rather are ruled by a few or even a single person" (Zhao et al. 2009, p. 269). Interestingly, Zhao claims to have always been interested in achieving democracy, but he felt that democracy could best be achieved through socialism. He came to understand, however, that while imperfect, parliamentary democracy is the only viable choice for a country hoping to "realize a modern market economy" (p. 270). Zhao's change in attitude did not mean that he thought the CCP should immediately give up power; instead, he advocated for a transitional period, during which time the party could "facilitate a smooth transition to a more mature, civilized, and democratic political system as economic, social, and cultural conditions change" (p. 271). At the same time, Zhao was convinced that movement toward a more open, democratic political system is an absolute necessity. "If we act with initiative," he concludes, "it will be beneficial to the Party, society, and the people. *Any other approach will be harmful*. The trend is irrefutable, that the fittest will survive. As Sun Yatsen said, 'Worldwide trends are enormous and powerful; those who follow them prosper, and those who resist them perish'" (p. 272; emphasis added).

Examining the evolution of Zhao's political attitudes reveals a lot. One can see, for example, that the views of the top leaders are not predetermined or fixed even in the confines of a strict one-party authoritarian system—where, I should add, the rational institutional perspective would suggest that his overarching interest should have been to stay in power. To be sure, Zhao's changing views on political reform were, as I noted earlier, generally self-interested and rational. Yet he interpreted his self-interest in a manner that led him to adopt a very different position than the majority of other leaders in the CCP. His primary motivation, it seems, was to ensure the success of the market reform process, whereas others wanted to ensure the dominance of the CCP itself and, presumably, their positions of power within the party. Zhao, moreover, was not alone: in the late 1980s, a sizable number of so-called soft-liners could be found, although too few to win the struggle over China's political path. Their presence raises an important question: What makes a soft-liner in the first place? For the most part, rational institutional analysis (and rational choice more generally) never explains why soft-liners exist, or under what conditions they will constitute a power-holding majority in a single-party system. Yet this point seems critical. The constructed actor model, by contrast, understands that individuals are shaped by a large current of social facts that push and pull actors down the same very wide path but that also leaves open the possibility for a range of perspectives. In Zhao's case, his position as party cadre and leader (he first joined the party in 1938) gave him a fundamental faith in the CCP, but he seemed to be driven by a larger concern for the economic and political "modernization" of China as a whole.

One can surmise that the views of many of China's soft-liners and reformers were shaped not only by objectively based self-interests (including material gain and self-preservation) but also by subjectively based ideals about, say, their historic role in leading China back to greatness or global preeminence. Notably, soft-liners, whether on economic or political matters (or both), always took a major risk in voicing their positions. Deng Xiaoping was the target of two purges, and Zhao Ziyang actually became a target of a half-dozen assassination attempts for his economic reformist views. In addition, as discussed above, after the Tiananmen Movement, Zhao was also forced to live under house arrest until his death. Given the risks involved in adopting reformist views, one should be surprised that China has had any soft-liners at all—especially during the Mao years and until the early 2000s. As market-based reforms began to enrich and strengthen China, however, the political space for reformist views has opened up. Thus, the risks of calling for political change and for democracy—while clearly still present—have eased, at least for leaders and others in the CCP.

In this "evolving" environment, individual actors, especially those who see deeper political reform as a necessity, will necessarily have to bring about political change. **Agency**, in short, matters. On this point, in a fact that is more than a little ironic, Maoism (Mao Zedong Thought) had, as one of its core principles, the idea of **voluntarism**, which is "the belief that human will ('volition') can be decisive in bringing about major historical changes" (Joseph 2010, p. 141). At the same time, the constructed actor models suggest in very clear terms that the scope of action is always subject to constraint. Mao, for example, wanted to build a viable, dynamic, and powerful socialist economy, but no amount of effort or voluntarism could make that happen. Still, the relatively strong turn toward the market beginning in 1978 was not predestined; as in North Korea, China could have stayed on the socialist "path to nowhere" for an indefinite period of time. Once the decision was made, though, a new set of institutional and structural forces began to take shape in China. Market-based economic reforms, as structuralists assert, necessarily reshaped Chinese society, gradually creating a counterbalance to the party-state. The imperatives of the market—the establishment of which marks a fundamental institutional change—have slowly transformed the broader decisionmaking environment: what is "rational" for China's leaders today may have been "irrational" thirty or forty or fifty years ago. Structural and institutional changes, in other words, make dramatic political reform more viable today than in the past. This point brings the conversation full circle, for to realize "dramatic political change," someone has to act to bring it about. Democracy will not just happen; it must be willfully created. And to create "democracy," China needs "democrats," that is, people who want democracy, whether for instrumental reasons (e.g., because it contributes to the economic growth of their own self-interests) or for normative reasons.

In the first decade or so of the twenty-first century, still not enough Chinese "want democracy." And as long as not enough people are behind the movement, no amount of structural and institutional change will necessarily turn China democratic. For an example that proves this point, just consider Singapore, one of the wealthiest capitalist countries on Earth with a (PPP) per capita income of around $61,800 in 2012, according to the **World Bank** (2013b). Politically, however, Singapore has long had a one-party system dominated by the People's Action Party. Opposition parties are not entirely banned in Singapore, but even in the early 2000s, "meaningful political contestation was completely absent from the island city-state . . . as opposition groups were highly marginalized and competed in only a minority of constituencies" (Ortmann 2011, p. 154). Since then, opposition parties have grown and are beginning to field stronger candidates with a more appealing message, but in the 2011 general elections, they still only managed to win six of ninety-nine seats in the Singapore parliament. Moreover, their potential to do significantly better is constrained by, as Stephan Ortmann puts it (2011), the country's "draconian legal system, which severely limits civil and political liberties and thwarts genuine political competition" (p. 154).

The upshot is that Singapore, at best, is a "competitive authoritarian regime" (Ortmann 2011, p. 153). China could very well head down the same path. On this point, though, one should note that Singapore has a number of distinctive characteristics, including a tiny overall population (around 5.2 million people) and a foreign worker population that constitutes almost 35 percent of Singapore's total workforce (Yeoh and Lin 2012). The large, nonresident, foreign worker population, in particular, makes maintenance of an authoritarian system easier for the Singaporean state. One reason, from a structural perspective, is clear: this population distorts class relations by allowing most Singaporeans to live relatively privileged lives in the middle class, while foreign migrants make up the bulk of the lower-paid, unskilled working class. With China's huge population, and equally huge labor force, the same scenario is unlikely. At some point, then, far stronger, more pervasive demands for democracy are likely to arise in China, with more people wanting democracy at the grassroots level. Within China's leadership circle, some "conservatives" will always likely emphasize the sort of "social stability," public order, and strong, unchallenged political rule the CCP provides, but a diversity—albeit within a fairly narrow range—of views has always been represented at the top of the CCP hierarchy. While one might not find any strong "normative democrats" (leaders who value the principles of democratic governance), a number of leaders are certainly "instrumental democrats." Whatever the case, their role will be critical.

As with the other approaches, the constructed actor model does not foreclose on the possibility of political change in North Korea. Ultimately, change will come through the decisions and actions of socially constituted actors, as is the case in all other countries. Individuals who "want democracy" are probably fewer in North Korea than anywhere else in the world. One salient reason for this shortage is the high degree of ideological-cultural and coercive control in the North, which remains extraordinarily robust despite showing signs of weakening in recent years. With few structural and institutional changes in the economy, this robustness is hardly surprisingly. Indeed, even those North Koreans who flee the country—an estimated 24,000 North Koreans now live in South Korea and many more in China—do so primarily for economic, and not political, reasons. According to Andrei Lankov and Peter Ward (2012), most of these refugees did not leave the North because they were unhappy with the political system, and few, if any, wanted to challenge or change it. Instead, they simply wanted to take advantage of opportunities to earn money in China, opportunities that are not available in North Korea. Of course, some political refugees are among the immigrant population—those fleeing persecution, soldiers, and regime officials—but these are few and far between. Worth noting, though, is that one of these individuals, Kim Duk Hong (a former high-ranking official in the North Korean regime) claimed, "Everyone wants to escape from North Korea. . . . [T]here would be a revolution by the people" if the United States helped the North Korean people directly (Public Broadcasting Service 2003).

The truth of Kim Duk Hong's statement is unclear (he fled North Korea in 1997), which underscores an unavoidable problem in analyses of North Korea. Namely, getting accurate information is difficult and sometimes impossible. But what one can safely conclude is that the prospect for political change is quite low for a number of reasons. First, I already mentioned the lack of market-based reform, which suggests that no structural changes have taken place within North Korea that would allow for a more balanced state-society relationship or even for the emergence of "instrumental democrats" or political reformers of any stripe. Second, observers know that the regime remains well insulated from outside influences and information, although less so than in the past. As a result, little information is available to leaders that can challenge the ideology of the regime. Third, the regime is one of the most ruthless in the world but is also largely immune from international pressures and sanctions. Fourth and finally, despite decades of economic difficulties, the regime not only survived but also avoided the debilitating factional infighting that often leads to internal collapse. Whether these factors will hold true into the future is anyone's guess.

Conclusion

In thinking about the prospects for political change in authoritarian regimes, one can all too easily assume that change is not possible. After all, those in power control the coercive assets of the country, and usually most of the economic assets. Authoritarian regimes usually construct sophisticated and pervasive systems for monitoring potential and actual dissidents and dealing with them in a manner that not only prevents them from achieving their goals but also dissuades others from joining their causes. Fear and coercion keep most of the population in line, but the strongest authoritarian regimes are also very good at co-opting potential rivals by providing privileges and material benefits. Still, history proves that even the strongest authoritarian regimes can and do fail. Understanding and explaining what makes that sort of change possible was a primary goal of this chapter. At the same time, in this chapter I explored how other authoritarian regimes resisted the forces of political change. In either case, one needs to look below the surface, especially to search for the key factors, processes, and relationships that indicate when change is likely and when it is not. In this regard, the examination of China and North Korea provided a very useful study in contrasts.

One lesson to take away from this chapter is that institutional arrangements are important, but they are not all-important. How does one know this? One reason is plain to see: China and North Korea shared a range of institutional features when they were first established, and while both countries are still single-party authoritarian states, or party-states, significant differences have developed that set them apart. China, of course, pursued the path of market reform, which set into motion important structural changes that make a political transition from authoritarianism to democracy more and more likely, but not inevitable. A second lesson is that, while structural processes cannot be ignored, cultural-ideological factors also need to be carefully considered and incorporated into any explanation of political change and continuity in the two countries. Why, for example, did China begin the process of market reform in the late 1970s? Almost certainly, the decision hinged on the views or beliefs of a handful of influential leaders in the CCP. Putting rational institutional, structural, and cultural-ideological factors together in a coherent explanation was the final step, which was accomplished using the constructed actor model (albeit in only a cursory fashion).

Notes

1. Shin's experience in the North Korean prison camp—known as "Camp 14"—is chronicled in the book, *Escape from Camp 14: One Man's Remarkable Odyssey from North Korea to Freedom in the West* (2012), written by Blaine Harden.

2. The statistics on "mass protests" need to be viewed with some caution, largely because the definition of what constitutes a mass protest or mass incident is very broad. As Freeman (2010) describes it, these can include "any kind of planned or impromptu gathering that forms because of 'internal contradictions', including mass public speeches, physical conflicts, airing of grievances or other forms of group behavior that may disrupt social stability"; in practice, moreover, no agreement can be found on the definition of a mass incident.

3. The higher figure of 210 million is based on a report by China's National Population and Family Planning Commission entitled "The 2010 Report on the Development of China's Floating Population" ("China's 'Floating Population' Exceeds 210m" 2010).

4. The information in the section on Shin comes from his interview on the *60 Minutes* television segment, "Three Generations of Punishment" (aired on May 19, 2013) with Anderson Cooper. Some information also comes from the *60 Minutes Overtime* segments, available at http://www.cbsnews.com/video/watch/?id=50136223n. I might also note that, while I have no reason to doubt Shin's story, parts of it do not always ring true; in particular, his ability to escape from the prison and travel to China on his own—without any geographic knowledge of his surroundings—raises questions.

8 East Asia as the New Immigrant Frontier?

Over the past several decades, a remarkable change has been taking place in East Asia. Specifically, Japan, South Korea, and Taiwan have all become increasingly significant destinations for migrants and immigrants from around the world. The numbers are still quantitatively small by international standards, but they are qualitatively large in terms of their impact on and meaning to these three societies, something that is particularly true for Japan and South Korea, which have long been viewed as extremely tight-knit, homogeneous nation-states, almost impervious to the pressures of racial and ethnic diversity and to the inclusion or even tolerance of a large number of outsiders in their respective societies. The influx of foreigners looking for work does not mean that East Asia has become a welcoming home to immigrants from around the world. This definitely is not the case. In all three countries, migrant and immigrant workers (primarily from South and Southeast Asia and China), in particular, are faced with daunting challenges. They are generally consigned to so-called 3-D jobs (dirty, difficult, and dangerous) and, despite some legal protections, are often subject to physical abuse, nonpayment of wages, harassment, a lack of medical care, social marginalization, and so on. One should not be surprised, however, since unskilled immigrant workers around the world suffer from the same issues. Indeed, this problem is pervasive as immigrant workers, especially those without legal authorization to work in their "host" countries, are typically unfamiliar with the language of the countries they are working in, afraid to bring attention to themselves, legally and socially disempowered, and therefore vulnerable to exploitation, even hyperexploitation. Notably, the increase in in-migration to East Asia is not only due to an apparent demand for more workers. South Korea and Taiwan, in particular, have also witnessed a "foreign bride" phenomenon starting in the early 1990s or so. Tens of thousands of women, primarily from Vietnam, the Philippines, and China, are also emigrating from their countries to marry South Korean and Taiwanese men. This trend, in turn, has led to a comparable increase in "multicultural children," a development that portends significant social change, especially with regard to questions of national identity and citizenship.

In this chapter, I examine both the phenomenon of increasing immigration to East Asia and its broader implications. The strong focus here is on cross-border worker migration, if only because the theoretical and empirical literature is best developed on this issue. This focus allows an exploration of the issue using the same basic frameworks of analysis that are used throughout this book. In the section that follows, I provide an extended overview of migration (both inter- and intranational) patterns in all five East Asian countries, though the primary focus of the chapter is on Japan, South Korea, and Taiwan.

International Migration in East Asia: Basic Facts and Issues

China

China is the world's largest country in terms of population with over 1.3 billion people. The country's working-age population (fifteen to sixty-four years old) made up 72.3 percent of the total population in 2006 and is expected to peak at 1.01 billion by 2016. The huge and growing working-age population has created pressures for continued strong economic growth in order to avoid the problem of massive unemployment. Already, by 2005, China had 10 million unemployed urban workers and 200 million "redundant farm laborers" (all figures cited in Surak 2011).

Uneven economic growth and industrialization in China has resulted in massive internal migration, which steadily expanded in the early 1980s, accelerated in the early 1990s, and then accelerated again in the first decade of the twenty-first century (K. Chan 2011). China has two types of internal migrants, those who have been authorized by the government (*hukou*), and those who migrate without authorization (non-*hukou*). *Hukou* migration has remained steady since 1980—between 17 and 21 million on an annual basis (these numbers mostly represent urban residents who moved within the same city or rural residents who moved within a single rural area). Non-*hukou* migration is far larger. In 2009, it involved almost 150 million people (all figures cited in Chan 2011).

In the nineteenth to mid-twentieth centuries, China was a major source of emigration: between 1850 and 1949, millions of Chinese migrants left China for destinations throughout the world. Most migrated to Southeast Asia, but large numbers also went to the United States, Spanish America, the Caribbean, the Pacific Islands, South Africa, and Australia. While many returned to China, by the outbreak of World War II, between 8.5 and 9 million Chinese lived outside of China. After the **communists** took control in 1949 and until 1978, out-migration was severely restricted (the one exception, of course, was the outflow of Chinese nationalists to Taiwan). In 1978, restrictions on internal migration and emigration were gradually lifted. In 1985, China's Emigration and Immigration

Law guaranteed the rights of Chinese citizens to travel outside China, including the right to emigrate (all figures cited in Skeldon 1996).

As I note in the following summaries of Japan, South Korea, and Taiwan, a large number of Chinese migrants are now moving to those countries for work and marriage, but Chinese emigrants are also moving to destinations in Southeast Asia, North Africa, the Middle East, Europe, and North America. In addition to worker and marriage migration, hundreds of thousands of Chinese students from the mainland and Hong Kong are migrating as students. The major destinations are all **OECD** countries (all figures cited in Surak 2011).

In-migration to China is limited, especially of unskilled or low-skilled workers. The government, however, first initiated programs to encourage skilled Chinese nationals to return to China in an effort to combat a potential "brain drain" resulting from well-educated and skilled workers emigrating to find better employment opportunities. These programs have recently been extended to ethnic Chinese and non-Chinese: in 2003, 90,000 skilled foreign migrant workers (including senior technicians, professionals, managers from large construction projects, and foreign teachers and researchers) arrived in China (all figures cited in Surak 2011).

Japan

During the **Meiji** era, Japan was primarily a sending country, with many Japanese immigrating to Hawaii, the West Coast of the United States (primarily California), South America, and other areas of Asia. In 2012, the largest concentrations of ethnic Japanese living outside of Japan were in Brazil (about 1.5 million), the United States (1.2 million), the Philippines (120,000), the United Kingdom (100,000), and Peru (90,000). Large-scale Japanese out-migration came to an end in the 1930s, primarily because of serious domestic labor shortages. As I discuss below, these shortages were largely met through "voluntary" immigration from Japan's colonial possessions, especially Korea, and a smaller number from China; during the war, many Korean immigrants were forcibly brought to Japan as workers.

Following the end of World War II until the 1980s, out- and in-migration were both limited. One should remember that US forces occupied Japan from 1945–1952, during which time as many as 58,500 US citizens worked in Japan for the US military. The United States established a network of military bases in Japan, with a particularly large concentration in Okinawa (thirty-nine military bases in Okinawa cover 40 percent of arable land on that island). Japan's rapid, postwar industrial expansion led, rather quickly, to renewed labor shortages. Initially, these shortages were addressed by (1) promoting greater automation, (2) encouraging more women and elderly to join the labor force, and (3) outsourcing industrial production. When these efforts failed to meet continuing demands for labor, Japanese officials permitted ethnic Japanese, primarily from

South America, to return to Japan. These immigrants were allowed to work in unskilled or low-skilled jobs while in Japan; however, Japanese immigration law to this day technically prohibits migrants other than ethnic Japanese from engaging in low-skilled work while in Japan. To get around this law, an "industrial training program" was also established, which allowed small and medium-size companies to bring in unskilled and low-skilled labor as "trainees." In 2007 and 2008, the number of new trainees peaked at more than 100,000; in 2009, the number fell by 20 percent, and then 2010 saw an additional 35 percent decline for a total of only 51,700 (the decline was primarily due to an economic downturn).

In 2006, according to the Regional Thematic Working Group (2008), about 2 million foreigners were living in Japan, the majority of whom were nonpermanent residents. In addition, in 2005, an estimated 207,000 migrants had overstayed their visas. The assumption is that most of these individuals are working illegally in Japan. The number of overstayers has gone up and down since 1990. At that time, the estimated number was 100,000; by 1993, that number had tripled to 300,000.

Another area in which significant growth in immigration has taken place is among foreign spouses. In 2002, 35,879 marriages were registered between a Japanese national and a foreigner (4.7 percent of all marriages); of these, 27,957 involved a foreign bride and 7,922 a foreign groom. About a quarter of these marriages involved a Japanese citizen and a South Korean permanent resident, but in 2002, Japanese men married more Chinese and Filipina brides than they did Koreans (figures cited in Regional Thematic Working Group 2008).

Beyond the labor shortage problem, the most important immigration issue facing Japan is its declining and aging population. Japan has one of the lowest fertility rates in the world (1.3 births per woman in 2007). The most salient implication of such a low fertility rate is a smaller working-age population (fifteen to sixty-four years old). As Japan's working-age population grows relatively and absolutely smaller and older, this shift will create increasing pressure to find a "demographic solution," which can involve a number of complementary options: (1) higher levels of "replacement migration," (2) increased productivity through automation and a transition to a post-Fordist (i.e., information-based) economy, and (3) reforms in pension and retirement policies.

North Korea

North Korea is a tightly controlled society about which solid data and information are difficult to obtain. Nonetheless, observers know that the country's long-term economic deterioration (beginning in the late 1970s) and disastrous floods and famines in the 1990s sparked an increase in unauthorized out-migration primarily to China (the North Korean government regards unauthorized emigration as an act of treason). Estimates on the total number of North Koreans who left for China are widely divergent—the US State Department, for example, puts the number at between 30,000 and 50,000, while some NGOs suggest at least 100,000 and as many as 300,000 North Koreans have emigrated as "refugees." Notably, the Chinese government does not regard North Korean migrants as refugees; instead, they are defined as unauthorized economic migrants and are therefore subject to deportation. China's refusal to recognize their status and provide a safe haven make up one reason why estimates are so soft (i.e., since North Korean migrants are afraid of being deported, they keep their presence in China hidden). A number of North Koreans who make it to China attempt to transit to other countries, including South Korea. Between 1990 and 2006, a total of 8,661 North Korean defectors were accepted by the South Korean government. Other North Korean migrants travel to Southeast Asia, especially Thailand and Vietnam, where they then receive assistance from the UN Refugee Agency (all figures cited in Tanaka 2008).

The North Korean government does allow for limited and carefully controlled worker migration to specific countries, including Russia, the Czech Republic, Poland, Bulgaria, Hungary, Mongolia, Qatar, and Kuwait. In November 2006, for example, about 400 women and 20 men from North Korea were employed in the Czech Republic in garment and leather factories; up to 20,000 North Koreans work in Russia's logging industry (Tanaka 2008). The North Korean government also allows for a small number of students (2,294 in 2006) to study abroad at the tertiary (university) level; interestingly, the majority were studying in New Zealand.

In-migration is severely restricted. Almost all involves temporary travel by business managers, investors, tourists, and government officials (including diplomatic personnel).

South Korea

Korea (both South and North) has a very large emigrant population of about 6.8 million people; the large proportion of Koreans, however, live in just three countries: China (2.8 million), the United States (2.0 million), and Japan (629,000). Much of the out-migration to China and Japan occurred prior to World War II, while the vast majority of Korean emigration to the United States took place after 1970. In the early years of industrialization—after **Park Chung Hee** came to power in 1961—South Korea was a labor-exporting country. South Korean workers were sent by their government and large business enterprises (the *chaebol*) to work on construction projects in the oil-producing countries of the Middle East. At this practice's peak in 1982, 197,000 South Korean construction workers were deployed overseas. Several thousands of South Koreans were also sent to Germany as nurses or miners in the 1960s; most returned to South Korea but about half stayed. Throughout the 1970s, they staged protests demanding the right to settle permanently in Germany. Ultimately, the West

German government under Helmut Schmidt allowed them to remain (Schön-wälder 2004).

By the mid-1980s, the number of Koreans deployed overseas had dropped sharply as South Korea made the transition from a labor-exporting country to a labor-importing one. As in Japan, the main reason for this transition was rapid industrialization and the attendant problem with labor shortages, which were concentrated in the small and medium-size business sector, particularly in un-skilled or low-skilled manufacturing and construction. Beginning in the late 1980s, migrant workers from China primarily (most of whom were also ethnic Koreans referred to as *joseonjok*), but also from South and Southeast Asia, began arriving in South Korea. Because South Korea's immigration law, as in Japan, did not permit unskilled immigrant labor, almost all of the new cross-border migrants worked in South Korea illegally. In these early years, stories of worker abuse, nonpayment of wages, and other problems were very common. In 1991, the South Korean government, following the Japanese model, intro-duced an industrial training program, which was ostensibly designed to provide training to workers from poorer countries, but which clearly was meant to pro-vide a back door for unskilled worker migration. A large proportion of cross-border migrants who entered South Korea as trainees ultimately left their positions to find better-paying jobs or stayed in South Korea after their visas expired. The number of overstayers peaked at 289,239 in 2002.

In 2004, the government introduced a guest worker program (the Employ-ment Permit System), which officially allowed for unskilled cross-border mi-grants to work in South Korea. The trainee program remained in place but was phased out and ultimately eliminated (in 2007, no new trainees were accepted into the program). The Employment Permit System allowed South Korean com-panies with fewer than 300 employees to bring in foreign workers (who had to be forty years old or younger) from selected countries (i.e., countries with which South Korea had signed a memorandum of understanding). The memorandum set out specific quotas and conditions; if workers from a certain country were found to have violated the conditions, the South Korean government could can-cel the memorandum with that entire country. Migrant workers were allowed to stay for three years (later, this limit was increased to just under five years); contracts could be renewed, but only if the worker left the country for at least one month. This provision prevented workers from obtaining the right to per-manent residency (which requires a five-year continuous stay). Under the Em-ployment Permit System, foreign workers were given the same labor rights as domestic workers.

In 2005, according to the Korea Immigration Service (2009a), 747,467 for-eigners were living in South Korea, including visa overstayers. Of that total, 283,030 were from China, including 167,589 *joseonjok*. In 2005, cross-border migrant workers accounted for about 2 percent of South Korea's total workforce.

In addition to foreign workers, a large number of foreign spouses have immigrated to South Korea, primarily women from Vietnam, China, Japan, and the Philippines. These marriages first began to take off in the early 1990s, when a large number of *joseonjok* women began marrying South Korean men: from a single marriage in 1990, the number grew to a cumulative total of 70,163 by the end of 2005. Between 1990 and 2006, the overall number of marriages between South Korean men and foreign women was 90,295. In 2005, 13.5 percent of all marriages in South Korea were between a Korean and non-Korean. In rural areas, the figure is even higher—upward of 40 percent (all figures cited in Lim 2010). Since 2005, a small decline has been seen in the proportion of international marriages—from 11.7 percent in 2006 to 10.5 percent in 2010 (cited in G. W. Jones 2012).

South Korea also has a very low fertility rate of about 1.26 children per woman (in 2012, this fertility rate was the sixth lowest in the world). Thus, as in Japan, the low fertility rate suggests that South Korea will be faced with increasing pressures to find solutions to a declining working-age population and an increasingly aged population. Higher levels of in-migration, both temporary worker migration and permanent settlement, are one of several options.

Taiwan

Taiwan has had a tumultuous experience with immigration, even if the view is limited to the postwar period only. As was discussed Chapter 6, following the victory by communist forces in the late 1940s, around 2 million Chinese mainlanders fled to Taiwan and essentially took control of the island under the **KMT**. During the 1960s and into the early 1970s, no significant in- or out-migration took place, but the country experienced a very large amount of internal (rural to urban) migration. Internal migration was sufficient to meet the country's labor demands through the 1970s, but by the mid- to late 1980s, Taiwan was beginning to feel the pressures of the migration transition. By 1987, large numbers of migrant workers, primarily from Southeast Asian countries, were arriving in Taiwan and finding work in the country's very large small-business sector. Almost all of these workers—estimated at 70,000 in 1987—came on tourist visas and worked illegally (Liu 1996). As in Japan and South Korea, Taiwan's immigration law did not permit any immigration by unskilled workers. Despite the large influx of "illegal" cross-border migrants, the Taiwanese government did not take steps to expel them, primarily because of a severe labor shortage. For example, employers faced no legal penalty for hiring foreign workers illegally, nor did the government attempt to pass any laws to that effect (Liu 1996).

In 1990, via an administrative order, the Taiwanese government decided to open the country's borders to low-skilled cross-border migrants. Initially, this order was limited to fourteen specific construction projects, but two years later, the program was formalized in the Employment Service Act (Surak 2011). While the act opened up many more areas of legal employment, the program was also tightly regulated and designed to better control the inflow and outflow of foreign workers. As in South Korea, strict time limits were set—initially, the maximum employment period was either one or two years—and the workers were explicitly prohibited from becoming permanent residents The law also imposed sanctions on employers who hired workers illegally. The first large-scale deportations were carried out in 1994, about two years after the introduction of the law. By 2009, the program had approximately 350,000 participants—a figure that was fixed through informal negotiations with unions. Of this total, Indonesians make up about 40 percent, with Thais, Vietnamese, and Filipinas (mainly women working as maids or in other "domestic" jobs) accounting for about 20 percent each (all figures cited in Surak 2011).

As in both Japan and South Korea, Taiwan also has an increasingly large number of international marriages, mainly foreign women marrying Taiwanese men. In the case of Taiwan, however, most men marry Chinese women from the mainland; nonetheless, international marriages involving a non-Chinese spouse accounted for 10 percent of all marriages in 2003 (by 2010, the figure had dropped substantially, to just 4 percent). Including ethnic Chinese spouses, the proportion of international marriages in Taiwan in 2003 was 32 percent and 13 percent of all marriages in 2010 (figures cited in G. W. Jones 2012).

Another major similarity between Taiwan and its two East Asian neighbors is an extremely low fertility rate, although among the three Taiwan is the clear "winner." In 2010, Taiwan's fertility rate actually dropped below 1.0, to an extraordinarily low 0.895 children per woman, although this low rate may have had something to do with the Chinese zodiac (2009 was the "Year of the Tiger," which is considered inauspicious for births). In 2011, the fertility rate recovered somewhat but was still only 1.16 (figures in R. Chan 2012). At this level, according to a projection by the CEPD (2012) of Taiwan, Taiwan's population of 23 million people will fall by almost 20 percent over the next fifty years.

Theories of International Migration and East Asia

Theories of immigration and migration abound. Douglas S. Massey and colleagues (2006) list five major theories on the "initiation of international migration" (i.e., **macroeconomic** theory, microeconomic theory, the new economics of migration, dual labor market theory, and world-systems theory), and another four theories on the "perpetuation of international movements" (i.e., network theory, institutional theory, cumulative causation, and migration systems theory). I do not endeavor to cover all these theories, in part, because the focus (in the first part of this chapter) is primarily on the issue of initiation. That is, I am concerned with two interrelated questions. First, why have Japan, South Korea, and Taiwan become significant destinations for immigration? Second, why have these three countries accepted more and more immigrants, especially from poorer areas? I also address, albeit only cursorily, the question of why China and North Korea have not. Theories on the initiation of international migration, I should emphasize, examine factors and forces that affect both source and destination countries. Despite the strong focus on Japan, South Korea, and Taiwan as destination countries, considering why individuals from source countries decide to migrate or emigrate is both useful and even necessary. After all, at one time, all three East Asian destination countries were primarily source countries themselves, and even today the region sees significant out-migration, especially from South Korea and Taiwan. With all this in mind, I begin with an examination of the two major neoclassical economic theories of migration, the macroeconomic and the microeconomic models.

Economic Models: Macroeconomic and Microeconomic Explanations

As late as the 1970s, most observers both inside and outside of East Asia thought the region was too socially insulated and culturally hidebound to accommodate large-scale migration and immigration. Foreigners, and especially poor foreigners, were simply not wanted and therefore would be prevented from moving to, still less settling in, the three most industrialized countries of East Asia—Japan, South Korea, and Taiwan. The clear implication was that culture and tradition, along with a strong dose of xenophobia, would act as impenetrable barriers to migration and immigration, regardless of economic, demographic, or other rational considerations. (In other words, the earliest explanations were largely culture based.) Macroeconomic theory, however, has long held that migration/immigration is primarily a function of classic principles of economics, especially of supply and demand. More specifically, according to macroeconomic theory, increasing labor cost in high-wage economies increases demand for "cheap labor," which of course is in ready supply in low-wage countries. In this view, whenever a large differential in wages develops between and among economies, workers from low-wage countries will invariably migrate to higher-wage countries. This theory and other primarily economic ideas underlie a broader range of "push-pull" theories. As Stephen Castles and Mark Miller (2003) explain, push-pull theories "perceive the causes of migration to lie in a combination of 'push factors,' impelling people to leave the areas of origin, and 'pull factors,' attracting them to certain receiving countries. 'Push factors' include demographic growth, low living standards, lack of economic opportunities and political repression, while 'pull factors' are demand for labour, availability of land, good economic opportunities and political freedoms" (p. 22).

Notably, the macroeconomic supply and demand theory does not directly address or incorporate push factors, nor does it explicitly include other demand factors except for the demand for labor. Other economists have provided a corrective by focusing on individual migrants and their rational choices. These microeconomic models of individual choice stress the importance of "human capital endowments" (i.e., the value of skills, knowledge, talents, and other capacities that human beings possess), which vary from person to person, but which can also be improved through migration. From this perspective, the decision to migrate is understood as a human capital investment: people will migrate "if the expected rate of return from higher wages in the destination country is greater than the costs incurred through migrating" (Castles and Miller 2003, p. 23, citing Chiswick 2000). More simply, as rational actors, migrants will decide to move across borders for work or other reasons on the basis of a cost-benefit calculation (also known as strategic calculation). In this scenario, as George Borjas (1989) explains, "individuals residing in any source country consider the possibility of remaining there or of migrating to a number of potential host countries. Individuals make the migration decision by considering the values of the various alternatives, and choosing the option that best suits them given the financial and legal constraints that regulate the international migration process" (p. 460). The "financial and legal constraints" are a crucial part of this calculation. Financially, for example, cross-border travel can be very expensive, so the choice of many migrants, especially those in search of work, to travel to neighboring countries, such as the large-scale migration between Mexico and the United States, makes sense. Legally, constraints can be even more imposing. Many countries impose stiff barriers to immigration, sometimes keeping immigrants out, sometimes keeping their own people in, or sometimes both. North Korea is a particularly good example of a country that allows for limited in- and out-migration. Importantly, though, this rigidity has never meant a total absence of cross-border migration and immigration. In the 1960s and 1970s, when China experienced serious economic problems (including a disastrous famine) and harsh rule under **Mao Zedong**, both Chinese and ethnic Koreans living in China migrated to North Korea. Then, in the 1980s and 1990s, when China was booming economically and North Korea was suffering serious economic problems (including its own famines), the flow reversed. In recent years, according to Andrei Lankov (2012), cross-border movement has been partly "regularized," with about 122,000 North Koreans crossing into China for work in 2011 (p. 2). This change suggests that even under totalitarian or near-totalitarian rule, individuals behave as rational actors. (Notably, with the exception of China, North Korea has been extremely effective at keeping out migrants/immigrants from other countries.)

In East Asia more generally, push-pull theories seem persuasive. Indeed, macroeconomic theory alone appears to explain increasing migration to East Asia. During the early periods of industrialization in South Korea, Taiwan, and

Japan, for example, demand for low-wage labor was easily met from a large and still largely untapped "surplus labor force" primarily from the countryside in all three countries. Taiwan illustrates this phenomenon quite clearly: between 1960 and 1973, the share of the labor force engaged in agricultural activities shrank from 50 percent to 30 percent, which indicated a massive rural-to-urban migration (Lin 1998). On this point, I should emphasize that internal migration is, in principle, no different from cross-border migration. Individuals are behaving rationally by seeking higher wages or a better selection of economic opportunities in urban areas compared to the countryside. In fact, this same process of rural-to-urban migration—on a much more massive scale—can be seen in China today.[1] Thus, as the macroeconomic model predicts, with ample domestic supply and scant demand for foreign labor, essentially no unskilled worker migration took place to East Asia in the 1950s through the 1970s, and even later in South Korea and Taiwan. As the surplus labor force dried up beginning in the late 1970s in Japan and mid-1980s in South Korea and Taiwan, and as unemployment levels dropped to historic lows, demand for additional workers began to ramp up. Wages, too, began to increase in each of the East Asian economies, which created a larger differential between East Asia and other regions. Predictably, then, by the late 1980s, all three East Asian economies were "importing" foreign workers, and despite some ups and downs over the years, the demand for foreign workers has remained relatively strong. The conclusion seems simple: culture and traditions are no barrier to the forces of supply and demand.

At the same time, and also in a manner ostensibly consistent with the push-pull model, during the early period of East Asian industrialization, some out-migration took place from East Asia to other, richer countries, something that was especially true for South Korea, which was a major labor-sending country until the mid-1980s. Between 1963 and the mid-1980s, approximately 2 million South Korean workers went overseas for strictly temporary employment, with the bulk going to oil-producing Middle Eastern countries to do construction work (Park 1997). In addition, beginning in the 1960s and accelerating into the 1970s, a large number of people from Taiwan and South Korea immigrated to the United States. By 1980, the population of Taiwan-born immigrants in the United States was about 75,000 (S. Lin 2010), whereas for Koreans the number was almost 290,000, a dramatic increase from only 11,171 in 1960 (Terrazas 2009).

Criticisms of Economic Models

Despite this seeming correspondence between theory and real-world migration patterns, when one looks a little deeper into the migration process in East Asia and elsewhere, macro- and microeconomic theories begin to lose some of their explanatory power. Indeed, economic models of migration have been subject to a wide range of criticism. Perhaps the most basic criticism is that push-pull models are too simplistic, especially with regard to international or cross-border migration (as opposed to domestic migration). This failing is especially true of the macroeconomic model, which cannot explain why some people in some poor countries migrate, while others in the same country or different but equally poor countries do not. Nor does the model explain the choice of destination country. After all, if demand for foreign workers is high and if the wage differential between poor and rich countries is large, then one should expect most people in poor countries to migrate until the wage differential equalizes. But this conclusion is not supported by trends in the real world.

Moreover, as I just noted, the macroeconomic model also cannot explain why migrants from certain countries tend to favor certain destination countries over others. In recent migration to Japan, Taiwan, and South Korea, significant differences can be identified with regard to the major immigrant groups. Japan is a particularly popular destination for Chinese, Brazilians, Filipinos, and Peruvians (Koreans constitute the second-largest nonresident population, but a large proportion are "historical residents," meaning that they arrived in Japan during the colonial period, sometimes by force). Taiwan, by contrast, has a very large Indonesian migrant population, followed in size by migrant populations from Vietnam, Thailand, and the Philippines. And in South Korea, while the largest group is also from China, the majority come from a particular area, the Yanbian region. The other large migrant populations in South Korea are from Vietnam, the Philippines, Thailand, and Mongolia (Figure 8.1 has additional details). Why do more Indonesians migrate to Taiwan than to Japan or Korea? Why does Japan attract migrants from South America, while neither Taiwan nor South Korea have any significant migration from that region? The answer to this last question is actually quite simple—most South American migrants to Japan are ethnic Japanese. In addition, the migrants from the Yanbian region in China who move to South Korea are ethnic Koreans. These facts suggest a strong ethnic component to migration. The ethnic component is an important (albeit not surprising) issue, which I come back to below.

Even more importantly, perhaps, macroeconomic theory does a poor job of explaining why, as a destination region, East Asia still has a relatively low level of worker immigration compared to other "economically developed" regions of the world. Japan especially is a case in point: the country saw a dramatic increase in wages between 1960 and 1971, during which time real manufacturing wages more than doubled (Allen 1981). According to the macroeconomic model, then, one should have expected Japan to have become a major destination country at least by the early 1970s. But even before 1960, the economic gap between Japan and most of its neighbors in Asia was already quite substantial, and yet very little in-migration took place at the time. In stark contrast to Japan, Germany had already begun a large-scale "guest worker" program,

Figure 8.1   Major Source Countries for Foreign Resident Groups in Japan, Taiwan, and South Korea, 2008

	Source Country				
Japan	China	Korea[a]	Brazil	Philippines	Peru
Population	655,377	589,239	312,582	210,617	59,723
Percentage[b]	29.6	26.6	14.1	9.5	2.7
Taiwan	Indonesia	Vietnam	Thailand	Philippines	
Population	123,905	101,592	80,484	79,901	—
Percentage[b]	28.3	23.2	18.4	18.3	
South Korea	China	Vietnam	Philippines[c]	Thailand	Mongolia
Population	556,517	84,763	46,894	45,198	32,206
Percentage[b]	48.0	7.3	4.0	3.9	2.8

Sources: Figures for Japan are cited in Koyama and Okamoto (2010), figures for Taiwan are cited in Kaneko (2009), and figures for South Korea are from Korea Immigration Service (2008).

Notes: Totals do not add to 100 percent since only the major source countries are shown.

a. Foreign residents from Korea include those who emigrated to Japan during the colonial period, before the peninsula was divided into two countries.

b. Percentage of total in-migration.

c. For South Korea, Japan is the third-largest source of foreign residents.

officially implemented in 1955, which brought millions of temporary workers into that country. In sum, the macroeconomic model is a very "blunt instrument." That is, it illustrates one reason cross-border migration exists, but it cannot explain specific patterns of migration, nor does it account for significant variations in the timing and degree of immigration among destination countries.

Microeconomic explanations are less blunt, but oversimplification is still a problem. Consider, on this point, a hypothetical situation: 100 individuals with similar human capital endowments, all equally poor, live in the same community. Three or four may decide to migrate to another country (usually the same one), while the rest remain. This typical scenario is likely, but in this scenario, the microeconomic explanation fails to capture and account for the divergence in individual decisionmaking. What motivated the three or four individuals to leave their home and travel to another country, sometimes thousands of miles away? Why did they choose to migrate to South Korea rather than Japan? Why did the others choose to stay or perhaps migrate to an urban area in their own country? Again, for the most part, microeconomic theory cannot provide answers to these questions. These questions are not meant to suggest that individual migrants do not engage in "cost-benefit calculations"; they almost certainly do. Rather, they underscore the point that cost-benefit calculations are—critics argue—only a piece of a larger, more complex social process. Castles and Miller (2003) sum up the issue nicely:

> Historians, anthropologists, sociologists and geographers have shown that mi-
> grants' behaviour is strongly influenced by historical experiences as well as
> by family and community dynamics. . . . Moreover, migrants have limited and
> often contradictory information, and are subject to a range of constraints (es-
> pecially lack of power in the face of employers and governments). Migrants
> compensate through developing cultural capital (collective knowledge of their
> situation and strategies for dealing with it) and social capital (the social net-
> works which organize migration and community formation processes). (p. 24)

In addition to this explanation, I add another from Hein de Haas (2008), who
points out that the "propensity to migrate crucially depends on the *aspirations*
of people, an element which is typically ignored by neoclassical . . . and push-
pull models—in which needs are somehow assumed to be constant—but is essential to explaining migration" (p. 11; emphasis added). Thinking about the
hypothetical case above, one can fairly easily imagine how individual aspirations play a role in the decisionmaking process; indeed, one might argue that
aspirations (a subjective concept), combined with cultural and social capital,
are more important than mere strategic calculation.

These issues are important, but as noted above, in this chapter I am primarily concerned with the factors or forces that have encouraged—or compelled, as the case may be—the East Asian countries to accept immigration,
particularly in light of their long-standing resistance to the inclusion of outsiders, whether on a short- or long-term basis, into their societies. Of course, I
have already examined one possible explanation, the macroeconomic supply-
and-demand model. But other explanations can be given, some of which come
from structure-based approaches.

Structural Approaches

Economic models are premised on rational decisionmaking. Structural approaches, as suggested in the foregoing discussions of economic and political
change and continuity, do not discount rationality, but they put far stronger emphasis on how underlying processes and forces define the limits or parameters
of individual choices. With this in mind, one particularly prominent theory that
falls into the structural category is known as the dual labor market theory, which
is most closely associated with the work of Michael Piore (1979). Piore specifically takes issue with the conventional economic assumption that cross-border
migration is primarily a function of wage differentials. As he puts it, "migrant
behavior can better be understood in terms of the specific attributes of the *jobs
available* to migrants and the *meaning attached* in the social context in which
work is performed" (p. 8; emphasis added). In this regard, Piore (1980) argues
forcefully that worker migration is essentially demand initiated and, in the
early years, demand controlled. "The workers," he explains, "are recruited by

employers in the industrial country to fill a particular set of jobs—jobs that national workers have rejected. Certain conditions abroad—population pressure and low incomes—are required for workers to respond to these recruitment efforts, but neither is the *cause* of migration" (Piore 1980, pp. 312–313; emphasis in original).

So what are the structural elements of the dual labor market theory, and what are the two parts of the labor market? I will begin with the second question: the "dual market" refers to the idea that the labor market is structurally divided into two distinct parts, a primary and a secondary segment. The two segments, as Michael Reich, David Gordon, and Richard Edwards (1973) explain, "are differentiated mainly by stability characteristics. Primary jobs require and develop stable working habits; skills are often acquired on the job; wages are relatively high; and job ladders exist. Secondary jobs do not require and often discourage stable working habits; wages are low; turnover is high; and job ladders are few" (pp. 359–360). Importantly, the two segments of the labor market are not contingent: that is, they are not simply an expendable aspect of capitalist economies. Instead, they reflect an embedded and essentially permanent part of modern capitalism, and this idea is the structural element of the argument. While a number of explanations could be given for why the segmented or dual labor market came about, Reich, Gordon, and Edwards (1973) provide a useful perspective. They suggest that the segmented labor market was a deliberate—but necessary strategy—by "monopoly capitalist corporations . . . to resolve the contradictions between the increased proletarianization of the work force and the growth and consolidation of concentrated corporate power" (p. 361). The segmentation of the labor market, in other words, allowed (and continues to allow) for the division of labor between a relatively privileged group and a more exploited, subordinate group. The purpose of this division is to undermine or prevent the working class as a whole from uniting based on their common experiences. The workers in the subordinate group do not have to be cross-border migrants—ethnic or racial minorities and women have also served this purpose—but migrant workers have always played a central role, if only because the supply of them is virtually never ending. In this regard, Piore (1979, 1980) suggests that the demand for immigrant labor has become a permanent feature in the economic structure of industrialized capitalist economies (cited in Massey et al. 2006).

Loosely associated with the dual labor market theory is the historical structural approach, which primarily reflects ideas found in world-systems theory. This approach does not necessarily dismiss the notion of a dual labor market but instead focuses on the dynamics of global capitalism as a whole. In this view, cross-border worker migration arises from the vastly unequal distribution of economic and political power in the world economy and from the world economy's trimodal structure composed of the core, semiperiphery, and periphery (see Figure 8.2). As with the dual labor market theory, the historical structural approach

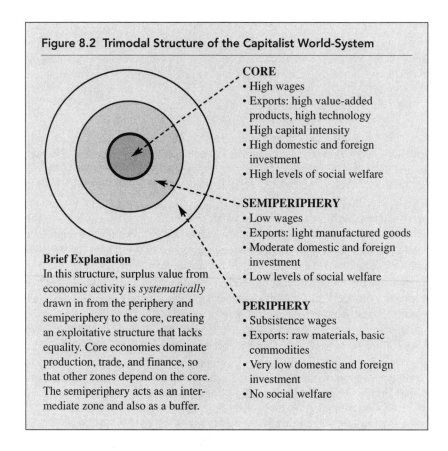

Figure 8.2 Trimodal Structure of the Capitalist World-System

CORE
- High wages
- Exports: high value-added products, high technology
- High capital intensity
- High domestic and foreign investment
- High levels of social welfare

SEMIPERIPHERY
- Low wages
- Exports: light manufactured goods
- Moderate domestic and foreign investment
- Low levels of social welfare

PERIPHERY
- Subsistence wages
- Exports: raw materials, basic commodities
- Very low domestic and foreign investment
- No social welfare

Brief Explanation
In this structure, surplus value from economic activity is *systematically* drawn in from the periphery and semiperiphery to the core, creating an exploitative structure that lacks equality. Core economies dominate production, trade, and finance, so that other zones depend on the core. The semiperiphery acts as an intermediate zone and also as a buffer.

considers demand from core economies to be an important determinant of cross-border worker migration; in this respect, both perspectives also agree that wage differentials among countries play, at best, a secondary role in explaining international migration. In the historical structural view, however, demand for labor is not the only issue; more important are the disruptive effects of capitalist penetration into peripheral regions. When capitalist **institutions** are introduced into nonindustrial societies, the indigenous economy is disrupted, sometimes dramatically so, and people are often disconnected or uprooted from their normal ways of earning a living. To survive, they often have to migrate, either to urban areas within their own countries or across borders if no work is available. Their labor becomes a commodity, and they become part of a world economy, within which their movements are largely determined by the needs and desires of the core economies.

Both of these structural arguments can find some—even a great deal of—support when applied to Japan, South Korea, and Taiwan. The relegation of "push" factors to secondary status and the focus on demand as the driving force in cross-border worker migration to the three countries is particularly relevant. In fact, international migration—especially of unskilled workers from poorer regions—was somewhat clearly initiated and effectively (albeit not perfectly) controlled by actors within the three East Asian countries. One can see this process, for example, in the selective pattern of immigration to each country (see Figure 8.1 above). Earlier I mentioned the major source countries of foreign residents (mostly unskilled workers) in Japan, South Korea, and Taiwan and followed up by pointing out the large number of ethnic Japanese Brazilians who immigrated to Japan and the large number of ethnic Koreans (known as *joseon-jok*) who immigrated to South Korea from the Yanbian region of China. Obviously, this outcome was not random but was instead a product of deliberate recruitment of specific workers by both Japan and South Korea, a trend predicted accurately by the dual labor market theory. On this point, notably, Japan had engaged in this process once before: during the colonial period and until Japan's defeat at the end of World War II, millions of Koreans were recruited to work in Japan's secondary labor market. In the early years, most Koreans went to Japan voluntarily, and the vast majority (almost 90 percent) were agricultural workers from Korea's three southern provinces. In Japan, they "engaged in manual and menial work, occupying—along with **burakumin** (descendants of premodern outcastes) and Okinawans—the lowest tier in the urban labor market" (Lie 2008, p. 4). Once the war began, severe labor shortages in Japan led to *forced* migration—between 1939 and 1945, 700,000 to 800,000 Koreans were made to work in Japan (Lie 2008, p. 5). This earlier instance of immigrant labor recruitment is worth learning about because it starkly underscores the demand-driven nature of cross-border labor migration. That is, when Japan needed immigrant workers, they were delivered into the country "by hook or by crook"; when Japan did not need immigrant labor, by contrast, the flow was stopped almost completely.

At the same time, once the door to unskilled worker migration was open in East Asia, immigrant workers from around the world began to arrive seemingly of their own accord, a conclusion that was made evident by the large number of unauthorized migration into all three countries. At its highest point in 2001, for example, more than 66 percent of all foreign workers in South Korea (255,206 out of 329,555 total immigrant workers) were in the country illegally (Seol and Skrentny 2004). In the same time period, in 2002, of the 710,000 foreign workers in Japan (who had arrived after 1980), at least 280,000 were classified as "illegal workers" (Usui 2006). The statistics for Taiwan are more difficult to find, but according to Taiwan's National Immigration Agency (2005), the number of "ferreted foreign illegal residents" in 2001 was 18,277 (I surmise that "ferreted" refers to illegal immigrants apprehended by authorities). The statistics suggest that the three East Asian **states** could not control the immigration process completely, a conclusion made even more apparent when one considers that many of the unauthorized migrants were from "untargeted" countries and regions. In South Korea, for example, a significant number of workers came from countries such as Bangladesh, Nepal, Sri Lanka, Pakistan, Nigeria, Ghana, and Egypt—all told, immigrants from as many as fifty-four countries were in South Korea by the early 2000s (Lim 2003), suggesting that push factors were not entirely irrelevant in this process. While valid, this observation does not necessarily obviate the main insights of the dual labor market theory.

Criticisms of Structural Approaches

Despite what appears to be an even stronger correspondence between dual labor market theory and real-world patterns of migration, not everyone is convinced. David Bartram (2000), for example, argues that dual labor market theory does a poor job of explaining the immigration process in Japan. First, he points out that Japan's dualism has been widely recognized—a point I discussed in Chapter 5.[2] Second, Bartram argues that if demand is the driving force behind the initiation of and increase in cross-border migration, migration to Japan should have started much earlier and, even more importantly, a much more significant amount of cross-border worker migration to Japan should have occurred, once it did start, than is the case. On this point, recall that Japan, as well as South Korea and Taiwan, have generally had much lower levels of worker migration than other countries with similar economic structures. In principle, this difference should not exist: if demand drives the need for immigrant labor, then once the door or recruitment channels are open, one should expect to see a flood of new immigrants until demand is fully sated, or the needs of capital are otherwise met.

Although I did not discuss the historical structural perspective in much detail, worth noting are some of the criticisms of this perspective as well. Castles and Miller (2003) sum up the main criticism in a rhetorical question: "If the logic of capital and interests of Western states were so dominant, how could the *frequent breakdown* of migration policies be explained, such as the unplanned shift from labour migration to permanent settlement in certain countries?" (p. 25; emphasis added). To clarify, Castles and Miller are pointing to a common occurrence in countries with significant immigration. Specifically, state and business leaders have generally crafted their immigration policies so that migrants would remain temporary; that is, they would be allowed into the country to work for a set number of years and then, when their time was up, would be forced to leave. In many countries, officials had no intention of allowing permanent settlement. In practice, however, these intentions have been frustrated, as is certainly apparent in Western countries and becoming a distinct possibility in East Asia. At a minimum, in East Asia, a process can be observed by which carefully constructed immigration policies have been effectively challenged and sometimes overturned. The high level of authorized immigration in all three countries, as I suggested above, is a good indication of this loss of control in that migrant workers defied authorities by (1) entering the country to find work without permission, (2) entering the county with a work permit, but then abandoning their approved positions, or (3) "overstaying," that is staying beyond the time permitted on their visas, often with the intention of continuing to work. A number of other important issues are left to examine, but before doing so, I want to look at one additional theoretical approach—an approach that has not received much attention in the mainstream literature on cross-border migration.

The Role of the State: An Institutional Perspective

In the previous section, I referred to a criticism of the dual labor market theory by David Bartram (2000). His main criticism, to repeat, is that the dual labor market theory and all other theories of cross-border migration cannot account for what he refers to as "negative cases" of immigration, or ones in which highly industrialized countries with clear labor shortages and a strong demand for additional workers continue to have low levels of cross-border labor immigration. Japan represents one such case, and both South Korea and Taiwan arguably fall into this category, too. On this point, Bartram refers to an alternative explanation that focuses on national identity and culture. In this argument, Myron Weiner (1995) posits that the resistance of some countries to significant in-migration can be explained by "differences in conceptions of national identity—specifically, whether a nation is built on the notion of cultural homogeneity or cultural diversity and whether the notion of pluralism extends from the political to cultural realm" (pp. 73–74). The argument, as Bartram points out, faces an immediate empirical problem: Weiner puts Germany and Japan in the same group of countries that emphasize cultural homogeneity, yet Germany has a very large proportion of immigrant workers in its economy, especially when compared to Japan (Bartram 2000). From 1960 to 1988, in fact, the proportion of foreign workers in Japan's total labor force never exceeded 0.8 percent, compared to a high of 8.2 percent in Germany. Bartram's analysis, notably, covers the 1960s and 1970s, when the labor shortage in Japan was most severe. In other words, despite needing hundreds of thousands or even millions of new workers (at one point, in 1971, the Japanese Labor Ministry estimated that there were as many as 2 million unfilled job openings [cited in Bartram 2000, p. 16]), only a few hundred thousand immigrant workers were allowed in the country.

Bartram's argument focuses on the role of the state as an autonomous—and very powerful—institutional actor, which is neither beholden to politicians and their parties nor to business. In this respect, Bartram largely echoes the arguments made by scholars who explain East Asia's economic rise as a product of the **developmental state**. As Bartram puts it, "Economic policy in Japan has

long been distinguished by the location of decisionmaking: most major decisions were made by bureaucracies, not by the **Diet**. . . . The bureaucrats generally concerned themselves less with the profitability of particular companies
and more with the long-term trajectory of the economy" (p. 24). The crux of
his argument is that the Japanese state (i.e., the bureaucracies in charge of economic policy) did not want immigration, and that those "who stood to benefit
most from imported labor [i.e., small and medium-size businesses] were systematically excluded from policy making" (p. 25). Bartram's points raise an obvious question: Why was the state opposed to immigrant labor? The short
answer, offered by Bartram, is that state bureaucrats thought a number of other
viable options would be better for the national economy in the long run. Thus,
the "solutions actually advocated by the government and adopted by employers
included automation and other means of increasing worker productivity and
output; exporting some types of production into the low-wage countries; has-
tening the mobilization of 'reserve' labor into the urban labor force; allowing
inflation to increase as labor shortages contributed to increasingly militant wage
demands; and . . . allowing the transfer of income from capital to labor" (p. 19).

Do the other two East Asian cases—South Korea and Taiwan—support Bartram's model? Before answering this question, one needs to ascertain if both are
"negative cases." The short answer is a qualified yes; high-speed industrialization
in South Korea and Taiwan produced labor shortages beginning in the late 1980s,
and although both countries began "importing" foreign labor around that time,
both also imposed limits that kept the number of cross-border migrant workers
relatively small (in proportion to the total labor force). A little less clear, however,
is whether limited cross-border worker migration was primarily a product of an
autonomous state or of limited demand from only certain industries (e.g., the
3-D sector), or of something else. I address these questions below. For now, one
can say that both South Korea and Taiwan, as already shown, had their own versions of a developmental state. Also fairly clear is that both states were—and
continue to be—active in shaping immigration policy to fit the needs of the national economy, with little concern for individual and human rights. In South
Korea, for example, the state created an industrial "trainee" program in 1991
modeled after a similar program in Japan, which was designed to accommodate
the growing demand for unskilled immigrant labor in the small-business sector
(where almost all 3-D jobs are located). This program was, however, a "trainee"
program only in name; the international migrants who participated in the program were not learning new skills, knowledge, and technical expertise to take
back to their home countries but instead were thrown into small factories and
businesses to do unskilled labor. The creation of the trainee program, though,
enabled the government to avoid amending the immigration law, which prohibited international migrants from entering the country to engage in unskilled work.

In Taiwan a slightly less cynical approach was used: in 1992, the Taiwanese
government legalized the recruitment of unskilled foreign labor through the

Employment Services Act. Under the act, strict quotas were set, and unskilled or low-skilled foreign workers were allowed to work only in certain industries—construction, manufacturing, and caregiving—but only "so long as they remained supplements to the native work force, did not delay economic upgrading, stayed only temporarily with no access to citizenship, and brought only minimal social costs" (Surak 2011, p. 2). In addition, the act barred foreign workers from getting married and becoming pregnant while in Taiwan. South Korea, notably, eventually followed the Taiwanese path and established its own "guest worker" program, known as the Employment Permit System, in 2004. In sum, that the East Asian developmental states were in charge of the immigration process from start to end certainly seems to be the case.

Bartram's model is an appealing argument and, as I noted already, one that dovetails nicely with the notion of the developmental state. It does have, however, a couple of potential problems or objections. First, Bartram himself acknowledges that Japan's major corporations had little need for immigrant labor, in part, because they could "better afford to pay higher wages to keep [their] . . . labor rolls filled and had a variety of means of ensuring labor market flexibility" (Surak 2011, p. 25). On the other hand, small businesses were severely squeezed by the shortage of labor, but they lacked the political and economic muscle to compel the Japanese state to act in their interests. Worth asking is, if the situation were reversed, would pressure from major corporations have led to a different result? Obviously, one cannot answer the question with any certainty, but posing counterfactual questions is useful since doing so can bring greater clarity to certain issues. After all, one can far more easily make an argument about the autonomy of the state when the interests of the state and big capital coincide. On this point, one should note that, in the early 1970s, one large and powerful association of Japanese businesses—the Nikkeiren (Japan Federation of Employers Association)—did begin to press the government to allow unskilled immigrant labor into the country. The power of the Nikkeiren is difficult to ignore, so the Japanese state would have likely accommodated the demands of the organization, at least to some extent. The recession following the first oil crisis in the early 1970s, however, rendered the issue moot since it temporarily reduced the demand for unskilled labor. Unfortunately, the shift in Japan's situation means that one cannot "test" Bartram's argument about the capacity of the Japanese state to dictate immigration policy in face of significant opposition from the business sector.

The Dual Labor Market and the Gendered Division of Labor in East Asia

A second possible objection to Bartram's argument focuses on the various bases of Japan's long-standing national dual labor market. Recall that immigrant labor is not necessary if the secondary labor market can be filled by other types of workers—in the case of Japan, these included women, older workers, and less educated workers and, in the prewar period, as discussed above, voluntary and coerced immigrant workers from Korea and China. In this situation, the interests of Japanese capital in maintaining a segmented or divided labor force were being met, thus the lack of pressure on the state to open the country's door to cross-border migrant labor. One should understand, on this last point, that Japan's dual labor market system was clearly designed to create two classes of workers along the lines of the primary and secondary segments discussed above. Women, in particular, occupied a central place in the secondary segment. Consider this description by H. J. Jones (1976–1977):

> In the 1970s, while women still account for almost half of the employees in textile-related industries, they hold the lowest positions, show the least rate of wage increase over the years, and one of the lowest in relation to male employees. . . . [I]n all areas of employment, a sex-based dual-track system developed which persists in postwar Japan despite legal reforms upholding equality of opportunity and denouncing discrimination on the basis of sex. (p. 591)

The foregoing account is a good depiction of a **gendered division of labor**, which continues to be of significance in Japan's employment system. Jones also notes that the secondary labor market in Japan was premised on the *dekasegi* concept: "a short-term labor pool that can be expanded and contracted in accordance with market demand, without security or welfare benefits" (p. 591). With this type of system in place, and with domestic women workers willing to fill positions in that system, Japan had little need for cross-border migrant workers. Significantly, the "reserve" supply of Japanese women was sufficient to meet the demand for unskilled, low-wage labor for all of the 1960s and into the early 1970s, a fact partly reflected in the employment statistics; the employment of Japanese women increased steadily during the 1960s and by 1972, for the first time since the 1930s, constituted half of the total labor force (H. J. Jones 1976–1977, p. 590). Fortuitously, around this time, the economic recession brought a temporary end to severe labor shortages (unemployment "shot up" from 1.1 percent in 1970 to almost 2.0 percent beginning in 1975), a condition that lasted until the mid-1980s. This train of thought leaves the question, was it the state or was it the dual labor market and a timely recession that minimized cross-border worker migration to Japan? To be sure, one can argue that the state helped to create the dual labor market in Japan, which is likely the case. But, even more important, this system benefited Japanese business first and foremost.

South Korea and Taiwan, one should recognize, also had their own versions of a gender-based dual labor market. To this day, for instance, South Korea has the largest wage gap between male and female workers among **OECD** countries (not coincidentally, Japan is second). In South Korea the wage gap in 2008 was 38 percent, more than two times the OECD average of 18.8 percent (Japan's wage gap was 31 percent). Thirty years earlier, not surprisingly, the gap was much worse: in 1988, South Korean women earned only 48 won to every 100 won earned by a South Korean male (Monk-Turner and Turner 2004); in Taiwan, the situation was not nearly as bad, but a large gap still existed as women earned about 64 to 68 percent of what men earned in 1988 (Zveglich and Rodgers 2004). On one level, nothing should be surprising about the disparity in pay between men and women, as gender wage gaps exist in almost all capitalist economies. Nonetheless, the situation in South Korea, and to a lesser extent in Taiwan, clearly reflects a dual labor market, one in which women served as the key labor element in the secondary segment.

A major part in the development of the secondary segment was the emergence of export manufacturing in the 1960s. Export manufacturing required a relatively unskilled, low-paid, and "flexible" labor force. From the standpoint of Korean and Taiwanese employers, women fulfilled these criteria perfectly. Thus, between 1960 and 1980, the two countries saw a dramatic rise in female manufacturing employment. As a percentage of the total manufacturing labor force, female participation climbed, in South Korea, from 26.5 percent in 1960 to 39.2 percent in 1980. In Taiwan, the increase was even more dramatic: from 11.6 percent in 1960 to 43.8 percent in 1980. Predictably, women were over-represented in light manufacturing industries (where pay was particular low and job advancement extremely limited), such as textiles, apparel and footwear, and plastics. In the apparel and footwear industries, women accounted for 78 percent of all employment in South Korea in 1980, and 74 percent in Taiwan in 1986 (all figures cited in Deyo 1989).

To repeat the key point: the ability to sustain a dual labor market with domestic workers obviated the need for large-scale cross-border worker migration. By the late 1980s, however, the "reserves" of women willing to take jobs in the secondary labor market began to wane, which, one might argue, led to the switch to cross-border workers. And while both states have endeavored to regulate the "inflow" of foreign workers—with some success—one can fairly say that regulation of the immigration process was never easy. In South Korea, especially, problems with "runaway" trainees, a very large population of illegal workers, and protests by the workers themselves, generally in alliance with civic organizations, forced the state to change course several times. Indeed, the implementation of the Employment Permit System is itself a product, at least in part, of protests by foreign workers who were unwilling to comply with the rules of the industrial trainee program (see Lim 2003).

The Role of Culture: The "Ethnic Bias" in Cross-Border Migration to Japan and South Korea

I have not said much about cultural factors yet, except to seemingly dismiss culture as a relevant variable, an approach that is unwarranted. Thus, although cultural forces were directly responsible for basic changes and shifts in immigration policy, they almost certainly played a role in terms of defining or shaping societal and political attitudes toward immigration policy and the immigrants themselves. Earlier, for example, I briefly mentioned the pronounced ethnic bias in the immigration policies of Japan and South Korea. In Japan, this bias has been manifested in the "privileged status" granted to the descendants of Japanese immigrants to Latin America (the *nikkeijin*), the majority of whom left for Brazil, but some also settled in Peru, Argentina, Bolivia, and Paraguay. The main privilege the *nikkeijin* enjoy is access to long-term resident status in Japan, which was only established in 1990. As Naoto Higuchi (2005) explains, this issue was complicated by a number of factors, most of which were not necessarily cultural. Ultimately, though, the fate of *nikkeijin* came down to a decision by a task force in the Japanese Ministry of Justice. The ministry regarded descendants of Japanese emigrants as "ethnic Japanese" and, therefore, in need of "special treatment" (p. 8). Ironically, this attitude arose because the task force had earlier engaged in a required review of the legal status of third-generation Koreans in Japan (a stipulation of the 1965 treaty that normalized relations between Japan and South Korea). Since the task force recommended that third-generation Koreans in Japan be given permanent resident status, "they felt it necessary to create a special status of residence for third-generation emigrants to adjust the balance between the two groups" (Higuchi 2005, p. 8).

The privileged status of *nikkeijin* did not automatically mean that they would become the major source of migrant labor to Japan—as Higuchi (2005) argues, the decision to grant long-term residency to *nikkeijin* had nothing to do with the demand for cross-border migrant labor. Nonetheless, they were the most obvious choice, especially for certain types of jobs in the secondary labor market, since they were the only unskilled migrant workers legally entitled to work in Japan. As a result, many were hired in the automobile and electric/electronic manufacturing industries (Goto 2007); not coincidentally, many of these jobs were on a subcontracted basis, which meant that the work was strictly temporary and that workers were treated as "flexible" and "disposable" commodities (Higuchi 2005). Between 1989 and the end of 1990, the number of *nikkeijin* from Brazil grew from around 30,000 to 100,000; by the end of 1991, the population had doubled to about 200,000. To be clear, cultural factors did not play a direct role in the rapid growth of the *nikkeijin* worker population in Japan in the early 1990s. As described before, however, Japanese attitudes toward ethnicity and belongingness helped to shape a change in immigration policy that gave *nikkeijin,* many if not most of whom were socially and culturally South American, rather than Japanese—and who were also citizens of Brazil, Peru, Argentina, Bolivia, and Paraguay—access to a right that nationals from other countries did and do not enjoy. I should emphasize that tremendous debate occurs on this issue, with many scholars arguing that economic interests, and not culture, have been the determining factors. Remember, though, in the cultural framework, economic or political interests, on the one hand, and cultural forces, on the other hand, are not mutually exclusive.

In South Korea, in fact, one can see this intersection of economic, political, and cultural forces even more clearly. Recall that South Korea has a disproportionate number of cross-border migrant workers from China, and more specifically from the Yanbian Korean Autonomous Prefecture (in Jilin Province), an area that runs along North Korea's border with China (see Figure 8.3). Because of the geographic proximity, Korean migration to the area has long taken place (and vice versa), but this migration accelerated during the colonial period; between 1881 and 1944, the Korean population grew from 10,000 to 1.6 million, although many Koreans subsequently returned to Korea after the end of the war and when the Chinese communists took power in 1949 (Kwon 1997). Today, about 2 million ethnic Koreans—known as *joseonjok*—live throughout China, with most residing in China's three northeastern provinces: Jilin (Yanbian), Liaoning, and Heilungjiang.

Attitudes among South Koreans toward the *joseonjok* are extremely conflicted. On the one hand, the *joseonjok* are "brothers and sisters" because they are understood to share a common ancestry and are connected through "blood," making them different from "other" peoples. On the other hand, the *joseonjok*

Figure 8.3 Map of China Showing Yanbian (Korean Autonomous Prefecture) in Jilin Province

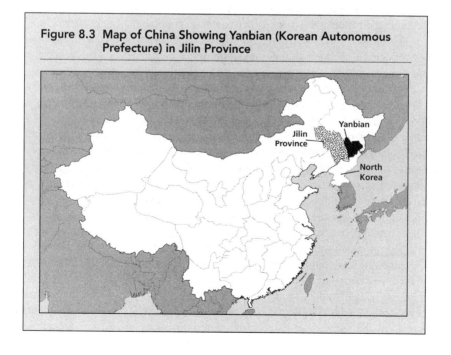

are citizens of a global and regional power, one with which South Korea has not always had good relations (South Korea did not have diplomatic relations with China until 1992). In addition, and equally important, the *joseonjok* are relatively poor: in the eyes of many South Koreans, their poverty means that they have less value to the country's economy and society. Taken together, economic interests and geopolitical concerns, Dong-Hoon Seol and John Skrentny (2009a) argue, have served to overrule "blood" in South Korea's treatment of the *joseonjok*. Seol and Skrentny are almost certainly correct; still, the South Korean government was faced with a dilemma in its treatment of the *joseonjok*. That is, it seemed unable to completely dismiss the historical, cultural, and ideological significance of the *joseonjok*: if their entry into South Korea had been prohibited, the government would have faced harsh criticism for not only abandoning "forgotten brothers, but also the heroes of the struggle for [Korean] independence" (H.-K. Lee 2010, p. 54). On the other hand, the government did not want to damage relations with China, which strongly disapproved of any policy that gave *joseonjok* citizenship rights in South Korea. The result was an ambiguous policy that allowed large-scale migration to unfold—for a short time, at least, a sense could be found that *joseonjok* would pose a minimal threat to South Korea's tight-knit social fabric—but which denied any special legal status to the *joseonjok*. Thus, in the early 1990s, the *joseonjok* vastly outnumbered all other migrant groups, composing 40.6 percent of all cross-border migrant workers in 1991 and 62.4 percent in 1992 (cited in Seol and Skrentny 2009a). From that point onward, the proportion of *joseonjok* steadily declined but generally constituted about one-fifth of the total population of migrant workers.

The ambiguous stance of the South Korean government toward the *joseonjok* reflected embedded attitudes about the significance of blood ties in Korean society and culture; while this cultural factor clearly did not determine policy—nor was it, in any way, the most powerful force—it played a meaningful role in explaining the large numbers of *joseonjok* who suddenly immigrated to South Korea in the early 1990s. Another area, however, where culture likely played a more prominent role was in the still strong resistance on the part of the South Korean government, and also the governments of Japan and Taiwan, to allowing large-scale permanent settlement by cross-border foreign migrants, particularly unskilled or low-skilled workers. Seol and Skrentny (2009b), in another article, posit that an elite political culture—one that prioritizes national economic goals above all else—is the primary **independent variable** explaining the lack of long-term or permanent settlement among unskilled cross-border migrant workers. This elite cultural view, the authors emphasize, is an outgrowth of the developmental state model, which over time has become much more than an objective set of institutions and policies; instead, it has become a mind-set, an ingrained way of understanding the world. In this view, policymakers see cross-border migrants as simply another **economic input**; they exist to serve the interests of the national economy, but once their utility to national economic development ceases, they should be discarded or replaced. This argument is interesting and makes a good deal of sense—although, as the authors themselves admit, "elite cultural hypotheses are hard to test" (p. 606). At the least, it reveals another way to think about the importance of culture in the immigration process. On this point, one needs to keep in mind that culture is not fixed; elite political cultural attitudes and practice can and do change. Thus, even if elites and others in East Asia view unskilled cross-border migrants as disposable commodities, this attitude will not necessarily remain the case in the future. Seol and Skrentny (2009b) seem to acknowledge as much when they point to the potential importance of international institutions and NGOs that espouse transnational values, especially human rights. Indeed, other scholars have argued that outside ideas about human rights and other norms are having a deep impact in East Asia.

Western Norms, Cross-Border Migration, and East Asia

In thinking about the role of culture, one should remember that traditional or indigenous culture is only part of the picture. Cultural variables and processes easily transcend borders and intersect with domestic values and political, institutional, and social arrangements. In addition, as Amy Gurowitz (1999) points out, transnational, generally Western norms—she defines norms "as standards of appropriate and legitimate behavior" (p. 417)—serve as a critical source of ideas for change in state policy and also are strategically used by activists and others to legitimize and empower their calls for political or social change. The results of this process are neither predictable nor uniform, but they are often significant. Thus, despite strong similarities in immigration policy and approaches among Japan, South Korea, and Taiwan, one can also see strong differences as well. For example, South Korea and Taiwan, as already discussed, both have adopted guest worker programs—that is, both countries officially allow the entry of unskilled migrant workers on a temporary basis. Japan, by contrast, continues to prohibit unskilled worker migration and instead relies on "backdoor" or "side-door" mechanisms, including the industrial trainee program and easier entry requirements for *nikkeijin*. Granted, cultural variables do not offer a full explanation. In Taiwan, the guest worker program, as noted above, is tightly constrained and still, one can argue, fundamentally reflects the values of the developmental state model. In South Korea, though, the switch to the guest worker program in 2004 represented a long-term struggle by cross-border migrant workers allied with South Korean NGOs to overturn what they portrayed as a inhumane and exploitative worker migration system that violated human dignity and human rights.

The strategy of the workers and South Korean NGOs was clear from a very early stage. In 1994, a small group of migrants from Bangladesh, Nepal, the Philippines, and Ethiopia staged a sit-in at the headquarters of one of South

Korea's most prominent rights-based organizations, the Citizens' Coalition for Economic Justice. During this sit-in, the migrants and the NGO framed the workers' plight as a human rights problem. This theme was repeated in 1995, when a different group of thirteen Nepalese "trainees" staged a sit-in at Seoul's Myeongdong Cathedral, which is a symbolic site for South Korea's prodemocracy and labor movements. In one joint statement, the workers from Nepal said, "We may be from a poor country and that's why we are working here in Seoul like slaves. But we have our basic human rights as well" (cited in Lim 2003, p. 435). The protest was otherwise extremely passive, as the workers simply sat in their tents, from which hung various signs with the following messages: "I lost three fingers on my right hand working in a factory. What will I do for the future?" Or "Please don't beat me," and "We are not slaves." These and other protests did lead to minor policy changes, but, more important, they changed the discourse surrounding foreign worker migration to South Korea. Prior to these protests, cross-border migrant workers were largely perceived as potential threats to the homogeneity and fabric of South Korean society. After the protests, they no longer could be seen as mere economic inputs to be exploited and then thrown away; instead, they were understood to be rights-bearing human beings. This change did not result in an immediate about-face in the state's immigration policy; however, with little doubt, even state bureaucrats understood that they could not completely ignore the rights of foreign workers. Even more, after these protests, dozens of civic organizations or NGOs in South Korea sprung up to support migrant workers and their rights. Over time, a number of important legal protections were extended to foreign workers, culminating in the creation of the Employment Permit System, which give foreign workers full rights as workers in South Korea. The story is far more complicated than I've presented—and the permit system, to many migrant workers, is still considered inadequate and unacceptably exploitative—but it does represent a significant change. Moreover, migrant workers are continuing to struggle and South Korean NGOs, which once ignored the issue of permanent settlement and political rights for foreign workers, have begun to change their perceptions and attitudes as well.

In Taiwan, by contrast, the existing system has seen relatively minor change since it was first established. One missing ingredient, perhaps, is a strong rights-oriented civil society, the kind that exists in South Korea. As was explored in an earlier chapter, Taiwan's path to democratization was relatively smooth, with the **authoritarian** state "managing" a gradual and largely peaceful transition to democracy. In this context, the opportunity for a strong, deeply rooted prodemocracy civil society to develop never fully emerged. Thus, while some organizations have aligned with foreign migrant groups, their influence is limited. As a result, as Kristin Surak (2011) notes, "the handful of NGOs struggling for migrants' rights [in Taiwan] has thus far achieved only 'paper victories' of the thinnest sort. In a state outside of the international community, and where civil society is embryonic, persuading the government to provide literature on migrants' rights in English is considered a triumph" (p. 4). Surak brings up an additional factor that makes Taiwan different from South Korea: pressure from the international community to conform to "universal norms." Taiwan's long-term diplomatic exclusion has made the country's leaders less concerned with and less subject to pressure from international or supranational organizations and the norms they promote and embrace. Thus, unlike South Korea, Taiwan's leaders are much less concerned with obtaining legitimacy through concordance with international agreements on human rights, nor can political activists (whether domestic NGOs or migrant groups) appeal to specific obligations to which Taiwan is a signatory: in fact, because Taiwan is not a member of the United Nations, it is categorically excluded from all UN covenants. According to Winston Hsiao (1995), as a result, Taiwan "has no legal duty to uphold many of the human rights that other nations have obligated themselves to maintain," including the Universal Declaration of Human Rights and the International Covenant on Civil and Political Rights (p. 184). Hsiao further argues that Taiwan's exclusion from this instrument is far from trivial: "The creation of legal obligations is at the core of international law and without them, the usual remedies for breaching these obligations are inapplicable" (p. 184). How much effect Taiwan's particular situation has had on its treatment of cross-border migrant workers is unclear, but it likely makes the use of international norms on human rights as instruments of empowerment far more difficult for domestic activists and workers themselves.

In Japan, the situation is different still. As in South Korea, many Japanese are sensitive to and concerned about the country's international image. As Gurowitz (1999) puts it, the "adoption of [international] norms is seen as the necessary price of existence in the outside world" (p. 422). But like Taiwan, many Japanese, especially state leaders and bureaucrats, see themselves as a "step removed from Western developed states in international society" (p. 424), especially in terms of Western norms on human rights. So, while Japan is a full-fledged member of the international community, Japan's ratification rate for international agreements on human rights was, in 1999, significantly lower than almost all other OCED countries—only Turkey and the United States had ratified fewer agreements. Since 1999, Japan has ratified only one additional human rights agreement. Given all this, one would not expect international norms to have much impact in Japan, particularly on the issue of immigrant rights. Indeed, already discussed is that the dominant norms related to the developmental state model have helped construct a highly exploitative immigration regime in Japan. Scholars, however, have demonstrated a countervailing trend in Japan, one that operates at the local level. Katherine Tegtmeyer Pak (2006), for instance, has shown that a number of Japanese municipalities have pursued a policy of "internal internationalization." Thus, even as the national government has held firm to "its stringent denial of Japan's emergence as an immigration country, internal internationalization rhetoric came to signal the development of incorporation policies by local government" (p. 66). This conflict in rhetoric and practice has led to efforts by cities to treat cross-border migrants as "local citizens." Consider this fairly typical statement by officials of Yokohama, a city of 3.7 million people and more than 74,000 foreign residents:

> Our goal is to encourage people from various cultural backgrounds living here to come together to recognize each other's culture so that they can revolutionize individual consciousness and change the community, thereby building a multicultural society that eliminates discrimination and prejudice against foreigners and protects basic human rights. (City of Yokohama 2012, cited in Tegtmeyer Pak 2006, p. 86)

That these efforts at creating local citizenship will change national immigration policy is not clear, but what is clear is that local governments and their supporters have embraced a more inclusive, rights-oriented set of values and norms, which has already brought a great deal of change to Japan. Among these changes is a new concept of local citizenship that, until recently, had never existed. The idea of local citizenship has, in this regard, opened a space for debate that has the potential of leading to stronger, more pervasive cultural, political, and social change throughout Japan.

Explaining the Rise of Cross-Border Marriages in East Asia

Marriage migration, as suggested above, has become a major new source of immigration in East Asia, and especially in South Korea and Taiwan. Some figures were provided earlier in the chapter, but looking at the numbers in more detail is worthwhile. In South Korea, international marriages have seen a steady rise from 4,710 in 1990, to 13,494 in 1995, to 15,913 in 2003, to a peak of 43,121 in 2005 (see Figure 8.4 below). Even more significant than the rise in

Figure 8.4 Marriages in South Korea (selected years)

	1990	1995	2000	2005	2006	2007
Total marriages	339,312	398,494	334,030	316,375	332,752	345,592
International marriages	4,710	13,494	12,319	43,121	36,690	38,491
Percentage of total	1.2	3.4	3.7	13.6	11.9	11.1

Source: National Statistics Office (South Korea), Marriage Statistics, 2007 (cited in Korea Immigration Service 2009b).

the number of marriages is the dramatic shift in terms of gender: in 1990, almost 87 percent of international marriages involved a South Korean woman and non-Korean man, but fifteen years later, this figure had virtually flipped. In 2005, more than 72 percent of international marriages involved a South Korean man and a non-Korean woman. Overall, as of October 2006, most of the foreign spouses were from China (54,079), and the majority of the Chinese nationals were *joseonjok* (34,660). The next largest sources of marriage migrants were, in order, Vietnam (13,987), Japan (6,656), the Philippines (4,246), Mongolia (1,581), Thailand (1,557), the United States (1,297), Russia (1,082), and Uzbekistan (1,047) (all figures cited in Seoul Immigration Control Office 2006).

In Taiwan, the proportion of international marriages has generally been even higher, although a significant degree of variation has occurred. Thus, in 1998, about 16 percent of all marriages involved a foreign spouse, a figure that steadily rose for the next five years, reaching a peak of 32.1 percent in 2003. Since then, however, a large decline has taken place, and in 2010, only about 13 percent of all marriages were international. The reason for this decline is clear: in 2004, the Taiwan government implemented a number of legal restrictions and penalties explicitly designed to curtail cross-border marriages and to inhibit marriage fraud (G. W. Jones 2012). The large majority of foreign spouses come from China, including Hong Kong and Macao, but large numbers of women also arrive from Vietnam and Indonesia (see Figure 8.5 for details).

The numbers suggest that something significant is happening in South Korea and Taiwan, but as usual they do not reveal why. Of course, one explanation is quite simple: a "shortage" of marriageable women in both countries. But why should eligible women be in short supply? After all, for decades there were apparently no problems. Then, seemingly overnight, thousands—even tens of thousands of men in both countries—were frantically searching overseas for a spouse. One particularly salient reason is a persistent sex imbalance in both countries, largely caused by selective abortion. In South Korea, the imbalance

Figure 8.5 Marriages in Taiwan (selected years)

	1998	2000	2001	2002	2003	2010[a]
Total marriages	145,976	181,642	171,283	172,655	171,283	139,000
International marriages	22,905	44,966	46,202	49,013	55,116	17,792
Percentage of total	15.7	24.8	27.1	28.4	32.1	12.8

Source: G. W. Jones (2012).
Note: a. The total marriage figure for 2010 is rounded; in addition, the number of international marriages is calculated using the rounded total, and the percentage figure is only for marriages involving a non-Taiwanese woman.

reached a peak of 1.16 boys to 1 girl in 1990 (the highest in the world at the time) but dropped to 1.07 in 2007 (Barot 2012). In Taiwan, the sex ratio was, at one point, even higher, reaching 1.19 in 1950. From this high point, the imbalance gradually declined to "natural" levels by the 1980s (the natural ratio is considered to be 1.05), but then the ratio again increased above 1.1 in the early 1990s ("Worldwide War" 2010); in 2011, it decreased again to 1.079. The sex ratio imbalance may play a role, but many more factors are clearly at play. Indeed, given the fact that no clear and consistent correlation can be found between the rate of international marriages and the sex ratio, an alternative explanation is necessary. Again, one can draw from the standard repertoire of theoretical perspectives.

From a neoclassical economic perspective, for example, one can usefully consider the "economics of cross-border marriage." To put it simply, once entrepreneurs realized that a viable (i.e., profitable) market for international marriages existed, they quickly began to exploit the opportunities. In both Taiwan and South Korea, in fact, large numbers of marriage brokers and other intermediaries flooded the cross-border marriage market beginning in the 1990s. By 2010, an estimated 1,250 marriage brokers or matchmakers were plying their trade in South Korea, charging an average of $9,900 for their services ("South Korea Cracks Down on Marriage Brokers"). For Taiwan, precise numbers are not available, but one study estimated that at least 246 Taiwanese-owned agencies operated in just Vietnam in the early 2000s (Wang and Chang 2002); their fees were about the same as in South Korea, $300,000 in New Taiwan dollars (or US$9,100).

The marriage agencies essentially made international marriages on a large scale possible. Until they came on the scene, men in either South Korea or Taiwan had extreme difficulty not only in finding a potential spouse but also in navigating the "international marriage bureaucracy." Obtaining and translating legal documents, understanding myriad immigration laws in multiple countries, arranging travel and meetings, and ensuring that everything is actually processed in a timely manner require professional expertise (Wang and Chang 2002; Seol 2006). Indeed, as Hong-zen Wang and Shu-ming Chang (2002) put it, "without a mediating mechanism offered by a profit-oriented agency, there would be no such mass personal movement" (p. 109); matching supply with demand, in short, could not have happened without these agencies. Thus, while profit-seeking market actors did not create the demand for foreign brides, they clearly played a central role in accelerating the process and in ramping up the total number of international marriages by efficiently matching demand with the available supply.[3]

The economics of international marriage, then, are undoubtedly relevant. As I have suggested, though, states likely played and continue to play an equal if not more significant role through their immigration and naturalization policies. In South Korea, international marriages between Korean men and *joseonjok* women began slowly in 1990 but built up speed fairly quickly. By 1994, concerns about these marriages were being raised by both the South Korean and Chinese governments. The South Korean government, in particular, was worried that *joseonjok* brides were using marriage migration as a way to circumvent tight restrictions on worker migration and family reunification—once married, the *joseonjok* brides could invite their parents to join them in South Korea (H.-K. Lee 2008). After several years of discussion, in 1996, South Korea and China concluded a memorandum of understanding that imposed stronger restriction on international marriages between Koreans and Chinese, although these restrictions were eased in 2003. Through the mid- and late 1990s, international marriages, while appreciably more common than in the first few years of the 1990s, were still less than 4 percent of all marriages. In 1998, however, the government introduced the International Marriage Brokerage Law, which led to a rapid increase in for-profit agencies; these quickly diversified their operations into other countries, including Thailand, Vietnam, Mongolia, and Russia.

Even before the 1998 law, however, local governments themselves played a key role in bringing together the forces of supply and demand for international marriages. The first organized effort was the appropriately named "Getting Rural Bachelors Married" project (H. M. Kim 2007), which eventually involved over sixty municipalities. The cities provided between $3,200 and $8,600 in aid to each South Korean bachelor (H. M. Kim 2007), which laid the groundwork for the for-profit international marriage broker industry to emerge and later take off. In this regard, Surak (2011) argues that the 1998 International Marriage Brokerage Law was a key piece of legislation: it provided accreditation for marriage agencies and created a more organized but still market-based framework for the industry as a whole. In an important sense, the South Korean government acted as a developmental state in helping to create and sustain the international marriage industry. The law, in particular, furthered the **commodification** of international marriages by essentially defining husbands as consumers and their foreign spouses as products—the consequence of designing the law as a consumer protection act (Surak 2011). After passage of the law, South Korean brokers started to "guarantee the bride": the married men were offered six- to twelve-month "sales warranties" on their transactions (H. M. Kim 2007); if they were dissatisfied, they were entitled to phone counseling, home visits, and, for their wives, Korean-language instruction. If they divorced, they were entitled to replacement services—in other words, another matchmaking trip on an expense-only basis and additional introductions to potential brides (H. M. Kim 2007). All of these "improvements" helped lead to a dramatic upsurge in marriages.

In the South Korean case, then, one can see how state action facilitated and—to some extent—made the market for international marriages possible. Of course, once the framework was created, private businesses and individuals dominated the process, but the state remained ever vigilant, although in the background, ready and able to step in to redirect, freeze, or further strengthen the market. In Taiwan, the state played much less of a role in developing the market for international marriages, but, as noted above, the Taiwanese state did not hesitate to intervene in the international marriage market when the numbers increased dramatically from 1999 to 2003. Beginning in 2004, Taiwan implemented a number of new restrictions and penalties designed to curtail cross-border marriages, especially fraudulent marriages taking place between Taiwanese and Chinese nationals. The Act Governing Relations Between Peoples of the Taiwan Area and the Mainland Area, for example, required more careful assessment of mainland Chinese spouses. The law was vigorously applied—in 2005, Taiwan's Immigration Office of the National Police Agency interviewed 85,726 mainland Chinese, and nearly one-third were deported (Y.-H. Chen 2008). In addition, legal recognition of all cross-border marriages was withheld until the couples could pass a face-to-face interview (Y.-H. Chen 2008). These and other regulations had an immediate major impact by significantly reducing the number of international marriages in subsequent years. I should also point out that, since a very large proportion of cross-border marriages in Taiwan are between a Taiwanese and a mainland Chinese national—at the end of 2007, the cumulative total of marriage migrants was 399,038, of which 66 percent were from China, Hong Kong, and Macao (Y.-H. Chen 2008)—one of the most important actions taken by the state was the lifting of martial law in 1987, followed by a stabilization of cross-strait relations. In particular, the easing of travel restrictions made cross-border marriages between the two countries possible on a larger scale.

Although not many structural analyses of cross-border marriage have been done, seeing how and where structural forces are at play in this phenomenon is fairly easy. Consider, for example, these facts. First, the dramatic rise in the number of cross-border marriages in South Korea and Taiwan closely corresponds to the economic rise of both countries. Increasing urbanization and a concomitant increase of women's participation in the formal economy (albeit typically in the secondary labor market) were a product of capitalist industrialization, as too was the declining fertility rate in both countries. These were structural changes that led to changing social dynamics; women as a group did not necessarily become less willing to marry, but they began to postpone marriage—in Japan, for example, between 1975 and 1995, the average age at first marriage increased from twenty-four to twenty-eight years for women and from twenty-eight to thirty-one for men. A similar increase has occurred in both Taiwan and South Korea. Second, capitalist industrialization generally requires more investment in human capital, which in practical terms means higher levels of education. Again, in all three East Asian countries, the educational level for men and women has tended to rise in concert with economic growth. This trend has led to a narrowing of the education gap between the sexes and has also contributed to the tendency of both women and men to marry later, often due to their pursuit of education into the tertiary level. Third, the rise in cross-border marriage also corresponds to structural change in the position of the East Asian economies: all three, but South Korea and Taiwan especially, did not become major destinations for "marriage migrants" until both moved up in the hierarchical structure of the global economy. Indeed, during the early stage of industrialization when both countries were relatively poor, they were predominantly a source of female marriage migrants. In this regard, that foreign spouses in East Asia come primarily from poorer countries and regions, China and Vietnam in particular, is clearly not coincidental. Fourth, in the previous discussion on the commodification of international or cross-border marriages, the rise of these types of marriages equally clearly reflects, at a basic level, the logic of capitalism.

Primarily for reasons of space, I am content with simply raising these structural issues rather than engaging in a more thorough analysis. Given readers' familiarity with the structural principles, this approach should not be a problem. I do the same with the discussion of cultural factors, although they likely play an especially prominent role in cross-border marriages. Their role can be seen, most saliently, in the strong tendency, especially among East Asian males, to choose spouses who ostensibly share common cultural traits. Yen-Fen Tseng (2010), for example, points out that cross-border marriages are not necessarily cross-cultural. "What has been happening in international marriages within Asia," Tseng writes, "is an increase of the type of spousal migration that involves marriages of the same ethnic or religious background. . . . Examples in East Asia are the preference from Taiwanese **Hakka** to marry Hakka women from Indonesia and Mainland China. . . . Another example is that South Korean men often marry members of their ethnic diaspora" (p. 43). Patriarchal norms are perhaps even more important. In Japan, for example, a patriarchal practice of requiring coresidency between daughter-in-law and mother-in-law (prevalent in the Tohoku Region in the northeastern part of Honshu island) has contributed to a regional "marriage squeeze" (i.e., the imbalance between the number of marriage-ready men and women), because increasingly large numbers of Japanese women—who have been influenced by a new set of norms—simply do not want to live in such a situation (Liaw, Ochiai, and Ishikawa 2010). This reluctance reflects a broader "value transformation" among women in Japan, South Korea, and Taiwan, a transformation that clashes with still strong patriarchal traditions, especially for married women.

This clash, Doo-Sub Kim (2010) surmises, plays a large role in the marriage squeeze since "women are well aware that their careers and self-realization will be compromised once they get married" (p. 131), and for this reason, they tend to postpone marriage. On this last point, one can find a related cultural factor: traditional norms in East Asia dictate that women marry by a certain age, and once they pass that age, they quickly lose their appeal as marriage partners. In Japan, for example, a twenty-five-year-old woman who had not yet married is referred to as a "Christmas cake"—that is, something to be thrown away on December

26. This norm was powerful, and one that is underscored in these statistics: in 1970, only 5.8 of Japanese women ages thirty-five to thirty-nine had never been married; in Taiwan the corresponding figure was 1.2 percent, while in South Korea, the figure was an astounding 0.4 percent. By 2005, however, the numbers had shot up to 18.4, 15.9, and 7.6 percent, respectively (G. W. Jones 2010). These numbers indicate a dramatic change, and one that cannot be easily explained solely or even mostly by economic, institutional, or structural variables.

Coming Back to Agency and the Socially Constituted Actor

From the discussion above, one could fairly say that rational-economic, institutional, and structural factors are all part of the explanation for the gradual but still significant transformation of Japan, South Korea, and Taiwan into "multiethnic" societies. To be sure, the transformation is still very limited from a comparative international perspective, but the changes should not be underestimated. Not so long ago, as was noted at the outset, the rigid sense of racial and ethnic homogeneity among East Asians suggested that no changes would ever take place, that all immigration, temporary and permanent, would be steadfastly rejected regardless of economic, demographic, and structural pressures. As has been demonstrated, though, these pressures cannot be ignored. But this fact does not mean culture is unimportant. As was also explored, an "elite political culture" (as well as a socially constructed notion of ethnic and racial purity) can help explain the lack of permanent settlement in all three countries and the still tight numerical restrictions on temporary migration. Yet, as I have repeatedly said, culture does not act alone; instead, culture interacts with political, social, and economic forces within specific contexts. This said, in this last section I focus primarily on the significance of **agency**, which was tacitly embedded in most of the analyses throughout this chapter. However, a more explicit discussion, I think, is necessary.

I did address agency earlier, in the discussion of migrant workers and NGOs in South Korea and their struggle to obtain rights as workers and, even more basically, as human beings (rather than just disposable commodities). These efforts were, in an important sense, remarkably successful, even if they failed to realize their most important goals. Also explored was how actors within municipal governments in Japan have made "local citizenship" a reality. One needs to understand that both these outcomes were ultimately a product of agency and, more specifically, of socially constituted actors struggling to bring about specific political and social changes. An agent-centered account not only focuses on actors in a generic manner but also examines the decisions and actions of specific actors. In South Korea, for example, not just "foreign workers" in general struggled for political and social change, but thirteen individuals from Nepal staged a sit-in with the help of specific activists within such organizations as the Citizens' Coalition for Economic Justice. Even more specifically, success and change came about through the efforts of people such as Anwar Hussein, Shakil, Bonogit Hussain, May Cordova, and many others.

Hussein and Shakil, for example, were cross-border migrant workers from Bangladesh who helped lead the Migrants' Trade Union in South Korea; Bonogit Hussain, an Indian national, was subjected to racial harassment on a public bus but then spoke out against racism and discrimination in South Korea; May Cordova was a "marriage migrant" from the Philippines who later became an outspoken critic of the assimilationist and integrationist assumptions of South Korean immigration policy. These are all individuals whose efforts were a meaningful part of the immigration process. Not all were successful in bringing about change, but all represent a concrete and essential element of agency. Similar examples can be found in Taiwan and Japan. One must also remember that, while many actors struggle for social, political, and economic change, others struggle just as mightily for preserving the status quo or for returning to some prior condition. Even more, those actors who endeavor to preserve the status quo almost always have significant economic, institutional, and structural advantages. The dynamics of struggles between and among actors with different interests must always be examined. The main point here can usefully be summed up by repeating a quote from Chapter 5: "Inert, invisible structures do not make democracies or dictatorships. People do" (McFaul 2002, p. 214). The same assertion applies, if not more powerfully, to social and political change in the realm of immigration.

Of course, one must continue to exercise caution and remember that agency is always constrained and enabled by institutional and structural processes. In Japan, South Korea, and Taiwan, as was previously discussed, the pressure for cross-border work migration arose directly from capitalist industrialization, and even the marriage squeeze can be tied to increasing economic growth and urbanization. One point that I did not discuss is the importance of democratic institutions. Democracy, as some scholars persuasively argue (see, for example, Joppke 2001), provides an essential set of values, laws, and procedures that make the expansion of immigrant rights possible. In democratic societies, even noncitizens have a political voice and implicit political rights, especially the right to have their grievances heard and adjudicated in the court system. Cross-border migrant workers and their domestic allies took full advantage of their legal rights in South Korea, winning a number of favorable court decisions that gradually and seemingly inexorably expanded their rights as workers. In Japan and Taiwan, the court system has not been as friendly to cross-border migrant workers, but the same basic principle still applies, which means that the possibility of greater political and social change remains. Contrasting the institutional environment of democratic political systems to that of an authoritarian or dictatorial system, with no in-built institutional recourse against state dictates, is important here.

Larger structural forces will always be important as well. Cross-border migrant workers necessarily occupy one of the most disadvantaged positions in the global economy. Exploitation and a lack of basic labor and even human rights has long been the fate of these workers. Still, even in a very weak, marginalized position, possibilities always exist to exercise agency. After all, the people who move thousands of miles from their homes, who take a major risk to improve their lives and the lives of their families, are already exercising tremendous agency. They are doing what relatively few of their compatriots are willing to do. Extraordinary bravery and determination to change personal circumstances, one should add, are found in both cross-border migrant workers and women who migrate for marriage. The women from "poor" Asian countries, in particular, are often assumed—by their husbands-to-be and future in-laws—to be subservient and "traditional" and are expected to be grateful for the opportunity to escape the poverty of their homeland. This stereotype may be true of some women, but it is certainly not true of all Asian women—much depends on how the women are socially constituted. Thus, many women see marriage to a Japanese, South Korean, or Taiwanese man as an opportunity to exercise greater independence. In fact, many are better educated and far more ambitious than the men they marry (Constable 2005). This clash of expectations (or of imagined realities) frequently sets the stage for conflict, not only between wives and husbands but also between the women and their new societies. Unlike supposedly temporary migrant workers, however, marriage migrants have the institutional advantage of "permanence." What this permanence means in practice is not always clear—in part because it depends on so many other variables—but it can create a different dynamic for the exercise of agency.

Continuing this discussion for many more pages would be possible, but the basic point is clear: a full account of the social, political, and economic changes revolving around the immigration process among the three capitalist societies of East Asia requires a constructed actor approach. The "dialectics" between structure and agency, the significance of institutions, the dynamics of capitalism, and the influence of culture are all necessary parts of comprehensive explanation.

In Closing

I have not written much about either North Korea or China. One reason for their omission in this chapter, especially in the case of North Korea, is simply the lack of significant social change with regard to immigration. North Korea remains a generally closed, insulated society. Tellingly, its leaders are extremely critical of South Korea for allowing both temporary cross-border worker migration and permanent marriage migration by peoples without "Korean blood." The North Korean leadership still hews closely to the ideal of racial and ethnic purity. Given the analysis in this chapter, however, one can argue that the country's leaders have a certain "luxury" in doing so. North Korea's anemic economy, which has created a labor surplus rather than shortage, is a long way from the migration transition. North Korea, in short, is still a labor exporter, although its ideological rigidity has limited the number of people allowed to leave the country for work. Of course, as North Korea is a **centrally planned**, nonmarket economy, one should not be surprised by North Korea's situation. In other words, the economic and underlying structural changes that have taken place in Japan, South Korea, and Taiwan (and which are currently taking place in China) will not unfold in North Korea unless and until it moves onto the path of capitalist industrialization. Several lessons can be drawn here. First, the absence of any pressure that might lead to a migration transition in North Korea underscores the importance of economic and structural processes in creating the basis or conditions for social change. Second, the capacity of the North Korean leadership to eschew capitalist industrialization for well over six decades reveals that even global structural forces can effectively be held at bay—perhaps not forever, but certainly for a very long time. The agency of North Korea's leadership, in short, cannot be ignored. Third, one can anticipate that institutional and cultural factors, which are clearly in play right now, will continue to be important should North Korea make the transition to capitalism and eventually face the pressures of the migration transition.

In China, with its huge working-age population, rapid industrialization has not yet created the basis for a migration transition. Nonetheless, the dual labor market in China has, remarkably, created labor shortages in some areas. In Guangdong Province, China's main production and export center (which accounts for one-third of the country's exports), economic officials reported a shortage of about 800,000 workers in early 2012. The key reason? Internal migrants have been increasingly reluctant to take jobs in Guangdong factories, in part because of better opportunities closer to their rural homes (Mitchell 2012). China's experience, therefore, reinforces the significance of economic and structural processes in forcing certain types of predictable changes and responses—such as labor shortages in rapidly growing economies. As long as China retains its internal "**reserve labor force**," these regional shortages will likely be solved through market-based incentives, especially higher wages and better working conditions. However, that China will start to import labor from other countries is not inconceivable, especially if domestic labor becomes too expensive in low-wage, export-based industries. Whatever the case, any good explanation will require that one brings together—into a single framework of analysis—rational-economic, structural, institutional, and cultural variables while maintaining an analytical focus on constructed actors.

Notes

1. In 2008, China's National Bureau of Statistics estimated that at least 140 million internal migrant workers were moving around in the country, fully one-tenth of China's population (Scheineson 2009).

2. Whether or not this criticism is fair is debatable. Dual labor market theory does not posit that secondary markets are created only through immigration but instead argues that immigrants are generally the primary source of workers for this segment.

3. Notably, though, in the case of South Korea, local governments helped to facilitate marriages between South Korean men and *joseonjok* women in the early 1990s (H.-K. Lee 2008).

9 Conclusion

Explaining change and continuity in Japan, China, South Korea, North Korea, and Taiwan is a complicated and difficult task. However, the task is made much easier if a systematic framework, based on both basic methodological and theoretical principles, is used as a guide. The overarching goal of this book, of course, was to introduce just such a framework. More importantly, the goal was to enable the reader to apply theory, **method**, and evidence to an examination of political, economic, and social change and continuity in the five East Asian countries. I hope I was successful. But even if some confusion or uncertainty remains as to "how to study change and continuity" in East Asia, I am certain that through this journey, the reader has developed a better, more substantial understanding of the myriad processes that have shaped, and which are continuing to shape, the five countries in the region. The competing-perspectives approach, in particular, was designed to reveal the value—even the necessity—of applying different modes of analysis to explain the same basic outcome (such as rapid capitalist industrialization or democratization). One can all too easily embrace a single, often narrowly focused approach. In some situations, using a single approach may be a perfectly reasonable thing to do, but when considering complex political, economic, and social processes, one faces a danger that important, even essential elements of the process will be entirely missed. A competing-perspectives approach is certainly not a panacea, but it is a corrective, especially for a novice researcher. At the same time, simply understanding that complex processes involve multiple factors and forces can end up sowing more confusion. Developing a sense of how to fit the pieces of a complex explanatory puzzle together is critical and the core reason for the constructed actor model. To repeat, the constructed actor model was meant to provide a way to bring insights from the competing perspectives together so that they could create a comprehensive but coherent explanation.

The intent, however, was not to create a sort of metatheory (that is, a theory that rises above or transcends all other theoretical approaches). Instead, the intent was to present a heuristic framework for the integration or synthesis of existing theoretical arguments. At a more general level, too, the constructed actor model was meant to allow one to move beyond dichotomous or either-or analysis (e.g., either markets are all-important, or they are not; either structural forces determine everything or they determine nothing). As noted in the introduction, a key purpose of the constructed actor model was to provoke and challenge students (and others) to think about different "theoretical possibilities." Taking seriously the idea of the constructed actor, as the many examples and cases throughout the book have demonstrated, requires one to do just that. With these general points in mind, this book can be usefully ended with a general discussion of emerging issues and trends for the five East Asian countries, both individually and as a whole.

An Asia-Centric World?

One of the most salient—albeit also somewhat trite—emerging issues is the question of East Asia's future role in the global political economy. For many decades, ever since the rapid rise of Japan, people have talked of an Asia-centric world: a world in which predominant economic, political, and even cultural power resides in East Asia rather than in the West. Japan's long-standing economic difficulties beginning in 1990 put to rest some of this talk, but China's almost simultaneous ascendance as a new and still-growing center of capital accumulation in the world economy immediately put Asia back on the map, so to speak. Quite unlike Japan, moreover, China does not eschew or downplay the importance of military power. In fact, China's military buildup, which has paralleled the country's economic rise, is a major concern for both Western and Asian countries alike. This trend does not mean, however, that China is on the verge of supplanting the United States as the world's dominant military power— most analyses put China at least a couple of decades behind the United States in terms of overall military capability—but it does mean that China will be, and already is, a significant counterweight to US military power in East Asia. In terms of nuclear weapons capability, moreover, China has developed a sufficiently potent arsenal to effectively cancel out the technological superiority of US conventional military power in the region. On this last point, worth noting is that China has made tremendous strides in its nuclear weapons program over the past few years, including its "strategic capacity" (that is, its capacity to deliver nuclear-armed missiles anywhere in the world). As the Center for Strategic and International Studies (2013), a US-based think tank, puts it, "in less than two decades, China has progressed from a limited and vulnerable nuclear ballistic missile capability to one of the world's most impressive nuclear and conventional ballistic missile programs" (p. 33). China's military potential is important to emphasize because it speaks to a crucial element of the US- or Western-centered global system, namely, military power. An Asia-centric world, in other words, will require not just economic dominance but significant military capability as well. Thus, if China continues along the same path—economically and militarily—one can imagine without difficulty an eventual shift from a world dominated by the United States, and the West more generally, to a world dominated by China and centered in East Asia.

Still, no one can guarantee that this recentering will happen. Even if such a shift occurs, what an Asia-centric world will look like, or what it will mean for the rest of the world, is not at all clear. Indeed, predicting future outcomes has not been a strong suit of the social sciences. Fortunately, one is not left completely or even mostly in the dark. To better "see" the possibilities, one can use the same theoretical and methodological principles—the same analytical framework—upon which this book is based. Hitherto, I have used the competing-perspectives approach and the constructed actor model primarily, albeit not exclusively, for retrospective analysis, that is, to explain how and why events and trends already have happened or unfolded in the manner that they did. Prospective analysis is also possible. Although I hesitate to go too far down this path, the exercise is useful as both an intellectual and practical exercise. Intellectually, it provides another opportunity to think about and consider the logic or reasoning of various theoretical approaches. Practically, it provides another opportunity to apply these approaches to real-world situations and cases. In the few remaining pages, then, I once again apply the competing-perspectives approach and the constructed actor model to an analysis of Asia's future. The discussion, however, is extremely broad and stylized; the objective is more to raise questions than to answer them.

China, East Asia, and the Global Economy: Three Competing Views

In the liberal economic view, markets are key. More importantly, of course, free markets are key and are central to any country's or region's future economic success. The extent to which East Asia's **states** allow or, even better, actively encourage their economies to become more strongly integrated into global networks of trade, finance, and production will, therefore, largely determine East Asia's future position in the global economy. Their role does not mean that states are only marginally important; the market-friendly version provides space for states (or national governments) to play a role in overcoming or dealing with **market failures** in particular. Yet the expectation is that as the East Asian economies mature or become more advanced, they will become less reliant on state intervention of any kind. Assuming greater integration into global markets and reduced state intervention, one can see a strong likelihood of a global recentering in East Asia and on China in particular. To be sure, China's unprecedented rapid growth since the mid-1990s will almost assuredly slow down over the coming decades, but as a still largely untapped market, the country will remain a major center of global investment and production. At the same time, neighboring East Asian countries—with high national savings rates and large earnings from foreign trade (given their own integration into world markets)—will be particularly well positioned to tap into China's immense labor market and burgeoning consumer and capital markets. The result will be a virtuous circle, in which China's receptiveness to global capital will continue to attract new flows of foreign investment, disproportionately from other East Asian economies, which will generate stronger growth, which in turn will attract more capital and lead to even stronger growth for China and the region as a whole.

However, one huge and extremely relevant caveat can be identified: should China rely too much on an interventionist state, it could fall victim to the "Japanese disease." In an important respect, this disease could be even more debilitating for China than it has been for Japan, since China relies so strongly on huge market-dominating but relatively (and sometimes woefully) inefficient, **SOEs**. The danger is particularly significant, as the **CCP** has shown little desire to release its grip on political control. Such control not only encourages continued intervention in the economy but also helps to breed corruption and **rent-seeking** behavior, which can be a bane to any still-developing economy. Yet, as China goes, so may the rest of East Asia.

In the statist view, by contrast, the lack of state intervention is the problem, especially in a more competitive, globalized world economy. A recentering of the global economy on China and East Asia, therefore, should be seen primarily as a political issue, that is, as a struggle for power, control, and influence in the region. In this regard, a particularly important issue is the trend toward stronger regional integration (or regionalism). Regional integration is a diverse phenomenon, but in a general sense it refers to a process by which individual states join together, usually through a formal agreement, to create a larger whole. On the surface, regional integration may seem innocuous, but under the surface it represents a serious threat to existing power dynamics. If the United States, for example, is excluded from regional agreements in Asia, it must then deal with a bloc of countries as opposed to a single state. Even if the United States is included, its power may be diluted. Conversely, if China, Japan, Taiwan, and South Korea join together, the regional agreement may become a fulcrum for the exercise of enhanced economic or strategic power. Not surprisingly, then, the United States has effectively torpedoed several regional proposals in the past. Recall that the United States used its power to prevent Japan from creating the **AMF** in 1997. The reason, to repeat, was clear: the establishment of the AMF would have resulted in a loss of influence for the United States in Asia, while simultaneously increasing the influence of Japan. Several years earlier, the United States also strongly opposed the East Asian Economic Caucus, first proposed by Malaysia in 1990. The organization would have included China and Taiwan along with the **ASEAN** countries, Japan, South Korea, Vietnam, and Hong Kong, but would have excluded the United States, Australia, and New Zealand. The United States put substantial diplomatic pressure, especially on Japan, to prevent the trade organization from developing (Davison 2012). At the same time, the United States has had no problem pursuing its own forms of discriminatory or closed regionalism, such as the North American Free Trade Agreement. China, for its part, has pursued regional initiatives such as the proposal for an ASEAN-China Free Trade Area, which was agreed to in 2002 and subsequently implemented on January 1, 2010.

China, notably, has had a much easier time developing regional agreements with the ASEAN countries, in large part because US influence over ASEAN is very limited compared to its influence over Japan and South Korea. Of course, control is precisely the issue: who will win the struggle for predominant influence in the region, China or the United States? For now, at least, the national interests of Japan and South Korea are still very much in remaining strongly aligned with the United States. Yet their interests certainly could change if (and I emphasize the *if*) China continues its economic ascendance. Doing so, however, will require that the Chinese state maintain a major role in guiding and protecting the economy. Fortunately for China's leaders, they are not reliant on the United States for security. China is an independent and growing military power, which means the country will not need to "kowtow" to the United States—as Japan certainly has had to do despite that country's significant economic power. With this in mind, the statist view might also conclude that the prospects for a recentering of the global economy—and global power—on China and East Asia is likely, although the United States will not go down without a fight. While the conclusion here is the same as in the liberal view, the reasoning is almost diametrically opposite.

In the structural view, the rise of East Asia was very much the product of the region's close relationship with the United States. In other words, the region's economic success was essentially a function of and dependent on the needs of the hegemonic power, at least in the initial stage. For a variety of reasons (recall the argument by Giovanni Arrighi [1996]), however, the East Asian economies—led by Japan—broke free of dependence on the United States and other core economies and developed an independent basis for sustained capital accumulation. Importantly, the ability of Japan, South Korea, and Taiwan (plus Hong Kong and Singapore) to break free of dependence on the United States was not primarily, still less solely, based on individual efforts by each country. Instead, their success was a reflection, first, of structural dynamics that caused an "overaccumulation" crisis in the Western core (including the United States) and, second, regional integration that, again, was put in motion by the United States. China's economic rise must also be viewed from this perspective. The incorporation of China into a regional system, to put it very simply, was necessary for the continued expansion of capitalism in East Asia and the world.

The inevitable emergence of China, however, has further deepened East Asia's economic independence and is remaking East Asia as the global center of capital accumulation. Writing in 1996, in fact, Arrighi had already come to this conclusion—before China had really begun its remarkable economic ascent. Thus, from the structural view, the recentering of the global economy on East Asia is not seriously in question anymore. The key remaining question is whether China can move into the core. Nonetheless, remnants of dependence are still remaining: in particular, Japan and South Korea have not yet broken free from their reliance on US military protection. But their independence, too, is just a matter of time. For just as China was reincorporated into the capitalist world-system, so too will North Korea be. The eventual integration of North Korea will significantly reduce whatever "security threat" still exists in East Asia, thereby rendering US military protection in the region largely irrelevant. Of course, China is generally portrayed as the most significant military threat within the region, but the structure of global capitalism today makes the use of military force within a regionally integrated economy relatively unlikely, at least as long the global economy is growing.[1] Once the need for US military protection disappears, the "rise of East Asia" will be completed.

The recentering of the global economy, however, is only one part of the structuralist picture. In Chapter 4, I discussed a number of other important implications tied to the rise of China in particular. The whole discussion does not need to be repeated; I only want to reemphasize that China's full integration into the capitalist world-system has a number of dire implications, not the least of which is a global environmental catastrophe. The second, more structural implication is related to the **global division of labor** and the instability that could result in wage levels as China's economy continues to advance. In this regard, the recentering of the global economy on East Asia may not last very long—certainly, not as long as the 500 or so years that Western dominance has lasted. Indeed, an Asia-centric globe may be little more than a blip in the history of the capitalist world-system.

The Constructed Actor Model and East Asia's Future

Global recentering seems as if it would be a quintessential macrolevel, structural process. To a significant extent, this is almost certainly the case. However, one must remember, in this regard, that East Asia's economic emergence as a center of global capitalism—and perhaps *the* center of global capitalism—has been part of a long process, which was itself initiated by the structural need for capitalism to expand and intensify; Japan was shoved onto the capitalist path by

Western imperialism, and more specifically by the United States, which demanded—by force of arms—that Japan open up to trade with the Western (i.e., capitalist) world. Japan's rapid industrialization, in turn, had its own expansionary tendency. Thus, Japan incorporated Korea, Taiwan, and parts of China into its economic sphere. Ultimately, this string of events led to direct military conflict with core capitalist powers, first with Russia and then the United States and its allies. Following the end of the Pacific War, however, the United States, in its role as hegemon, implicitly understood that cooperation among the major capitalist economies was far more effective than conflict. This understanding meant not only a reverse course in Japan but also an invitation to develop. As Japan moved ahead, expansion was still necessary: instead of colonization, however, Japan, with the help of the United States, established a tightly integrated but still hierarchic regional economy, first with South Korea and Taiwan, and then with the Southeast Asian economies. Regional integration was integral to the success of all three economies (Japan's, South Korea's, and Taiwan's), but their continued success depended on even further expansion. While this expansion was able to proceed without China for a while, as soon as China made its inevitable turn to capitalism, the final (or at least most important) piece was in place.

The structural account, however, is seriously incomplete for a variety of reasons. The most important of these reasons were already carefully covered in Chapter 2, so repeating that discussion is unnecessary here. Suffice it to say that, just as the earlier stages of East Asia's economic rise crucially depended on the purposeful action of many socially constituted actors (within and outside the state), on the construction of effective **institutions** (including the **developmental state**) to mediate market processes, on cultural constructions, and so on, so too will a recentering of global power in East Asia. Thus, while the structural approach, in general, portrays this recentering as practically a fait accompli, the constructed actor model suggests that recentering is far from inevitable. One reason is immediately apparent: Structural forces may create opportunities and possibilities, but those opportunities and possibilities must be activated. Even more, they must be intentionally, strategically, and often rigorously exploited by socially constituted actors. Most important, perhaps, structural forces should not be seen as completely or even primarily autonomous from human society; they are part of the world and are themselves subject to change through purposeful human/social action. The contrast between capitalism in Japan and in China, for example, demonstrates very clearly that capitalism itself is subject to significant variation at the domestic level. The foregoing discussion of regionalism suggests, in turn, that capitalism at a regional or international level is likewise amenable to significant, even profound change (although, to be sure, this change has not yet been realized).

The key point is as follows: an Asia-centered world must be constructed from the ground up. The foundation has been laid, but the edifice, for the most part, must still be built. Socially constituted actors in all the East Asian countries will play a role in this process, but arguably, state and nonstate actors in China will play the lead role. Again, for the purposes of this concluding chapter, a detailed and in-depth discussion of just what this role might be is not provided. Instead, I conclude with just a few general and selective points. First, a recentering on East Asia will require the East Asian economies, and especially China, to maintain strong and consistent records of economic growth; this task will not be easy, especially as the United States and the European Union will likely endeavor to maintain their positions of economic power. The United States, in particular, has pursued a policy of **neoliberal** globalization, which serves to undermine the developmental state, and has used the **IMF** as a tool to impose neoliberal economic policies around the world. China and to a lesser extent Japan—because of their vast reserves of foreign exchange—are in a good position to resist IMF pressure. Second, a recentering on East Asia will likely require, at least to some extent, that the term *East Asia* not only or primarily be a geographic label but also a sign of closer political and security-based regional unity or integration, rather than just economic integration. Political and security integration, however, has not been a strong suit of the East Asian countries, so this requirement remains a key obstacle.

Third, a recentering on East Asia also requires a capacity and willingness to project influence and power outside the region. Japan, South Korea, and Taiwan have all attempted to do this to some extent, but China has likely made the strongest inroads. One of the most salient of China's efforts has been its involvement in Africa, which goes back to the 1950s but took off in the early 2000s. Since 2000, in particular, China has committed $74 billion to African projects, spread throughout the African continent (Moss 2013). Demonstrating the importance of Africa to China, **Xi Jinping** visited three African states very shortly after assuming leadership of the CCP in November 2012. According to Trefor Moss (2013), moreover, "Africa is not the only place from which China looks appealing. Its soft power also draws people in Latin America, Eastern Europe and parts of Asia, where the popular impression of China might contrast favorably with the general perception of the West, or where Beijing might be seen as a welcome partner in tough financial times, or as a trusted long-time ally." The success of these ventures remains to be seen; what is already very clear, though, is that such efforts are part and parcel of a larger process designed to empower China and East Asia more generally.

This list could be extended, but the few examples cited are enough to reinforce the overarching point that a one-dimensional analysis of East Asia's future can provide only a partial glimpse into a far more complex and multidimensional process. The constructed actor model, by contrast, provides a comprehensive and coherent framework tailor-made for understanding and explaining the possibilities for a future global recentering on East Asia, or for other complex political, economic, and social processes and outcomes.

Notes

1. *Regional integration* in the structural view is not necessarily the same as the earlier use of the same term. In the structural view, the economic integration of East Asia was a largely "organic process," that is, the product of the demands of global capitalism. At the same time, the integration of the East Asian economies also reflected purposeful effort on the part of Japanese and US policymakers; they had to institutionalize the connections among and between the economies, especially in the integration of Japan, South Korea, and Taiwan. In this regard, the two uses of *regional integration* overlap.

Glossary

The entries included here correspond to words that appear in **boldface** *in the main text. Items in* SMALL CAPITALS *in the glossary are cross-references to main glossary entries.*

$\star\ \star\ \star$

agency. Often contrasted with the concept of STRUCTURE, the term *agency* implies that actors, whether acting individually or collectively, have an ability to affect or shape the larger social environment in which they live. Although a seemingly common-sense assertion, many scholars argue that all human action is, to at least some degree, constrained or otherwise shaped by broader forces, which can derive from INSTITUTIONS, culture, the economic system, or other overarching structures.

ahistorical analysis. The dictionary definition of *ahistorical*—"lacking historical perspective or context"—presupposes that historical perspective or context is important in or even central to developing an adequate understanding of certain issues, concepts, or events. On this point, however, intense disagreement can be found among scholars.

amakudari. Literally meaning "descent from heaven," *amakudari* is at its most basic a Japanese term that refers to the process by which high-level bureaucrats "retire" to senior management positions in private enterprises. See Figure 6.6 for further discussion.

AMF. See ASIAN MONETARY FUND.

ancien régime. *Ancien régime* is a French term that means "old order." Although it technically refers to the political and social system of France prior to the French Revolution, it is used more generally to refer to any traditional political and social system.

Arab Spring. This term is one of many used to describe the series of uprisings and antigovernment protests, both violent and nonviolent, that took place throughout the Arab world (centered in the Middle East and North Africa), beginning in December 2010. The uprisings began in Tunisia and then spread to Algeria, Egypt, Jordan, Yemen, Libya, Syria, Bahrain, Oman, and several other countries in the region. In some cases, long-standing authoritarian regimes were overthrown (e.g., Egypt, Tunisia, Yemen, and Libya), but in other places, the protests were quickly put down.

area studies. Area studies began in the United States after World War II as an interdisciplinary academic field; as the term implies, researchers in this field focused on specific geographic areas, the most common being East Asia, Southeast Asia, the Middle East, Africa, Latin America, and Western Europe. Ever since its inception, however, the field of area studies has been subject to criticism. In the early years, critics alleged that the discipline of area studies was too closely connected to the national security goals and interests of the US government, and especially to intelligence agencies, including the CIA. The problem, in this view, is that the field could not help but be tainted by its close association with the US national security bureaucracy. More recent criticisms focus on the lack of methodological and theoretical rigor in the field.

ASEAN. See Association of Southeast Asian Nations.

Asian Financial Crisis. Colloquially known as the Asian Contagion or the IMF Crisis, after the International Monetary Fund, this major financial crisis had a particularly hard impact on Thailand, Indonesia, Malaysia, and South Korea. The crisis began in Thailand, with the dramatic devaluation of the Thai baht in July 1997, and then spread—like a contagion—to other economies in Asia. The Asian Financial Crisis is discussed in Chapter 3.

Asian Monetary Fund (AMF). First proposed by the Japanese government during the Asian Financial Crisis, the AMF was meant to provide an alternative to the International Monetary Fund. The Japanese proposal, however, was strongly opposed by the United States.

asset bubble. An asset bubble is financial development in which the price of a particular type of asset (e.g., securities, gold, houses, real estate) rises to a level that appears to be well above the asset's "fundamental value." All asset bubbles eventually burst, which typically results in widespread economic difficulties.

Association of Southeast Asian Nations (ASEAN). ASEAN was established in 1967 by Indonesia, Malaysia, the Philippines, Singapore, and Thailand. Since then, its membership has expanded to include Brunei, Myanmar, Cambodia, Laos, and Vietnam. The organization was designed to promote economic growth and to maintain regional peace and stability by helping to moderate relations between and among its five founding members. See Helen S. Nesadurai (2008) for an extended discussion of ASEAN's activities since its founding.

autarky. *Autarky* means self-sufficiency, and it typically refers to the idea that a country can and should be self-sufficient economically, producing everything it needs internally, without the need to engage in international or cross-border trade.

authoritarianism. Authoritarianism is a political system in which political power is highly concentrated and centralized but does not necessarily reside in the hands of a single individual. In an authoritarian system, the regime typically governs through a political party, which is used to mobilize people around the goals of the regime. See Autocracy for a comparison.

autocracy. Although the word *autocracy* is often used interchangeably with the word *authoritarianism,* the two are quite clearly different. Autocracy is a form of government in which one person, in a literal sense, is the supreme power within a country. An autocracy is synonymous with an absolute monarch. See Authoritarianism for a comparison.

bafuku. A Japanese term literally meaning "tent office," *bafuku* more generally refers to the military-led government of a shogun. Three major periods of *bafuku* rule occurred in Japan: (1) the Kamakura *bakufu* from 1192–1333, (2) the Muromachi *bakufu* from 1338–1573, and (3) the Tokugawa *bakufu* from 1603–1867.

bailout. A bailout refers to the policy of rescuing a firm or industry from potential or imminent financial insolvency, usually by extending credit to which the failing firm or industry would otherwise not have access. While credit can be extended by the private sector, most commonly it is extended or guaranteed by a government or international financial institution, such as the International Monetary Fund.

burakumin. An outcast group in traditional Japanese society, the *buraku* people (*min* means "people") engaged in occupations that were considered impure or unclean, such as working as butchers, tanners, undertakers, and executioners. Although the class was formally eliminated during the Meiji era, discrimination against the *burakumin* remained severe even in the postwar period. Even today, Japan's family registration makes determining if a family has *buraku* ancestors easy.

Bushido. Bushido, which can be translated as the "way of the warrior," refers to the code of conduct that governed the lives of Japan's samurai class. Bushido is not a fixed set of values, as it has changed. Bushido has often been influenced by broader cultural currents over the many centuries of its existence, its origins dating back to the Kamakura period (1192–1333). In very general terms, though, it espouses obedience to authority, obligation, loyalty, and fearlessness.

capitalist roader. This term was used during the MAO era in China to refer to members of the CHINESE COMMUNIST PARTY accused of harboring antirevolutionary thoughts about the value of capitalism.

cat principle (or theory). This principle is based on DENG XIAOPING'S famous quip, "It does not matter if the cat is black or white, as long as it catches mice." The meaning behind this statement was clear: Deng was an advocate of "pragmatic" and effective economic policies, even if those policies appeared to contradict the ideals of MARXISM-LENINISM and Maoism. Made in 1962, Deng's comment came when MAO ZEDONG was open to market-based economic reforms. Later, however, the statement was used as evidence to show that Deng was a "CAPITALIST ROADER."

CCP. See CHINESE COMMUNIST PARTY.

central planning. In central planning, basic economic decisions (what industries should be built, what prices of goods will be, how much of certain products will be produced, etc.) are made by nonmarket actors (e.g., government bureaucrats or officials). Central planning, in this regard, can be seen as the antithesis of a free market.

chaebol. Also spelled *jaebol* or *jaebeol,* the *chaebol* is the Korean equivalent of the Japanese *ZAIBATSU* (*chaebol* and *zaibatsu* use the same Chinese characters). Most generally, the *chaebol* are large, family-owned conglomerates. They have dominated the South Korean economy since its early years but became particularly prominent under PARK CHUNG HEE'S administration, in large part because they were given preferential access to scarce economic resources controlled by the government. The most prominent *chaebol* include Hyundai, LG (originally Lucky-Goldstar), Samsung, and SK Group.

Charter 08. In December 2008, 303 Chinese activists issued a petition—dubbed "Charter 08"—calling for greater human rights and the establishment of democratic freedoms in China. Liu Xiaobo, a prominent intellectual and critic of the CCP, wrote the petition. A year later, he was sentenced to eleven years in prison by Chinese authorities.

Chen Yun (1905–1995). Chen was one of the most influential "elders" within the CHINESE COMMUNIST PARTY. During the 1950s, he was credited with helping to stabilize the Chinese economy and was widely considered China's leading economic planner. Chen, however, was a "conservative" and therefore not in favor of many of the market-based reforms introduced by DENG XIAOPING.

Chiang Kai-shek (1887–1975). Chiang was the president of the Republic of China (Taiwan) from 1948 to 1975 and was one of the leading figures in the KUOMINGTANG (KMT), the Chinese Nationalist Party. In 1925, after the death of Sun Yat-sen (another major figure in postimperial China, often referred to as the Father of the Nation), Chiang became leader of the KMT and commander in chief of the revolutionary army, a position he used to help unify China in the 1920s. In 1931, however, the Japanese seized MANCHURIA and threatened to invade the rest of the country. Chiang, however, remained focused on his main internal enemies, the COMMUNISTS, who had retreated to the rural areas. As the Japanese threat grew, Chiang was literally forced to concentrate on fighting the Japanese: he was kidnapped by one of his generals, who demanded he face the Japanese threat. Chiang agreed, but fighting the Japanese meant forging a united front with the communists. Not surprisingly, the alliance between the KMT and the communists broke down after the Japanese were defeated, but by this time, the communists had regrouped and become a much more powerful force—a force that the KMT could not defeat. In 1949, the KMT was forced to flee the mainland; Chiang and about 2 million nationalists and others moved to Taiwan and set up a new government in exile on the island. Chiang formally resumed his duties as president of the Republic of China on March 1, 1950, a position he held until his death in 1975.

Chiang Mai Initiative (CMI). The CMI was a direct product of the ASIAN FINANCIAL CRISIS and of efforts by the United States and INTERNATIONAL MONETARY FUND to prevent the establishment of the ASIAN MONETARY FUND, first proposed by Japan. It was announced by the ASEAN+3 (that is, the membership of the ASSOCIATION OF SOUTHEAST ASIAN STATES plus China, Japan, and South Korea) in May 2000 and indicated the group's intention to cooperate in four areas: monitoring capital flows, regional surveillance, swap networks, and personnel training.

Chinese Communist Party (CCP). The CCP (also known as the Communist Party of China) was founded in 1921 and has been the sole ruling party of China since 1949. Before coming to power, the CCP fought a long war against the KUOMINGTANG and was also engaged in a struggle against the Japanese. The CCP is the world's largest political party, with a membership of around 76 million.

Chongryon. Chongryon is an abbreviation for the General Association of Korean Residents in Japan, which is an organization comprised of ethnic Koreans living in Japan. The members of Chongryon generally support or have ties with the North Korean government. Most members either came to Japan during the colonial period as voluntary migrants or as conscripted labor or are descendants of the former. Another organization, known as Mindan, represents the interests of ethnic Koreans in Japan who chose South Korean nationality.

class struggle. A Marxist concept that portrays the relationship between dominant and subordinate social classes as one that is defined by constant struggle or conflict. According to this concept, a new society can be built through class struggle. MAO ZEDONG not only embraced the concept of class struggle but also argued that it continues even after the capitalist class has been defeated. Mao's ideas about class struggle were partly the basis for the CULTURAL REVOLUTION.

clientelism. Clientelism refers to a type of social relationship between a "patron" and "client." A patron is someone who controls valuable resources, while the client is someone who receives a resource controlled by the patron. In a political system, the patron will often provide resources in exchange for votes (or political campaigning).

CMI. See CHIANG MAI INITIATIVE.

Comintern. Comintern, an abbreviation of Communist International, was founded by leading members of the Communist Party in Russia in 1919. The aim of the Comintern was to fight "by all available means, including armed forces, for the overthrow of the international bourgeoisie and for the creation of an international Soviet republic as a transition stage to the complete abolition of the STATE" (Report and Discussion of Statutes of the Communist International" 1921 [1977]).

command economy. A command economy is typically associated with COMMUNIST countries such as the former Soviet Union, China (prior to 1979), or North Korea today. In a command economy, major economic decisions are controlled by STATE authorities, who may determine what products to produce and how much, what the prices of the products will be, how income will be distributed, and so on. In other words, a command economy is one in which market forces, especially the forces of supply and demand, are made subservient to state policies and goals. In general, command economies have proven to be highly flawed. At the same time, the East Asian economies have demonstrated that some centralized planning (an important aspect of a command economy) can be beneficial.

commodification. This term refers to the transformation of an object or activity into a commodity, that is, a good or service that can be bought or sold (usually for profit). In Marxism, commodification is an alienating process: it reduces everything—friendship, knowledge, sex, the environment, even human beings—to a monetary value.

commune. In China, the commune was a type of very large rural organization—typically involving between 5,000 and 25,000 families—introduced during the GREAT LEAP FORWARD. Communes, meant to be the basic unit of China's COMMUNIST system, were designed to be largely self-reliant, producing not just agricultural goods but also industrial goods. The commune system, however, failed to achieve its objectives and was soon scaled back and given greater autonomy.

communist (communism). In classic Marxist theory, communism is a specific stage in the historical development of human society, one that can be reached only after society achieves the capacity to produce and sustain a huge surplus of material wealth. More simply, it is the stage that succeeds capitalism. Importantly, classical Marxism argued that on the basis of the material surplus produced by capitalism, a communist society—in other words, a society that is classless and stateless—can emerge. In popular usage, by contrast, communism refers to a totalitarian system of government in which a single party controls the major means of production. As should be apparent, these two definitions of *communism* are contradictory; indeed, profound disagreement can be found on how to define the term. For current purposes, keeping in mind that the popular understanding is not the only, nor the best way to define *communism* is enough.

comparative advantage. Comparative advantage is an economic principle first introduced by David Ricardo (1772–1823), one of the most influential of the classical economists. The concept of comparative advantage is fairly simple, although the implications are profound. Basically, Ricardo argued that international trade allows all countries to benefit (to be better off), even if one country enjoys an absolute advantage in the production of any given product. The key to understanding the significance of comparative advantage is the following: in any situation of trade, one country can always produce a good or service at a lower opportunity cost (the value of what is given up) than another. In other words, every country has a comparative advantage in some area, which further means that trade is always mutually beneficial.

conditionality. Conditionality, in general, simply refers to the conditions a bank or lending INSTITUTION places on the borrower in exchange for a loan. More commonly, however, it refers specifically to the conditions placed by the INTERNATIONAL MONETARY FUND (IMF) or WORLD BANK on individual countries in return for a loan provided or approved by the IMF. The IMF defines *conditionality* as follows: "When a country borrows from the IMF, its government agrees to adjust its economic policies to overcome the problems that led it to seek financial aid from the international community. These loan conditions also serve to ensure that the country will be able to repay the Fund so that the resources can be made available to other members in need. In recent years, the IMF has streamlined conditionality in order to promote national ownership of strong and effective policies." IMF conditionality is extremely controversial, as many developing countries view the IMF as an institution controlled by the major Western economies, especially the United States, which uses conditionality as a way to gain control over other countries' domestic economies.

Confucianism. An East Asian ethical and philosophical system developed mostly upon the teachings of Confucius (traditionally 551 B.C. TO 479 B.C.). Confucianism remained the mainstream Chinese orthodoxy for 2,000 years, until the beginning of the twentieth century, when the CHINESE COMMUNIST PARTY first began to exert influence in Chinese politics. Outside of China, Confucian ideas have influenced a variety of Asian societies, including Korea, Japan, Taiwan, Singapore, and Vietnam.

coup d'état. Most commonly referred to simply as a "coup," a coup d'état is a sudden and decisive use of force in politics. Most often, it involves the forceful overthrow of a sitting government through the use of violence (or the threat of violence) by a small group, almost always from the military.

Cultural Revolution. The Cultural Revolution is more formally known as the Great Proletarian Cultural Revolution. Most basically it was a political campaign and mass movement instigated by MAO ZEDONG to rid China of its traditional-cultural elements, bureaucratism, and capitalist tendencies. Lasting approximately from 1966 to 1976 (Teiwes 2010), it produced disastrous results.

debt-to-equity ratio. A measure of a company's financial leverage, debt-to-equity ratio is calculated by dividing a company's total liabilities by stockholders' equity. If a company has a long-term debt of $1 million and shareholders' equity of $1 million, the debt-to-equity ratio is 1. Debt (or "leverage") is not necessarily a bad thing: it is an effective and cost-efficient way to fund further investments. A very high debt-to-equity ratio, however, can lead to serious difficulties, including bankruptcy, if a company does not have enough funds to pay its obligations.

Deng Xiaoping (1904–1997). Deng Xiaoping was a prominent leader within the CHINESE COMMUNIST PARTY during the MAO ZEDONG years and the decades following Mao's death. The de facto leader of China from 1978 to the early 1990s, Deng is most known for his championing of market-based economic reforms. He is often credited with China's successful transition from a rigid socialist economy, based on CENTRAL PLANNING, to a fast-growing capitalist economy. Deng also played an instrumental role in helping China recover from the GREAT LEAP FORWARD.

dependent variable. In a causal or social scientific analysis, the dependent variable is that variable the researcher seeks to explain. It is the result or effect in a causal relationship and is expected to change when another variable—the INDEPENDENT VARIABLE—is changed (thus the name).

developmental state. The developmental state is a particular type of STATE distinguished by its high capacity to promote and facilitate rapid industrial development. The concept has been around for several decades, and one of the most influential early works was Chalmers Johnson's *MITI and the Japanese Miracle* (1982). The developmental state is discussed in depth in Chapter 2.

Diet. The Diet is Japan's national assembly or parliament, which is composed of the House of Representatives and the House of Councilors (originally the House of Peers). Although the term *Diet* was officially replaced with *Kokkai* under the 1947 Constitution, it is still commonly used to refer to Japan's national assembly.

dirigiste (or *dirigisme* as a noun). A French term that typically refers to a capitalist economy in which the STATE plays an important role (over and above simple regulation). To a certain extent, one can argue that all capitalist economies have some form of dirigisme, but the label has been specifically applied to countries such as Japan, South Korea, France, and China.

discount rate. The discount rate is the interest rate that a depository banking INSTITUTION is charged to borrow short-term funds directly from the Federal Reserve Bank (or a central bank more generally). Loans based on the discount rate are limited, but the rate is significant because it indicates the direction in which the Federal Reserve is trying to push the broader economy. A low interest rate, for example, typically indicates that the Federal Reserve is trying to promote growth, while a high discount rate shows that the Federal Reserve is concerned about inflationary pressures.

dollar-peg scheme. When a country "pegs" its currency to the dollar, the value of the domestic currency—say the Thai baht—adjusts according to changes in the value of the dollar. If the dollar rises in value, so does the baht, and vice versa. In this type of fixed exchange-rate policy, the value of the local currency is fixed to a specific value of the dollar. In practice, a country will peg its currency to a certain dollar range, allowing for some degree of flexibility.

dual economy. A larger economy is divided into two distinct sectors. One sector is characterized by a high level of productivity, technology, and high wages, while the other sector is characterized by low levels of productivity, low technological development, and low wages.

economic inputs. Economic inputs are used to produce economic outputs. Thus, labor, energy, capital (money), land, and entrepreneurship are all considered inputs.

economies of scale. In general, as a firm or factory produces more of the same product, the cost per unit of output decreases. The reduction in the average per-unit cost of output is known as the economy of scale. See ECONOMIES OF SCOPE for a comparison.

economies of scope. Economies of scope are related to ECONOMIES OF SCALE. In the latter, higher levels of production of a single product lead to a reduction in the average unit cost; in the former, the average production cost of multiple products is reduced when a firm diversifies its product line, as long as certain fixed costs remain largely the same. Consider Apple's iPhone. If the same factory produces only iPhones, but produces millions of units, it will benefit from economies of scale. However, if the same factory can also produce iPads using some of the same fixed costs (building, machinery, land), it now benefits from economies of scope.

enclave development. In economic terms, an enclave refers to the portion of the economy devoted to the manufacturing or assembly of products for export. In addition, foreign firms usually control all or most production within the enclave, which is used primarily to take advantage of low labor and resource costs. Economic growth that results from enclave development, therefore, primarily benefits foreign firms and not the local economy.

ethnocentrism. Referring to the act of assessing different cultures and societies by one's own standards, values, and expectations, ethnocentrism can lead to misunderstanding and biased research.

ethnography (ethnographic method). Ethnography is an in-depth study of a particular human community; today, it is primarily based on an immersive method of fieldwork, whereby the researcher essentially becomes part of a community and participates in the everyday life of the people whom the researcher is studying.

FDI. See FOREIGN DIRECT INVESTMENT.

federalism. A type of political system in which sovereignty or governing authority is constitutionally divided between a central or national government and constituent political units. The US political system, for example, is based on federalism.

Federation of Korean Trade Unions. Formed after the military COUP D'ÉTAT in 1961, the Federation of Korean Trade Unions was created by the PARK CHUNG HEE regime in an effort to co-opt labor. During the AUTHORITARIAN period, it was the sole, legally authorized trade union.

filial piety. Filial piety is a CONFUCIAN principle, which can be generally defined as a virtue of respect for one's parents and ancestors.

foreign direct investment (FDI). FDI is a type of cross-border investment in which, first, a direct inflow of funds goes from one country into a different country, and, second, those funds are used for building, machinery and equipment, or other physical assets. For example, a Japanese company might use its own money to build a factory in China or invest in a joint partnership with a Chinese company. Today, FDI can also take the form of investment in a joint venture, a strategic alliance, the direct acquisition of a foreign firm, and so on. For many countries, FDI is a major source of economic growth.

free ride (free rider). An important concept in rational choice analysis, the "free ride" theory is based on the assumption that an individual will not voluntarily contribute to the cost of a good, service, resource, and so on, available to anyone without restriction. Free riding, it is important to add, is rational behavior. The existence of free riding, however, poses a problem: if it is rational to free ride, why would anyone voluntarily participate, for example, in a prodemocracy movement? If the protest is successful, the free rider will still reap all the benefits from a more democratic political system whether or not he or she participated.

Gang of Four. This name refers to a small group of "radicals" within the CHINESE COMMUNIST PARTY, including MAO ZEDONG's wife, who rose to power during the CULTURAL REVOLUTION. Although criticized by Mao himself, the Gang of Four was largely protected until Mao's death in 1976. After his death, however, the Gang of Four lost power; the members were arrested and convicted of political crimes. All received long prison sentences, including Jiang Qing (Mao's wife), who initially received a suspended death sentence, which was later reduced to life imprisonment.

GDP. See GROSS DOMESTIC PRODUCT.

gendered division of labor. As the phrase implies, a gendered division of labor refers to the tendency for certain types of work and job categories to be divided along gender lines. Although, on the surface, a gendered division of labor may seem "natural," as in the tendency for women to engage in child-care work, feminist scholars argue the cruciality of recognizing that the gendered division of labor is socially constructed and not a universal given. Indeed, one of the most important implications of the gendered division of labor is that women dominate the unpaid work category, often because women have little opportunity to engage in paid work. However, even when women engage in paid work, their earnings are typically much less than those of men, in part because they are involuntarily consigned to low-paying job categories but also because of discriminatory payment schemes: women are generally paid less than men doing exactly the same work with the same level of experience and productivity.

Gini coefficient. Also known as the Gini index or Gini ratio, the Gini coefficient is a basic measure of income inequality. A Gini coefficient of zero (0.0) indicates perfect equality—that is, a situation in which all the income in a given society is distributed equally to all members—and a coefficient of 1.0 indicates perfect inequality. A ratio of 0.2 to 0.3 is generally considered to represent strong equality, while a ratio above 0.5 represents strong inequality.

global (or international) division of labor. The division of labor, in general, refers to a process by which the production of a given product is broken down into specific or specialized tasks to maximize efficiency. In principle, the division of labor can take place within a single factory, but increasingly the process has been globalized, taking place in locations around the world. Unfortunately, this process, according to many critics, exacerbates inequality by locating low-value, low-skilled tasks in the poorest countries, while locating higher-value, higher-skilled tasks in wealthier countries.

Great (Kanto) Earthquake. The Great Earthquake struck the Kanto region (which includes Tokyo and Yokohama) on September 1, 1923. It was the deadliest earthquake in Japanese history (with an estimated 142,800 deaths) and the most powerful earthquake ever recorded in the region to that point. The significance of the earthquake, however, was not just limited to devastation from the quake itself. Instead, it also became known as a key source from which ethnic violence and repression sprang. In the aftermath of the earthquake, rumors spread that Koreans were taking advantage of the disaster, which quickly led to mob violence. Thousands of Koreans were killed, as well as hundreds of Chinese citizens who were mistaken for Korean. To add to the chaotic situation, the Imperial Army used the ethnic violence as an excuse to round up political dissidents.

Great Leap Forward. The Great Leap Forward was an economic program launched by MAO ZEDONG in 1958 in an effort to accelerate China's industrialization and to catch up with the West. The program was tremendously disruptive and damaging, as it was not only designed to speed up industrialization but also based on the principle of collectivization, even if by force, which required farmers and peasants to give up their land. During the Great Leap Forward, private property was virtually eliminated from the countryside. The excesses of the Great Leap Forward contributed to major famines and an industrial depression.

gross domestic product (GDP). GDP is the monetary value of all finished goods and services produced within a country's borders in a specified time period (usually a calendar year); it includes all private and government consumption, public spending, investments, and exports less imports. See also PER CAPITA GDP.

guanxi. In general, *guanxi* refers to a system of social networks and strong personal relationships based on mutual commitment and reciprocity that exist in Chinese societies. Literally, *guanxi* can be translated as "relationships" or "connections," although that simple translation cannot do proper justice to the term. See Chapter 2 for additional discussion.

Hakka. The Hakka are Han Chinese but are considered an ethnic minority group in China. The word *Hakka* means "people from guest families"; it is assumed that the Hakka migrated from "somewhere else." The Hakka people also have a distinct spoken language known simply as Hakka.

Han Chinese. The Han Chinese are the dominant ethnic group in China, constituting about 92 percent of the country's population (and 19 percent of the world's population). In addition, 98 percent of Taiwan's population is Han Chinese, although most (86 percent) are descendants of early Han immigrants, known as native Taiwanese. The term *Han* comes from the Han dynasty, whose first emperor was known as Han Zhong. As with any ethnic label, the term *Han Chinese* is a fluid and socially constructed concept.

Homo economicus. Literally meaning the "economic man," the term is used to refer to a pure economic actor, that is, a theoretical human being who has complete information and acts in a consistently self-interested, rational manner. As an ideal type, it is understood that *Homo economicus* does not actually exist, but many (albeit not all) economists believe that the concept can still be used as a basis for theorizing about real-world economic outcomes.

Hu Jintao (b. 1942). Hu became general secretary of the CHINESE COMMUNIST PARTY in 2002 (and president in 2003); he stepped down in 2012. During his term in office,

Hu sought to address some of the more deleterious aspects of China's rapid economic growth through his promotion of a "harmonious society." At the same time, he was not an advocate of major political reform and continued China's hard-line policy toward political dissidence.

Hu Yaobang (1915–1989). Hu was a protégé of DENG XIAOPING who played a key role in rehabilitating victims of the CULTURAL REVOLUTION and in promoting economic and political reform. Hu was also known for his relatively tolerant attitude toward "liberal" intellectuals in the late 1980s. In fact, Hu's death helped spark the 1989 TIANANMEN MOVEMENT.

Hua Guofeng (1921–2008). To the surprise of many, Hua was selected by MAO ZEDONG to succeed Zhou Enlai as premier in January 1976. He played an instrumental role in the arrest of the GANG OF FOUR. The removal of the Gang of Four provided space for reformers, led by DENG XIAOPING (who had been temporarily purged), to take control of China's economic policy. In 1980, Hua resigned the premiership but retained a seat on the CHINESE COMMUNIST PARTY'S Central Committee until 2002.

hukou **(system).** A system of population registration and control, the Chinese *hukou* provides the principal basis for establishing identity, citizenship, and proof of "official status." The system plays a particularly important role in controlling internal migration from China's countryside to urban areas.

IMF. See INTERNATIONAL MONETARY FUND.

import-substitution industrialization (ISI). This economic strategy was premised on reducing the need for imports by expanding and increasing production of domestically produced goods. Typically, an ISI strategy requires heavy STATE involvement in the national economy. For example, to create the minimal foundation for ISI, the state must prohibit certain imports and provide financial assistance (for example, a subsidy) to import-substituting firms and industries.

independent variable. An independent variable is one that influences another variable, called a DEPENDENT VARIABLE. Informally, the independent variable can be thought of as the cause of a particular outcome. Consider the following simplified statement, "Democratization in East Asia resulted from a shift in class power made possible by self-organization on the part of the working class." In this example, self-organization is the independent variable.

industrial policy. Related to the concept of INDUSTRIAL TARGETING, industrial policy refers to purposeful and strategic efforts on the part of state or national governments to encourage the development of specific sectors of the national economy. The focus on specific sectors differentiates industrial policy from MACROECONOMIC policy, the latter of which is based on broad, economy-wide policies. Industrial policy characterizes interventionist or DEVELOPMENTAL STATES, as opposed to LAISSEZ-FAIRE ECONOMICS.

industrial targeting. This government policy is based on targeting certain industries or industrial sectors for future development. Typically, once an industry is targeted, it will receive preferential treatment (e.g., tax breaks, low-interest loans, subsidies, and protection from foreign competition).

infant industry. In an already established and internationally competitive industrial sector, an infant industry is one that emerges relatively late. As a newcomer, the infant industry normally cannot operate on the same scale and, therefore, at the same level of competitiveness and efficiency as its more established international competitors. Thus, some argue that STATES should be allowed to protect and nurture their infant industries until those industries have time to "grow up."

information asymmetry. Simply put, information asymmetry refers to a situation in which one party to a transaction has more or better information than the other party (or parties). In a free market, information asymmetry can undermine the mutually beneficial aspect of market transactions, since the party with more or better information can "take advantage of" or "cheat" the other party.

institution. Traditionally, institutions are equated with concrete public and private organizations or agencies, such as the legislature, the presidency, the STATE as a whole, or a corporation. The traditional definition is still relevant and frequently used, but the term has other, more expansive, and arguably more important meanings as well. One of these more expansive definitions describes institutions as "systems of established and embedded social rules that structure social interactions," where rules are understood as "socially transmitted and customary normative injunctions" (Hodgson 2006, pp. 17–18). In other words, rules tell us what is right or wrong.

International Monetary Fund (IMF). See WORLD BANK AND INTERNATIONAL MONETARY FUND (IMF).

intersubjectivity. One way to understand this concept is to break it down. *Inter-* as a prefix simply means "between, among, or within a group." *Subjective* (or *subjectivity*) means "dependent on the mind or on the individual's perception for its existence." Thus *intersubjectivity* might be defined as "the perceptions people share among themselves about the world."

Iron Triangle. The Iron Triangle has been used to describe, in general terms, the very strong triangular relationship among legislative, bureaucratic, and corporate interests. This relationship is assumed to be mutually reinforcing, as each element of the triangle benefits from the close ties. In Japan, it refers to the same basic relationship, although it is more specifically among LIBERAL DEMOCRATIC PARTY politicians, big business, and the leading bureaucratic agencies.

ISI. See IMPORT-SUBSTITUTION INDUSTRIALIZATION.

Jiang Zemin (b. 1926). Jiang replaced ZHAO ZIYANG after the TIANANMEN MOVEMENT and served as the general secretary of the Chinese Communist Party from 1989 to 2002, as well as president of China from 1993 to 2003. After DENG XIAOPING died in 1997, Jiang became the "paramount leader." One of his major reforms was a privatization plan introduced in 1997, which was designed to reduce the number of STATE-OWNED ENTERPRISES. Jiang also helped to improve US-China relations. In 2002, he became the first Chinese leader to voluntarily step down as president after serving two five-year terms. He was succeeded by HU JINTAO as general secretary and president.

Kaohsiung Incident. This event in 1979, which occurred during the period of AUTHORITARIAN rule in Taiwan, started out as a Human Rights Day celebration by opposition groups (led by the prodemocracy *Formosa Magazine*). It turned into a major civil disturbance when KUOMINTANG officials attempted to disperse the crowd. Using the chaotic situation as an excuse, the authorities rounded up leaders of the opposition; fifty-one opposition figures were arrested, and several were tried in military court. They received sentences ranging from twelve years to life imprisonment. The incident is pointed to as a watershed in Taiwan's prodemocracy movement.

keiretsu. A specific type of business organization in Japan, a *keiretsu* is composed of a group or set of companies that are linked together through both formal and informal mechanisms, including cross-shareholding, interlocking directorates, joint affiliation with commercial and investment banks, and "presidents' club" meetings. Several major types of *keiretsu* can be identified, but the two most important are the horizontal or intermarket *keiretsu* and the vertical *keiretsu*. The horizontal *keiretsu* are typically formed around a bank and include firms from a range of industries. A vertical *keiretsu* is formed around a lead company, usually a major manufacturer such as Toyota, Hitachi, or Nippon Steel. Members of a vertical *keiretsu* may produce different parts of a product, which are manufactured for the lead company.

Keynesianism. An economic approach based on the work of John Maynard Keynes (1883–1946). One of Keynes's most salient contributions to economic theory was the idea that aggregate demand (total spending in the economy, including spending by the government) does not necessarily equal aggregate supply; in other words, Keynes challenged the then prevailing idea that markets are self-regulating and self-correcting (i.e., that supply and demand will always come into equilibrium via a free market). The logical conclusion of this argument was that government intervention in the economy is sometimes necessary to ensure full employment and price stability. For example, Keynes argued that, during recessionary periods, governments should "spend against the wind" to boost aggregate demand. This spending was necessary, Keynes argued, because aggregate spending by consumers goes down during a recession, which further exacerbates poor economic conditions: consumers spend less, businesses invest less, profits fall, more workers are laid off, and consumer spending decreases even more. To stop this vicious cycle, governments have to spend more.

Kim Il-sung (1912–1994). Kim was the leader of North Korea from its establishment as the Democratic People's Republic of Korea in 1948 until his death in 1994. Before helping to create North Korea, Kim was part of the Korean guerrilla resistance against the Japanese occupation of Korea during the 1930s. A major part of Kim's legitimacy when he returned to the northern part of Korea after the end of the Pacific War stems from his anti-Japanese activities.

Kim Jong-il (1941–2011). The son of KIM IL-SUNG, the younger Kim officially succeeded his father as the "supreme leader" of North Korea in 1997. The North Korean people referred to Kim as "Dear Leader," while his father was called "Great Leader." As with his father, Kim Jong-il died of natural causes.

Kim Jong-un (b. 1983). Kim Jong-un is the son of KIM JONG-IL and the grandson of KIM IL-SUNG. He is the current supreme leader of North Korea (as of September 2013).

KMT. See KUOMINTANG.

Kondratieff cycle (or wave). Named after Nikolai D. Kondratieff, the Kondratieff cycle (or wave or most simply, K-wave), refers to an economic cycle that tends to occur every fifty years or so. These cycles consist of alternating periods of high sectoral growth (the "A-phase") and periods of relatively slow growth (the "B-phase"). The A-phase of K-waves is typically associated with the development of basic innovations (e.g., electric power and steel, electronics and automobiles, information technology) that launch technological revolutions.

Korean People's Army. Also known as the Inmin gun, the Korean People's Army is the official designation for the armed forces of North Korea.

Korean War. This war took place on the Korean peninsula between June 1950 and July 1953. While ostensibly a war between North and South Korea, two of the main combatants were the United States, allied with the South, and China, allied with the North. The United Nations was also involved, and contingents from a wide range of countries—the United Kingdom, Turkey, Australia, Canada, France, Greece, Colombia, Thailand, Ethiopia, and eight other countries—fought on behalf of South Korea. The war ended in a stalemate, with the two sides ending up in exactly the same position they started. Estimates on the total number of casualties vary widely. The United States lost about 40,000 soldiers, and South Korea about 46,000. The Pentagon estimates that over 400,000 Chinese soldiers were killed, while North Korea lost about 215,000.

Korean Workers' Party. Also known as the Workers' Party of Korea, the Korean Workers' Party is the ruling political party of North Korea, a position the party has held since the country was founded. KIM IL-SUNG completely controlled the party until his death in 1994; after that, leadership of the party was assumed by KIM JONG-IL, although three years passed between the elder Kim's death and Kim Jong-il's formal appointment as general secretary. After Kim Jong-il's death in 2011, KIM JONG-UN was appointed head of the party.

Kuomintang (KMT). Also spelled as *Guomindang,* the KMT can be translated as the Chinese Nationalist Party; it ruled over Taiwan for most of the postwar era under the leadership of CHIANG KAI-SHEK. The KMT, however, was founded much earlier on mainland China (in 1919) and was originally led by Sun Yat-sen. After being defeated by COMMUNIST forces during the Chinese civil war, the KMT and its supporters fled to Taiwan, where leaders of the KMT established a single-party AUTHORITARIAN system that lasted until 1991 (the year that martial law was finally lifted).

Kwangju Uprising. Also spelled *Gwangju,* the Kwangju Uprising in May 1980 was a major antigovernment protest that took place in the city of Kwangju, located in South Korea's South Cholla Province—the stronghold of the prominent opposition leader, Kim Dae-jung. The uprising took place in the context of military rule under Chun Doo-hwan, who had seized power after the assassination of PARK CHUNG HEE. It was triggered by the use of deadly force against a student demonstration that took place on the morning of May 18. Subsequently, even larger demonstrations took place, which eventually led to a citizen takeover of the entire city. For a few days, protestors governed the city, but on May 27, troops from five divisions moved into the city and quelled the uprising, again using deadly force.

Kyoto Protocol. The name refers to the Japanese city in which the United Nations Framework Convention on Climate Change was negotiated. The protocol set binding obligations on industrial countries to reduce their emissions of greenhouse gases with the goal of stabilizing "the greenhouse gas concentrations in the atmosphere at a level that would prevent dangerous anthropogenic interference in the climate system" (United Nations Framework Convention on Climate Change 1997).

laissez-faire economics. The loose translation of *laissez-faire* from French is "leave it alone," where "it" refers to the market. Laissez-faire economics, then, is based on the idea that markets should be free from government intervention.

land reform. In practical terms, land reform refers to a redistribution, by force if necessary, of agricultural land, from large landholders to smaller landholders (e.g., individual farmers and peasants). The motivations behind land reform are generally more political than economic; that is, land reform has typically been used by STATES to abolish feudal relationships by undercutting the power of the landlord class, thereby "freeing" peasants from subjugation and dependence.

LDP. See LIBERAL DEMOCRATIC PARTY.

Li Peng (b. 1928). Li held numerous high-level positions, including chairman of the National People's Congress. As chairman of the National People's Congress, Li played a key role in shaping the Chinese government's response to the TIANANMEN MOVEMENT. Specifically, he was instrumental in ensuring a violent crackdown on the protestors by convincing most of the other senior CCP officials and DENG XIAO-PING of the need to act. Li officially declared martial law on May 20, 1989, and subsequently ordered the military to move in and crush the movement.

Li Xiannian (1909–1992). Li was a veteran of the Long March and a self-taught economist who favored the STALINIST MODEL of economics. (The Long March was a 6,000-mile trek of the CHINESE COMMUNIST PARTY that resulted in the relocation of the COMMUNIST revolutionary base from southeastern to northwestern China.) He also played an important role in helping China recover from the GREAT LEAP FOR-

WARD. Following the death of MAO ZEDONG, Li eventually sided with DENG XIAO-PING and stayed on as one of the five members of the CCP POLITBURO STANDING COMMITTEE until 1987.

Liberal Democratic Party (LDP). The LDP, a major political party in Japan, was originally formed in 1955 with the merger of the conservative Liberal Party and the Democratic Party. The LDP dominated Japanese politics for most of the postwar period, holding a majority in the DIET for thirty-eight straight years between 1955 and 1993.

liberalization. Liberalization has many meanings depending on the context; in terms of liberalizing trade, however, it refers to a relaxation or elimination of barriers to free trade. Concretely, liberalization of trade would mean lowering or eliminating tariffs, ending subsidies, ensuring that any regulations apply equally to domestic and foreign firms, and so on. Liberalization is also associated with deregulation and privatization.

Liu Shaoqi (1898–1969). Liu was president of the People's Republic of China from 1959 to 1966 and a chief "theoretician" for the CHINESE COMMUNIST PARTY. At one point, he was considered the heir to MAO ZEDONG but was purged as a CAPITALIST ROADER during the CULTURAL REVOLUTION.

macroeconomics. Macroeconomics is concerned with dynamics of the economy as a whole, as opposed to the behavior of individuals and individual firms (which is the domain of microeconomics). The focus of macroeconomics is on major economic factors or indicators, such as GROSS DOMESTIC PRODUCT, unemployment rates, balance of payments, and price trends (inflation or deflation).

Manchuria. Geographically, Manchuria is a large region in Northeast Asia that consists of three provinces: Liaoning, Jilin, and Heilongjiang. In addition, the northeastern portion of Inner Mongolia is sometimes included as part of Manchuria. Importantly, the area is bounded by Russia (northwest) and Korea (to the south); Japan lies to the east across the Sea of Japan. Partly because of its geographic position, Manchuria has played a central role in East Asian politics. Disputes over Manchuria, for example, led to the Russo-Japanese War of 1904; in 1931, Japan invaded Manchuria and in 1932 created the puppet STATE of Manchukuo. Manchukuo was used as a base for Japan's subsequent expansion into other parts of Asia.

Mao Zedong (1893–1976). Also referred to as *Mao Tse-tung, Mao,* or *Chairman Mao,* Mao Zedong was the founding father of the People's Republic of China and presided over the country from its inception on October 1, 1949, to his death on September 9, 1976. His rise to power began as one of the founders of the CHINESE COMMUNIST PARTY in 1921. He gradually rose through the ranks of the CCP and became part of the top leadership in 1934–1935 during the Long March. Despite a number of severe missteps while ruling China, including the GREAT LEAP FORWARD and the CULTURAL REVOLUTION, Mao remains a revered figure.

market failure. A market failure occurs when a freely functioning market cannot produce an efficient outcome. Although a market failure can have many possible causes, one of the most important has to do with PUBLIC GOODS. A public good is something that provides a benefit to people but, once it is created, is available to everyone whether they pay for it or not. A good example of a public good is a lighthouse: those who built and maintain the lighthouse cannot control which ships benefit from it and which do not. The problem with market failures is clear: if everyone benefits, but no one has to pay, no public goods would ever be created. In this scenario, then, a nonmarket actor such as the STATE must step in to create these goods.

Marxism-Leninism. Marxist-Leninist Thought, or Marxism-Leninism, as the name implies, represents the thinking of both Karl Marx and Vladimir Lenin (as well as

Frederick Engels). Lenin, unlike Marx, actually led a revolution, one that toppled the AUTOCRATIC government of Tsar Nicholas II of Russia. Lenin later became the first leader of Soviet Russia. While Lenin agreed with the fundamental precepts of Marxism, he argued that the expansion of COMMUNISM around the world would require struggles of national liberation that began not with the working class (as Marx posited) but with a "vanguard party" of the proletariat comprised primarily of intellectuals rather than workers.

Meiji oligarchs (oligarchy). The term used to describe the relatively small group of men who governed Japan during the MEIJI RESTORATION. The Meiji oligarchs were strong proponents of economic and social change and used their positions of power and influence to push through major reforms for the "modernization" of Japan.

Meiji Restoration. The Meiji Restoration refers to a turbulent period of Japanese history that saw the fall of a long-lived feudal system, known as the TOKUGAWA SHOGUNATE or *BAKUFU* (1600–1869) and the rise of a new, Western-oriented regime that oversaw rapid industrialization, modernization, and far-reaching social change throughout Japan. During this period, imperial rule was "restored" to Japan with the emperor assuming a supreme position (during the Tokugawa period, by contrast, the shoguns or "great generals" ruled). The new emperor took the name Meiji, which means "enlightened rule," as his reign name (during his rule, he was known as Emperor Mutsuhito). The Meiji era lasted from 1868 to 1912, when the Meiji emperor died.

mercantilist (mercantilism). Mercantilism is an economic doctrine that emphasizes the centrality of STATE power in the world economy. In its original form, mercantilism stressed the necessity for states to play a major role in foreign trade, since mercantilists equated national wealth with the possession of precious metals, such as gold and silver. To maximize national wealth, states would enact protectionist policies designed to maximize exports and minimize imports.

method. In the social sciences, method (or a research method) refers to the specific techniques or procedures researchers use to study a subject. Methods guide researchers by identifying the types of evidence needed and the manner in which that evidence must be obtained, evaluated, and analyzed. The goal is to use a method to substantiate or invalidate a particular argument, hypothesis, or theory. The types of methods social scientists use vary widely, although a basic division exists between quantitative methods and QUALITATIVE METHODS.

middle class. The middle class is an ambiguous term subject to a great deal of debate. However, some agree that, in contemporary capitalist societies, the middle class is composed of nonmanual occupational groups (small-business owners, "white-collar" professionals, managers, and so on). The middle class is considered important insofar as the interests of those who constitute this class differ from the interests of those in the upper and working classes. Additional discussion can be found in Chapter 7.

military-first policy. See SONGUN.

moral hazard. This term is used in situations where an individual or an INSTITUTION (such as a corporation or bank) is shielded from the full consequences and responsibilities of its actions. In the United States, for example, the notion that some banks are "too big to fail" may encourage those banks to engage in extremely risky financial behavior. Why? Because bank managers may assume that, if they make the wrong decisions, the US government will step in to bail them out.

mutually constitutive. A mutually constitutive relationship refers to a situation in which both parts of the relationship depend on each other in a fundamental way. Part A cannot exist independently of Part B, and vice versa. In addition, the existence of both is necessary to sustain the relationship.

neoliberalism. Most simply, neoliberalism refers to a set of economic policies that stress a return to the "rule of the market." These policies include deregulation, privatization of functions normally undertaken by governments (e.g., allowing private firms to operate prisons), trade LIBERALIZATION, and a general reduction or elimination of any form of government intervention in markets. Neoliberalism is also a philosophy based on the idea that the only legitimate purpose of the STATE is to safeguard individual liberty, and that the most important freedoms are market freedoms.

OECD. See ORGANISATION FOR ECONOMIC CO-OPERATION AND DEVELOPMENT.

one-child policy. Officially named the family planning policy, the one-child policy was enacted in 1979 as a way to mitigate the social, economic, and environmental strains caused by China's huge population. Although not as draconian as often portrayed in the Western media—the policy allowed for several exceptions (e.g., if a couple's first child is a girl or disabled, they are allowed to have a second child)—it likely did have a significant impact on reducing population growth, although not everyone agrees that the policy is the primary reason. It is clear, however, that the policy has had negative social consequences, including a serious gender imbalance: in 2010, there were 119 boys for every 100 girls at birth, which created a "surplus" of 41 million boys between 1983 and 2010 (Mu 2013). The gender imbalance, moreover, is partly if not largely a product of female infanticide and selective abortions.

operationalize. This process involves defining a concept empirically so that it can be measured. In qualitative analysis, the emphasis on empirical specification is not strictly followed, but the key to operationalizing a concept is the ability to translate it into a consistent measurement of some kind.

Organisation for Economic Co-operation and Development (OECD). The OECD is an international economic organization founded in 1961 (although it originated in 1948 as the Organisation for European Economic Co-operation, the OEEC). The OECD defines itself as an organization "to promote policies that will improve the economic and social well-being of people around the world." To accomplish this goal, it provides a "forum in which governments can work together to share experiences and seek solutions to common problems" (OECD 2013). When it was first established, however, the OECD had only twenty members, eighteen European countries plus the United States and Canada. By 2012, membership had expanded to thirty-four countries, including Japan (1964), South Korea (1996), and Mexico (1994).

overdeveloped state. *Overdeveloped state* is a term used by scholars to describe the type of governmental structure that many former colonies were bequeathed after independence; an overdeveloped state has a powerful military-bureaucratic apparatus that allows it to thoroughly control and subordinate civil society.

Park Chung Hee (1917–1979). Park Chung Hee came to power through a military COUP D'ÉTAT carried out on May 16, 1961. He continued to rule South Korea as president until his assassination on October 26, 1979.

After initially training to be a primary school teacher, Park embarked on a military career—with the Japanese Imperial Army. He enrolled in the Manchukuo Imperial Army Academy in 1940 and in 1942 was selected for officer training at the Army Staff College in Japan. Eventually he rose to the rank of first lieutenant. After the war, Park entered the Korean Military Academy and became implicated in a COMMUNIST-inspired plot for which he was sentenced to die. Fortunately for Park, he was pardoned and allowed to rejoin the military; during the KOREAN WAR he rose to the rank of brigadier general.

Park is often credited with creating the basis for South Korea's rapid and sustained industrialization; indeed, until Park took control, South Korea's economy was in shambles, so one can hardly dismiss his contributions to national economic growth. In particular, Park was instrumental in pushing South Korean industry toward export-based manufacturing; at the same time, he pushed forward major infrastructural projects and brought large-scale heavy industry—particularly steel manufacturing—to South Korea. To achieve these goals, however, Park was also well known for his repressive AUTHORITARIAN policies and tactics, which included severe restrictions on political activity along with the use of media censorship and outright torture and imprisonment of political opponents. Political oppression under Park, however, did not emerge immediately: for the first decade of his rule, between 1963 and 1972, South Korea had a semblance of an electoral democracy, but even this semblance ended in 1972 with the imposition of the Yushin system, based on the YUSHIN CONSTITUTION, which gave Park almost unlimited power.

parliamentary system. A system of government in which the power to make and execute laws is held by a parliament or legislature. Typically, parliamentary systems are headed by a prime minister (who is selected by the parliament) rather than a popularly elected president.

party-state system (or single-party state). This term refers to a type of political system in which a single political party completely controls all key elements of the STATE apparatus such that the distinction between the political party and the state is largely lost. North Korea and China are two examples of party-state systems.

path dependence. In economics and the social sciences more generally, path dependence refers to the tendency of historical or traditional practices or preferences to continue even if better alternatives are found. As Douglas Puffert (2010) explains, "in a path dependent process, 'history matters'—it has an enduring influence. Choices made on the basis of transitory conditions can persist long after those conditions change. Thus, explanations of the outcomes of path-dependent processes require looking at history, rather than simply at current conditions of technology, preferences, and other factors that determine outcomes."

People's Liberation Army (PLA). The PLA is China's combined military force, consisting of the army, navy, air force, the Second Artillery Force, the Armed Police Force, and the reserves. Established in 1927 as the military arm of the CHINESE COMMUNIST PARTY, in terms of sheer numbers, the PLA is the largest military force in the world, with approximately 3 million members (including an active standing army of 2.24 million).

per capita GDP. Per capita GDP simply takes total GROSS DOMESTIC PRODUCT (GDP) and divides it by the number of people in the country. Compared to total GDP, per capita GDP is often considered a better indicator of a country's economic standing—although, in China's case, this is not necessarily true. For example, based on total GDP, China is the second-richest country in the world (in 2011, China's GDP was $9.1 trillion in PPP terms); on a per capita basis, however, China is ranked only about 124th.

PLA. See PEOPLE'S LIBERATION ARMY.

plutocracy. Plutocracy is rule by the wealthy.

Politburo Standing Committee. The Politburo Standing Committee is the most powerful leadership organization within the CHINESE COMMUNIST PARTY. The term *politburo* comes from the Soviet system and means "political body." The Standing Committee is composed of nine members who are selected by the twenty-five-member Politburo. In November 2012, XI JINPING replaced HU JINTAO as general secretary of the Standing Committee.

political liberalization. Political liberalization is a primarily Western concept that refers to the process by which individual rights and liberties are strengthened within a political system.

PPP. See PURCHASING POWER PARITY.

predatory state. On one level, a predatory state is a STATE that "preys" on its citizens, "terrorizing them, despoiling their common patrimony, and providing little in the way of services in return" (Evans 1995, p. 45). One should understand, however, the one factor that makes this situation possible: a lack of institutional mechanisms that can substitute for personalistic connections. Put another way, a predatory state is characterized by a dearth of bureaucracy (Evans 1995).

protectionism. Protectionism is an effort by governments to protect domestic businesses from foreign competition by imposing restrictions or barriers to trade. A tax on imported goods (known as a tariff) is one of the most common types of protectionist policies, but governments may also protect domestic industries with quotas, subsidies, and so-called nontariff barriers, such as complicated regulations or "red tape" designed to slow down the importation of or increase the costs of foreign goods.

public good. In technical terms, a public good is (1) nonexcludable and (2) nonrivalrous. Nonexcludable means that, once the good is produced, no one can be excluded from "consuming" that good. Nonrivalrous means that the consumption of a particular good does not reduce availability to others. A lighthouse is an example of a public good, but other public goods include clean air, national defense, or a flood control system. One can also find many quasi-public goods: the highway system, an educational system, fire protection, and TV and radio broadcasting (these are goods that may have only one characteristic of a public good or that may, in practice, be nonexcludable).

purchasing power parity (PPP). Most simply, PPP is used to show how much money would be needed to purchase the same goods and services in different countries. In principle, this calculation allows for more accurate cross-national comparisons of income. PPP is also an economic principle and method used to determine the relative value of currencies; in principle, it can show when currencies are over- or undervalued.

qualitative method. This type of METHOD places strong emphasis on understanding and interpreting data or information that cannot be adequately or meaningfully quantified (i.e., expressed in numbers). An interview of a high-ranking official or peasant farmer, close observation of factory workers, a careful analysis of historical records and documents, and so on, are all types of qualitative method.

rent seeking. The word *rent* stems from Adam Smith's division of incomes into profit, wage, and rent. A rent is, most simply, the excess value that can be generated from a product due to scarcity or exclusivity. Put differently, it is the amount that can be earned from a product in a noncompetitive environment. Rent seeking, therefore, is simply the effort to obtain economic rents (as opposed to profit seeking). Rent seeking is commonly associated with monopolies, since a monopoly's total control of a resource or product allows it to charge far more than it could earn in a competitive market. However, rent seeking is also associated with corruption. Consider a scenario in which a business attempts to bribe a public official in order to gain special privileges within a market. This bribery is an example of rent seeking.

reserve army of labor. See RESERVE LABOR FORCE.

reserve labor force. Also known as the reserve army of labor (or industrial reserve army), the reserve labor force is a Marxist concept that refers to the mass of unemployed and underemployed workers that constitute a necessary part of the capitalist system. A reserve army of labor is necessary to keep production and overall labor costs low, especially in times of overproduction. With a constant source of unemployed and underemployed workers from which to draw, capitalist firms do not have to increase wages in order to attract workers.

Rhee, Syngman (1875–1965). Also spelled *Yi Seungman*; in general, when we refer to Asian names (Korean, Chinese, and Japanese), the family name or surname is listed first. In the case of Syngman Rhee, however, Rhee is the family name. Rhee was South Korea's first elected president and held office from August 1948 to April 1960. A major reason for his election stems from his activities as a leader of Korea's independence movement when the country was under Japanese rule (1910–1945). During this time, he helped form a provisional Korean government, which was based in Shanghai. Rhee was elected as the president of the provisional government, although he spent a large part of his time in the United States lobbying for Korean independence. He was eventually pushed out of this position in 1939 (in the mid-1920s, he was impeached for abuse of his authority, but Rhee refused to recognize his impeachment). Because of his connections in the United States, Rhee was able to return to Korea at the end of World War II before other members of the provisional government, an advantage that he used quite effectively to build up a political organization and undercut potential rivals.

Rice Riots. The Rice Riots broke out in 1918 in Japan as a response to wartime inflation and other deteriorating economic conditions resulting from rapid industrialization. They were sparked, however, by a rapid increase in the price of rice due to speculation and were the largest popular protests Japan had ever seen.

Saemaul Undong. The Saemaul Undong, or "New Community Movement" (also known as the Rural Reconstruction Campaign), was a program of the South Korean government in the 1970s. It was designed to address continuing and endemic poverty in South Korea's rural areas by building infrastructure and creating a new "can-do" spirit within the rural population (Asian Development Bank 2012). More recently, the principles of Saemaul Undong have been revived by the South Korean government as a way to promote economic growth in developing countries (more information on Saemaul Undong can be found at this South Korean government website: http://www.saemaul.or.kr/english/default.asp).

SEZs. See SPECIAL ECONOMIC ZONES.

SII. See STRUCTURAL IMPEDIMENTS INITIATIVE.

single-party state. See PARTY-STATE SYSTEM.

social structure. See STRUCTURE.

SOEs. See STATE-OWNED ENTERPRISES.

Songun. Also spelled *Seon' gun,* Songun, or "military first," is an official policy of the North Korean regime that gives the KOREAN PEOPLE'S ARMY ultimate priority within the North Korean political and economy system.

special economic zones (SEZs). Also known as export processing zones, these specific areas of a country are set up to attract foreign investment for the production or assembly of products meant only for the export market. To encourage foreign investment, a range of incentives is offered, including low rents, tax holidays, and freedom from normal labor or environmental regulations. Typically, too, the STATE ensures access to low-cost labor. In China, the SEZs were established in the coastal regions, areas with easy access to ports.

Stalinist model. As an economic system, the Stalinist model is based on CENTRAL PLANNING by the STATE. In Soviet Russia, the Stalinist model was put into place in the early 1930s and was later introduced into Eastern Europe by Soviet occupation forces in the late 1940s and early 1950s. In the simplest terms, this model was premised on the state, through the Communist Party, directing the economic activities for the national economy. In other words, the state decides what to produce, how to produce, how much to produce, and for whom. The Stalinist model required that the state create an economic bureaucracy not only for planning but also for general oversight and monitoring.

Standing Committee. See POLITBURO STANDING COMMITTEE.

state. Perhaps the simplest definition of a state is a political entity or INSTITUTION possessing sovereignty (that is, not subject to any higher political authority). Most scholars agree that another fundamental characteristic of the state is its monopoly on legitimate violence in a particular geographic area. The terms *state, country,* and *government* are often used interchangeably, although their meanings are different.

state-owned enterprises (SOEs). As the term implies, these companies are owned and operated by the government (including local governments). In market-oriented economies, SOEs are still fairly common, not only in China but also in Russia, Brazil, Taiwan, and many other countries. SOEs generally receive special protections or advantages from the STATE (compared to full private companies), but many SOEs are also compelled to compete in international markets.

Structural Impediments Initiative (SII). The SII was a negotiation between the United States and Japan designed to reduce their bilateral trade imbalance. US negotiators demanded "structural changes" rather than simple tariff reductions because US business leaders believed that the imbalance was due, in part, to the manner in which the Japanese economy was organized. An agreement was reached in 1990 that revolved around changes in Japan's retailing practices (e.g., its prohibitions on large retailers), land use, and investment in public works. The United States for its part promised to increase domestic saving and reduce its budget deficit.

structure. The everyday meaning of structure is akin to the framework of a building or some other artifact. Structure also refers to the interrelations or arrangements of parts in a complex entity. In the social sciences, both meanings are reflected in the concept of social structure, which might be most easily defined as any relatively enduring pattern of social relationships. The existence of a social structure implies that human action (or AGENCY) is at least partly influenced by the structure within which that action takes place.

Super 301. A trade law provision under which the US trade representative identifies, in an annual report, those "priority foreign country practices" that, if eliminated, have the greatest potential for the expansion of US exports. Section 301 of the Trade Act of 1974, as added by Section 1302 of the Omnibus Trade and Competitiveness Act of 1988, required the US trade representative in 1989 and 1990 to identify trade LIBERALIZATION priorities and to initiate Section 301 investigations with respect to such priority practices in all countries where these liberalization priorities had not been met (Womach 2005, p. 249).

supreme commander for the Allied Powers. This title was held by General Douglas MacArthur during the occupation of Japan following the end of World War II, a position he remained in until 1951. The term *supreme commander for the Allied Powers* also referred to the offices of occupation, which included a staff of several hundred US civil servants and military personnel.

Taisho period. Following the death of the Meiji emperor in 1912, his son and designated successor, Crown Prince Yoshihito, became the emperor of Japan. As is customary in Japan, the emperor takes on a posthumous name; in the case of Crown Prince Yoshihito, this name was Taisho, which translates as "great righteousness." The Taisho period dated from July 30, 1912, to December 25, 1926—a relatively short period owing, in large part, to the emperor's ill health (as an infant, he suffered from cerebral meningitis, which left him with lifelong brain damage). The Taisho era saw Japan's first, but unsuccessful, experiment with liberal democracy—appropriately known as Taisho democracy.

terms of trade. This term denotes the value of a country's exports relative to that of its imports. Generally speaking, the more valuable a country's exports are relative to its imports, the better off that country will be.

TFP. See TOTAL FACTOR PRODUCTIVITY.

third world. A term coined during the Cold War to differentiate three categories of countries: (1) those that were aligned with the United States and other Western countries, (2) those that were aligned with the Soviet Union, and (3) those that were "nonaligned." Over time, however, the term began to be used almost exclusively to refer to poor and underindustrialized countries. In this sense, *third world* took on a pejorative meaning. Partly for this reason, other terms have been proposed as replacements. These terms include, among others, the *South* (or the *Global South*), *less developed countries,* and *developing countries.* Of these alternatives, the most common are the *Global South* (often abbreviated to the *South*) and *developing countries.*

three pillars. The concept of the three pillars in the Japanese employment system was first introduced by James Abegglen (1958), in his book *The Japanese Factory: Aspects of Its Social Organization.* The three pillars are enterprise-based union, seniority-based wages and promotion, and lifetime employment.

Three Principles of the People. Also known as the San-min Doctrine, the Three Principles of the People were espoused by Sun Yat-sen and are based on (1) nationalism, (2) people's power or democracy, and (3) people's welfare or livelihood. They have been put forward as the ideological basis for the KUOMINTANG.

Tiananmen Movement. Taking place in 1989, this movement was the largest popular protest in China. Initially, Chinese citizens, mainly students, began to congregate in Tiananmen Square to commemorate the death of HU YAOBANG, who died of a heart attack on April 15, 1989. The commemoration of Hu, however, soon morphed into a movement for greater political freedom. More and more citizens began to join the protestors, who had set up camp in Tiananmen Square; at one point, an estimated 1 million-plus citizens were involved in the movement. The Chinese Communist Party eventually cracked down, sending in military units to clear the square and surrounding areas. The CCP's actions led to violent clashes in which well-armed soldiers killed scores of civilians.

Tokugawa shogunate (or *bakufu*). The Tokugawa era (also known as the Edo *BAFUKU*) refers to the feudal regime established in 1603; it lasted more than 250 years, until 1867. As might be expected from a regime that lasted so long, the Tokugawa period was marked by a high degree of political stability and relatively slow—but not necessarily insignificant—economic and social change. Politically, one of the most important aspects of this period was the concentration of political authority. Edwin O. Reischauer (one of the leading scholars of Japanese history until his death in 1990) coined the term *centralized feudalism* to describe the form of government that dominated this era. The terms *shogunate* and *bakufu* provide additional insight into the nature of the Tokugawa system. The term *shogunate* denotes the rule of the shogun or "military commander," whereas *bakufu* means "military government."

total factor productivity (TFP). TFP is an index used to measure the efficiency of all inputs that contribute to the production process. Economists use TFP, in particular, as a way to measure an economy's long-term technological change or technological dynamism. Among economists, however, serious disagreement exists as to the utility or validity of TFP. Some economists, in fact, argue that TFP fails to measure anything useful.

228 Incident. Referring to a large antigovernment uprising in Taiwan, the 228 Incident began on February 28, 1947, against the KUOMINTANG (KMT), which was then governing the island under the rule of Chen Yi (the KMT was allowed to take control of Taiwan after the Japanese surrender on October 25, 1945; Chen himself accepted the Japanese surrender instrument). The incident—or massacre—was triggered by a dispute between a cigarette vendor and a representative of the Office of Monopoly. This small incident turned into an open rebellion, which was put down with massive violence. While no reliable figure can be found, estimates range between 10,000 and 30,000 mostly civilian deaths. The incident also marked the beginning of the so-called White Terror period in Taiwan, during which thousands of Taiwanese were killed, imprisoned, and tortured by the KMT. Until Taiwan's democratization, the 228 Incident was never officially acknowledged.

unit of analysis. The unit of analysis is the "who" or "what" of a researcher's examination, such as an individual (e.g., peasant, business owner, political leader), an organization (e.g., firm, INSTITUTION, society, or STATE), or some other type of complex social entity (e.g., *keiretsu*). Any particular research study may contain any number of units of analysis, and although general correspondence should exist between the unit of analysis and the level of analysis, the two terms are not the same. For example, a researcher might be interested in examining the dynamics of global capitalism (macrolevel of analysis) but be focused on states (the primary units of analysis).

voluntarism. Not to be confused with volunteerism, voluntarism is a social scientific and philosophical concept premised on the idea that voluntary action—the exercise of free will or human AGENCY—plays a central role in human society. Voluntarism can be contrasted with the structural approach, which argues that a great deal of human action is determined by larger forces over which individuals have limited control.

Weibo. Also known as Sina Weibo, Weibo is a Chinese microblogging website (http:// us.weibo.com/gb) and one of the most popular websites in China. In 2012, according to the British Broadcasting Corporation, it had over 300 million registered users. As with the US site Twitter, Weibo allows users to post up to 140 Chinese characters—the equivalent of seventy to eighty words—in individual messages (Hewitt 2012).

Wen Jiabao (b. 1942). Along with HU JINTAO, Wen was a key part of the CHINESE COMMUNIST PARTY's "Fourth Generation" leadership circle. As premier (2003–2012), Wen played a key role in restructuring China's heavily indebted banking system and in continuing reforms to the STATE-OWNED ENTERPRISE section.

Westernization. The "West" (which typically means Western European countries and North America) is characterized by a range of ideological/cultural, economic, political, and social features and practices, including individualism, rationalism, capitalism, liberal democracy, Christianity, and political and social equality. Thus, Westernization is the process by which these and other values and practices have expanded to and influenced other parts of the world. Consider something as mundane as clothing: in most countries today, people dress largely along Western lines. Within the West, this process may seem unremarkable, but it can be the source of tremendous tension and conflict in other parts of the world, as Western values and practices often clash with and disrupt long-standing social, political, and economic relationships.

World Bank and the International Monetary Fund (IMF). The World Bank and its sister INSTITUTION, the IMF, were established in 1944; together, they are known as the Bretton Woods Institutions. The World Bank and the IMF were carefully constructed to serve complementary roles in the world economy. The World Bank, which was formally known as the International Bank for Reconstruction and Development, is responsible for "financing economic development." In other words, it provides long-term funding for large-scale, usually infrastructural projects. The Bank's first loans were extended to the war-ravaged economies of Western Europe, although in recent decades almost all its lending goes to "developing economies." The IMF, by contrast, is designed to promote international monetary cooperation. The IMF also engages in lending but on a short-term basis only. IMF loans (and loan guarantees) are meant to solve temporary balance-of-payment problems faced by member countries who cannot otherwise obtain sufficient financing. In this sense, the IMF is an international "lender of last resort." Both the World Bank and the IMF have been subject to intense criticism. Critics are mainly concerned with the "CONDITIONALITIES" imposed on borrower countries. These conditions typically require borrowers to liberalize their economies and cut government spending. The problem, critics charge, is that LIBERALIZATION and austerity often make economic conditions worse. For further information, see the discussion at the Bretton Woods Project website (http://www.brettonwoodsproject.org/item.shtml?x=320869).

Xi Jinping (b. 1953). Xi is part of China's "Fifth Generation" of leaders, meaning in part that he is relatively young. He became part of the POLITBURO STANDING COMMITTEE in 2007, which helped to solidify his position as the leading candidate to replace HU JINTAO after the end of his second five-year term in 2012. In fact, Xi was elected general secretary of the CHINESE COMMUNIST PARTY on November 15, 2012.

yangban. The *yangban* were part of Korea's traditional ruling class during the Joseon (or Chosun) dynasty. Unlike other traditional ruling classes, however, *yangban* status was not strictly determined by heredity; instead, any male who passed a government-sponsored civil service examination based principally on CONFUCIAN classics and history could obtain the title of *yangban.* Thus, the *yangban* was often assigned a government post.

yuan. For practical purposes, *yuan* can be translated as the equivalent of "branch," as in the Executive Yuan (executive branch), the Legislative Yuan (the legislative branch), or the Judicial Yuan (judicial branch). Taiwan's constitution designates five *yuan.*

Yushin Constitution. Also spelled *Yusin,* the Yushin Constitution was adopted in October 1972 under PARK CHUNG HEE. The Korean meaning of *yushin* is "renewal" or "restoration." The new constitution was an effort to legitimize Park's dictatorial rule. It allowed for the unlimited reelection of the president to six-year terms and gave the president the authority to appoint a large portion of the national assembly (thus ensuring that all laws proposed by the president would be passed). It also allowed the president to declare emergency measures, which gave the president authority to promulgate laws without ratification by the assembly.

zaibatsu. A Japanese term meaning "financial clique," more concretely, the term *zaibatsu* refers to large, family-controlled conglomerates that emerged during the MEIJI era. The *zaibatsu* were not a single company but instead were a network of hierarchically organized firms that generally consisted of a holding company on top (a holding company owns shares of other companies), a banking subsidiary (which provided financing), a trading company (known as *shoga shosa*), and several industrial subsidiaries. The major *zaibatsu* of the prewar era were Sumitomo, Mitsui, Mitsubishi, and Yasuda. (Sumitomo and Mitsui were founded in the TOKUGAWA period.) Following Japan's defeat in World War II, US occupation authorities ordered the complete dissolution of sixteen *zaibatsu.* This order was not completely carried out; still, technically, no *zaibatsu* remain in Japan. However, within a few years after the purported breakup of the *zaibatsu,* a new corporate organization emerged, the *KEIRETSU.*

zaiteku. *Zaiteku* is an abbreviation for the term *zaimu tekunorjii,* which itself is a hybrid Japanese-English word. *Zaimu* means "financial dealings," while *tekunorijii* is simply the Japanese pronunciation of "technology." Taken together, the term can be translated as "financial techniques," and refers to a range of financial practices by Japanese corporations to boost profits by investing in securities, real estate, and other speculative instruments. The term came into vogue after 1984, when the Japanese financial market was deregulated.

zero-sum. This term refers to a situation, such as an argument or game, in which, in an interaction between two players, a gain for one side means an exactly equal corresponding loss for the other side. Thus, the payoff from the interaction is zero. Zero-sum arguments are often criticized as unrealistic, especially in discussions of economic growth, since even the loser in an economic transaction may be better off than before the transaction took place.

Zhao Ziyang (1919–2005). Zhao was a close associate of DENG XIAOPING and played a central role in implementing China's market-oriented reforms beginning in 1978. Zhao, however, lost favor with Deng during the TIANANMEN MOVEMENT in 1989 (due, in part, to the machinations of his rival, LI PENG) and was forced out of the CHINESE COMMUNIST PARTY. He lived out the rest of his life under house arrest.

Bibliography

Abegglen, James G. 1958. *The Japanese Factory: Aspects of Its Social Organization.* Glencoe, IL: Free Press.

Aggarwal, Raj. 2002. "Bubble Economy." Pp. 51–54 in *Encyclopedia of Japanese Business and Management,* edited by A. Bird. New York: Routledge.

Akamatsu, Kaname. 1935. "Wagakuni Yomo Kogyohin No Susei [Trend of Japanese Trade in Woollen Goods]." *Shogyo Keizai Ronso* [Journal of Nagoya Higher Commercial School] 13:129–212.

Alemán, José. 2008. "Labor Market Deregulation and Industrial Conflict in New Democracies: A Cross-National Analysis." *Political Studies* 56(4):830–856.

Allen, G. C. 1981. *A Short Economic History of Modern Japan.* New York: St. Martin's.

Amsden, Alice H. 1989. *Asia's Next Giant: South Korea and Late Industrialization.* New York: Oxford University Press.

Aoki, Masahiko, and Ronald Dore, eds. 1996. *The Japanese Firm: Sources of Competitive Strength.* Oxford: Oxford University Press.

Armstrong, Charles K. 2011. "Trends in the Study of North Korea." *Journal of Asian Studies* 70:357–371.

Arrighi, Giovanni. 1996. "The Rise of East Asia: World Systemic and Regional Aspects." *International Journal of Sociology and Social Policy* 16(7–8):6–44.

Arrighi, Giovanni, Po-Keung Hui, Ho-Fung Hung, and Mark Selden. 2003. "Historical Capitalisms, East and West." Pp. 259–333 in *The Resurgence of East Asia,* edited by G. Arrighi, T. Hamashita, and M. Selden. New York: Routledge.

Ashton, David. 2002. "Explaining Change in National HDR Strategies: The Case of the Three Asian Tigers." *European Journal of Development Research* 14(1):126–144.

Asian Development Bank. 2012. *The Saemaul Undong Movement in the Republic of Korea: Sharing Knowledge on Community-Driven Development.* Mandaluyong City, Philippines: Asian Development Bank.

Baerwald, Hans H. 1987. "Early SCAP Policy and the Rehabilitation of the Diet." Pp. 133–156 in *Democratizing Japan: The Allied Occupation,* edited by R. E. Ward and Y. Sakamoto. Honolulu: University of Hawaii Press.

Banister, Judith. 2009. "Health, Mortality, and Longevity in China Today." Paper presented at the Twenty-Sixth IUSSP International Population Conference, September, Marrakech, Morocco. http://iussp2009.princeton.edu/papers/90481.

Bank of Korea. 2012. "Gross Domestic Product Estimates for North Korea for 2011." Seoul: Bank of Korea. http://www.bok.or.kr/contents/total/eng/boardView.action?menuNaviId=634&boardBean.brdid=11043&boardBean.menuid=634&boardBean.rnum=2.

Barot, Sneha. 2012. "A Problem-and-Solution Mismatch: Son Preference and Sex-Selective Abortion Bans." *Guttmacher Policy Review* 15(2). http://www.guttmacher.org/pubs/gpr/15/2/gpr150218.html.

Barraclough, Solon L. 1999. "Land Reform in Developing Countries: The Role of the State and Other Actors." Discussion Paper No. 101. United Nations Research Institute for Social Development, Geneva. http://www.unrisd.org/unrisd/website /document.nsf/(httpPublications)/9B503BAF4856E96980256B66003E0622?Open Document.

Bartram, David. 2000. "Japan and Labor Migration: Theoretical and Methodological Implications of Negative Cases." *International Migration Review* 34(1):5–32.

Beech, Hannah. 2006. "School Daze." *Time* (online), April 5. http://www.time.com/time /asia/features/asian_education/cover.html.

Beeson, Mark. 2007. *Regionalism and Globalization in East Asia: Politics, Security and Economic Development.* Basingstoke, UK: Palgrave Macmillan.

Bello, Walden. 2006. "The Capitalist Conjuncture: Over-Accumulation, Financial Crises, and the Retreat from Globalisation." *Third World Quarterly* 8:1345–1367.

Biggs, Tyler S. 1988. *Financing the Emergence of Small and Medium Enterprise in Taiwan: Heterogeneous Firm Size and Efficient Intermediation.* Cambridge, MA: Employment and Enterprise Policy Analysis Project.

Bird, Kelly, and Hal Hill. 2010. "Tiny, Poor, Land-Locked, Indebted, but Growing: Lessons for Late Reforming Transition Economies from Laos." *Oxford Development Studies* 38(2):117–143.

Blechinger, Verena. 2000. "Corruption Through Political Contributions in Japan." Paper presented at the TI [Transparency International] Workshop on Corruption and Political Party Funding, October, La Pietra, Italy. http://unpan1.un.org/intradoc /groups/public/documents/APCITY/UNPAN013118.pdf.

Bleiker, Roland. 2005. *Divided Korea: Toward a Culture of Reconciliation.* Minneapolis: University of Minnesota Press.

Board of Foreign Trade (Taiwan). 2001. "Taiwan Joins the WTO: Trade and Investment Opportunities Presented by Taiwan's Accession to the World Trade Organization." http://www.gio.gov.tw/taiwan-website/4-oa/wto/wto01.htm.

Borjas, George J. 1989. "Economic Theory and International Migration." *International Migration Review* 23(3):457–485.

Bosworth, Barry, and Susan M. Collins. 2008. "Accounting for Growth: Comparing India and China." *Journal of Economic Perspectives* 22(2):45–66.

Breen, Michael. 2010. "Park Got Dictatorial Powers with Yushin Constitution in 1972." *Korea Times* (online), Seoul, October 31. http://www.koreatimes.co.kr/www/news /nation/2010/10/116_75537.html.

Caballero, Ricardo J., Takeo Hoshi, and Anil K. Kashyap. 2008. "Zombie Lending and Depressed Restructuring in Japan." *American Economic Review* 98(5):1943–1977.

Caballero-Anthony, Mely. 2007. "The Philippines in Southeast Asia: An Overview." Pp. 1–17 in *Whither the Philippines in the 21st Century?* edited by R. C. Serverino and L. C. Salazar. Singapore: Institute of Southeast Asian Studies.

Cai, Fang, Albert Park, and Yaohui Zhao. 2008. "The Chinese Labor Market in the Reform Era." Pp. 167–214 in *China's Great Economic Transformation,* edited by L. Brandt and T. G. Rawski. Cambridge: Cambridge University Press.

Calder, Kent E. 1993. *Strategic Capitalism: Private Business and Public Purpose in Japanese Industrial Finance.* Princeton, NJ: Princeton University Press.

Calder, Kent E., and Min Ye. 2010. *The Making of Northeast Asia.* Stanford, CA: Stanford University Press.

Camdessus, Michel. 1999. "Crisis, Restructuring, and Recovery in Korea." Paper presented at the Conference on Economic Crisis and Restructuring, December 2, Seoul, South Korea. http://www.imf.org/external/np/speeches/1999/120299.htm.

Castles, Stephen, and Mark J. Miller. 2003. *The Age of Migration.* New York: Guilford.

Center for Strategic and International Studies. 2013. *Nuclear Weapons and U.S.-China Relations: A Way Forward.* Washington, DC: Center for Strategic and International Studies.

Central Intelligence Agency (CIA). 2013. "East and Southeast Asia: Japan." *The World Factbook.* https://www.cia.gov/library/publications/the-world-factbook/geos/ja.html.

Cha, Seong Hwan. 2003. "Myth and Reality in the Discourse of Confucian Capitalism in Korea." *Asian Survey* 43(3):485–506.

Cha, Victor. 2012. *The Impossible State: North Korea, Past and Future.* New York: HarperCollins. http://books.google.com/books?id=x3ksdpZsUJwC&source=gbs_navlinks_s.

Chan, Kam Wing. 2009. "The Chinese Hukou System at 50." *Eurasian Geography and Economics* 50(2):197–222.

———. 2011. "Internal Migration in China: Trends, Geography and Policies." Pp. 81–109 in *Population Distribution, Urbanization, Internal Migration, and Development: An International Perspective,* edited by United Nations Department of Economic and Social Affairs. New York: United Nations.

Chan, Rachel. 2012. "Taiwan's Fertility Rate Edges Up." *Taiwan Today* (online). http://taiwantoday.tw/ct.asp?xItem=188075&CtNode=448.

Chang, Ha-Joon, Hong-Jae Park, and Chul Gyue Yoo. 1998. "Interpreting the Korean Crisis: Financial Liberalisation, Industrial Policy, and Corporate Governance." *Cambridge Journal of Economics* 22:735–46.

"Change." 2013. *Cambridge Dictionaries Online.* Retrieved December 11. http://dictionary.cambridge.org/us/dictionary/american-english/change_1.

Chen, An. 2002. "Capitalist Development, Entrepreneurial Class, and Democratization in China." *Political Science Quarterly* 117(3):401–422.

Chen, Edward K. Y. 1979. *Hyper-Growth in Asian Economies: A Comparative Study of Hong Kong, Japan, Korea, Singapore, and Taiwan.* New York: Holmes and Meier.

Chen, Jie, and Chunlong Lu. 2011. "Democratization and the Middle Class in China: The Middle Class's Attiudes Toward Democracy." *Political Research Quarterly* 64(3):705–719.

Chen, Yi-Chi. 1998. *Asian Crisis Project.* "Country Report on Taiwan." University of Washington, Seattle. http://faculty.washington.edu/karyiu/Asia/booklet/tn-report.pdf.

Chen, Yu-Hua. 2008. "The Significance of Cross-Border Marriage in a Low Fertility Society: Evidence from Taiwan." *Journal of Comparative Family Studies* 39(3): 331–352.

Cheng, Tun-Jen. 1989. "Democratizing the Quasi-Leninist Regime in Taiwan." *World Politics* 41(4):471–499.

Cheng, Tun-Jen, and Gang Lin. 2008. "Competitive Elections." Pp. 161–184 in *Political Change in China: Comparisons with Taiwan,* edited by B. Gilley and L. Diamond. Boulder, CO: Lynne Rienner.

"China's 'Floating Population' Exceeds 210m." *China Daily,* June 27. http://www.chinadaily.com.cn/china/2010-06/27/content_10024861.htm.

Chiswick, Barry R. 2000. "Are Migrants Favorably Self-Selected? An Economic Analysis." Pp. 61–76 in *Migration Theory: Talking Across Disciplines,* edited by C. D. Brettell and J. F. Hollifield. New York: Routledge.

Choi, Jang Jip. 1993. "Political Cleavages in South Korea." Pp. 13–50 in *State and Society in Contemporary Korea,* edited by H. Koo. Ithaca: Cornell University Press.

———. 2005. *Democracy After Democratization: The Korean Experience.* Translated by L. Kyung-hee. Seoul: Humanitas.

Choi, Myeong-Hae. 2011. "The DPRK-PRC Joint Projects in Rason and Hwanggumpyong." *SERI Quarterly* 4(4):130–136.

Chou, Yangsun, and Andrew J. Nathan. 1987. "Democratizing Transition in Taiwan." *Asian Survey* 27(3):277–299.

Chu, Yin-wah, and Siu-lun Wong. 2010. "East Asia's New Democracies: An Introduction." Pp. 1–21 in *East Asia's New Democracies: Deepening, Reversal, Non-Liberal Alternatives,* edited by Y. W. Chu and S. L. Wong. New York: Routledge.

Chu, Yun-han. 1998. "Taiwan's Unique Challenges." Pp. 133-146 in *Democracy in East Asia,* edited by L. Diamond and M. Plattner. Baltimore: Johns Hopkins University Press.

Chung, Young Chul. 2004. "North Korean Reform and Opening: Dual Strategy and 'Silli (Practical) Socialism.'" *Pacific Affairs* 77(2):283–304.

Ciorciari, John D. 2011. "Chiang Mai Initiative Multilateralization: International Politics and Institution-Building in Asia." *Asian Survey* 51(5):926–952.

City of Yokohama. 2012. "Foreign Residents." *A Statistical Look at Yokohama.* http://www.city.yokohama.lg.jp/ex/stat/jinko/non-jp/1207-e.html.

Colignon, Richard, and Chikako Usui. 2001. "The Resilience of Japan's Iron Triangle: Amakudari." *Asian Survey* 41(5):865–895.

Congressional-Executive Commission on China. 2012. "China: List of Political Prisoners Detained or Imprisoned as of October 10, 2012." http://www.cecc.gov/sites/china commission.house.gov/files/documents/20121010_CECC%20Pris%20List_148 4%20rec.pdf.

Constable, Nicole. 2005. "Introduction." Pp. 1–16 in *Cross-Border Marriages: Gender and Mobility in Transnational Asia,* edited by N. Constable. Philadelphia: University of Pennsylvania Press.

Constitution of the Empire of Japan. 1889. Hanover Historical Text Project. Retrieved on December 7, 2013. http://history.hanover.edu/texts/1889con.html.

"Continuity." 2013. *Oxford Dictionaries* (online). Retrieved December 11. http://www .oxforddictionaries.com/us/definition/american_english/continuity?q=continuity.

Copper, John F. 2003. "Taiwan: Consolidating Its Democracy?" *China: An International Journal* 1(2):326–338.

Council for Economic Planning and Development (CEPD). 2012. "Taiwan Statistical Data Book 2012." Taipei: Executive Yuan (Taiwan).

Cox, W. Michael, and Richard Aim. 2007. "Creative Destruction." In *The Concise Encyclopedia of Economics,* edited by D. R. Henderson. Indianapolis: Liberty Fund. http://www.econlib.org/library/Enc/CreativeDestruction.html.

Croissant, Aurel. 2011. "Civilian Control over the Military in East Asia." EAI Fellows Program Working Paper Series No. 31, September. http://www.eai.or.kr/data/bbs /kor_report/201109091057148.pdf.

Cumings, Bruce. 1984. "The Origins and Development of the Northeast Asian Political Economy: Industrial Sectors, Product Cycles, and Political Consequences." *International Organization* 38(1):1–40.

———. 1993. "The Corporate State in North Korea." Pp. 213–246 in *State and Society in Contemporary Korea,* edited by H. Koo. Ithaca: Cornell University Press.

———. 2012. "The Kims' Three Bodies: Communism and Dynastic Succession in North Korea." *Current History* 111(746):216–222.

Dahl, Kathleen. n.d. "Culture." Retrieved December 1, 2013. https://docs.google.com /viewer?a=v&pid=sites&srcid=ZW91LmVkdXxrYXRobGVlbi1kYWhsfGd4OjM yOTM4NDFlNjdhZTJhZWU.

Dahl, Robert A. 1956. *A Preface to Democratic Theory.* Chicago: University of Chicago Press.

———. 1972. *Polyarchy: Participation and Opposition.* New Haven, CT: Yale University Press.

Dasgupta, Jyotirindra. 2001. "India's Federal Design and Multicultural National Construction." Pp. 49–77 in *The Success of India's Democracy,* edited by A. Kohli. Cambridge: Cambridge University Pres.

Davison, Rémy. 2012. "Globalization Versus Regionalism in the Asia Pacific?" Pp. 176–203 in *The New Global Politics of the Asia Pacific,* edited by M. K. Connors, R. Davison, and J. Dosch. New York: Routledge.

de Haas, Hein. 2008. "Migration and Development: A Theoretical Perspective." Working papers, International Migration Institute, University of Oxford, Oxford.

Deyo, Frederic C. 1987. "State and Labor: Modes of Political Exclusion in East Asian Development." Pp. 182–202 in *The Political Economy of the New Asian Industrialism,* edited by F. C. Deyo. Ithaca: Cornell University Press.

———. 1989. *Beneath the Miracle: Labor Subordination in the New Asian Industrialism.* Berkeley: University of California Press.

Director-General for Policy Planning (Statistics Bureau). 2009. "Table 2-1 Population by Sex, Population Increase and Decrease (1872–2009)." In *Historical Statistics of Japan: Population and Households* (online). Ministry of Internal Affairs and Communications (Japan). http://www.stat.go.jp/english/data/chouki/02.htm.

Dirlik, Airf. 1998. "Introduction: Pacific Contradictions." Pp. 3–14 in *What Is in a Rim? Critical Perspectives on the Pacific Region Idea,* edited by A. Dirlik. Boston: Rowman and Littlefield.

Dodhia, Rahul. 2007. "The Misuse of Statistics." *Raven Analytics.* http://www.stats consult.com/Articles/Misuse%20of%20statistics.pdf.

Dressel, Björn. 2011. "The Philippines: How Much Real Democracy?" *International Political Science Review* 32(5):529–545.

Dreyer, June Teufel. 2003. "Taiwan's Evolving Identity." *Asia Program Special Report* (114):4–9.

Durdin, Peggy. 1947. "Terror in Taiwan." *The Nation,* May 24, pp. 626–627.

Durdin, Tillman. 1947. "Formosa Killings Are Put at 10,000." *New York Times,* March 29, p. 6.

Duus, Peter. 1976. *Feudalism in Japan.* New York: Alfred A. Knopf.

Duverger, Maurice. 1980. "A New Political System Model: Semi-Presidential Government." *European Journal of Political Research* 8(2):165–187.

Eberstadt, Nicholas. 1992. "Taiwan and South Korea: The 'Democratization' of Outlier States." *World Affairs* 155(2):80–89.

Eisenhower, Dwight D. 2005 [1954]. "Dwight D. Eisenhower 1954: Containing the Public Messages, Speeches, and Statements of the President, January 1 to December 31, 1954." *The Public Papers of the Presidents of the United States.* Ann Arbor, MI: University of Michigan Library. http://quod.lib.umich.edu/p/ppotpus/4728402 .1954.001?view=toc.

Elgie, Robert. 2007. "Varieties of Semi-Presidentialism and Their Impact on Nascent Democracies." *Taiwan Journal of Democracy* 3(2):53–71.

———. 2010. "Variations on a Theme. Pp. 292–305 in *Debates on Democratization,* edited by L. Diamond, M. F. Plattner, and P. J. Costopolous. Baltimore: Johns Hopkins University Press.

Elliot, John. 1980. "Marx and Schumpeter on Capitalism's Creative Destruction: A Comparative Restatement." *Quarterly Journal of Economics* 95(1):45–68.

Elwell, Frank W. 2002. "The Sociology of C. Wright Mills." Unpublished paper. Rogers State University, Claremore, OK. http://www.faculty.rsu.edu/users/f/felwell/www /Theorists/Mills/SocMills.htm.

Erturk, Korkut A. 2001–2002. "Overcapacity and the East Asian Crisis." *Journal of Post Keynesian Economics* 24(2):253–275.

Evans, Peter. 1995. *Embedded Autonomy: States and Industrial Transformation.* Princeton, NJ: Princeton University Press.

Fabienne, Peter. 2010. "Political Legitimacy." *The Stanford Encyclopedia of Philosophy,* edited by E. N. Zalta. http://plato.stanford.edu/archives/sum2010/entries/legitimacy/.

Farrell, Diana, Ulrich A. Gersch, and Elizabeth Stephenson. 2006. "The Value of China's Emerging Middle Class." *McKinsey Quarterly,* June, pp. 61–69.

Fingleton, Eamonn. 2011. "The Myth of Japan's 'Lost Decades.'" *Atlantic,* February 26. http://www.theatlantic.com/international/archive/2011/02/the-myth-of-japans-lost-decades/71741/.

Firn, Mike. 2012. "Kim Jong-un 'Planning China-like Reforms in North Korea.'" *Telegraph* (online), August 6. http://www.telegraph.co.uk/news/worldnews/asia/north korea/9455190/Kim-Jong-un-planning-China-like-reforms-in-North-Korea.html.

Fisher, Daniel. 2010. "The Global Debt Bomb." *Forbes Magazine* (online), January 21. http://www.forbes.com/forbes/2010/0208/debt-recession-worldwide-finances-global-debt-bomb.html.

Freeman, Will. 2010. "The Accuracy of China's 'Mass Incidents.'" *Financial Times* (online), March 2. http://www.ft.com/intl/cms/s/0/9ee6fa64–25b5–11df–9bd3-00144 feab49a.html.

Friedman, Benjamin. 2000. "Japan Now and the United States Then: Lesson from the Parallels." Pp. 37–56 in *Japan's Financial Crisis and Its Parallels to U.S. Experience,* edited by A. S. Posen and R. Mikitani. Washington, DC: Peterson Institute for International Economics.

Frost, Ellen L. 2008. *Asia's New Regionalism.* Boulder, CO: Lynne Rienner.

Fukuyama, Francis. 1995. "The Primacy of Culture." *Journal of Democracy* 6:7–14.

Gao, Bai. 2001. *Japan's Economic Dilemma: The Institutional Origins of Prosperity and Stagnation.* Cambridge: Cambridge University Press.

———. 2002. *Economic Ideology and Japanese Industrial Policy: Developmentalism from 1931 to 1965.* Cambridge: Cambridge University Press.

Garon, Sheldon M. 1987. *The State and Labor in Modern Japan.* Berkeley: University of California Press.

Garvey, Gerald T., and Peter L. Swan. 1992. "The Interaction Between Financial and Employment Contracts: A Formal Model of Japanese Corporate Governance." *Journal of the Japanese and International Economies* 6(3):247–274.

Gasiorowski, Mark J., and Timothy Power. 1998. "The Structural Determinants of Democratic Consolidation: Evidence from the Third World." *Comparative Political Studies* 31(6):740–771.

Geddes, Barbara. 1999. "What Do We Know About Democratization After Twenty Years?" *Annual Review of Political Science* 2:115–144.

Gill, Stephen. 1999. "The Geopolitics of the Asian Crisis." *Monthly Review* 50(10):1–9.

Gilley, Bruce. 2004. *China's Democratic Future: How It Will Happen and Where It Will Lead.* New York: Columbia University Press.

———. 2010. "Deng Xiaoping and His Successors (1976 to the Present)." Pp. 103–128 in *Politics in China: An Introduction,* edited by W. A. Joseph. Oxford: Oxford University Press.

Glassman, Ronald M. 1995. *The Middle Class and Democracy in Socio-Historical Perspective.* Leiden, Netherlands: Brill.

Gold, Thomas B. 1997. *State and Society in the Taiwan Miracle.* Armonk, NY: M. E. Sharpe.

Goto, Junichi. 2007. "Latin Americans of Japanese Origins (*Nikkeijin*) Working in Japan—A Survey." *World Bank Policy Research Working Paper 4203,* April. http://elibrary.worldbank.org/doi/pdf/10.1596/1813-9450-4203.

Gurowitz, Amy. 1999. "Mobilizing International Norms: Domestic Actors, Immigrants, and the Japanese State." *World Politics* 51(3):413–445.

Haggard, Stephen, and Marcus Noland. 2007. *Famine in North Korea: Markets, Aid, and Reform.* New York: Columbia University Press.

Hahn, Bae-Ho, and Kyu-Taik Kim. 1963. "Korean Political Leaders (1952–1962): Their Social Origins and Skills." *Asian Survey* 3(7):305–323.

Halliday, Jon. 1981. "The North Korean Model: Gaps and Questions." *World Development* 9(9–10):889–905.

Hamilton, Gary G. 1998. "Culture and Organization in Taiwan's Market Economy." Pp. 41–77 in *Market Cultures: Society and Morality in the New Asian Capitalisms,* edited by R. W. Hefner. Boulder, CO: Westview.

Hamilton, Gary G., and Nicole Woosley Biggart. 1997. "Market, Culture, and Authority: A Comparative Analysis of Management and Organization in the Far East." Pp. 111–150 in *The Economic Organization of East Asian Capitalism,* edited by M. Orrù, G. G. Hamilton, and N. W. Biggart. Thousand Oaks, CA: Sage.

Han, Sungjoo. 1978. "South Korea's Participation in the Vietnam Conflict: An Analysis of the U.S.-Korean Alliance." *Orbis* 21:893–912.

Hane, Mikoso. 1986. *Modern Japan: A Historical Survey.* Boulder, CO: Westview.

Harden, Blaine. 2012. *Escape from Camp 14: One Man's Remarkable Odyssey from North Korea to Freedom in the West.* New York: Viking.

Hart-Landsberg, Martin. 2004. "The South Korean Economy and U.S. Policy." *Asian Perspective* 28(4):89–117.

Heiden, Peter Thomas in der. 2011. "Chinese Sectoral Industrial Policy Shaping International Trade and Investment Patterns—Evidence from the Iron and Steel Industry." Duisburg Working Papers on East Asian Studies. Institute for East Asian Studies, University of Duisburg-Essen, Duisburg, Germany.

Henderson, David R. 1997. "Lessons of East Asia's Economic Growth." *Orbis* 41(3): 427–443.

Henderson, Gregory. 1968. *Korea: The Politics of the Vortex.* Cambridge: Harvard University Press.

"Heuristic." 2013. *Dictionary.com.* Retrieved December 11. http://dictionary.reference.com/browse/heuristic?r=75&src=ref&ch=dic.

Hewitt, Duncan. 2012. "Weibo Brings Change to China." *BBC World Service* (online), July 31. http://www.bbc.co.uk/news/magazine-18887804.

Higuchi, Naoto. 2005. "Brazilian Migration to Japan: Trends, Modalities and Impact." Paper presented at the Expert Group Meeting on International Migration and Development in Latin America and the Caribbean, Mexico City, November 30–December 2.

Hill, Steven. 2010. "We Need a Case of 'Japan Syndrome.'" *Los Angeles Times,* July 29, p. A-21.

Hirschman, Albert O. 1958. *The Strategy of Economic Development.* New Haven, CT: Yale University Press.

Ho, Ming-sho. 2010. "Manufacturing Loyalty: The Political Mobilization of Labor in Taiwan, 1950–1986." *Modern China* 36(6):559–588.

Hobday, Michael. 1995. *Innovation in East Asia: The Challenge to Japan.* Aldershot, UK: Edward Elgar.

Hodgson, Geoffrey M. 2006. "What Are Institutions?" *Journal of Economic Issues* 15(1):1–25.

Hong, Ihk-pyo. 2002. "A Shift Toward Capitalism? Recent Economic Reforms in North Korea." *East Asian Review* 14(4):93–106.

Hood, Steven J. 1997. *The Kuomintang and the Democratization of Taiwan.* Boulder, CO: Westview.

Hoshi, Takeo, and Anil K. Kashyap. 2004. "Japan's Financial Crisis and Economic Stagnation." *Journal of Economic Perspectives* 18(1):3–26.

Howard, Mike. 2011. "Samsung Electronics Is the Most Competitive DRAM Company." *IHS iSuppli Market Research* (online), March 14. http://www.isuppli.com/memory -and-storage/marketwatch/pages/samsung-electronics-is-the-most-competitive -dram-company.aspx.

Howell, David L. 1992. "Proto-Industrial Origins of Japanese Capitalism." *Journal of Asian Studies* 51(2):269–286.

Hsiao, Hsin-Huang Michael, and Ming-Sho Ho. 2010. "Civil Society and Democracy-Making in Taiwan: Reexamining the Link." Pp. 43–64 in *East Asia's New Democracies,* edited by Y.-W. Chu and S.-L. Wong. New York: Routledge.

Hsiao, Winston. 1995. "The Development of Human Rights in the Republic of China on Taiwan: Ramifications of Recent Democratic Reforms and Problems of Enforcement." *Pacific Rim Law and Policy Journal* 5(1):161–204.

Hu, Zuliu, and Mohsin S. Khan. 1997. *Why Is China Growing So Fast?* Economic Issues (8). http://www.imf.org/EXTERNAL/PUBS/FT/ISSUES8/INDEX.HTM.

Huang, Teh-fu, and Ching-hsin Yu. 1999. "Developing a Party System and Democratic Consolidation." Pp. 85–100 in *Democratization in Taiwan,* edited by S. Tsang and H. M. Tien. New York: St. Martin's.

Huber, Evelyne, Dietrich Rueschemeyer, and John D. Stephens. 1993. "The Impact of Economic Development on Democracy." *Journal of Economic Perspectives* 7(3): 71–86.

Huntington, Samuel P. 1991. "Democracy's Third Wave." *Journal of Democracy* 2(2): 12–34.

Hutchison, Michael M., Takatoshi Ito, and Frank Westermann. 2006. "The Great Japanese Stagnation: Lessons for Industrial Countries." Pp. 1–32 in *Japan's Great Stagnation: Financial and Monetary Policy Lessons for Advanced Economies,* edited by M. M. Hutchison and F. Westermann. Cambridge, MA: MIT Press.

Hwang, Eui-Kak, 1993. *The Korean Economies: A Comparison of North and South.* Oxford: Clarendon Press.

Im, Hyug Baeg. 1987. "The Rise of Bureaucratic Authoritarianism in South Korea." *World Politics* 39(2):231–257.

International Monetary Fund (IMF). 2012. "IMF Members' Quotas and Voting Power, and IMF Board of Governors." http://www.imf.org/external/np/sec/memdir/members .aspx.

———. 2013. "IMF Conditionality." *Factsheet.* http://www.imf.org/external/np/exr/facts /conditio.htm.

Jain, Purnendra C. 1993. "A New Political Era in Japan: The 1993 Election." *Asian Survey* 33(11):1071–1082.

James, William E., Seiji Naya, and Gerald M. Meier. 1989. *Asian Development: Economic Success and Policy Lessons.* Madison: University of Wisconsin Press.

Janelli, Roger I., and Dawhnee Yim. 1999. "The Mutual Constitution of Confucianism and Capitalism." Pp. 107–124 in *Culture and Economy: The Shaping of Capitalism in Eastern Asia,* edited by T. Brook and H. V. Luoung. Ann Arbor: University of Michigan Press.

Jansen, Marius B. 2000. *The Making of Modern Japan.* Cambridge, MA: Belknap.

Japan Institute for Labor Policy and Training. 2013. *Dairokkai Kinrouseikatsu Nickansuru Chousa (2011)* [The Sixth Survey Research on Working Life (2011)]. Tokyo: Japan Institute for Labor Policy and Training.

Jeon, Jei Guk. 2000a. "North Korean Leadership: Kim Jong Il's Balancing Act in the Ruling Circle." *Third World Quarterly* 21(5):761–779.

———. 2000b. "The Politics of Mourning Ritual in North Korea (1994–1997)." *World Affairs* 162(2):126–136.

Jeong, Dae Yong, and Ruth V. Aguilera. 2007. "The Evolution of Enterprise Unionism in Japan: A Socio-Political Perspective." *Social Science Research Network*. http://papers.ssrn.com/sol3/papers.cfm?abstract_id=981173.

Jeong, Dong-Young. 2012. "The IT Industry in Northeast Asia: Present and Future." *SERI Quarterly* 5(1):13–21.

Jin, Jingyi. 2012. "Prospects for Reform in North Korea." *SERI Quarterly* 5(4):114–120.

Joffe, Ellis. 1996. "Party-Army Relations in China: Retrospect and Prospect." *China Quarterly* (146):299–314.

Johnson, Chalmers. 1982. *MITI and the Japanese Miracle: The Growth of Industrial Policy, 1925–1975*. Stanford, CA: Stanford University Press.

———. 1995. *Japan: Who Governs? The Rise of the Developmental State*. New York: W. W. Norton.

Jones, Gavin W. 2010. "Changing Marriage Patterns in Asia." Asia Research Institute Working Paper Series, No. 131. http://www.ari.nus.edu.sg/docs/wps/wps10_131.pdf.

———. 2012. "International Marriage in Asia: What Do We Know, and What Do We Need to Know?" Asia Research Institute Working Paper Series, No. 174. http://www.ari.nus.edu.sg/docs/wps/wps12_174.pdf.

Jones, H. J. 1976–1977. "Japanese Women and the Dual-Track Employment System." *Pacific Affairs* 49(4):589–606.

Jones, Leroy P., and Il SaKong. 1980. *Government, Business, and Entrepreneurship in Economic Development: The Korean Case*. Cambridge, MA: Council on East Asian Studies, Harvard University.

Joppke, Christian. 2001. "The Legal-Domestic Sources of Immigrant Rights: The United States, Germany, and the European Union." *Comparative Political Studies* 34(4):339–365.

Joseph, William A. 2010. "Ideology and Chinese Politics." Pp. 129–164 in *Politics in China: An Introduction*, edited by W. A. Joseph. Oxford: Oxford University Press.

Joshi, Devin. 2012. "Does China's Recent 'Harmonious Society' Discourse Reflect a Shift Toward Human Development?" *Journal of Political Ideologies* 17(2):169–187.

Jowett, A. J. 1984. "The Growth of China's Population, 1949–1982 (with Special Reference to the Demographic Disaster of 1960–61)." *Geographical Journal* 150(2):155–170.

Jung, Hae Gu, and Ho Ki Kim. 2009. "Development of Democratization Movement in South Korea." *Stanford Korea Democracy Project*. Stanford University, Freeman Spogli Institute for International Studies, Palo Alto. http://iis-db.stanford.edu/pubs/22591/Development_of_Democratization_Movement_in_South_Korea-1.pdf.

Jupp, James. 1995. "From 'White Australia' to 'Part of Asia': Recent Shifts in Australian Immigration Policy Towards the Region." *International Migration Review* 29(1):207–228.

Kalinowski, Thomas, and Cho Hyekyung. 2009. "The Political Economy of Financial Liberalization in South Korea: State, Big Business, and Foreign Investors." *Asian Survey* 49(2):221–242.

Kamal-Chaoui, Lamia, Edward Leman, and Zhang Rufei. 2009. "Urban Trends and Policy in China." OECD Regional Development Working Papers, Organisation for Economic Co-operation and Development, Paris.

Kane, John, Hui-Chieh Loy, and Haig Patapan. 2010. "Introduction to the Special Issue: The Search for Legitimacy in Asia." *Politics and Policy* 38(3):381–394.

Kaneko, Kenji. 2009. "Foreign Migrants in Taiwan and Japan: A Comparative Analysis." *Asian Journal of Global Studies* 3(1):22–36.

Kang, Myung Hun. 1996. *The Korean Business Conglomerate: Chaebol Now and Then.* Berkeley: Institute of East Asian Studies.

Kasahara, Shigehisa. 2004. "The Flying Geese Paradigm: A Critical Study of Its Application to East Asian Regional Development." United Nations Conference on Trade and Development. http://ideas.repec.org/p/unc/dispap/169.html.

Kay, Christóbal. 2002. "Why East Asia Overtook Latin America: Agrarian Reform, Industrialisation and Development." *Third World Quarterly* 23(6):1073–1102.

Kennedy, John James. 2010. "Rural China: Reform and Resistance." Pp. 225–249 in *Politics in China: An Introduction,* edited by W. A. Joseph. Oxford: Oxford University Press.

Kharas, Homi. 2010. "The Emerging Middle Class in Developing Countries." OECD Development Centre Working Paper, No. 285, Organisation for Economic Cooperation and Development, Paris. http://unpan1.un.org/intradoc/groups/public/documents/UN-DPADM/UNPAN044413.pdf.

Kikkawa, Takeo. 2005. "Toward the Rebirth of the Japanese Economy and Its Corporate System." *Japan Forum* 17(1):87–106.

Kim, Byung-Kook. 1992. "Economic Policy and the Economic Planning Board (EPB) in Korea." *Asian Affairs* 18(4):197–213.

———. 1998. "Korea's Crisis of Success." Pp. 113–132 in *Democracy in East Asia,* edited by L. Diamond and M. Plattner. Baltimore: Johns Hopkins University Press.

Kim, Byung-Yeon, Suk Jin Kim, and Keun Lee. 2007. "Assessing the Economic Performance of North Korea, 1954–1989: Estimates and Growth Accounting Analysis." *Journal of Comparative Economics* 35:564–582.

Kim, Choong Soon. 1992. *The Culture of Korean Industry: An Ethnography of Poongsan Corporation.* Tucson: University of Arizona Press.

Kim, Doo-Sub. 1994. "The Demographic Transition in the Korean Peninsula, 1910–1990: South and North Korea Compared." *Korea Journal of Population and Development* 23(2):131–154.

———. 2010. "The Rise of Cross-Border Marriage and Divorce in Contemporary Korea." Pp. 127–156 in *Asian Cross-Border Marriage Migration: Demographic Patterns and Social Issues,* edited by W. S. Yang and M. C. W. Lu. Amsterdam: Amsterdam University Press.

Kim, Eun Mee. 1997. *Big Business, Strong State: Collusion and Conflict in South Korean Development, 1960–1990.* Albany: State University of New York Press.

Kim, Hyun Mee. 2007. "The State and Migrant Women: Diverging Hopes in the Making of 'Multicultural Families' in Contemporary Korea." Paper presented at the Knowledge Production and Challenges of Feminisms in the Glocal Era, Ewha Womans University, Seoul.

Kim, Suk H. 2001. "Asian Financial Crisis of 1997: The Case of Korea." *Multinational Business Review* 9(1): 50–58.

Kim, Tongy-hyung. 2010. "Samsung Founder's Dream Closer than Ever." *Korea Times,* February 4. http://www.koreatimes.co.kr/www/news/biz/2010/05/123_60330.html.

Kim, Yoo Hyang. 2004. "North Korea's Cyberpath." *Asian Perspective* 28(3):191–209.

Klein, Sidney. 1962. "The Land Reform Policies of the Chinese Communist Party, 1928–1958: A Brief Economic Analysis." *Agricultural History* 35(2):59–64.

Kohli, Atul. 2001. "Introduction." Pp. 1–20 in *The Success of India's Democracy,* edited by A. Kohli. Cambridge: Cambridge University Press.

Kondo, M. James, William W. Lewis, Vincent Palmade, and Yoshinori Yokoyama. 2000. "Reviving Japan's Economy." Pp. 19–37 in *The McKinsey Quarterly 2000 Special Edition: Asia Revalued*. Washington, DC: McKinsey Global Institute.

Koo, Hagen. 1989. "The State, Industrial Structure, and Labor Politics: Comparison of Taiwan and South Korea." Pp. 561–580 in *Taiwan: A Newly Industrialized State*, edited by H.-H. M. Hsiao and W.-Y. Cheng. Taipei: National Taiwan University.

Korea Immigration Service (Ministry of Justice). 2008. "Classified by Nationality and Age." Seoul: Ministry of Justice.

———. 2009a. *Ch'ulip-Guk Weigukin Chongch'aek T'onggye Yonbo* [Report on the Arrival and Departures of Foreigners]. Seoul: Ministry of Justice.

———. 2009b. *The First Basic Plan for Immigration Policy 2008–2012*. Seoul: Ministry of Justice.

Koyama, Kaoru, and Masataka Okamoto. 2010. "Introduction: Migrants, Migrant Workers, Refugees and Japan's Immigration Policy." Pp. 3–6 in *NGO Report Regarding the Rights of Non-Japanese Nationals, Minorities of Foreign Origins, and Refugees in Japan*, edited by Solidarity Network with Migrants Japan. Tokyo: Solidarity Network with Migrants Japan.

Krauss, Ellis S., and Robert J. Pekkanen. 2010. "The Rise and Fall of Japan's Liberal Democratic Party." *Journal of Asian Studies* 69(1):5–15.

Krugman, Paul. 1994. "The Myth of Asia's Miracle." *Foreign Affairs* 73(6):62–78.

———. 1998. "What Happened to Asia?" *The Official Paul Krugman Web Page* (online). Retrieved December 1, 2013. http://web.mit.edu/krugman/www/DISINTER .html.

———. 2001. "It's Baaack: Japan's Slump and the Return of the Liquidity Trap." *Brookings Papers on Economic Activity* 10(2):137–187.

Kuo, Cheng-Tian. 1995. *Global Competitiveness and Industrial Growth in Taiwan and the Philippines*. Pittsburgh: University of Pittsburgh Press.

Kwon, Tai-Hwan. 1997. "International Migration of Koreans and the Korean Community in China." *Korea Journal of Population and Development* 26(1):1–18.

Lam, Danny, and Jeremy T. Paltiel. 1994. "The Confucian Entrepreneur? Chinese Culture, Industrial Organization, and Intellectual Piracy in Taiwan." *Asian Affairs: An American Review* 20(4):205–217.

Landes, David. 2000. "Culture Makes Almost All the Difference." Pp. 2–13 in *Culture Matters: How Values Shape Human Progress*, edited by L. E. Harrison and S. P. Huntington. New York: Basic.

Lankov, Andrei. 2012. "North Korea's Busy Border." *Asia Times* (online), June 21. http://www.atimes.com/atimes/Korea/NF21Dg02.html.

Lankov, Andrei, and Peter Ward. 2012. "North Korean Refugees Leave Intrigue Behind." *Asia Times* (online), December 8. http://www.atimes.com/atimes/Korea/NL08Dg01 .html.

Lee, Grace. 2003. "The Political Philosophy of Juche." *Stanford Journal of East Asian Affairs* 3:105–112.

Lee, Hy-Sang. 1988. "North Korea's Closed Economy: The Hidden Opening." *Asian Survey* 28(12):1264–1279.

Lee, Hye-Kyung. 2008. "International Marriage and the State in South Korea: Focusing on Governmental Policy." *Citizenship Studies* 12(1):107–123.

Lee, Sook-Jong, and Taejoon Han. 2006. "The Demise of 'Korea, Inc.': Paradigm Shift in Korea's Developmental State." *Journal of Contemporary Asia* 36(3):305–324.

Lee, Sunny. 2007. "US Cartoons 'Made in North Korea.'" *Asia Times* (online), March 14. http://www.atimes.com/atimes/Korea/IC14Dg03.htm.

Lee, Youngjae. 2005. "Law, Politics, and Impeachment: The Impeachment of Roh Moo-hyun from a Comparative Constitutional Perspective." *American Journal of Comparative Law* 53 (Fordham Law Legal Studies Research Paper No. 97):403–432.

Lewis, James A. 2007. *Building an Information Technology Industry in China: National Strategy, Global Markets.* Washington, DC: Center for Strategic and International Studies.

Li, Cheng. 2008. "Introduction: Assessing China's Political Development." Pp. 1–24 in *China's Changing Landscape: Prospects for Democracy,* edited by C. Li. Washington, DC: Brookings Institution Press.

Li, Minqi. 2005. "The Rise of China and the Demise of the Capitalist World-Economy: Exploring Historical Possibilities in the 21st Century." *Science and Society* 69(3): 420–448.

Li, Wei, and Dennis Tao Yang. 2005. "The Great Leap Forward: Anatomy of a Central Planning Disaster." *Journal of Political Economy* 113(4):840–877.

Li, Weiye, and Louis Putterman. 2008. "Reforming China's SOEs: An Overview." *Comparative Economic Studies* 50:353–380.

Liaw, Kao-Lee, Emiko Ochiai, and Yoshitaka Ishikawa. 2010. "Feminization of Immigration in Japan: Marital and Job Opportunities." Pp. 49–86 in *Asian Cross-Border Marriage Migration: Demographic Patterns and Social Issues,* edited by W. S. Yang and M. C. W. Lu. Amsterdam: Amsterdam University Press.

Lie, John. 1998. *Han Unbound: The Political Economy of South Korea.* Stanford, CA: Stanford University Press.

———. 2008. *Zainichi (Koreans in Japan): Diasporic Nationalism and Postcolonial Identity.* Berkeley: University of California Press.

Liebowitz, Stan J., and Stephen E. Margolis. 1999. "Path Dependence." In *Encyclopedia of Law and Economics,* edited by B. Bouckaert and G. D. Geest. Cheltenham, UK: Edward Elgar. http://encyclo.findlaw.com/0770book.pdf.

Lim, Linda. 1998. "Whose 'Model' Failed? Implications of the Asian Economic Crisis." *Washington Quarterly* 21(3):25–36.

Lim, Timothy C. 1996. "Competition, Markets, and the Politics of Development in South Korea, 1945–1979." Doctoral dissertation, University of Hawaii at Manoa, Honolulu.

———. 2001. "Bringing Competition In: A New Perspective on Capitalist Development in South Korea." *Competition and Change* 5:103–133.

———. 2003. "Racing from the Bottom in South Korea? The Nexus Between Civil Society and Transnational Migrants." *Asian Survey* 43(3):423–442.

———. 2010. *Doing Comparative Politics: An Introduction to Approaches and Issues.* 2nd ed. Boulder, CO: Lynne Rienner.

Lin, Ji-Ping. 1998. "Labor Migration in Taiwan." Doctoral dissertation, School of Geography and Geology, McMaster University, Hamilton, Ontario, Canada. Open Access Dissertations and Theses. http://digitalcommons.mcmaster.ca/open dissertations/2725/.

Lin, Justin Yifu, and Zhiyun Li. 2006. "China's SOE and Financial Reforms: 1978–2002." China Center for Economic Research, Peking University, Beijing.

Lin, Serena Yi-Ying. 2010. "Taiwanese Immigrants in the United States." *Migration Information Source: US in Focus* (online). http://www.migrationinformation.org/us focus/display.cfm?ID=790.

Lincoln, James R., Michael L. Gerlach, and Christina L. Ahmadjian. 1996. "*Keiretsu* Networks and Corporate Performance in Japan." *American Sociological Review* 61(1):67–88.

Lincoln, James R., Michael L. Gerlach, and Peggy Takahashi. 1992. "*Keiretsu* Networks in the Japanese Economy: A Dyad Analysis of Intercorporate Ties." *American Sociological Review* 57(5):561–585.

Linden, Greg. 2004. "China Standard Time: A Study in Strategic Industrial Policy." *Business and Politics* 6(3):1–26.

Lintner, Bertil. 2004. "North Korea, Shop Till You Drop." *Far Eastern Economic Review,* May 13, pp. 14–19.

Linz, Juan J. 1990. "The Perils of Presidentialism." *Journal of Democracy* 1(1):51–69.

Linz, Juan J., and Alfred Stepan. 2010. "Toward Consolidated Democracies." Pp. 3–22 in *Debates on Democratization,* edited by L. Diamond, M. F. Plattner, and P. J. Costopolous. Baltimore: Johns Hopkins University Press.

Lipscy, Phillip Y. 2003. "Japan's Asian Monetary Fund Proposal." *Stanford Journal of East Asian Affairs* 3(1):93–104.

Little, Daniel. 2005. "Causal Mechanisms in Comparative Historical Sociology." Paper presented at the Social Science History Association, Portland, Oregon, November 3–6.

Liu, Dorothy. 1996. "The 1992 Employment Service Act and the Influx of Foreign Workers in Taiwan (and Translation of the 1994 Implementary Provisions)." *Pacific Rim Law and Policy Journal* 5(3):599–637.

Lockwood, William W. 1968. *The Economic Development of Japan.* Princeton, NJ: Princeton University Press.

Lukauskas, Arvid. 2002. "Financial Restriction and the Developmental States in East Asia: Toward a More Complex Political Economy." *Comparative Political Studies* 35(4):379–412.

Lum, Thomas, Patricia Moloney Figliola, and Matthew C. Weed. 2012. "China, Internet Freedom, and U.S. Policy." CRS Report for Congress. Washington, DC: Congressional Research Service. http://www.fas.org/sgp/crs/row/R42601.pdf.

Maddison, Angus. 2008. "The West and the Rest in the World Economy: 1000–2030." *World Economics* 9(4):75–99.

Malkiel, Burton G., Jianping Mei, and Rui Yang. 2005. "Investment Strategies to Exploit Economic Growth in China." CEPS Working Paper. Center for Economic Policy Studies, Princeton University, Princeton, NJ.

Mansourov, Alexandre. 2011. "North Korea on the Cusp of Digital Transformation." *Nautilus Institute Special Report,* October 20. http://nautilus.org/wp-content/uploads/2011/12/DPRK_Digital_Transformation.pdf.

Manyin, Mark E., and Dick K. Nanto. 2011. "The Kaesong North-South Korean Industrial Complex." CRS Report for Congress. http://www.fas.org/sgp/crs/row/RL34093.pdf.

Martin, Ron. 2012. "(Re)Placing Path Dependence: A Response to the Debate." *International Journal of Urban and Regional Research* 36(1):179–192.

Marx, Karl. [1848] 1998. *The Communist Manifesto: A Modern Edition.* Introd. by Eric Hobsbawn. London: Verso.

——. [1852] 2008. *The 18th Brumaire of Louis Bonaparte.* Rockville, MD: Wildside.

Masaki, Hisane. 2005. "China and the Legacy of the Plaza Accord." *Asia Times* (online), September 21. http://www.atimes.com/atimes/Global_Economy/GI21Dj01.html.

Mason, Edward S., Mahn Je Kim, Dwight H. Perkins, Kwang Suk Kim, and David C. Cole. 1980. *The Economic and Social Modernization of the Republic of Korea.* Cambridge, MA: Harvard University Press.

Massey, Douglas S., Joaquín Arango, Graeme Hugo, Ali Kouaouci, Adela Pellegrino, and J. Edward Taylor. 2006. "Theories of International Migration: A Review." Pp. 34–61 in *The Migration Reader: Exploring Politics and Policies,* edited by G. Lahav and A. M. Messina. Boulder, CO: Lynne Rienner

Mastanduno, Michael. 1992. "Framing the Japan Problem: The Bush Administration and the Structural Impediments Initiative." *International Journal* 47(2):235–264.

Matveerva, Anna. 1999. "Democracy, Legitimacy and Political Change in Central Asia." *International Affairs* 75(1):23–44.

McCormick, Thomas J. 1995. *America's Half-Century: United States Foreign Policy in the Cold War and After.* Baltimore: Johns Hopkins University Press.

McFaul, Michael. 2002. "The Fourth Wave of Democracy *and* Dictatorship: Noncooperative Transitions in the Postcommunist World." *World Politics* 54:212–244.

McNeill, David. 2009. "North Koreans Dare to Protest as Devaluation Wipes Out Savings." *The Independent* (online), August 25. http://www.independent.co.uk/news/world/asia/north-koreans-dare-to-protest-as-devaluation-wipes-out-savings-1833156.html.

Mehmet, Ozay. 1995. *Westernizing the Third World: The Eurocentricity of Economic Development Theories.* London: Routledge.

Mikami, Satoru. 2008. "Popular Support for Democracy and Democratic Governance of the State: An Empirical Analysis Based on the World Values Survey Data." Pp. 121–153 in *Between Structures and Institutions: Evolving Conflict over Regime Change,* edited by T. Ito. Tokyo: Shobunsha.

Mikami, Satoru, and Inoguchi Takahashi. 2010. "Diagnosing the Micro Foundation of Democracy in Asia: Evidence from the Asia Barometer Survey, 2003–2008." Pp. 246–292 in *East Asia's New Democracies: Deepening, Reversal, Non-Liberal Alternatives,* edited by Y.-W. Chu and S. L. Wong. London: Routledge.

Mill, John Stuart. [1843] 1967. *A System of Logic: Ratiocinative and Inductive.* Toronto: University of Toronto Press.

Mills, C. Wright. [1956] 2000. *The Power Elite.* New York: Oxford University Press.

_____. 1958. *The Causes of World War Three.* London: Secker and Warburg.

Ministry of Strategy and Finance (MOSF). 2013. "About MOSF: History." Retrieved December 1, 2013. http://english.mosf.go.kr/.

Mitchell, Tom. 2012. "No Place Like Home for Migrant Workers." *Financial Times* (online), February 25. http://www.ft.com/intl/cms/s/0/d813512a-223b-11df-9a72-00144feab49a.html#axzz24xUMX3qV.

Monk-Turner, Elizabeth, and Charlie Turner. 2004. "The Gender Wage Gap in South Korea: How Much Has Changed in 10 Years?" *Journal of Asian Economics* 15:415–424.

Moon, Chung-in, and Jae-Ok Paek. 2010. "Defense Innovation and Industrialization in South Korea." *Study of Innovation and Technology in China* (Policy Brief No. 14). http://igcc.ucsd.edu/assets/001/500879.pdf.

Moon, Ihlwan. 1998. "It's Not Just the Chaebol That Are Squeezed." *Businessweek,* February 16, p. 54.

Moore, Ray A., and Donald L. Robinson. 2002. *Partners for Democracy: Crafting the New Japanese State Under MacArthur.* New York: Oxford University Press.

Moriguchi, Chiaki, and Hiroshi Ono. 2004. "Japanese Lifetime Employment: A Century's Perspective." Working Paper, No. 205. http://swopec.hhs.se/eijswp/papers/eijswp0205.pdf.

Morrison, Wayne M. 2009. "China's Economic Conditions." *CRS Report for Congress.* Washington, DC: Congressional Research Service.

Morton, Katherine. 2009. *China and the Global Environment: Learning from the Past, Anticipating the Future.* Double Bay, New South Wales: Lowry Institute for International Policy.

Moss, Trefor. 2013. "Soft Power? China Has Plenty." *Diplomat* (online), June 4. http://thediplomat.com/2013/06/04/soft-power-china-has-plenty/comment-page-3/?all=true.

Mu, Guangzong. "Tackling Gender Imbalance." *Women of China* (online), December 4. http://www.womenofchina.cn/html/womenofchina/report/167797-1.htm.

Munck, Ronaldo. 1999. "Deconstructing Development Discourses: Of Impasses, Alternatives, and Politics." Pp. 196–210 in *Critical Development Theory: Contributions to a New Paradigm,* edited by R. Munck and D. O'Hearn. London: Zed.

Myers, Ramon Hawley, Mark R. Peattie, and Ching-chih Chen, eds. 1984. *The Japanese Colonial Empire, 1895–1945.* Princeton, NJ: Princeton University Press.

Myint, H. 1960. "The Demand Approach to Economic Development." *Review of Economic Studies* 27(2):124–132.

Nanto, Dick K., and Emma Chanlett-Avery. 2008. "The North Korean Economy: Leverage and Policy Analysis." CRS Report for Congress. Washington, DC: Congressional Research Service. http://www.fas.org/sgp/crs/row/RL32493.pdf.

Nathan, Andrew. 1997. *China's Transition.* New York: Columbia University Press.

National Bureau of Statistics of China. 2012. "Statistical Communiqué on the 2011 National Economic and Social Development." http://www.stats.gov.cn/english/news andcomingevents/t20120222_402786587.htm.

National Diet Library (Japan). 1947. "The Constitution of Japan." Retrieved on December 7, 2013. http://www.ndl.go.jp/constitution/e/etc/c01.html.

National Immigration Agency (Ministry of the Interior, Taiwan). 2005. "Foreign Residents and Ferreted Illegal Foreign Residents." Retrieved on December 10, 2013. http://www.moi.gov.tw/english/english_news/news_detail.aspx?sn=97&type_code=.

National Public Radio. 2002. "'Keep on Moving' Speech." *Morning Edition,* January 21. http://www.npr.org/templates/story/story.php?storyId=1136695.

Naughton, Barry. 1995. *Growing Out of the Plan: Chinese Economic Reform, 1978–1993.* New York: Cambridge University Press.

———. 2007a. *The Chinese Economy: Transitions and Growth.* Cambridge, MA: MIT Press.

———. 2007b. "China's Transition: Predatory State or Developmental Autocracy?" *Rule of Law in China: Chinese Law and Politics.* http://www.fljs.org/sites/www.fljs.org /files/publications/Naughton_pb3%25231%2523.pdf.

———. 2008. "A Political Economy of China's Economic Transition." Pp. 91–135 in *China's Great Economic Transformation,* edited by L. Brandt and T. G. Rawski. Cambridge: Cambridge University Press.

Nesadurai, Helen S. 2008. "The Association of the Southeast Asian Nations (ASEAN)." *New Political Economy* 25(2): 225–239.

Noland, Marcus, Sherman Robinson, and Tao Wang. 1999. "Famine in North Korea: Causes and Cures." Institute for International Economics. http://www.piie.com /publications/wp/99–2.pdf.

O'Donnell, Guillermo. 2010. "Illusions About Consolidation." Pp. 23–40 in *Debates on Democratization,* edited by L. Diamond, M. F. Plattner, and P. J. Costopolous. Baltimore: Johns Hopkins University Press.

Office of the Registrar General (India). 2002. "Data on Workers and Their Categories: An Insight." In *eCensusIndia.* Retrieved on February 28, 2002. http://www.census india.net.

Ogden, Suzanne. 2002. *Inklings of Democracy in China.* Cambridge, MA: Harvard University Asia Center.

Oh, Chang-gyu. 2010. "Next 10 Years." *Munhwa Ilbo,* March 19. Reprinted in *Korea Focus.* http://www.koreafocus.or.kr/design2/layout/content_print.asp?group_id=102972.

Oh, John Kie-chiang. 1968. *Korea: Democracy on Trial.* Ithaca, NY: Cornell University Press.

Okimoto, Daniel I. 1989. *Between MITI and the Market.* Stanford, CA: Stanford University Press.

Ono, Hiroshi. 2005. "Lifetime Employment in Japan: Concepts and Measurements." Stockholm School of Economics. http://www.japanfocus.org/data/Ono.pdf.

Organisation for Economic Co-operation and Development (OECD). 2012. *FDI in Figures*. Paris: Organisation for Economic Co-operation and Development. http://www.iccmex.mx/correos/2012/agosto/FDI%20in%20figures.pdf.

———. 2013. "The Organisation for Economic Co-operation and Development (OECD): Our Mission." http://www.oecd.org/about/.

Orlik, Tom. 2011. "Unrest Grows as Economy Booms." *Wall Street Journal* (online), September 26. http://online.wsj.com/news/articles/SB10001424053111903703604576587070600504108.

Ornatowski, Gregory K. 1996. "Confucian Ethics and Economic Development: A Study of the Adaptation of Confucian Values to Modern Japanese Economic Ideology and Institutions." *Journal of Socio-Economics* 25(5):571–590.

Ortmann, Stephan. 2011. "Singapore: Authoritarian but Newly Competitive." *Journal of Democracy* 22(4):153–164.

Ozawa, Terutomo. 1993. "Foreign Direct Investment and Structural Transformation: Japan as a Recycler of Market and Industry." *Business and the Contemporary World* 5(2):129–150.

Paprzycki, Ralph, and Kyoji Fukao. 2004. "Overcoming Economic Stagnation in Japan: The Importance of Total Factor Productivity and the Potential Contribution of Foreign Direct Investment." Hi-Stat Discussion Paper Series, No. 39. Hitotsubashi University Research Unit for Statistical Analysis in Social Sciences, Tokyo.

Park, Chung Hee. 1962a. *Our Nation's Path: Ideology of Social Reconstruction*. Seoul: Hollym Corporation Publishers.

———. 1962b. *The Country, the Revolution, and I*. Seoul: Hollym Corporation Publishers.

Park, Han S. 2002. *North Korea: The Politics of Unconventional Wisdom*. Boulder, CO: Lynne Rienner.

———. 2007. "Military-First Politics (Songun): Understanding Kim Jong-il's North Korea." *KEI Academic Paper Series* 2(7):1–8.

Park, Sang Mi. 2010. "The Paradox of Postcolonial Korean Nationalism: State-Sponsored Cultural Policy in South Korea, 1965–Present." *Journal of Korean Studies* 15(1):67–94.

Park, Sang Yong. 2001. "Asian Financial Crisis: South Korea's Experiences." Pp. 25–57 in *Taiwan, East Asia and Copenhagen Commitment*, Vol. 1, *UN NGO Policy Series*, edited by L. C. Chiu. Taipei: Chung-Hua Institution for Economic Research.

Park, Young-bum. 1997. "Issues Papers from the Republic of South Korea." In *Migration Issues in the Asia Pacific* (online). Paris: United Nations Educational, Scientific, and Cultural Organization. http://www.unesco.org/most/apmrnw12.htm.

Peattie, Mark R. 1984. "Introduction." Pp. 3–26 in *The Japanese Colonial Empire, 1895–1945*, edited by R. H. Myers and M. R. Peattie. Princeton, NJ: Princeton University Press.

Pei, Minxin. 1998. "The Fall and Rise of Democracy in East Asia." Pp. 57–78 in *Democracy in East Asia*, edited by L. Diamond and M. Platter. Baltimore: Johns Hopkins University Press.

———. 2006. *China's Trapped Transition: The Limits of Developmental Autocracy*. Cambridge, MA: Harvard University Press.

Pempel, T. J. 1999. "The Enticement of Corporatism: Appeals of the 'Japanese Model' in Developing Asia." Pp. 26–53 in *Corporatism and Korean Capitalism*, edited by D. L. McNamara. London: Routledge.

————. 2005. "Introduction: Emerging Webs of Regional Connectedness." Pp. 1–30 in *Remapping East Asia: The Construction of a Region,* edited by T. J. Pempel. Ithaca, NY: Cornell University Press.

Peng, Xizhe. 1987. "Demographic Consequences of the Great Leap Forward in China's Provinces." *Population and Development Review* 13(4):639–670.

Piore, Michael J. 1979. *Birds of Passage: Migrant Labor and Industrial Societies.* Cambridge: Cambridge University Press.

————. 1980. "Comment." *Industrial and Labor Relations Review* 33(3):312–314.

Posen, Adam S., and Ryoichi Mikitani. 2000. *Japan's Financial Crisis and Its Parallels to US Experience.* Washington, DC: Peterson Institute of International Economics.

Powell, Benjamin. 2002. "Explaining Japan's Recession." *Mises Daily* (online), November 19. http://mises.org/daily/1099.

Price, John. 1997. *Japan Works: Power and Paradox in Postwar Industrial Relations.* Ithaca, NY: Cornell University Press.

Public Broadcasting Service (PBS). 2003. "Kim Duk Hong: Interview with a North Korean Defector." *Frontline.* http://www.pbs.org/wgbh/pages/frontline/shows/kim/them/defector.html.

Puffert, Douglas. 2010. "Path Dependence." *EH.net Encyclopedia.* http://eh.net/encyclopedia/article/puffert.path.dependence.

Putzel, James. 1999. "The Survival of an Imperfect Democracy in the Philippines." *Democratization* 6(1):198–223.

Pye, Lucian W. 1993. "How China's Nationalism Was Shanghaied." *Australian Journal of Chinese Affairs* (29):107–133.

Pyo, Hak K. 1999. "The Financial Crisis in South Korea." Pp. 151–170 in *Asian Contagion: The Causes and Consequences of a Financial Crisis,* edited by K. D. Jackson. Boulder, CO: Westview.

Ragin, Charles. 1987. *The Comparative Method: Moving Beyond Qualitative and Quantitative Strategies.* Berkeley: University of California Press.

Ramstad, Evan. 2012. "North Korea Leader Says Military Is Priority." *Wall Street Journal* (online), April 16. http://online.wsj.com/article/SB10001424052702304818404577345282956384006.html.

————. 2012. "A Rather Flimsy Firewall." *Economist* (online), April 7. http://www.economist.com/node/21552210.

Rauhala, Emily. 2013. "Kim Jong Un's Purge of His Uncle May Test Ties with China." *Time* (online), December 9. http://world.time.com/2013/12/09/kim-jong-uns-purge-of-his-uncle-may-test-ties-with-china/.

Reed, Edward. 2010. "Is Saemaul Undong a Model for Developing Countries?" Paper presented at the International Symposium in Commemoration of the Fortieth Anniversary of Saemaul Undong, September 30. http://asiafoundation.org/resources/pdfs/SaemaulUndongReedSept2010FINAL.pdf.

Regional Thematic Working Group on International Migration Including Human Trafficking. 2008. *Situation Report on International Migration in East and South-East Asia.* Bangkok: International Organization for Migration, Regional Office for Southeast Asia.

Reich, Michael, David M. Gordon, and Richard C. Edwards. 1973. "Dual Labor Markets: A Theory of Labor Market Segmentation." *American Economic Review* 63(2):359–365.

"Report and Discussion of Statutes of the Communist International: Evening Session of August 4." [1921] 1977. In *Minutes of the Second Congress of the Communist International,* trans. Bob Archer. London: New Park. Reproduced online. http://www.marxists.org/history/international/comintern/2nd-congress/ch10a.htm.

Richardson, Bradley. 1997. *Japanese Democracy: Power, Coordination, and Performance.* New Haven, CT: Yale University Press.

Riethmuller, Paul, and Joseph Chai. 1999. "Japan's Large Scale Retail Store Law: A Cause of Concern for Food Exporters?" Paper presented at the International Agribusiness Marketing Association Conference, Florence, Italy, June 13–16.

Roberts, Dexter. 2012. "China's State Enterprises Have to Pay Up." *Bloomberg Businessweek* (online), May 17. http://www.businessweek.com/articles/2012-05–17 /chinas-state-enterprises-have-to-pay-up.

Rothbard, Murray N. 2007. "Free Market." *The Concise Encyclopedia of Economics.* http://www.econlib.org/library/Enc/FreeMarket.html.

Rueschemeyer, Dietrich, Evelyne Huber Stephens, and John Stephens. 1992. *Capitalist Development and Democracy.* Chicago: University of Chicago Press.

Rueschemeyer, Dietrich, and John D. Stephens. 1997. "Comparing Historical Sequences—A Powerful Tool for Causal Analysis." *Comparative Social Research* 16:55–72.

SaKong, Il. 1993. *Korea in the World Economy.* Washington, DC: Institute for International Economics.

Sally, Razeen. 2011. "Chinese Trade Policy After (Almost) Ten Years in the WTO: A Post-Crisis Stocktake." ECIPE Occasional Paper, European Centre for International Political Economy (ECIPE), Brussels.

Samsung. 2009. *Sustainability Report, 2008–2009: Samsung Electronics.* Gyeonggi-do, Korea: Samsung Electronics. http://www.samsung.com/us/aboutsamsung/sustain ability/sustainabilityreports/download/2009/2009Environmentalnsocialreport .pdf.

Samuels, Richard J. 1987. *The Business of the Japanese State: Energy Markets in Comparative and Historical Perspective.* Ithaca, NY: Cornell University Press.

Sarkar, Sumit. 2001. "Indian Democracy: The Historical Inheritance." Pp. 23–46 in *The Success of India's Democracy,* edited by A. Kohli. Cambridge: Cambridge University Press.

Sayer, Andrew. 1992. *Method in Social Science: A Realist Approach.* 2nd ed. London: Routledge.

Scalapino, Robert A. 1968. "Elections and Political Modernization in Prewar Japan." Pp. 249–292 in *Political Development in Modern Japan,* edited by R. E. Ward. Princeton, NJ: Princeton University Press.

Schaffer, Scott E. n.d. "Analytical Tools: Levels of Analysis." Retrieved December 10, 2013. http://www.millersville.edu/~schaffer/courses/LOA.htm.

Schedler, Andreas. 2001. "Measuring Democratic Consolidation." *Studies in Comparative and International Development* 36(1):61–87.

———. 2010. "What Is Democratic Consolidation?" Pp. 59–74 in *Debates on Democratization,* edited by L. Diamond, M. F. Plattner, and P. J. Costopolous. Baltimore: Johns Hopkins University Press.

Scheiner, Ethan. 2005. *Democracy Without Competition in Japan: Opposition Failure in a One-Party Dominant State.* Cambridge: Cambridge University Press.

Scheineson, Andrew. 2009. "Backgrounder: China's Internal Migrants." *Council on Foreign Relations,* May 14. http://www.cfr.org/china/chinas-internal-migrants /p12943.

Schönwälder, Karen. 2004. "Why Germany's Guestworkers Were Largely Europeans: The Selective Principles of Post-War Labour Recruitment Policy." *Ethnic and Racial Studies* 27(2):248–265.

Schuman, Michael. 2010. "What Asia Can Really Teach America." *Time* (online), February 4. http://www.time.com/time/business/article/0,8599,1959065,00.html.

Schumpeter, Joseph. [1942] 1975. *Capitalism, Socialism, and Democracy.* New York: Harper.

Schurmann, Franz. 1974. *The Logic of World Power; An Inquiry into the Origins, Currents, and Contradictions of World Politics.* New York: Pantheon.

Scobell, Andrew. 2006. *Kim Jong Il and North Korea: The Leader and the System.* Carlisle, PA: Strategic Studies Institute.

"Secret Sauce." 2009. *Economist* (online), November 12. http://www.economist.com/node/14844987.

Seol, Dong-Hoon, and John D. Skrentny. 2004. "Joseonjok Migrant Workers' Identity and National Identity in Korea." Paper presented at the Korean Identity: Past and Present conference, Yonsei University, Seoul, South Korea, October 28–29.

———. 2006. "International Matchmaking Agencies in Korea and Their Regulation." Paper presented at the Asia Culture Forum: Transformation and Prospect Toward a Multiethnic, Multiracial, and Multicultural Society, October 26.

———. 2009a. "Ethnic Return Migration and Hierarchical Nationhood: Korean Chinese Foreign Workers in South Korea." *Ethnicities* 9(2):147–174.

———. 2009b. "Why Is There So Little Migrant Settlement in East Asia?" *International Migration Review* 43(3):578–620.

Seoul Immigration Control Office. 2006. "Establishment of International Marriages."

Sharma, Basu. 1985. *Aspects of Industrial Relations in ASEAN.* Singapore: Institute for Asian Studies.

Shen, Jianming. 2000. "Sovereignty, Statehood, Self-Determination, and the Issue of Taiwan." *American University International Law Review* 15(5):1101–1161.

Shepard, Kevin. 2010. "Buying into the Hermit Kingdom: FDI in the DPRK." *Korea Economic Institute Academic Paper Series* 5(11):1–10.

Shieh, Gwo-shyong. 1992. *Boss Island: The Subcontracting Network and Micro-Entrepreneurship in Taiwan's Development.* New York: Peter Lang.

Shin, Doh Chull, and Jason Wells. 2005. "Is Democracy the Only Game in Town?" *Journal of Democracy* 16(2):88–101.

Shin, Gi-Wook, and Daniel C. Sneider. 2007. *Cross Currents: Regionalism and Nationalism in Northeast Asia.* Stanford, CA: Shorenstein APARC.

Shin, Jang-Sup, and Ha-Joon Chang. 2005. "Economic Reform After the Financial Crisis: A Critical Assessment of Institutional Transition and Transition Costs in South Korea." *Review of International Political Economy* 12(3):409–433.

Shugart, Matthew Søberg. 2005. "Semi-Presidential Systems: Dual Executive and Mixed Authority Patterns." Unpublished paper, University of California, San Diego.

Skeldon, Ronald. 1996. "Migration from China." *Journal of International Affairs* 49(2): 434–453.

So, Alvin Y., and Stephen W. K. Chiu. 1995. *East Asia and the World Economy.* Thousand Oaks, CA: Sage.

Sohn, Chan-Hyun. 2002. "Korea's Corporate Restructuring Since the Financial Crisis: Measures and Assessments." Paper presented at Promoting Growth and Welfare: Structural Changes and the Role of Institutions in Asia. Rio de Janeiro, Brazil, April 29–May 3.

Solinger, Dorothy J. 2008. "The Political Implications of China's Social Future: Complacency, Scorn, and the Forlorn." Pp. 251–266 in *China's Changing Political Landscape: Prospects for Democracy,* edited by C. Li. Washington, DC: Brookings Institution Press.

"South Korea Cracks Down on Marriage Brokers After Death of Foreign Woman." 2010. *Taipei Times* (online), August 1. http://www.taipeitimes.com/News/world/archives/2010/08/01/2003479279.

"State Capitalism's Global Reach: New Masters of the Universe." 2012. *Economist* (online), January 21. http://www.economist.com/node/21542925.

Stone, Katherine V. W. 2009. "Flexibility in Japan: New Institutions of Work and New Conceptions of the Social Contract." http://www.law.yale.edu/documents/pdf/Intellectual_Life/Stone_FlexibilityinJapan.pdf.

Stubbs, Richard. 2005. *Rethinking Asia's Economic Miracle*. Basingstoke, UK: Palgrave Macmillan.

Subramanian, Arvind. 2011. "Is China Already Number One? New GDP Estimates." *Real Time Economic Issues Watch* (Peterson Institute for International Economics), January 13. http://www.piie.com/blogs/realtime/?p=1935.

Suh, Dae-Sook. 1995. *Kim Il Sung: The North Korea Leader*. New York: Columbia University Press.

Suh, Sang Chul. 1975. "Development of a New Industry Through Exports: The Electronics Industry in Korea." Pp. 95–120 in *Trade and Development in Korea*, edited by W. Hong and A. O. Krueger. Seoul: Korean Development Institute.

———. 1978. "Foreign Capital and Development Strategy in Korea." *Korean Studies* 2:67–93.

Surak, Kristin. 2011. "States and Migration Industries in Taiwan, Japan, and South Korea." EUI Working Papers. European University Institute, Florence, Italy. http://cadmus.eui.eu/bitstream/handle/1814/18137/MWP_Surak_2011_12.pdf.

"A Survey of Taiwan: In Praise of Paranoia." 1998a. *Economist* (online), November 7. http://www.economist.com/node/174726.

"A Survey of Taiwan: The Survivor's Tale." 1998b. *Economist* (online), November 7. http://www.economist.com/node/174771.

Szamosszegi, Andrew, and Cole Kyle. 2011. "An Analysis of State-Owned Enterprises and State Capitalism in China." Washington, DC: US-China Economic and Security Review Commission.

Tabuchi, Hiroko. 2009. "In Japan, Secure Jobs Have a Cost." *New York Times* (online), May 19. http://www.nytimes.com/2009/05/20/business/global/20zombie.html.

Takayoshi, Matsuo. 1966. "The Development of Democracy in Japan—Taisho Democracy: Its Flowering and Breakdown." *Developing Economies* 4(4):612–632.

"Taking Lessons from Japan." 2012. *Economist* (online), July 7. http://www.economist.com/blogs/buttonwood/2012/03/economic-growth.

Tanaka, Hiroyuki. 2008. "North Korea: Understanding Migration to and from a Closed Country." *Migration Information Source*. http://www.migrationinformation.org/Profiles/display.cfm?ID=668.

Tegtmeyer Pak, Katherine. 2006. "Making Immigrants Local Citizens: Social Integration Programs in Japanese Cities." Pp. 65–96 in *Local Citizenship in Recent Countries of Immigration: Japan in Comparative Perspective*, edited by T. Tsuda. Lanham, MD: Lexington.

Teiwes, Frederick C. 2010. "Mao Zedong in Power (1949–1976)." Pp. 63–102 in *Politics in China: An Introduction*, edited by W. A. Joseph. Oxford: Oxford University Press.

Terrazas, Aaron. 2009. "Korean Immigrants in the United States." *Migration Information Source*, January. http://www.migrationinformation.org/usfocus/display.cfm?ID=716.

Thongswasdi, Tarnthong. 2008. "Military Intervention in Thai Parliamentary Democracy." Pp. 163–172 in *Parliaments as Peacebuilders in Conflict-Affected Countries*, edited by M. O'Brien, R. Stapenhurst, and N. Johnston. Washington, DC: World Bank.

"Three Generations of Punishment." 2012. Narr. Anderson Cooper with Shin Dong-hyuk. *Sixty Minutes*, May 19. http://www.cbsnews.com/videos/north-korean-prisoner-escaped-after-23-brutal-years-50147159/.

Tija, Paul. 2012. "Inside the Hermit Kingdom: IT and Outsourcing in North Korea." *Communications of the ACM* 55(8):22–25.

Tilly, Charles. 2007. *Democracy.* Cambridge: Cambridge University Press.

Tseng, Wanda, and Harm Zebregs. 2002. "Foreign Direct Investment in China: Some Lessons for Other Countries." IMF Policy Discussion Paper. International Monetary Fund, Washington, DC.

Tseng, Yen-Fen. 2010. "Marriage Migration to East Asia: Current Issues and Propositions in Making Comparisons." Pp. 31–48 in *Asian Cross-Border Marriage Migration: Demographic Patterns and Social Issues,* edited by W. S. Yang and M. C. W. Lu. Amsterdam: Amsterdam University Press.

Tuan, Hoang Anh. 2009. "Doi Moi and the Remaking of Vietnam." *Global Asia: A Journal of the East Asia Foundation* 4(3). http://www.globalasia.org/V4N3_Fall_2009 /Hoang_Anh_Tuan.html.

Tucker, Vincent. 1999. "The Myth of Development: A Critique of a Eurocentric Discourse." Pp. 1–26 in *Critical Development Theory: Contributions to a New Paradigm,* edited by R. Munck and D. O'Hearn. London: Zed.

Twomey, Brian. 2009. "The Plaza Accord: The World Intervenes in Currency Markets." *Investopedia,* November 12. http://www.investopedia.com/articles/forex/09/plaza -accord.asp.

Unger, Jonathan. 2006. "China's Conservative Middle Class." *Far Eastern Economic Review,* April, pp. 27–31.

United Nations. 1971. UN General Assembly, 26th Session. "Resolution 2758: Restoration of the Lawful Rights of the People's Republic of China and the United Nations." http://www.un.org/en/ga/search/view_doc.asp?symbol=a/res/2758(xxvi)& lang=e&area=resolution.

———. 2011. *World Economic Situation 2012: Global Economic Outlook.* New York: United Nations. http://www.un.org/en/development/desa/policy/wesp/wesp_current /2012wesp_prerel.pdf.

United Nations Framework Convention on Climate Change. 1997. "Article 2: Objective." In *Full Text of the Convention.* http://unfccc.int/essential_background /convention/background/items/1353.php.

US Department of State. 1948. *Foreign Relations of the United States, 1948. The Far East and Australasia,* Vol. 6. http://digital.library.wisc.edu/1711.dl/FRUS.FRUS 1948v06.

US Department of Treasury. 2011. "Major Foreign Holders of Treasury Securities." http://www.treasury.gov/resource-center/data-chart-center/tic/Documents/mfh.txt.

Usui, Chikako. 2006. "Japan's Demographic Future and the Challenge of Foreign Workers." Pp. 37–64 in *Local Citizenship in Recent Countries of Immigration: Japan in Comparative Perspective,* edited by T. Tsuda. Lanham, MD: Lexington.

Van Arkadie, Brian, and Raymond Mallon. 2003. *Vietnam: A Transition Tiger?* Canberra: Australian National University E-Press.

Vernon, Raymond. 1966. "International Investment and International Trade in the Product Cycle." *Quarterly Journal of Economics* 80(2):190–207.

Vorontsov, Alexander V. 2006. "North Korea's Military-First Policy: A Curse or a Blessing?" *Policy Forum* (online). Nautilus Institute for Security and Sustainability, Berkeley, CA. http://nautilus.org/napsnet/napsnet-policy-forum/north-koreas -military-first-policy-a-curse-or-a-blessing/#axzz2eVloj3SX.

Wade, Robert. 1990. *Governing the Market: Economic Theory and the Role of Government in East Asian Industrialization.* Princeton, NJ: Princeton University Press.

Wallerstein, Immanuel. 1974. "The Rise and Future Demise of the World Capitalist System: Concepts for Comparative Analysis." *Comparative Studies in Society and History* 16(4):387–415.

————. 2008. "The Depression: A Long-Term View" *MRZine,* October 16. http://mrzine .monthlyreview.org/2008/wallerstein161008.html.

Wampler, Robert. 2010. "Seeing Human Rights in the 'Proper Manner': The Reagan-Chun Summit of February 1981." *The National Security Archive.* http://www.gwu .edu/~nsarchiv/NSAEBB/NSAEBB306/index.htm.

Wang, Alex. 2012. "China's Environmental Tipping Point?" Pp. 112–133 in *China In and Beyond the Headlines,* edited by T. B. Weston and L. M. Jensen. Lanham, MD: Rowman and Littlefield.

Wang, Helen H. 2010. "Defining the Chinese Middle Class." *Forbes* (online), November 24. http://www.forbes.com/sites/helenwang/2010/11/24/defining-the-chinese-middle -class/.

Wang, Hong-zen, and Shu-ming Chang. 2002. "The Commodification of International Marriages: Cross-Border Marriage Business in Taiwan and Viet Nam." *International Migration* 40(6):93–116.

Wang, Zhengxu. 2006. "Explaining Regime Strength in China." *China: An International Journal* 4(2):217–237.

Ward, Robert E. 1978. *Japan's Political System.* Englewood Cliffs, NJ: Prentice-Hall.

Weber, Max. 1964. *The Theory of Social and Economic Organization,* edited by T. Parsons. New York: Free Press.

Weiner, Myron. 1995. *The Global Migration Crisis: Challenge to States and Human Rights.* New York: HarperCollins College.

Weiss, Linda.1998. *The Myth of the Powerless State.* Ithaca, NY: Cornell University Press.

————. 2000. "Developmental States in Transition: Adapting, Dismantling, Innovating, Not 'Normalizing.'" *Pacific Review* 13(1):21–55.

Weiss, Linda, and John M. Hobson. 1995. *States and Economic Development: A Comparative Historical Analysis.* Cambridge, UK: Polity.

Williams, David. 1994. *Japan: Beyond the End of History.* London: Routledge.

Winckler, Edwin A. 1994. "Cultural Policy in Postwar Taiwan." Pp. 22–46 in *Cultural Change in Postwar Taiwan,* edited by S. Harrell and H. Chun-chieh. Boulder, CO: Westview.

Winters, Jeffrey A. 1999. "The Determinants of Financial Crisis in Asia." Pp. 79–97 in *The Politics of the Asian Economic Crisis,* edited by T. J. Pempel. Ithaca, NY: Cornell University Press.

Womach, Jasper. 2005. "Agriculture: A Glossary of Terms, Programs, and Laws, 2005 Edition." *CRS Report for Congress.* Washington, DC: Congressional Research Service.

Woo, Jung-en. 1991. *Race to the Swift: State and Finance in Korean Industrialization.* New York: Columbia University Press.

Woo-Cumings, Meredith. 1998. "National Security and the Rise of the Developmental State in South Korea and Taiwan." Pp. 319–340 in *Behind East Asian Growth: The Political and Social Foundations of Prosperity,* edited by H. S. Rowen. London: Routledge.

————. 2002. "The Political Ecology of Famine: The North Korean Catastrophe and Its Lessons." ABD Research Paper, No. 31. Asian Developmental Bank Institute, Tokyo. http://www.adbi.org/files/2002.01.rp31.ecology.famine.northkorea.pdf.

World Bank. 1993. *The East Asian Miracle: Economic Growth and Public Policy.* Oxford: Oxford University Press.

World Bank. 2013a. "Foreign Direct Investment, Net Inflow (BoP, Current US$)." *World Bank Data* (online). http://data.worldbank.org/indicator/BX.KLT.DINV.CD.WD.

————. 2013b. "GDP per Capita, PPP (Current International $)." *World Bank Data* (online). http://data.worldbank.org/indicator/NY.GDP.PCAP.PP.CD.

World Trade Organization (WTO). 2013. "About the WTO—A Statement by Former Director-General Pascal Lamy." http://www.wto.org/english/thewto_e/whatis_e /wto_dg_stat_e.htm.

"The Worldwide War on Baby Girls." 2010. *Economist* (online), May 4. http://www .economist.com/node/15636231.

Wu, Rong-I, and Chung-Che Huang. 2003. "Entrepreneurship in Taiwan: Turning Point to Restart." *Entrepreneurship in Asia: Playbook for Prosperity* (online), edited by MCPA. Washington, DC: Maureen and Mike Mansfield Foundation. http://www .mansfieldfdn.org/backup/programs/entrepreneurship.htm.

Wu, Yu-Shan. 2007. "Taiwan's Developmental State: After the Economic and Political Turmoil." *Asian Survey* 47(6):977–1001.

Yeoh, Brenda S. A., and Weiqiang Lin. 2012. "Rapid Growth in Singapore's Immigrant Population Brings Policy Challenges." *Migration Information Sources: Country Profiles.* http://www.migrationinformation.org/feature/display.cfm?ID=887.

Yu, Keping. 2008. "China's Governance Reform from 1978 to 2008." Duisburg Working Papers on East Asian Studies, No. 76. Institute for East Asian Studies, University of Duisburg-Essen, Duisburg, Germany. http://hdl.handle.net/10419/40964.

———. 2009. *Democracy Is a Good Thing: Essays on Politics, Society, and Culture in Contemporary China.* Washington, DC: Brookings Institution.

Yun, Ji-Whan. 2010. "The Myth of Confucian Capitalism in South Korea: Overworked Elderly and Underworked Youth." *Pacific Affairs* 82(2):237–259.

Zhao, Suisheng. 1998. "A State-Led Nationalism: The Patriotic Education Campaign in Post-Tiananmen China." *Communist and Post-Communist Studies* 31(3):287–302.

Zhao, Ziyang, Pu Bao, Renee Chiang, Adi Ignatius, and Roderick MacFarquhar. 2009. *Prisoner of the State: The Secret Journal of Zhao Ziyang.* New York: Simon and Schuster.

Ziltener, Patrick. 2007. "East Asia: Structure and Formation of a World Region." Pp. 111–146 in *Regional and Local Shaping of World Society,* edited by M. Herkenrath. Piscataway, NJ: Transactions Publishers.

Zveglich, Joseph E., and Yana van der Meulen Rodgers. 2004. "Occupational Segregation and the Gender Wage Gap in a Dynamic East Asian Economy." *Southern Economic Journal* 70(4):850–875.

Zweig, David. 2010. "China's Political Economy." Pp. 192–224 in *Politics in China: An Introduction,* edited by W. A. Joseph. Oxford: Oxford University Press.

Index

Abortion: selective abortion and international marriages, 327–328
Accountability: China's provincial corruption, 166
Acheson, Dean, 71
Africa: China's economic involvement, 344
Agency: characteristics of democracy, 186–187; circumstances of China's economic transformation, 167; constructed actor, 17–21; democratic consolidation, 263; democratic transition and reversal, 188; individual and collective structure and, 124; individual decisions and actions in political change, 224–226; levels of analysis, 19(fig.), 20; migration theories, 332–334; mutually constitutive relationships, 19–21; North Korea's economic decline, 142–143; political change in authoritarian states, 289, 291; role of human agency in China's economic transformation, 175–176; states and individuals, 83; Taiwan's "managed" democratic transition, 200–205. *See also* Constructed actor model
Agents of change, 1
Agreement on Joint Development and Management of the Rason Economic and Trade Zone, 136–137
Agriculture: China's collectivization, 151–152, 156; China's decollectivization, 161–162; land reform, 152(fig.); North Korea's limited reforms, 136; push-pull theories of migration, 307; South Korea's democratic reversal, 255; Tokugawa era treatment of peasants, 224–225

Ahistorical analysis, 23
Ai Weiwei, 268(fig.)
Allied Powers, 114
Amakudari (elite movement), 256, 257(fig.)
Analysis, levels of, 19(fig.)
Anglo-Japanese Alliance, 191(fig.)
Arab Spring, 189
Arduous march, period of the (North Korea), 136
Area studies, 30
Aritomo, Yamagata, 49
Arrighi, Giovanni, 69, 73–74, 76
Asia-centric world, 338–339, 343–344
Asian Barometer Survey Project, 264(n3)
Asian Financial Crisis: Asian Monetary Fund as response to, 121–122; beginning of, 90–91; capitalist factors, 118; causes of Japan's decline, 94–95; CMIM currency reserve, 123; Japan's economic recovery preceding, 110; liberal view of, 101–103; MOFE response to, 86(n5); South Korea's corporate restructuring, 103–104; South Korea's market liberalization policy, 107–108; South Korea's recovery, 103; statist explanations, 105–111; Taiwan's ability to weather, 92–94, 104–105, 127(n2)
Asian Games, 211
Asian Monetary Fund (AMF), 121–123, 340–341
Aspirations of immigrants, 310
Asset bubble: China's SOE corporatization, 166; Japan's, 95, 97–98, 111, 123; statist view of, 109–110
Association of Southeast Asian Nations (ASEAN), 13, 74, 122–123, 340–341

About the Book

This systematic, innovative introduction to the dynamic politics and political economies of China, Japan, North Korea, South Korea, and Taiwan teaches students how to think analytically, critically, and independently about the most significant developments in the region.

The text offers in-depth coverage of the unique experiences of each country, all within the framework of an explicit comparative perspective. Throughout, the five countries are contrasted with one another to maximize opportunities for learning. Covering the intertwined issues of politics, economics, and culture, this book is ideally suited for assignment in any social science course on East Asia.

Timothy C. Lim is professor of political science at California State University, Los Angeles. He is author of *Doing Comparative Politics: An Introduction to Approaches and Issues.*